THE ROUTLEDGE RE
COMPANION TO TRAV

Showcasing established and new patterns of research, *The Routledge Research Companion to Travel Writing* takes an interdisciplinary approach to scholarship and to travel texts themselves. The volume adopts a thematic approach, with each contributor considering a specific aspect of travel writing – a recurrent motif, an organising principle or a literary form. All of the essays include a discussion of representative travel texts to ensure that the volume as a whole represents a broad historical and geographical range of travel writing. Together, the 25 essays and the editors' introduction offer a comprehensive and authoritative reflection of the state of travel writing criticism and lay the ground for future developments.

Alasdair Pettinger is an independent scholar based in Glasgow, Scotland. He has published on travel literature, the cultures of slavery and abolitionism, and representations of Haiti. His books include the anthology *Always Elsewhere* (1998) and *Frederick Douglass and Scotland, 1846* (2018).

Tim Youngs is Professor of English and Travel Studies at Nottingham Trent University. His books include *The Cambridge Companion to Travel Writing* (edited with Peter Hulme, 2002), *The Cambridge Introduction to Travel Writing* (2013) and *The Cambridge History of Travel Writing* (edited with Nandini Das, 2019).

THE ROUTLEDGE
RESEARCH COMPANION
TO TRAVEL WRITING

Edited by Alasdair Pettinger and Tim Youngs

Routledge
Taylor & Francis Group

LONDON AND NEW YORK

First published 2020
by Routledge
2 Park Square, Milton Park, Abingdon, Oxon OX14 4RN

605 Third Avenue, New York, NY 10017

First issued in paperback 2021

Routledge is an imprint of the Taylor & Francis Group, an informa business

Publisher's Note

The publisher has gone to great lengths to ensure the quality of
this reprint but points out that some imperfections in the original
copies may be apparent.

British Library Cataloguing-in-Publication Data
A catalogue record for this book is available from the British Library

Library of Congress Cataloging-in-Publication Data
A catalog record has been requested for this book

ISBN 13: 978-1-03-209078-8 (pbk)
ISBN 13: 978-1-4724-1792-3 (hbk)

Typeset in Bembo
by Swales & Willis Ltd, Exeter, Devon, UK

CONTENTS

FIGURES

CONTRIBUTORS

James R. Akerman (PhD, Geography, Pennsylvania State University) has been Director of the Hermon Dunlap Smith Center for the History of Cartography at the Newberry Library (Chicago) since 1996 and the Newberry's Curator of Maps since 2011. His research and publications primarily concern the history of travel mapping and atlases. He is the editor or co-editor of five collections of scholarly essays, including *The Imperial Map: Cartography and the Mastery of Empire* (2009) and *Decolonizing the Map: Cartography from Colony to Nation* (2017).

Eve Tavor Bannet is George Lynn Cross Professor (Emeritus) at the University of Oklahoma. Her monographs include: *Empire of Letters: Letter Manuals and Transatlantic Correspondence, 1688–1820* (2005), *Transatlantic Stories and the History of Reading 1720–1810: Migrant Fictions* (2011) and *Manners of Reading: Print Culture and Popular Instruction in the Eighteenth-Century British Atlantic World* (2017). She is editor of *British and American Letter Manuals 1680–1810*, 4 vols (2008) and, with Susan Manning, *Transatlantic Literary Studies, 1640–1830* (2012).

Clare Brant is Professor of Eighteenth-Century Literature and Culture at King's College London, where she co-directs the Centre for Life-Writing Research. Her book *Eighteenth-Century Letters and British Culture* (2006) won the ESSE Book Award for 2008. She has published widely on literature, culture and gender, including *Balloon Madness: Flights of Imagination in Britain, 1783–1786* (2017).

Michael G. Brennan is Professor of Renaissance Studies at the School of English, University of Leeds. He has published extensively on English travellers on the Continent between 1500 and 1700, including *The Travel Diary of Robert Bargrave, Levant Merchant* (1999) and *The Origins of the Grand Tour* (2004), and is currently working on English travellers to Venice. He is also the author of books on the Sidneys of Penshurst, Graham Greene, Evelyn Waugh and George Orwell.

Angela Byrne is Research Associate at Ulster University and in 2018–19 Historian-in-Residence at EPIC The Irish Emigration Museum. She has previously held research and lecturing positions at the Royal Irish Academy, University of Toronto and University of Greenwich.

She is author of *Geographies of the Romantic North: Science, Antiquarianism, and Travel, 1790–1830* (2013) and *A Scientific, Antiquarian and Picturesque Tour: John (Fiott) Lee in Ireland, England and Wales, 1806–07* (Routledge for Hakluyt Society, 2018).

Benjamin Colbert is Reader in English Literature at the University of Wolverhampton and co-editor of *European Romantic Review*. He is the author of *Shelley's Eye: Travel Writing and Aesthetic Vision* (2005) and the online bio-bibliographical database *Women's Travel Writing, 1780–1840* (2014–18). His edited works include *Women's Travel Writing in Post-Napoleonic France* (4 vols, 2012), *Travel Writing and Tourism in Britain and Ireland* (2012) and, with Jan Borm, *Foreign Correspondence* (2014).

Michael Cronin is Professor of French (Chair) 1776 in Trinity College Dublin. He has published widely on questions of translation, language, mobility and identity. He is a Member of the Royal Irish Academy and the Academia Europaea. He is an Officer in the Ordre des Palmes Académiques and is a former Irish-language Literature Advisor to the Arts Council of Ireland. His most recent book is *Eco-Translation: Translation and Ecology in the Age of the Anthropocene* (2017).

John Culbert teaches in the French programme and the Department of English at the University of British Columbia, Vancouver. He is the author of *Paralyses: Literature, Travel, and Ethnography in French Modernity* (2010), as well as numerous articles on travel, tourism, postcolonialism and cultural politics.

Charles Forsdick is James Barrow Professor of French at the University of Liverpool. He is currently Arts and Humanities Research Council theme leadership fellow for 'Translating Cultures'. He has published on travel writing, colonial history, postcolonial and world literature, and the memorialisation of slavery. Recent publications include *The Black Jacobins Reader* (2016) and *Toussaint Louverture: Black Jacobin in an Age of Revolution* (2017). He is a member of the Academy of Europe.

Sarah Jackson is Associate Professor in Literature at Nottingham Trent University. Her publications include *Tactile Poetics: Touch and Contemporary Writing* (2015) and *Pelt* (2012), which won the Seamus Heaney Prize and was longlisted for the *Guardian* First Book Award. She is a BBC/AHRC New Generation Thinker and her current project, *Crossed Wires: Literature and Telephony*, is funded by an AHRC Leadership Fellows grant.

Kevin J. James is Professor of History at the University of Guelph, Canada, where he is founder of the Tourism History Working Group. His publications include *Tourism, Land, and Landscape in Ireland: The Commodification of Culture* (Routledge, 2014) and articles in *Studies in Travel Writing* and *Journeys: The International Journal of Travel and Travel Writing*. His research focuses on international hotel history.

Kathryn N. Jones is Associate Professor of French at Swansea University. Her research focuses on representations of conflict, memory and travel in contemporary French and German cultures, and gender and transnational studies. Her publications include *Journeys of Remembrance* (2007) and articles on travel narratives by François Maspero, Leïla Sebbar, Anne Brunswic and Caroline Riegel. She is co-investigator on the AHRC project 'European Travellers to Wales: 1750–2010'.

Innes M. Keighren is Reader in Historical Geography at Royal Holloway, University of London. He has research interests in geography's disciplinary and discursive histories, in book history, and in the history of science. He is the author of *Bringing Geography to Book: Ellen Semple and the Reception of Geographical Knowledge* (2010) and co-author of *Travels into Print: Exploration, Writing, and Publishing with John Murray, 1773–1859* (2015).

Christina Laffin is Associate Professor and Canada Research Chair in Premodern Japanese Literature and Culture at the University of British Columbia. Her publications include the monograph, *Rewriting Medieval Japanese Women: Politics, Personality, and Literary Production in the Life of Nun Abutsu* (2013); the co-edited collection of essays and translations, *The Noh Ominameshi: A Flower Viewed from Many Directions* (2003); and the multi-volume anthology *Gender and Japanese History* (1999; managing editor).

Elizabeth Leane is Professor of English at the University of Tasmania, where she holds a research fellowship split between the School of Humanities and the Institute for Marine and Antarctic Studies. She has published three monographs, most recently *South Pole: Nature and Culture* (2016); the co-edited collection *Considering Animals* (2011); chapters in books, including *Cinematic Canines, Screening Natures* and *Engaging with Animals*; and articles in journals such as *Studies in Travel Writing* and *Anthrozoös*.

Maria Lindgren Leavenworth is Associate Professor of English at the Department of Language Studies, Umeå University, Sweden. Her research with a focus on travel literature, nordicity and the Arctic has resulted in articles on nineteenth-century travellers Selina Bunbury, Bayard Taylor and S. H. Kent, as well as on contemporary fictional works by Ursula K. Le Guin, Dan Simmons and Michelle Paver.

Lynn Mastellotto is Assistant Professor in English Language Teaching at the University of Bolzano, Faculty of Education. She has a PhD in English from the University of East Anglia, a PGCE in English and French Foreign Language Teaching from the University of Oxford, and a BA and MA in English from McGill University.

David Murray took English and a PhD on Modern American Poetry at King's College, London. He taught at the University of Kent and University of Nottingham, where he is Emeritus Professor of American Studies. His publications include *Speech, Writing and Representation in North American Indian Texts* (1991), *Indian Giving: Economies of Power in Early Indian–White Exchanges* (2000) and *Matter, Magic, and Spirit: Representing Indian and African American Belief* (2007).

Aedín Ní Loingsigh is a Lecturer in French and Translation Studies at the University of Stirling. She has published widely on travel writing in the context of francophone sub-Saharan Africa, including *Postcolonial Eyes: Intercontinental Travel in Francophone African Literature* (2009). She is currently working on the translations of the North American scholar and diplomat Mercer Cook.

Heidi Oberholtzer Lee teaches in the English department at Eastern University, in St. Davids, Pennsylvania. She specialises in early American literature, travel writing, religion and literature, and food studies. Her work has appeared in publications such as *Food and Faith in Christian Culture, Christian Scholar's Review, Journal of Narrative Theory, Early American Studies* and *Religion & Literature*.

Alasdair Pettinger is an independent scholar based in Glasgow, Scotland. He has published on travel literature, the cultures of slavery and abolitionism, and representations of Haiti. His books include the anthology *Always Elsewhere* (1998) and *Frederick Douglass and Scotland, 1846* (2018).

Paul Smethurst is Honorary Associate Professor at the University of Hong Kong where he taught theory, contemporary fiction and travel literature until he retired in 2016. His books include *The Postmodern Chronotope* (2000), *Travel Writing and the Natural World* (2013) and *The Bicycle: Towards a Global History* (2015). He is co-editor of three collections of essays on travel writing, including, with Julia Kuehn, *New Directions in Travel Writing* (2015). His first retirement project is a new book on nature writing.

Margaret Topping is Professor of French Literary and Visual Cultures at Queen's University, Belfast. Her research trajectory has developed from an early disciplinary focus on one of France's canonical writers, Marcel Proust, to a firmly interdisciplinary approach to debates linked to travel, tourism and migration, and to the ethics and aesthetics of cross-cultural representation. Particular focal points are the ethical role and responsibilities of public spaces such as museums and archives in negotiating diversity, as well as the possibilities for creating enhanced connectivity, cohesion and social wellbeing in post-conflict or postcolonial societies through community-based initiatives such as cultural festivals or urban art projects.

Tom F. Wright is Senior Lecturer in English at the University of Sussex. He is the author of *Lecturing the Atlantic: Speech, Print and an Anglo-American Commons* (2017) and editor of *The Cosmopolitan Lyceum: Lecture Culture and the Globe in Nineteenth Century America* (2013). He has published widely on nineteenth-century literature and oratory, and is currently working on a book on the history of 'charisma'.

Tim Youngs is Professor of English and Travel Studies at Nottingham Trent University, where he established and continues to direct the Centre for Travel Writing Studies. His books include *The Cambridge Companion to Travel Writing* (ed. with Peter Hulme, 2002), *The Cambridge Introduction to Travel Writing* (2013) and *The Cambridge History of Travel Writing* (ed. with Nandini Das, 2019). He is founding editor of the journal *Studies in Travel Writing*. His debut poetry pamphlet, *Touching Distance*, was published in 2017.

INTRODUCTION

Alasdair Pettinger and Tim Youngs

I

Travel writing 'presents a problem for academic studies', claims Steve Clark, introducing his influential edited collection on *Travel Writing and Empire* (1999). The reason for this, according to Clark, is that the genre 'seems too dependent on an empirical rendition of contingent events [. . .] for entry into the literary canon, yet too overtly rhetorical for disciplines such as anthropology, sociology, geography or history'.[1] Despite that problem, or more likely because of it, and despite a continuing suspicion about the status of the genre, academics have turned to travel writing in increasing numbers. Some dissenting voices aside, it is now firmly established as a subject of serious study. Its seemingly competing strands of the empirical and the rhetorical, the scientific and the literary, the documentary and the artful, the objective and the subjective, are in fact among the main elements that continue to generate scholarly inquiry and debate.

Clark's collection was published at approximately the midway point between the start of the new academic scrutiny of travel writing and our own *Research Companion* introduced here. By common consensus it is since the 1980s that travel writing has received sustained critical attention. Kuehn and Smethurst summarise concisely the late twentieth-century 'impetus for travel writing studies as a discipline' which, as they put it,

> came in the 1980s when a counter-traditional wave swept through the humanities. In literary studies, interest began to turn from the canon to 'minor texts', alternative voices and *petits récits* in a war against grand narratives. As Leavisite notions of a 'great tradition' were deconstructed by strategies of 'writing back' and new localisms, a much wider range of texts were made available for scrutiny. Travel writing then emerged from the margins as a significant resource. When the 'theory' revolution took hold in the late 1980s, travel writing proved especially adaptable and responsive to the application of cross-cultural, post-colonial, gender and globalization studies. Cultural historians, geographers and those working in literary studies found in travel writing an endless supply of texts reaching back into antiquity and across all cultures.[2]

A pioneering text from that decade is Peter Hulme's *Colonial Encounters* (1986), although the movement towards analyses of power, 'race' and ideology in travel texts is usually seen to have gained its impetus from Edward Said's *Orientalism* (1978).[3] It should be noted that neither of these works focused on travel writing but travel writing was a significant vehicle for the representations they discuss. In the introduction to a collection of new essays in 2014, Charles Forsdick, Corinne Fowler and Ludmilla Kostova share a widespread view when they comment that '[t]he study of travel writing has emerged rapidly over the past three decades as a thriving cross-disciplinary field.'[4] The boundaries and moral frame of the genre may be contested, but those, too, are part of the discussion about it.

Subsequent to the wave of scholarly activity on travel writing, dating in particular from postcolonial- and feminist-inflected works of the 1980s and 1990s, overviews of the field have become numerous enough for them to survey not only the primary material and some of the more specialised scholarly works, but to comment on one another. This attention has intensified, attracting academics from across disciplines as well as coinciding with or even stimulating highly self-reflexive work from practitioners of the craft themselves. It has given rise to journals dedicated to the subject, critical introductions and anthologies, conferences, seminar series, websites, at least one centre of study, and university courses in many countries. In 2018, for example, the year we write this Introduction, the journal *Studies in Travel Writing* is in its twenty-second year of publication and the conference series *Borders and Crossings* celebrates its twentieth anniversary. Like much of the literature with which it deals, this body of critical activity does not simply add to what has come before; rather, it often points to its own characteristics. The title of Kuehn and Smethurst's 2015 edited volume, *New Directions in Travel Writing Studies*, attests to both the establishment of the field and the impulse to strike out on a distinctive path – just as travel writers themselves often emphasise the distinctiveness of their own approaches, and just as this Introduction and volume will attempt to do.[5]

Introductions to travel writing collections and single-authored surveys form a genre in themselves. Typically they note that '[t]ravel writing studies is a burgeoning field of academic enquiry'. They cite the foundational works by Edward Said, Peter Hulme, Mary Louise Pratt, Sara Mills, Mary Baine Campbell, James Buzard and (usually disapprovingly because of his neglect of women writers and his nostalgia for an age of slower, less standardised travel before mass tourism) Paul Fussell. The introductions observe that in the twenty-first century, as Thompson puts it, 'travel writing studies have proliferated, diversified and grown more historically nuanced and theoretically sophisticated'.[6] They identify ways in which previous work is deemed deficient and the work on offer remedial, and they end with the caveat that the work being introduced is not meant to be 'exhaustive and all-encompassing',[7] but that the editors or authors hope it will 'be a spur to further research and scholarship, and [. . .] provide models and resources that can assist in these ongoing enquiries'.[8] Just as with travel writing itself, so these introductions may arrive at a common destination while revealing something of their individual starting points. For example, in the opening to *Travel Narratives in Translation*, Alison Martin and Susan Pickford compare travel with translation:

> While travel writing is associated with recasting the foreign textually and visually for readers back home, translation is similarly concerned with transporting the foreign into the target language and culture and adapting it to meet the target audience's expectations [. . .] the translator and the traveler are [. . .] figures moving between languages and cultures in comparable ways.[9]

Opening their collection, James Duncan and Derek Gregory make a similar comparison to that made by Martin and Pickford, underlining the role of travel writing as an act of translation that constantly works to produce a tense 'space in-between' [. . .] In re-presenting other cultures and other natures, then, travel writers 'translate' one place into another, and in doing so constantly rub against the hubris that their own language-game contains the concepts necessary to represent another language-game.[10]

Duncan and Gregory observe that there are losses and gains in this process, but that 'even in its most imperial gestures, by virtue of its occupation of that "space in-between" [. . .] travel writing can also disclose an ambivalence, a sense of its own authorities and assumptions being called into question'.[11] This is analogous with the body as the site of translation between the material and inner worlds, the environment and the self. It is in this regard that the senses, which are the subject of Part III of the present volume, perform a mediating role. They help determine whether external objects are perceived favourably or negatively as markers of difference. They are signifiers of culture as much as of individuality. They indicate and even shape how one travels and how effective and open is the interpretation one makes.

The act of translation that Duncan and Gregory describe is managed through the manner of the writing. Each literary form has its own characteristics, though often these are cognate versions of features found in others, and all transport the travel experience to the reader. (This holds true also for private and unpublished work that remains available for subsequent reading and that has carried the experience away from the place and moment it records.) Yet Duncan and Gregory are geographers and they introduce their collection by warning against readings that are

vulnerable to the accusation of textualism: they tell us much about the constitution of authors as subjects through the process of writing, and about the relations between their own strategies of representation and the wider cultural formations of which they were a part, but they often say very little about the places these travellers encountered or the physical means through which they engaged them.[12]

Duncan and Gregory 'fear that some critical readings fail to register the production of travel writings by corporeal subjects moving through material landscapes'.[13] The two editors' priorities may reflect their disciplinary remit but this is not the complete picture: they and their contributors discuss literary texts, while some in literary studies, including those who study refugees' narratives, might also disfavour an emphasis on the textual over experience and place.

The present volume attends both to the textual and to the physicality of the subject moving across and within material landscapes. Through the various types of traveller as well as through the different approaches to their writings that are presented here, we intend our volume to extend the range of what is normally considered to be travel writing and of ways of reading it. We hope that our examples serve to illustrate the heterogeneous nature of the field. Any omissions underline this. Diversity exists even within what superficially may seem to be a discrete group of travellers who produce texts with shared themes and concerns. Thus, for example, in his book on African American travel narratives in the age of segregation, Gary Totten reminds us that

not all African American travelers share the same ideological agendas or enact the same cultural interventions. Indeed, there is a significant heterogeneity generally found in travel literature that can also be found in African American travel literature during this time.[14]

This is true not only of the lack of uniformity in travel writing in general, but is also a useful corrective to those discussions that posit a uniform set of counter-narratives in opposition to dominant, imperial ones. Travel writing is often radical and oppositional, challenging political, social and generic conventions, but to expect radicalism solely on the basis of ethnicity or gender or sexuality or other characteristics is to stereotype in its own way.

II

As we add our own introductory essay to the corpus of introductions to edited collections, we too, then, claim for it some distinctiveness while pointing to the common ground it shares with its predecessors. Our volume follows the general, though not universally agreed-upon principle that travel writing consists of the narrative of an actual journey told by the person or persons who undertook it. We do not disagree with the tenor of the bold statement by the editor of one anthology that 'the biggest fiction, in the end, is travel writing's own claim to being an objective genre', or with the import of his accompanying rhetorical question: 'What does anyone really know about a foreign place that isn't partly his or her own creation?', but we do not go so far as to include in our definition, as that editor does, works that are 'obviously fiction'. We find in our supposedly non-fiction works what Raphael Kadushin observes in the range of his contributors' stories: the knowledge of 'how to use the trip as a metaphor, or a frame'.[15] Alongside analysis of texts that knowingly treat the journey metaphorically, one of the important accomplishments of criticism, however, has been the exposure of texts that do so unconsciously. Accordingly, travel writers' symbolic use of aspects of their journeys, whether intended or not, is discussed in many of the chapters that follow. That symbolism operates on the personal and collective level. Indeed, the appeal of travel metaphors is apparent in literary criticism and theory, as noted by Kuehn and Smethurst, who see travel as 'provid[ing] a rich source of metaphor in theory-based critical practice' following the 'spatial/geopolitical turn in the humanities'.[16]

If, as Jaś Elsner and Joan Pau Rubiés remark, 'the literature of travel not only exemplifies the multiple facets of modern identity, but it is also one of the principal cultural mechanisms, even a key cause, for the development of modern identity since the Renaissance',[17] it is important to generate new approaches towards an understanding of this mechanism. In attempting to do so we attend to form, context and content, and to the textual and the bodily. Editors of essay collections perform something of an analogous role to those translator-travellers described above, journeying into the field, selecting voices and material, and offering an interpretive frame. As do some of the texts it discusses, then, this Companion aims to inspect the terrain and to offer its own approach while building on previous accounts. The volume identifies established and emerging patterns of research and examines critical reflection, in scholarly publications as well as in travel texts themselves. It strives both to assess theoretical models and terminologies where they have been deployed with some regularity and to map areas of newer concern where the analytical tools have yet to be developed.

Our volume adopts a thematic approach. Contributors were asked to consider a specific aspect of travel writing – a recurrent motif, an organising principle, a literary form – and to identify and evaluate the scholarly resources that have been used to understand it. In some cases, there was a substantial body of research to survey and question. In others, where the aspect assigned remains relatively unexplored, our authors' task was to indicate some of the key theoretical challenges ahead and how they might be confronted. In all cases, contributors were asked to illustrate their discussion with examples of travel texts, ensuring that the volume as a whole includes reference to a broad historical and geographical range of travel writing. In turn, this procedure allows readers to gain their own sense of which features may be specific to a period or region and which may transcend specific contexts.

Our contributors were chosen so as to reflect something of the historical, linguistic and geographical dimensions of travel writing scholarship today. They were expected to draw on examples from their own areas of expertise but were encouraged to consider material from sources sufficiently varied to have them bring a comparative perspective to bear on the topic.

The volume is divided into five main sections that between them focus on matters of textual and contextual detail. We hope that, taken together, they suggest the importance of the inter-relationship of various facets of the travel experience, taking in the reasons for and the impulses to travel; forms and characteristics of travel writing; the role of the senses; interactions between traveller and travellee (to use Pratt's term);[18] and paratexts.

**

In Part I, 'Framing travel', we present seven chapters that discuss and reflect on the ways in which different kinds of journey – distinguished by how one travels and for what purpose – shape the language and structure of the narratives that recount them. The journeys considered here include those undertaken to acquire knowledge of the unknown or reassess one's relation-ship with the familiar, to flee danger or simply seek a better life, and those that engage with other travel writers, whether they be companions and co-authors or precursors whose itineraries the later writers attempt to duplicate.

The late eighteenth and early nineteenth centuries saw a rapid growth of the European acqui-sition of 'new' global knowledge, often associated with explorers such as James Cook, George Vancouver, Alexander von Humboldt and Mungo Park. Angela Byrne chooses to examine two lesser-known figures to show how the category of 'scientific traveller' could encompass a wide range of participants. The on-the-spot research of Thomas Pennant in Scotland and Sarah Bowdich in West Africa involved intensive first-hand observation and information-gathering from local residents, and their accounts have much to tell us of the complex power relations of the imperial contact zones in which these encounters took place.

In the next chapter Paul Smethurst examines how nature writing helped shape ideas of nature in the West, and explores the ecological perspectives that inform the so-called 'new nature writing' of Robert Macfarlane and others. He describes how although Romanticism and scenic tourism sought to bring their subjects closer to nature at a time of urbanisation and materialism, they both ended up, through 'aestheticisation and sentimentalisation', dis-tancing the natural environment from the site of human habitation and labour. Smethurst welcomes ecocriticism's scrutiny of our exploitation of the natural world in contrast to the celebratory tone of much traditional nature writing. He sees in the new nature writing 'a new poetics that [. . .] aims to bridge the gap between human society and the biosphere that enfolds and supports it'.

The early twenty-first century has seen a growth of interest in the writings of undocumented migrants who make often hazardous journeys fleeing persecution, famine, war and poverty. Aedín Ní Loingsigh considers the ways in which the veracity of their accounts has been con-tested by reviewers and critics, and how such potential incredulity can determine the form in which the accounts are published. Examining the contrasting cases of *Soif d'Europe* (2008) by Omar Ba and *Dem ak xabaar* (2012) by Mahmoud Traoré and Bruno Le Dantec, Ní Loingsigh asks what makes one account supposedly more reliable than another and pursues the themes of trust and mistrust as they are addressed in the texts themselves.

If some migrants are impelled to travel under duress, others – often dubbed 'expatriates' – freely choose to live elsewhere because they are driven by what Lynn Mastellotto describes as an ethical impulse to pursue a vision of 'the good life'. Comparing two very different kinds of 'expatriate memoir' – Susanna Moodie's *Roughing It in the Bush* (1852) and Frances Mayes' *Under the Tuscan Sun* (1996) and its two sequels – Mastellotto indicates the range of variation of their authors' 'cosmopolitan engagement' with their new homes, from radical self-invention to a more detached flirtation with cultural difference.

Although the authors of travel books are often assumed to travel alone, many do so with companions who also record their experiences, sometimes publishing them in collaboration. Kathryn N. Jones considers two Francophone texts, each jointly authored by two women, *Aux pays des femmes soldats* (1931) by Suzanne de Callias and Blanche Vogt, and *Vacances en Iran* (1961) by Caroline Gazaï and Geneviève Gaillet. While the narration of the first alternates between the two authors, the voices of the second are generally merged in a single 'we', a contrast that allows Jones to explore the way in which collaborative works try to steer 'a tricky path between the solipsism of individually narrated travelogues and the erasure of difference that can result from collective narrative perspectives'.

A significant group of travel narratives record journeys made in the footsteps of earlier travellers. Of particular interest to Maria Lindgren Leavenworth are what she calls 'second journeys', those that directly engage with the texts written by such predecessors. While there are many possible ways in which the accounts of second journeys respond to the first, the motifs of nostalgia, authenticity and oversaturation figure frequently. Key issues raised by 'footsteps' travel are highlighted in Lindgren Leavenworth's reading of the postmodern travelogue *Expeditionen* (2013) by Bea Uusma, which tracks an 1897 expedition to the Arctic. Lindgren Leavenworth foregrounds the author's inability to duplicate her precursor's experience and sharply reminds us how knowledge comes to be structured differently over time.

If the most common direction of movement in travel writing is horizontal, we might also speak of significant traditions of what has been called 'vertical travel'. As Charles Forsdick explains, this might be literal (involving an upward or downward trajectory) or figurative (remaining within a fairly restricted area, subjecting it to various practices of microspection). Drawing on the work of twentieth- and twenty-first-century writers, including Georges Perec, Robert Macfarlane and Karl Whitney, he discusses two distinctive characteristics of 'the poetics of verticality' – its fondness for 'detailed, even exhaustive, enumeration' and a 'multisensory rediscovery of the everyday'.

**

Travel writing is characterised by its generic range and mixture. The six chapters in Part II, 'Modes of writing', examine some of the most commonly used literary forms and rhetorical modes, and explore their possibilities and limitations. The forms covered here include the epistolary, the diary, the guidebook and tourist brochure, narrative, and the lecture. Modes of description are also considered. An aim of this section is to raise awareness of, and foster debate about, the influence of literary form on the telling of the travel experience. Although there can be no fixed answer about the extent to which travel accounts are shaped by the vehicle of their narration, attention to form increases our sense of the mediation that occurs between the act of travel and a reader's (or auditor's) reception of tales of it. If, as Peter Hulme has stated, travel writing is *made* rather than made up (because that would mean it were fiction),[19] then recognition of how it is made underlines the layers that are interposed between the event and its relation, between the actor and the narrator.

Eve Tavor Bannet's chapter examines travel letters. It points to their 'intrinsically fragmentary' nature, which makes them 'like a snapshot or a still', and to their status as a kind of speech-utterance. Bannet's focus is on the eighteenth century, and in particular on 'polite and sociable travel letters', though her observations apply more generally. Letters are, of course, affected by the identity and expectations of the addressee, such that a correspondent might represent a place very differently to different recipients. Bannet also notes that travel letters move and change shape: perhaps more than other forms, except possibly the diary, they are modified or extracted (and often not by the authors themselves) for various texts, contexts and readerships.

Japanese vernacular travel diaries from the tenth to the fourteenth centuries provide the focus for Christina Laffin's scrutiny of the journal genre. Most of those produced in the premodern period were authored by women. The chapter moves from the emergence of poetic travel journals to later examples of how content and style were shaped by literary conventions. Laffin offers her discussion as a way of rethinking some of the assumptions about travel writing that derive from the field's concentration on Anglophone and modern texts. She notes that in the Japanese tradition, travel writing and poetry were closely linked. The conventions of the former demanded that writers cite previous travellers and their images, thus inscribing themselves into a tradition and emphasising homogeneity and lineage rather than novelty.

With the emergence of modern tourism in the nineteenth century, many travel writers marked their distance from those they disparaged for following the 'beaten track', of which the guidebook was a comic symptom. And yet, as Alasdair Pettinger argues, if the formal organisation and stylistic features of travel books and travel guides seem to be sharply distinct from each other, the rhetoric of practical advice, with its characteristic moods and pronouns, plays an important role in narrative travel writing, not only as an object of parody. Pettinger's discussion of accounts of journeys to Italy by D. H. Lawrence and Edith Wharton, and of *Guadeloupe* (1988) by Maryse Condé, suggests different ways in which the autobiographical co-exists with a concern to prescribe a certain 'art of travel'.

Accounts of travels very often take narrative form, but like narratives of any sort, fictional or otherwise, their authors must choose which events to narrate, how often, at what speed and in what order. Choosing where to *begin* is often of special significance, as John Culbert's discussion of the opening of Bronislaw Malinowski's *Argonauts of the Western Pacific* (1922) demonstrates. If the male narrator of that work tends to disavow the colonial apparatuses that make the anthropologist's work possible, the explicitly 'postcolonial' writing of Jamaica Kincaid offers a contrast. In the accounts she provides of her botanical collecting tours in *Among Flowers* (2005) and elsewhere, Kincaid's awareness of the colonial genealogy of such activity structures the way she narrates origins and departures.

If scholars can benefit from a rich body of narratological theory that helps them understand how travel writers tell stories, the techniques of description by means of which those writers try to capture the immediacy of the moment are much less understood. Benjamin Colbert examines how several writers describe the Wye Valley in eighteenth- and nineteenth-century texts, from William Gilpin's *Observations on the River Wye* (1782) to Louisa Anne Twamley's *An Autumn Ramble on the Wye* (1838). Colbert is especially interested in their attempts to convey the particularity of a subjective experience while constrained by aesthetic and scientific conventions, often encoded in previous descriptions of the same place by earlier authors and visual artists.

Alongside written travelogues – and predating them – is a long tradition of travellers returning to recount their experiences before a live audience. Tom F. Wright considers the flourishing of this tradition in Britain and the United States in the half-century or so before the rise of the cinema, dwelling on three celebrated travel lecturers – Albert Smith, Bayard Taylor and Esther Lyons – in order to show how the genre developed over time and made use of new technologies. His chapter pays particular attention to the performative elements of the lectures, which were often delivered with theatrical flair and supported by visual aids such as panoramas and coloured slides.

**

The five chapters of 'Sensuous geographies' examine our current understanding of the roles of each of the five senses in travel narratives and of the kinds of knowledge and emotional response they encourage or inhibit. Scholars of travel writing, particularly those influenced by Mary Louise Pratt's *Imperial Eyes* or John Urry's *The Tourist Gaze*, have emphasised the part played by sight and looking in travel. These approaches have tended to stress domination, appropriation or recognition. In recent years this ocularcentrism has been attacked for its privileging of one sense over the others but also for its ableist assumptions. In Veit Erlmann's words, 'it makes scientific sense to conceive of the senses as an integrated and flexible network but also, and more importantly [. . .] arguments over the hierarchy of senses are always also arguments over cultural and political agendas'.[20] Part III of our volume, then, places the senses alongside one another to show how all are important to travel, and to suggest how critical approaches to the literary treatment of them may enhance our understanding of travel writing.

Margaret Topping's chapter, focusing on charity and gap-year tourism, examines the ethics and power relations involved in seeing. Noting the dominance of vision in travel narratives, Topping considers the relationship between seeing and being seen. Basing her discussion on Jean-Christophe Perrot's and Diego Audemard's 2007 *Tandems africains* in which the authors rely on blind or partially sighted local guides during their journey across sub-Saharan Africa, Topping outlines how the writers' experience is thus mediated by the non-seeing guides. Although the gap-year travellers share 'something of the discourses of discovery and domination associated with seeing and thus knowing', their 'journey of self-discovery' affects them and has a lasting impact on the travellees through media coverage and donations from the book's profits.

The dominance of vision in studies of travel writing is also noted by Tim Youngs. In his chapter, Youngs contends that although hearing might be considered the most objective of the senses, its presence in travel narratives can be profoundly symbolic. How sounds are reported may tell us much about the traveller's subjectivity. Through a discussion of a range of twentieth- and twenty-first-century texts, with a focus on H. V. Morton's *In Search of England* (1927), Amryl Johnson's *Sequins for a Ragged Hem* (1988) and Iain Sinclair's *London Orbital* (2002), Youngs examines how sound transmits ideas about the past and present, nature and technology, and cultural identity.

In her chapter Sarah Jackson challenges the neglect of touch in travel writing studies. Stressing the importance of developing an aesthetics of touch, she investigates the representation of touch in the Antarctic. Jackson takes as her case studies Apsley Cherry-Garrard's *The Worst Journey in the World* (1922) and Sara Wheeler's *Terra Incognita* (1996), texts which, she contends, show the significance of tact in an extremely inhospitable region. Jackson considers the 'texturality' of the texts; that is, how they 'are themselves "textured" by expressions of touch and feeling'. Attention to the haptic, Jackson states, 'enables us to consider the multi-sensory quality of geographical experience'.

As Heidi Oberholtzer Lee observes, travellers often interpret their experiences through what she calls a 'hermeneutic of appetite' in which the sensation of taste is mediated by broader cultural assumptions about 'foodways'. In a close reading of two early American texts – William Bartram's *Travels* (1791) and the *Journals* (1803–1806) of Meriwether Lewis and William Clark – Oberholtzer Lee shows how they articulate two forms of 'gastronomical heroism', the first primarily concerned with the relationship between human and natural economies, the second more geared to the project of imperial expansion. In both cases, the vocabulary used to convey the flavour and texture of food is not exclusively gustatory, but is flexible enough to evoke complex responses to the social relationships in which their encounters were embedded.

Clare Brant shows how the insights of the relatively new field of olfactory studies, which emerged in the 1980s, can be applied to the study of travel writing. She examines several motifs, including the conjunction of rage and malodours in D. H. Lawrence's *Sea and Sardinia* (1923) and the way naming smells serves not only to convey a sense of place but also to indicate the limits of cultural identity (in Jay Griffith's *Wild*, 2008), or to offer compensation to a disoriented traveller (in Paul Theroux's *Happy Isles of Oceania*, 1992 and George Orwell's *Road to Wigan Pier*, 1937). Brant also suggests that accounts by blind travellers, such as Nicola Naylor's *Jasmine and Arnica* (2001), may help critics reassess long-established hierarchies of the senses.

**

Many travel writing studies devote considerable space to analyses of the construction of self and other in travel texts. In the main, these involve differentiation along the lines of ethnicity, nation, gender or cultural practice. Often the critical focus is on ideologies of power or psychological processes of individuation or affiliation. The four chapters in Part IV, 'Interactions', may share some of these concerns but in considering some of the different kinds of encounter that punctuate travel narratives, and that often form the rhetorical bedrock of their cross-cultural judgements, they combine to point to the broader types of interaction that occur. As with the other sections, the coverage in this one is not encyclopaedic but offers illustrative case studies. Its subjects are hospitality, the exchange of material objects, interlingual meetings and communication (or attempts at it), and the relationships between humans and other animals.

Hospitality involves relations of power (between hosts and guests) and codes of conduct, often given legal form. 'Cultures of hospitality' vary considerably, even in the same locale, with standards improving or declining over time, as travel writers often observe. Referring to texts such as James John Hissey's *The Charm of the Road* (1910), Kevin J. James shows how late nineteenth- and early twentieth-century travel books about Britain commonly resorted to rhetorical contrasts in which the homely English 'inn' was set in opposition to the impersonal American 'hotel' on the one hand and the spartan, poorly managed accommodations in Ireland, Scotland and Wales on the other. He concludes with suggestive remarks on the figures of the landlord and landlady in travel narratives, and on their descriptions of meals.

David Murray's chapter focuses on the exchange of material objects and its representation. In particular, Murray is fascinated with how in early modern accounts of cross-cultural contact, exchange may involve 'radical challenges to the ideas of value on which each side is operating'. He argues that while power relations are more obvious in colonial and imperial exploration (his case studies are Columbus, Raleigh, John Smith, Cook and de Lapérouse), power is 'a constant in travel and travel writing'. Close attention to exchange reveals its complexity, exposing often 'submerged ideological and cultural agendas, and power-relations' that remain present in modern encounters.

In his chapter Michael Cronin challenges critics' neglect of the relationships travellers have to other languages and consequently to their own. Cronin notes that how travellers deal with other languages 'has clear implications for their capacity to engage with or interpret the realities they encounter'. He discusses Patrick Leigh Fermor's *A Time of Gifts* (1977), written in a major language; and Pádraig Ó Fiannachta's *Ó Mháigh go Fásach* [From Plain to Desert] (1977), in a minor language, Irish Gaelic. Cronin argues that as migration increases linguistic diversity, 'the question of language difference will be an inescapable dimension to writing about travel and places'.

While most travel narratives record encounters with non-human beings to some degree, Elizabeth Leane argues that these encounters and interactions have attracted relatively little scholarly interest, much of it tending to treat animals as metaphors for human qualities rather than exploring the complex interactions involved. She proposes a possible typology of animal roles in travel accounts – as quest object (such as the emperor penguin in Apsley Cherry-Garrard's *Worst Journey in the World*, 1922), instrument of travel (in Robert Louis Stevenson's *Travels with a Donkey*, 1879, or Robyn Davidson's *Tracks*, 1980) and companion (the author's dog in John Steinbeck's *Travels with Charley*, 1962) – which reveals how animal studies can shed new light on familiar travel accounts which, in turn, can further our appreciation of human–animal encounters.

**

Finally, Part V, 'Paratexts', goes beyond the body of the text to examine the additional material that often frames or accompanies the travel narrative as well as the wider context of the editing, publishing and marketing of travel accounts. One of our purposes here is to encourage a view of travel narratives not as a given or as the product of any one individual, but rather to restore awareness of some of the layers and choices involved in the process by which they appear in print.

Editors of travel texts often face considerable difficulty in ascertaining the authorship, purpose and intended audience of the documents they examine – all of which informs the decisions they make concerning the form the introductory material, scholarly apparatus and supplementary material will take. They must also meet the often specialised requirements of their own readers. Focusing on modern editions of sixteenth-century texts, Michael G. Brennan pays particular attention to the accounts of the Spanish Armada (1588) and the Cadiz expedition (1596) compiled by Richard Hakluyt, analysing Hakluyt's own choices as editor as well as those made in subsequent republications of his *Principal Navigations*, including the latest edition prepared by Oxford University Press.

James R. Akerman discusses the different ways maps are deployed (or not) in travel texts, perhaps most consistently in guidebooks and in accounts of exploration. He considers two main types: detailed strip-maps and smaller-scale maps in which a route is plotted across a much larger area of land or sea – before outlining a history of the integration of maps and text and the development of printing techniques that made this possible. His examples range from the accounts of the earliest European transatlantic voyages to the books aimed at tourists visiting the battlefields of World War I, with a sidelong glance at the inclusion of fictitious maps in narratives of imaginary voyages such as Robert Louis Stevenson's *Treasure Island* (1883).

While Basil Hall's *Account of a Voyage of Discovery to the West Coast of Corea* (1818) is relatively familiar to students of nineteenth-century travel writing, its publishing history is not. Innes Keighren offers a close analysis of the differences between the first edition, an expensive quarto, the second, a cheaper duodecimo, and even cheaper subsequent editions, showing how narrative, technical data and illustrations are expanded, corrected or removed, and demonstrating that travel books of the period were 'dynamic entities, being subject to textual emendation (during and after their publication) and periodic repositioning within an expanding and fast-changing literary marketplace'.

III

Together, these twenty-five chapters offer what we believe to be a wide-ranging reflection of the state of travel writing criticism while laying the ground for future developments. Our volume is not intended to be the last word – research is a journey that continues – and we recognise that there will be divergences from its approaches, interpretations and assumptions. But we hope that the chapters here will further an appreciation of the complexity of the genre. They address some of the factors that mediate between the experience of travel, the communication of it and the reception of the travel story. These include physical, psychological, social and, of course, textual aspects. Although many texts are covered here, there are other types and aspects of travel writing that remain understudied or less noticed in scholarship on the field. Among these are travel writing in languages other than English, especially in those other than the major European ones,[21] Indigenous travel narratives, travel writing (and its criticism) that is not ableist, and aesthetically innovative or experimental travel writing. Some of these are discussed by our contributors but each of them deserves its own several volumes.

The role of travel writing in helping promote imperialism and colonialism, studies of which, as we have seen, helped generate the academic scrutiny of the genre from the late 1970s onward, should not be understated. Yet to associate travel writing predominantly with empire and 'race' is to take a narrower view of it than of, for example, the novel, which has existed in its recognisable form for a fraction of the time that travel writing has been in existence and examples of which are no less culpable in transmitting racist views than are some travel texts. Moreover, what has rightly been gained in exposing the lack of objectivity, reliability and disinterestedness in texts that purport to possess these qualities has resulted in an overlooking of travel writing within and outside the West that does not have empire as its frame of reference. In addition to expanding ways of approaching travel writing, then, we hope that this Companion will help extend the sense of what travel writing is, where it is produced and by whom.

It is more than the texts themselves and their subjects that travel, too. As Ottmar Ette notes, '[n]ot only the places described, but also the places of writing and the places of reading are in reciprocal as well as in independent movement'. The same might be said of the relationship of our contributors to one another and to ourselves as editors. Readers, Ette reminds us, 'also move constantly', and 'we only rarely read a longer book in the same place'.[22] This fact introduces another element into the layers between the act of travel, its recitation and its readership. Although our volume does not explicitly consider the last stage of the process that Ette describes, we invite our readers to contemplate whether and how their own places of reading affect their responses to its content as well as to travel texts themselves.

As we approach the third decade of the twenty-first century, what do we predict that travel writing and its criticism will look like as the century wears on? We might expect that in response to the diffusion of critical studies and the elaboration of theories, travel writing itself may more openly question some of its own premises. Certainly, there is and has been for some time a greater awareness of its historical role in shaping negative attitudes towards other peoples and in reinforcing gender constructs. Some travel writers have expressed concern about this and are conscious of the broader ethical implications of their activities, but the distance between academics' and practitioners' views has not narrowed as much as one might anticipate. What Fowler, Forsdick and Kostova describe as 'the possibility of an alliance between the practices of criticism and travel writing' has yet to be realised on any meaningful scale.[23] It may be that with the huge growth in creative writing courses in universities, and in particular with the growing popularity of creative-critical PhDs, the gap between the practice and the criticism of travel writing will narrow. It will not be the only factor in any convergence: there is a widespread awareness among travel writers, in whatever form they work, of the racial, colonial and gendered politics of earlier examples of the genre and a desire to be more ethically responsible. That said, in the words of Fowler, Forsdick and Kostova, 'the open, active, and enabling engagement of studies in travel writing with questions of ethics remains largely undeveloped'.[24] Of course, travel writing has survived and developed quite independently of academics, and perhaps the most obvious way in which it will continue to evolve is through its presence on the internet, whose technology allows people to upload and publish their travel accounts while on the move. The main features of this are the *immediacy* of publication; the *democratisation* of publication such that anyone with access to the internet and a smartphone, tablet or laptop can disseminate their stories; and *individualisation* – the potential for more original and individual voices to emerge as one may reach audiences directly without the intervention of editors who are influenced by their conception of the market. But in truth, the provision of formal templates in combination with the weight of previous narratives and representations means that there is not in practice the amount of innovativeness one might hope for.

A benefit of the internet is that it provides local, including Indigenous, communities with the opportunity to present themselves to prospective visitors. While this primarily involves tourism rather than travel writing, it does help shape views of the place and community to which visitors may be travelling. Yet the internet does also allow for new voices to be heard and it facilitates new groupings. Thus, for example, the freely available online magazine, *Panorama: The Journal of Intelligent Travel*, a quarterly launched in autumn 2016 under the general editorship of Amy Gigi Alexander, brings together contributors and editors from around the world with a mission to 'draw attention to every part of the scene, so that we are able to see and hear the images and voices excluded from the conventional, narrow travel narrative'.[25] At the time of writing it is planning an East African issue (for 2019 publication) with a requirement that its contributors be at least East African-born.

The importance of travel and of the internet cannot be overstated at a time of nationalist retrenchment, tighter border controls and the distortion of 'migrant' into a pejorative term. Our aim for the present volume is to help convey a sense of the multifacetedness of travel writing and of diverse, if complementary, ways of reading it. Far from being only or predominantly a record of colonial expansion and imperial rule, travel writing narrates the whole spectrum of human journeys. It is a record of meetings, exchanges and movements towards the comprehension of oneself and of others as much as it is a record of domination, exploitation and violence. Perhaps travel writing studies will fully have come of age when companions and introductions need only be to very specific types and features of the genre. We hope that this volume points the way to some of these.

Notes

1 Steve Clark, 'Introduction', in *Travel Writing and Empire: Postcolonial Theory in Transit*, ed. Steve Clark (London: Zed Books, 1999), 2.

2 Julia Kuehn and Paul Smethurst, 'Introduction', in *New Directions in Travel Writing Studies*, ed. Julia Kuehn and Paul Smethurst (Basingstoke: Palgrave Macmillan, 2015), 1.

3 Peter Hulme, *Colonial Encounters: Europe and the Native Caribbean 1492–1797* (London: Methuen, 1986); Edward W. Said, *Orientalism* (London: Routledge & Kegan Paul, 1978).

4 Charles Forsdick, Corinne Fowler and Ludmilla Kostova, 'Introduction: Ethics on the Move', in *Travel and Ethics: Theory and Practice*, ed. Corinne Fowler, Charles Forsdick and Ludmilla Kostova (New York: Routledge, 2014), 1.

5 Julia Kuehn and Paul Smethurst, eds, *New Directions in Travel Writing Studies* (Basingstoke: Palgrave Macmillan, 2015). Of course, it is in the nature of much academic work that it should remark on its connections with and departure from precursors, but the similarity between the narrators of several travel texts and several critical works on those texts appears very close in this regard.

6 Both quotations are from Carl Thompson, 'Introduction', in *The Routledge Companion to Travel Writing*, ed. Carl Thompson (Abingdon: Routledge, 2016), xvi. (The present volume was commissioned by Ashgate as the *Ashgate Research Companion to Travel Writing* but retitled by the publisher following Routledge's takeover of Ashgate.)

7 Thompson, 'Introduction', xix. Cf. Kuehn and Smethurst's '[t]his is not, and could not be, a complete survey of theoretical/thematic approaches', Kuehn and Smethurst, 'Introduction', 3; Martin and Pickford's 'No single work can hope to offer a comprehensive account of the translation, circulation, and consumption of non-fictional travel writing in late eighteenth- and early nineteenth-century Europe', Alison E. Martin and Susan Pickford, 'Introduction', in *Travel Narratives in Translation, 1750–1830: Nationalism, Ideology, Gender*, ed. Alison E. Martin and Susan Pickford (New York: Routledge, 2012), 8; and Crowley, Humble and Ross's 'This collection aims to analyse a range of texts that involve travel and intercultural reflection and that are representative of different periods and locations across the Mediterranean. No attempt is made to anthologize or supply an exhaustive overview, instead this volume [on Mediterranean travels] seeks to furnish comparative contexts that might contribute to further debate within the field of travel studies', Patrick Crowley, Noreen Humble and Silvia Ross, 'Introduction: The Mediterranean Turn', in *Mediterranean Travels: Writing Self and Other from the Ancient World to Contemporary Society*, ed. Patrick Crowley, Noreen Humble and Silvia Ross (London: Modern Humanities Research Association and Maney Publishing, 2011), 4–5. Such caveats may be seen to echo travellers' comments on the limitations of their narratives.

8 Thompson, 'Introduction', xix–xx. Cf. Kuehn and Smethurst's announcement that their volume 'augments and complements' regional and historical surveys, 'author-based approaches', 'collections organized around particular themes or sub-genres' and 'companions, handbooks and introductions' as well as being 'intended to provide a theoretical touchstone for further travel-related criticism' (2); and Martin and Pickford's 'aim to stimulate further research in the area of non-fictional travel writing in translation that will open up new and exciting perspectives both for scholars of Travel Writing and Translation Studies' (8).

9 Martin and Pickford, 'Introduction', 1–2.

10 James Duncan and Derek Gregory, 'Introduction', in *Writes of Passage: Reading Travel Writing*, ed. James Duncan and Derek Gregory (London: Routledge, 1999), 4.

11 Duncan and Gregory, 'Introduction', 5.

12 Duncan and Gregory, 'Introduction', 5.

13 Duncan and Gregory, 'Introduction', 5.

14 Gary Totten, *African American Travel Narratives from Abroad: Mobility and Cultural Work in the Age of Jim Crow* (Amherst, MA: University of Massachusetts Press, 2015), 5.

15 Raphael Kadushin, 'Introduction', in *Wonderlands: Good Gay Travel Writing* (Madison, WI: The University of Wisconsin Press, 2004), 5. Kadushin's laudable aim is to show writers 'not conforming to any defined style' and 'leap[ing] boundaries' (5). For an example of a critical work that focuses on travel in fiction see Alexandra Peat, *Travel and Modernist Literature: Sacred and Ethical Journeys* (New York: Routledge, 2011).

16 Kuehn and Smethurst, 'Introduction', 1–2, 1. See also Tim Youngs, 'Where Are We Going? Cross-Border Approaches to Travel Writing', in *Perspectives on Travel Writing*, ed. Glenn Hooper and Tim Youngs (Aldershot: Ashgate, 2004), 175–78.

17 Jaś Elsner and Joan Pau Rubiés, 'Introduction', in *Voyages and Visions: Towards a Cultural History of Travel*, ed. Jaś Elsner and Joan Pau Rubiés (London: Reaktion, 1999), 4.

18 Mary Louise Pratt, *Imperial Eyes: Travel Writing and Transculturation* (London: Routledge, 1992), 7. Unless quoting from US publications we use British English spelling for this and other terms.

19 Peter Hulme and Tim Youngs, *Talking about Travel Writing: A Conversation between Peter Hulme and Tim Youngs* (Leicester: English Association, 2007), 3.

20 Veit Erlmann, 'But What of the Ethnographic Ear? Anthropology, Sound, and the Senses', in *Hearing Cultures: Essays on Sound, Listening, and Modernity*, ed. Veit Erlmann (Oxford: Berg, 2004), 4.

21 For more on these, see for example Thompson, *The Routledge Companion to Travel Writing* and Nandini Das and Tim Youngs, eds, *The Cambridge History of Travel Writing* (Cambridge: Cambridge University Press, 2019).

22 Ottmar Ette, *Literature on the Move*, trans. Katharina Vester (Amsterdam: Rodopi, 2003), 10.

23 Forsdick, Fowler and Kostova, 'Introduction', 7.

24 Forsdick, Fowler and Kostova, 'Introduction', 3.

25 *Panorama: The Journal of Intelligent Travel*, accessed 11 May 2018, www.panoramajournal.org/mission.

PART I

Framing travel

1

THE SCIENTIFIC TRAVELLER

Angela Byrne

This chapter discusses the role of natural history and the sciences in travel and exploration, before responding in more detail to the themes of interactions between the local and the global, and the significance of gender. The term 'scientific traveller' is used here in a broad sense, to refer to any travellers or explorers with an evident interest in gathering and disseminating scientific information. I emphasise the status of their travel as a scientific activity, and of their travel accounts as scientific discourse. Recognition of these factors may deepen our understanding of the ways in which women and outsiders participated in the sciences in the eighteenth and nineteenth centuries, following Carl Thompson's important reappraisal of the travel writer Maria Graham as not just 'a scrupulous eye-witness' but rather as a serious contributor to scientific knowledge.[1]

This chapter focuses on the mid-eighteenth to mid-nineteenth centuries, a period of rapid European acquisition of new global knowledge. All over the world, specimens were collected, maps made and temperatures tabulated, all for publication, communication and display to a European public eager for new and exciting details. While the connection between natural history and empire stretches back to the seventeenth century, the figure of the 'scientific traveller' is bound together with the intellectual, imperial and cultural contexts of late eighteenth-century European exploration.[2] Scientific travel was fundamental to European imperialism and the acquisition of colonies in the period 1760–1850. In 1768–9, international teams of scientists travelled from several countries to Tahiti, Baja (California), Hudson Bay and St Petersburg to observe the Transit of Venus, a rare astronomical event with the potential to assist calculations of the distance between Earth and the sun and the size of the solar system. The period saw the initiation of the large-scale, state-sponsored scientific expedition with Cook's Pacific voyages (the *Endeavour*, 1768; the *Resolution* and *Adventure*, 1772–5; the *Resolution*, 1776–80) and the publication of their 'discoveries' of unfamiliar animals like the kangaroo.[3] The expedition also, of course, launched its botanist, Joseph Banks, as one of Britain's pre-eminent gentlemen of science.[4] Of the first expedition, to witness the Transit of Venus at Tahiti, one Royal Society fellow noted, 'No people ever went to sea better fitted out for the purposes of Natural History.'[5] Around the same time, Hudson's Bay Company (HBC) fur traders in Rupert's Land (Canada) communicated their findings on the geography and natural history of the sub-Arctic.[6] By 1798, the hydrographer George Vancouver (1757–98) would remark, 'Although the ardour of the present age, to discover and delineate the true geography of the earth, had been rewarded with uncommon and unexpected success [. . .] yet not all was completed.'[7] Research continued in the early nineteenth century with Alexander von Humboldt's excursions, which were published as *Travels to the Equinoctial Regions . . . 1799–1804* (1819–29), receiving great attention and laying the foundations for his career as the eminent naturalist of the age. Almost contemporaneous were Mungo Park's excursions into West Africa to ascertain the source and course of the Niger in 1795–7 and 1805–6; his account of the first expedition was a bestseller.[8] In the 1810s, the much-lauded British Arctic expeditions of 1818–45 were foregrounded by the pioneering meteorological and oceanographic observations of the whaler and scientist William Scoresby the younger (1789–1857). Michael Bravo has demonstrated how Scoresby, despite participating in the sciences by collecting specimens while engaged in a private whaling enterprise and the recognition his studies in natural history earned in French circles, was viewed as a mere 'accomplished artisan' by the Royal Navy.[9] James Cook and Joseph Banks are the subjects of so many studies that they have assumed the status of canonical scientific travellers, despite Cook's lack of a formal education. This chapter focuses on the less popularly known but no less important figures of Thomas Pennant and Sarah Bowdich, demonstrating that the category 'scientific traveller' admits a broad range of participants. The focus here on the eighteenth and nineteenth centuries reflects the intersections of European imperial and territorial expansion, romantic fascination with extreme climates and indigenous peoples, and the interdependency of scientific activity and travel.

Empire and scientific travel

As indicated in the introduction above, empire forms the cultural, social and intellectual backdrop to the activities studied in this chapter and the dominant critical frameworks employed in their study. Late nineteenth-century European high imperialism was foreshadowed by learned societies' privately sponsored expeditions, such as the African Association's searches for the sources of the Nile and Niger rivers, and competitive, ill-prepared expeditions in the Australian interior prompted by inter-settler colony rivalries, like Robert O'Hara Burke and William Will's infamous 'dash for Carpentaria' in 1860–1. These expeditions cemented intersections of national pride, imperial expansion and international trade. While contemporaries idealised scientific travel as disinterested, it was crucial to the delineation, control and exploitation of colonial territories.[10]

In the latter decades of the twentieth century, postcolonial approaches offered fresh critiques of the imperial contexts within which scientific travellers, their research and their writings functioned. Edward Said's *Orientalism* (1978) and Mary Louise Pratt's concept of the 'contact zone' have provided the basis for the dominant analytical frameworks for the study of travel and exploration in broad terms since the 1980s and 1990s.[11] Similarly, Pratt's vision of natural history as fundamental to the acquisition of colonies has been hugely influential as a framework for studying the links between natural history, travel narratives and an imperial, systemising vision of nature. Pratt demonstrates how:

> Like the rise of interior exploration, the systematic surface mapping of the globe correlates with an expanding search for commercially exploitable resources, markets, and lands to colonize [. . .] It is not, then, simply a question of depicting the planet as it was.[12]

The political uses and imperial imperatives underpinning mapping and surveying projects around the globe have been particularly effectively demonstrated.[13]

Since the late 1990s, scholarship has to a large extent turned towards examining the intellectual frameworks that underpinned and sustained Europe and North America's expanding empires in the eighteenth and nineteenth centuries. Global knowledge networks emerged as far-flung naturalists communicated their findings to centralised repositories in state and university botanic gardens.[14] Conceptualisation of the dynamic operations of these networks that emerged from the intersections of science, exploration and empire is largely indebted to Bruno Latour's vision of natural history as a means of shipping things (specimens, records, drawings) back to the 'centres of calculation' where power and knowledge reside.[15] This transmission of observations and specimens made colonial natural history 'a world-making activity, which mediated colonial natures through their more portable forms'.[16] Through sustained critical engagement with Pratt's and Latour's frameworks, a rich picture has emerged of transnational scientific networks mediated through learned societies, institutions and individuals located in European centres – such as the collections amassed at the British Museum and the Royal Botanic Gardens at Kew through Joseph Banks's tireless promotion of colonial science, and his use of his own network to expand the museum's collections[17] – as well as satellite nodes dotted around the imperial world. This is also exemplified in the work of Thomas Pennant, discussed in detail below. The notion of circulation has extended to the transformative power of interactions across different locations, and has itself come to be considered a type of production, taking such forms as local (re)appropriation.[18] Raposo, Simões, Patiniotis and Bertomeu-Sánchez have usefully framed eighteenth- and nineteenth-century Greek, Portuguese and Spanish scientific travellers in terms of 'moving localities', arguing that these travellers were *of* Europe and retained an eye on Europe, but functioned through mobile and responsive 'connections, allegiances and commitments' that travelled with them and created mobile intellectual spaces.[19]

Environmental history and ecocriticism have, since the 2000s, begun to uncover the role of travel and exploration in the elaboration of what is now known as environmental consciousness and ecological thought. In a two-part 2006 article, Richard Grove and Vinita Damoradan provided a detailed outline of the long history of global environmental history.[20] Richard Grove's *Green Imperialism* (1996) memorably traced these developments to the observations of travelling naturalists like Johann Reinhold Forster (1729–98), whose observations during the *Resolution* voyage of 1772–5 demonstrate a clear vision of human agency over climatic and ecological conditions, particularly the impact of Europeans on South Pacific island ecology. Specifically, Forster was concerned about the potential climatic impact of any deforestation on Tahiti, as without the protection of the thick tree cover the soil would be exposed to the heat of the tropical sun.[21] Most famously, Alexander von Humboldt elucidated a vision of interdependent and interlinking organisms and habitats that would revolutionise scientific understanding of the interconnected lives of humans, animals, plants and geological matter. His exposition of the climatic influence of altitude (rather than latitude) also fundamentally altered understandings of climate, meteorology and plant and animal biology, displacing eighteenth-century theories like the French naturalist Comte de Buffon's that had connected climate to culture based on a north–south dichotomy. The global, comparative vision employed by travelling scientists was made possible by their exposure to and rigorous observation of natural phenomena, geological features and the circumstances of existence of all forms of life, in a variety of environments.[22]

Scientific travel has played a key role in the history of Western science itself, as important conceptual breakthroughs arose from observations made on expeditions. The Swedish botanist Carl Linnaeus's (1707–78) revolutionary method of plant identification was translatable and transferable for use in any colonial or imperial territory. Delineated in his *Systema Naturae* (1735), it provided a methodological basis for the twenty or so 'apostles' who emulated the mode of scientific travelling Linnaeus practised in Scandinavia in 1732.[23] These 'apostles' included Daniel Solander (1733–82) and Anders Sparrman (1748–1820), who travelled on Cook's first and second Pacific expeditions respectively. Scientific travel accounts of 'new' lands had a lasting impact on British literary culture, with exciting accounts of 'new plants, new animals, and new men' prompting fresh literary – and, as demonstrated in the following section, scientific – responses to domestic nature.[24]

Domestic scientific travel in Britain

The global knowledge generated by imperial science informed the emerging genre of domestic British scientific description from the 1770s, exemplified in the publications of the Welsh-born naturalist Thomas Pennant (1726–98).[25] While he never travelled to India or the Arctic, his *Indian Zoology* (1769) – the first natural history of India published in English – and *Arctic Zoology* (1784) were masterful syntheses of the most up-to-date accounts of European colonial acquisitions, rendered comprehensible and meaningful across diverse regions through the unifying language of the Linnaean taxonomy. In the same way that Comte de Buffon compiled his encyclopaedic thirty-six-volume *Histoire naturelle* (1749–88), Pennant received detailed accounts of the latest discoveries from global informants. *Arctic Zoology* incorporated the observations of the naturalist and Hudson's Bay Company fur trader Samuel Hearne (1745–92), whom Pennant met in England in the winter of 1782–3; this, however, did not prevent Hearne from alerting readers of his *A Journey from Prince of Wales's Fort in Hudson's Bay to the Northern Ocean* (1795) to an error in Pennant's *Arctic Zoology*.[26] Andrew Graham (*c.* 1733–1815), also a naturalist and Hudson's Bay Company fur trader, sent specimens and information on new fish species to the eminent naturalist Johann Reinhold Forster (1729–98), evidently just before the latter's engagement to Cook's second Pacific expedition in 1772–5; Forster then published the information in the form of a letter to Pennant, supported by the scientific apparatus of detailed illustrations and a Latin written description.[27]

Pennant initially conceived *Arctic Zoology* as a North American zoology, but the loss of the American colonies (he referred to the new United States as a 'mortifying sight', 1:cc) together with the new information gathered by Cook, by fur traders in North America, and by the German botanist Peter Simon Pallas in Siberia (1768–74), convinced him to reconceptualise the work in a broader way.[28] The result was a dynamic vision of northern (not only Arctic) animal and human life, a vision that transcended national borders. Pennant pointed to the tides that connected Iceland with Europe and North America, bringing driftwood to the isolated island's shores (1:xliv); the migrations and movements of peoples and animals that transformed the environmental and cultural characteristics of the region (1:xlii–xliii, l–li); and the trade winds and Gulf Stream that deposit exotic fruits, seeds and leaves on Europe's northwestern shore (1:xlix). Pennant introduced his book as a 'voyage' through the region, a concept carried through to his emphasis on the importance of European exploratory and scientific expeditions as sources: 'the fruits of their labors have been liberally communicated to a public thirsting for knowledge. The[ir] names [. . .] will ever be held in respect, for adding to the stock of natural knowledge' (1:cxiv). Throughout, the reader is guided around each continent by celebrated explorers; the existence of new lands and new species comes second to the celebration of their discovery. The intersections of time, space and experience are carried through the book in Pennant's rich cross-references to his other publications, the whole forming an interdependent assemblage.[29]

Pennant placed Britain's northern fringe – the Scottish coast and islands, and the northern Irish coast – within the broader, global context of imperial science, revealing the region in a new light. Unlike *Indian Zoology* (1769) and *Arctic Zoology* (1784), his *A Tour in Scotland* (1771) and *A Tour in Scotland and Voyage to the Hebrides* (1774) were based on his own observations made during two tours of Scotland in 1769 and 1772. Having previously toured the Continent, he decided to become better acquainted with Britain. In the preface to the first edition of *A Tour in Scotland*, he compared himself to a literary figure who 'discovered that in order to see a country to best advantage it was infinitely preferable to travel by day than by night', shining the light of his scientific eye on the landscape of North Britain.[30]

Pennant's respect for, and extensive use of, on-the-spot observations made by residents in and travellers to the Arctic and India was also a feature of his books on Scotland, in which he drew on valuable, previously untapped fonts of local information on natural history and antiquities. The *Tour in Scotland*, his account of his first tour made in June–September 1769, teems with detail and is characteristic of the antiquarian–scientific tour of the age. It juxtaposes descriptions of country seats and their art collections, agricultural prices and an eye for landscape honed on Burke's prescription of the sublime and the beautiful, and William Gilpin's definition of the picturesque. The entrance to the Highlands was 'awefully [sic] magnificent; high, craggy, and often naked mountains', and nearby Dunkeld offered gardens with 'the most beautifull [sic] and picturesque views of wild and gloomy nature that can be conceived' (74–5). The narrative is enriched with observations on Highland culture and everyday life, expert descriptions, illustrations and lists of flora and fauna, and geological detail. Much of what he observed he treated as 'curiosities'; for instance, a 'very singular phenomenon' related to him by 'some very intelligent fishermen' at Scarborough, whereby fish spawning rendered the water 'saturated with a thick jelly' (20). He was precise in crediting his sources, and took care to prove his account authentic and reliable by, for example, alerting the reader to the fact that his accounts of Highland rituals were 'communicated to [him] by gentlemen resident on the spot where they were performed' (90).

Pennant's second tour of Scotland, encompassing the Hebrides as well as the Scottish mainland and undertaken in May–October 1772, makes more claims to the status of a scientific tour. On this occasion, his tour resembled a mini-expedition, accompanied as he was by the Gaelic scholar Reverend John Stuart (1743–1821) and the botanist John Lightfoot (1735–88; Lightfoot would in 1773 accompany Banks on a botanical tour of Wales). The resultant two-volume *A Tour in Scotland and Voyage to the Hebrides* was dedicated to Banks, to whom Pennant expressed his gratitude for 'making [him] the vehicle for conveying to the public the rich discovery of your last voyage'. This is a reference to Banks having granted Pennant permission to publish for the first time Banks's observations on the striking basalt columns at Staffa, incidentally also taken in 1772, in August.[31] (Pennant himself was prevented from recording detailed observations at Staffa due to rough seas.) Impressionistic illustrations of the scene, produced from sketches supplied by Banks, are also included (vol. I, facing pp. 304, 305). The book is the result of a collaborative effort between naturalists with local and global expertise. It also directs readers to Pennant's previous publications, especially *British Zoology* (1768–70) (e.g., 1:217, 227, 314).

Pennant's Scottish volumes were epistemologically grounded in, and had at their heart, well-established principles of statistical enquiry. He used a seventy-two-point questionnaire to gather information on Scotland's place names, history and antiquities, local customs, industry and trade, topography, geology, and natural resources from local landowners and clergy. The questions were circulated in advance of Pennant's first tour 'with a view of exciting them to favor the World with a fuller and more satisfactory Account of their Country, than it is in the Power of a Stranger and transient Visitant to give' (287–98). In the spirit of disinterestedness, and possibly in the hope of encouraging others to complete similar surveys, Pennant's list of queries was published as an appendix to *A Tour in Scotland*, but he neglected to mention in the book's first edition that his questionnaire was based on one previously published by James Theobald of the Royal Society of Antiquaries in 1754.[32] This slip aside, as Adam Fox notes, the collaborative nature of such questionnaires was an important facet of 'scientific antiquarianism' from the late sixteenth century onwards.[33] Furthermore, David Livingstone has demonstrated how the practice of providing 'heads' or guiding questions was one means of guaranteeing the quality of the information provided, and the trustworthiness of the observer.[34]

Pennant published advertisements in Scottish newspapers in advance of his second tour, requesting that locals bring to his attention sites and sights of note.[35] This seems to have invited a wider range of informants than the circulars that had been addressed to landowners and clergy three years previously. Throughout, *The Tour in Scotland* contains repeated use of the phrases, 'I was informed' and 'I was told', while the *Tour in Scotland and Voyage to the Hebrides* contains more precise references to named informants. These include the Carlisle MP and antiquary Humphrey Senhouse (?1731–1814); Norman MacLeod of Dunvegan, chief of clan MacLeod (1705–72); a schoolmaster at Comrie named MacNab; the historian and classicist John Gillies of Brechin (1747–1836); one Gillander, agent on the Isle of Lewis; and the print collector and biographer Rev. James Granger (1723–76), to 'whose liberal disposition' Pennant acknowledged himself 'often indebted'.[36] Pennant also acknowledged John Stuart's contribution to the book's treatment of Erse language and Highland and island traditions.[37] The preface or 'advertisement' to his *Tour in Scotland and Voyage to the Hebrides* listed, from south to north, seventeen local informants who 'favored me at different times with accounts and little histories of the places of their residence, or their environs'.[38] Seven of the twenty appendices to the book were copies of communications from local residents, including John Maxwell of Broomholme, Thomas Marshall of Perth, Rev. George Rainy of Kincardine and Rev. Donald MacQueen of Kilmuir. In *The Tour in Scotland*, Pennant explained his rationale for reproducing such communications: 'As I am unable to satisfy the curiosity of the Reader from my own observation, I shall deliver in the Appendix the informations I could collect.'[39]

Sensitivity to the local is central to Pennant's experience and scientific interpretation of Scotland and the Hebrides. His interest in the local is embedded in his project from the outset, through his employment of the questionnaire and the open invitation to contribute. With his focus on 'the particularity of nature and with individual identity', Pennant's published accounts embody Romantic science, which was itself a response to the literary and aesthetic concerns of the late eighteenth and early nineteenth centuries.[40] Paul Smethurst has demonstrated how Pennant's contribution to the genres of scientific travel writing and domestic British travel writing lies in his reproduction of the natural world as 'an abstract spatiality' that brought 'disparate identities and topographies into a common imaginative frame', unifying Scotland and the rest of Britain by seeking out a shared history, integrating the fragments of the Scottish past into a larger British narrative.[41] Furthermore, Pennant's attention to the local enabled him to grant agency to traditional ways of knowing in the form of local landscape mythologies that were used for generations to explain unusual or prominent topographical features. For example, he reports that local tradition in Argyleshire holds that

> a deep circular hollow, in the form and size of a large cauldron [. . .] was one of the vatts frequent in the highland turberies, from which the old natives drew an unctuous substance, used by them to dye their cloth black

and mentions 'the tradition of its [Killin] having been the burial place of Fingal'.[42] As an expression of British history and natural history, Pennant's domestic travels in Scotland and Wales form one of the most important interventions of the age, not least for the variety of contributors who helped to shape them.

Scientific travelling women

The development of travel writing – one of the most published genres in English in the eighteenth century – for and by women is well known.[43] In brief, women were prolific travellers and travel writers, forming an important constituency of production and consumption in the very popular literary and scientific genre of travel writing. Women made important contributions to geographical knowledge by publishing travelogues, geographies and geographical primers in an international and intergenerational current of knowledge exchange. This occurred during a period in which travel became synonymous with the advancement of scientific knowledge. Travel enabled women to undertake fieldwork, to infiltrate and create scientific networks, to construct and maintain learned identities, and to publish their findings in a format and genre that admitted both personal and empirical observations, operating within the *habitus* of what Alice Walters has termed 'polite science'. Characterised by conversation – and, I would add, epistolary and associational sociability – polite science is essential to understanding the means by which eighteenth- and nineteenth-century women 'locate[d] and legitimize[d] scientific discourse within polite society', and helps to locate the contributions of women whose work does not conform to twentieth- and twenty-first-century general ideas of what science 'really' was or is.[44]

There is truth in Pratt's assessment of nineteenth-century natural history as the assertion of 'an urban, lettered, male authority over the whole of the planet'.[45] However, until recently, the assumption of women's exclusion from imperial activities and from the sciences effectively sidelined all but a minority of so-called 'exceptional' women from historical studies. There has been a welcome and overdue rehabilitation of women's contributions to the sciences, particularly in the eighteenth and nineteenth centuries. The persistent notion that women were unable to contribute and participate in travel and in the sciences – or that they were unwilling to, due to conventions of modesty and privacy – has been challenged by women's history and feminist history since the 1980s.[46] With the development of a more holistic view of what constituted 'science' in the past, including the roles played by outsider collectors, observers and writers, there is growing acknowledgement of women's gathering, production and dissemination of scientific knowledge in the eighteenth and nineteenth centuries.

Sarah Bowdich's West African travels and ichthyology are an exemplar of women's agency in scientific travel and publishing, and the ways in which scientific travel provided a means for women to negotiate institutional and socio-cultural barriers and give voice to their work and experiences. Mary Orr's work has rehabilitated Bowdich's published contributions to ichthyology, geology and scientific biography, and has reconstructed her international scientific networks.[47] Bowdich and her husband Edward collaborated with Georges Cuvier (1769–1832) at the Jardin des Plantes in Paris in 1819–22, where a number of women were employed as assistants, and Sarah had a lifelong friendship with Cuvier.[48] Bowdich packaged her account of her and her husband's journey – published after Edward's death from fever during the expedition – as an edition of Edward's scientific observations and travel narrative, prioritising his 'excursions' in the title. However, she made substantial contributions to the work as the narrator of the journey from Madeira to the River Gambia, and she sketched, on the spot, almost all of the volume's geological plates and illustrations.[49] She dedicated the book to Earl Bathurst in the hope that it counted among the 'attempts towards the extension of general knowledge' that he encouraged (iii). The book intertwines narrative and scientific information – for example, her entertaining account of the chaotic mode of living at the slave trader Manoel Martin's crowded house on Boa Vista, Cape Verde Islands (180–8), shortly followed by her description of the island's geology and an account of her attempts to gather specimens (189–90) – with botanical, entomological and linguistic appendices, all compiled by Bowdich herself. In The Gambia, she found the new settlement of McCarthy (now Janjanbureh) 'a very desirable residence for the scientific traveller, who would there be able to form some rich collections, and make some very valuable observations on an unknown part of Africa' (206). She compiled detailed zoological lists, including dozens of 'new species' that she positively claimed as her own discoveries, and attempted to identify a previously unknown mammal, 'a very interesting little beast' (221–31). The figures, drawn by her own skilled hand, included a 'Crab, or new species of Planes' (15, facing 16). Her authority is further asserted in her references to an array of scholarship, including the works of renowned naturalists, such as Pierre Joseph Bonnaterre (e.g., 123), the botanist and East India Company surgeon Francis Hamilton (121), Karl Ludwig von Willdenow (267) and of course Cuvier. Her appendices are detailed, based on meticulous scholarship and research, but she qualified her discoveries with the postscript: 'I presume that some of the above species have never yet been discovered, but I by no means flatter myself with having made any very important discoveries' (231). Later, she was more forthright:

> With regard to those [specimens] which I profess to have determined, I offer them with some degree of confidence, for, since my return, I have re-examined my notes, and the remnants of my specimens, amid the collection in the Jardin du Roi, and have scarcely had a single instance to alter.
>
> *(266–7)*

Sarah Bowdich's subversive manipulation of the 'modesty topos' – the means by which travel writers commonly apologised to their readers for lacking the skills that their books actually demonstrated – functioned within the text to grant her agency and authority in her own right. Mary Orr has demonstrated how,

> [d]espite the mock-humility in Bowdich's appeal to her readers, the Gambia section is where the range of her scientific knowledge, interests, and expertise is most fully apparent and where she is keenest to contribute to the forefront of European scientific knowledge.[50]

Bowdich's subsequent publications (under the name Mrs Robert Lee, after her second marriage) referred back to her experiences in West Africa. *Elements of Natural History* (1844) directly references her observations in The Gambia, and in *Trees, Plants, and Flowers* (1854), she stated that '[v]ery little idea of the abundance of [fossilised] vegetation can be formed, unless the reader should have visited equatorial regions'. Her collection of tales for children, *Stories of Strange Lands; and Fragments from the Notes of a Traveller* (1835), combined tales of Gambian life and customs with her deep knowledge of the region expressed in detailed footnotes occupying 96 of the book's 367 pages.[51]

Sarah Bowdich's continued absence from the canon of 'great' scientific travellers may be explained by the appeal and simplicity of more straightforward 'uncluttered tales of heroic accomplishment', like the lives of Cook or Darwin.[52] In other words, long-standing institutional and cultural blocks to women's participation in the sciences, travel and exploration veiled their contributions, as they were forced to employ what Orr terms 'tactics of survival' such as the use of a male pseudonym or husband's name.[53] The silencing of Sarah's voice arguably began with Edward's 'Sketch of Gaboon, and Its Interior', his account of his first mission in 1815–18.[54] Even though Sarah joined him there with their infant daughter in 1816, her presence is not recorded. All of Edward's experiences and observations are related in the first-person singular, even though Sarah's *Stories of Strange Lands* evinces that she was present. While hardly to the forefront of the book, the depth of her engagement with West African life and customs is also attested in the *Excursions*, particularly in her references to traditional medicine (250, 254, 267) as complementary to the catalogues of flora and fauna she compiled for the region. By contrast with Pennant, however, the *Excursions* contains little reference to information gathered from local informants. One explanation lies in her account of the people of the region (207–12), which demonstrates her disdain for local customs, and for some groups of people. A second explanation lies in her own admission that she could not afford to pay 'the fishermen and peasantry to bring me specimens of all the fishes, birds, &c., they knew, or might meet with' and that 'no museum had furnished me with spirits and cases to preserve them [specimens] in' (121). Finally, while not usurping all references to the vernacular, her self-assertion as an expert privileged metropolitan European ways of knowing.

Conclusions

The sciences operated, until the mid-nineteenth century, not in the vacuum of the laboratory, but 'in the field' – informed and inspired by direct experience. On-the-spot observation was key. Scientific travellers like Sarah Bowdich and Thomas Pennant knew this, and they understood the necessity of developing new methodologies to maximise knowledge gathering and production in response to local contingencies. Ichthyology demanded rapid and accurate recording of the specimen from the instant of its extraction from the water, with only moments to spare before the colour of the fish deteriorated. In response, Bowdich devised techniques to make records with accuracy and speed on the riverbanks of England and of West Africa. The same diligence and commitment to the field are evident in her remarkably fast production of her and her husband's observations on Madeira and The Gambia – completed in just one month – and in her hand-painting of all fifty copies of *Fresh-Water Fishes of Great Britain* (1828–38). It is possibly a little better known that Mary Kingsley returned from her second African expedition in December 1894 to November 1895 with specimens of eighteen new species of reptile and sixty-five of fish, three of which were named after her.[55] Bowdich, and dozens of other nineteenth-century women – like the plant hunter and botanic illustrator Charlotte Wheeler Cuffe, who identified three new plant species in the mountains of Burma; the Anglo-Canadian popular natural history writer for children and adults, Catherine Parr Traill; and the translator Elizabeth Helme – demonstrate the extent to which travel and travel writing offered a vital avenue for participation in and contribution to the sciences.[56]

Interactions between the global and the local were central to the exercise of scientific travel from the 1770s onwards. The roles of empire and networks in scientific travel having been well studied, one of the next challenges is to further develop a more meaningful scholarly engagement with the ways in which European observers integrated traditional ways of knowing into their work[57] – that is, to do more than simply chart any overt references to traditional knowledge, and to conceive of knowledge as the product of the 'contact zone', as something not just translated or communicated, but as a fluid entity. Thomas Pennant set out to record observations on Scottish geology and antiquities, but was unable to do so without reference to local mythologies. He recorded such information along with assurances to the reader that they were mere superstitions, but he still included in his published texts tales like that of a hag who was exorcised from the Highland moors near Arnisdale.[58] That his text swells with his retelling of those stories does not dilute its scientific value, but rather emphasises the extent to which his exposure to the local in Scotland and the Hebrides transformed his experience and understanding of the natural world into one that was richer, more compelling and more relevant to the circumstances of life in that locality. By contrast, and as discussed above, Bowdich appears to have relied less on local informants, with her text emphasising the collection and identification of new species as part of the construction of her scientific self.

The figure of the scientific traveller embodies many of the contradictions inherent in eighteenth- and nineteenth-century travel accounts themselves. They looked simultaneously towards the local contingencies that made the gathering of new knowledge possible and to the imperatives imposed by the metropolitan audience and epistemological context. Scientific travellers were mediators – of forms of knowledge, of cultures, of language and expression – who spoke to and wrote for both 'professionals' in the sciences and outsiders and, most especially, whose words and illustrations mediated between the human and natural world. Ruth Barton has demonstrated how 'amateur status did not imply inferior science' (until the twentieth century), an important reminder of the value of the assemblages of information produced by scientific travellers like Pennant and Bowdich, who operated as part of local and global networks.[59] Their deep understanding and direct experience of life in all its forms, in all kinds of environments, made their travel accounts both scientifically valuable and masterful literary texts.

Notes

1   Carl Thompson, 'Earthquakes and Petticoats: Maria Graham, Geology, and Early Nineteenth-Century "Polite" Science', *Journal of Victorian Culture* 17.3 (2012): 329–46. The term outsider is used here in preference to 'amateur', which is open to misapplication and misinterpretation; see H.S. Torrens, 'Notes on "The Amateur" in the Development of British Geology', *Proceedings of the Geologists' Association* 117 (2006): 1–8.

2   See Sarah Irving, *Natural Science and the Origins of the British Empire* (London: Pickering and Chatto, 2008).

3   The literature on Cook's voyages is extensive; for contrasting viewpoints, see Gananath Obeyesekere, *The Apotheosis of Captain Cook: European Mythmaking in the Pacific* (Princeton, NJ: Princeton University Press, 1992) and Marshall Sahlins, *How 'Natives' Think: About Captain Cook, for Example* (Chicago, IL: University of Chicago Press, 1995).

4   Neil Chambers (ed.), *The Scientific Correspondence of Sir Joseph Banks, 1765–1820*, 6 vols (London: Pickering and Chatto, 2007).

5   Quoted in J.C. Beaglehole, *The Life of Captain James Cook* (Stanford, CA: Stanford University Press, 1974), 146.

6   See Angela Byrne, 'Scientific Practice and the Scientific Self in Rupert's Land, c. 1770–1830: Fur Trade Networks of Knowledge Exchange', in *Spaces of Global Knowledge: Exhibition, Encounter and Exchange in an Age of Empire*, ed. Diarmid A. Finnegan and Jonathan J. Wright (Aldershot: Ashgate, 2015), 79–95.

7   George Vancouver, *A Voyage of Discovery to the North Pacific Ocean, and Round the World* (London: G. G. and J. Robinson, 1798), 1:vii.

8   Mungo Park, *Travels in the Interior Districts of Africa: Performed under the Direction and Patronage of the African Association, in the Years 1795, 1796, and 1797* (London: W. Bulmer and Co., for the author, 1799).

9   Michael Bravo, 'Geographies of Exploration and Improvement: William Scoresby and Arctic Whaling, 1782–1822', *Journal of Historical Geography* 32.3 (2006): 512–38.

10 As Deborah Allen states, Jefferson for one was 'keenly aware that European sponsors of exploratory expeditions used the disinterested language of science in order to conceal the extent to which these ventures were driven by a political and commercial agenda'. Deborah Allen, 'Acquiring "Knowledge of Our Own Continent": Geopolitics, Science, and Jeffersonian Geography, 1783–1803', *Journal of American Studies* 40.2 (2006): 210. Mary Louise Pratt also notes: 'On the one hand, dominant ideologies made a clear distinction between the (interested) pursuit of wealth and the (disinterested) pursuit of knowledge; on the other hand, competition among nations continued to be the fuel for European expansion abroad.' Mary Louise Pratt, *Imperial Eyes: Travel Writing and Transculturation* (London: Routledge, 1992), 18.

11 Edward Said, *Orientalism* (London: Routledge & Kegan Paul, 1978); Pratt, *Imperial Eyes*.

12 Pratt, *Imperial Eyes*, 30; for more, see chapter 2, 'Science, Planetary Consciousness, Interiors' (15–37).

13 See Deepak Kumar, 'The Evolution of Colonial Science in India: Natural History and the East India Company', in *Imperialism and the Natural World*, ed. John M. MacKenzie (Manchester: Manchester

University Press, 1990), 51–66; M.H. Edney, *Mapping an Empire: The Geographical Construction of British India, 1765–1843* (Chicago, IL: Chicago University Press, 1997); Suzanne Zeller, *Inventing Canada: Early Victorian Science and the Idea of a Transcontinental Nation* (Toronto: University of Toronto Press, 1987).

14 See Joseph Gascoigne, *Science in the Service of Empire: Joseph Banks, the British State and the Uses of Science in the Age of Revolution* (Cambridge: Cambridge University Press, 1998).

15 Bruno Latour, *Science in Action: How to Follow Scientists and Engineers through Society* (Cambridge, MA: Harvard University Press, 1987).

16 Alan Bewell, 'Romanticism and Colonial Natural History', *Studies in Romanticism* 43.1 (2004): 17.

17 See Neil Chambers, *Joseph Banks and the British Museum: The World of Collecting, 1770–1830* (London: Pickering and Chatto, 2007).

18 See Lissa Roberts, 'Situating Science in Global History: Local Exchanges and Networks of Circulation', *Itinerario* 33.1 (2009): 9–30; Kapil Raj, *Relocating Modern Science: Circulation and the Construction of Knowledge in South Asia and Europe 1650–1900* (Basingstoke: Palgrave Macmillan, 2007).

19 Pedro M.P. Raposo, Ana Simões, Manolis Patiniotis and José R. Bertomeu-Sánchez, 'Moving Localities and Creative Circulation: Travels as Knowledge Production in 18th-Century Europe', *Centaurus* 56.3 (2014): 167–88.

20 Richard Grove and Vinita Damoradan, 'Imperialism, Intellectual Networks, and Environmental Change: Origins and Evolution of Global Environmental History, 1676–2000: Part I', *Economic and Political Weekly* 41.41 (2006): 4345–54; Richard Grove and Vinita Damoradan, 'Imperialism, Intellectual Networks, and Environmental Change: Origins and Evolution of Global Environmental History, 1676–2000: Part II', *Economic and Political Weekly* 41.42 (2006): 4497–505.

21 See Richard Grove, *Green Imperialism: Colonial Expansion, Tropical Island Edens and the Origins of Environmentalism* (Cambridge: Cambridge University Press, 1995), 314–25.

22 Comte de Buffon, *Barr's Buffon. Buffon's Natural History*, 10 vols (London, 1797); Alexander von Humboldt, *Cosmos: A Sketch of a Physical Description of the Universe*, trans. E.C. Otté, 2 vols (New York, 1850). Recent work on Humboldt includes *Studies in Travel Writing* 15.1 (special issue, ed. Peter Hulme), *Alexander von Humboldt and America* (2011) and Laura Dassow Walls, *The Passage to Cosmos: Alexander von Humboldt and the Shaping of America* (Chicago, IL: University of Chicago Press, 2009).

23 Michael Robinson, 'Linnaeus, Carl', in *Literature of Travel and Exploration: An Encyclopedia*, ed. Jennifer Speake (New York: Fitzroy Dearborn, 2003), 2:723–6.

24 La Condamine, 1748, quoted in Bewell, 'Romanticism and Colonial Natural History', 6.

25 Pennant is the subject of a major AHRC-funded project, 'Curious Travellers: Thomas Pennant and the Welsh and Scottish Tour, 1760–1820', at the University of Wales Centre for Advanced Welsh and Celtic Studies (CAWCS) and the University of Glasgow, accessed 5 September 2017, http://curioustravellers.ac.uk; the website includes links to digitised originals of some of Pennant's correspondence. The first volume of essays dedicated to Pennant was *Enlightenment Travel and British Identities: Thomas Pennant's Tours in Scotland and Wales*, ed. Mary-Ann Constantine and Nigel Leask (London: Anthem Press, 2017).

26 Stuart Houston, Mary Houston and Tim Ball, *Eighteenth-Century Naturalists of Hudson Bay* (Montréal: McGill-Queen's University Press, 2003), 85–6; Bewell, 'Romanticism and Colonial Natural History', 20.

27 John Reinhold Forster, 'An Account of Some Curious Fishes, Sent from Hudson's Bay; By Mr. John Reinhold Forster, F.R.S. in a Letter to Thomas Pennant, Esq; F.R.S.', *Philosophical Transactions* 63 (1773–4): 149–60. Graham was listed in the acknowledgements to Pennant's *Arctic Zoology*.

28 Ryan Tucker Jones, *Empire of Extinction: Russians and the North Pacific's Strange Beasts of the Sea, 1741–1867* (Oxford: Oxford University Press, 2014), 170–95.

29 On assemblage, see David Turnbull, 'Local Knowledge and Comparative Scientific Traditions', *Knowledge and Policy* 6 (1993–4): 29–54.

30 Thomas Pennant, *A Tour in Scotland* (Chester: John Monk, 1771), iii.

31 Thomas Pennant, *A Tour in Scotland and Voyage to the Hebrides*, 2 vols (Chester: John Monk, 1774), 1.299–309.

32 Adam Fox, 'Printed Questionnaires, Research Networks, and the Discovery of the British Isles, 1650–1800', *The Historical Journal* 53.3 (2010): 613.

33 Fox, 'Printed Questionnaires', 594.

34 David N. Livingstone, *Putting Science in Its Place: Geographies of Scientific Knowledge* (Chicago, IL: University of Chicago Press, 2003), 147.

35 Penny Fielding, *Scotland and the Fictions of Geography: North Britain, 1760–1830* (Cambridge: Cambridge University Press, 2009), 9.

36 Pennant, *A Tour in Scotland and Voyage to the Hebrides*, 2:98, 163, 441, 131.

37 Pennant, *A Tour in Scotland and Voyage to the Hebrides*, 2:43.

38 Pennant, *A Tour in Scotland and Voyage to the Hebrides*, 1:iii–iv.

39 Pennant, *A Tour in Scotland*, 179.

40 Noah Heringman, 'The Commerce of Literature and Natural History', in *Romantic Science: The Literary Forms of Natural History*, ed. Noah Heringman (Albany, NY: State University of New York Press, 2003), 3. For more on 'Romantic science', see Noah Heringman, *Romantic Rocks, Aesthetic Geology* (Ithaca, NY: Cornell University Press, 2004).

41 Paul Smethurst, *Travel Writing and the Natural World, 1768–1840* (London: Palgrave, 2012), 110–11.

42 Pennant, *A Tour in Scotland and Voyage to the Hebrides*, 1:12, 1:20.

43 See 'Women's Travel Writing, 1780–1840: A Bio-Bibliographical Database', accesssed 10 August 2016. www4.wlv.ac.uk/btw

44 Alice Walters, 'Conversation Pieces: Science and Politeness in Eighteenth-Century England', *History of Science* 35 (1997): 122. See also Thompson, 'Earthquakes and Petticoats', 329–46.

45 Pratt, *Imperial Eyes*, 38.

46 See, for example, Pnina G. Abir-Am and Dorinda Outram (eds), *Uneasy Careers and Intimate Lives: Women in Science, 1789–1979* (New Brunswick, NJ: Rutgers University Press, 1989); Patricia Phillips, *The Scientific Lady: A Social History of Women's Scientific Interests 1520–1918* (London: Weidenfeld and Nicolson, 1990); Ann B. Shteir, *Cultivating Women, Cultivating Science: Flora's Daughters and Botany in England 1760–1860* (Baltimore, MD: Johns Hopkins University Press, 1996); *Natural Eloquence: Women Reinscribe Science*, ed. Barbara T. Gates and Ann B. Shteir (Madison, WI: University of Wisconsin Press, 1997); Barbara T. Gates, *Kindred Nature: Victorian and Edwardian Women Embrace the Living World* (Chicago, IL: University of Chicago Press, 1998); Ruth Watts, *Women in Science: A Social and Cultural History* (London: Routledge, 2007). Specifically in relation to scientific travel, see Sara Mills, *Discourses of Difference: An Analysis of Women's Travel Writing and Colonialism* (London: Routledge, 1991); Lila Marz Harper, *Solitary Travelers: Nineteenth-Century Women's Travel Narratives and the Scientific Vocation* (London: Associated University Presses, 2001). See also Thompson, 'Earthquakes and Petticoats'.

47 See Mary Orr, 'New Observations on a Geological Hotspot Track: "Excursions in Madeira and Porto Santo" (1825) by Mrs T. Edward Bowdich', *Centaurus* 56.3 (2014): 135–66; 'Fish with a Different Angle: "The Fresh-Water Fishes of Great Britain" by Mrs Sarah Bowdich (1791–1856)', *Annals of Science* 71.2 (2013): 1–35.

48 Orr, 'New Observations', 148–9.

49 *Excursions in Madeira and Porto Santo, during the Autumn of 1823, while on his Third Voyage to Africa; by the Late T. Edward Bowdich . . . To which is added, By Mrs Bowdich, I. A Narrative of the Continuance of the Voyage to its Completion . . . II. A Description of the English Settlements on the River Gambia. III. Appendix: Containing Zoological and Botanical Descriptions, and Translations from the Arabic. Illustrated by Sections, Views, Costumes, and Zoological Figures* (London: George B. Whittaker, 1825); Orr, 'New Observations', 150.

50 Mary Orr, 'Pursuing Proper Protocol: Sarah Bowdich's Purview of the Sciences of Exploration', *Victorian Studies* 49.2 (2007): 281.

51 Mrs R. Lee, *Elements of Natural History, for the Use of Schools and Young Persons* (London: Longman, Brown, Green and Longmans, 1844), 32, 107, 248, 289; Mrs R. Lee, *Trees, Plants, and Flowers: Their Beauties, Uses, and Influences* (London: Grant and Griffith, 1854), 2; Mrs R. Lee, *Stories of Strange Lands; and Fragments from the Notes of a Traveller* (London: Edward Moxon, 1835).

52 Harper, *Solitary Travelers*, 24.

53 Orr, 'Pursuing Proper Protocol', 278.

54 T. Edward Bowdich, *Mission from Cape Coast Castle to Ashantee* (London: John Murray, 1819), 422–52.

55 Alison Blunt, *Travel, Gender, and Imperialism: Mary Kingsley and West Africa* (New York: The Guilford Press, 1994), 53.

56 See Nuala C. Johnson, 'Global Knowledge in a Local World: Charlotte Wheeler Cuffe's Encounters with Burma 1901–1902', in *Spaces of Global Knowledge: Exhibition, Encounter and Exchange in an Age of Empire*, ed. Diarmid A. Finnegan and Jonathan J. Wright (Aldershot: Ashgate, 2015), 19–38; and Angela Byrne, '"My Little Readers": Catharine Parr Traill's Natural Histories for Children', *Journal of Literature and Science* 8.1 (2015): 86–101. On women scientific illustrators, see: Barbara Maria Stafford, *Voyage into*

Substance: Art, Science, Nature, and the Illustrated Travel Account (Cambridge, MA: MIT Press, 1984) and Suzanne Le May-Sheffield, 'Gendered Collaborations: Marrying Art and Science', in *Figuring It Out: Science, Gender, and Visual Culture*, ed. Ann B. Shteir and Bernard Lightman (Hanover, NH: Dartmouth College Press), 240–60. On women and scientific translation, see Alison E. Martin, 'Outward Bound: Women Translators and Scientific Travel Writing, 1780–1800', *Annals of Science* 73.2 (2016): 157–69.

57 This approach is exemplified in Daniel W. Clayton, *Islands of Truth: The Imperial Fashioning of Vancouver Island* (Vancouver: University of British Columbia Press, 2000), and in Julie Cruikshank, *Do Glaciers Listen? Local Knowledge, Colonial Encounters and Social Imagination* (Vancouver: University of British Columbia Press, 2005).

58 Pennant, *A Tour in Scotland and Voyage to the Hebrides*, 2:397.

59 Ruth Barton, '"Huxley, Lubbock, and Half a Dozen Others": Professionals and Gentlemen in the Formation of the X Club, 1851–1864', *Isis* 89.3 (1998): 428. See also Ruth Barton, '"Men of Science": Language, Identity and Professionalization in the Mid-Victorian Scientific Community', *History of Science* 41.1 (2003): 73–119.

2

NATURE WRITING

Paul Smethurst

This chapter examines the role of nature writing in shaping dominant ideas of nature in the West, and then explores ecological perspectives that inform 'new' nature writing. The genre provides a historical record of the natural world and evidence of changing attitudes to nature and the environment. It is therefore highly relevant to contemporary discussions of climate change and environmental degradation. Since the late twentieth century, the legacy of nature writing in shaping dominant ideas of human–nature relations has been scrutinised, with the result that ecological issues and perspectives are now at the forefront of recent criticism. Ecocriticism offers a corrective to the long tradition of nature writing, which through a wide spectrum of fictional and non-fictional prose and poetry has tended to celebrate the wonders of nature and to classify natural objects and phenomena without turning a critical eye on how humanity has exploited the natural world.

Forms of nature writing can be found in most cultures, and in most periods, but the late eighteenth century was an especially productive period in Britain and parts of Europe, where natural history, global exploration, scenic tourism and Romanticism all contributed to its profusion, with the effect of distancing humans from the natural world. The scientific objectivity inherent in projects of natural history and global exploration presumed a vantage point outside nature from which humans might protect or destroy a natural world to which they would be essentially exterior. Adding to this sense of abstraction, scenic tourism and Romanticism evidence a desire to bridge the gap with nature in an age of increasing urbanisation and materialism, and yet both gave rise to the aestheticisation and sentimentalisation of nature, further distancing the natural environment from the place where humans live and work.

This exteriorisation of nature created a realm no longer constituted in everyday social life, but to suggest that there was a golden age when nature was an inclusive space and the primary site of social bonding can lead to nostalgia and regression. Yet a significant shift undoubtedly occurred in Britain between the end of the eighteenth and the early nineteenth century. Henceforth, largely urban-based societies would regard the natural world as an abstract space detached from a real environment now open to unchecked exploitation by social and economic forces. In *Contested Natures*, Phil Macnaghten and John Urry argue that the '"social" dimensions of nature have been significantly under-examined'.[1] Despite numerous attempts by society to preserve parts of the natural world since the nineteenth century, the larger sense of social responsibility implied by the notion of stewardship has been in competition with the global exploitation of natural resources to advance human society. Nature writing, which includes some key travel texts, reveals traces of this tension.

Since the 1960s, as the extent of the damage to the natural world from human intervention has become apparent in depleted forests, bleached coral reefs, rising sea levels, polluted rivers and oceans, poor air quality and loss of species, so an ecocritical perspective has understandably become the dominant theme in nature writing and criticism. 'New' nature writing laments the loss of wildlife habitats and the negative impact of human activity on the natural world, rather than waxing lyrical about the wonders of nature. It also shifts its focus from merely witnessing natural sites and objects to scrutinising interfaces and interactions between human and non-human forces in the environment as a whole. One effect of this is to question the very idea of 'natural' as a category for phenomena. In the twenty-first century, the extent and impact of environmental degradation are all too evident. Globalisation has undoubtedly accelerated this process, but for some writers it also provides a larger canvas on which to draw attention to the crisis. In one particularly striking example, a container ship loaded with rubber ducks, trainers and other consumer goods shed its cargo, which was later to be found washed up on remote beaches across the globe. This provided a scientific register for the distribution of waste through the oceans' currents, and also a metaphor for the global intrusion of the inorganic into the organic detritus of nature – a rebinding of human and non-human realms, which has become a major theme in new nature writing. In *Findings* (2005), Kathleen Jamie is struck by the odd juxtaposition of the natural ('seals' vertebrae and whalebones, driftwood') and the unnatural, yet strangely familiar domestic waste on a remote beach in the Orkney Isles of Scotland:

> The cleavages between sand dunes [. . .] were choked with plastic [. . .] Among the dunes and bent grass, at the mouths of rabbit holes, trapped in every cove, were tangles of rope and plastic bottles, shoes and aerosol cans.[2]

This compelling image of the organic and the plastic, the local and global, illustrates the 'rubber duck effect', which like the 'butterfly effect' describes the non-linear global impact of local events on the dispersal of waste and weather systems.

Unsurprisingly, concern over climate change, the loss of wildlife habitats and environmental crises have forced a critical and more urgent tone in nature writing in the twenty-first century. The genre has also been pushed into self-reflection since it would now seem that its historical role in framing views of nature as 'other' was a factor in the disconnection between nature and society, and in dividing human from non-human realms.

The production of nature and the great divide

Nature writing is a very diverse genre, which does not exactly map onto the equally diverse genre of travel writing that is the subject of this volume. It also has national connotations: in Britain it can sometimes be restricted to studies of local natural history; whereas in the United States it refers to any form of writing about nature, or simply the experience of being in nature. This wider definition would also allow for discussion of nature writing from beyond Western centres of knowledge, in Asia and Africa for example, where nature was often the object of scrutiny for Western traveller-scientists who paid little attention to how indigenous people might have regarded it. Some forms of nature writing record Western exploration beyond Europe, while others have tightly circumscribed local ambits. The distance travelled might affect the content and the reception of the writing, but the journey itself is not always prominent. In this chapter, nature writing is taken to include any account of a journey undertaken to encounter, observe and meditate on the natural world. This would range from reports by naturalists on James Cook's first voyage to the South Seas between 1768 and 1771 to Gilbert White's biore-gional expeditions from his doorstep in the English village of Selbourne (1789), to William Wordsworth's *Guide Through the Lake District of England* (1810) and Henry David Thoreau's *Walden* (1854). Only in the first of these examples is the physical journey remarkable, yet all have gathered information about the natural world with the aim of enhancing our perception and understanding of nature. The naturalists on Cook's expeditions were, like Charles Darwin on *HMS Beagle*, conscious of taking part in epic journeys that would lay the foundations for understanding nature as a planetary system, as suggested by Alexander von Humboldt in his *Cosmos: Sketch of a Physical Description of the Universe* (1850–52). At the other end of the scale, White delved into the minutiae of a local ecosystem to explore the microcosms underlying the visible natural world.

As well as describing landscapes, wildlife and ecosystems, certain forms of nature writing also record personal responses to nature, while others invoke Nature (capitalised) as a transcendental signifier and a mysterious force that drives the biosphere and ultimately the cosmos. At its most capacious, the genre includes classical texts, medieval religious writings, Renaissance literature, the journals of explorers, naturalists and scenic tourists, Romantic travel writing, topographical descriptions, essays on natural history and guidebooks. Broadly, we can distinguish between three main historical forms: (1) philosophical, moral and religious writings on Nature; (2) secular and scientific descriptions of landscapes, habitats, flora and fauna; (3) personal narratives of encounters with and reflections on the natural world. The first is associated with formative ideas, myths and interpretations which have defined relations between Nature and humankind since antiquity, and continue to resonate in representations of pastoral idylls and quasi-religious spaces. The second form is associated with the project of natural history exemplified in Carl Linnaeus's *Systema Naturae* (1735), and Comte de Buffon's *Histoire Naturelle* (1749–78).[3] The third form presents observations and reflections of natural phenomena in prose narrative. Such narratives were sometimes considered dichotomous with scientific writing since they were sub-jective and apparently more concerned with impressions than facts. Yet it was not unusual in the late eighteenth and nineteenth century to find both forms combined in the notebooks of travellers, with the narrative of the journey complemented by appendices and sketches contain-ing observations. This was how Alexander von Humboldt presented his account of his travels in South America between 1799 and 1804.

In his *Personal Narrative* (1814–29), Humboldt distinguishes between the different forms available to him, and the desire for a 'unity of composition' which would convey that sense of nature writ large he strove for in all his work:

> A historical narrative covers two quite different aims: whatever happens to the travel-ler; and the observations he makes during his journey. Unity of composition [. . .] can be sought only when the traveller describes what he has seen with his own eyes, and when he has concentrated on [. . .] the great phenomena of nature.[4]

For Humboldt, the history of nature could not be conveyed by recording passing impressions; it must contain informed scientific study of phenomena in the field and their connections and interactions. These he aimed to present in totalising visions which accounted for such global phenomena as the worldwide distribution of plants, and the effect of climate on this distribution. Even his *Personal Narrative* contained voluminous charts and appendices which caused critics at the time to complain that it was neither 'personal' nor 'narrative'.[5] And yet, influenced by

German Romanticism, Humboldt was also interested in how representations of nature might impress themselves on and expand human consciousness through 'insight into the harmonious and concurrent action of different powers and forces of Nature'.[6]

There is some synergy between Humboldt's project and that of the English Romantics, though Wordsworth describes a more self-indulgent form of insight in his *Guide Through the Lakes* (1810), which addresses 'the *Minds* of Persons of taste, and feeling for landscape'.[7] This work describes local and proximate nature through the learnt aesthetic protocols of the picturesque and the sublime with the aim of finding correspondence between natural and mental landscapes. Although one effect of this framing is to produce general and idealised templates of the natural world, it also insinuates a new aesthetics of nature into actual landscapes which others could visit either physically or vicariously through the text. He certainly created a 'taste' for the Lake District in the vulgar sense of a site for touristic consumption, although he was opposed to mass tourism, urging his like-minded visitors to look beyond a 'superficial entertainment of the eye' to communicate with 'The Soul of Objects' in nature, and campaigning against the railway line to Kendal, now a tourist centre for the region.[8]

By contrast with the grandiose aims of Humboldt and Wordsworth, others would look at nature from a progressive, utilitarian perspective, advocating draining, soil improvement and other measures to improve the productivity of the land and, in doing so, the economy of the nation and its colonies. For example, in Daniel Defoe's *A Tour Through the Whole Island of Great Britain* (1724–26), and in Thomas Pennant's *A Tour in Scotland* (1771), wild nature is not something to be celebrated, but is evidence of a 'regressive milieu',[9] and plenty of examples could be found in the peripheries of Britain. Pennant, who like Defoe promotes the idea of British nationhood through representations of British topography, discovers a literal translation of the idea of the primitive swamp in the Highlands of Scotland (only recently incorporated into the 'Island of Great Britain'). He associates the boggy valleys hindering the traveller's progress with a backward culture of vagabonds and thieves, whereas General Wade's military roads 'symbolise the civilizing and progressive force of Georgian modernity'.[10]

In *Voyage into Substance* (1984), Barbara Maria Stafford argues that scientific, utilitarian and Romantic forms of travel writing are dialectical in that demands for objectivity were a reaction against sentimental and quasi-religious attitudes to nature.[11] We could also say that German Romanticism subsequently derived some of its impetus from a perceived need to counter overly scientific approaches to the natural world. We have already seen how Humboldt attempts to combine approaches, but a more striking illustration can be found in the journals of George Forster, a naturalist on James Cook's second voyage to the South Seas. The influence of Kant can be found when Forster admits that

> our observations [of natural objects] will frequently be foreign to each other [because] the different branches of science which we have studied, our turns of mind, our heads and hearts have made such a difference in our sensations, reflections, and expressions.[12]

His description of Cascade Cove in New Zealand then shows a remarkable synthesis of scientific and Romantic sensibility. At times he regards the cascade through the lexicon of Romantic nature writing, as in 'the great beauty and grandeur before us' and 'the first object that strikes the beholder', where he makes nature active and the observer a passive receptor of impressions. But he is also precise in his measurements and analyses of rocks and minerals and in his classification of fauna and flora. This scientific interest is then enhanced by a strong sense of presence as he verbally sketches the visual and aural qualities of 'this wild and romantic spot'.[13] In allowing the scientific analysis of natural objects to buttress impressions and reflections that nature can induce in the informed observer, Forster introduced a method which has been adopted by some 'new' nature writers, as well as, more immediately, by Humboldt.

By the nineteenth century, industrialisation and urbanisation made the sense of loss a common theme in nature writing. A trend then emerged to idealise and sentimentalise the countryside and the wilderness as alternate loci where escape from the real world might be found, as in Thoreau's *Walden* (1854). The sense of personal renewal and redemption become more pronounced in the twentieth century with a stronger suggestion of healing after each of the two World Wars. Such privileging and deification of the natural world, typically by male writers, such as D.H. Lawrence, would help secure the divorce of nature from social development through the willed act of escaping into it.

From the eighteenth century onwards, a pastoral revival was further enhanced by a collective nostalgia for a perceived loss of 'organic communities' as traditional social ties with the countryside were severed. Yet, as Raymond Williams has pointed out, there was nothing new in this nostalgia for a better rural world nestling in the folds of recent history. The habit of positive retrospection reaches all the way back to Eden and the Golden Age of Hesiod's *Theogony*, sometimes cited as the first example of nature writing in the West.[14] But in modernity, rural nostalgia is undercut with lamentation for the actual loss of countryside and wilderness areas to industrialisation, to the point where truly wild nature unaffected by human intervention is hard to find. Until fairly recently, nature writing has not overtly criticised those activities that are now seen to have led to the destruction of nature, but has instead eulogised particular landscapes still thought to be immune and pristine, for example the Highlands of Scotland or the mountains of California.[15] Here wild and sublime nature might be found by the many followers of Thomas Pennant, William Gilpin and John Muir, although the threat from loggers, railways and urban tourists, who travelled en masse (the 'sooty hordes', as Wordsworth called them) to visit this 'disappearing nature', is already foreshadowed. With the rise of environmental awareness in the twenty-first century, we can see more clearly Muir's warning about the destruction of wilderness areas in California in 1911, even though his writings are more often cited as celebrations of the design and perdurance of wild nature.

As nature is removed from everyday experience for burgeoning urban populations, the nature–culture opposition, already seen in Defoe's and Pennant's utilitarian approaches, adds further to the 'othering' of nature. Unsurprisingly, this construct has been a target of recent ecocriticism and has led to some reassessment of the tradition of nature writing. In *The Song of the Earth* (2000), Jonathan Bate asks 'why the recovery of the repressed "Others" of woman and black in cultural criticism since the 1960s has not generally been accompanied by a recovery of "nature", the original Other'.[16] The comparison is not particularly helpful since it crosses into differently politicised fields, but given the concomitant rise of deconstruction and geopolitics, the recovery of nature as other might have come sooner. It has, of course, taken the politics of climate change to trigger the recovery, yet attempts to reintegrate the realm of nature into social affairs are proving problematic. Academic debate so far has revolved around opposing positions that draw on theories of eco-Marxist instrumentalism, Heideggerian phenomenology and deconstructionist ecocriticism.[17] The problem with each of these is that 'nature' is perhaps a term with such diverse connotations that its recovery is inevitably fraught. What does nature mean in the twenty-first century? Perhaps we need to accept finally that humans are part of nature and move beyond the opposition to consider instead the ways in which human and non-human realms interact through an inclusive planetary ecosystem. This is at least a starting point for new nature writing and for reconsidering traditional nature writing.

Nature writing, criticism and the Anthropocene

Scholarly approaches to nature writing in the late twentieth century point to a paradigm shift in Western understanding of and feeling towards the natural world from about 1800, when social, economic and cultural forces combined to other nature, and redefine it for a modern world. In *Man and the Natural World* (1983) Keith Thomas describes the prehistory of this shift through a detailed analysis of attitudes to nature in England from 1500–1800. In the Tudor and Stuart periods, he explains, most people believed that the Creator intended every living thing to 'serve some human purpose, if not practical, then moral or aesthetic'.[18] Theological writings on nature in the sixteenth and seventeenth centuries consistently defined humans' special status, and justified their rule over other living things. At the same time, it was understood that human civilisation throughout medieval Europe depended not only on deifying Nature, but also on the progressive exploitation of plants and animals for food, fuel, labour, clothing and transport.[19] The stewardship of Nature, which might include protecting and conserving the natural world, gradually shifted to a role of domination and conquest, conveniently gelling with European colonialist ideology. In this analysis, contemporary moves to establish 1950 as the beginning of the Anthropocene might be reconsidered. The era of human-directed change on a geological scale seems to have begun far earlier.

Between 1500 and 1800, men and women at different social levels would understand the natural world in ways we would recognise now and develop attachments to it that are still prevalent today. In Britain, the aristocracy would remain rural-based, and retain an intense interest in the natural world both on estates at home and on colonial plantations. Many of the elite, including George III, had a passion for the science of natural history, helping to make it one of the most fashionable pursuits of the eighteenth century. Beyond simply a fashion, capitalism, the coming of private property and trade, would make the study and exploitation of the natural world a matter of public and national interest. As nature is subsumed into the processes of production, capital and labour, a transformation occurs, which from a Marxist perspective would be described as a shift from 'first nature' to 'second nature', where labour is conjoined with natural production.

A dichotomy between the social and the natural is also evident in Henri Lefebvre's *The Production of Space* (1974), which resigns itself to the gradual disappearance of nature in the wake of modernity. While nature has not vanished, it has lost its social significance. It becomes the 'background of the picture' and, emptied of the dialectics of social production, its primary function in modernity is one of registering loss and absence.[20] But even if we accept the premise that a transformation from first nature to second nature occurred as a result of the rise of private property and industrial capitalism, we must acknowledge that first nature never disappeared. It is still a force to be reckoned with, as we are constantly reminded when second nature, as the realm of human intervention, is powerless to control first nature in the form of wild tornadoes and hurricanes.[21] The presence of first nature also stalks the future imaginary of climate change dystopia, as we begin to see how the wild might begin to reassert itself.

The supposed disappearance of first nature/wild nature in the wake of modernity is also put in doubt when we recognise that sensibilities remained firmly attached to the natural world in Britain. Indeed, anxieties about the intrusion of society on the natural world and the need for nature conservation were already evident in the nineteenth century. Clubs and societies for nature field studies were a feature of Victorian society and, as Thomas points out, with the acquisitiveness inherent in amateur collecting, 'feelings were engendered which would ultimately produce the legislation in the late nineteenth and twentieth centuries for nature conservation and the protection of wild creatures'.[22] Furthermore, English and Scottish landowners were responsible for conserving large areas of woodland, streams and heath for the preservation of wild nature for hunting, shooting and fishing. Clearly second nature was already wrought with social relations, whether in the countryside or wilderness areas, yet these have been ignored in favour of the continuing fiction that wild nature exists as a realm outside human history.

By the early twentieth century, the natural world would also be recast through sentimental depictions of the countryside in nature writing for adults and children. Here, objects in the natural world are given plenty of 'human significance' in the form of anthropomorphic appropriation, with toads, moles, bears and donkeys acquiring a moral compass and the received English of their middle-class audience. The sentimentalisation of nature has become a target for contemporary nature writing informed by ecological perspectives, but it is persistent, as can be seen in Roger Deakin's description of the evening antics of the badgers of Castle Carey:

> I had witnessed a posse of badgers sauntering nonchalantly along the street beneath Lodge Hill, knocking the tops off dustbins like teenagers and rifling them, even pausing to tip over the ice-cream sign outside the newsagents. Emerging early from the snouting dingles of the town at dusk, they went their rounds with impatient efficiency, jogging from house to house like council workers on some lucrative bonus scheme.[23]

The double anthropomorphism (badgers as both teenagers and council workers) can be read as an example of late twentieth-century social realism, but it also re-invokes the very human-centred approach that new nature writing ostensibly opposes.

Interest in the writing of Deakin and other 'new' nature writers over the last few decades can be largely attributed to the emergence of concerns about ecological crisis and climate change, and for the need to rethink our relations with nature. This has led to increased scholarship in the field and a rash of books on ecological thought, the end of nature, second nature, ecocriticism and the environmental imagination, and to the historicisation from an ecological viewpoint of earlier writing about the natural world. To this end, new college courses on literature and the environment regularly encourage 'green readings' of works by Alexander von Humboldt, Charles Darwin, William Wordsworth, Gilbert White, Henry David Thoreau and John Muir. This comes alongside a proliferation of new nature writing from writers with academic connections such as Robert Macfarlane whose ecocritical views are openly professed.

Interest in nature writers of the eighteenth and nineteenth centuries, such as those already mentioned, follows attempts to trace the beginnings of ecological thinking. Romanticism is an obvious starting point, given its privileging and deification of wild nature and its ideological opposition to the progressive forces of industrial capitalism. Jonathan Bate was one of the first to make this connection in his *Romantic Ecology: Wordsworth and the Environmental Tradition* (1991), followed by Laurence Coupe's *Green Studies Reader: From Romanticism to Ecocriticism* (2000). But, in his *Green Imperialism* (1995), Richard Grove puts the origins of environmentalism a century earlier. It has not always been recognised that naturalists could see beneath the symbolic veneer of paradise in an island like Tahiti to appreciate the fragile ecosystem underlying it. The island is not then a natural idyll, but utterly dependent on sophisticated irrigation methods devised and maintained by Tahitian farmers. The naturalists on Cook's voyages would soon realise how unsustainable were the demands of European visitors on an agricultural system, recast through classical allusion as paradise in the works of Rousseau and other European philosophers.[24] Recent ecological perspectives such as Grove's not only give a lead to new nature writers, but also provide an opening for the 'greening' of postcolonial studies and the revisioning of the work of naturalists. In the critical milieu of the 1980s and 90s, travelling naturalists were commonly tarred with the same brush: 'agents of empire'.[25] The reputation of writers such as Humboldt, Alfred Russel Wallace and Darwin might well benefit from a reassessment from ecological perspectives. There is no doubt that Humboldt, a major influence on Darwin, demonstrated an ecological and planetary consciousness in his major works, *Aspects of Nature* (1849) and *Cosmos* (1845–62). His interests were holistic and, according to Grove, he always sought 'to promulgate a new ecological concept of relations between man and the natural world'.[26] Humboldt's holistic thinking helped to synthesise and visualise disparate components of a planet-wide ecosystem. He was probably the first naturalist to see all aspects of nature such as the biosphere, atmosphere, lithosphere and hydrosphere operating with a high degree of interaction and interdependency. This informed an ecological viewpoint through which he predicted environmental degradation as the result of logging, farming and mining.[27]

New nature writing: a double erasure

Having examined the historical record of nature writing and the ways in which traditional ideas of nature were first shaped by this and then affected by recent ecocriticism, the remainder of this chapter looks at the way contemporary writing resists the tradition. 'New nature writing' is a term coined by *Granta* in 2008. In his introduction to a special edition on the subject, Jason Cowley identifies 'new' nature writers: Mark Cocker, Roger Deakin, Kathleen Jamie, Richard Mabey and Robert Macfarlane, who

> share a sense that we are devouring our world, that there is simply no longer any natural landscape or ecosystem that is unchanged by humans. But they don't simply want to walk into the wild, to rhapsodize and commune: they aspire to see with a scientific eye and write with literary effect.[28]

Expressed in this way, the novelty of this approach is questionable given that anxieties about human disconnection from natural processes have been at the forefront of nature discourse since it gained prominence in the environmental movement of the 1970s.[29] And I would argue that if there is to be a new eco-poetics, it needs to produce compelling images with 'literary affect', not, as Cowley suggests, 'literary effect', a term which suggests instrumentalism and too direct a link with the radical politics of environmentalism, although perhaps there is nothing new in this either, since combining literary affect with a scientific eye is not unlike the approach taken by Forster and Humboldt. A different formulation, one I think most new nature writers are following, is a new poetics that articulates a revised semiotics of nature that aims to bridge the gap between human society and the biosphere that enfolds and supports it. This requires a new understanding of relations between the human and non-human and a more nuanced idea of what constitutes 'nature in the wild'. As we shall see, Jamie's strategy of finding and framing wild nature within mundane domestic realms goes some way towards this by imbricating human life with wildness.

Before looking at particular examples of new nature writing, it is worth considering the upsurge in interest in nature writing in the last few years, with many book stores in the UK now promoting bestsellers in nature writing in their windows. The trend can be traced back to the 1990s when *The Norton Book of Nature Writing* (1990) appeared, soon to be superseded by a new edition in which a broadening of what constituted nature writing was apparent (the US editors wanted to redress the dominance of white, male, Anglo-American writers in the first edition, although they did so by widening the 'tradition' somewhat to include fiction writers). In Britain, Richard Mabey's collection, *The Oxford Book of Nature Writing* (1995), begins in classical literature and contains more examples from the European tradition of natural history and exploration, as well as more contemporary, ecologically aware nature writing. His chapters are thematic rather than chronological or geographical, and the sequence of his headings suggests ways in which the genre is now being historicised from an ecological viewpoint: 'Out of the Dark Ages', 'Watching Narrowly', 'The Romantics', 'Wonders and Creation', 'Weeds and Wilderness', 'New Naturalists' and 'Fellow Creatures'. Each category connects with major themes of contemporary ecocriticism: the conflicting history of religious, scientific and Romantic approaches to the natural world; a reappraisal of wilderness; and resistance to anthropocentric attitudes to nature.

Another starting point for 'new' nature writing was the formation in the UK of Common Ground which began in 1983 with two main objectives:

> to promote the importance of common plants and animals, familiar and local places, local distinctiveness and our links with the past; and to explore the emotional value these things have for us by forging practical and philosophical links between the arts and the conservation of nature and landscapes.[30]

Localist and environmentalist aims are expressed here, but there is also a determined attempt to use words and images to inspire people to visit the countryside and engage in actual encounters with nature. The ecological perspective is expressed through an eco-poetics that installs affective relations with nature, connecting with but going beyond the realpolitik of environmentalism.

The problem with the aesthetic is how to distinguish it from the now discredited fetishisation and re-enchantment of a disappearing nature that might resemble a revival of Romanticism in postmodern pastiche. John Fowles addresses the problem in his essay for *Second Nature*:

> Nature is a sort of art sans art; and the right human attitude to it ought to be, unashamedly, poetic rather than scientific. Such a bald statement may sound dangerously like the Romantic Movement's theory of nature – Nature with a capital as an evoker of beautiful and noble sentiments [. . .] a theory memorable when transmitted by genius but only too repulsive when couched in the purple prose of debased 'Nature Corner' journalism. We are not the age for beautiful, noble sentiments about anything, let alone nature. For all that, I think we, in our present vilely polluted world, had better think twice before we sneer the Romantic theory into oblivion.[31]

We cannot rely on scientists alone to defend wildlife. As Fowles puts it, 'Science may understand nature; but it can never understand what nature requires of man'; it is through a combination of poetry and 'direct experience' with nature that we might learn to recognise and mesh with the natural world.[32] As with other contemporary nature writers, Fowles sees the 'wild' as something we have sought to entrap, either literally or metaphorically in 'cages of banality, or false parallels, of anthropomorphic sentimentality'.[33] He suggests we learn to recognise the wild through a *'poetry of survival'*, the subjects of which would include forms of life found in the commonplace, in city gardens, cellars, cracks in the pavement, domestic spaces and even within us.[34] So the wild is not tamed; it is not even dichotomous with the tame; it is made intimate as a route to survival.

In *What Is Nature?*, Kate Soper shows that an opposition between nature and culture has been 'axiomatic to Western thought'.[35] She makes a useful distinction between two different approaches to the 'end of nature' scenario: the first is a direct response to the 'human plunder and destruction' of the environment, 'politically directed at correcting that abuse'; the second is 'focused on the semiotics of nature', and directed at the idea of nature as a social construct that has been used historically to 'legitimate social and sexual hierarchies and cultural norms'. In stark, binary terms, she identifies 'nature-endorsing' and 'nature-skeptical' discourses: the first is more instrumentalist with clear-sighted aims to protect the environment from exploitation; the second takes a semiotic approach to question and ultimately to reject nature as a cultural construct, shifting emphasis instead to the idea of the wild as a category that bridges human and non-human realms.[36]

Especially salient to deconstructivist strategies in nature writing are the deep-rooted gendering of Nature as female, and the gender implications of 'man–nature' interactions, both of which inform Carolyn Merchant's *The Death of Nature: Women, Ecology and the Scientific Revolution* (1979). Nature-sceptical discourses acquire further significance when they include feminist critiques of the historical embedding of gender in nature. The idea of Nature being opposed to 'Man' privileges men in active relations with the natural world, while implicitly feminising nature and reducing the role of women. The development of an exclusively male ego through and against wild nature, as typically occurs in a great deal of exploration journals and Romantic nature writing, overshadows the extensive history of women's actual and often more intimate dealings with nature (see for example the works of Sarah Hazlitt, Helen Maria Williams, Mary Wollstonecraft and Dorothy Wordsworth, and more recent works by Nan Shepherd, Kathleen Jamie and others).[37] Meanwhile, the symbolic association between women and nature intimates that both are driven by wild and unruly forces wanting social control. Wilderness is then set aside for the banishment of untamed women, as well as providing a 'liminal site for male self-fulfillment'.[38] Eco-feminists argue that the exclusively male ego in this opposition with nature needs replacing with a more relational sense of self, a subject that is more transpersonal and potentially transhuman in its interactions.[39]

Although it is not travel writing *per se*, the pioneering example of nature-endorsing discourse is Rachel Carson's *Silent Spring* (1962), widely cited as a 'wake-up call' (through association with the absent 'dawn chorus') to the devastating ecological damage caused by pesticides. Yet in negating the Romantic allusion to spring as a time of bird song, she is also operating through the semiotics of nature in a nature-sceptical sense, invoking the loss of an idealised form. In travel writing, Peter Matthiessen's *The Snow Leopard* (1978), Robyn Davidson's *Tracks* (1980) and Barry Lopez's *Arctic Dreams* (1986) are overtly nature-sceptical in revisiting and problematising historical constructions of nature. Each response explicitly displaces Western traditions through the presentation of Buddhist (Matthiessen), Aborigine (Davidson) and Inuit (Lopez) perspectives of nature, which challenge anthropocentrism, Western landscape aesthetics and the opposition of nature and culture.

Nature-sceptical discourses might seem arcane amid the widespread destruction of the natural world, yet challenges to the aestheticisation of rural life, the sentimentalisation of the natural world and the othering of nature are all necessary to the development of an environmental imagination for the twenty-first century. In *Arctic Dreams*, Lopez shows how the aesthetics of landscape shape attitudes to the environment: 'To a Western imagination that finds a stand of full-crowned trees heartening, that finds the flight and voice of larks exhilarating, and the sight of winds rolling over tall grass agreeable, Pingkok seems impoverished'. He admits that he too first saw this Arctic terrain through prejudiced eyes as bleak and desolate, a place to ignore, or worse: 'It is in a place like this that we would unthinkingly store poisons or test weapons'.[40] Lopez's argument is that we should look at landscape differently by forgetting learnt responses – forgetting the prejudices of eighteenth-century aesthetics, Romanticism and utilitarianism.

This willed amnesia about what nature actually *is* might allow us to consider the environment and our place in it from different perspectives. Lopez's revisioning is helped by learning to see the Arctic through the eyes of indigenous people (albeit a constructed and potentially romanticised view), through the sense-terrain of the Arctic fox – the non-human, 'creaturely' perspective – and through the eyes of a botanist who concentrates on microhabitats of the tundra, a bio-region containing a wealth of living and dead organisms in a single tussock.[41]

In *Landmarks* (2015), Robert Macfarlane tackles the semiotics of nature to save similarly under-represented and previously unloved landscapes. He begins with an account of the controversy over building a wind farm on the remote Isle of Lewis in Western Scotland. The planned desecration of the island's ecology by the installation of 234 wind turbines was justified by the planners because, they argued, there was nothing of particular scientific, economic or aesthetic value on Brindled Moor.[42] It was described by the company applying for planning permission as a wasteland, a wilderness, a '*terra nullius*, "a vast, dead place: dark brown moors and black lochs under a grey sky, all swept by a chill wet wind"' (29). The argument hinged on the received idea that this was a kind of wilderness retaining no intrinsic, human or social value. The scientists would not defend it and few locals were directly affected by it. It had no value attached to it through representation in picturesque or sublime words and images – unlike the nearby Isle of Skye and the Scottish Highlands with their many Romantic literary and artistic connections. The victim of under-representation and scientific indifference, the moor's fate appeared sealed until the islanders found a way of establishing its local relevance by unearthing its rich cultural history of art, writing and linguistics. The establishment of a 'Peat Glossary' that records dialect words specific to the region helped to re-inscribe social history into the natural landscape. This values the wilderness by reintegrating it with culture, and with the moor recovered from social and cultural oblivion the planning application was rejected (29–32). Macfarlane continues his etymological and socio-linguistic defence of the environment in *Landmarks* by compiling glossaries of disappearing local dialect 'place-words'. His approach is both nature-affirming in effecting direct action to protect the environment and nature-sceptical in disrupting received ideas and learnt responses to nature through semiotic strategies.

In his earlier book, *The Wild Places* (2007), Macfarlane sets out from his Cambridge home to explore places in Britain that are remote and detached from human habitation. This looks like a regression, since the wilderness is once more the liminal site for masculine self-fulfilment and semiotic appropriation. Kathleen Jamie seizes on this in her review of the book, 'A Lone Enraptured Male', rejecting appropriation by:

> A white, middle-class Englishman! A Lone Enraptured Male! From Cambridge! Here to boldly go, 'discovering', then quelling *our* [emphasis added] harsh and lovely and sometimes difficult land with his civilized lyrical words.[43]

She finds 'an awful lot of "I"' in Macfarlane's encounters with wild places, and connects this with a kind of semiotic colonialism through his English translation of *her* homeland, Scotland. But after some regionalist tub-thumping and grudging admiration of his 'lovely honeyed prose',[44] she accepts that Macfarlane's main objective, much like her own, is to dispose of the older constructs of wilderness where men boldly went. In my reading, Macfarlane actually installs this traditional androcentric idea of 'wild places' outside human history with some irony, and with the intention of subverting it, as he ends the book with a contemporary revision of the idea of 'wildness'. In common with Roger Deakin, Nan Shepherd and Edward Thomas, whose paths he follows literally and figuratively in *The Old Ways* and again in *Landmarks*, Macfarlane not only considers landscape as a reflection of ourselves and an influence on what we think and how we think, but also what it is 'to be thought *by* place'.[45] Unlike post-Romantic dialogues where self resonates with nature and is articulated through a kind of human ventriloquism, place here initiates the communication, because it has a voice (or a meaningful silence); it is capable of thinking us. As Macfarlane puts it, 'wild places' are 'self-willed' (30–31). It follows that 'wildness' is not only to be found in a separate space where human activity is diminished or non-existent; it is not something 'hived off from human life, but [. . .] exist[s] unexpectedly around and within it: in cities, backyards, roadsides, hedges, field boundaries or spinnies' (226).

Macfarlane borrows Gary Snyder's distinction between circumscribed wilderness as an alternative space and a ubiquitous 'wildness' which, as Fowles notes, meshes us with nature. In *The Practice of the Wild*, Snyder claims that 'Wilderness' makes up no more than '2 percent of the land of the United States', and this is formally set aside as public space, and includes those 'shrines saved from all the land that was once known and lived on by the original people, the little bits left as they were, the last little places where intrinsic nature totally wails, blooms, nests, glints away'. In *Findings*, Jamie reflects on this kind of secondary wilderness in the Central Highlands of Scotland, where ancient pasturelands and shelters – the 'shielings' – are barely perceptible in the glen except as 'mossy ruins' sinking back into the earth. 'Wilderness' is not the word for places like this, abandoned two centuries ago; 'it is an affront to those many generations who took their living on that land. Whether their departure was forced or whether that way of life fell into abeyance, they left such subtle marks'.[46]

The trope of old dwellings recolonised by nature is not new, of course; this is a staple of Romantic nature writing and the picturesque. But from an ecological (nature-sceptical) perspective, nature and society are brought within the same frame to deconstruct a false opposition between wild nature and culture. Edward Thomas often finds crossovers between wild nature and culture, and although he might have preceded the ecological wave, in drawing compelling images of the corners of wildness that mesh with human life, he provides a model for new nature writers. In *The South Country* (1909), he writes of a cottage that seems to have risen out of its natural surroundings:

> if the field happens to be without a crop, the earth is of the same colour as the thatch, and the cottage looks as if it were the work – like a mole-hill – of some creature that has worked underground and risen up just there and rested, peering out of the two dark windows upon the world.[47]

The occupant of this cottage is regarded in the same light, a man who has grown so close to wild nature it is as though it inhabits his being:

> His fingers, his limbs, his face, his silence, suggest crooked oak timber or the gnarled stones of the many times polled ash. It is barely credible that he grew out of child, the son of a woman, and not out of the earth itself, like the great flints that work upwards and out on to the surface of the fields.
>
> *(176)*

While this man seems formed from nature, another is folded into nature, having been discarded by society; the itinerant 'umbrella man', wounded in the war and cast out from society, wanders the old tracks of Southern England, gradually returning 'to a primeval wildness and simplicity' (170).

Human intervention in nature doesn't go away, but sometimes wild nature intervenes in the human and this aids the deconstruction of nature–culture and human–non-human oppositions. But we must not confuse wildness with wilderness. Wilderness as an alternative topos is disappearing fast. It has morphed into a social space now, an area set aside and managed. At this point in the human-saturated Anthropocene, it might be appropriate to put both 'nature' and 'wilderness' under erasure and consider, as does Snyder, the ubiquity of 'wildness' instead:

> it [wildness] is everywhere: ineradicable populations of fungi, moss, mold, yeasts, and such that surround and inhabit us [. . .] deer bounding across the freeway, pigeons in the park, spiders in the corners [. . .] Exquisite complex beings in their energy webs inhabiting the fertile corners of the urban world in accord with the rules of wild systems.[48]

Wilderness as a self-organising space of nature, untouched by human activity, has dwindled and barely exists as a present reality, but wildness is persistent, constant and ubiquitous. The spectre of wilderness might stalk the planet, waiting for the demise of the Anthropocene, but there will be no return to a pristine planet, because of the permanent damage we have done. As Snyder puts it, when wilderness returns, 'it will not be as fine a world as the one that was glistening in the early morning of the Holocene'.[49]

Dispensing with wilderness as a form of place to focus instead on an inclusive and pervasive sense of wildness is a common theme in new nature writing. In *Findings*, Jamie's main theme is the suturing of separate realms, of human and non-human, organic and inorganic, wild and domestic, natural and unnatural. Although the details of her domestic life sometimes verge on the banal, she undoubtedly brings wild nature close to home. Furthermore, in writing about a condition that has afflicted her husband, and about the various specimens she finds in the collection of the Royal College of Surgeons in Edinburgh, she identifies the wild in the micro-organisms of the human body: 'We consider the natural world as "out there", an "environment", but these jars show us the forms concealed inside, the intimate unknown'.[50]

Wild nature has become desecrated by centuries of human activity, while the once transcendental signifier, 'nature', with all its historical baggage, gets in the way of writing about the natural world. So let us finish by putting the word under erasure to signify doubly deleted real and semiotic realms. Let us consider the idea of 'ecology without nature', as Timothy Morton proposes.[51] Out of the ruins of the Anthropocene might then emerge 'wildness' as an inclusive principle that meshes the organic being that inhabits us with the environment that surrounds us.

Notes

1 Phil Macnaghten and John Urry, *Contested Natures* (London: Sage, 1998), 4.
2 Kathleen Jamie, *Findings* (London: Sort Of, 2005), 59.
3 Paul Lawrence Farber, *Finding Order in Nature* (Baltimore, MD: Johns Hopkins University Press, 2000); Paul Smethurst, *Travel Writing and the Natural World, 1768–1840* (Basingstoke: Palgrave Macmillan, 2013), 29–33.
4 Alexander von Humboldt, *Personal Narrative*, ed. and trans. Jason Williams (1814–29, Harmondsworth: Penguin, 1995), 11.
5 Smethurst, *Travel Writing and the Natural World*, 92–7.
6 Alexander von Humboldt, *Aspects of Nature*, trans. Mrs Sabines (1808; London: Longmans and John Murray, 1850), vii.
7 William Wordsworth, *A Guide Through the Lakes of the North of England* [1810], in *The Prose Works of William Wordsworth,* ed. W.J.R. Owen and J.W. Smyser (Oxford: Clarendon Press, 1974), 2:151.
8 Wordsworth, *Guide*, 2:306.

9   Smethurst, *Travel Writing and the Natural World*, 117.
10 Smethurst, *Travel Writing and the Natural World*, 117.
11 Barbara Maria Stafford, *Voyage into Substance: Art, Science, Nature, and the Illustrated Travel Account, 1760–1840* (Cambridge, MA: MIT Press, 1984).
12 George Forster, *A Voyage Round the World*, ed. Nicholas Thomas and Oliver Berghof (1777; Honolulu, HI: University of Hawai'i Press, 2000), 1:7–8.
13 Forster, *Voyage*, 1:90–91.
14 Raymond Williams, *The Country and the City* (1973; repr. London: Hogarth, 1993), 21.
15 A tradition which begins in the Scottish Highlands with Thomas Pennant's *A Tour in Scotland and Voyage to the Hebrides* (Chester: John Monk, 1774) and William Gilpin's *Observations, Relative Chiefly to Picturesque Beauty . . . Particularly the High-Lands of Scotland* (London: Blamire, 1789), and continues in the mountains of California with John Muir, a displaced Scotsman; Muir, *The Mountains of California* (New York: Century, 1894) and *My First Summer in the Sierra* (Boston, MA: Houghton Mifflin, 1911).
16 Jonathan Bate, *The Song of the Earth* (London: Picador, 2000), 35.
17 For an account of this debate, see Bate, *Romantic Ecology* (London: Routledge, 1991) and *The Song of the Earth* (2000); Lawrence Buell, *The Environmental Imagination* (Cambridge, MA: Harvard University Press, 1995) and *Writing for an Endangered World* (Cambridge, MA: Harvard University Press, 2001); Adrian Franklin, *Nature and Social Theory* (London: Sage, 2002); Graham Huggan, 'Postcolonial ecocriticism and the limits of Green Romanticism', *Journal of Postcolonial Writing* 45.1 (2009): 3–14.
18 Keith Thomas, *Man and the Natural World* (New York: Pantheon, 1983), 19.
19 Thomas, *Man and the Natural World*, 25.
20 Henri Lefebvre, *The Production of Space*, trans. Donald Nicholson-Smith (1974; Oxford: Blackwell, 1991), 30–31. See also Smethurst, *Travel Writing and the Natural World*, 199–200 and Kate Soper, *What Is Nature?* (Oxford: Blackwell, 1995), 185.
21 Buell, *Writing for an Endangered World*, 5.
22 Thomas, *Man and the Natural World*, 283–4.
23 Roger Deakin, *Wildwood: A Journey Through Trees* (London: Hamish Hamilton, 2007), 95.
24 Smethurst, *Travel Writing and the Natural World*, 80.
25 See for example Mary Louise Pratt, *Imperial Eyes: Travel Writing and Transculturation* (New York: Routledge, 1992) and David Phillip Miller and Peter Hans Reill, eds, *Visions of Empire: Voyages, Botany and Representations of Nature* (Cambridge: Cambridge University Press, 1996).
26 Richard H. Grove, *Green Imperialism: Colonial Expansion, Tropical Island Edens and the Origins of Environmentalism* (Cambridge: Cambridge University Press, 1995), 11.
27 Smethurst, *Travel Writing and the Natural World*, 88–108.
28 Jason Cowley, 'Editors' letter: The new nature writing', *Granta* 102 (2008): 9.
29 Joe Moran, 'A cultural history of the new nature writing', *Literature and History* 23.1 (Spring 2014): 49.
30 Susan Clifford and Angela King, 'Preface', in *Second Nature*, ed. Richard Mabey (London: Cape, 1984), vii.
31 John Fowles, 'The Blinded Eye', in Mabey, *Second Nature*, 84.
32 Fowles, 'Blinded Eye', 86.
33 Fowles, 'Blinded Eye', 88.
34 Fowles, 'Blinded Eye', 89.
35 Soper, *What Is Nature?*, 38.
36 Soper, *What Is Nature?*, 3–4.
37 Sarah Hazlitt, 'Sarah Hazlitt's journal of my trip to Scotland' [1822], *University of Buffalo Studies* 24 (1959): 185–252; Helen Maria Williams. *A Tour in Switzerland*, 2 vols (London: G. G. and J. Robinson, 1797); Mary Wollstonecraft, *Letters Written During a Short Residence in Sweden, Norway and Denmark* (London: 1796); Dorothy Wordsworth, 'Recollections of a Tour Made in Scotland A.D. 1820', in *The Journals of Dorothy Wordsworth*, ed. E. de Selincourt (London: Macmillan, 1941), 1:195–409; Nan Shepherd, *The Living Mountain* (1977; Edinburgh: Canongate, 2011).
38 Buell, *Writing for an Endangered World*, 33.
39 Robin Morgan, *The Anatomy of Freedom* (New York: Anchor/Doubleday, 1982).
40 Barry Lopez, *Arctic Dreams* (1986; New York: Random House, 2001), 255.
41 Lopez, *Arctic Dreams*, 267, 259.
42 Robert Macfarlane, *Landmarks* (London: Hamish Hamilton, 2015), 27. Subsequent references are included parenthetically in the text.

43 Kathleen Jamie, 'A lone enraptured male', *London Review of Books* (6 March 2008): 7, accessed 4 September 2016, www.lrb.co.uk/v30/n05/kathleen-jamie/a-lone-enraptured-male.

44 Jamie, 'Lone enraptured male', 5.

45 Robert Macfarlane, *The Old Ways* (London: Penguin, 2013), 193.

46 Jamie, *Findings*, 126.

47 Edward Thomas, *The South Country* (1909; repr. Wimborne Minster, Dorset: Little Toller Books, 2009), 172. Subsequent references are included parenthetically in the text.

48 Gary Snyder, *The Practice of the Wild* (1990; repr. Berkeley, CA: Counterpoint, 2010), 15–16.

49 Snyder, *Practice of the Wild*, 16.

50 Jamie, *Findings*, 141.

51 Timothy Morton, *Ecology Without Nature: Rethinking Environmental Aesthetics* (Cambridge, MA: Harvard University Press, 2007).

3

MIGRANT NARRATIVES

Aedín Ní Loingsigh

Mis/trusting migrants: travel writing, lies and undocumented migrancy

Whatever the motivations and consequences of lies in travel writing, critics must first identify them. Their priority, argues Percy G. Adams, is 'to ferret them out and determine their extent'.[1] This is precisely the approach French journalist Benoît Hopquin appears to adopt when he exposes what he claims to be the bogus nature of *Soif d'Europe*, a first-hand description of illegal travel to Europe by Senegalese author and essayist Omar Ba.[2] In his account, Ba describes leaving Senegal by boat in September 2000 and landing in the Moroccan coastal town of Dakhla following a failed attempt to reach the Canary Islands.[3] Following months of low-paid work in Morocco, he takes a trans-Saharan route to Chad via Mauritania, Mali and Niger and then onwards to the North African coast. His journey, however, is never straightforward, and rather than progressing in any geographically logical fashion, arrest and deportation by border police in Chad, Morocco and Italy mean Ba moves back and forth across the Sahara and North African coast as he unsuccessfully attempts to penetrate fortress Europe. Eventually he returns to Dakhla where, in November 2002, he makes it to the Canary Islands following a traumatic crossing in an over-crowded boat. Unable to repatriate this undocumented traveller, the Spanish border agency transfers him to Barcelona. The text ends with a description of Ba's illegal entry into France and his ignominious deportation to Senegal by the French authorities.

By the time the 'truth' behind this journey is revealed by Hopquin, Ba was becoming an outspoken critic of immigration policy in France and Senegal and had just published a successful essay on this topic.[4] At the outset of his article, Hopquin notes with some irritation the increasing media 'visibility' of this 'irregular migrant' ['un clandestin très visible'] before outlining the 'inconsistencies and chronological errors' ['incohérences et anachronismes'] that prove Ba's narrative to be a fabrication. The *Le Monde* reporter also reveals the fact that Ba had been registered as a student in Africa and France during much of the period of travel described in the book. He then further undermines the African's credibility by alluding to more serious criminal accusations that were pending investigation at the time.

How are readers to respond to the content of *Soif d'Europe* once Hopquin identifies its 'lies'? One reaction is to see the text's fabricated content as invalidating the account of irregular travel and divesting its author of the authority normally associated with the empirically minded western travel writer. The search for a more reliable method for documenting the irregular migrant's journey might then lead to the 2012 text, *Dem ak xabaar/Partir et raconter.*[5] In this instance, the Wolof title and its French translation are the first indicators of the particular form of collaboration that sees the French author and journalist Bruno Le Dantec co-author with the unknown Senegalese migrant Mahmoud Traoré a detailed account of the latter's three-and-a-half-year clandestine journey to Europe. Like his compatriot Omar Ba, Traoré's overland travel is along the beaten tracks established by trans-Saharan traders in earlier centuries. However, prior to departure, Traoré fixes a clear route to which he sticks, even when arrest and abandonment force him to double back significant distances. A sickle-shaped trajectory thus takes him east from Senegal to Mali and Niger, then curves gently north-eastwards through the Sahara to Libya before heading westwards across North Africa to Morocco. There, Traoré participates in the infamous October 2005 collective attempt to scale the border fence of the Spanish territory of Ceuta when a number of migrants were shot dead by police.[6]

In his preface to the co-authored account of illegal travel, Le Dantec insists that *Dem ak xabaar* 'is not a tale, but an authentic personal account that has been scrupulously compiled' ['N'est pourtant pas un conte, mais un témoignage authentique, scrupuleusement établi'] (14). This suggests a desire to influence the reception of the text by reassuring readers of its legitimacy. The near absence of a critical reception to *Dem ak xabaar* could then suggest that its content did not arouse the type of suspicion prompted by *Soif d'Europe* and that the nature of Le Dantec and Traoré's partnership succeeds in restoring credibility to the migrant narrative. It would be a mistake, however, to read the later publication as forming a corrective to the perceived failings of Ba's text. For all their very different narrative strategies and critical fates, *Soif d'Europe* and *Dem ak xabaar* can be read alongside each other in order to examine the ways in which each calls attention to the place of mis/trust in narratives of migrant journeys and their reception. For his harshest critics, mistrust in Ba the messenger appears to have undermined the value of the message of *Soif d'Europe*. However, this instantly dismissive approach ignores the manner in which strategic invention shapes *all* discourse. More importantly, condemnation of Ba's act of fabrication obscures the complex logic of mis/trust in the context of undocumented migrant journeys where moral and legal boundaries are frequently ignored or non-existent.

This is not to say that questions of mis/trust have been absent from critical considerations of migration. From the 1990s, an extensive scholarly literature began to elaborate on the significance of migrant mobility and geographical displacement. This was particularly evident in postcolonial studies, the theoretical field that has done more than any other to shape critical approaches to travel writing. Indeed, as Andrew Smith argues, the very legitimacy of postcolonial studies is centred on 'the idea that the relationship between narrative and movement takes on a new and qualitatively different significance in the context and aftermath of colonialism'.[7] Much of this 'newness', particularly in the postcolonial era of mass migrations, has been associated with the cultural accommodations of various travelling figures and groups – migrants, exiles, nomads, diasporas. These emerging processes of identity formation have in turn been theorised via terms that invariably evoke mobility-related spaces and behaviours – rootlessness, restlessness, hospitality, borders, contact zones.[8] And whether or not they are explicitly referenced, notions of mis/trust have necessarily been at the centre of 'the negotiation of [the] incommensurable differences' that for Homi K. Bhabha characterise the 'new transnational world and its hybrid names'.[9]

However, at the same time as 'migration' has come to be increasingly deployed as a trusted trope for explaining postcolonial writing of cultural difference, other critics have signalled disquiet at increasing metaphorical uses of the term.[10] Particularly vexing for materialist critics has been the development of a poetics of relocation that can 'entail forgetfulness about that other, economically enforced dispersal of the poor from Africa, Asia, Latin America'.[11] This has prompted concern regarding the persistence of dematerialised readings of borders and border crossings, and disapproval of the neglect of undocumented migration within cultural criticism more generally. To be sure, much of this emerging work has focused on asylum rather than on the position of irregular economic migrants. Nonetheless, it has insisted on the need 'to retain a nuanced conception of forced migration' whilst at the same time highlighting the key issue for this chapter of European 'anxieties over authenticity' and the way in which these are used to adjudicate truth claims.[12]

Both *Soif d'Europe* and *Dem ak xabaar* devote sections of their narratives to describing the travails of the economic migrant who must negotiate an inhospitable Europe in order to find work and accommodation. In this respect, aspects of what they describe accord with an earlier and substantial body of textual and cinematic representations of economic migrants who 'arrived' legitimately and in many cases 'settled' – however uncertainly – and subsequently saw their children inherit the tensions between homeland and host land. In the Francophone context that is the main focus here, it would be inaccurate to say that critics have forgotten the material circumstances that shape these diasporic groups' negotiation of difference.[13] However, it is also fair to say that despite a growing body of literary and filmic work exploring the singular journeys of irregular migrants *on the move* from West Africa to Europe, critical attention has been cursory.[14] This is as true of travel writing scholarship as it is of critical commentary on other areas of cultural production.

Consequently, this chapter concentrates on the substantial sections of both *Soif d'Europe* and *Dem ak xabaar* that are encoded as travel narratives in the more conventional western understanding of the term. I return below to the value of regarding such texts as integral to travel writing's critical project. For the moment, however, suffice to say that these texts' self-description as non-fictional prose accounts of journeys that were actually undertaken by their narrators fully justifies their inclusion under the generic understanding of travel writing. It should also be made clear that like many readings of travel writing, this chapter's initial discussion of trust and mistrust as tropes and themes of undocumented migrancy willingly tolerates any 'lies' or traveller's 'tales'. It does so on the understanding that the selective view of these retrospective accounts of journeying inevitably results in suppressions and distortions. The final section on authorship and trust, however, returns in particular to the question of Ba's alleged impropriety and explores more critically the implications of his 'lies' on the reception of *Soif d'Europe*. It also asks what questions Ba's actions raise about the dual authorship of *Dem ak xabaar* and the factors, if any, that might suggest this account to be more trustworthy than *Soif d'Europe*.

Trusting travellers

Although feelings of suspicion and uncertainty frequently threaten to overwhelm the narrative in *Soif d'Europe* and *Dem ak xabaar*, they do not mark the journey experience exclusively. Like any travelling figure embarking on an international journey as uncertain as that undertaken by irregular migrants, the decision to travel must rest to some degree on trust. For without trust the migrant is immobilised. It should come as no surprise, then, that both texts begin with a strong sense that the decision to opt for an alternative life in Europe has been undertaken precisely in a spirit of confidence. The self-assurance (or trust in themselves) both travellers exhibit, and their related ability to reciprocate trust in the context of some of their travelling encounters, never fully dissipates and is evident most clearly in the unwavering determination to make it to Europe. Both narrators understand that this journey is a gamble: they know they are likely to be tricked, abused and arrested and that they may even die. Nonetheless, they are clearly willing to wager against these odds. Where do this confidence and self-belief come from and how far do they actually sustain the clandestine migrant traveller?

Although in both cases the complex push and pull factors of economic realities unquestionably influence decisions to leave home, there is arguably a critical myopia in seeing them as the only explanation. In other words, if the journeys in these texts, and those of many irregular migrants (as opposed to refugees), are made for economic reasons, they are also prompted by a desire for adventure and the opportunity to test strength and courage. For example, it is possible to interpret the undeniable impulse of self-confidence informing attitudes to travel in *Soif d'Europe* and *Dem ak xabaar* as evidence of a connection to a recognised literary tradition of adventure travel that frames the figure of the self-assured, self-abnegating male traveller. This is certainly a thread in Le Dantec's introduction to *Dem ak xabaar*, where he insists on associations between the migrant's heroic 'odyssey' and established characters and motifs of classical Greek adventure narratives. Of course, this comparison can just as easily be extended to an historically more recent context that allows us to see the migrant as globalisation's equivalent of the 'heroic' explorer or adventurer of so much western travel writing.

Needless to say, there are important critical advantages to using the critical frame of travel writing in order to draw parallels between the journeying of more established western traditions of travel and the so-called 'displacement' of the modern-day irregular migrant: it can secure his/her place in a broader history of travel; it can highlight the specific ways in which migrant narratives impose their own form of the recognised basics of travel writing; it can underscore the way in which the former's choice to experience travel is affirmation of a self-assured travelling identity rather than evidence of powerless victimhood. However, such comparisons, because they risk being decontextualised, are also capable of undermining our ability to grasp fully the complexity and anxieties of migrant mobility. Needless to say, such concerns fit into the above-mentioned mistrust of dematerialised critical approaches to travel. Thus, it is important to remember that although the traveller may demonstrate confidence and an ability to trust when travelling, these are not necessarily qualities acquired for the first time when on the move. Social and cultural interactions at home also play their part. This means that any openness to adventure detected in *Soif d'Europe* and *Dem ak xabaar*, and any resilience and resourcefulness displayed en route, must be understood by looking more closely at the specific cultural origins of the migrant travellers.

Ba's initial determination to overcome fear and 'to leave no matter what might happen' ['Je veux partir quoi qu'il advienne'] (5) and Traoré's confident dismissal of the 'pessimism of those who are too tired to embark on an adventure' ['Le pessimisme de ceux qui sont trop fatigués pour faire l'aventure'] (20) certainly echo the adventurous spirit of established travelling precursors. However, certain forms of social interaction that create a sense of predictability, stability and solidarity also shape their approach to setting out on their journeys. In this regard it is significant that the respective departures of *Soif d'Europe* and *Dem ak xabaar* are set against what could be described as ritualised send-offs organised by close friends and family. These certainly share the symbolic significance that Barbara A. Misztal attributes more generally to 'rites of transition and other group rituals [that] can be seen as contributing to members' self-confidence and mutual trust within the group as well as to mapping out whom to trust outside the group'.[15]

In Traoré's case, the ritual marking his departure involves the preparation by his cousin of a 'sacrificial' dish of bread. Once they have eaten it together, the family members wash their hands in water which is then thrown outside the threshold to ensure a safe journey. It is noteworthy, too, that as Traoré's journey progresses, and as the ability to trust is continuously challenged, italicised passages in the text indicate breaks in a narrative structure that is otherwise faithful to the chronological and spatial progress of the journey. Many of these interruptions are reflections on routinised practices relating to childhood play, work and interpersonal relationships. For example, during a particularly arduous section of his journey between Niger and Libya when he and a group of fellow migrants are abandoned in the desert and forced to follow an untrustworthy guide on foot, we learn that from the age of six Traoré and his friends were taken to the fields to divide their days between work and fun. This routine, he suggests, prepared them to be flexible in their expectations and to savour the pleasures that inevitably followed tough physical exertion. Later, in an illegal immigrant camp on the North African Mediterranean coast, the narrative digresses to describe the solidarity of village life in the face of poor harvests. Recalling how any surplus produce was shared with the most badly affected families, Traoré explains that this practice provided assurance of mutual assistance should it be subsequently required.

Such habits or 'patterning' of social life, as Misztal describes it, 'can be seen as playing the same role as trust'.[16] Routine and a spiritual faith that, as Traoré explains, trusts in a 'God [who] will provide' ['Dieu y pourvoira'] (24) allow the unpredictable to be managed, and, crucially, 'facilit[ate] the taking of a risk'.[17] In Traoré's case, the stoicism that this patterning encourages appears more durable than in the case of Ba. Unlike the latter, who largely travels alone, Traoré begins his journey with a close friend, Bambo. Although the pair subsequently separate, Traoré continues to establish important friendships – and in Algiers a potentially romantic relationship – that sustain him through some of the most uncertain moments. His seemingly ineradicable optimism can also be explained by the many instances where his predisposition to trust in others is repaid by the arbitrary expressions of kindness he benefits from en route. Arguably this ability to trust to the end is most forcefully expressed by the cooperative exchange with Le Dantec and the resulting textualisation of his own story.

Ba's departure is also marked in what could be described as a ritualised manner. He is sent on his way with symbolic gifts from his parents that include a copy of the *Koran* and two talismans intended to ensure courage and protection. One caustic online commentator of *Soif d'Europe* sees this as a blatant example of exoticisation designed to appeal to a western readership and, consequently, yet more reason to mistrust Ba's motives.[18] Nonetheless, as in *Dem ak xabaar*, the emphasis on such a ritual is striking. It serves as another reminder of how a secure sense of personal and cultural identity – and the related ability to trust in oneself and others – is strengthened by strong positive personal and cultural bonds. The importance of solidarity with fellow migrants is also underlined by Ba, who notes very early on in his journey how a commonality of purpose can unite these travellers and provide protection. As with Traoré, family, as well as wider networks of trust based on shared national and cultural affiliations, can also provide important sources of material and psychological support to the migrant on the move. Key here are the many migrants who have already made it to Europe and whose stories of success, seemingly supported by generous remittances, help to establish the pathways used by subsequent migrants.

Ultimately, however, although *Soif d'Europe* presents notable overlaps with *Dem ak xabaar* in terms of its representation of the material conditions of the migrant's journey, the psychological trajectory described does not map so easily on to Traoré's more stoic attitude. In this respect, Ba's ultimate spiralling into cynicism and suspicion cautions against the naïve suggestion that close personal relationships and strong cultural ties guarantee the continued preservation of trust. As his journey becomes a series of failures and disappointments, Ba becomes increasingly critical of the societal and familial pressure on migrants to leave for Europe as a matter of course. Rather than celebrate, as Traoré's narrative digressions do, a durable ability to trust in himself and others, he becomes more resentful and critical of his country for failing to provide an alternative to emigration. Ba's growing difficulty in reciprocating trust with those he encounters en route is also explained by the complex realisation that if migration is a 'family affair', it is one defined by betrayal rather than solidarity. This development is underlined during a phone call home to his aunt, who praises him profusely as she reminds him of the hope (clearly financial and status-related) he represents for his family. This time, however, his family's apparent faith in him does not embolden him but causes him to mistrust their intentions as well as his own. Their belief in his ability to complete the journey then says little positive about him but rather indicates how the 'notions of failure and success have been displaced from them to me' ['Les notions d'échec et de réussite se sont déplacées d'eux vers moi'] (70). If Ba does not express that he has been lied to, his anxieties about his future and his critical attitude to 'home' point to a crucial distinction between the ultimately fragile confidence of the clandestine migrant and what Patrick Holland and Graham Huggan identify as the 'assertive individualism' of western travel writers whose 'experiences of travel are predicated on the possibility of return'.[19]

Mistrusting travellers

Mistrust is a near permanent factor shaping travel in *Soif d'Europe* and *Dem ak xabaar*. Frequently, when the migrant narrators of the texts are not being seen to mistrust, they are themselves mistrusted. For example, in Libya, a country where Traoré feels others' mistrust of him more acutely than elsewhere, a shared religious identity does nothing to counter what he sees as a fundamental dismissal of black Africans as spiritually damned and sexually threatening. Indeed, throughout the journey, Traoré is made increasingly aware of how his migrant identity can often subsume others (national, ethnic, religious) and provoke the suspicions and animosity of 'hosts'. He learns to 'guess people's intentions from their opening gestures. If they avoid your gaze or start to gesticulate at your approach, it's a bad sign' ['Tu en viens à deviner les intentions des gens dès leurs premiers gestes'] (149). The automatic suspicion towards the migrant described here signals a much wider public perception in Europe, but also in transit countries, which sees noncitizens invariably 'treated as potential offenders without regard to their personal situation'.[20] This pervasive mistrust also risks shifting emphasis onto the 'criminality' of the irregular migrant. The fear that they can be betrayed at any moment means the narrators of *Soif d'Europe* and *Dem ak xaabar* travel in a state of constant tension because, as Thomas Nail observes, 'all of society increasingly functions "like a border", where surveillance is a constant'.[21]

The migrant's mistrust of others arises almost immediately after departure and is frequently related to financial transactions. In Ba's case, for example, the initial decision to take the shortest route to Europe by sea means travelling by pirogue from Senegal to the Canary Islands. Departure is from a nondescript beach under cover of darkness in a craft that seems barely seaworthy. Despite this, the boat continues its course north along the coast, increasing its passenger numbers from a recommended thirty to over eighty individuals. All the while, an unconcerned 'captain' accepts this overloading in return, the reader deduces, for the high sums of money his passengers willingly hand over. Concerned about his safety and his chances of reaching his destination, Ba finally opts to disembark in Dakhla. (Despite this interruption to the journey, he receives no refund and subsequently spends an unforeseen and lengthy period of time working to finance his costly overland route.)

This is the first of repeated instances in *Soif d'Europe* and *Dem ak xaabar* where the unscrupulous 'business' practices of smugglers undermine the trusted system of exchange on which financial transactions normally depend. In stable societies, and also in the secure travel conditions we associate with first-world travellers, 'money is "a promise" that exchange will be honoured'.[22] In certain respects, the 'business' practices that profit from clandestine migration do appear to mirror those of legitimate travel agencies that are trusted to deal with the practical arrangements of travel and, crucially, to provide the traveller with security. Thus, for example, the providers of counterfeit travel documents, the drivers and guides who promise to deliver migrants to the next stage of the journey, and the 'chairmen' who welcome migrants into the unofficial 'foyers' and camps that exist along key routes seem to offer the type of reassurance and comfort that a western traveller expects in return for payment. Time and again, however, trust in the 'promise' thought to be provided by such payment is abused by drivers, guides and 'officials' who twist the 'trusted' principles of the law to profit from the alternative economy of irregular migration.

Any hope that the highly organised camps, ghettos and 'foyers' might function as sub-stitute spaces of sovereignty for vulnerable noncitizens is also proved false. Migrants may well be received into these spaces on the basis of national and cultural identity. However, despite their own forms of 'parliamentary' rule and 'justice', these alternative embassies have no desire to protect the interests of migrants. Like the corrupt officials 'protecting' borders with whom they collude, their interest is in controlling and perpetuating the circulation of migrants across borders whilst at the same time extracting a profit. Traoré's description of the notorious Maghnia migrant ghetto on the Algerian-Moroccan border makes this racketeering ethos patently clear:

> Here you don't pay for the right to enter, but the right to leave. Once you are in the ghetto, you are fleeced in order to pay for passage over the border. If you have the means, you can go to Rabat in a truck. If you are poor, you go on foot, guided by a smuggler. But whatever you do, you've got to 'pay up'.
>
> [Ici, tu ne payes pas un droit d'entrée, mais un droit de sortie! Une fois dans le ghetto, on te rançonne pour financer le passage de la frontière. Si tu as les moyens, tu vas jusqu'à Rabat en camion. Si tu es pauvre, tu traverses à pied, guidé par un passeur. Mais quoi que tu fasses, tu dois 'dépocher'.]
>
> *(131)*

Where notions of mistrust and insecurity are concerned, a final word on the conditions endured by female migrants is necessary. Although Ba's text only fleetingly mentions encounters with female migrants, Traoré devotes a relatively lengthy passage to the particular challenges faced by them. This is prompted by an encounter with four women who all claim to be Cameroonian 'so they won't be separated during identity checks or border crossings' ['pour ne pas être séparées lors des contrôles ou des passages de frontière'] (104). On the one hand, this serves as an impor-tant reminder of the recent feminisation of global patterns of undocumented migration. More disturbingly, however, this brief reference points to the particular vulnerabilities of women trav-elling unaccompanied and without recourse to legal protection. Earlier, in the Nigerien transit hub of Agadez, Traoré is exposed to this reality when a female migrant from Ghana is sexually assaulted by a police officer (36). Traoré's retrospective narrative allows him to conclude that whatever the violence faced by male migrants (and neither he nor Ba shirk from describing it), their female counterparts have even less protection from physical and psychological abuse.[23]

Authorship and mis/trust

In an interview with Mathieu Leonard in *Article 11*, 21 November 2012, Bruno Le Dantec notes the frustrating efforts to have *Dem ak xabaar* published. Just as noteworthy, however, is the way in which his description of the reception of migrant journey narratives reveals the literary establishment's mistrust of migrants:

> The first impression I had when I submitted the manuscript [of *Dem ak xabaar*] was that it didn't tick the right box. Some publishers told me they would have published it had it been literature, a novel inspired by this story. Others would have been more comfortable had it been a political essay on the theme of irregular immigration [. . .]
>
> The second reason for publishers' misgivings is surely due to previous attempts at autobiographical accounts by clandestine migrants. In 2008, there was the case of a fake, *Soif d'Europe*: the Senegalese author, Omar Ba, admitted to having appropriated firsthand accounts of experiences he had not lived himself. This bogus example cast a shadow of doubt over everything that followed, as if one case was enough to disqualify all the rest [. . .]
>
> After this fake, there was *Migrant au pied du mur* in 2010 by Cameroonian Fabien Didier Yene who decided on a fictionalised form even though he had experienced what he described. It's the opposite of Omar Ba: Yene had to disguise the narrative form even though his story was true [. . .] In the end, his book went unnoticed.
>
> [La première impression que j'ai ressentie en présentant le manuscrit, c'est qu'il n'entrait pas dans les cases. Certains éditeurs me disaient qu'ils l'auraient publié si ça avait été de [la] littérature, un roman inspiré de cette histoire. D'autres, au contraire, auraient été plus à l'aise s'il s'était agi d'un essai politique sur le thème de l'immigration clandestine [. . .]
>
> Cela dit, la seconde raison de cette méfiance des éditeurs est sûrement due aux antécédents de tentatives de récits autobiographiques de clandestins. Il y a eu le cas d'un faux, *Soif d'Europe*, en 2008: l'auteur, Omar Ba, un Sénégalais, a reconnu avoir usurpé des témoignages qui n'étaient pas de sa propre expérience. Ce cas de bidonnage a jeté l'ombre du doute sur tout ce qui a suivi. Comme si un cas avait suffi à disqualifier le reste [. . .]
>
> Après ce faux, il y a eu *Migrant au pied du mur*, en 2010, du Camerounais Fabien Didier Yene, qui a fait, lui, le choix d'une forme romancée alors qu'il avait réellement vécu ce qu'il décrivait. C'est l'inverse d'Omar Ba: Yene a dû déguiser la forme de son récit alors que son histoire est authentique [. . .] Son bouquin est finalement passé inaperçu.][24]

Le Dantec's explicit reference to *Soif d'Europe* appears initially to concur with Benoît Hopquin's assessment of Ba's literary misconduct and the dismissal of his travel account as bogus. Closer examination, however, reveals that the situation is more nuanced than the outright assertion of the Senegalese author's 'guilt' suggests. In the first instance, an unnamed publisher is also guilty of double standards. It uses the apparent infraction committed by the literary 'pretender' Ba as the basis for establishing borders and deciding whether and how migrant narratives of travel are to be admitted. Whilst 'the shadow of doubt' cast by Ba's text may offer some explanation for the paucity of published accounts of '*bona fide*' migrant travel, Le Dantec suggests that the arbitrary application of generic criteria plays an equally significant role. In some cases, the truth of migrant narratives is required to be fictionalised in the novel form. However, this strategy is no guarantee that the migrant's travel 'tale' will be heard, as the reference to Fabien Didier Yene's already out-of-print 2010 novel underlines. In other situations, publishers expressly seek fact, yet this 'truth' must not be framed by the supposedly 'authentic' experience of autobiography or travel writing but by a discursive form that depends on detached, objective analysis. This of itself would not be such an issue were it not clear that the genres of writing characterised by such an approach (in particular the essay form) are frequently the domain of those with power and influence rather than those who can claim genuine 'ownership' of the migrant's story, i.e. the status-less migrants themselves. (In this respect it is interesting that Ba adopts the essay form only after he has attempted entry into French literary circles via *Soif d'Europe*.)

Returning, then, to Hopquin's disapprobation in respect of Ba's behaviour, the question of literary borders and their policing emerges more clearly. To be clear, there is no suggestion here that the 'inaccuracies' in Ba's text revealed by Hopquin should be suppressed. However, they are hardly sanctionable literary crimes. More interesting is the more general anxiety over authenticity that weighs upon the French journalist's investigation and the way in which his sleuthing recalls certain legal practices used to question migrant credibility. As Shahram Khosravi explains, the 'illegal traveller' who wishes to cross the border must be able to master 'Eurocentric juridical language' because 'in seeking the "truth", the hearing system checks and rechecks facts to find contradictions and inconsistencies in the applicant's narrative'.[25] More significant for the present context is Khosravi's contention that the need to protect their own and others' safety means 'asylum seekers usually do not reveal all the details of their journey, Accordingly, the part of any asylum seeker's story in which it is easiest to find discrepancies is the story of his or her journey'.[26]

Ultimately, however, Hopquin's approach to text-based evidence of unethical behaviour lacks the kind of rigorous 'ferreting out' one might expect from journalism in the scandal-breaking mould. Just as relevant in this context is Hopquin's failure to reveal that the mistrust of Ba's narrative and intentions does not originate with his investigation but was being widely discussed online since *Soif d'Europe* was first published. Indeed, in the comments posted in response to an article by Eric Mettout in *L'Express* on 10 July 2009, this fact is brought to the attention of French readers by one Senegalese commentator who claims that

> like most of my compatriots we knew from the beginning that [Ba's] story was untrue [. . .] We didn't stop ourselves from saying it was untrue online [. . .] That was last year. So *Le Monde* has uncovered nothing. It has reported an investigation conducted by the Senegalese diaspora.[27]

Perusing these online reactions, it would seem that 'ferreting out' the fabricated content of *Soif d'Europe* was in fact no more difficult than identifying the many explicit admissions in the narrative itself of lying for practical reasons (for example, to smugglers in order to travel more cheaply, and to family and friends to hide the truth of the migrant's situation). Consequently, the response of commentators who are supportive of Ba points to a much more complex under-standing of the latter's actions. In the final analysis, they see Ba's political message as taking priority over his means of communicating it.

As for Ba himself, an open letter published in *Le Parisien* on 11 July 2009 offers a brief and unrepentant response to Hopquin's accusations. He explains that in addition to personal experience, his account is also based on 'incidents experienced by others, anonymous individuals whose voice is too often silenced. I rearranged my life story because I felt it would have more impact' ['des drames vécus par d'autres, des anonymes dont la voix est souvent tue. J'ai arrangé ma biographie parce que je pensais que cela aurait plus d'impact'].[28] Moreover, by quoting the epigraph from Pablo Neruda's memoir – 'perhaps I didn't live just in myself; perhaps I lived the lives of others' – Ba reminds us of the space between fiction and truth where all supposed factual writing, including travel writing, is situated. His emphasis on 'impact' and his desire to have the voiceless, subaltern migrants heard by the greatest possible number also suggests, ironically, that he may well have identified a *succès à scandale* as a tactical manoeuvre to overcome the interests of those who police the borders of genre.[29]

Whatever Ba's intentions – and his answer fails to satisfy fully – his methods raise important questions about the legal and literary operations that strive to silence undocumented migrants. This, in turn, invites us to take a closer look at *Dem ak xabaar* and Le Dantec's role in the written record of Traoré's clandestine journey. It is important to emphasise that there is no impugning the former's motivations here: his sympathies with the marginalised and silenced are unambiguously demonstrated in his introduction and afterword, and research also reveals him to be an outspoken critic of hostile immigrant policy.[30] Consequently, what interests me here is the context within which Le Dantec's collaborative role can be examined and what it reveals about any perception of the trustworthiness of *Dem ak xabaar*.

The text's title page credits Le Dantec with the translation and re-writing of Traoré's story. However, there is no mention in the text of how interviews were conducted, how the inevitable challenges of translation were dealt with and what the nature of any re-writing or re-ordering of the journey narrative entailed. In other words, the text assumes that the reader will trust in the accuracy and truthfulness of Le Dantec's translation and re-writing of a journey he has not undertaken. Yet to the extent that translation and re-writing, and indeed collaboration, are no longer seen as neutral practices, it is worth looking more closely at a fuller description given by Le Dantec in the above-mentioned interview with Mathieu Leonard regarding the precise nature of his collaboration with Traoré:

> Given the power of this story [. . .] we decided that it had to be told in a way that would mean it would be heard by a maximum number of people. Consequently, we both reached an agreement. He trusted me to write his story, to make it accessible whilst avoiding any temptations to embellish. And I trusted what he told me whilst verifying wherever possible facts, dates, places.
>
> [Étant donné la puissance de cette histoire [. . .] on s'est dit qu'il fallait la raconter de manière à ce qu'elle touche le maximum de gens. On a donc passé un accord tous les deux. Il me faisait confiance pour rédiger son récit, pour en faire quelque chose d'accessible, tout en évitant les pièges de l'embellissement. Et moi, je me fiais à ce qu'il me racontait, tout en vérifiant, autant que faire se peut, les faits, les dates, les lieux.][31]

Le Dantec goes on to describe the role of Sonia Retamero Sánchez, Traoré's original interlocutor it would seem, who conducted and recorded interviews and is said to have brought her own curiosity and sensitivity to bear on aspects of the narrative. This description repeats what is already evident from Ba's explanation of his actions: in order for the story of irregular migrancy to penetrate the literary domain and to be widely read, consideration must be given to the *way* it is told. It also suggests that mistrust is as significant to understanding the narrative project of *Dem ak xabaar* as it is to reading the 'lies' of *Soif d'Europe*. The critical silence surrounding *Dem ak xabaar* is certainly in marked contrast to the high-profile negative reception of Ba's text and might therefore suggest it is entirely trustworthy. Le Dantec's account of his collaboration with Traoré, however, implies something more complex. Even if it eventually gives way to trust, there is clearly some mistrust between both authors at the outset: Traoré fears his co-author may embellish the 'truth'; Le Dantec, for his part, admits to verifying the facts of what he is being told by his co-author. However, unlike *Soif d'Europe*, where lies and mistrust are arguably hidden in plain view of the narrative, in *Dem ak xabaar* they are absorbed, behind the text, by the transformational practices – interviewing, translation, re-writing – that make this story of irregular migrancy 'accessible'. Any residual doubts are likely to be dismissed subsequently by the confident, authoritative voice of an introduction and postface that reassures: in other words, Le Dantec provides a mediating voice that can be trusted.

Conclusion

This chapter's framing of *Soif d'Europe* and *Dem ak xabaar* as travel writing allows light to be shed on the material and psychological conditions under which undocumented African economic migrants travel to Europe. Both texts reveal some of the 'push and pull' factors that underpin the decision to travel. Well-established routes followed by undocumented migrants are traced, complex networks of transport and hospitality are described and attention is drawn to the strategies necessary for negotiating hostile borders. Reading these narratives as travel writing also undermines understandings of migrant travellers as disempowered, passive movers focused entirely on their European destination and closed off to the contingent, salutary experiences that usually define western understandings of travel. Both Ba and Traoré demonstrate that an 'adventurous', open mind-set is required to embark on what are more often than not uncertain and arduous journeys. Some ability to trust themselves and others is therefore seen as essential to making progress along routes that stretch out over time and place.

However, as both *Soif d'Europe* and *Dem ak xabaar* reveal, a culture of lies and mutual mistrust invariably comes to dominate the travel experience of these texts' undocumented economic migrants. The pattern of these journeys highlights practices designed to exploit and criminalise the migrant narrators, whether in the informal 'business' of people-smuggling or in the official sphere of border control and law enforcement. This further accentuates elements of doubt and disparities of power inherent in a travel practice that is viewed as 'illegal'. This prevalence of mistrust also informs a view of migrants as lacking credibility.

This pattern of lies and mistrust also manifests itself in a literary context. As this chapter has shown, questions of trust and credibility translate themselves in concerning ways into the production, circulation and reception of the texts studied here. Ba's 'fabrication' of his migrant journey narrative was already acknowledged within the Senegalese diasporic community when a journalistic *exposé* in *Le Monde* transformed it into a literary scandal. In doing so, the article in the reputable, 'credible' French newspaper arguably silenced the political arguments of *Soif d'Europe*. It also appears to have wanted to transform its African author into an opportunist whose merging of fact and fiction, a long-established strategy of European travel writing, discredited him as a trustworthy author. In a troubling echo of the legal context in which undocumented migrants seek to have their stories heard, the *Le Monde* article might also be said to highlight a certain adversarial relationship between the would-be African author of a migrant narrative and a cultural/literary establishment that seeks to exclude him. This, then, might explain how a collaborative writing strategy, such as that employed by Bruno Le Dantec and Mahmoud Traoré in *Dem ak xabaar (Partir et raconteur)*, could be used to reassure a distrusting readership. In this instance, doubts about the veracity of Traoré's version of events are arguably assuaged by the corroborating, mediating voice of his French co-author.

In the end, any discussion of the textualisation of undocumented migrant travel must not forget there are real lives at stake and real consequences when a culture of lies and mistrust is allowed to take hold. At the same time, if travel writing and its criticism are to continue to open up to divergent voices, experiences and forms, they must retain a sophisticated understanding of the history of lies in travel writing and the prejudices that can perpetuate a culture of mistrust.

Notes

1 Percy G. Adams, *Travelers and Travel Liars 1660–1800* (New York: Dover, 1980), 14.
2 Benoît Hopquin, 'Contre-enquête sur un affabulateur', *Le Monde*, 8 July 2009, accessed 14 March 2015, www.lemonde.fr/societe/article/2009/07/07/contre-enquete-sur-un-affabulateur_1216190_3224.html.

3 Omar Ba, *Soif d'Europe: Témoignage d'un clandestin* (Paris: Editions du Cygne, 2008). All further references to this work will be given parenthetically.

4 Omar Ba, *Je suis venu, j'ai vu, je n'y crois plus* (Paris: Max Milo editions, 2009). A year later he published a further essay, *N'émigrez pas! L'Europe est un mythe* (Paris: JC Gawsewitch, 2010).

5 Bruno Le Dantec and Mahmoud Traoré, *Dem ak xabaar (Partir et raconter)* (Fécamp: Nouvelles Editions Lignes, 2012). All further references to this work will be given parenthetically.

6 The 2007 documentary *Victimes de nos richesses*, directed by Malian Kal Touré, provides an insight into the 2005 Cueta crossing, as well as that at Melilla some weeks earlier, from the perspective of survivors. For more on deadly border crossings in this area, see Tabea Alexa Linhard, 'At Europe's End: Geographies of Mediterranean Crossings', *Journal of Iberian and Latin American Research*, 22.1 (2016): 1–14.

7 Andrew Smith, 'Migrancy, Hybridity, and Postcolonial Literary Studies,' in *Postcolonial Literary Studies*, ed. Neil Lazarus (Cambridge: Cambridge University Press, 2004), 242.

8 See Edward Said, 'Reflections on Exile', in *Reflections on Exile and Other Essays* (Cambridge, MA: Harvard University Press, 2000), 173–86; Rosemary Marangoly George, *The Politics of Home: Postcolonial Relocations and Twentieth-Century Fiction* (Oakland, CA: University of California Press, 1999); Rey Chow, *Writing Diaspora: Tactics of Intervention in Contemporary Cultural Studies* (Bloomington, IN: Indiana University Press, 1993); Mireille Rosello, *Postcolonial Hospitality: The Immigrant as Guest* (Stanford, CA: Stanford University Press, 2001).

9 Homi K. Bhabha, *The Location of Culture* (London: Routledge, 1994), 218.

10 For one of the best-known critiques of this tendency, see Janet Wolff, 'On the Road Again: Metaphors of Travel in Cultural Criticism', *Cultural Studies*, 7.2 (1993): 224–39.

11 Benita Parry, 'Directions and Dead Ends in Postcolonial Studies', in *Relocating Postcolonialism*, ed. David Theo Goldberg and Ato Quayson (Oxford: Blackwell, 2002), 72.

12 Agnes Woolley, *Contemporary Asylum Narratives: Representing Refugees in the Twenty-First Century* (Basingstoke: Palgrave Macmillan, 2014), 11. For a related study, see David Farrier, *Postcolonial Asylum: Seeking Sanctuary before the Law* (Liverpool: Liverpool University Press, 2011).

13 See for example Rosello, *Postcolonial Hospitality*; and Dominic Thomas, *Black France: Colonialism, Immigration and Transnationalism* (Bloomington, IN: Indiana University Press, 2006).

14 For an exception to this, see Alessandro Triulzi and Robert L. McKenzie (eds), *Long Journeys: African Migrants on the Road* (Leiden: Brill, 2013). For a fuller account of this literature in the Francophone context, see Hakim Abderrezah, 'Burning the Sea: Clandestine Migration and the Strait of Gibraltar in Francophone Moroccan "Illiterature"', *Contemporary French and Francophone Literature*, 13.4 (2009): 461–9 and Carla Calargé, 'Clandestine or Conquistadores? Beyond Sensational Headlines, or a Literature of Urgency', *Research in African Literatures*, 46.2 (2015): 1–14. There is also an important body of French-language cinematic representations of irregular migrant journeys that includes Abderrahmane Sissako, *En attendant le Bonheur* (2002) and Moussa Touré's *La Pirogue* (2012).

15 Barbara A. Misztal, *Trust in Modern Societies: The Search for the Bases of Social Order* (Cambridge: Polity Press, 1996), 117.

16 Misztal, *Trust*, 105.

17 Misztal, *Trust*, 106.

18 See Bathie Ngoye Thiam, 'Soif d'Europe: l'imposture d'un immigré', *Wal Fadjiri*, 16 July 2009.

19 Patrick Holland and Graham Huggan, *Tourists with Typewriters: Critical Reflections on Contemporary Travel Writing* (Ann Arbor, MI: University of Michigan Press, 1998), 5.

20 Nora V. Demleitner, 'The Law at a Crossroads: The Construction of Migrant Women Trafficked into Prostitution', in *Global Human Smuggling: Comparative Perspectives*, ed. Kyle David and Rey Koslowski (Baltimore, MD: Johns Hopkins University Press, 2001), 262.

21 Thomas Nail, 'Violence at the Borders: Nomadic Solidarity and Non-Status Migrant Resistance', *Radical Philosophy Review*, 15.1 (2012): 242.

22 Misztal, *Trust*, 51.

23 For more on female experiences of undocumented travel, see Demleitner, 'The Law at a Crossroads' and Woolley, *Contemporary Asylum Narratives*.

24 Mathieu Leonard, 'Clandestins: l'odyssée invisible. Entretien avec Bruno Le Dantec,' *Article 11*, 21 November 2012, accessed 24 May 2015, www.article11.info/?Clandestins-l-Odyssee-invisible.

25 Shahram Khosravi, *'Illegal' Traveller: An Auto-Ethnography of Borders* (Basingstoke: Palgrave Macmillan, 2010), 33. See also Catherine Farrell's identification of what she terms a 'culture of disbelief' in relation to asylum claimants amongst certain Glasgow-based solicitors, *Asylum Narratives and Credibility*

Assessments: An Ethnographic Study of the Asylum Appeal Process in Scotland, PhD Thesis (Glasgow: University of Glasgow, 2012).

26 Khosravi, *'Illegal' Traveller*, 112.

27 Eric Mettout, 'Omar Ba nous a tous bernés, ou pourquoi il faut être sceptique', *L'Express*, 10 July 2009, accessed 24 May 2015, http://blogs.lexpress.fr/nouvelleformule/2009/07/10/djeuner_avec_ma_copine_anne.

28 Omar Ba, 'Lettre Ouverte d'Omar Ba à ses Lecteurs, à la Presse et à tous ses détracteurs', *Le Parisien*, 11 July 2009, accessed 24 May 2015, http://etoile.touteleurope.eu/index.php/post/2009/07/20/Omar-Ba-%3A-je-persiste-et-signe.

29 It is interesting to compare such a strategy with the aims of the Latin American *testimonio*, another form that has seen its credibility questioned. See John Beverly, '*Testimonio*, Subalternity, and Narrative Authority', in *A Companion to Latin American Literature and Culture*, ed. Sara Castro-Klaren (Oxford: Wiley Blackwell, 2013), 571–83.

30 See for example the articles Le Dantec has published with the publication CQFD, http://cqfd-journal.org/Bruno-Le-Dantec, and also a radio interview recorded after the publication of the co-authored text with Traoré where the French journalist's sympathies are very clear: www.radiogrenouille.com/antenne/partir-et-raconter-mahmoud-traore-et-bruno-le-dantec.

31 See Note 24. With regard to translation and re-writing, see André Lefevere, *Translation, Rewriting and the Manipulation of Literary Fame* (London: Routledge, 1992). Questions of motive and legitimacy in collaborative writing projects have been discussed by scholars in a variety of contexts. See for example Beverly, '*Testimonio*, Subalternity, and Narrative Authority' and Jenny Siméus, 'Collaboratively Writing a Self: Textual Strategies in Margaret McCord's *The Calling of Katie Makanya: A Memoir of South Africa*', *Research in African Literatures*, 46.2 (2015): 70–84.

4

THE EXPATRIATE LIFE

Lynn Mastellotto

Dwelling in difference

The global flow of people, capital, goods, services and ideas helped characterise the twentieth century as a 'century of migrations',[1] with the emphasis on the plural noun signalling how the defining experience of flux is embedded in a wide range of material and aesthetic practices, which have continued in the twenty-first century. Though emigration is commonly understood as a one-way movement – leaving one's homeland for an adopted home, usually in pursuit of an improved quality of life – it is, in fact, a spectrum of different forms of displacement, including exile, voluntary relocation, sojourn and resettlement, which occupy different positions in a complex and often overlapping field of mobilities. 'Expatriation', which derives etymologically from the Latin *ex* (out of) and *patria* (country, fatherland), is commonly understood as a voluntary form of migration by individuals searching for greater freedom, economic opportunity, self-determination or other lifestyle advantages through relocation abroad. It has long co-existed with 'exile', a term deriving from the Latin *exilium* (expulsion, banishment), which is generally associated with political migration (voluntary or enforced) related to war, poverty or persecution. Neither is a particularly new migratory phenomenon, but both grew exponentially in the twentieth century as forms of voluntary and involuntary displacement increased as effects of modernity.

Easy access to leisure travel and occupational mobility for middle-class Westerners in contemporary society often masks the privilege inherent in such ease of movement; the recent migrant crisis in Europe serves as a reminder that mobility is not always a matter of individual choice. This chapter does not address the migration narratives of those who suffer displacement through political upheavals and migrate under extreme duress; for a discussion of the recent responses in Europe to the migrant crisis, see Aedín Ní Loingsigh's chapter in this volume. Nor does it discuss literary expatriates on the move in the early twentieth century – the well-documented experiences of interwar writers like Gertrude Stein and Ernest Hemingway in 1920s Paris, of D.H. Lawrence in Italy and Lawrence Durrell in Greece, of W.H. Auden and Christopher Isherwood in 1930s Berlin, of Richard Wright and James Baldwin in 1950s France – in search of freedom through escape to continental outposts or European cultural capitals from social, racial, sexual and artistic limitations imposed at home. Instead, this chapter seeks to expand an understanding of 'expatriate' by examining the defining choice to live elsewhere as one guided not only by aesthetic concerns but also by an ethical impulse to remake one's life in accordance with a particular vision of 'the good life'; in other words, expatriation as a deliberate act of displacement and a long-term process of self-transformation centred on the question, 'How should I live?' Conveying interior journeys towards greater self-knowledge and identity reformation, these narratives follow a quest pattern in Youngs's sense of 'travelling in search of meaning, purpose and belonging'.[2]

Displacement as a theme in Western culture is a familiar terrain of analysis, particularly in relation to literary modernism and the central role of the exile and émigré writer in experimentations with language, perspective and form. Critics such as Anders Olsson point to the centrality of the exilic experience in the development of Western literature, from Dante Alighieri's *Divine Comedy* to Albert Camus's *L'Étranger*, and signal the connection of modernist exile writing to witness literature in twentieth-century narrative.[3] Edward Said's well-known claim that 'modern Western culture is in large part the work of exiles' and that, consequently, the past century can be called 'the age of the refugee, the displaced person, mass immigration', identifies displacement as *the* existential and cultural condition of the twentieth century.[4] Although expatriate writers are often labelled as 'self-imposed exiles' or 'voluntary exiles',[5] and their works studied through the exilic lens of a metaphorical loss of origins and its aesthetic implications for modernist narration, this chapter takes a slightly different perspective by surveying expatriation through a wider lens, one which opens up the modernist treatment of expatriation beyond a focus on formal tropes and figures (organicism, primitivism, exoticism, hedonism) to take into account the affective and ethical dimensions of the expatriate life in the mid-nineteenth and late twentieth centuries.

Recognising expatriation as a form of 'dwelling-in-traveling', as James Clifford does, requires a mobility paradigm in which routes and roots are not inherently oppositional but, instead, co-exist, overlap, contest and, at times, complement each other.[6] Justin Edwards and Rune Graulund refer to this expanded mobility paradigm in their discussion of the simultaneously 'orienting and disorienting' practices of travel.[7] The tension between the impulse to move (flux) and the impulse to stay put (fixity) in the expatriate experience is a productive one: even when migration is voluntary, it does not follow a seamless path from A to B since uprooting oneself and re-routing the course of one's life involve a cultural accommodation that is neither simple nor straightforward. Whilst some expatriates are short-stay travellers who move mainly within compatriot enclaves, never seeking integration in the host country, others become residents who engage more deeply with locals and local culture over time. For the latter type, expatriation can be an indelibly diasporic condition of ontological displacement characterised by multiple senses of belonging and not belonging, not easily resolved through repatriation to the home country or through permanent resettlement abroad.

This chapter will examine Susanna Moodie's expatriate memoir about her mid-nineteenth-century emigration to the New World and Frances Mayes's account of her own late twentieth-century resettlement in Europe in order to illuminate issues related to identity and belonging that characterise the expatriate life as it evolves in overlapping stages of intercultural confrontation, negotiation and accommodation, in different locations at different moments in time. The search for the 'good life' – for improved economic security, enhanced freedom of self-expression and self-definition, peace and tranquillity, greater work–life balance, and other attributes generally associated with greater well-being – has unfolded on an ever-expanding horizon in the modern period as transportation, telecommunications, trade and commerce, education, and tourism have been transformed by what John Tomlinson calls a 'rapidly developing and ever-densening network of interconnections and interdependences' that make a range of lifestyle options accessible to voluntary migrants.[8] The constant factor linking expatriates across this wide continuum is choice: expatriation is a privilege pursued by a minority of migrants at any historical moment, those with the education, money and means to voluntarily relocate in order to overcome perceived limitations at home and pursue presumed lifestyle advantages abroad. As Bruce Robbins notes, cosmopolitans' independent means and globe-trotting ways give them 'the choice to live abroad and return home if/when it suits them'.[9]

Postcolonial critics have rightly pointed to the problems associated with cosmopolitan privilege; that is, with élite travellers enjoying the Western cultural legacy from a dominant position over the past 500 years.[10] The term 'expatriate' conjures images of élites – young nobles on extended Grand Tours in the late seventeenth and eighteenth centuries; British colonial officials in India, Africa and other outposts of empire in the age of imperial expansion; nineteenth-century Romantics fleeing the effects of urban industrialisation for less developed lands – enjoying the local heritage in exotic locales whilst deriding the locals encountered. While it is true, as Ghose notes, that white, middle-class women, 'albeit marginalized, are nevertheless participants in the dominant culture', it is also true that the discursive practices of self-examination and self-transformation prompted by travel are especially resonant in travel narratives by women, as revealed in an analysis of Moodie's and Mayes's resettlement accounts below.[11] As Patrick Holland and Graham Huggan claim, women's travel writing more explicitly interrogates the identity of the travelling subject, 'a subject recognized as being constituted by the complex interactions of gender, race, and class'.[12] This chapter seeks an expanded understanding of expatriation, offering a more generous reading of its contribution to cultural representation, by drawing on conceptualisations of cosmopolitanism that decouple the term 'expatriate' from its reductive association with mobile, rootless élites, recognising, instead, the possibility for transnationals' ethical engagement with cultural difference.[13]

Drawing on Marilyn Papayanis's view that expatriation is 'a significant mode of apprehending some important life good', I argue that expatriation can be read as a quest for the articulation of value, for a meaningful way of living in a disenchanted world, and that expatriate writing deserves serious consideration rather than dismissal as necessarily 'colonialist/ neo-colonialist'.[14] Reading contemporary resettlement accounts as a form of ascesis, of a disciplined meditation on the self, a significant component of self-artistry, the central theme of identity reformation emerges as an ethical imperative: these are stories of individuals struggling to be true to a mode of meaningful existence through discursive and life practices.[15] Expatriate women writers like Moodie and Mayes are deeply engaged in forms of 'identity work' as they negotiate national, gender and class identities through the experience of geographical displacement and the intercultural encounters it affords.[16] They develop points of identification and attachment with subject positions constructed through these new life practices; their narratives then present a reflection on this process of self-transformation, grounded in the subjective experiences of their embodied selves transformed through long-stay resettlement.

The philosophical focus on selfhood and identity draws on a vast literature which recognises that the process of identity-making involves continual self-overcoming and self-transformation in which alterity plays a pivotal role since identities are dialogically constructed through difference: one defines oneself based on the recognition of what one is not in relation to the Other.[17] Encounters with others facilitated through travel provide opportunities for individuals to engage in the modern project of reforming personal identities in ways that do not simply reproduce a fixed self/other logic but which, instead, treat these terms as dynamic and socially constructed.[18] This links expatriate writing to broader debates about the ethical value of narrative and its enabling of perspective-taking, empathy, moral inclusiveness and respect for Others.[19]

Close readings of two expatriate memoirs bring these ethical issues to light by revealing a migrating sensibility in the authors' accounts of expatriate life as they dwell in difference over time.[20] First, *Roughing It in the Bush* (1852) by Susanna Moodie, an English-born emigrant whose memoir details her experiences as a settler in Upper Canada as the wife of a military retiree lured to this colonial outpost by the promise of a reduced cost of living and better quality of life.[21] Moodie's excitement about building a new life in a new land gives way to disillusionment as she chronicles the hardships of a pioneering life in a subjective style that increasingly registers a modern consciousness of heterogeneity through her encounters with indigenous inhabitants and European settlers. Second, Frances Mayes's *Under the Tuscan Sun* (1996), the first memoir in her Tuscan trilogy, recounts her flight from metropolitan life in San Francisco and pursuit of a 'slow life' in rural Italy in the 1990s.[22] The self-help *cogito* underpinning this book – eat-pray-love and home-renovate your way to personal happiness – accounts for the cool critical reception of her popular memoir, yet it should be read as an initiation story, part of a multipart series in which Mayes's intercultural consciousness develops over time.

At first glance, there seems little in common to connect a middle-class military wife from Sussex coming to terms with life in the Canadian wilderness in the first half of the nineteenth century and an American academic from San Francisco seeking to downshift in rural Tuscany in the late twentieth century. Indeed, differences and discontinuities in their historical contexts, reasons for migrating, experiences of acculturation and narrative modes of representation will be examined below. Yet, these multipart memoirs are linked by a common thread – the desire for greater freedom, self-determination and self-expansion that travel often affords women – which leads in both cases to a deliberate act of displacement and a prolonged process of cultural accommodation. These are stories with a long span, since for both Moodie and Mayes expatriation is a life project with affective and ethical dimensions that deeply engages them in place through a process of identity reformation over time.

Expatriate life in rural Upper Canada, mid-1800s

In the introduction to her two-volume memoir, *Roughing It in the Bush: A Life in Canada*, first published in 1852, Susanna Moodie (née Strickland) notes how the great tide of emigration flowed westward in the 1830s as 'Canada-mania' pervaded the middle ranks of British society. Enticed by advertisements in public newspapers and by private letters extolling the advantages to be derived from resettlement in this supposedly 'highly-favoured region', many military families 'rich in hope and poor in purse' chose emigration to the colony in the hope of bettering their material conditions (1: ix). Counting herself among migrants misled by overblown and romanticised accounts of life in Upper Canada – 'its salubrious climate, its fertile soil, commercial advantages, great water privileges, its proximity to the mother country, and last not least, its almost total exemption from taxation' (1: xi) – Moodie rails against marketers' portrayal of the colony as the British emigrant's utopia, then sets down her own corrective version, detailing the realities of life without the sentimentalism or triumphalism characteristic of heroic tales of colonial adventure.

Before she emigrated, Moodie's publisher, Richard Bentley, encouraged her to write a settler's guide to the colony, prompting her to record her resettlement experience in a journal. Moodie's account presents a cautionary tale for would-be emigrants of her day, offering a frank depiction of the difficulties inherent in the pioneering life in early Canada, over two volumes which span the nineteen years of her residency there. Beginning with her reluctant departure from England in 1832, she chronicles her family's early struggles with the harshness of the land and climate, the lack of familiar cultural customs and comforts, their general inexperience and unpreparedness for backwoods farming, and their strained interactions with meddlesome 'Yankee' neighbours. Noting that 'a large majority of the higher class [of emigrants] were officers of the army and navy, with their families – a class perfectly unfitted by their previous habits and education for contending with the stern realities of emigrant life' (1: xi), Moodie signals class-based aspirational and experiential differences inherent in the migration story.

As the middle-class wife of a retired army officer seeking to prosper economically through a colonial posting, Moodie explains that

> the half-pay of a subaltern officer, managed with the most rigid economy, is too small to supply the wants of a family [in England]; and if of a good family, not enough to maintain his original standing in society [. . .] In such a case, it is both wise and right to emigrate.
>
> *(1: 209)*[23]

Hers is clearly a case of voluntary relocation in pursuit of lifestyle advantages, yet she eschews the notion of having had any freedom of choice, stating:

> In most cases, emigration is a matter of necessity, not of choice; and this is more especially true of the emigration of persons of respectable connections, or of any station or position in the world. Few educated persons, accustomed to the refinements and luxuries of European society, ever willingly relinquish those advantages, and place themselves beyond the protective influence of the wise and revered institutions of their native land, without the pressure of some urgent cause.
>
> *(1: vii)*

Her claim that she is especially hard done by as a middle-class emigrant because she is accustomed to the advantages of a certain social status and lifestyle conveys the kind of class blindness that postcolonial critics point to as pervasive in travel narratives from the age of empire.[24] Though Moodie's perspective is not static but evolving, with her sensibility shifting notably across the span of two volumes written over two decades, similar to Fanny Parkes in India, the cosmopolitan openness to difference marked by Moodie's later observations is not in evidence in the earlier part of her narrative.[25]

Upon stopping at Grosse Isle during her initial journey up the St Lawrence River in August 1832, Moodie remarks on the unruliness and insolence of the locals, using the rhetoric of negation identified by David Spurr as a narrative device through which colonial writers ascribe negative values to others in order to create distance from them.[26] She especially condemns the Irish and Scottish emigrants she encounters for their incivility: their shouting in 'uncouth dialect', violent gesturing and lack of 'common decency' by walking around 'almost naked' cause her to shrink 'with feelings almost akin to fear, from the hard-featured, sun-burnt harpies, as they elbowed rudely past' (1: 11). This passage also deploys the rhetoric of abjection and defilement, which Spurr associates with a colonialist view of the Other in presenting a stereotypical depiction of Irish and Scottish emigrants.

Further noting that these 'vicious, uneducated barbarians who form the surplus of over-populous European countries, are far behind the wild man in delicacy of feeling or natural courtesy', Moodie simultaneously paints indigenous peoples as 'noble savages' imbued with a kind of intrinsic grace: 'the Indian is one of Nature's gentlemen, he never says or does a rude or vulgar thing' (1: 11). Though seeming to praise non-European inhabitants, this form of naturalisation draws on the Rousseauian ideal of natural man as representative of 'original freedom and the absence of artifice, dissimulation, or repression'.[27] Thus, in her first contact with others in the new world, Moodie denies them equality by portraying them as one-dimensional rather than as real, complex and embodied.

Such rhetorical distancing gestures are prevalent in her early sketches as she initially confronts cultural difference through a colonialist lens. It is important to read these as part of an initiation story that unfolds in a multipart account over time, revealing Moodie's evolving sensibilities and rhetorical forms. Her two-volume memoir maps out an arc of accommodation as she moves through various phases of acculturation that characterise the gradual process of building a new home in a new land: first, a confrontation with place that focuses on cultural difference and novelty; second, a negotiation with place that juxtaposes contrasting cultural paradigms; third, an accommodation with place that involves deep and sustained engagement in local community.[28] These phases should be understood as cyclical, not linear: as new situations arise, patterns of confrontation and negotiation repeat themselves; consequently, Moodie's memoir does not describe a teleological progression towards integration, but rather an ongoing process of cultural accommodation.

Peter Hulme refers to this third phase as 'deep immersion', noting that as travel writers immerse themselves in foreign cultures and languages for extended periods they acquire 'the sort of intimate knowledge which gives them access to people and places unknown to short-stay travellers, let alone tourists'.[29] For Moodie and for other long-stay expatriates, there is no moment of definitive arrival or complete integration in the adopted homeland, nor do their texts reproduce the archetypal pattern of return to the place of origin and re-integration in society there. Long-term expatriates occupy a liminal position, living between two cultures and maintaining a foot in both worlds. Robbins signals how transnationals develop a 'density of overlapping allegiances' by cultivating multiple identifications between their home and host countries, affinities that are not resolved over time but rather accrue and give rise to complex identities.[30]

This tension is evident in Moodie's expression of nostalgia for England when she writes:

> Keenly for the first time I felt that I was a stranger in a strange land; my heart yearned intensely for my absent home. Home! The word had ceased to belong to my present – it was doomed to live for ever in the past; for what emigrant ever regarded the country of his exile as his home?
>
> *(1: 31)*

She observes that emigration, even when freely chosen, can feel a lot like exile: 'an act of severe duty, performed at the expense of personal enjoyment, and accompanied by the sacrifice of those local attachments which stamp the scenes amid which our childhood grew, in imperishable characters, upon the heart' (1: vii). Yet, she simultaneously seeks to be open-minded about Canada and its possibilities, admonishing readers and would-be emigrants: 'Beware of drawing disparaging contrasts between the colony and its illustrious parent. All such comparisons are cruel and unjust; you cannot exult the one at the expense of the other without committing an act of treason against both' (1: 20–1). Her affective ambivalence about her adopted home rubs up against an ethical impulse to remain open to its cultural differences.

Her early interactions with neighbours are, at best, strained as Moodie shrinks from their 'rude, coarse familiarity' whilst they, in turn, view her as an interloper 'who wished to curtail their independence by expecting from them the kind of civilities and gentle courtesies of a more refined community' (1: 212). The Moodies are treated with insolence despite their class superiority because, in the new world, this is permissible. She reports one neighbour's spiteful words to her: 'I rejoice to see you at the washtub, and I wish that you may be brought down upon your knees to scrub the floor' (1: 141). In England, necessity compelled the compliance of the lower classes in a system of homage to rank and education, however insincere, whereas in Upper Canada 'they are free, and the dearest privilege of this freedom is to wreak upon their superiors the long-locked-up hatred of their hearts' (1: 213–14). Irritated at first, she gradually comes to see herself from their point of view, and she sees their irreverence as 'better than a hollow profession of duty and attachment urged upon us by a false and unnatural position' (1: 215). This shift in sensibility indicates her growing ability to negotiate between two sets of customs as she accommodates to local life.

In addition to losing their social standing in Canada, the Moodies lose their economic advantage as their fortunes suffer through emigration; far from prospering in the colony, they are reduced to poverty after being swindled in property deals that deplete their savings. Moreover, unaccustomed to 'bush-farming', they expend their scarce resources in hiring labourers to work the land. Moodie notes that much of her time in this early period is spent 'abusing the place, the country, and our own dear selves for our folly in coming to it' (1: 85), recounting how, like other destitute emigrants, they cannot even pay for a return passage to England. It is clear that the Moodies have lost the social and economic privilege conventionally associated with expatriates: their situation is a far cry from the independent means and globe-trotting ways expatriates are presumed to possess, as well as from the presumed choice they have 'to live abroad and return home if/when it suits them', as posited by Robbins.[31]

Perhaps even harder to accept than their downward social mobility and financial ruin is the fading connection to England experienced through their prolonged absence. Moodie notes:

> After seven years' exile, the hope of return grows feeble, the means are still less in our power, and our friends give up all hope of our return; their letters grow fewer and colder, their expressions of attachment are less vivid; the heart has formed new ties, and the poor emigrant is nearly forgotten. Double those years, and it is as if the grave had closed over you, and the hearts that once knew and loved you know you no more.
>
> *(1: 122)*

While she seeks to keep alive her connection to England and simultaneously nurture a connection to Canada, such dual allegiance is not shared by her compatriots back in England whom she claims lack understanding of the diasporic condition. Moodie fully belongs to neither the place she has left nor the one she has arrived at; instead, she maintains affective bonds to both and acquires a plural sense of 'home'.

The sense of painful separation from England eases once she starts building a community in her adopted home. She gradually develops a close and affectionate friendship with several neighbours, including two indigenous women she calls Mrs Muskrat and Snow-storm, who occasionally borrow Moodie's canoe, admiring her pluck in managing house, farm and children whilst her husband is away for long periods with his regiment. Upon visiting their encampment, they teach her how to dry venison, read the clouds for changes in weather and paddle with the current to cross the lake and gain headland (2: 267–9). This latter skill is arguably a metaphor for Moodie's acculturation process: over time, she develops the practical and social skills needed to steer her way in a new environment by assimilating local knowledge through close interactions with locals and through engagement in local practices.

As the years pass, Moodie reaches an accommodation with her new life, claiming:

> Now, when not only reconciled to Canada, but loving it, and feeling a deep interest in its present welfare, and the fair prospect of its future greatness, I often look back and laugh at the feelings with which I then regarded this noble country.
>
> *(1: 83)*

However, when a reversal of fortune enables their sudden departure, she bids a frank farewell to pioneering life, stating:

> I have given you a faithful picture of a life in the backwoods of Canada, and I leave you to draw from it your own conclusions. To the poor, industrious working man it presents many advantages; to the poor gentleman, none!

(2: 290)

The lack of sentimentalism and resounding cautionary tone in this final address reveal the negative conclusion Moodie herself seems to have drawn about expatriate life in Canada.

Expatriate life in rural Tuscany, late 1990s

In contrast to Moodie, there is little affective ambivalence in Frances Mayes's account, as she ostensibly sees no downside to expatriate life in rural Tuscany. Escape from the pressures of urban living in California lead her to Cortona in 1990 where she acquires a 300-year-old stone villa, 'Bramasole', whose name means 'to yearn for the sun' (*TS*, 15). This aptly captures the impulse that draws Mayes to its doorstep: both a literal longing for sunshine and a metaphorical desire for a better quality of life. She states at the outset of her bestselling memoir, *Under the Tuscan Sun* (1996), that the allure of a foreign place is about imagining new possibilities for selfhood, imagining what it would be like to 'be extant in another version' (*TS*, 28). This potential for self-transformation is also what makes relocation writing so compelling for readers. Blending conventions of travel writing and life writing, these hybrid accounts offer readers a touristic escape by gazing vicariously on exotic landscapes whilst simultaneously satisfying their penchant for gazing into interior spaces and the mundane details of domestic life lived elsewhere through the personal accounts of transnational writers like Mayes who have built homes abroad.

At the outset, Mayes repeatedly invokes her urban life in San Francisco as a counterpoint to her life in rural Tuscany as she renovates the hillside ruin with a view: the household objects and practices which characterise her Tuscan life gather meaning in opposition to those associated with her American life. This recalls Susanna Moodie's early tendency to compare the customs she left behind in Sussex to ones in the colony, albeit to opposite effect. Whilst Moodie is initially dismayed by her new surroundings and she experiences cultural differences mainly as irritants or obstacles, Mayes enthusiastically embraces each novelty in Tuscany with an idealising impulse. This marked difference in their initial responses to their adopted homes is perhaps indicative of the varying degrees of choice each exercised in the decision to relocate: while Mayes's decision is motivated by individual will and self-interest, Moodie is bound by the socio-economic and cultural conventions of her time to follow her husband to the new world.

Tuscan Sun is filled with Mayes's early impressions of the place and its people rendered through the objects of material culture – house, garden, food and culinary practices – which act, initially, as portals to greater understanding of foreign place and local practices. Her journey of becoming 'at home' in Italy involves moving beyond this immediate domestic sphere of home renovation and culinary exploration to engage with place through a local–global nexus of social relations. As with Moodie, Mayes's impressions accrue over time; however, unlike Moodie who lacks the means to return to England, Mayes maintains two homes and eventually retires in Tuscany. Across the twenty years chronicled in her trilogy, her status shifts from an intermittent resident whose initial engagement with locale is mostly touristic, to a fixture in the community whose engagement moves towards the dialogical. After several years in Italy, Mayes begins to understand events unfolding around her, leading her to claim: 'Now that I know this one place a little, I read with doubled perception' (*TS*, 152). Later, in her second memoir, *Bella Tuscany*, she claims: 'It's a lifetime quest, finding out who "the other" is, and how life is lived outside your own thin skin' (*BT*, 203).

Although she becomes gradually more adept at reading place and understanding others, her initial readings of Tuscany and of Tuscans present a monological interpretation of cultural difference. Wendy Parkins observes that Mayes's characters tend to serve as 'heuristic devices', or 'exemplars of eternal verities', not as 'subjects with whom to connect in community'.[32] Her tendency to idealise and essentialise Italians is poignantly displayed in her initial description of Placido, a neighbour, who appears episodically across her trilogy:

> I have begun to idealize his life. It is easy for foreigners to idealize, romanticize, stereotype, and oversimplify local people [. . .] but what I idealize is that Placido seems utterly happy [. . .] I have the feeling that he could have lived in any era; he is independent of time there in his stone house on the olive terraces with his peaceable kingdom. To reinforce my instinct, he has appeared, my Rousseau paradigm neighbour, at our door with a hooded falcon on his wrist [. . .] This sport certainly does nothing to subtract from my impression that Placido lives across time. I see him on the white horse, falcon on his wrist, and he is en route to some medieval joust or fair.
>
> (TS, 198–9)

In this portrayal, Placido is paradigmatically a–modern: existing outside time as a kind of 'noble savage' who communes with falcons and horses, lives in a stone hut and appears perennially 'happy' in his peaceable kingdom. Even though Mayes attaches a positive value to Placido's uncultured simplicity, to his uncorrupted natural way of being outside modernity, her construction closes off the possibility for complexity and ambiguity in his representation, as did Moodie's early depiction of indigenous people in Upper Canada. Parkins notes that Mayes's poetic image of the peasant Other serves her artistic purpose of portraying Italy 'as an Arcadian backdrop against which the existential dilemmas of modernity [can] be illuminated and explored by subjects from elsewhere'.[33]

A subtle shift in narrative sensibility and rhetorical style is demonstrated in Mayes's third memoir after a twenty-year period of sustained residency in Cortona. When she re-introduces Placido in *Every Day in Tuscany* (2010), she gives a more rounded impression of the man. The sense of alarm she experiences when he falls from his horse and spends several months recovering in hospital is real and palpable; she worries about the person, not the poetic image. Upon seeing him again, she finds him 'thinner, with a crease on either side of his smile, but he's [still] Placido' (*ED*, 28). His creased smile is a significant shift in detail from the previous straw portrayal of the 'utterly happy' Rousseauian figure and marks a post–lapsarian turn in Mayes's text: Placido becomes humanised through suffering. Mayes notes: 'In the months of his illness, we faced how unbearable it was to imagine Cortona without Placido. For us, he's a great love and the essence of Tuscan life' (*ED*, 28). The unthinkable loss of her friend helps Mayes render a more human portrayal:

> Every morning, all year, he's having coffee at Banchelli's, often a second with another group of friends. He's a husband, in the old sense, to his land and animals, tending his falcon, horse, chickens, rabbits, and guinea hens. With his friend Lucio, he combs secret areas to find more porcini mushrooms than anyone. He makes archery shields

and pouches out of leather [. . .] Always on his porch there's a bird or owl he's rescued. The cages he makes for their recoveries are works of folk art. A merlo, blackbird, with a crushed wing has lived in a jolly yellow and red house for fifteen years. It whistles as Placido passes.

(ED, 28)

The qualities of 'slow living' are clearly evoked through his everyday way of living: convivially in a close-knit community, a husband to his farm, a forager who knows the land, an artisan who crafts objects of great beauty, a modern-day St Francis who lives close to nature and whom the creatures praise in song. Although his portrayal is more layered in this passage than in earlier constructions, Mayes cannot quite resist the tendency to idealise Placido, rendering him symbolic of Tuscan authenticity; he appears as a real, embodied person in her text, but still functions as an exemplar of an idealised rural past.

Her nostalgia for the past causes Mayes to misread her environment, as illustrated in a significant episode relayed in *Bella Tuscany*. Her bucolic description of the countryside as one of 'hummocky hills, cypress-lined road, cerulean skies with big baroque clouds that look as if cherubs could peer from behind them' (*TS*, 54) emphasises how rural Tuscany – in opposition to hyper-modern California – serves her purpose as a poetic image. This picturesque portrait does not reveal the region's complex culture, though, as Tuscany is not just a rural idyll for transnationals seeking escape from modernity in uncontaminated landscapes: it is a real place in which traditional and modern practices intersect and postmodern subjects interact. This tension is made explicit when Mayes confronts an aspect of the Tuscan landscape at odds with her poetic idyll:

> In this blissful landscape we are suddenly stunned to see a tall African woman, dressed in tight striped pants and a revealing red shirt, standing on the roadside. Around the next bend we see another, this one equally statuesque and curvaceous. She stares. Every few hundred feet these women are stationed along the road. They stand or sit on wooden crates. One eats a bag of potato chips. Then we see a parked car, with no woman near her crate. This is surreal. Prostitutes out in rural Italy [. . .] Bizarre and disturbing because this makes no sense in the Arcadian valley of the upper Tiber, which appears in the backgrounds of paintings, this dreamy route known as the Piero della Francesca trail.

(BT, 90–1)

This tableau 'makes no sense' to Mayes, neither at the time of observing it nor subsequently when reporting it, because she fails to fully analyse the dynamics of globalisation in the region: how global flows of people and capital result in her own presence there, as an affluent American second-home owner, as well as the presence of African sex-workers.

Mayes's account too often elides the ways in which her construction of the 'good life' in Arcadia is an idealised one shaped by a selection of white, middle-class affinities. Jeffrey Folks suggests that Mayes surrenders to a 'Mediterranean myth' that posits Tuscany as 'a dream-world of charming expatriate experience – dinners on the veranda, shopping for local crafts, encounters with warm-hearted locals'.[34] This critique is partially valid since, despite acknowledging their presence, she sees the prostitutes as intruders who disturb the bucolic integrity and peaceable authenticity of the Tiber valley, as though it exists as a place outside time. Silvia Ross notes that this insistence on Italy's timelessness is a form of nostalgia for a sanitised version of the past.[35] She claims that Mayes's repeated references to the 'country's ancient roots, mythological figures, and the art of centuries gone by' are a means of preserving the trope of renewal and rebirth associated with Renaissance Tuscany, of ensuring that Tuscany continues to function as a rural idyll in her aesthetic representations.[36] Though Mayes might prefer rural Tuscany to remain a retreat from modernity and its influences, the presence of African prostitutes subverts its construction as a coherent Renaissance tableau: it is not a bucolic refuge from modernity or an 'ideal community' inhabited by coherent and homogeneous locals (among whom Mayes counts herself), but instead is a postmodern space marked by heterogeneous influences.[37]

Later, when a stranger leaves a hand grenade on her lawn at Bramasole, Mayes's Tuscan idyll collapses and she is forced to confront the fact that it does not provide immunity from the modern world: her retreat to a country villa near Cortona no longer offers peace and solace from the 'craziness and violence and downright surreal aspects of America' (TS, 88) since rural Tuscany is also contaminated by the anxieties of contemporary life. Although the grenade is disposed of and no one is injured, Mayes suffers an existential crisis as she is forced to confront crime and its implications on her own doorstep: Bramasole is not the shelter or refuge from modernity she had posited. The grenade incident, similar to her previous sight of the prostitutes, but not as easily ignored, so disrupts her idyllic construction that she considers leaving Tuscany altogether; her 'peaceable kingdom' feels hostile and inscrutable, and she lacks the ability to interpret complex layers of local history to make sense of her situation and surroundings.

Her decision to stay marks a defining moment in her twenty-year process of accommodation; thereafter, she divides her Italian life in two periods: *before* (the grenade) and *after* (the grenade). These are also useful tags for charting the development of a cosmopolitan consciousness in her social interactions – *before* (tourist/outsider) and *after* (settler/insider). The event marks a dramatic shift not only in how she perceives her environment but also in how she is perceived by those in it. She notes:

> What became clear over the ensuing months was that our [Mayes's and her husband's] relationship to the town changed. From the day we arrived, we were overwhelmed by friendliness and hospitality. We'd always felt totally welcome. But while we'd felt a belonging before, we got the sense that the people just now knew we really belonged, that we were here to stay, and that since we knew the worst, we could become not just *residenti elettivi*, elective residents, but familial. '*Cari, siete cortonesi.*' My dears, you're of Cortona [. . .] I didn't even know I was on the outside looking in until I was suddenly on the inside looking out.
>
> (ED, 90)

By experiencing community on a completely different level, she realises that 'Learning from another culture is one of those mysterious movements of the psyche [. . .] you learn what you need to unlearn' (ED, 282–3). After spending her adult life in San Francisco learning to be 'monumentally self-reliant' (TS, 274), Mayes must learn to be part of a community in Cortona, its cycle of obligations and favours.

This shift requires her to move from a position of disengaged observation to one of engaged participation, in Beck's sense of cosmopolitanism as a practice of the 'dialogical imagination' that is deeply rooted in engagement with difference.[38] Though Mayes states towards the end of her third memoir, 'I came to Italy for the art, the cuisine, landscapes, history, architecture, wine, and the ineffable beauty. I stayed for the people' (ED, 179), one is left with the sense that she spends too long cataloguing the lifestyle advantages of Tuscany and arrives belatedly at 'the people'. In fact, following the grenade incident, she buys another rustic house to renovate, a mountain refuge further removed from town (hence from the encroachments of modernity) where she hopes to encounter 'deep-country Tuscans' (*ED*, 6). Whilst an index of change is revealed across her trilogy, it is a modest form of cosmopolitanism that shies away from fully dialogical encounters with difference. Perhaps surrendering too readily to a Mediterranean myth, her relocation trilogy falls short of rendering what Folks refers to as a full 'meeting of self and place', which he identifies as the secret to good travel writing, noting: 'travel writing – all writing, in fact, if it is to be any good – is not *about* the place but *of* it'.[39]

Conclusion

As long-term expatriates, Moodie and Mayes address the local/global dynamics inherent in relocation with varying degrees of intra-subjective awareness and inter-subjective engagement as they seek an accommodation with foreign place over time. Defining cosmopolitanism as 'an intellectual and aesthetic openness to divergent cultural experiences' in which a 'willingness to engage with the Other' is demonstrated through a 'search for contrasts rather than uniformity',[40] Hannerz signals openness and engagement with diversity as core values in this ethical orientation. Vered Amit proposes that the consonance or disjuncture of cosmopolitan consciousness is not a simple either/or question: 'the issue becomes less a matter of the simple presence or absence of inclusive consciousness but of the degree of inclusiveness, self-awareness and the consonance or disjuncture between this consciousness and the actual experiences of travel', and he questions 'the degree to which [cosmopolitan] privileges can blunt the edge of full engagement with difference'.[41] This question is central to understanding whether and how white, middle-class travellers like Moodie and Mayes can overcome the circumscriptions associated with their class status to achieve self-transformation, the kind of self-transcendence that Gerard Delanty identifies as central to cosmopolitan engagement.[42]

The two cases presented in this chapter reveal varying degrees of cosmopolitan engagement with cultural difference. Bronislaw Szerszynski and John Urry claim that cosmopolitan predispositions involve 'a willingness to take risks by virtue of encountering the Other'.[43] Though Moodie loses her economic privilege and social status through emigration, she develops rich loyalties and attachments in the local community for survival and support. Her life in Upper Canada is filled with risk and her memoirs chart a deepening engagement with place through situated readings of life in Upper Canada over two decades (1832–1850), accounts that move away from a colonial subject's totalising certainty towards a settler's recognition of complexity and ambiguity. Moodie's memoir charts a shifting sensibility as she develops self-awareness and critical reflection through accommodation to foreign place over time.

Mayes arguably experiences less risk in relocation as she maintains a life in California; her initial engagement with Tuscan space is consequently more touristic. The view she offers of Italy and Italians is not at ground level but from a more detached point of view, one which enables her to construct an idyll of rural Tuscany based on a circumscribed selection of self-referential affinities. She is an 'ideal observer' in Maria Lugones's sense of a post-cultural subject who observes and essentialises other cultures while remaining 'pure, unified and simple so as to occupy the vantage point and perceive unity amid multiplicity'.[44] Mayes's interactions avoid risk-taking by remaining detached and reducing multiplicity and complexity through idealisation, thus blunting the edge of full engagement with difference. Hers is a modest form of cosmopolitanism: the narrative point of view across her trilogy remains largely fixed and unchanged, a free-floating cultural connoisseur more focused on displaying an Italianate self and the cultural accoutrements acquired through a transnational lifestyle than in engaging deeply with cultural differences. Mayes's expatriate story is more makeover than self-transformation: the ethical project of living 'an examined life' evoked at the outset of *Tuscan Sun* is circumscribed by the consumer discourse running through her narrative reconstructions of life abroad. Her connection with cultural difference is more strategic in Michael Skey's sense of furthering her own instrumental goals rather than progressive aims or values.[45]

In both cases, travel fulfils the axiomatic imperative of 'broadening the mind' with which it is conventionally associated, since the experience of relocation enables both writers to acquire an expanded sense of the world through the experience of foreign place. Yet their experiences of dwelling in difference reveal varying degrees of cosmopolitan engagement through their attachments, place-based interactions, processes of self-interrogation, cultural inclusiveness and meaning formation. Unmoored from ontological certainty, Moodie's subjective persona is fundamentally reconstituted through relocation; Mayes's memoirs, instead, present a subject who gains epistemological awareness of cultural diversity yet remains constant and unified, not radically transformed through migration. Expatriate writing by those who seek an accommodation with foreign place over time provides powerful examples of the ways in which identities can be dialogically reconstructed through contact with difference in a globalised world.

Notes

1 James Clifford, *The Predicament of Culture* (Cambridge, MA: Harvard University Press, 1988).

2 Tim Youngs, *The Cambridge Introduction to Travel Writing* (Cambridge: Cambridge University Press, 2013), 90.

3 Anders Olsson, 'Exile and Literary Modernism', in *Modernism*, ed. Ástráður Eysteinsson and Vivian Liska (Amsterdam: John Benjamins, 2007), 735.

4 Edward W. Said, *Reflections on Exile and Other Essays* (Cambridge, MA: Harvard University Press, 2000), 173–74.

5 Peter Nicholls, *Modernisms: A Literary Guide* (Berkeley, CA: University of California Press, 1995).

6 James Clifford, 'Traveling Cultures', in *Cultural Studies*, ed. Lawrence Grossberg, Cary Nelson and Paula Treichler (New York: Routledge, 1992), 108.

7 Justin D. Edwards and Rune Graulund, *Mobility at Large: Globalization, Textuality and Innovative Travel Writing* (Liverpool: Liverpool University Press, 2012), 3.

8 John Tomlinson, *Globalization and Culture* (Cambridge: Polity Press, 1999), 2.

9 Bruce Robbins, 'Comparative Cosmopolitanism', *Social Text* 31/32 (1992): 177.

10 See, for example, Edward W. Said, *Orientalism* (London: Routledge & Kegan Paul, 1978); Gayatri Chakravorty Spivak, 'Can the Subaltern Speak?', in *Colonial Discourse and Post-Colonial Theory: A Reader*, ed. Patrick Williams and Laura Chrisman (New York: Columbia University Press, 1994), 66–111.

11 Indira Ghose, *Women Travellers in Colonial India: The Power of the Female Gaze* (Delhi: Oxford University Press, 1998), 6.

12 Patrick Holland and Graham Huggan, *Tourists with Typewriters: Critical Reflections on Contemporary Travel Writing* (Ann Arbor, MI: University of Michigan Press, 1998), 20.

13 See, for example, Ulrich Beck, 'Cosmopolitan Realism: On the Distinction between Cosmopolitanism in Philosophy and the Social Sciences', *Global Networks* 4.2 (2004): 131–56; David Held, 'Democracy and the New International Order', in *Cosmopolitan Democracy: An Agenda for a New World Order*, ed. Daniele Archibugi and David Held (Cambridge: Polity Press, 1995), 96–120.

14 Marilyn Adler Papayanis, *Writing in the Margins: The Ethics of Expatriation from Lawrence to Ondaatje* (Nashville, TN: Vanderbilt University Press, 2005), 6.

15 Papayanis, *Writing in the Margins*, 10–11.

16 The term 'identity work' is used by Walseth to address the socially constructed status of identities, drawing attention to the ways in which identities are dynamic, contested and contextualised as opposed to

essentialist or natural. Kristin Walseth, 'Young Muslim Women and Sport: The Impact of Identity Work', *Leisure Studies* 25.1 (2006): 75–94.

17 See, for example, Jane Bennett, *The Enchantment of Modern Life* (Princeton, NJ: Princeton University Press, 2001); Anthony Giddens, *Modernity and Self-Identity: Self and Society in the Late Modern Age* (Cambridge: Polity Press, 1991); Alexander Nehamas, *The Art of Living: Socratic Reflections from Plato to Foucault* (Berkeley, CA: University of California Press, 1998); Martha C. Nussbaum, *Love's Knowledge: Essays on Philosophy and Literature* (New York: Oxford University Press, 1990); Charles Taylor, *Sources of the Self: The Making of the Modern Identity* (Cambridge, MA: Harvard University Press, 1989).

18 See, for example, K. Anthony Appiah, 'Identity, Authenticity, Survival: Multicultural Societies and Social Reproduction', in *Multiculturalism: Examining 'The Politics of Recognition'*, ed. Amy Gutmann (Princeton, NJ: Princeton University Press, 1994), 149–64; Luke Desforges, 'Traveling the World: Identity and Travel Biography', *Annals of Tourism Research* 27.4 (2000): 926–45; Stuart Hall and Paul du Gay, *Questions of Cultural Identity* (London: Sage, 1996).

19 See, for example, Frank Hakemulder, *The Moral Laboratory: Experiments Examining the Effects of Reading Literature on Social Perception and Moral Self-Concept* (Amsterdam: John Benjamins, 2000); Lynn Hunt, *Inventing Human Rights* (New York: W.W. Norton, 2008); Martha Nussbaum, *Not for Profit: Why Democracy Needs the Humanities* (Princeton, NJ: Princeton University Press, 2010).

20 My notion of 'dwelling in difference' builds on Clifford's conceptualisation of 'traveling-in-dwelling' and 'dwelling-in-traveling' in global cosmopolitanism: see Clifford, 'Traveling Cultures'.

21 Susanna Moodie, *Roughing It in the Bush: Or Life in Canada* (1852; repr. Cambridge: Cambridge University Press, 2011). Subsequent citations will be provided parenthetically in the text.

22 Frances Mayes, *Under the Tuscan Sun* (London: Bantam, 1996); *Bella Tuscany: The Sweet Life in Italy* (London: Bantam Books, 1999); *Every Day in Tuscany* (New York: Broadway Books, 2010). Subsequent references will be included parenthetically in the text, identified as TS, BT and ED respectively.

23 Moodie further explains that in 1832 a military half-pay stipend amounted to approximately £100 per annum of Canadian currency, which was sufficient to supply the family with food and to pay for the clearing of land for wheat and hay for cattle (1: 288).

24 See, for example, Holland and Huggan, *Tourists with Typewriters*; Caren Kaplan, *Questions of Travel: Postmodern Discourses of Displacement* (Durham, NC: Duke University Press, 1996); Debbie Lisle, *The Global Politics of Contemporary Travel Writing* (Cambridge: Cambridge University Press, 2006); Mary Louise Pratt, *Imperial Eyes: Travel Writing and Transculturation* (London: Routledge, 1992).

25 Fanny Parkes, *Wanderings of a Pilgrim: In Search of the Picturesque, During Four-and-Twenty Years in the East . . .* (London: Pelham Richardson, 1850).

26 David Spurr, *The Rhetoric of Empire: Colonial Discourse in Journalism, Travel Writing, and Imperial Administration* (Durham, NC: Duke University Press, 1993), 76.

27 Spurr, *Rhetoric of Empire*, 157.

28 I am drawing on Edward C. Knox's use of the term 'literature of accommodation' in his study of twentieth-century nonfiction by American writers in France who 'accommodate' to their new cultural context by recognising and making allowances for 'a new norm'. See 'A Literature of Accommodation', *French Politics, Culture & Society* 21.2 (2003): 95–110.

29 Peter Hulme, 'Travelling to Write: 1940–2000', in *The Cambridge Companion to Travel Writing*, ed. Peter Hulme and Tim Youngs (Cambridge: Cambridge University Press, 2002), 97.

30 Bruce Robbins, *Feeling Global: Internationalism in Distress* (New York: New York University Press, 1999), 250.

31 Robbins, 'Comparative Cosmopolitanism', 177.

32 Wendy Parkins, 'At Home in Tuscany: Slow Living and the Cosmopolitan Subject', *Home Cultures* 1:3 (2004): 262–3.

33 Parkins, 'At Home', 258.

34 Jeffrey J. Folks, 'Mediterranean Travel Writing: From Etruscan Places to Under the Tuscan Sun', *Papers on Language and Literature* 40.1 (2004): 103.

35 Silvia Ross, 'Home and Away: Tuscan Abodes and Italian Others in Contemporary Travel Writing', *Studies in Travel Writing* 13.1 (2009): 50.

36 Ross, 'Home and Away', 49.

37 On the dream of an 'ideal community' that tends to erase difference in seeking mutual recognition see Iris Marion Young, *Justice and the Politics of Difference* (Princeton, NJ: Princeton University Press, 1990), 300.

38 Ulrich Beck, 'The Cosmopolitan Society and Its Enemies', *Theory, Culture and Society* 19.1–2 (2002): 18.

39 Folks, 'Mediterranean Travel Writing', 105–6.

40 Hannerz, 'Cosmopolitans and Locals', 239.

41 Vered Amit, 'Circumscribed Cosmopolitanism: Travel Aspirations and Experiences', *Identities: Global Studies in Culture and Power* 22.5 (2015): 553, 556.

42 Gerard Delanty, 'The Cosmopolitan Imagination: Critical Cosmopolitanism and Social Theory', *British Journal of Sociology* 57.1 (2006): 25–47.

43 Bronislaw Szerszynski and John Urry, 'Cultures of Cosmopolitanism', *Sociological Review* 50.4 (2002): 470.

44 Maria Lugones, 'Purity, Impurity, and Separation', *Signs* 9.2 (1994): 464–5.

45 Michael Skey, 'What Does It Mean to Be a Cosmopolitan? An Examination of the Varying Meaningfulness and Commensurability of Everyday Cosmopolitan Practices', *Identities: Global Studies in Culture and Power* 20.3 (2013): 241.

5

TRAVELLING IN PAIRS

Kathryn N. Jones

Textual travel companions: negotiating joint-authored journeys

Although travel writers are seldom alone when they travel, and their journeys always entail a certain degree of dependence on others, from the late eighteenth century onwards with the emergence of more subjectivist Romantic travelogues, modern travel writing has been characterised by its constructions of individualism.[1] The recent success of works such as Sylvain Tesson's *The Consolations of the Forest: Alone in a Cabin on the Siberian Taiga*, winner of the 2014 Dolman Best Travel Book Award, and Sarah Marquis's *Wild by Nature: From Siberia to Australia, Three Years Alone in the Wilderness on Foot*, attests to the continued prevalence and popularity of the lone-traveller narrative.[2]

Moreover, even if the journeys themselves were not in fact solitary undertakings, their retrospective narratives frequently filter the travel experience through a single lens, with the travel companion represented as a blurred and marginal presence at best.[3] Graham Greene's *Journey without Maps* (1936) offers one of the most prominent examples of such occlusion, with the writer's cousin and co-traveller in Liberia, Barbara Greene, conspicuous by her absence from his narrative.[4] Such widespread solipsistic tendencies and power imbalances led to the call by James Clifford for 'new representational strategies' to allow for the emergence of a 'long list of actors' previously relegated to the margins of travel writing.[5]

Yet although relatively unusual, alternative modes of narration do exist. Co-authored travel narratives constitute an important sub-trend within the genre which raise salient questions regarding mobility and agency, textual ownership and authorship. Indeed, the study of certain periods and cultures reveals a significant tradition of jointly authored travel accounts. Kris Lackey has observed a pre-Second World War tradition of 'kintrips' in American nonfiction transcontinental narratives, frequently undertaken by married couples and often whole families.[6] Margot Irvine notes that whereas contemporary feminist studies prefer to focus on the solitary woman traveller, most nineteenth-century female travellers in fact undertook their journeys as part of a couple.[7] Moreover, numerous twentieth- and twenty-first-century French travel writers embark on *des voyages à deux* [joint journeys] with companions of the same or opposite sex. Indeed, Irvine contends that the subgenre of the *voyage à deux* is particularly French, and that such dual departures have significant repercussions for the form of the travel narrative produced.[8] In the late twentieth century, Sylvain Tesson's joint exploits with Alexandre Poussin, *On a roulé sur la terre* (1996) and *La marche dans le ciel* (1997), headed bestseller lists in France.[9] Travelogues by Carol Dunlop and Julio Cortázar (*Les Autonautes de la cosmoroute*), and by François Maspero with photographers Anaïk Frantz (*Les Passagers du Roissy-Express*) and Klavdij Sluban (*Balkans-Transit*), have been critically acclaimed as offering innovative, alternative approaches to travel and its representation.[10] Indeed, the proliferation of joint-authored travel narratives, in particular by married couples such as Marie-Hélène and Laurent de Cherisey, as well as numerous journeys across the world undertaken as part of a family unit, represent a striking recent trend in French-language travel literature, and suggest a re-emergence of the 'kintrip' in a different cultural context.[11]

Nevertheless, collaborative travel narratives have not often been the object of detailed academic study. This chapter analyses two French joint-authored travelogues written thirty years apart which offer insights into 'the strategies of accommodation, coordination and resistance that are required when two (or more) individuals share a conventionally unitary space of authorship'.[12] As Charles Forsdick has observed, parallel accounts of shared journeys have hitherto been most frequently analysed in terms of identifying gender differences in travel writing,[13] and it is necessary to widen the field of enquiry and examine writing partnerships by travellers of the same gender, in addition to narratives by LGBTQ and gender-fluid authors. Sara Mills has argued that travel narratives by women tend to be characterised by a 'less authoritarian stance vis-à-vis narrative voice', and this chapter will consider whether Mills's claim can also be applied to travelogues that use collective narrative viewpoints.[14]

The present analysis of two contrasting female literary partnerships explores the ways in which the travellers' relationships are inscribed or erased in their joint-authored work. The travelogues offer divergent approaches to the construction of individual and collective narrative perspectives, with one adopting a multi-vocal approach and the other a fusion model. Nevertheless, the reasons why these writers have come together are not thematised explicitly, meaning that the processes of collaborative writing remain largely hidden in these texts. Lorraine York is critical of the 'fusion' model of analysis that characterised much earlier feminist scholarship in this field, which celebrates and idealises women's collective acts, whilst effectively abolishing questions of individual creative property and authorial difference.[15] My chapter situates these works along the fusion/difference scale identified by York,[16] whilst drawing attention to ways in which they eschew such polarities.

Aux pays des femmes soldats [In the Countries of Female Soldiers] (1931) by Suzanne de Callias and Blanche Vogt recounts the authors' journey to Finland, Estonia, Lithuania, Germany and Denmark by boat, train and airplane in the summer of 1930.[17] Their travelogue was the sixth to be published in Fasquelle's *Collection Voyageuses de lettres* (1930–1949), a ground-breaking series devoted to female-authored literary travelogues in French, which featured some of the most prominent and prolific authors of 1930s France.[18] *Aux pays des femmes soldats* is the only joint-authored work contained in the twenty-volume collection, and also the only travelogue to feature a female travel companion. In *Vacances en Iran* [Holidays in Iran] (1961), journalists Caroline Gazaï and Geneviève Gaillet travel in the summer of 1960 in a Citroën 2 CV from France to Iran, where they stay for a period of three months.[19] Their travelogue is one of the few female-authored contributions to the popular 1950s and 1960s subgenre of Citroën 2 CV travel narratives.[20]

Although they undertake shared itineraries initially, by the conclusion of both works the travellers have chosen to continue their journeys separately, and the present chapter considers the ways in which this rupture is reflected in the collective text. Both sets of female travellers selected here encounter comparatively few obstacles during their journeys, although family obligations do curtail Gazaï's stay in Iran (246). For de Callias and Vogt, the only restriction on their ability to travel is the vast amount of bureaucratic paperwork to be completed prior to departure. De Callias and Gaillet in particular were experienced travellers, and the *voyageuses* [female travellers] shared similar journalistic backgrounds. Their profession means that they are perceived as valued visitors, and in the case of Gazaï and Gaillet, their status as Western journalists opens many doors that remained closed to Iranian women.[21] Vogt makes extensive use of the services of foreign ministries and French embassies, which supply her with numerous contacts and guides, whereas Gazaï's familial connections due to her Iranian husband allow her to live amongst and observe Iranian women in the private sphere.[22] In addition to a marked interest in issues concerning women, the travelogues under discussion offer incisive portrayals of political change in the 'new Europe' of the early 1930s and the 'new Iran' of the early 1960s.

Aux pays des femmes soldats

Aux pays des femmes soldats is a polyphonic travelogue composed of two alternating *cahiers* [notebooks], by 'Lucienne' on the one hand and 'Claire' on the other. Their journey is undertaken following a meal in the Eiffel Tower restaurant, when the two close friends express their desire to see the 'new Europe', and in particular 'these new Nordic republics' ['ces nouvelles républiques nordiques'] (10), with their own eyes.[23] Claire wishes to 'be displaced, see completely new people in new countries' ['me transplanter, voir des gens absolument nouveaux dans des pays neufs'] (9), whereas Lucienne wants to 'get a bit of fresh air' ['m'aérer un brin'] (12).

De Callias and Vogt choose to adopt fictional narrative personae in order to provide distinct yet intertwined accounts of their journey together to Finland and then on to Estonia. Nevertheless, this fictionalisation would have been futile as a means of masking their true identities, as it would have been abundantly clear to contemporary readers and reviewers that 'Lucienne' is de Callias, and 'Claire' is Vogt. Suzanne de Callias was renowned as a novelist, whose works (in particular *Jerry* [1923] and *Lucienne et Reinette* [1925]) were notorious for their sympathetic portrayals of homosexuality, and as a feminist journalist and caricaturist. 'Lucienne', like de Callias, has a fluent command of German, and is a caricaturist (55). Blanche Vogt was one of the most prominent and acclaimed French female journalists of the interwar years, writing numerous investigative reports for the newspapers *L'Oeuvre* and *L'Intransigeant*, in which she had a daily column. She was also a popular novelist and the author of numerous fictional works for children. In *Aux pays des femmes soldats*, 'Claire' undertakes numerous interviews with key political and military figures, and visits several national projects in order to fulfil her journalistic work and thereby finance her journey (103).

The reasons for their invention of fictional personae are not thematised explicitly, and it could be argued that the use of this device has a depersonalising and distancing effect. The only implicit explanation could be found in the fact that Claire's decision to travel also resulted from a desire to escape from her marital difficulties, which Vogt may not have wished to discuss openly. Claire's statement that 'I have never wanted to escape from Paris so much' ['jamais, je n'ai eu autant envie de fuir Paris'] is followed by 'melancholy confidences' ['de mélancoliques confidences'] (8) and ruminations on the incompatibility of men and women by Lucienne. Travel is thereby used as a means to assert individual agency and escape from confining domestic situations, and this freedom is extended to the creation of new identities.

Furthermore, the two alternating notebooks function as a highly effective device which allows the very distinctive individual voices of the traveller-narrators to resonate in the text. At the close of the first entry in her notebook, Lucienne writes: 'But it would be unfair for only one of the two travellers to express her point of view. I'll pass my pen to Claire' ['Mais il serait injuste qu'une seule des deux voyageuses exposât son point de vue. Je passe la plume à Claire'] (13).

This desire for equality between the narrative voices is also echoed intermedially in the first of the seven sketches by de Callias included in the travelogue, with the other sketches all portraying travellees encountered during the journey. The first sketch portrays the two travellers sitting side-by-side on a bench, watching a group of female soldiers march past against a backdrop of fir trees. The faces of both travellers are viewed in profile; they have similar bobbed hairstyles and are of the same height. Both women look up attentively; Lucienne is sketching, and Claire has her hand raised, as if she were pointing out some detail to her companion. The sketch thereby conveys the impression that the two are equal observers, whose joint journey is guided by the same shared aims and desire for similar experiences. Although Claire's account is given significantly more textual space in the travelogue, Lucienne's sketches act as a visual bridge between the *cahiers*, and these drawings, along with Lucienne's more forthright opinions, ensure that Claire's narrative voice is not allowed to dominate.[24]

The two notebooks have strikingly different tones, and the accounts also diverge in their choice of subject matter. A portrayal emerges of the at times fractious yet close relationship between the enthusiastic and good-humoured Claire, and her more melancholic and irritable travel companion Lucienne. Claire seeks out encounters with travellees more readily, and her account contains numerous conversations with a wide range of interlocutors.[25] She is assigned the task (by Lucienne) of providing detailed descriptions of the landscapes they visit (69), but as a journalist she is also concerned with 'social investigation' ['l'enquête sociale'] (70), and is not afraid to tackle issues such as the nature of Finnish democracy (111) and the true extent of the communist threat in northern Europe. Claire is more open to new ideas and experiences, and readier to praise the innovations, values and behaviour of travellees, for example the honesty, spirit of cooperation and respect for communal laws she encounters in Denmark (170–3). By contrast, Lucienne is far less easily impressed, and the following filmic metaphor describing her stay in Finland suggests her disengagement from her surroundings: 'In the documentary film that we have just lived for three weeks, I find that only Viborg merited a long pause' ['Dans le film documentaire que nous venons de vivre pendant trois semaines, je trouve que seul Viborg méritait une longue pause'] (77). Although she is strongly critical of national stereotypes (155), Lucienne is also prone to universalising tendencies, and in her descriptions of Helsinki, Tallinn and Riga she insists on pointing out Russian and Germanic influences and continuities rather than recognising national differences. However, although a more reserved figure, she also proves to be an incisive observer of other travellers and of political realities. When visiting Berlin in 1930, she predicts that the mounting economic crisis will trigger a fundamental conflict between the emerging National Socialists and the Weimar Republic.

The travellers' intertwining accounts create a fascinating dialogue about the countries visited, the travellees encountered and the values they represent. As each voice takes up the narrative thread, it becomes apparent that this dialogue is a conflicting one, as the notebooks portray the palpable tensions and overt disagreements that arise between the travellers. As Rebecca Pope observes in her discussion with Susan Leonardi: 'After all, when our lips speak together, as often as not they disagree'.[26] In *Aux pays des femmes soldats*, on occasion one narrative voice fills in the silences and omissions in the other traveller's account. Claire mischievously informs the reader: 'Lucienne may grumble about the banality of Helsinki, whose contours all fail to tempt her pencil. However, I know that she is not averse to resting her eyes on so many handsome fellows' ['Lucienne peut maugréer contre la banalité d'Helsinki, dont aucun contour ne tente son crayon. Je sais, moi, qu'elle n'est pas fâchée de reposer ses yeux sur tant de beaux gars'] (33).

The titular female soldiers function as a leitmotif, yet they also constitute the greatest source of conflict between the travellers, and this discord was noted by contemporary reviewers. De Callias and Vogt's interest in and disagreement about the *Lottas* extends across several countries and notebook entries. Finland's female auxiliary army, the *Lottas-Svard*, was formed in order to stave off the threat of communism and Russian invasion. Following their meeting with the Finnish head of the *Lottas*,[27] an argument ensues between the travellers: 'Lucienne explodes: "Really Claire, what do you think of all these women who are proud to imitate soldiers? In a world of progress, is it tolerable that a woman helps to kill?"' ['Lucienne éclate: "Enfin, Claire, comment juges-tu toutes ces femmes orgueilleuses d'imiter des soldats? Est-il tolérable, dans un monde de progrès, qu'une femme aide à tuer?"'] (Claire, 41–2). Whereas Lucienne takes a resolutely pacifist and internationalist stance, Claire attempts to contextualise and understand Finnish militarism, and in her notebook she implies that Lucienne's stance is politically naïve: 'Dear Lucienne, who fervently believes that soldiers are the ones who declare war!' ['Chère Lucienne, qui croit dur comme canon que ce sont les soldats qui déclarent la guerre!'] (Claire, 47). The beginning of Lucienne's next *cahier* seems at first glance to suggest a new-found agreement between the two, as she states: 'I agree with Claire about everything she has just written' ['Je suis d'accord avec Claire sur tout ce qu'elle vient d'écrire'] (55). However, she does not in fact concur here with Claire's views on militarism, but rather on Finnish cleanliness. It is indicative of the travelogue's dialogical qualities that it is precisely this source of unresolved tension between the authors that provides the title of the work.

By contrast to her focus on the gender of the *Lottas*, Lucienne in particular does not explicitly thematise her own identity as a female traveller, nor does she refer to the reactions of those they encounter to herself and Claire. Conversely, Claire is more aware of the impression that she makes on travellees, and constructs the travelling self as an exotic other, though the curiosity of travellees is perhaps due more to her inappropriately warm attire in the summer heat of Helsinki than to her identity as a female traveller: 'People turn around in the streets in order to look at my fur coat. A half-naked Tahitian woman under her fringed umbrella in a Paris street in January would not have excited more curiosity' ['Dans les rues, les gens se retournent pour regarder mon manteau de fourrure. Une Tahitienne à demi nue sous son ombrelle à franges dans une rue de Paris au mois de janvier n'aurait pas plus grand succès de curiosité'] (61). Lucienne's greater experience as a solitary female traveller is portrayed as a key difference between the two women. On disembarking at Helsinki, Claire notes that she searches for 'a helping hand for my assembled luggage. Lucienne manages alone and makes the brusque remark: "You can really see that you are used to travelling with a man!"' ['une main secourable pour mes valises rassemblées. Lucienne se débrouille toute seule, elle me jette: "Comment on voit bien que tu as l'habitude de voyager avec un homme!"'] (25). Claire's reliance on Lucienne as her German-language interpreter quickly becomes an undeniable source of irritation for the latter. Lucienne begins the second entry in her notebook by expressing her admiration for Claire as a 'magnificent travel companion' ['magnifique compagne de voyage']: 'She is pleased with everything; she finds things to be astounded by and admire everywhere. Her journalist's eyes are always searching; she observes the country with all her senses' ['Elle est contente de tout; elle trouve partout à s'ébaubir et à admirer. Ses yeux de journaliste sont toujours en quête; elle est là qui observe le pays avec tous les sens'] (27). Yet she swiftly tires of her companion's dependence on her, whilst questioning Claire's ability to cope without her. Lucienne describes how Claire watches her strenuous efforts to make hotel staff in Helsinki speak to her in German: 'The positively school-girl sentences that I utter fill my friend with ease; she watches the performance from her seat in the stalls, and believes that this is how it will go on all the time' ['Des phrases bien scolastiques que je leur débite remplissent d'aise mon amie; elle assiste à la représentation, assise dans un fauteil d'orchestre, et croit que ça va durer tout le temps comme ça'] (28).

Indeed, the travellers spend an increasing amount of time on separate activities. In Tallinn, Claire notes, not without a sense of annoyance: 'Lucienne has left me again in order to go and sketch some old church. I keep myself busy interviewing female members of parliament and male politicians' ['Lucienne m'a encore quittée pour aller dessiner je ne sais quelle vieille église. Moi, je m'occupe de mon côté. Je prends des interviews avec des femmes-députés, des hommes politiques'] (Claire, 85). Around halfway through *Aux pays des femmes soldats* the travellers go their separate ways, exchanging 'heartfelt hugs and kisses, recommendations' ['embrassades émues, recommandations'] (97). It is not stated explicitly whether this separation was planned from the outset. Lucienne travels on alone to Latvia, and after a comparatively brief stay moves on to Berlin, the capital of Weimar Germany. Claire returns to Finland to carry out interviews, and then travels on to Denmark, before returning to France on the first ever scheduled flight from Copenhagen to Paris. Inevitably, as the notebooks begin to describe solo journeys instead of a shared itinerary, the impression of a continued travel-dialogue decreases, the narration becomes more monological and the transition between the notebooks becomes more abrupt.

Paradoxically, it is also implied that the travellers' viewpoints come closer together when they are apart. By the end of the work, Claire shares Lucienne's frustration with the limits placed on travellers by bureaucracy: 'I am beginning to understand why Lucienne, who is always on the road, on each return to France disembarks with increased revolutionary tendencies' ['Je commence à comprendre pourquoi Lucienne, qui est toujours en route, débarque en France, à chaque retour, avec des tendances révolutionnaires accrues'] (185). The travellers keep in touch through letter and telegram. References to this correspondence at the beginning and end of notebook entries conjure up the presence of the absent interlocutor. They also plan to meet for lunch on the day after their separate returns to Paris. The narrative thereby travels full circle. The travelogue ends with the prospect of another shared journey, as Lucienne observes that the next world congress on moral reform is taking place in Moscow: 'This promises to be curious . . . Moscow! What if I talked to Claire about it?' ['Ceci promet d'être curieux . . . Moscou! Si j'en parlais à Claire?'] (190). The ellipsis implies an ongoing process and continuing dialogue about travel, and the polyphonic text illustrates ways in which a joint travelogue can accommodate conflicting views.

Vacances en Iran

By contrast, the second work under discussion, *Vacances en Iran*, offers a far more harmonious representation of the shared journey and the process of collective writing, which is narrated for the most part using the merged collective 'nous' [we] form. Geneviève Gaillet and Caroline Gazaï's journey from Paris to Iran in the summer of 1960 began with a casual suggestion by one friend to another: '"Do you want to come to Iran?" // "Iran, why not?"' ['"Veux-tu venir en Iran?" // "En Iran, pourquoi pas?"'] (7).[28] The first chapter, entitled 'Excursion for beginners', explicitly thematises their identities as *voyageuses*, and implies that their journey should be characterised as a feminist undertaking, rather than a classic search for adventure or a desire for displacement (7). Defiantly mocking preconceptions of women as inferior travellers, they assert: 'Setting off on our own to a country where women have no rights was reason enough for us. We wanted to know if so-called "grand tourism" is an exploit, or if we, as feeble women, could undertake it' ['Partir seules dans un pays où les femmes n'ont aucun droit, pour nous c'était une raison suffisante. Nous voulions savoir si le "grand tourisme" est un exploit, ou si nous, faibles femmes, pouvions le réaliser'] (7). Gaillet and Gazaï therefore present themselves as role models from the outset, and in their afterword 'If you want to go' ['Si vous voulez partir'], they invite others to follow in their footsteps by providing details of 'everything it's good to know' ['tout ce qu'il est bon de savoir'] (259). Their self-portrayal as pioneering female travellers is reinforced by a keen awareness of how the duo are perceived by travellees. As they travel past Samsun in Turkey, they declare that 'men and women watch us more out of curiosity and terror than animosity [. . .] For them [the sight of] these two free women was certainly an extraordinary spectacle' ['des hommes et des femmes nous regardent avec plus de curiosité et d'effroi que d'animosité [. . .] C'était certainement pour eux un spectacle extraordinaire que celui de ces deux femmes en liberté'] (25). Unaccompanied by a male chaperone, the *voyageuses* become more conspicuous the further eastwards they travel, noting that the residents of the Turkish town of Eregli 'gaze at us in awe' ['nous dévisagent stupéfaits'] (20).

In a conscious break with earlier female travellers, such as Isabelle Eberhardt, who chose to wear masculine clothes in order to be less conspicuous, Gaillet and Gazaï endeavour to draw attention to their feminine appearance through their choice of attire: 'We did not want to put on trousers and disguise ourselves as "explorers". Throughout our travels, we were determined to wear clean and chic dresses, which we ironed during breaks in the journey' ['Nous n'avons pas voulu adopter le pantalon et nous déguiser en "exploratrices". Tout au long du parcours, nous avons tenu à porter des robes fraîches et pimpantes, que nous faisions repasser aux étapes'] (25). Elizabeth Hagglund makes the telling observation that although 'travel is often thought of as an escape from home and domesticity [. . .] travellers – both men and women – spend much of their time in a kind of displaced home-making, creating and re-creating temporary home spaces'.[29] In a contrast to other 2 CV narratives, rather than concentrating their efforts on traversing the greatest amount of terrain in the quickest possible time, the travelogue's attention shifts gradually from portraying reactions to the *voyageuses* to a focus on intercultural encounters. Rather than the boat or airplane, these travellers choose the car not for its speed, but for its slowness, in order to 'handle transitions carefully, and to approach this far-off country gradually in order to understand it better' ['ménager les transitions, et d'aborder peu à peu ce lointain pays pour mieux le comprendre'] (8).[30]

Vacances en Iran combines traditional touristic descriptions of the travellers' 'astonishing journey' ['voyage stupéfiant'] through a country in the grip of a 'revolution' ['révolution'] (97) with keen socio-political observations. On their arrival in Iran, they observe that 'the hurried traveller can only return from this country very disappointed' ['le voyageur pressé ne peut revenir que très déçu de ces pays'] (42–4), and emphasise the need to 'know how to take your time, and simultaneously adopt the ancestral customs of the inhabitants' ['savoir prend son temps, et simultanément adopter les habitudes ancestrales des habitants'] (44). This desire for deceleration and interpersonal/intercultural encounters corresponds closely to James Clifford's notion of 'dwelling-in-traveling'.[31] Yet this shift from the space of the journey on the road in their 'winged' 2 CV (36) to a return to a familial, domestic setting and its patriarchal social structures also leads to the protagonists becoming increasingly unobtrusive figures who are much less confident in their identities as *voyageuses*. Gazaï is perceived by her Iranian family-in-law as an object of curiosity, 'this daughter-in-law who came from France all by herself' ['cette belle-fille venue toute seule de France'] (190). Iranian patriarchal norms thereby negate the agency of her female travel companion Gaillet as a traveller in her own right. For her part, Gaillet is unwilling to venture on a solo car journey without her travel companion, thus suggesting their interdependence: '"By car, without Caroline? Alone on these deserted roads? Out of the question!" Geneviève had refused point-blank' ['"En voiture, sans Caroline? Seule sur ces routes désertes? Pas question!" Geneviève avait été très catégorique'] (206).

Yet the narrators themselves also choose not to thematise their own identities as female travellers following their arrival in Iran. This change is represented and reflected paratextually in the striking contrast between the authors' photographs inside the front and back covers. The front-cover photographs are individual studio portraits which depict the beaming authors in close-up, wearing Western 1960s clothes, short hairstyles and make-up. In the back-cover photograph (taken by Gaillet in Iran), the authors are covered by black and floral-print *tchadors* (a full-length cloth outer garment worn by many Iranian women), with one sitting on the side of the road and the other standing next to their 2 CV. Both women hold their hands up in order to secure their *tchadors*, and offer timid smiles. The accompanying caption states: 'Caroline and Geneviève wore the national *tchador* in order to discover this old civilisation, a country with incredible riches' ['Caroline et Geneviève ont revêtu le *tchador* national pour découvrir ce pays de vieille civilisation, aux richesses incroyables'] (n.p.). In contrast to their determination not to disguise their identities as female travellers during their journey from France to Iran, the narrators conform to patriarchal dress codes and don the *tchador*, noting that in places such as the narrow streets of the *vieille ville* of Tehran, 'it is better not to walk alone and dress as a European woman' ['il vaut mieux ne pas se promener seule et habillée à l'européenne'] (64). The 'extraordinary spectacle' of 'these two free women' (25) becomes hidden from view after reaching their destination.

The far more muted portrayal of the dynamics between the travellers, and the emphasis on their interdependence, could be read as a direct result of their choice of narrative perspective. In contrast to *Aux pays des femmes soldats*, the majority of this joint-authored travelogue takes a more unified and ultimately homogenising fusion approach towards the process of collaborative writing. Most chapters are narrated using the collective 'nous' [we] form, and on a few occasions the narrators refer to themselves in the third person as the protagonists 'Caroline' and 'Geneviève', though their distinctive personalities do not come to the fore. The adoption of these narrative perspectives leads to a more harmonious representation of a shared itinerary, suggesting a far greater element of collaboration than between de Callias and Vogt. Catharine Mee contends that 'the use of "we" for companions brought from home tends [. . .] to efface them from the text. "We" absorbs companions, making them invisible and denying them the separate identity afforded by the third person'.[32] In *Vacances en Iran*, the collective 'nous' minimises any difference of opinion between the travellers, and this united front is deployed to construct a predominantly eulogistic portrayal of their destination and its landscape, social practices and culture. Gazaï in particular is anxious that their travelogue not be construed as critical of Iran: 'If some people believe they can detect disparaging remarks in our pages, what can we do? That was not our intention' ['Si certains croient déceler des propos désobligeants dans nos pages, que pouvons-nous? Tel n'était pas notre dessein'] (31).

Nevertheless, the use of the collective 'nous' is not universal, and it is in the individually narrated passages that a more critical note emerges in both text and images, most notably regarding the treatment of Iranian women. Although for the majority of the travelogue it is not possible to discern which author has written each chapter or section, in a few instances the singular 'je' [I] is used to narrate accounts of separate activities and diverse experiences. Moreover, Gaillet narrates the twelfth, final chapter alone, as she remains in Iran after Gazaï returns to Paris in order to supervise her children's return to school (246). Gaillet also takes the majority of the photographs included in the travelogue (the others being agency images), many of which feature the travellers and their car, and human figures (including numerous women), thereby directing its visual narrative.

The abrupt transition between the travelogue's collective and individual narrative voices is illustrated at the beginning of the ninth chapter:

> One day, all the same, we had to separate for a few days. We still had too many things to see [. . .] Geneviève went off to discover the 'tribes' of the south, whilst Caroline, needed by her family-in-law, headed up north.

As a Western woman, I was going to be suddenly submerged into a universe in which women still only have relatively little freedom.

[Un jour, tout de même, nous dûmes nous séparer pour quelques jours. Nous avions encore trop de choses à voir [. . .] Geneviève partait à la découverte des 'tribus' du sud, pendant que Caroline, réclamée par sa belle-famille, remontait vers le nord.

Occidentale, j'allais brusquement être plongée dans un univers où les femmes ont encore bien peu de liberté].

(189)

Through her familial connections, Gazaï is able to offer an insider/outsider's perspective on Iranian society, and its women in particular. Married to an Iranian man living in Paris, Gazaï's stay with her family-in-law fuels her desire to 'document the condition of women in the twentieth century, a condition which would be my own if I lived in this country' ['me documenter sur la condition de la femme au xxe siècle, condition qui serait la mienne si je vivais dans ce pays'] (194).[33] Impassioned by this question, Gazaï investigates by attending meetings, clubs and women's dinners, and seeking out the president of the *Society for the Awakening of Iranian Women* in Tehran (194). She constructs a polyphony of contrasting male and female perspectives on why so many Iranian women still choose to wear the *tchador* despite its abolition in 1933, ranging from protection from sensationalist foreign photographers in search of oriental beauty to a means of hiding poverty (199–202). Gazaï highlights the work of the nascent Iranian feminist movement and its demands for the introduction of civil law and a revision to Koranic law. She chronicles the sweeping changes in the fields of women's literacy and education, women's work outside the home in all professions and their adaptation to modern life through the acquisition of a driver's licence. However, she also draws attention to persisting inequalities, such as the denial of women's right to vote.

The section entitled 'Femme-objet' [Woman-Object] offers a particularly powerful intermedial dialogue between text (by Gazaï) and image (by Gaillet). Following an interrogation of the practices of repudiation and polygamy in Iran, Gazaï criticises the prevalent treatment of women as commodities:

Here the woman is all too often an object bought by the man, as the future husband deposits the dowry which will be paid to the family in the event of repudiation. When the object no longer pleases he discards it, chooses another wife or [else] gets rid of it.

[Ici la femme est encore trop souvent un objet que l'homme s'achète, puisque le futur mari dépose la dot qui sera versée à la famille en cas de répudiation. Lorsque l'objet a cessé de plaire, il le met au rebut, choisit une autre femme ou bien s'en débarrasse].

(202)

The accompanying full-page photograph shows a human form covered completely by a black *tchador*, sitting alone on the floor of a busy airport next to the baggage claim area. Men in suits stand around in groups and hurry past the shrouded figure, and a woman wearing a Western-style blouse and floral skirt waits for an arrival in the background. The caption of the photograph proclaims: 'Watch out sir! This little black heap is a woman' ['Attention monsieur! Ce petit tas noir est une femme'] (203). In *Vacances en Iran*, the shift towards individualised narrative perspectives allows room for critical dialogues and facilitates the representation of female travellees in particular.

Conclusion

The joint-authored travelogues under discussion in this chapter demonstrate the manifold opportunities afforded by collaborative travel writing, as well as its inherent challenges. By departing from conceptions of travel as an individualistic and solitary undertaking, collaborative travel narratives illuminate and probe the boundaries of the relationship between mobility and agency, textual ownership and authorship. Joint-authored travelogues endeavour to negotiate a tricky path between the solipsism of individually narrated travelogues and the erasure of difference that can result from collective narrative perspectives.

Though de Callias and Vogt's *Aux pays des femmes soldats* and Gazaï and Gaillet's *Vacances en Iran* may seem at first glance to embody a clear-cut distinction between alternating '*je*/I' and joint '*nous*/we' modes of narration, these dividing lines are not universal, and become more ambiguous as the works progress. On the one hand, the multi-vocal approach deployed by de Callias and Vogt allows each author to retain her distinctive narrative perspective, and functions as a strategy of resistance and assertion of textual ownership. Distinguishing between narrative voices becomes especially significant when the authors are divided by profession and approach, as is the case in *Parallel Worlds*, which recounts anthropologist Alma Gottlieb and writer Philip Graham's journey to Côte d'Ivoire.[34] Conversely, the usual singular authority of the solo traveller's voice is undermined within the text, as the competing alternating 'I' accounts of shared experiences relativise the other's style and point of view. Indeed, it could be suggested that as a result of their conflicting views, the dual narrators of *Aux pays des femmes soldats* choose to maintain their divergent individual interests at the expense of the shared journey, suggesting an incompatibility of co-travelling, but not co-authorship in this case.

In *Vacances en Iran*, Gazaï and Gaillet portray themselves as role models for other female travellers from the outset, yet they mask their female travelling identities and European appearance following their arrival in Iran. Their individual views on their destination become largely submerged and homogenised due to their choice of a collective narrative perspective, and the fusion of their voices functions as a strategy of coordination in order to present a unified view of Iran.[35] Nevertheless, on occasion the narrating 'I' is deployed to depict different experiences, and diverse viewpoints enter the work through the interplay between words (by Gazaï) and photographs (by Gaillet). Other travel writers have also sought to avoid the limitations of the 'I/we' binary through formal experimentation, creating travel texts that rely on generic diversity to incorporate multiple viewpoints. The innovative intermediality of W.H. Auden and Louis MacNeice's travel collage *Letters from Iceland* (1937), and W.H. Auden and Christopher Isherwood's *Journey to a War* (1939), offered a radical departure from the prevalent monologism of the travel *reportage* of the 1930s.[36] The generic diversity or 'untidiness' of *Journey to a War*, which comprises poems by Auden and a 'travel diary' reworked by Isherwood from both men's diaries and articles written during and after the journey, is inextricably tied to its subject matter of the Sino-Japanese war, as Auden observes: 'War is untidy, inefficient, obscure and largely a matter of chance'.[37]

The fictionalisation of travellers' identities is a further approach used by collaborative authors to foreground the relationship between co-travellers and to allow for the inclusion of multiple narrative perspectives. *Moon Country: Further Reports from Iceland* (1996), by poets Simon Armitage and Glyn Maxwell, was conceived as a self-conscious attempt to follow in the footsteps of Auden and MacNeice. Their homage is particularly evident in their assembling of different genres, from a three-act verse drama to an interview with the Icelandic President Vigdís Finnbogadóttir.[38] However, they diverge from their British predecessors by choosing to fictionalise their own identities in the *reportage* sections of the work. While on the one hand they highlight their authorial individuality by ascribing textual ownership in the work's index, conversely they dissimulate their national identities through the invention of the generic Scandinavian-sounding travelling personae Petersson (Armitage) and Jamesson (Maxwell), whose [mis]adventures are narrated in a self-deprecating tone. Simultaneously introducing a distance between author-narrator and traveller, as is also the case in *Aux pays des femmes soldats*, this fictionalisation serves to disrupt the power dynamics and binaries of the traveller/travellee relationship. The ambiguity of this device destabilises what Debbie Lisle has termed the genre's 'authorian sureness'.[39]

Other travel writers have deployed an omniscient narrator and referred to both travellers in the third person in order to foreground the presence of co-travellers and travellees. In François Maspero's *Roissy-Express*, by portraying the narrator-traveller as a character called 'François', 'the travelling *I* is decentred', thus placing Maspero on an equal footing with his collaborator, the photographer Anaïk Frantz, and facilitating 'the inclusion of other viewpoints, voices and intertexts'.[40] This novelistic approach might seem at odds with the assertion of the traveller's authorial authority, but several more recent collaborative travelogues have been read as postmodern responses to the predominant monologism of travel literature. In his analysis of Stephen Muecke and Paddy Roe's *Reading the Country* (1984), Tim Youngs observes: 'The notion of joint authorship contrasts with the individualistic narration of most travel writing and is a symptom [. . .] of trends in contemporary literary theory that stress the desirability of multivocality and collaboration'. Youngs argues that the 'collaborative nature of the book is crucial to its politics', as Muecke aims to restore multiple perspectives on the histories of place and travel.[41]

Indeed, didactic, political or ideological aims may often lie behind the decision to narrate in a collective voice. Youngs contends that W.H. Auden's designation of 'hundreds of anonymous Icelanders, farmers, fishermen, busmen, children' as 'the real authors of this book'[42] in his preface to *Letters from Iceland* is 'in keeping with Auden's left-wing politics of the time'.[43] Similarly, in both *Aux pays des femmes soldats* and *Vacances en Iran*, it is noteworthy that the travelogues are at their most conflictual and dialogical when contentious contemporary socio-political issues such as militarism and gender equality come to the fore. Furthermore, Debbie Lisle draws attention to the transformative potential of co-authored travel texts as a means of deconstructing the authorial function and questioning 'the automatic hierarchy of power between author and other'.[44] Lisle argues that the dual authorship of Julio Cortázar and Carol Dunlop's *Les Autonautes de la cosmoroute* 'unsettles the "monarch-of-all-I-survey" position of the travel writer' and 'provides a model for how travel writing might be transformed in a context of globalisation, mobility and deterritorialisation'.[45]

Conversely, Bill Ashcroft has questioned the possibility of achieving collaborative subjectivity in travel literature. In his consideration of travel writing as a means of bearing witness, despite noting that in some cases testimony 'speaks for a collective subject', Ashcroft contends that 'collective subjectivity is something to which the travel writing can never bear witness', as it is 'excluded from the experience of trauma'.[46] Yet I would argue that not only is it possible, indeed it is imperative for travel writing to cease perpetuating a stance of splendid isolation. The adoption of dialogical approaches to travel and its narrative reconstruction would facilitate a full acknowledgement of the contribution made by 'travellees' and co-travellers in various guises, and allow the genre to move towards a more accurate and inclusive reflection of the shared 'human landscapes' of many journeys.[47] The exploration of alternative modes of narration should play a prominent role in the current ethical turn in contemporary travel writing, as questions of not only where we travel, but why, how and with whom become increasingly pressing concerns.[48] As 'the fundamental division amongst the inhabitants of our world remains between those who can travel and those who cannot',[49] more collective and collaborative textual dialogues about travel and mobility, and their significance, implications and representation, need to be held.

Notes

1   See Carl Thompson, *Travel Writing* (London: Routledge, 2011), 117.

2   Sylvain Tesson, *The Consolations of the Forest: Alone in a Cabin on the Siberian Taiga*, trans. Linda Coverdale (London: Penguin, 2013); Sarah Marquis, *Wild by Nature: From Siberia to Australia, Three Years Alone in the Wilderness on Foot* (Crows Nest: Allen & Unwin, 2016).

3   See Catharine Mee's stimulating discussion of the role of travel companions, 'Accompanying', in *Interpersonal Encounters in Contemporary Travel Writing: French and Italian Perspectives* (London: Anthem, 2014), 127–46.

4   Graham Greene, *Journey without Maps* (London: Heinemann, 1936); cf. Barbara Greene, *Too Late to Turn Back: Barbara and Graham Greene in Liberia* (1936; London: Settle Bendall, 1981).

5   James Clifford, *Routes: Travel and Translation in the Late Twentieth Century* (Cambridge, MA: Harvard University Press, 1997), 25.

6   Kris Lackey, *RoadFrames: The American Highway Narrative* (Lincoln, NE: University of Nebraska Press, 1997), 26.

7   Margot Irvine, *Pour suivre un époux: Les récits de voyages des couples au dix-neuvième siècle* (Québec: Éditions Nota bene, 2008), 8.

8   Irvine, *Pour suivre un époux*, 10.

9   Alexandre Poussin and Sylvain Tesson, *On a roulé sur la terre* (Paris: R. Laffont, 1996); *La marche dans le ciel* (Paris: France loisirs, 1997).

10 Carol Dunlop and Julio Cortázar, *Les Autonautes de la cosmoroute: ou, un voyage intemporel Paris-Marseille* (Paris: Gallimard, 1983); François Maspero, *Les Passagers du Roissy-Express*, photographies d'Anaïk Frantz (Paris: Seuil, 1990); François Maspero, *Balkans-Transit*, photographies de Klavdij Sluban (Paris: Seuil, 1997). Amongst the prominent forebearers for these textual/visual partnerships is John Steinbeck and Robert Capa's *Russian Journal* (New York: Viking Press, 1948).

11 Marie-Hélène and Laurent de Cherisey, *Passeurs d'espoir: 1. Une famille à la rencontre des bâtisseurs du XXIe siècle* (Paris: Presses de la Renaissance, 2005).

12 Marjorie Stone and Judith Thompson, 'Contexts and Heterotexts: A Theoretical and Historical Introduction', in *Literary Couplings: Writing Couples, Collaborators, and the Construction of Authorship*, ed. Marjorie Stone and Judith Thompson (Madison, WI: The University of Wisconsin Press, 2006), 25.

13 Charles Forsdick, 'Peter Fleming and Ella Maillart in China: Travel Writing as Stereoscopic and Polygraphic Form', *Studies in Travel Writing* 13.4 (2009): 294. For example, Valerie Kennedy emphasises the contrast between the 'masculine' and 'feminine' styles of Graham and Barbara Greene in their respective accounts of their travels in Liberia in the 1930s. Valerie Kennedy, 'Conradian Quest Versus Dubious Adventure: Graham and Barbara Greene in West Africa', *Studies in Travel Writing* 19.1 (2015): 48–65.

14 Sara Mills, *Discourses of Difference: An Analysis of Women's Travel Writing and Colonialism* (New York: Routledge, 1991), 21.

15 Lorraine York, *Rethinking Women's Collaborative Writing* (Toronto: University of Toronto Press, 2002), 7, 21, 59.

16 York, *Rethinking*, 134–5.

17 Suzanne de Callias and Blanche Vogt, *Aux pays des femmes soldats: Finlande - Esthonie - Danemark – Lithuanie* (Paris: Fasquelle, 1931). All references are to this edition and will be placed in parenthesis in the body of the text.

18 The series is also noted for its publication of Ella Maillart's first travelogue, *Parmi la jeunesse russe* [Among Russian Youth], in 1932.

19 Caroline Gazaï and Geneviève Gaillet, *Vacances en Iran* (Paris: Berger-Levrault, 1961). All references are to this edition and will be placed in parenthesis in the body of the text.

20 For a discussion of this subgenre, including *Vacances en Iran*, see Charles Forsdick, *Travel in Twentieth-Century French and Francophone Cultures: The Persistence of Diversity* (Oxford: Oxford University Press, 2005), 106–33.

21 To take one example, they observe that they are the only representatives of their sex present at a large reception hosted by the Iranian emperor to celebrate Iran's technological progress (175).

22 Caroline Gazaï also co-directed (with Georges Bourdelon and Louis Dalmas) a 1963 travel *reportage* entitled *L'Empire de la rose*, which focused on Iranian women.

23 All translations from the French are my own.

24 Lucienne's *cahier* only makes up 63 out of the work's 190 pages.

25 The term 'travelee' was coined by Mary Louise Pratt, *Imperial Eyes: Travel Writing and Transculturation* (London: Routledge, 1992), 133.

26 Susan Leonardi and Rebecca Pope, 'Screaming Divas: Collaboration as Feminist Practice', *Tulsa Studies in Women's Literature* 13.2 (1994): 259–70.

27 Perhaps due to linguistic barriers, both travellers have a tendency to judge the female military leaders and politicians they encounter primarily on their appearance and dress; for instance, Claire observes that the head of the Finnish *Lottas* 'is not a stylish woman' ['n'est pas une femme coquette'] (37), and describes her uniform in detail.

28 Biographical information about the authors has not been located to date, therefore all information about the authors and their trip is from the text itself.

29 Elizabeth Hagglund, 'Travel Writing and Domestic Ritual', in *Seuils et traverses: enjeux de l'écriture du voyage*, 2 vols, ed. Jean-Yves Le Disez and Jan Borm (Brest: Centre de Recherche Bretonne et Celtique, 2002), 2:89.

30 The semantic link here between 'ménager' [to handle, make room for] and 'ménage' [household] reinforces the renewed domestic framework of this journey.

31 Clifford, *Routes*, 36.

32 Mee, *Interpersonal Encounters*, 130.

33 This probability is underlined when she notices a significant change in her husband's attitude towards her after he joins her in Iran. Unlike in Paris, he forbids her from leaving the house alone, and she is obliged to wear a *tchador* when they go out for the evening (190, 193).

34 Alma Gottlieb and Philip Graham, *Parallel Worlds: An Anthropologist and a Writer Encounter Africa* (New York: Crown, 1992).

35 Richard Price and Sally Price's *Equatoria* (New York: Routledge, 1992) provides a further example of a jointly authored travelogue which chooses to merge the individual authors' accounts.

36 W.H. Auden and Louis MacNeice, *Letters from Iceland* (London: Faber and Faber, 1937); W.H. Auden and Christopher Isherwood, *Journey to a War* (London: Faber and Faber, 1939).

37 Auden and Isherwood, *Journey*, 202; see Tim Youngs, 'Auden's Travel Writings', in *The Cambridge Companion to W.H. Auden*, ed. Stan Smith (Cambridge: Cambridge University Press, 2004), 76, 78.

38 Simon Armitage and Glyn Maxwell, *Moon Country: Further Reports from Iceland* (London: Faber and Faber, 1996).

39 Debbie Lisle, *The Global Politics of Contemporary Travel Writing* (Cambridge: Cambridge University Press, 2006), 271.

40 Kathryn N. Jones, '*Le voyageur étonné*: François Maspero's Alternative Itineraries', *Studies in Travel Writing* 13.4 (2009): 338.

41 Tim Youngs, 'Making It Move: The Aboriginal in the Whitefella's Artifact', in *Travel Writing, Form and Empire: The Poetics and Politics of Mobility*, ed. Julia Kuehn and Paul Smethurst (New York: Routledge, 2009), 150.

42 Auden and MacNeice, *Letters*, 11.

43 Youngs, 'Auden's Travel Writings', 68.

44 Lisle, *Global Politics*, 271.

45 Lisle, *Global Politics*, 271.

46 Bill Ashcroft, 'Afterword: Travel and Power', in *Travel Writing, Form and Empire: The Poetics and Politics of Mobility*, ed. Julia Kuehn and Paul Smethurst (New York: Routledge, 2009), 238.

47 The phrase 'human landscapes' is taken from Turkish poet Nâzim Hikmet's poem 'Paysages humains', written in 1941 during his imprisonment in Bursa for disseminating communist propaganda. Nâzim Hikmet, *Paysages humains* (Paris: La Découverte, 2002).

48 See *Travel and Ethics: Theory and Practice*, ed. Corinne Fowler, Charles Forsdick and Ludmila Kostova (New York: Routledge, 2014).

49 'Reste ce clivage fondamental [...] parmi les habitants de notre monde, il y a ceux qui peuvent voyager et ceux qui ne le peuvent pas'. François Maspero, *Transit & Cie* (Paris: Quinzaine Littéraire/Louis Vuitton, 2004), 33.

6

FOOTSTEPS

Maria Lindgren Leavenworth

The travelogue as map: second journeys

In discussions about contemporary forms of journeying and travel writing, the argument that these are times of belatedness and oversaturation (of destinations as well as book-shelves) and that travellers can do nothing but repeat has almost become a truism.[1] Still, this is a logical starting point for a chapter that focuses on reiterative travel writing, and on overt connections between works. Travel as a mode and travel writing as a genre are intertextual in the sense that information is continuously sought and re-circulated and different forms of preparatory readings guide the journeying subject to the correct site, in some cases instructing her or him in how to respond to it. The textual filter constituted by previous representations can be perceived as limiting when travellers turn to chronicling their own experiences, but modern travelogues in the popular footsteps genre not only explicitly acknowledge sources of inspiration, but are structurally contingent on them. This chapter examines a sub-genre of footsteps travel: what I call second journeys.[2] The second journey form hinges on the presence of two travelogues: a first and a second text as material artefacts. The first journey supplies an itinerary which the second traveller repeats, and the first travelogue is continuously used in the second journey narrative for purposes of comparison and contrast. Stated motivations vary: the second journey may be embarked upon to seek answers to unresolved mysteries, 'rescue' travel writers risking obscurity, pay homage, or simply spring from a wish to stand in the exact spot of a predecessor. In any case, the first text becomes an explicit map to the past and serves 'both as pretext and pre-text'.[3]

The first section of this chapter outlines recent scholarship on second journeys with a focus on ambiguities, strategies, and tensions in the travelogues that the critics address. To contextualise the form, the second section explores affinities between second journeys and more broadly defined reiterative travels, highlighting notions of authenticity, nostalgia, and the impossibility of chronicling the novel. Second journeys profit from being seen in relation to textual experimentations in other postmodern genres, particularly tendencies to productively blur the boundaries between 'original' and 'copy', and David Cowart's notion of 'literary symbiosis' is especially fruitful when examining the combination of overt intertextuality and subversion at play in the form.[4] Bea Uusma's second journey *The Expedition* (2013) illustrates unusually frank renditions of the motivations behind and consequences of the obsession to repeat; the third section gives a close-reading of this text as an example of literary symbiosis.

Review of scholarship

Journeys retracing previous itineraries constitute an attractive option for many contemporary travel writers. Tim Youngs has recently called retracings 'the most common kind of travel writing at present', and notes in particular two aspects of the production: 'the gimmick and the tag that appeal to publishers' marketing departments and to readers', and the suggestion 'that foreignness exists in the past'.[5] Peter Hulme similarly comments on the usefulness of the connection with previous 'usually better-known travellers' as a 'marketing device' and on the possibility of 'mark[ing] the historical gap between the two moments'.[6] Stacy Burton, finally, notes 'the surprising number of writers who seek to recapitulate famous journeys [. . .] as though the imprimatur of a more pristine time will guarantee the quality of the experience'.[7] These brief comments highlight potentially problematic aspects of the second journey form: one crass, one more ideologically fraught, imbricating the repetition in uncritical idealisations of exoticism and Otherness. All three critics offer examples of successful negotiations of past and present, but they collapse second journeys into the broader category of footsteps travel.

In a 1997 article, Hulme performs a more sustained analysis of the second journey form, or what he calls, borrowing a term from Charles Nicholl, an 'ambulant gloss'.[8] At focus is an early, rare, example: Frederick Albion Ober's 1893 *In the Wake of Columbus*. Hulme's outline of the retracing sub-genre branches off in three directions. One form is concerned with solving the mysteries of disappeared travellers and thus strives to repeat a voyage without having access to the exact itinerary. Another form concerns the replication of a 'usually disputed' route, and a third revolves around a 'literary variant', exemplified by what I have called the biographical second journey.[9] What Hulme finds to be of particular interest are 'hybrid texts' that mix 'homage', 'self-examination', 'scholarly investigation', and a 'search for relics'. The 'secondary nature' of these hybrid texts is apparent, but the story the modern traveller tells bears an 'asymptotical relationship to the "original"'.[10] First and second journey become increasingly intertwined, the one seen as a reflection in the other and 'epiphanic moment[s]' occur when past and present seem to completely amalgamate.[11]

Hulme expresses a guarded optimism regarding the sub-genre's ability to problematise the relationship with the past, arguing that 'an increasing awareness of the limits of representation and of the responsibility of writers to gauge their own relationship to the past they analyse' may be the result of careful ambulant glossing.[12] Although it may seem as if the recourse to the past through an emulation may predictably uphold hierarchies prevalent in that past and enforce outdated notions of Otherness, a productive distance may thus instead be articulated between past and present, resulting in closer ties to 'more general postcolonial and postmodern developments within the travel genre in which the awareness of the self and the inability to represent encountered Others are [. . .] addressed'.[13] That is, it is not despite but because of the emulation that second journeys can contribute to an increased understanding of the problems of representation, provided that attention is paid to gaps and discrepancies. Christopher Keirstead builds his genre-analysis of footsteps travel writing on a similar argument. Rather than automatically resulting in reiterations of hegemonic structures, he claims, the form can produce 'a deeper awareness and critical understanding of the politics of travel [as] borders of self and other [. . .] become permeable, reinforcing how much the traveler is always written on by others'.[14] The distance between first and second journey may thus productively problematise the already-influenced perspective of the observer.

The reliance on a previous text as a map may present significant problems, however, and preclude travellers' critical assessment of their projects. In the last section of '"Innlandsisen, våre lengslers mål"' ['"The Inland Ice, Goal of Our Longings"'], Henning Howlid Wærp examines second journeys that have resulted from expedition tourism duplicating Fritjof Nansen's cross-ing of Greenland in the late 1880s. The trip itself is fairly easy to emulate, Wærp maintains, but crucial to Nansen's narrative are the sections outlining the period before the explorer even gets to Greenland and its depictions of encounters with indigenous people. Second travellers are commonly brought to the island by air, rendering a sense of anticipation moot, and very little is said about contemporary interpersonal exchanges, since these would foreground contempo-rary conditions. The Norwegian explorer's status as role model and a dogged determination to repeat circumscribe second travellers, since when you 'go, so to speak, by the book', looking to faithfully repeat experiences, you 'risk [. . .] closing yourself to the new'.[15] Preoccupied with the past journey, and with emulating the feats of a national icon, Wærp's sample second travellers do not subject themselves to experiences of their own; rather, they suppress or ignore events and impressions that do not 'agree' with the first journey narrative.[16]

A long list of prescriptive regulations, potentially closing the traveller off from her or his con-temporary context, need to be adhered to also in what A.V. Seaton terms the 'metempsychotic journey'. The metempsychotic journey is defined as 'an act of impersonation that requires a contemporary traveller to role-play the behaviour of a previous traveller'.[17] Overshadowing the restrictions imposed by the rules to be followed is how the template of a previous journey offers the possibility of avoiding feelings of both spatial and temporal strangeness.[18] 'Though physically displaced', Seaton states, metempsychotics 'are entering a psychological space colonised by the perceptions of their quarry [and] though they are entering a new time, it is a partly known one, that of the original traveller.'[19] Familiarity also extends beyond time and place as the role-playing project builds on the reiteration of a trip that has already acquired a high 'degree of public or social meaning'.[20] In other words, oversaturation is not problematic in this context; instead, the more popular and known a traveller, the more metempsychotic second journeys will be.

To travel writer Rolf Potts, on the other hand, repeated emulations render a new project superfluous. In the foreword to *Marco Polo Didn't Go There* (2008), he states that '[j]ourneys in the footsteps of others [have] become the travel-literature equivalent of cover music' and then notes with some dismay that several others have already followed his titular explorer.[21] This is not the only reason for a change of plans, however. Rather, Potts stresses that globalisation has rendered a replication of the thirteenth-century journey impossible and that, in line with both Seaton and Wærp, the 'thematic vessel' of a footsteps-emulation can preclude the traveller from engaging fully with the encountered present.[22]

Idealised images of the past and an overtly problematic relation with an ongoing imperialism are examined in Christy Collis's chapter 'Walking in Your Footsteps' (2010). With a focus on second journeys into the Australian desert, Collis investigates the perpetuation of 'exploration spatiality' and the non-Indigenous desire for 'a filial Australian connection to Empire origins' in the aftermath of the Land Acts in the 1970s and 80s.[23] A spatial anxiety was produced in non-Indigenous groups by the transfer of control and ownership of areas to Aboriginal cultures, Collis claims, resulting in attempts to re-reclaim the land by travelling through it, in the footsteps of white ancestors. The texts examined thus illuminate particularly aptly problematic aspects of not only physical but ideological reiteration. In close-readings of Graham McInerney and Alec Mathieson's *Across the Gibson* (1978) and Kelvin Hogarth's video *Conquering the Outback* (1990), Collis examines articulations and perpetuations of sameness. Firstly, she notes the 'repeatedly asserted [. . .] continuing accuracy of the original explorers' spatial production', and secondly, she draws attention to the tendency 'to reinforce the imperial fantasy of desert stasis' that neatly elides sometimes disastrous developments in the areas.[24] The imperial narrative is perceived as unbro-ken, with later generations seeing and experiencing the same emptiness that once seemingly justified the explorers' discursive structure of the space as open to conquest and to colonisation.

In her article 'Travel Across Time' (2005), Dafna Zur's larger project is to challenge the Eurocentrism of much travel criticism. Her focus on Korean travellers to China questions various forms of hierarchies. Pak Chiwŏn's late eighteenth-century *Yŏrha Ilgi* (*Diary of Yŏrha*) exemplifies how the encounter with Chinese culture, perceived by Pak as more evolved than the Korean, leads him to reflect on his own identity and on the socioeconomic aspects of his home environment. A distinctly different process of Othering emerges, along with alternative forms of self-representation. Zur examines three modern appropriations of Pak's travelogue, by Ko Misuk (2003), Ch'oen Inhun (1976), and Yi Kuyt'ae (1997), in order to tease out how themes and motifs resonate with Pak's followers, and how each new rendition invites alternative, contemporary explorations of power and identity. Zur structures her discussion around the literary and musical notion of 'theme-and-variation' (more positive than Potts' 'cover music'). 'What is it', she asks, 'about a familiar theme that impels a writer to remain rooted in a story and yet excavate it for new meaning? And how do [musical] variations impart new meaning to the theme?'[25] Central for Zur, as for the majority of critics discussed in this section, is that sustained analyses of journeys made with a previous travelogue as a map to follow must involve examinations of how the past as well as the present are interrogated, and of what gains and losses are involved in the process.

Affinities: nostalgia, authenticity, and oversaturation

Second journeys concretely invoke the past by their reliance on a previous text and in doing so forge affinities with other forms of reiteration. Religious and secular pilgrimages revisiting destinations prominent in the world's faiths hark back to past texts in the wide sense of the term; teachings and biographies of founding figures are as important as concrete writings. The Grand Tour guided the traveller, book-in-hand, to the appropriate destinations and to 'correct' emotions. Literary heritage trips trace past works of fiction as well as literal and figurative paths of an author's life. In all these cases, a route is more or less strictly followed and being present at a destination previously only encountered in texts is touted as bringing something extra to the experience. The 'kind of data' amassed through the physical reiteration is, in the words of second traveller Charles Nicholl, 'different from the evidence of the documents: this is evidence you have felt on the surface of your skin'.[26] The attainment of a sense of authenticity thus emerges as central in repetitive travels and travel writing, as a counter to textual exhaustion and sometimes complex figurations of nostalgia.

Different eras and travel trajectories produce different types of oversaturation: of travellers at a destination, of previous travel texts to contend with, or of ways of depicting various encounters. Forms of belatedness may result in an acute sense of nostalgia: a desire for a past time providing access to exclusivity and originality. Engaging with the notion that the past can be figured as a foreign country, Debbie Lisle examines how non-Western destinations and their inhabitants are figured as problematically occupying a place farther back in the Western construct of the historical queue.[27] Nostalgia for the past in which 'real' travel is thought possible consequently becomes imbricated in problematic gestures that either celebrate what may be the result of various forms of oppression or overlook features that may be positive effects of modernisation. Lisle's close-reading of Gavin Bell's 1994 second journey *In Search of Tusitala* is a case in point: it demonstrates how the author's 'utopian fantasy' of the Pacific as an unspoilt Paradise on Earth is undone by the touristified present, and how he therefore 'relocates the *real* South Pacific' in the past of first traveller Robert Louis Stevenson.[28] Lisle identifies two intertwined problems in Bell's narrative. Firstly, colonial relations structuring the first narrative go relatively unexamined; secondly, Bell 'does not question [. . .] the assumptions behind [the narrative's] nostalgia and elegiac fantasies'.[29] Uncritically reading the past as better thus entails overlooking modern developments that threateningly move the destination to a place in the historical queue, closer to the comparison point: the second traveller's own culture.

A common strategy in second journeys, when the traveller is unable to escape to less 'evolved' sites, is to juxtapose the disappointing experience with an example that brings into focus unaltered aspects of the encountered environment. In *Blood River*, Tim Butcher offers a complex illustration. Aiming to duplicate Henry Morton Stanley's nineteenth-century journey, Butcher cannot align his first sight of the Congo River with his forebear's 'lyrical description' of it.[30] What is more, there are no longer any signs of the bustling river traffic that post-dates Stanley's time, but that nevertheless is part of Butcher's expectations. However, a pirogue suddenly appearing on the water creates a shift in emotions and results in 'a feeling of connection with Stanley. It was no different in design from those he would have seen [. . .] when he first reached the Congo River at a spot not far from where I was standing'.[31] Over the course of three pages, Butcher thus notes disappointment stemming from modernity, from the collapse of elements of that modernity, and how an unaltered feature conjures up the past.

The appearance of the pirogue produces a moment of what Ning Wang (1999) has termed 'existential authenticity', denoting how events, sites, or experiences, regardless of how staged they may be, can produce a sense of emotional fulfilment. Instead of relying solely on objective authenticity measured by 'an absolute and objective criterion', or on authenticity as a social construct where meaning is always 'relative, negotiable', foregrounding the 'potential' of a subjective experience entails that questions about how or by whom the authentic is judged no longer apply.[32] Butcher's sighting of the pirogue carries a particular meaning for him, in the precise moment he sees it: he does not authenticate the object for anyone else. But the promise of more communal forms of existential authenticity is used by branches of the tourist industry, as Barbara Schaff demonstrates in a semiotic analysis of contemporary literary tourism. Certain places, she argues, 'promise the experience of a holistic and possibly sublime experience, in which the individual and the context of author and work amalgamate'.[33] These sites can often be staged and modernity masked, but the literary tourist's individual engagement may still result in instances of existential authenticity.

Places specifically signposted in the first journey may hold out to the second traveller the promise of a heightened existential authenticity, but sites that first travellers see little reason to foreground can also accrue meaning to the later traveller because of the latter's disposition and motivation. In *Terra Incognita* (1996), Sara Wheeler experiences an increasing closeness to several Antarctic explorers by travelling in their footsteps and by reading their texts in situ. The shelter at Cape Crozier described in Apsley Cherry-Garrard's *The Worst Journey in the World* (1922) takes on a specific importance and Wheeler is driven by a desire to lie a little while in what remains of it. The closeness she experiences to the first traveller is predicated not only on this physical reiteration but also on an admiration for his approach to hardship. All individuals may have their own 'personal Crozier' in the sense of individual difficulties, Wheeler argues, whether this is 'summiting without oxygen [or] telling someone you love them', but when undertaken 'with dignity and loving kindness', the difficulty can be surmounted.[34] Cherry-Garrard's life philosophy is thus experienced strongly when Wheeler is physically in the spot where he was convinced that he would perish and several aspects align to produce a specific, individual, and authentic experience.

Site-specificity is highly relevant to Romantic literary pilgrimages in which authors' graves were the original point of interest, growing into more extended itineraries delineating sites of importance to authors' biographies or their literary production.[35] Paul Westover argues that the concrete practice of visiting graves and monuments, in conjunction with reading a book, was perceived as creating a profound connection with an earlier time. Conjured up by the fictional or factual book itself, and intensified by proximity to sites of particular importance, 'ideal presence' reduces or eliminates the distance between one age and another, and the author's voice is perceived as speaking directly to the reading subject.[36] Experiences were 'described [. . .] in terms of time travel', the designated site as 'a portal to a vanished era', and 'metaphors [such as] conversation, resurrection and nearness' testify to the desire of establishing manifest connections to another age and to long since dead authors.[37]

The long Romantic period sees these travels to meet the dead consolidated into a cultural practice, and echoes of it are clearly heard in second journeys, particularly in formulations that underline direct communication. Caroline Alexander had planned for a trip to West Africa for a long time when she by chance came across Mary Kingsley's 1897 tome in her local library. The voice of the first traveller 'sparkled from the pages', Alexander writes, and the closing words of the preface to *Travels in West Africa* – 'if you go there you will find things as I have said' – encourages her to do just that.[38] Towards the end of her trip, Alexander notes that she has relied on the first traveller's 'companionship and guidance' and that being on her own produces a sense 'of arbitrariness as to where I should go next'.[39] In Richard Holmes' *Footsteps*, Robert Louis Stevenson's route in the Cevennes is recreated and at the very end of it, after a nap under a chestnut tree, Holmes wakes up with the palpable feeling that he is now 'alone: Stevenson had departed'.[40] The almost physical presence of the first travellers can only be sustained as long as it can be substantiated by what they wrote. When Alexander parts ways with Kingsley and when Stevenson's *Travels with a Donkey* ends, the conversations are brought to a halt.[41]

As Westover demonstrates, literary tourism in what he calls the 'necromantic' era is synthesised from other strands of travel history, predominantly devotional pilgrimages and the European Grand Tour. While not assuming absolute affinities between these practices and literary tours (and for our purposes, second journeys), religious pilgrimages 'offered a template for memorial practices [and] fostered the cultural habit of establishing hierarchies of significant space', whereas the 'on-the-spot engagement with the dead', characterising the Grand Tour, encouraged travellers to imagine canonised authors and their works in a previous state.[42] In these processes, as in figurations of the historical queue, the present encountered culture is screened out. In the Christian pilgrimage, for example, 'Palestine's [. . .] genuine existence lies in a transcendent identity as the Holy Land' and the comparative modernity of the region needs to be ignored so that the destination continues to belong to a specifically Western Christian tradition.[43] The Bible, in this case, becomes a representational filter which structures the journey and supplies a template for how sights are to be viewed, in effect enabling the negation of modernity.[44] The Grand Tour saw a combination of factual and fictional texts providing a similar structure. Previous travelogues worked as road-maps whereas novels and poems functioned as maps to the correct emotion,[45] but the journeying subject was at times asked to suppress the present and imagine the studied authors alive, and the depicted structures as whole rather than in ruins.

However, preparatory readings posed concrete problems when the traveller aimed at a publication of his or her own; the 'prison of prior texts' constituted a structure travel writers eagerly sought to escape.[46] These problems, needless to say, persist. As a backdrop to her analyses of contemporary novelists who subvert the format of the travelogue, Alison Russell notes that 'travel writers have been faced with a problem much like that of fiction writers [. . .] a sense of exhaustion of the planet and exhaustion of the forms we use to write about it'.[47] She draws attention to a number of strategies employed to rejuvenate experiences as well as writing about them, and among these are destinations, routes, and modes of travel that can strike the reader as unusually dangerous and difficult. Second travellers rarely employ formal experimentation, and are unlikely to see the previous text as a prison (although the travel tradition may still be perceived as such). But with some regularity, attention is drawn to potential dangers, many of which are generated by the destinations. David Grann, retracing Perry Fawcett's Amazonian trek in the 1920s, is highly aware of the dangers associated with the region and states that to follow the original expedition he has 'taken out an extra [life] insurance policy'.[48] *The Lost City of Z* also starts in the rainforest, and with the author staring at a map that he hopes will 'lead [him] out of the Amazon, rather than deeper into it'.[49] Butcher explicitly refers to his mode of journeying as 'ordeal travel' giving him a 'feeling of superiority' over individuals who have not been through the same strenuous exertions as he has.[50] He also travels through an area which in itself is associated with instability and the preface sees him wake up in Kalemie in the early morning proclaiming: 'Outside was the Congo and I was terrified'.[51] Opening lines and paragraphs in these cases work to situate the second traveller in a foreign environment, already way into the reiteration, and highlight a personal, emotional experience that attests to the distinctiveness of the projects.

Bea Uusma's symbiotic expedition

Bea Uusma's 2013 book *The Expedition: My Love Story* (*Expeditionen: Min kärlekshistoria*), which traces a failed 1897 Swedish expedition in the Arctic region, is given a close-reading in this section against the backdrop of David Cowart's notion of postmodern symbiotic texts. Cowart's focus is on works of fiction that enter into an 'epistemic dialogue' with precursors, emulating some aspects of the host text while simultaneously subverting many of its assumptions.[52] As every text is an expression of 'the climate of perception within a culture at a particular historical moment' (Michel Foucault's *epistemè*), symbiotic attachments between guest and host highlight differences between forms of knowledge production in different times, as well as between discourses structuring representations.[53] As a specific form of intertextuality, 'the franker sphere of symbiosis' on the one hand illustrates an awareness that all texts are circulated and re-used, and on the other that recycling of themes, tropes, and entire narratives can be conducive to development.[54] Both aspects are highly relevant to second journeys, which cannot exist without a first journey, and to a particular postmodern development of the sub-genre.

The first journey in Uusma's case is an expedition led by Samuel August Andrée, the aim of which was to fly a hydrogen balloon over the North Pole, drop a buoy, and continue to the mainland across the Atlantic. However, the vessel was only airborne for a little less than three days and Andrée and his colleagues Nils Strindberg and Knut Fraenkel never returned. In August 1930, a camp and the remains of the expedition members were found on Kvitøya (White Island) in the Svalbard archipelago. What caused their death remains a mystery – provisions, ammunition, and medicines were left behind and the climate is not described as unusually harsh in their journals. Subsequent conjectures are reminiscent of those surrounding other fated polar trips with commentators variously proposing lead poisoning from the tinned foods, speculating about botulism or scurvy, or suggesting ennui-induced violence among the group members.

More than a century after the ascent of the balloon, Uusma finds a book at a dull party: the collected and edited diaries of Andrée's expedition *Med Örnen mot polen* (*Andrée's Story*). She becomes deeply engrossed in it and leaves the party with the book in her possession. A few weeks afterwards, she visits the Andrée exhibit at Grenna Museum and has a strong reaction when she sees what remains of the expedition's equipment; objects that normally, she indicates, would have no emotional impact on her. The epistemic dialogue between one age and another is represented as initiated by these two moments: when the voices of the expedition members seem to speak to her from the past and when she is in the presence of the exhibited remains of a failed quest. A fifteen-year-long obsession is sparked off. 'I tried to talk sense into myself', Uusma writes, 'but I was like a vampire tasting human blood for the first time. It became *my* expedition'.[55]

The ostensible motivation is to solve the mystery and Uusma peruses all available texts and artefacts surrounding the expedition. Initially text-focused, she has a desire to 'get behind the words on the crumbling pages of their journals' with the intention of better understanding what happens to individuals, physically and psychologically, when isolated and exposed to the elements (14). To accomplish this, however, entails her being present in the same conditions as the first travellers and penetrating the landscape itself: 'to go into the ice, beneath the snow crust' (14). When Uusma is way into a medical career (an occupational choice she attributes to her obsession) she states: 'I have to get inside their cells. Inside the nuclei of their cells. Inside the double helixes of their DNA' (91). Forms of inquest thus move from figurative to literal levels, and no detail is too small (or too difficult) to be left unexamined.

On another level, however, this quest is a device framing a project of self-examination. Never conclusively answering the question 'why am I doing this', *The Expedition* instead foregrounds issues of misgivings and doubt. Cowart argues that the symbiotic text produces 'a statement about the modern temper as contrasted to the spirit of the age that produced' the host.[56] The first expedition members are enthusiastic about being the first to fly across the North Pole in the modern hydrogen balloon, and hopeful that they will accomplish something bringing fame to themselves as well as to the nation. Andrée asks in his journal: 'How soon, I wonder, will we have successors?'[57] This spirit of adventurousness and exploration of the unknown is juxtaposed with Uusma's anxieties about driving forces that are difficult to explain (to herself and others) and with the ever-present knowledge of the belatedness of the project. She opens her text by stating that she 'hate[s] being cold', closes it by noting that she is '[d]efinitely no adventurer', and repeatedly writes that she is too late (3, 250). The epistemic dialogue between the late nineteenth and the early twenty-first centuries consequently illuminates past discourses as well as aspects significant for our times and for the contemporary traveller; belatedness is so deeply ingrained in *The Expedition* that it becomes part of its aesthetic.

The difference between enthusiasm and doubt is one of many examples of 'thematic revision' in *The Expedition*, a salient feature of postmodern literary symbiosis.[58] Another prominent example comes in the form of science. The scientific pretext of past expeditions was at times used to mask aims for individual or national glory. Closely conforming to the practices of their time, the Andrée expedition took careful notes about the climate, the landscape, and the (decreasing) height of the balloon, and collected samples and specimen once stranded on the ice. On board a boat during one of her trips north, Uusma each day chooses colour swatches that correspond to nuances of the ice but the pseudo-scientific process is accompanied by Uusma's pronouncement that she 'hold[s] onto details, of the seemingly meaningless kind', and by the comment that the research she carries out is: 'Real, and yet, make-believe' (70).[59] Her sentences are a word-by-word repetition of how she has previously summarised the first travellers' activities, engaged in until the very end. Their research, 'real, and yet, make-believe', is used to create a sense of purpose, but Uusma's revision highlights the meaninglessness of conforming to the discourse.

Thematic, or perhaps rather perceptual, revision is also visible in how the North Pole is apprehended. It constitutes the ultimate goal for the Andrée expedition although its members never plan on actually setting foot on it. Influenced by nineteenth-century discourses as well as by the many failed attempts at reaching it, it is figured as surrounded with mystery. Although the remoteness of the Pole is more easily negotiable with modern means of transportation, the absence of landmass underneath and the fact that it is never constituted by the same ice from one year to the next create an unreal, insubstantial feeling. To situate her readers as well as herself in this strange environment, Uusma writes: 'On a globe, we would now be underneath the round plastic disc at the top, the one you have to unscrew to change the light bulb' and continues by noting that before reaching the Pole proper, she will first 'have to pass the giant letters reading MADE IN TAIWAN and the enormous screw anchoring the power cord' (84). The imagery of the regular desk globe creates familiarity but its Earth-size produces an estrangement effect. These depictions encapsulate how Uusma, despite being physically present at the Pole, needs to translate the site without losing its peculiarities.

White Island constitutes the end of the Andrée expedition. To Uusma the place has been loaded with meaning since the start of her obsession. When she is finally close to the island, the expected sense of exhilaration is undercut by the realisation that '[i]n two hours and three minutes' time, the life [she has] lived for the last fifteen years, *before White Island*, will end and another life, *after White Island*, will begin' (236, original emphases). The temporal transition entails that Uusma will no longer be able to carry a sense of anticipation and that the experience at the already-established end point will change her identity predicated on the quest in a definite way. Finally on land, she writes: 'I have carried this place inside me for so long, and now that I am here it is as though I am wandering around inside myself' (238). Each reading of a text represents an individual interpretation, in Cowart's words, each 'symbiont defines itself in terms of how it reorders or revises' the host text.[60] In Uusma's case, a notable sense of isolation is the result of the revision process. Her obsession and solitary quest have meant a very particular assemblage of details and readings and it is thus on a level approaching the literal that she is, indeed, journeying inside herself.

Despite reaching White Island, Uusma does not come to a full understanding of the men she has followed, and although she presents an answer to the mystery as plausible as any other, her project does not end as conclusively as she would have wished. 'The more I learn about the Andrée expedition, the more unsure I feel about what really happened', she writes. 'I thought I could follow them, but I never get close enough' (250). Starting in questions, the second journey project has led to more; it has relativised what Uusma thought she knew and her experiences and conclusions compete with others. However, the dead ends she has encountered and the sense of never quite catching up are used to highlight a similarity between herself and the first travellers. Andrée, Frænkel, and Strindberg made excruciatingly slow progress because the ice they traversed moved with the current in the opposite direction. Uusma is exhausted from following clues that lead nowhere and frustrated because of the inherent impossibility of the project: to connect physically and psychologically with individuals who lived more than a hundred years ago. This frustration and the figurative similarity of movement in opposition to the current are finally used as binding agents: 'We belong together', Uusma finishes the narrative part of her text; 'The expedition and I' (250).

Two final comments from Uusma's text anchor them within the framework of the symbiotic text. Firstly and as earlier noted, she describes her obsession as a kind of vampirism. Secondly, she remarks upon the peculiarity of the colour of ice. On the one hand, the ice contains 'all the colours you can't see'; on the other, as the effect is achieved in the brain, '[c]olour itself isn't created until someone is there to see it' (71). The vampire metaphor, initially aimed at self-characterisation, also suggests a re-birth and a continued existence. Uusma draws sustenance from the Andrée expedition, but interest in it may be (re)awakened in readers – Andrée, Frænkel, and Strindberg are figuratively brought back to life. Similarly, as long as no one sees the ice, or the first text, it does not exist. By seeing the first journey, Uusma ensures that it continues to exist, not only for her but for readers of *The Expedition*. In Cowart's biological nomenclature, the most productive category of symbiosis is 'mutualism, in which both host and guest seem to gain [. . .] in meaning or significance'.[61] I read Uusma's text, along with many other examples of second journeys, as profoundly mutualistic. While it seems a given that second journeys gain inspiration, structure, or impetus, first journeys also profit, as revisions and reworkings productively problematise their processes of meaning-making and (re)actualise their significance.

Conclusion: where to now?

With increasingly detailed divisions into genres and sub-genres of travel literature come possibilities of asking precisely what each form does, what it does not do, and what questions each raises or answers. Although, as established, there are several affinities between second journeys and more broadly defined reiterative travel, a distinction should be upheld to account for the particularities of the sub-genre, predominantly the existence of two material artefacts and the overt, symbiotic attachments between them. Systematic analyses of the epistemic dialogue between host and guest move issues beyond simply acknowledging similarities and contrasts and instead highlight the discourses that structure knowledge differently in one age and another. Continued sustained analyses of the sub-genre at large, and of careful considerations of isolated works in the broader contexts of ethics, postmodernism, and globalisation, have the potential to highlight what questions are raised and answered by second journeys, and what aspects they fail to address: both are equally important for the continued mapping of the complex genre of travel literature. A limitation in the present discussion is the focus on anglophone writers following travellers from their own linguistic and sometimes cultural background (and a Swede following other Swedes). To identify and examine second journeys following textual maps produced in other cultures and languages would diversify considerations of epistemic dialogues further.

With few exceptions, the second travellers referred to in this chapter journey in the late twentieth and early twenty-first centuries and engage with nineteenth-century travelogues. In fact, texts from the 1800s are overrepresented in second journey narratives generally. In part, this can be explained by the cultural significance the travelogues have accrued through being critically examined and widely read; in part, the era sees the flourishing of forms of adventurous travel and exploration that are particularly attractive to emulate. It is also a past far enough from the second traveller to produce differences, close enough to enable examinations of similarities. The 1893 ambulant gloss on Columbus's fifteenth-century journey, discussed by Hulme above, rather yields insights into discourses separated by four centuries, and in addition separated from our own. Time specificity, regarding both first and second journeys, thus appears fruitful to investigate further when examining instances of epistemic dialogue.

I have argued that two material artefacts are required for a second journey to *be* a second journey, but what is to be made of the extensive virtual options existing for travellers and travel writers today? In the concluding remarks in *Necromanticism* Westover writes that virtual affordances 'raise questions about the relationship between the real and the simulated', and user participation 'reveals tensions (but also productive collaborations) between amateur and professional practices'.[62] Youngs similarly draws attention to how online environments allow travel without, necessarily, spatial movement, and provide access to those who are privileged with computer skills and equipment.[63] The interactive website *Literary Traveler* offers a venue for the publication of short texts that read a contemporary place through the filter of a previous text. Although the filter is most often fictional or biographical, there are also examples of second journeys in the strict definition.[64] Articles are commonly illustrated with appropriate photographs; by clicking on hyperlinks the reader is transported to external pages that supply additional information, and she or he can also leave comments. As such, the website attests to the continued interest in various forms of footsteps travel, and academic attention could usefully be paid to the interplay between texts, objects, and images, to blurred lines between the real and the simulated, to dialogic contributions to meaning-making, and to how reiterations are negotiated in ways different from (or similar to) traditionally printed texts.

Notes

1 Different times and destinations contend with different forms of oversaturation, discussed in the second section of this chapter. James Hamilton-Paterson's tellingly entitled 'The End of Travel' provides a personal look at how mass tourism has altered conditions. *Granta* 94 (2006): 221–34.

2 Maria Lindgren Leavenworth, *The Second Journey: Travelling in Literary Footsteps* (Umeå: Studier i språk och litteratur från Umeå universitet, 2010). References are to the second, revised edition of my 2000 dissertation.

3 Jacinta Matos, 'Old Journeys Revisited: Aspects of Postwar English Travel Writing', in *Temperamental Journeys: Essays on the Modern Literature of Travel*, ed. Michael Kowalewski (Athens, GA: University of Georgia Press, 1992), 215.

4 David Cowart, *Literary Symbiosis: The Reconfigured Text in Twentieth-Century Writing* (Athens, GA: University of Georgia Press, 1993).

5 Tim Youngs, *The Cambridge Introduction to Travel Writing* (Cambridge: Cambridge University Press, 2013), 184, 185.

6 Peter Hulme, 'Travelling to Write (1940–2000)', in *The Cambridge Companion to Travel Writing*, eds. Peter Hulme and Tim Youngs (Cambridge: Cambridge University Press, 2002), 98.

7 Stacy Burton, *Travel Narrative and the Ends of Modernity* (Cambridge: Cambridge University Press, 2014), 86.

8 The term is taken from Charles Nicholl's second journey tracing Sir Walter Ralegh's search for El Dorado. Cognisant of '[t]he scale of difficulty, of expectation, of the unknown' which separates his own journey from his sixteenth-century predecessor, Nicholl prefers to see his journey as 'an ambulant gloss on that earlier journey, made in the belief that history should be learned on foot [...] as much as by studying books and documents'. Charles Nicholl, *The Creature in the Map* (1995; repr. New York: William Morrow and Company, Inc., 1996), 6. Comparisons and contrasts in this way become an evolving commentary.

9 Peter Hulme, 'In the Wake of Columbus: Frederick Ober's Ambulant Gloss', *Literature and History* 6.2 (1997): 18. See Lindgren Leavenworth, *The Second Journey*, 153–85.

10 Hulme, 'In the Wake of Columbus', 18, 19.

11 Hulme, 'In the Wake of Columbus', 24.

12 Hulme, 'In the Wake of Columbus', 20.

13 Lindgren Leavenworth, *The Second Journey*, 188. The second travellers who are the focus of *The Second Journey*, Caroline Alexander, Nicholas Rankin, Roger Mear, and Robert Swan, exemplify to varying extents these contemporary tendencies, especially in problematisations of traditional notions of adventure and heroism and in self-reflexive comments on the representational nature of their projects.

14 Christopher Kierstead, 'Convoluted Paths: Mapping Genre in Contemporary Footsteps Travel Writing', *Genre* 46.3 (2013): 286, 287. Kierstead sees footsteps travel as a narrow enough definition, but he is explicitly interested in '[j]ourneys undertaken with the deliberate aim of retracing the routes of earlier travelers' (285).

15 Henning Howlid Wærp, '"Innlandsisen, våre lengslers mål" Om Fridtjof Nansen: *På ski over Grønland* (1890) – og noen andre bøker i hans spor', *Norsk Litteraturvitenskapelig Tidsskrift* 10.2 (2007): 112, my translation.

16 Tellingly, the most successful second journey in Wærp's estimation is *Over den store bre. Alene i Nansens spor* [*Across the Great Glacier: Alone in Nansen's Tracks*] (Oslo: Cappelens, 1988) in which Carl Emil Petersen does not strive for complete fidelity to Nansen and therefore opens himself up to experiences of his own.

17 A.V. Seaton, 'In the Footsteps of Acerbi: Metempsychosis and the Repeated Journey', in *Tutkimusmatkalla pohjoiseen: Giuseppe Acerbin Nordkapin matkan 200-vuotissymposiumi*, eds. Eero Jarva, Markku Mäkivuoti, and Timo Sironen (Oulu: Oulun yliopisto, 2001), 122.

18 Seaton's primary sources can all be categorised as second journeys as a previous travelogue constitutes the template to be used. His examples are all male and he claims in an aside that '(so far there have been

no metempsychotic texts by or about women)'. In the same article, there is a footnote reference to Tim Severin's series of books repeating famous first journeys (some actual, some fictional), and Severin is used as an example of 'serial metampsychosis' [sic]: A.V. Seaton, 'Tourism as Metempsychosis and Metensomatosis: The Personae of Eternal Recurrence', in *The Tourist as a Metaphor of the Social World*, ed. Graham M.S. Dann (Cambridge, MA: CABI Publishing, 2002), 135, 164, note 2. Caroline Alexander's *One Dry Season* (1989), *The Endurance* (1993), and *The Way to Xanadu* (1998), to mention but a few of her second journeys, seem to make her not only a good example of a female metempsychotic, but a serial one to boot.

19 Seaton, 'Tourism as Metempsychosis', 138.

20 Seaton, 'In the Footsteps of Acerbi', 124.

21 Rolf Potts, *Marco Polo Didn't Go There: Stories and Revelations from One Decade as a Post-Modern Travel Writer* (Palo Alto, CA: Travelers' Tales, 2008), xiii.

22 Potts, *Marco Polo Didn't Go There*, xvi.

23 Christy Collis, 'Walking in Your Footsteps. "Footsteps of the Explorers" Expeditions and the Contest for Australian Desert Space', in *New Spaces of Exploration: Geographies of Discovery in the Twentieth Century*, eds. Simon Naylor and James R. Ryan (London: I. B. Tauris, 2010), 224, 228.

24 Collis, 'Walking in Your Footsteps', 235, 236.

25 Daphna Zur, 'Travel Across Time: Modern "Rewrites" of Pak Chiwŏn's *Yŏrha Ilgi*', *Acta Koreana* 8.2 (2005): 50.

26 Nicholl, *The Creature in the Map*, 6.

27 Debbie Lisle, *The Global Politics of Contemporary Travel Writing* (Cambridge: Cambridge University Press, 2006), 203–14.

28 Lisle, *The Global Politics of Contemporary Travel Writing*, 228, original emphasis.

29 Lisle, *The Global Politics of Contemporary Travel Writing*, 229.

30 Tim Butcher, *Blood River: A Journey to Africa's Broken Heart* (London: Chatto & Windus, 2007), 179.

31 Butcher, *Blood River*, 181.

32 Ning Wang, 'Rethinking Authenticity in Tourism Experience', *Annals of Tourism Research* 26.2 (1999): 351, 352.

33 Barbara Schaff, '"In the Footsteps of . . .": The Semiotics of Literary Tourism', *KulturPoetik* (2011): 171.

34 Sara Wheeler, *Terra Incognita* (New York: Random House, 1996), 152, 151.

35 Nicola J. Watson, *The Literary Tourist: Readers and Places in Romantic and Victorian Britain* (Houndmills: Palgrave Macmillan, 2006), 5.

36 Paul Westover, *Necromanticism: Traveling to Meet the Dead, 1750–1860* (Houndmills: Palgrave Macmillan, 2012), 17–30.

37 Westover, *Necromanticism*, 19, 17.

38 Mary Kingsley, *Travels in West Africa: Congo Français, Corisco and Cameroons* (1897; repr. Boston, MA: Beacon Press, 1988), xxi. Caroline Alexander, *One Dry Season: In the Footsteps of Mary Kingsley* (London: Bloomsbury, 1989), 6.

39 Alexander, *One Dry Season*, 192.

40 Richard Holmes, *Footsteps: Adventures of a Romantic Biographer* (1985; repr. New York: Vintage Departures, 1996), 63.

41 In *Saddled with Darwin*, Toby Green resurrects the titular scientist in an all but manifest way when plagued by increasing loneliness on the plains of South America. He has long conversations with the 'extremely affable' Darwin riding next to him, and who seems as perplexed as anyone about Green's second journey: '"Still following me, eh? I thought you'd have given up long ago."' (London: Weidenfeld & Nicolson, 1999), 306, 305.

42 Westover, *Necromanticism*, 34, 39.

43 Burton, *Travel Narrative and the Ends of Modernity*, 168.

44 For a discussion about the Bible as textual filter, see Maria Lindgren Leavenworth, 'Destinations and Descriptions: Acts of Seeing in S. H. Kent's *Gath to the Cedars* and *Within the Arctic Circle*', *Studies in Travel Writing* 15.3 (2011).

45 Rosemary Sweet, *Grand Tour: The British in Italy, c. 1690–1820* (Cambridge: Cambridge University Press, 2012), 9–15.

46 James Buzard, *The Beaten Track: European Tourism, Literature, and the Ways to 'Culture', 1800–1918* (Oxford: Clarendon Press, 1993), 170.

47 Alison Russell, *Crossing Boundaries: Postmodern Travel Literature* (New York: Palgrave, 2000), 9.

48 David Grann, *The Lost City of Z* (London: Simon & Schuster, 2009), 3.

49 Grann, *The Lost City of Z*, 3.

50 Butcher, *Blood River*, 216, 268.

51 Butcher, *Blood River*, xi.

52 Cowart, *Literary Symbiosis*, 1. Among the primary sources Cowart analyses are Jean Rhys's *Wide Sargasso Sea* (in conversation with Charlotte Brontë's *Jane Eyre*) and David Henry Hwang's play *M. Butterfly* (in dialogue with Puccini's opera).

53 Cowart, *Literary Symbiosis*, 150.

54 Cowart, *Literary Symbiosis*, 16.

55 Bea Uusma, *The Expedition: A Love Story*, trans. Agnes Broomé (London: Head of Zeus Ltd., 2014), 6, original emphasis.

56 Cowart, *Literary Symbiosis*, 16–17.

57 Samuel August Andrée, *Andrée's Story: The Complete Record of His Polar Flight, 1897*, trans. Edward Adams-Ray (New York: The Viking Press, 1930), 308.

58 Cowart, *Literary Symbiosis*, 1. In Cowart's study, 'formal [...] revision' (1) is of equal interest, but the present discussion will be confined to noting that Uusma's text is formally dissimilar to the first journey through its unchronological structure, its constant mix of text forms (written and visual), and with different type faces and font sizes used to make distinctions between different materials.

59 In the original Swedish edition of *The Expedition*, a drawing of these swatches is represented along with time, date, latitude, and longitude which even further underscores how the protocols of science are followed. Bea Uusma, *Expeditionen: Min kärlekshistoria* (Stockholm: Norstedts, 2013), 87.

60 Cowart, *Literary Symbiosis*, 150.

61 Cowart, *Literary Symbiosis*, 5.

62 Westover, *Necromanticism*, 172–3.

63 Youngs, *The Cambridge Introduction to Travel Writing*, 178–82.

64 See for examples Katherine Gypson's 'Freya Stark's Afghanistan' (posted 25 February 2012), accessed 10 June 2019, www.literarytraveler.com/articles/freya-starks-afghanistan/; and Klas Lundström's 'Man's Last Chance: Impressions of Central America' (posted 3 September 2012 and engaging with Bruce Chatwin's *In Patagonia*, the travels of Darwin, and Paul Theroux's novel *The Mosquito Coast*) accessed 10 June 2019, www.literarytraveler.com/articles/mans-last-chance-impressions-of-central-america/.

7

VERTICAL TRAVEL

Charles Forsdick

When the surface of the world is overloaded with competing narratives, with shrill boasts hung from every blue fence and plastered over buses and police cars and refuse trucks, there is an understandable impulse to go underground.[1]

Strive to picture yourself, with the greatest possible precision, beneath the network of streets, the tangle of sewers, the lines of the Métro, the invisible underground proliferation of conduits (electricity, gas, telephone lines, water mains, express letter tubes), without which no life would be possible on the surface.

Underneath, just underneath, resuscitate the eocene: the limestone, the marl and the soft chalk, the gypsum, the lacustrian Saint-Ouen limestone, the Beauchamp sands, the rough limestone, the Soissons sands and lignites, the plastic clay, the hard chalk.[2]

Going underground

The variables that have traditionally been deployed in the analysis of travel writing are primarily socio-cultural ones, ranging from gender and sexual orientation to class and ethnicity. These categories relate to the identity and status of the traveller, but often have clear implications also for the shape and general conditions of the journey itself that the traveller undertakes. These aspects remain, in the majority of travelogues, the *sine qua non* of a distinctive narrative. As Susan George's concept of 'fast castes' makes clear, the speed and ease of travel are often linked to social class, and the gendering of the journey can also have profound implications for access to – and experience in – the field, as well as for the ways in which the itinerary is subsequently transformed into a narrative.[3] The various forms of policing of the field of travel mean that certain routes and spaces are not available to certain travellers, with the result that at times – as a specific historical case such as the underground railroad in the nineteenth-century United States makes eloquently clear – journeys can veer off their conventionally horizontal (even horizontalist) axes, roughly in parallel to the crust of the earth, and follow alternative, often hidden and even clandestine itineraries.[4]

What Iain Sinclair describes, in the quotation chosen as one of the epigraphs to this chapter, as 'going underground' relates more generally to a range of types of contemporary travel that may be seen along these lines as variously 'vertical'. Such vertical tangents, veering away from a horizontal norm, can adopt literal or figurative forms, reflecting unorthodox practices of physical descent (and, at times, of ascent), or using metaphors of verticality to betoken forms of attention to place that rely on microspection to reveal the fractal diversity of what is otherwise seen as everyday. Some of these contemporary journeys – such as those explored by Sinclair in the essay from which the quotation is drawn – involve actual excavation and descent; others relate more figuratively to the modes of deceleration and recovery of the quotidian that characterise other works by Sinclair himself, including *London Orbital* (2002), his account of a journey on foot around London's M25.[5]

The specific term of 'vertical travel', which might be deployed to describe such modes of journeying, is a practice named and explored by Michael Cronin in *Across the Lines: Travel, Language and Translation* (2000), where he claims:

> Horizontal travel is the more conventional understanding of travel as a linear progression from place to place. Vertical travel is temporary dwelling in a location for a period of time where the traveller begins to travel down into the particulars of place either in space (botany, studies of micro-climate, exhaustive exploration of local landscape) or in time (local history, archaeology, folklore).[6]

Broadly understood in these terms, 'vertical travel' constitutes a general challenge to the topographical and environmental defaults with which many conventional forms of journeying are associated. Verticality contrasts and even clashes, therefore, with the horizontal axes often traced by travel narratives, although it is to be recognised (in contrast with acceleration) as key to now mainstream forms of mobility such as air travel, which may be seen to combine both vertical and horizontal vectors. At the same time, its emphasis on microspection, on deceleration (associated with Cronin's concept of 'temporary dwelling' or 'denizenship') and (at times) on forms of physical confinement may be associated with a relationship to the lived environment that reasserts the fact that, in Tim Ingold's analysis, 'life is lived at such close proximity to the earth's surface that a global perspective is unobtainable'. This is, in other words, a perspective that opposes surface with depth, or to borrow further from Tim Ingold, that challenges the horizontalism of a world '*on* which we dwell' with the vertical perspective of one '*within* which we dwell'.[7]

When the vertical movement inherent in such forms of travel is literal, implying a movement downwards and underground, clandestine or otherwise, it permits a discovery of elements of everyday space otherwise deliberately concealed or ignored by emphases on horizontal, seemingly superficial ways of encountering space and its contents. As such, it is exemplified by the text from Perec with which this chapter opens, where the author imagines a shift of axis, away from the surface of the street, into those urban underworlds of tunnels, sewers and other utilities that are attracting increasing attention (not least in the context of Urban Exploration or Urb-Ex),[8] and then beyond into the geographical substrata that have attracted other travellers' attention (as works such as Ian Vince's *The Lie of the Land* or Ted Nield's *Underlands* make clear).[9] Or, as has been noted above, 'vertical travel' can be more figurative, directing attention and a degree of curiosity more often associated with non-domestic cultures towards the detail of everyday contexts, and encapsulating the fresh curiosity regarding often unanticipated detail that emerges from slowing down, from adopting an alternative mindset, from looking, listening and sensing differently. The French sociologist Jean-Didier Urbain claims: 'Banality is not in the world; it is in the gaze', but much vertical travel – with its interest in soundscapes and smellscapes – seeks also to disrupt the connection between horizontalism and ocularcentrism, and to suggest that the microspection it entails is a process of multisensory rediscovery of the everyday.[10]

Such distinctions between horizontalism and verticality, between ocularcentrism and multisensory approaches to elsewhere, underpin the specific critique developed by Urbain of late twentieth-century travel writing, and especially of the work of the *Pour une littérature voyageuse* group. He targets in particular Michel Le Bris, the author and founder in 1990 of the *Étonnants voyageurs* literary festival in Saint-Malo. Le Bris identified, in a 1992 volume of essays entitled *Le Grand Dehors* [The Great Outdoors], a practice of travel and engagement with space characterised by a range of parameters that vertical travelling seeks to subvert: horizontal expansiveness; a yearning for wilderness free of traces of humanity; solipsism redolent of much Romantic travel; and a traveller's self-positioning that may be understood in terms of what Mary Louise Pratt, in *Imperial Eyes* (published in the same year as Le Bris's volume), called the 'monarch-of-all-I-survey trope'.[11] Engaging with these neo-Romanticist sentiments and practices, Urbain juxtaposes – in his *Ethnologue, mais pas trop* [Ethnologist, but not excessively] (2003) – the 'tyrannie agoraphile' [agoraphiliac tyranny] of much contemporary travel writing with an 'ironie claustrophile' [claustrophiliac irony], by which he understood the identification of different modes of travel, of ways of relating to space, and of textualising a relationship to space that no longer fetishises the 'exotic' (understood in a reductively geographical sense), but explores instead the 'endotic' or everyday.[12]

In generating this binary relationship, and in deploying these terms, Urbain reveals his debt to Georges Perec, and in particular to the author's reflections on this subject in the essay 'Approches de quoi?' [Approaches to what?]: 'What's needed perhaps is to found our own anthropology, one that will speak about us, will look in ourselves for what for so long we've been pillaging from others. Not the exotic any more, but the endotic.'[13] As a retort to those he critiqued, Urbain draws on Perec's concept of the 'endotic' to identify a number of contemporary 'voyageurs de l'immédiat' [proximate travellers], travellers drawn – to borrow again from Perec – to the 'choses communes' [shared objects] of the infra-ordinary, who adopt this mode of 'ironie claustrophile' [claustrophiliac irony] in order to re-engage with the everyday. As examples, he cites accounts of decelerated journeys through French locations that are customarily dismissed, following Marc Augé's designation, as *non-places*, foregrounding forms of domestic travel that atomise and defamiliarise everyday spaces, and encourage attention to their unexpectedly fractal details. Urbain cites Julio Cortazar and Carole Dunlop, who in *Les Autonautes de la cosmoroute* [Autonauts of the Cosmoroute] (1983) treat the *Autoroute du Soleil* (between Paris and Marseilles) not as a means of accessing elsewhere, but as a site of travel in its own right; and also François Maspero and Anaïk Frantz, who in *Les Passagers du Roissy-Express* [Roissy Express] (1990) travel the RER-B line in a southerly direction, away from Roissy Charles-de-Gaulle airport, and thus become unlikely explorers of the *banlieue*.[14] Although cognate to Perecquian practices, these examples owe as much to other forms of engagement: not only to the idea of interstitial travel, in which any distinction between point of departure and point of arrival becomes hazy, and where space is encountered through a practice of microspection; but also to the disruption of the traditional dynamics of ethnography. The second of these is indebted also to the reverse exoticism of Montesquieu and his *Lettres persanes* [Persian Letters], an approach evident more recently in the essays of Marc Augé focused on locations such as the Paris Métro, whereby the domesticity of French culture and society is exoticised via a series of actively foreignising strategies.[15]

To explain the mechanics of these journeys, Urbain deploys the metaphor of travel down into the catacombs, using the subterranean, even katabatic journeying this involves to re-inscribe verticality and other forms of burrowing down into the everyday.[16] As such, from a French and Francophone perspective, he contributes – without explicitly deploying the term – to recent discussions of 'vertical travel' alluded to above. Cronin was not the first to evoke the concept, and it appears slightly earlier in Kris Lackey's study of the American highway narrative, where he contrasts '"horizontal" books' (in which the emphasis is on the progression of the journey and not on attention to the field crossed) with '"vertical" travel' (evident in texts such as Dos Passos's *State of the Nation*, which 'downplay the travel itself and dwell on the knotty particulars of some local conflict').[17] For Lackey, this distinction relates to environmental ethics, and in particular to tensions between the rapid turnover of impressions often evident in the narratives of motorised travel (particular examples of which might be Michel Butor's *Mobile* [1960] or Jean Baudrillard's *Amérique* [1986]). He identifies a closer attention to place more common in travelogues based on slower modes of transport.[18] As such, without adopting this specific vocabulary, Lackey links vertical journeys to the dialectics of 'dwelling' and 'travelling' as explored by James Clifford in *Routes* (1997), suggesting the ways in which an apparent state of (relative) motionlessness on a horizontal axis might be viewed very differently should an emphasis on horizontality be replaced by attention to verticality.[19]

Verticality and the geometries of place

As the term suggests, central to 'vertical travel' – whether understood metaphorically or literally – is an interest in the geometry of the journey. Discussions of the structure of Perec's *Espèces d'espaces* [Species of Spaces] (1974) often focus on the concentric circles through which the text unfolds, passing from the bed, bedroom and apartment, via the street, *quartier* and town, to the country (France), the continent (Europe) and then the World.[20] In developing practices central to the discussion in this chapter, Perec uses this structure to privilege the close focus of microspection, and to survey – with a marked sense of discontinuity – various degrees of spatial granularity as he toys with the variable distance between observing subject and observed space. The aim of the text, as Michael Sheringham explores in his *Everyday Life* (2006), is to 'play cat and mouse with organised forms and procedures of knowledge'.[21] What is particularly striking about *Species of Spaces* (and about the numerous experiments it has engendered) is the extent to which these may be perceived – in retrospect – as part of the elaboration of a post-war, neo-humanist geography, situated at a point where semiotics, anthropology and literary creation converge. This forms part of an effort shared with his contemporaries as diverse as Jean-Luc Godard and Michel de Certeau not only to challenge the ways in which people are increasingly alienated from the spaces in which they live, but also to reveal how immanent in those spaces is potential material for a searching critique of everyday life as well as the resources for new forms of dwelling together.[22]

Perec's principal call was for new ways of viewing and engaging with urban space, rooted not least in new approaches to spatial literacy – a point underlined by the fact that *Espèces d'espaces* opens in fact not with a focus on the bed (for Perec, 'the individual space *par excellence*, the elementary space of the body'), but – self-referentially – with attention to the literary page. Mindful of the fact that our passage through everyday life leaves endless written traces – evident not least in the forms of listing central to much of Perec's work ('almost everything', he notes pre-digitally, 'passes through a sheet of paper') – Perec privileges the act of writing. He presents it as a means, via practices such as cartography and toponymy, of bringing spaces into being; but he also sees his own writing as a geometrically informed spatial practice in its own right: 'I write. I inhabit my sheet of paper, I invest it, I travel across it. I incite *blanks, spaces* (jumps in the meaning, discontinuities, transitions, changes of key)'.[23] Writing is seen even as a colonisation of paper: – 'I write: I trace words on a page [. . .] a fairly strictly horizontal line is set down on the blank sheet of paper, blackens the virgin space, gives it a direction, vectorises it: from left to right, from top to bottom', and this is a process that Perec accordingly describes in terms of geometry, evoking not only vectorisation, this movement performed (in Western scripts at least) habitually from left to right, but also, in this section in the original text, writing calligrammatically to highlight the tensions between the verticality and the horizontality of the page.[24]

The suggestion that writing is a form of journey across the space of the page ('I travel across it') encourages focus on the ways in which Perec's interest in the geometric dimensions of writing converges with very similar issues in travel itself – and more specifically in travel literature. As I suggested at the outset of this chapter, there is often a surprising absence, from the variables by which travel is analysed, of questions of geometry: most notably axes (verticality *versus* horizontality), and vectors (the specific direction of the journey, and issues of velocity associated with it). With some notable exceptions, such as the sub-genre of accounts of journeys based around mountaineering, it might be argued that travel writing has a tendency towards an 'embedded horizontalism' that may be seen to downplay verticality, and does not fully entertain the multi-levelled nature of travellers' engagement with space.[25] These are issues present in an author such as Victor Segalen, whose major 1914 archaeological journey across China was dubbed 'la Grande Diagonale' [Great Diagonal]. Segalen's *Équipée* [Escapade], which draws in part on the same journey, highlights additionally questions of ascension and descent, and his *René Leys* also reveals a geometric interest in the urban texture of early twentieth-century Beijing. Much travel writing tends, however, to be concerned more with the exclusively horizontal journeying that any vertical travel seeks to disrupt.

What is notable, however, is the specific *downwards* vector with which much 'vertical' travel is associated, as Cronin's early emphasis on movement 'down into the particulars of place' makes clear. Attention to the intersection of axis and direction is accordingly paramount, for although the direction of horizontal travel – according to the cardinal points – can have major implications for the ways in which the field of travel is experienced, these are usually less significant than the upward and downward movements encompassed by vertical travel. In an article helpfully entitled 'Ups and Downs of Vertical Travel', Daisann McLane uses the experience of dining with an acrophobic colleague in a high-rise shopping mall in Kowloon to reflect on the increasing presence of ascent in contemporary travel. 'Great travellers', McLane notes, 'follow the path in whatever direction it may lead. Most of the time that means straight ahead in a horizontal line, across deserts and oceans into the setting sun. But often our travels go vertical, too.'[26] Tall buildings have created this new verticalism in urban space, a tendency whose aesthetic implications have been explored in the photography of Horst Hamann, which eschews the default horizontalist geometry of a landscape format to present the city along axes perpendicular to the street.[27]

One of the implications of such cityscapes is the emergence of the elevator as a means of transport. A vehicle for travel in an upwards direction, replacing the stairwell, the lift was linked to the 'rearrangement of vertical space in the building's interior', and was responsible externally, by enabling the seemingly exponential growth in the height of buildings, for the emergence of a new 'vertical consciousness' linked to modern urban skylines.[28] Urban verticality has fascinated not only architects and planners (Le Corbusier in particular sought to imagine the 'vertical city'), but also the authors of science fiction, for whom vertical metaphors have often served as a means of exploring social inequalities and disaggregation.[29] As Lucy Hewitt and Stephen Graham have suggested, however, dominant understandings of urban geography have tended to privilege 'a flat, planar or horizontal imaginary of urban space over a volumetric or vertical one'.[30] Where verticality has been acknowledged, it has often been associated with the critique of elevated perception and human abstraction from the everyday, as articulated by Michel de Certeau in his influential analysis of the view from the World Trade Center in *The Practice of Everyday Life* (1980).[31] It is important nevertheless to stress that there are notable exceptions to such political understandings of verticality. *Mount London: Ascents in the Vertical City* (2014) is, for instance, a collection of short travel narratives which seek to describe journeys in the city – up hills and up buildings – whose role is nevertheless to reveal a landscape (mythological, historical and actual) obscured beneath the everyday city: 'the bedrock of the city repeatedly bursts through its concrete crust, disturbing [the] experiences of the built environment with its own underlying geography and history'.[32] Borrowing the disruptive conceit of mountaineering in the city, the authors manage to discover subtle new perspectives and reveal aspects of space and place that remain otherwise undiscerned.

Verticality, speed and vision

Although the contributions to *Mount London* challenge the idea that the default movement of vertical travel is a downwards one, the forms of looking and engaging with space central to this practice tend to privilege instead engagement with the everyday as a form of descent. Vertical travel is often manifested through forms of microspection, and even through associated processes of re-enchantment. In the extreme and often transgressive activity of Urban Exploration, vertical journeying – whilst not a term used by proponents of the practice – may arguably be seen to adopt complementary vectors, going underground into sewers, tunnels and other sites to which public access is customarily forbidden, but also ascending to the city's heights to view vistas from the top of buildings or cranes.[33] It is clear, as a result, that 'vertical travel' may be seen to operate increasingly as a federating term to describe a range of modes of travel, linked not only to Urb-Ex, but also to other practices such as the Situationist-inspired psychogeography, to 'deep topography' and to other modes of (re)visiting what Robert Macfarlane calls the 'detrital and neglected'.[34] It is important at the same time to historicise the concept, not least in relation to the rich tradition of room travel or 'voyages autour de ma chambre', exemplified by Xavier de Maistre, but certainly not restricted to his work.[35] A distinction is necessary here, however, for whereas this nineteenth-century tradition that emerged from de Maistre's work came to be associated with a certain *ennui*, with a parody of grand tour narratives and with a disillusionment with the mechanisation and democratisation of travel, the countercultural and counter-visual intention of modern vertical travel lie elsewhere, and may be seen – as the logic of Urb-Ex, or the guidebooks to everyday exploration by authors such as Keri Smith or the Wrights and Sites collective, make clear – as a form of re-empowerment for those seeking re-engagement with their own everyday surroundings.[36]

The majority of these approaches to vertical journeys encompass the various forms of descent to which Cronin and Lackey allude, and that Urbain implied in his specific evocation of the catacombs. This predominantly downward movement foregrounds the microscopic to the detriment of the macroscopic, the worm's-eye view as opposed to the bird's-eye view, and consequently tends to intensify the relation of the traveller to their environment, rather than rendering them apart or aloof from it.[37] Such approaches assume a certain relationship to speed and sensation. Vertical travel in its figurative sense, exemplified by the work of authors such as William Least Heat-Moon, depends on a predominant mode of deceleration. This is not necessarily associated with an antagonistic relationship with mechanical transport (the examples above from the work of Maspero and Cortazar make it clear that verticality can be embedded in motorised and otherwise mechanised itineraries), but one nevertheless in which the slowness – indeed, the often-imperceptible movement – of self-propulsion is key. Much vertical travel depends as a result on walking, with its dual emphasis on physical proximity to place, as well as on forms of multisensory engagement in which the shells and screens of vehicles no longer serve as a barrier to direct contact.[38]

In such understandings, Nick Papadimitriou's notion of 'deep topography' becomes an essential point of reference, for it explicitly associates verticality and depth, and — with its emphasis, in a text such as *Scarp* (2012) on the edgelands between the urban and the rural — underlines the importance of poetics and practice over any focus on specific locations or sites.[39] Although, with their Perecquian influences, vertical journeys are often understood to be predominantly urban, they may also be associated with particular approaches to nature. Jacques Lacarrière, a travel writer associated with Mediterranean journeys in the footsteps of Herodotus and walking journeys across France, undertook a radical form of vertical travel in *Le Pays sous l'écorce* (1980), a work in which he describes the microspection involved in observing the unseen life beneath the bark of a tree. The static nature of this form of extreme dwelling is illustrated also in Elisabeth Tova Bailey's *The Sound of a Wild Snail Eating* (2010), her account of watching a snail in a vivarium whilst, bedridden, she recovers from a debilitating neurological disorder.[40]

Vertical travel and the poetics of enumeration

Forms of vertical travel in the natural environment are also explored by Robert Macfarlane in his study of language and landscape, *Landmarks* (2015). Macfarlane's previous book, *The Old Ways*, had deployed walking as a means of re-engaging with place and rediscovering its often-lost contours. *Landmarks* is in many ways a continuation of this project, although central to it is a specific focus on the ways in which a reduced vocabulary relating to the natural world may be seen to reflect the impoverishment of the human relationship to the environment, with over-investment in the technoscape leading to disengagement from landscape and absorption into a 'blandscape' (23). It is in this context that Macfarlane quotes from 'The Parish and the Universe' (1967), an essay by the poet of the Irish everyday Patrick Kavanagh, and suggests that the genealogies of any contemporary reflection on 'vertical travel' merit scrutiny, not least because of the ways in which the practice extends, as is suggested above, beyond the urban, and also relates to poetics as well as to praxis:

> To know fully even one field or one land is a lifetime's experience. In the world of poetic experience it is depth that counts, not width. A gap in a hedge, a smooth rock surfacing a narrow lane, a view of a woody meadow, the stream at the junction of four small fields — these are as much as a man can fully experience.[41]

Macfarlane is of interest in the context of 'vertical travel' not so much because he raises questions about 'nature writing' and its relationship to this practice, or about the respective roles of 'vertical travel' in urban and rural contexts, but because, via Kavanagh, he relates an emphasis on *depth-not-width* to the specific questions of detailed, even exhaustive, enumeration and cataloguing that seem essential to a certain poetics of verticality. Macfarlane's particular interest is in lexical loss, in language deficit and in the role of word lists in the establishment of a relationship between individual and place. His subjects are 'particularisers', those who seek, in their engagement with the locations through which they travel, 'precision of utterance as both form of lyricism and a species of attention' (11). Among them is the Scottish poet Nan Shepherd, 'a localist of the best kind' (56), in whose work Macfarlane discerns a complementary dynamic of depth and proximity central to understandings of vertical travel: 'she came to know her chosen place closely, but that closeness served to deepen rather than limit her vision' (56). Shepherd's work focused on mountains, but it is 'mountain literature', not 'mountaineering literature' (63). It eschews emphasis on the ascent of a summit and the panoramic views this might afford for intense attention to an 'area of territory that she loved, walked and studied over time such that concentration within its perimeters led to knowledge cubed rather than knowledge curbed' (63).

Although little critical attention has been paid to the phenomenon, the practice of enumeration on which Macfarlane's vertical travelling depends – manifest in the list, the catalogue or the inventory – is relatively common in travel literature, and suggests ways in which the practices and poetics of vertical travel might be understood in a wider history of travel writing. Outside travel literature, the literary and cultural uses of listing have attracted considerable attention: Robert Belknap has analysed the historical and epistemological diversity of what he calls the 'literary list' as well as the poetics that listing implies; Bernard Sève offered in 2010 an exploration of what he calls the 'philosophy of lists'. One of the most searching recent explorations was provided, however, by Umberto Eco who – in 2009 – was invited to curate a series of events at the Louvre entitled *Vertige de la liste*, an activity that led to his own 2009 study, *The Infinity of Lists*.[42] In this book, Eco ranges from Homer to Joyce to explore enumeration as it manifests itself transhistorically, across media, and with a range of specific functions (pragmatic and poetic, panegyric and scientific, accumulative and commemorative). Eco reflects on the list and spatiality, and coins the spatial term 'list-city' to describe rhizomatic, decentred urban sprawls such as Los Angeles. At the same time, considering lists in modern and postmodern literature, he identifies two main trends: lists that assemble items 'deliberately devoid of any apparent reciprocal relationship', characterised by 'chaotic enumeration' (exemplified by Jorge Luis Borges, James Joyce and Jacques Prévert, who seek to 'chaoticize' order and 'reshuffle the world'); and those lists, such as Perec's *Je me souviens* [I remember] (1978) or his *Tentative d'épuisement d'un lieu parisien* [Attempt at exhausting a place in Paris] (1975), that are 'coherent by excess [. . .] put[ting] together entities that have some sort of kinship among them'.[43]

As Eco suggests, lists proliferate throughout Perec's work, in particular in his vertical, topographic writings, but the extent to which they adhere neatly to this binary remains unclear, for they often accumulate everyday detail linked by spatial co-ordinates, whilst at the same time reshuffling the ways in which these phenomena are customarily related to each other. Central to Perec's fiction (notably *La Vie mode d'emploi* [Life, a user's manual]) (1978), they are also a key part of his travels in the everyday, where they play an instrumental role in the construction of what Joshua Armstrong has called 'empiritexts', by which he means 'empirically-bound texts [that] allow *invention* to spring from *attention*'. Such works permit the author – from a practice of vertical travel – to 'take the literary text out into the real world and challenge it to find its content and form'.[44] As the practical exercises included in *Espèces d'espaces* make clear, this *invention-springing-from-attention* relies heavily on enumeration and listing: 'You must set about it more slowly, almost stupidly. Force yourself to write down what is of no interest, what is most obvious, most common, most colourless'.[45]

Michael Sheringham presents *Tentative d'épuisement*, the transcript of notes taken across three successive days in the Place Saint-Sulpice in October 1974, as 'Perec's single most significant contribution to the exploration of the *quotidien*', and the work has already attracted considerable attention.[46] The text is a striking example of experimental fieldwork in which the author eschews the obvious tourist (and other) attractions in his chosen location – e.g., 'a fountain decorated with the statues of four great Christian orators (Bossuet, Fénelon, Fléchier and Massillon)' – and concentrates instead on 'that which is generally not taken note of, that which is not noticed, that which has no importance: what happens when nothing happens other than the weather, people, cars and clouds'.[47] The result is a work of vertical travel dependent on a range of modes of engagement with the everyday, prominent among which are microspection and enumeration. Across three days and from several locations around the square (most notably the Tabac Saint-Sulpice and the Café de la Mairie), Perec observes people, buses and pigeons;

he notes vehicles and their trajectories; he enumerates words and numbers inscribed in the built environment as well as on moving objects, and also utterances and other noises in the sound-scape surrounding him.

Perec's initial attempt on the first day of notation is to discover patterns and to impose some form of typology, but as – across the three days – the catalogue of people and phenomena observed becomes increasingly baroque, he finds himself drawn instead to the subtle differences, linked to variables such as climate, time of day and his own subjectivity, through which these observations are filtered. Towards the end of the text, as the often highly amusing fragments of observations accumulate, there is a moment of potentially escapist re-enchantment of the everyday:

> By looking at only a single detail, for example rue Férou, and for a sufficiently long period of time (one or two minutes), one can, without any difficulty, imagine that one is in Étampes or in Bourges, or even, moreover, in some part of Vienna (Austria), where I've never been.[48]

The reader is left, however, with a sense of frustration over Perec's seemingly inconclusive enumerations, and even a feeling of melancholy at the inevitable failure of any attempt at exhaustive description.

A free-standing text, the *Tentative d'épuisement* is nevertheless to be understood in the frame of the wider – and incomplete, existing only as an archive – project of *Lieux*. This was an exemplary 'vertical travel' initiative of which Perec spoke on numerous occasions, the broad rationale of which depended on describing twelve Parisian sites across twelve years, with each catalogued in the field and from memory. In *Mémoires du quotidien*, Derek Schilling has explored in detail the ways in which the five extant fragments of this work appeared in a number of fora, most notably in periodicals and in a production for the Atelier de Création Radiophonique. The listing on which these works rely depends on a spontaneous field recording, textual or oral, whose detail illustrates the approach outlined in *Espèces d'espaces*: 'Force yourself to see more flatly'.[49] The extent to which flatness of description is achieved is limited, however, for while Perec's lists do not contain any thicker description, or do not lead to the retrospective narrative often associated with the literary elaboration of notes captured in the field, their seemingly factual, unvarnished style yields to significant variability, revealing a range of forms of enunciation.[50] Not only do they encapsulate clear formal variation, with movement between different modes of enumeration and description, and also with a layout shifting between vertical stacking and horizontal sequencing; but they also track the subjectivity of the vertical traveller, whose text is shaped by attention to certain objects, to the ebb and flow of particular features, whose enumeration of the everyday is, on occasion, disrupted by personal memories and even the arrival of acquaintances – drawing on the subtle distinctions between noting, noticing and merely glimpsing.

Perec's lists form part of a more general and formal experimentation, seen in the development of fractal texts evident throughout his *oeuvre*, manifest across his fictional, autobiographical and ludic work, and providing a clear indication of the search for form central to the work of OuLiPo.[51] Texts such as the *Tentative d'épuisement* belong primarily, however, to the 'sociological' strand of Perec's production, and demonstrate the potential of what Michael Sheringham calls in *Everyday Life* the 'recourse to enumeration'.[52] These texts reveal the ways in which listing serves as both praxis and form, aspects which – in the context of 'vertical travel' – are creatively and inextricably linked. Perec's use of the list is thus associated in part with what Michael Cronin has called a 'politics of microspection', an interest in the detail of 'micro-modernity' that seeks – by revealing the local to be 'endlessly and tantalizingly distinctive' – a 'way of re-enchanting a world grown weary of the jeremiads of cultural entropists'.[53] At the same time, Perec's use of observational catalogues challenges any understanding of them as 'subsumptive' forms that identify a thing by subordinating it under a particular category; instead, his lists articulate what is observed very differently. Arranging, combining and ordering words, observations and things sequentially not only subverts categorical hierarchies, but also has positively generative qualities in creating new orderings of knowledge.

Perecquian legacies: vertical travel now

The legacy of Perec as vertical traveller is evident in a number of examples of contemporary Perecquian writing. Sean Borodale's *Notes for an Atlas* (2003), a 370-page topographical work, was composed whilst its author walked around London and engaged in stream-of-consciousness-type microspection, transcribing things seen, heard and read.[54] It is also present in a series of experimental, project-based guides to city spaces that seek to recast the rapport between urban environments and those who travel through and dwell in them, inviting engagement with the depth, not breadth, of spaces traversed, and suggesting approaches to place that are more vertical than horizontal. Richard Phillips has analysed such works in his research on the development of experimental fieldwork practices, underlining the extent to which they defamiliarise everyday settings and seek 'space for curiosity'.[55] The popularity of vertical travel is evident in new approaches to everyday fieldwork, evident in the work of artists and writers such as Keri Smith in key works such as *How to Be an Explorer of the World*, where a Perecquian emphasis on the endotic manifests itself in increasing attention to the quotidian. This illustrates – through practices of exoticisation, de-familiarisation and re-enchantment – Cronin's 'travel[ling] down into the particulars of place'.[56]

Karl Whitney's *Hidden City* (2014) – subtitled *Adventures and Explorations in Dublin* – exemplifies recent developments in accounts of urban journeying that seek to apply the various practices of vertical travel to uncover aspects of the everyday ('secret places and untold stories') that are, for various reasons, obscured.[57] Whitney's narrative begins in the edgelands of Dublin as he cycles up the Dublin Mountains, the extension of the Wicklow Mountains, towards the capital. This opening panoramic view provides the author with an opportunity to 'test the continuity of a city that [he] had long viewed as broken into barely connected fragments, a place where the urban, the suburban and the rural interacted in unexpected ways' (2). The account begins with its author's claim that he is 'not a good climber' (1), but the aim of Whitney's narrative following the ascent of his first chapter is re-descent into a city 'defined more by its margins than by its centre, and more by its hidden places than by its obvious landmarks'. Observing that cities 'tend to expand laterally at their margins and vertically in the centre' (13), the author notes the emphasis in Dublin on the former, a tendency that leads him to burrow down into place, exploring with members of the council's drainage services the hidden underground rivers of the Liberties, or to visit Poolbeg Peninsula, 'where the necessary functions of the city – container port, electricity generation, sewage treatment – go to hide' (100). Here, he does not observe the iconic chimneys admiringly from afar, but suggests ways – as did Perec in *Species of Spaces* – of digging down into the materiality of the place.

Whitney's engagement with urban space does not exclusively involve literal descent, but also leads him to find new and often ludic ways of exploring urban sites in ways that disrupt their existing codification. A clear example of this is the development of a new type of literary tourism, visiting every house in which James Joyce lived in Dublin, but in chronological order and in a single day. He also develops the 'Bus Game', an activity very similar to some of the experimental travel initiatives of Latourex, in which he sees how far he can travel, and on how many different buses, using a Travel 90 ticket. Whitney is knowingly aware of the influences on his work, especially Situationist and Perecquian, 'two approaches to the city that had ended in boredom and failure' (146). His project is, however, ultimately a different one, using attention to verticality to grasp contemporary urban space as a palimpsest in which the 'New Dublin', especially since the financial crash, is a thin veneer on the 'Old'. Whitney has a clear affection for his object of study, the city where he had spent most of this life, but is driven by a curiosity to discover a place whose intricacies have been disguised not only by familiarity, but also by various forms of civic marketing and identity construction. The verticality he adopts in order to pursue this aim is both spatial and perspectival, dependent not only on 'haunt[ing] the vast suburban housing estates, the waste ground between buildings, the sewers and underground rivers' (14), but also on adopting ingenious modes of engagement with those sites that steer him away from stereotypes of the city. Such a manoeuvre allows him to discover otherwise obscured juxtapositions, of older landscape in the modern cityscape, and of the urban and rural in the peripheral edgelands. Central to his approach is a quality of looking learnt in part from Perec: 'if I looked hard enough, an industrial estate could be more interesting than a meadow' (28). Summarising the outcome of such an approach, Colm Toíbín (in an early review of the book) describes the recovery by Whitney of 'bits of monasteries and medieval walls and ancient river beds lurking uneasily among all the concrete and urban expansion'. He concludes by recommending *Hidden City* above other guidebooks or other literary vade mecums such as *Ulysses*, suggesting that it might allow access to 'the city's underground rivers and its great unfinished estates, not to speak of the strange bus routes and the many holes in the ground, the hidden and essential life of Dublin'.[58]

The debt to Perec of the vertical travel practices explored by contemporary authors such as Whitney is clear. Commenting on the English translation of *Tentative d'épuisement*, Whitney writes: 'Here, Perec is moving away from the notation of things as they happen towards a commentary on his task, a critical examination of what draws and escapes our attention in the crowded sensory field of the city.'[59] As in Whitney's own work, the microscopic attention to details otherwise ignored is not merely a matter of archiving the everyday, but also a means of reflecting on the forms of travel (and travel writing) most appropriate for its (re)exploration. Generically indeterminate, the lists of Perec's texts were significantly associated with the *tentative*, a term that cannot but resonate with the *essai* – and more particularly with the peripatetic practice of essayism. Central to Adorno's reflections in 'The Essay as Form' is an emphasis on fragmentation, an eschewal of rootedness and an allegiance with what we may see as a more rhizomatic mode: 'accentuating the fragmentary, the partial rather than the total'.[60] Interrogating the literary list, Robert Belknap acknowledges that the form has 'no requisite force of closure', but acknowledges nevertheless that it 'has a load limit of what it can skilfully hold'.[61] In *Penser/classer* [Thoughts of sorts], Perec elaborates on this tension: 'In every enumeration there are two contradictory temptations. The first is to list everything, the second is to forget something. The first would like to close off the question once and for all, the second to leave it open.'[62]

Such a reflection on the (im)possibility of closure is directly linked to questions of (in)exhaustibility with which Perecquian listing is associated, and to the ultimate openness with which both the practice and form are closely linked in the art of vertical travel. This is not so much – to return to Eco's analyses – a contrast between different systematised modes of accumulation ('chaotic enumeration' *versus* 'coherence by excess'). It is instead an acknowledgement that enumeration of the everyday remains an unfinishable project. This is in part as a result of the ever-increasing detail to which the microspection inherent in vertical travel permits access, in part because of the multiple deformations and defamiliarisations that repeated listing generates.

Travel writing is increasingly seen as a mode of translation and re-translation of place (Michael Cronin's discussion of 'vertical travel' is indeed a study exploring that interconnection). The practice of enumeration central to the *Tentative d'épuisement* – as well as to subsequent cognate projects, such as François Bon's *Paysage fer*, or Jacques Roubaud's *Tokyo infra-ordinaire* – may itself be related to questions of (un)translatability.[63]

(In)exhaustibility at the heart of vertical travel is accordingly to be understood in the light of Barbara Cassin's definition of the *intraduisible*, relating to a condition of unfinishedness and unfinishability.[64] Vertical travel reflects the experimental potential of travel writing to propose new and often defamiliarising ways of viewing and engaging with elsewhere. It combines physical descent (and, on occasion, ascent), disruptive of the horizontal emphases of many journeys, with the more metaphorical understandings of verticality evident in acts of microspection. This mode of travel permits formal literary experimentation, whilst revealing the capacity of the genre to discern heterogeneity and fractal detail in a world increasingly understood as homogenised. In the early twentieth century, Victor Segalen described an entropic levelling of the field of travel associated with the acceleration of transport, the rise of tourism and the introduction of new technologies of mechanical reproduction. In his *Essai sur l'exotisme* [Essay on Exoticism], he nevertheless points to a residual persistence of 'Diversity':

> the increasing fusion, the destruction of barriers [. . .] must of their own accord compensate themselves by means of new partitions and unforeseen lacuna, a system of very fine filigree striated through the fields that one initially perceived as an unbroken space.[65]

The practices of vertical travel, and the poetics with which these are associated, exemplify the approaches to such divisions and gaps, and underline the extent to which this striation of the seemingly horizontal and monotonous depends on physical and metaphorical burrowing down – that is, on Sinclair's 'impulse to go underground'.

Notes

1 Iain Sinclair, 'Into the Underworld', *London Review of Books*, 22 January 2015.
2 Georges Perec, *Species of Spaces and Other Places*, trans. John Sturrock (London: Penguin, 1999), 53–4.
3 Susan George, *Lugano Report: On Preserving Capitalism in the Twenty-First Century* (London: Pluto Press, 1999), 179.
4 'Horizontalism' is deployed here not in the traditional political or economic sense relating to the equitable distribution of power and resources, but to designate a set of spatial assumptions that privilege the horizontal over the vertical and may be seen to foreground surface to the detriment of depth.
5 Iain Sinclair, *London Orbital: A Walk Around the M25* (London: Penguin, 2003).
6 Michael Cronin, *Across the Lines: Travel, Language and Translation* (Cork: Cork University Press 2000), 19.
7 Tim Ingold, 'Globes and Spheres', in *The Perception of the Environment: Essays on Livelihood, Dwelling and Skill* (London: Routledge, 2000), 209, 213.
8 On Urban Exploration, see Tim Youngs, 'Urban Recesses: Memory, Nature and the City', in Françoise Besson, Claire Omhovère and Héliane Ventura, eds, *The Memory of Nature in Aboriginal, Canadian and American Contexts* (Newcastle-upon-Tyne: Cambridge Scholars Press, 2014), 31–42.
9 Ian Vince, *The Lie of the Land: An Under-the-Field Guide to Great Britain* (London: Boxtree, 2010), and Ted Nield, *Underlands: A Journey through Britain's Lost Landscape* (London: Verso, 2014). There is an increasing corpus of well-illustrated volumes exploring the undergrounds of specific cities, suggesting a growing contemporary appetite for (often vicarious) access to such spaces. See Jim Moore, *Underground Liverpool* (Liverpool: Bluecoat Press, 1998); Caroline Archer with Alexandre Parré, *Paris Underground* (New York: Mark Batty, 2005); Julia Solis, *New York Underground: The Anatomy of a City* (New York: Routledge, 2005); and Keith Warrender, *Underground Manchester: Secrets of the City Revealed* (Altrincham:

Willow Publishing, 2007). For a recent anthological approach to a range of different locations, see Paul Dobraszczyk, Carlos López Galviz and Bradley L. Garrett, *Global Undergrounds: Exploring Cities Within* (London: Reaktion, 2016). There is also an interest in historical approaches to such underground spaces. See David L. Pike, *Subterranean Cities: The World Beneath Paris and London, 1800–1945* (Ithaca, NY: Cornell University Press, 2005); Céline Knidler, *Le Paris souterrain dans le littérature* (Saarbrücken: Editions universitaires européennes, 2010); and Siobhan Carroll, 'Underworlds', in *An Empire of Air and Water: Uncolonizable Space in the British Imagination, 1750–1850* (Philadelphia, PA: University of Pennsylvania Press, 2015).

10 Jean-Didier Urbain, *Secrets de voyage: menteurs, imposteurs, et autres voyageurs invisibles* (Paris: Éditions Payot & Rivages, 1998), 27.

11 Mary Louise Pratt, *Imperial Eyes: Travel Writing and Transculturation* (London: Routledge, 1992), 201. See Michel Le Bris, *Le Grand Dehors* (Paris: Payot, 1992).

12 Jean-Didier Urbain, *Ethnologue, mais pas trop* (2003; Paris: Payot & Rivages, 2008), 171–234.

13 Perec, *Species of Spaces*, 210.

14 For a discussion of these accounts, see Charles Forsdick, 'Projected Journeys', in *The Art of the Project: Projects and Experiments in Twentieth-Century French Culture*, ed. Johnnie Gratton and Michael Sheringham (Oxford: Berghahn, 2005), 51–65.

15 Marc Augé, *Un ethnologue dans le métro* (Paris: Hachette, 1986).

16 See Urbain, *Ethnologue, mais pas trop*, 202–19.

17 Kris Lackey, *RoadFrames, The American Highway Narrative* (Lincoln, NE: University of Nebraska Press, 1997), 53.

18 Michel Butor, *Mobile* (Paris: Gallimard, 1962); Jean Baudrillard, *Amérique* (Paris: Editions Grasset & Fasquelle, 1986). On slow travel, see Janet Dickinson and Les Lumsdon, *Slow Travel and Tourism* (London: Earthscan, 2010), and Dan Kieran, *The Idle Traveller: The Art of Slow Travel* (Basingstoke: AA Publishing, 2012). Examples of the genre include Dan Kieran and Ian Vince, *Three Men in a Float: Across England at 15 MPH* (London: John Murray, 2008).

19 James Clifford, *Routes: Travel and Translation in the Late Twentieth Century* (Cambridge, MA: Harvard University Press, 1997).

20 This approach is not unique to Perec, and is to be found, for instance, at the opening of D.H. Lawrence's *Mornings in Mexico*, in which the narrator shifts from the macro to the micro in his focus. For a commentary on this, see Tim Youngs, *The Cambridge Introduction to Travel Writing* (Cambridge: Cambridge University Press, 2013), 72–3.

21 Michael Sheringham, *Everyday Life: Theories and Practices from Surrealism to the Present* (Oxford: Oxford University Press, 2006), 49.

22 Derek Schilling, *Mémoires du quotidien: les lieux de Perec* (Villeneuve d'Ascq: Presses universitaires du Septentrion, 2006), 128.

23 Perec, *Species of Spaces*, 11.

24 Perec, *Species of Spaces*, 9.

25 Andrew Harris, 'Vertical Urbanisms: Opening Up Geographies of the Three-Dimensional City', *Progress in Human Geography* 39.5 (2014): 601–20.

26 Daisann McLane, 'Ups and Downs of Vertical Travel', *National Geographic Traveler*, November 2012, accessed 19 July 2016, http://travel.nationalgeographic.com/travel/traveler–magazine/real-travel/traveler-highs.

27 Horst Hamann, *New York Vertical* (Kempen: Te Neues, 2000), and *Paris Vertical* (Kempen: Te Neues, 2005).

28 Andreas Bernard, *Lifted: A Cultural History of the Elevator*, trans. David Dollenmayer (New York: New York University Press, 2014), 36, 92. See also Nick Paumgarten, 'Up and Then Down: The Lives of Elevators', *New Yorker*, 21 April 2008.

29 Lucy Hewitt and Stephen Graham, 'Vertical Cities: Representations of Urban Verticality in 20th-Century Science Fiction Literature', *Urban Studies* 52.5 (2014): 923–37.

30 Hewitt and Graham, 'Vertical Cities', 924.

31 See Michel de Certeau, 'Walking in the City', in *The Practice of Everyday Life*, trans. Stephen Rendall (1980; Berkeley, CA: University of California Press, 1988), 156–63.

32 Tom Chivers and Martin Kratz, *Mount London: Ascents in the Vertical City* (London: Penned in the Margins, 2014), 8.

33 For an illustration of the tensions between these complementary vectors, compare Bradley L. Garrett, *Subterranean London: Cracking the Capital* (London: Prestel, 2014) with Bradley L. Garrett, Alexander Moss and Scott Cadman, *London Rising: Illicit Photos from the City's Heights* (London: Prestel, 2016).

34 Robert Macfarlane, *Landmarks* (London: Penguin, 2015), 232. Subsequent references will be inserted parenthetically in the text.

35 See Bernd Stiegler, *Traveling in Place: A History of Armchair Travel*, trans. Peter Filkins (Chicago, IL: University of Chicago Press, 2013).

36 See, for example, Keri Smith, *How to Be an Explorer of the World* (New York: Perigee; Penguin, 2008); Stephen Hodge, Simon Persighetti, Phil Smith, Cathy Turner and Tony Weaver, *An Exeter Mis-Guide* ([Exeter]: Wrights & Sites, 2003).

37 Robert Macfarlane describes, in the work of Roger Deakin, a 'frog's-eye view' (*Landmarks*, 97).

38 For a discussion of walking, see Rebecca Solnit, *Wanderlust: A History of Walking* (London: Verso, 2002).

39 Nick Papadimitriou, *Scarp* (London: Sceptre 2012).

40 Jacques Lacarrière, *Le Pays sous l'écorce* (Paris: Seuil, 1980), and Elisabeth Tova Bailey, *The Sound of a Wild Snail Eating* (Dartington: Green Books, 2010).

41 Quoted in Macfarlane, *Landmarks*, 63. The exact source of the original quotation is unclear.

42 Umberto Eco, *The Infinity of Lists*, trans. Alastair McEwen (London: MacLehose Press, 2009).

43 Eco, *The Infinity of Lists*, 254.

44 Joshua Armstrong, 'Empiritexts: Mapping Attention and Invention in Post-1980 French Literature', *French Forum*, 40.1 (2015): 95, 105.

45 Perec, *Species of Spaces*, 50.

46 Sheringham, *Everyday Life*, 261.

47 Georges Perec, *An Attempt at Exhausting a Place in Paris*, trans. Mark Lowenthal (Cambridge, MA: Wakefield Press, 2010), 3.

48 Perec, *An Attempt at Exhausting*, 46.

49 Perec, *Species of Spaces*, 51.

50 On 'thick description', see Clifford Geertz, 'Thick Description: Toward an Interpretive Theory of Culture', in *The Interpretation of Cultures: Selected Essays* (New York: Basic Books, 1973), 3–30.

51 The OuLiPo (short for Ouvroir de littérature potentielle) is a group of authors and mathematicians committed to creating texts under constrained writing techniques. Whilst not a founder, Perec was amongst its most prominent members.

52 Sheringham, *Everyday Life*, 63.

53 Michael Cronin, *The Expanding World: Towards a Politics of Microspection* (Winchester: Zero Books, 2011), 71, 7.

54 Sean Borodale, *Notes for an Atlas* (n.p.: Isinglass, 2003).

55 Richard Phillips, 'Space for Curiosity', *Progress in Human Geography*, 38.4 (2014): 493–512.

56 Cronin, *Across the Lines*, 19.

57 Karl Whitney, *Hidden City: Adventures and Explorations in Dublin* (London: Penguin, 2015), 14. Subsequent references will be included parenthetically in the text.

58 Colm Tóibín, 'Hidden City: Adventures and Explorations in Dublin by Karl Whitney', *The Guardian*, 26 September 2014.

59 Karl Whitney, 'What Happens When Nothing Happens?' *3:AM Magazine*, 17 November 2010. www.3ammagazine.com/3am/what-happens-when-nothing-happens.

60 T.W. Adorno, 'The Essay as Form', trans. Bob Hullot-Kentor and Frederic Will, *New German Critique*, 32 (1984), 157.

61 Robert E. Belknap, *The List: The Uses and Pleasures of Cataloguing* (New Haven: Yale University Press, 2004), 30, 31.

62 Perec, *Species of Spaces*, 198.

63 François Bon's *Paysage fer* (Paris: Verdier, 2000) and Jacques Roubaud's *Tokyo infra-ordinaire* (Paris: Tripode, 2014).

64 Barbara Cassin, ed., *Vocabulaire européen des philosophies: dictionnaire des intraduisibles* (Paris: Seuil, 2004), xv.

65 Victor Segalen, *Essay on Exoticism: An Aesthetics of Diversity*, trans. Yaël Schlick (Durham, NC: Duke University Press, 2002), 57–8.

PART II

Modes of writing

8

LETTERS

Eve Tavor Bannet

Travel letters: eighteenth-century correspondence from Britain and America

When eighteenth-century travel writing took epistolary form, it was subordinated to epistolary norms. Features characteristic of travel writing in other forms (listed below) were abandoned or adapted to scribal letter-writing conventions; adapted again when handwritten travel letters were collected and turned into printed books; and often adapted again when letters, or travel material extracted from letters, were integrated into other print genres. There were family resemblances among travel letters designed for different audiences and different purposes in different media, as we shall see; but the travel letter as such was an outlier in 'the bewildering diversity of forms, modes and itineraries' which constructed travel as 'a journey, a movement through space', and travel writing as 'the story of the voyage'.[1]

Other seventeenth- and eighteenth-century forms of travel writing – the 'relation', the journal, the memoir or the autobiographical 'history' of 'Life and Sufferings' abroad – were essentially narrative. They might be sketchy or episodic. There might be chronological gaps, or divisions by date or chapter. But, as scholars have shown, they were emplotted as pilgrimages, quests or inner journeys, or shaped as 'arguments' distinctive to sub-genres of travel writing such as the sea voyage, the captivity narrative or the castaway's tale.[2] In other words, successive movements away from home and back were connected, and given narrative coherence and continuity, by standard trajectories, recurrent topoi, ongoing themes, overarching goals and a modicum of causality. This is what turned mere movement into a journey, and a chronicle, log or diary into a travel story.

The letter, by contrast, was an intrinsically fragmentary, discontinuous and miscellaneous form. Letters could certainly be collected and connected to provide a semblance of continuity; and in print culture, they often were. A story or narrative could also be 'thrown into' a series of letters, or 'digested into familiar letters'.[3] This was possible, in part, because letters had no more difficulty in accommodating travel narrative and description than they had in accommodating reported dialogue, commentary, reflections, political or theological argument, thematic essays, commercial or administrative reports, military or diplomatic dispatches, and travel information that complied with contemporary scientific, historical or ethnographic investigative and discursive norms. But the letter was still traditionally conceived as 'silent speech', and correspondence as 'written conversation'[4] – in other words, every letter was a speech act addressed to others in an ongoing conversation that could always change course. The letter–writer was under no obligation to continue any subject from letter to letter, and had some interest in not doing so – in print culture, because 'variety' was a selling point, and in scribal culture, because the knowledge that posted letters might never reach their destination made it foolish to write letters which depended upon the reception of other letters for their intelligibility. As a classical genre of writing modelled on the oration, moreover, each letter-utterance had a well-defined beginning, middle and end: the form of address and *captio benevolentia* at the beginning, and the signal of impending conclusion, salutation and subscription at the end, framed a largely self-contained unit of speech. Thus, if the narrated journey was like a movie, emplotted and 'never statuesque',[5] each handwritten travel letter was like a snapshot or a still. It issued from its particular place and date. It conveyed some of what had impressed the writer about his/her environment, experiences and encounters with unfamiliar people and/or peoples at that halting point in his/her movements. It began and ended *in medias res*.

Pioneering work on printed letters as a vehicle for travel writing has been done by Charles Batten, who demonstrated how thoroughly eighteenth-century writers 'achieved a generic blending of factual information and literary art' which confounds modern distinctions between factual and fictional texts, and by Amy Elizabeth Smith, who concentrated on issues of quality and authenticity.[6] Particularly helpful is William Sherman's classification of travel letters by the various groups of early modern people concerned: pilgrims, knights errant, merchants, explorers, colonisers, captives and castaways, ambassadors, pirates and scientists.[7] If we substitute emigrants and tourists for pilgrims, a broader range of government officials for ambassadors, and soldiers for knights, it becomes apparent that the same groups continued to travel the British Atlantic throughout the eighteenth century, and that they often wrote about their travels by letter and in their own hand. By rightly emphasising both the utilitarian character of much of this travel writing and its bewildering variety, Sherman invites further research into each group's practices. His own study of the published letters and epistolary reports about the America of early modern explorers and conquistadores delineates the repurposing and distortions to which their writings were subjected by successive printers and editors.[8] Otherwise, observations about travel letters as a form tend to be spasmodic and connected to work on a particular literary travel writer or text. Jean Viviès, for instance, concludes his analysis of Smollett's *Travels through France and Italy* (1766) by observing that the letter 'establishes a context of mock communication' which permits the writer to 'connect various thematic fragments' and combine 'public and private utterances', while endowing the writing with an 'intimacy' which also gives it 'a quality of immediacy and authenticity'.[9] This is true – and equally true of letters that have nothing to do with travel.

One problem at present, as Zoë Kinsley points out, is that modern studies of the travel writing of this period too often ignore manuscript works.[10] This distorts the generic and historical picture, especially for travel letters, since scribal publication was still widely practised. Individually or collected in manuscript volumes, handwritten travel letters were circulated within coteries or across connected social groups for long periods before – or without – finding their way into print. The generic and historical picture is also distorted when travel letters are subsumed under a now discredited New Critical view of literary history, which opposes Enlightenment 'objectivity' to Romantic/modern 'subjectivity', and separates the 'non-literary' texts of most travellers from belletrised 'literary' travel texts produced by men or women of letters who had not necessarily travelled themselves. Letter-writers had at their disposal a graduated spectrum of options for representing subjectivity and describing the external world throughout the long eighteenth century. The travel letters we consider 'literary' were not a species apart.

The focus in this chapter is on those polite and sociable travel letters that were most frequently written, circulated in manuscript, printed, imitated in print and/or belletrised. The section below describes and illustrates the conventions for sociable travel letters, and some of the ways in which manuscript letters were altered and adapted when revised for print publication. The following section addresses an important but sometimes overlooked issue, which also bears on interpretation, by showing why travel letters secreted hidden subtexts and how they alerted attentive readers to their presence.

Sociable travel letters in manuscript and print

Technically a 'Letter of Advice, News or Intelligence' which doubled as a 'Letter of Friendship',[11] the polite and sociable travel letter was the kind of travel letter that one wrote to friends and acquaintances while abroad. It was used by diverse classes of traveller – from ladies and gentlemen travelling for improvement, pleasure or health, to surveyors, factors, soldiers, sojourners, minor government officials and literate women of diverse ranks. It differed both in function and in content from the more obviously utilitarian 'Letters of Advice, News or Intelligence' that some of the same people (a surveyor, officer, factor or government official abroad, for instance) might write in their professional capacity to a superior at home. The function of sociable travel letters was primarily phatic – to safeguard relationships and one's place in society and to remind erstwhile companions of the value of their absent friend by once again interesting, informing and entertaining them.

Sociable travel letters drew unobtrusively on one or more of the topics listed in the 'Instructions to travellers' which the Royal Society and learned men began to disseminate during the seventeenth century: topography, geography, natural history, husbandry and agriculture, trade and commerce, government and laws, religion, manners and customs, military installations and ports, the 'traditions of all particular things relating to the country, such as are either peculiar to it, or at least uncommon elsewhere'.[12] Since the cost of postage was paid by the recipient, and politeness precluded trespassing on his/her patience too much, each letter had at its disposal only a single, folded, sheet of paper, or at most two – writers exceeding this apologised for turning their letter into a journal. Sociable letter-writers therefore favoured miscellaneous anecdotes, descriptions and aperçus, or sometimes focused on a single metonymic scene or situation, in order to convey, vividly and in short order, what seemed to them characteristic and 'curious' or 'remarkable' about a foreign place and people, or about time spent in the vehicle that carried them there.

Because correspondence was considered 'written conversation', sociable travel letters were subject to the rules of polite conversation. Avoid 'the folly of talking too much' about yourself – your 'affairs can have no more weight with other men than theirs have with [you]'. Conversation is 'the Art of pleasing or doing good to one another', so your conversation should be 'pleasing' and 'profitable' to others, and designed to 'inform and entertain' those whom you address. Speak of subjects on which you are 'best versed', but avoid any 'imputation of pedantry', for 'we live in a world of common men, and not of Philosophers'.[13] In sociable travel letters, these rules shaped writers' representations of the external world and their displays of subjectivity in ways that both obeyed and ducked official instructions on how travellers should report empirical information about foreign lands. As Jason Pearl notes, instructions to travellers 'subordinat[ed]' travellers 'to the observed environment' by directing them to record their observations, not their subjective thoughts or feelings, and by instructing them to provide 'simple perceptible facts' without commentary or 'romantic embellishment'.[14] Denuded of 'pedantry' and with talk of self limited or suppressed, the observed environment became the principal focus of attention in sociable travel letters too. But it was an observed environment filtered, and discreetly person-alised, through the character and conversation of the writer, who was using the letter both to inform and entertain its readers and to make the writer's absence felt. The first-person singular, together with implicit or explicit commentary, was necessary to that end. This is well illustrated in the following missive, which was written during the Revolutionary War by a Scottish soldier in America to the friend in Scotland who was keeping an eye on his farm:

> You'll pardon incorrectness. I write you from the middle of a wood bit to death with all kinds of Flyes. I had a long passage of fourteen-weeks[,] landed on Staten Island[.] When I joined the Army we had above five hundred men taken on the passage[.] We assembled on this Island by Degrees and to the amount of two thousand men[.] Notwithstanding the rain the Enemy posted themselves so strongly at New York and on Long Island and occupied such Strengths up Hudson River[,] Howe found it not prudent to make two attacks on them. He therefore determined to make the first trepass [sic] on Long Island. Some got them flat bottom'd Boats [. . .] and we landed the 22nd of August on Long Island without the loss of men – however we march'd a few miles up the Country we found them strongly posted on Flatbush Heights and they had thrown up a work across the Road leading to Brookland March where they had a Chain of Forts [. . .] which they meant as a Defence to their principal Fort at Brookland Ferry which commands New York[.] [T]hey likewise occupied the high ground all covered with wood from Flatt bush to the Narrow where our shipping lay [. . .] which prevented our shipping favouring us [. . .] I am very much harried. Go to my wife poor woman[,] make as light of war as you can.[15]

The factual details show the writer's penetrating intelligence, his grasp of what they mean. For they have been carefully selected to convey and document his judgement that the Americans were better organised, and better strategists, than anyone in Britain had anticipated, and that Howe was already finding them hard to beat. There is also a suggestion that he expected Howe to lose significant numbers of men (including perhaps himself) from this too-small army in the attempt.

Letter-manuals provided standard models for travel letters. The *Secretaries*, which flourished from the 1680s to the 1740s, offered examples at different levels of difficulty, from the most laboured, 'objective' and devoid of subjectivity to the most elegantly shaped by a gentleman-wit's ironic voice and personality. But by mid-century, polite tastes had changed. The most popular manual of the second half of the eighteenth century, *The Complete Letter-Writer* (1755), demoted the wit's epistolary style by parodying it in a schoolgirl letter, and offered two 'Elegant Letters' instead. The first, a 'Letter from a Young Lady in one of the Canary Islands to her Sister in England describing the Beauties of the Place', culled from Eliza Haywood's *Epistles to the Ladies* (1749), showed what could be done with nature descriptions – 'we wander thro' the *Jessamin* Lanes, or sit in *Orange* Bowers, where Fruits ripe, and in Blossom, charm our Smell and Taste' – and how these could be integrated into a letter on family subjects. The other specimen – a long composite letter 'From Mr. George Farquhar abroad in Holland to his Friend in England' – showed what could be done with the 'Instructions to Travellers' list of topics:

> I find, very much to my Wonder, that the Accounts I have had of this Country are very different from the Observations that may be made upon the Place. Some general Remarks there are indisputably certain, as that nothing can parallel the *Dutch* Industry, but the Luxury of *England* [. . .][16]

For those too indolent to adapt this to the most commonly visited destinations, *The Accomplished Letter-Writer* (1779) offered 'Letters from Mr. Gray to his Friends, containing the Particulars of a Tour through Part of France and Italy'. Here travel letters by highly prized authors – a novelist, a dramatist and a poet – were presented as blueprints for others.

In practice, like conversation, epistolary models had to be adapted to the circumstances of the writer and to the tastes of addressees – to please as well as inform, inditers had to ensure that *what* and *how* they wrote about their travels corresponded to the interests, concerns and understanding of the intended recipient(s). The same writer might therefore portray the same location to different addressees in very different terms. Elizabeth Montagu's letters from her travels to Scotland in 1766 are a case in point. Both to her friends and to her husband, Elizabeth Montagu mentioned that 'all the literate and polite company in Edinburgh pay me all kinds of attentions' or that 'I am so kindly entertain'd by all people I believe I shall fancy myself a person of extraordinary merit before I leave this place'. But what she described at length and in greatest detail were the 'prospects' provided by each castle of each Scottish lord who entertained her, as well as 'the beautiful prospects I have seen about Edinburgh, where ye [the] sweetness of a cultivated Country is intermixd with ye sublime beauties of rocks and mountains an assemblage unknown to us'. To her husband, she would add a few more personal touches ('I find the Society here very agreeable. The Gentlemen are learned and the Ladies more so than with us'), say something anodyne about the people he knew and throw out the occasional literary allusion ('The Castle of Edinburgh is a most romantick thing, and brings to ones mind the Castles of Tasso and Ariosto, in which Giants are lodged and Captive Knights imprisoned.').[17] Giving her correspondents information about the external appearance of Scottish lords' estates and Edinburgh's natural and historic beauties entertained them with a superior kind of gossip about the nobility and flattered their fashionable aesthetic tastes.[18] It also indirectly represented Montagu as a great lady, and woman of letters and taste, whose standing had been properly acknowledged by Scotland's aristocratic and intellectual elite. Montagu wrote very differently to her sister:

> but to another time I must reserve all description of Edinburgh. Ld Kaimes author of ye Elements of Criticism suppd with us last night. I am invited to sup at Sir Gilbert Elliots tonight, in the afternoon he and his Lady carry me to see some things in ye Environs of ye Town. Tomorrow Ld Chief Baron Ord and his family carry me to see Woston House [. . .] I have just been at Holy rood House, but reserve ye acct of it to more lei- sure. Dr. Gregory having only lodgings for himself and family his House not being yet finish'd I have hired a lodging which is here called a flatt, but that you may not think it so flatt as to be damp I can tell you there are eight stories below me there are indeed six above me each of these flatts contains a family. I have but one pair of stairs to ascend, but was I to take it into my head to jump out of ye window, I shd be at least half as long in getting to ye bottom as ye man in ye moon wd if he took a leap to us.[19]

Intrinsically relational, travel letters often tell us as much about their addressees and about the latter's relationship to the writer as about the writers themselves.

Letters conveying information about the writer's private life or private feelings were thus functions of the relationship between interlocutors. The 'first person' was 'the little hero of each tale',[20] and subjectivity governed the eighteenth-century traveller's account, primarily in 'Letters of Advice, News or Intelligence' addressed to someone who did take a close personal interest in the letter-writer's affairs – usually a trusted family member, sometimes an intimate friend. These intimate letters often give us invaluable information about places, people, historical circumstances and travel conditions. But like the standard supplementary subjects for such letters (the writer's health, financial and family business, difficulties in epistolary communication), topics from the 'Instructions to Travellers' list appeared here only as relevant to the writer's personal experience and immediate concerns. This, for instance, is William Mylne writing to his beloved sister Nany from Georgia in May 1774 at the beginning of a two-year 'ramble' in America, while he still thought of becoming a planter:

> I have now lived above three months in the woods by myself. I have only been twice in Augusta in all that time, sometimes I am eight-ten days without seeing a human creature. I have had time to think about my situation [. . .] A planter's life is that I would prefer. Before I turned so much recluse I have been at pains to enquire the produce and profits, they are great; yet the planters are mostly poor, the reason of this is the great prices they are obliged to pay to the storekeepers for cloaths and necessaries for themselves and families. They have no manufacture in the country, the tabbaco they grow goes to England and Scotland and comes out to them again in snuff etc. Hemp and flax the same, unless it is some cotton they plant which their wives and daughters spin and weave, for the men does nothing but minds their plantations and hardly that, if they get as much as puts over the year they care for no more; this is with regard to the original settlers, but there are a set of industrious planters coming fast in from Virginia, North Carolina, Pensilvania and New England, these bring in with them a good number of negroes, they buy the plantations of the old settlers.[21]

A mason and architect bankrupted by faults in a bridge he had built in Edinburgh, Mylne made it clear to Nany that he spent much of his time in America hiding from other Scots – having 'a mind cut and slashed by the villainy of mankind' and 'not wishing to be embarrassed that way, it would be no credit to Bob [his successful brother] and vexatious to me, were I known'. From Nany, Mylne concealed neither his misanthropy nor his shame. He described places and events both from the outside and the inside as they affected him – sometimes literally, as when he depicted the exterior appearance of his small cabin, and how snugly he had disposed the furniture within. What mattered about an unexpected May frost was less the surprisingly wintery appearance of suddenly leafless trees than that 'my cucumbers, water & musk melons and several other vegetables were destroyed', the devastation of wheat and Indian corn on neighbouring plantations, and its effects on the food supply. When he travelled up the coast from Charleston to New York ('Although this is usually done by sea, yet as I have a horse I intend to ride it, if I sold my horse here I would not get nigh what he is worth, the market being overstocked at present'[22]) Mylne described, along with the scenery and towns along the way, getting lost for hours trying to find the right path through snowy, unpeopled woods. This simultaneously insider/outsider view, and communication of subjective thoughts, hopes, plans and feelings, distinguished intimate travel letters from merely sociable ones.

Printed travel letters that were based on sociable correspondences varied considerably in their fidelity to their sources. Some, like Mary Ann Hanway's *A Journey to the Highlands of Scotland by a Lady* (1777) or Mary Morgan's *Tour of Milford Haven in the Year 1791* (1795), simply collected and edited sociable letters written to diverse correspondents during their author's travels. These volumes preserve the fragmentary, discontinuous and miscellaneous character of the original letters, and rely for coherence primarily on gathering them together in one place. As Morgan explained: '[b]ecause I could not write to every friend at one and the same time, they all separately desired to have my Tour complete, which could not be done but by committing it to the

Press'.[23] More often, printed letters tried to combine this with a larger 'instructions-to-travellers' kind of view of the locations visited. As William Eddis put it in his *Letters from America* (1792):

> The former part of these letters will be found to give a description of the country, government, trade, manners and customs of the inhabitants; the latter, the rise and gradual progress of civil dissention, which is not perhaps so well known, at least so far as the province of Maryland is concerned.[24]

In practice, supplying this larger view often meant including thematic letters, and organising some letters like an essay that brought together under one head the variety of observations and experiences that had led the writer over time to the reflections about the foreign place which the letter conveyed. As in Edmund Burt's *Letters from a Gentleman in the North of Scotland to his Friend in London; Containing The Description of a Capital Town in that Northern Country; with an Account of some uncommon Customs of the Inhabitants; Likewise an Account of the Highlands with the Customs and Manners of the Highlanders* (1754), this could mean abandoning in short order any pretence that the letters followed the sequence of any single actual travel experience. At the extreme, it could lead to a series of learned, topical, scientific letters, as in William Smith's *A Natural History of Nevis and the rest of the English Leeward Charibee Islands in America* (1745) – without, for all that, entirely obliterating the personal 'voice', experience and perspective that were intrinsic to the sociable travel letter.

Printed travel letters edited out, along with the other party to the correspondence, what was particular to the writer or the writer's friends, and what was merely *fortuitous* about their travels, rather than what was subjective or personal. This distinction holds even for Charles Batten's much-cited example of Addison's supposedly characteristic Enlightenment objectivity. When Addison replaced this sentence in a handwritten sociable letter – 'I am just now arriv'd at Geneva by a very troublesome journey over the Alps where I have bin for some days together shivering among the Eternal Snows' – with this sentence in his printed *Remarks* – 'I came directly from Turin to Geneva, and had a very easie journey of mount Cennis, though about the beginning of December, *the snows having not yet fallen*'[25] – he was not depersonalising his trip. He was substituting information about what readers could generally expect in good weather for what happened to Addison in particular because he was foolish enough to venture across in deep snow. Viewing travel through the writer's personal experience and perspective, suitably generalised for the benefit of 'the generality of readers', was an essential part of the appeal of printed versions of sociable letters. Printed sociable travel letters therefore shared with handwritten ones the convention of conveying the writer's conversation and 'character' – where 'character' still meant the 'social I', the figure a person cut in the eyes of the world, the position, public persona and reputation they adopted, cultivated and sought to preserve in their social and professional life.

Printed travel letters used title pages, prefaces and/or the initial letters to ensure that the reading public knew in which character writers had travelled and in what capacity they 'showed' themselves in the letters: William Smith had 'spent five happy years as Rector of St. Johns', pursuing scientific interests which connected him to the Royal Society; Hanway was a 'lady' and 'a young author' who kept in touch with 'the scene of my accustomed conversation' during her travels to the 'interior' of the Highlands by resolving to 'accommodate my friends with information'. Eddis was both 'Late Surveyor of the Customs at Annapolis' and a member of Maryland Governor Eden's staff, and thus in a position to 'bec[o]me intimately acquainted with the leading characters of every party, and with every event that occurred subsequent to his own arrival'.[26] Besides authenticating the letters' contents, indications of the character in which authors wrote situated their letters, to show the public who was addressing them and how to read the writer's words as a result.

Secrecy, concealment and disguise

In printed letters, indications of the character and situation in which the correspondent wrote helped to clue readers in to the presence of subtexts. The polite, easy and colloquial style considered proper to eighteenth-century letters gave them a semblance of openness or sincerity, which in reality they often lacked. As Hugh Blair told the naïve British readers of 1782 (and naïve American readers shortly after), though 'we expect [. . .] to discover somewhat of [the writer's] real character', it is 'childish indeed to expect that in Letters we are to find the whole heart of the Author unveiled. Concealment and disguise take place, more or less, in all human intercourse'.[27] Concealment and disguise were all the more necessary in letters because these were subject to political surveillance and laws of seditious libel, opened in transit by the government's Secret Office or by American Patriots at the Post, and liable to be read to or by almost anyone. The most interesting part of eighteenth-century travel letters is often what they dared not openly say.

Edmund Burt, for instance, published his *Letters from a Gentleman in the North of Scotland* anonymously and never explained what brought him to the Highlands.[28] He only intimated that his letters 'might create Inconveniences for me in my present situation' (1:2), and 'give Offence' (1:3), observing that because 'in Publick, all Mankind act more or less in Disguise' (1:4), so 'in Prudence to myself' (1:11) it was foolish to 'expose' matters 'quite out of my Road to Profit and Preferment' (1:113). The indication provided by 'The Editor to the Reader' (1:iii) that the anonymous 'Gentleman' (1:iv) in question was 'an Officer of the Army or Revenue' (1:8) writing with 'caution' (1:112) was essential to uncovering what Burt hid among such descriptions as one might expect from a 'travelling Spectator' (1:120), notably his account of Highlanders' concerted resistance to the foreign, English army of occupation of which he was part, and his critique of the English government's Scotland policy. Scattered among objective descriptions of 'dirt, poverty, barbarity and superstition' (1:153) are mentions of Scottish resentment: people said Burt was a spy, that his job should have been given to a Scotsman and that the English were causing exorbitant rises in prices.[29] Interspersed among objective accounts of Scottish manners and mores are depictions of Scottish hostility and recalcitrance to English rule: prisoners repeatedly escaped from the Tolbooth prison in Inverness with the 'Connivance' of their keepers and as 'a Consequence [. . .] of Clan Interest' (1:34); Scottish magistrates and merchants were cold and 'shy' (1:43) of any intimacy with Englishmen like Burt; ordinary people were rebuked by other Scots for 'unguarded expressions' (1:120) or said they 'speak no Saxon (or English)' (1:151) to avoid answering English questions; a minister refused to baptise a 'Regimental bastard' (1:157); when forced to entertain English soldiers, one Highland laird gave them a taste of good French wine and then insultingly replaced it with cheap ale; another made a habit of getting them so drunk that 'his guests soon lose their guard, and then – I need say no more' (1:161).

Using the rhetorical figure which affirmed by denying, Burt asserted that he would 'not make any Remarks how much it is incumbent on the Rulers of Kingdoms and States (who are to the People what a Father is to his helpless Family) to watch over this Source of Human Convenience and Happiness' (1:36). But he made it clear that his letters' 'design is to show you by Example, the melancholy Consequence of the Want of Manufactories and foreign Trade, and most especially with respect to the Common People whom it affects to the Want of Necessaries' (1:37). This could be taken as an Englishman's self-congratulatory allusion to the wealth and luxury accruing to England from her commercial empire, and as an empirical demonstration from Scotland's counter-example of England's superior economic and political policies. But it read quite differently if one recalled that poverty had driven Scotsmen to agree to Union with England in 1707 in the belief that Scottish participation in England's commercial empire through their own manufactures and foreign trade would enrich Scotland too. Burt's observation that the wretched circumstances he found in the Highlands 'continually excite in me the painful Passion of Pity' (1:44) suggests that he designed every detailed account of 'the extreme Indigence of Country People' to arouse in English readers his own feelings of pity and shame, and that he intended every objective description of the 'Indolence' produced by a lack of 'Encouragement' of Scottish Trade as a reproach to English rulers for failing to act as fathers to the Scottish people.

Manuscript letters too tried to alert their addressees to concealment and disguise. Writing of his travels up the coast from the relative safety of New York in 1775, Mylne informed his sister:

> I wrote all this from my memory for I durst not keep a journal, in many places they talked of spies being out, I was afraid I might be taken for one, if a journal had been found I should have been tarred and feathered, an honour the Mobility sometimes confers on those they apprehend are friends to Government. As to politicks I think most of the people are mad, In South and North Carolina, Virginia, Maryland, they muster and are everywhere learning the exercise as if they were going to be attacked.[30]

This told Nany why even in New York, Mylne chose to 'remember' only a largely unpeopled landscape or the external appearance of towns, and kept the locations of those musterings vague.

Sometimes the alert consisted of code-switching, and changing one's style. Writing to his brother Donald from Oxford, Maryland in 1774, William McLeod explained how it came about that his Scottish firm moved him there from Queenstown to run the company store, pronounced himself 'comfortably situated with respect to the place and [. . .] the people', and continued: 'The present situation of this Country is very alarming to people in Trade. For my own part I am much afraid the property of foreigners is on a very precarious footing.' This signalled that what followed was not mere 'information', but something affecting the future prospects of people like himself. William showed even greater caution by switching to a neutral third-person, objective and generalising style for the lengthy explanation that followed about 'the Congress in Philadelphia', 'the inflamed state of the peoples minds', his anticipation of a non-importation agreement and its likely consequences for British companies in the transatlantic trade.[31] William thus disguised what he was telling his brother: that he did not expect to be able to establish himself in America as they had hoped, and through no fault of his own.

Sometimes the alert to concealment in travel letters depends on understanding the occasion, the significance of a passing remark and differences in subject or style from other letters to the same correspondent(s). For instance, writing from Scotland to her husband – a notable member of the Parliamentary Opposition – Montagu mentioned in passing that 'no one speaks of politics here'. An odd remark in 1766 when England was still brutally suppressing the Highlands after the Jacobite insurrection of 1745, this warned him that she would not touch on politics. It explained why her letters were silent on her favourite topics (the sufferings of the poor, philanthropy, national characters, political personalities and philosophies) and why they only portrayed the idyllic external appearance of Highland castles peacefully ensconced in magnificent unpeopled landscapes. All was well in Scotland; Montagu's travels were perfectly innocent, the pastime of a fashionable lady; there was no secret 'intelligence' for the post office to intercept here. Anything political Montagu saw, heard and thought was more prudently said when she got home. Her letters from France were likewise studiously clichéd and politically correct.[32] She was not unique in this respect. In letters home from England while her husband was American plenipotentiary to European courts, Abigail Adams likewise often substituted 'outsider' travelogues for her usual acute insider-discussions of political manoeuvring, complaining that 'the London ladies walk a great deal', and describing such things as 'the Foundling Hospital, decorum at the Concert Hall, or London's elegant squares'.[33] In travel letters such as these, the topoi and 'observed environment' of the 'travelling Spectator' filled the writer's silence about other things, and mutely profiled what had to be left unsaid.

Concealment and disguise figured differently in print culture when travel letters were belletrised by the adoption of literary devices that were designed to lend an air of novelty to accounts of places already much visited and much described.

One device was to exaggerate the 'character' needed to personalise sociable travel letters, into what, in literary periodicals like *The Spectator* or *The Idler*, is called an 'eidolon'. Unlike the more rounded 'persona', an eidolon was a person-like mask with a few notable quirks or eccentricities that could be assumed by diverse authors. It served at once to link miscellaneous and otherwise discontinuous texts, to protect real authors from prosecution by concealing their identities and to tease public curiosity about the real identity of their author(s). Here what was concealed in full public view was the true messenger, rather than the true message. As a form of concealment, the eidolon disguised through a blatant, but misleading authorial presence rather than through the full or partial absences of silence, hints or evasions. Standard eidolons such as 'the splenetic traveller', the 'picturesque traveller' or 'the suffering traveller' were signifiers of the 'literary' – some, like the character of 'the infirm traveller' adopted by Henry Fielding, went as far back as Horace's *Journey to Brundisium*.[34] As an assumed and ventriloquised character, the eidolon was almost anti-autobiographical – it was a mask that could be brandished, examined or satirised by anyone. Crèvecoeur, the sophisticated, European writer of *Letters from an American Farmer* (1782) who theorised about 'What is an American' and described his travels in British-America and the Caribbean, was no more his gently satirised and soon abandoned eidolon – James, the simple American farmer who had to be taught how to write a letter – than Benjamin Franklin was Silence Dogood, the reproving wife of a Puritan minister, even if Crèvecoeur did spend some years farming in America and Franklin did grow up in Puritan Boston.

Another literary device sometimes appropriated by literary travel writers was exaggeration of intimate letters centred on the 'I' into expressions of what William Coombe in 1803 dismissively called 'strong feelings'.[35] This is now associated with Romantic sensibility and modern subjectivity; but in England, the subjective shaping of experience in letters, accompanied by passionate expressions of strong feelings, had been signifiers of 'the literary' since *The Love Letters of a Portuguese Nun* (1668) and Aphra Behn's *Letters from a Nobleman to his Sister* (1684). Publication of desires, acts and feelings that modesty, morality and decorum dictated should be concealed was a longstanding mark of sensational literature – and a major source of its appeal. Early modern and Romantic literary writers both expressed strong subjective feelings. What separated them was a change in taste which enabled Romantics to dismiss the earlier florid style for expressing strong feelings as purple prose. This can complicate our readings. For instance, when Hanway, the 'young author', introduced a passage of purple prose into an otherwise formal sociable travel letter in 1777, was she imitating 'Romantic' contemporaries like Charlotte Smith, or invoking long-dead predecessors like Haywood and Behn?

Letter locations

There were family resemblances between all these different travel letters because there was constant interplay between scribal and print culture. Printed letters reflected scribal practices in significant ways, but manuscript writers also borrowed from printed materials – and not only because handwritten travel letters that were printed in manuals, periodicals and volumes of travel writing served as models for other handwritten letters, and shaped people's sense of the possibilities of the genre. Handwritten letters sometimes contain stylistic set-pieces or micro-genres copied from, or modelled on, printed matter. William McLeod's letter to his brother, for instance, included a paragraph copied from a travel guide describing Oxford, Maryland, and a mini-disquisition on trade. And women who collected their manuscript travel letters into manuscript 'books' for circulation among friends began in this period to add a table of contents or an index to make their handwritten volumes more like a printed book.

But the differences are equally or more important, especially as they related to the location, or successive locations, in which any given travel letter appeared. Travel letters were shape-changers – they were freely revised or extracted for different readerships, different purposes and different outlets, whether by their original authors, by the author's descendants or by successive editors. During this period, pragmatic re-use of extant handwritten or printed material by adapting or changing it to suit a different need, occasion, audience or print outlet was common, acceptable – and authentic each time.[36] Letters also often appeared singly, rather than blended into a continuous correspondence. Archived collections of 'Papers' often contain a few single letters from more or less obscure individuals, and short, obviously incomplete bits of correspondence, which were initially retained by their recipient(s) for reasons that are rarely explored. The editors of miscellanies, magazines and letter-manuals created a similar situation by culling and reprinting single letters, or small groups of letters, from correspondences and printed collections of travel letters. Even aside from any alterations made to the letters themselves, changing the location and thus the context of a letter changed its signification. As 'Et tu, Brute' means differently when read as Caesar's dying words in a play, as a quotation in a letter of reproach or as an example of the vocative in a Latin grammar book, so a travel letter means differently in a collection of single-authored travel letters, a miscellany of diverse travel writings, an archive, an epistolary novel, a magazine, a letter-manual or a commonplace book. By the same token, the travel letters cited in this chapter do not signify the same things, embedded in a modern academic analysis of past travel-writing practices, that they signified to an eighteenth-century 'armchair traveller' who periodically interspersed the reading of newspapers and sermons with the casual perusal of a few printed travel letters, or eagerly opened a missive in a familiar hand from a travelling friend.

Notes

1 Carl Thompson, *Travel Writing* (London: Routledge, 2011), 1–2; Philip Edwards, *The Story of the Voyage: Sea Narratives in Eighteenth-Century England* (Cambridge: Cambridge University Press, 1994).

2 Tim Youngs, *The Cambridge Introduction to Travel Writing* (Cambridge: Cambridge University Press, 2013); Barbara Korte, *English Travel Writing from Pilgrimages to Postcolonial Explorations* (Houndmills: Macmillan, 2000); Alfred Bendixen and Judith Hamera, eds., *The Cambridge Companion to American Travel Writing* (Cambridge: Cambridge University Press, 2009). Paul Smethurst proceeds on a different principle, but he too equates form with 'organizing metaphors [. . .] unifying structures [. . .] ordering codes'. Paul Smethurst, 'Introduction', in *Travel Writing, Form and Empire: The Poetics and Politics of Mobility*, ed. Julia Kuehn and Paul Smethurst (London: Routledge, 2009), 2.

3 For 'digested' see, for instance, *The Entertaining Correspondent, or Curious Relations, digested into familiar Letters and Conversations* (London, 1739) or *The Curious Traveller, being a Choice Collection of very remarkable Histories, Voyages, Travels etc. digested into Familiar Letters* (London, 1742); for 'thrown into', see Smollett's letter to John Moore, cited in Jean Viviès, *English Travel Narratives in the Eighteenth Century: Exploring Genres* (Aldershot: Ashgate, 2002), 55.

4 Jonathan Goldberg, *Writing Matter: From the Hands of the English Renaissance* (Stanford, CA: Stanford University Press, 1990).

5 Peter Hulme cited in Youngs, *Cambridge Introduction*, 3.

6 Charles L. Batten Jr., *Pleasurable Instruction* (Berkeley, CA: University of California Press, 1978), 5–6. See also Lennard J. Davis, *Factual Fictions: The Origins of the English Novel* (Philadelphia, PA: University of Pennsylvania Press, 1996); Amy Elizabeth Smith, 'Travel Narratives and the Familiar Letter Form in the Mid-Eighteenth Century', *Studies in Philology* 95.1 (1998): 77–96; and 'Naming the Un-"Familiar": Formal Letters and Travel Narratives in Late Seventeenth- and Eighteenth-Century Britain', *Review of English Studies* 45.214 (2003): 180.

7 William H. Sherman, 'Stirrings and Searchings (1500–1712)', in *The Cambridge Companion to Travel Writing*, ed. Peter Hulme and Tim Youngs (Cambridge: Cambridge University Press, 2002), 24–30. Sherman shows, contrary to Katherine Turner's *British Travel Writers in Europe 1750–1800* (Aldershot: Ashgate, 2001), that there were 'middle-class' – and indeed lower-class – travellers from the first.

8 William H. Sherman, 'Distant Relations: Letters from America, 1492–1677', *HLQ* 66.3–4 (2003): 225–45. The letters of scientists have garnered most attention to date. See, for instance, Susan Scott Parrish, *American Curiosity: Cultures of Natural History in the Colonial British Atlantic World* (Chapel Hill, NC: University of North Carolina Press, 2006).

9 Viviès, *English Travel Narratives*, 57–8.

10 Zoë Kinsley, *Women Writing the Home Tour, 1682–1812* (Aldershot: Ashgate, 2008), 13.

11 For the different classes of letter, see Eve Tavor Bannet, *Empire of Letters: Letter Manuals and Transatlantic Correspondence, 1688–1820* (Cambridge: Cambridge University Press, 2005), 55–63.

12 Robert Boyle, 'General Heads for the Natural History of a Country, Great and Small', in *The Philosophical Works of the Hon. Robert Boyle Esq.* 3 vols (London, 1725), 3:6.

13 Jonathan Swift, 'Hints towards an Essay on conversation', in *The Works of Dr. Jonathan Swift*, 2 vols (London, 1762), 1:199, 200, 202; Henry Fielding, 'Essay on Conversation', in *Miscellanies by Henry Fielding Esq.* 3 vols (London, 1743), 1:121, 123, 130.

14 Jason Pearl, 'Geography and Authority in the Royal Society's Instructions to Travellers', in *Travel Narratives, the New Science and Literary Discourse, 1569–1750*, ed. Judy A. Hayden (Aldershot: Ashgate, 2012), 73. See also the essays by Daniel Carey and Judy Hayden in the same volume; and Barbara Shapiro, *A Culture of Fact: England 1550–1720* (Ithaca, NY: Cornell University Press, 2000).

15 National Library of Scotland, MS 6410, f. 13. W. Erskine to Sir John Halkett, Bart, 9, 1776.

16 *The Complete Letter-Writer* (London, 1756), 111, 138.

17 The Huntington Library, MO 2625, Elizabeth to Edward Montagu [Aug. 12, 1766]; MO 2623 [Aug. 9, 1766].

18 See Elizabeth A. Bohls, *Women Travel Writers and the Language of Aesthetics, 1716–1818* (Cambridge: Cambridge University Press, 1995) and Nigel Leask, *Curiosity and the Aesthetics of Travel Writing, 1770–1840* (Oxford: Oxford University Press, 2002).

19 The Huntington Library, MO 5841, Elizabeth Montagu to Sarah Scott [Aug. 5, 1755].

20 Mary Wollstonecraft, *Letters Written during a Short Residence in Norway, Sweden and Denmark* (London, 1796), Advertisement.

21 *Travels in the Colonies in 1773–1775: Described in the Letters of William Mylne*, ed. Ted Ruddock (Athens, GA: University of Georgia Press, 1993), 25–6.

22 *Travels in the Colonies*, 55, 76, 56.

23 Quoted in Kinsley, *Home Tour*, 51.

24 William Eddis, *Letters from America, historical and descriptive, comprising occurrences from 1769–1777 inclusive* (London, 1792), Introduction A2–A3.

25 Batten, *Pleasurable Instruction*, 18.

26 Smith, 'Dedication', 1; Hanway, Title page, 'Dedication', and vii; Eddis, title page and 'Introduction', A2; Burt, 'The Editor to the Reader', iv, Letter I.

27 Hugh Blair, *Lectures on Rhetoric and Belles Lettres*, 2 vols (Carbondale, IL: Southern Illinois Press, 1965), II: 64.

28 [Edmund Burt,] *Letters from a Gentleman in the North of Scotland* (London: 1754), 2 vols. Subsequent page references will be inserted parenthetically.

29 David Stevenson, 'Burt, Edmund', ODNB (2004). www.oxforddnb.com/view/article/4118.

30 *Travels in the Colonies*, 75.

31 The National Library of Scotland, ms 19297, William McLeod to Donald McLeod of Geanies, October 1st, 1774.

32 Emma Major, 'Femininity and National Identity: Elizabeth Montagu's Trip to France', *ELH* 72:4 (2005): 901–18.

33 See for instance Abigail Adams' letters to her sister, Mary Cranch, in July 1784.

34 Batten, *Pleasurable Instruction*, 72, 44 and Carl Thompson, *The Suffering Traveller and the Romantic Imagination* (Oxford: Clarendon, 2007).

35 Thompson, *Suffering Traveller*, 79.

36 For changes to travel writing in general, see Matthew Day, 'Travelling in New Forms: Reissued and Reprinted Travel Literature in the Long Eighteenth Century', *Memoirs du livre/Studies in Book Culture* 4.2 (2013): 1–18. See also Eve Tavor Bannet, *Transatlantic Stories and the History of Reading* (Cambridge: Cambridge University Press, 2012).

9

DIARIES AND JOURNALS

Christina Laffin

Introduction: premodern Japanese travel diaries

This chapter will provide an overview of Japanese vernacular travel diaries, focusing on works from the tenth to eleventh centuries, when the first poetic travel journals emerged, followed by examples from the thirteenth and fourteenth centuries, which show the significant role literary conventions played in determining both style and content. Despite notable exceptions, scholarship in English on travel writing has tended to focus on examples from Europe and the United States and has often ignored other geographical areas, with the exception of journeys recorded by Anglophone writers. Examining literary records of travel written in Japanese before the modern period, with particular attention to early works by women, may offer inroads into rethinking prevailing assumptions about travel writing.

Travel is integral to the literature produced in Japan before the modern period; that is, to the body of poetry, diaries, tales, and other genres written in classical Japanese and Sino-Japanese before the nineteenth century. Scholars have argued that by the twelfth century, nearly every Japanese literary work included references to journeys.[1] Journals and memoirs offer one of the main forms of travel literature – in the examples below, the *Tosa Journal* features a journey as the backbone of the work, and *The Kagerō Diary* represents a pilgrimage as the turning-point in the author's life and literary account. *The Sarashina Diary* highlights the disappointment literary sojourners felt when their experiences of travel did not measure up to poetic ideals. *The Diary of the Sixteenth Night Moon* shows how poetic convention determined the route, famous locations, and literary response expected of a travel writer.

The particular historical and cultural developments that took place after script was introduced from China to Japan resulted in women being the main producers of literary works written in the vernacular. Thus, the majority of premodern diaries in the Japanese literary canon have been written by female authors. These women recorded their experiences of accompanying patrons on imperial processions, journeying with family members on official travel to the provinces, and undertaking pilgrimages to shrines and temples. The numerous extant literary examples of travel by premodern women have led one scholar to characterise the paradigm of Japanese travel as an 'ovular journey', undertaken by women who remain within the body politic, in contrast to the 'spermatic journey' of a European male traveller to a foreign country.[2] While only a small fraction of the women of tenth- and eleventh-century Japan were literate, noblewomen and members of the imperial family were skilled at writing poetry and prose that enabled them to produce the body of works that have come to be known as 'women's-style diary literature' (*joryū nikki bungaku*).

In the remainder of this chapter I shall trace how travel writing developed together with journals, diaries, and memoirs (all covered by the Japanese term '*nikki*'; literally, a 'record of days') and how the genre is linked to the production of poetry. While sketching out a history of early Japanese travel literature through early sources and Japanese secondary literature, I shall draw occasionally from scholarship on Anglophone sources to show the ways in which Japanese travel diaries may corroborate or challenge current perspectives on travel writing.

Travel literature in Japan before the nineteenth century encompasses poetry, letters, tales, and other forms but it is primarily associated with a genre known as *kikō* (literally, 'records of travel'), described by Herbert Plutschow as 'short accounts in prose and poetry about journeys usually starting from the capital (Kyoto)'.[3] Travel writing developed in tandem with autobiographical forms of literature like the journal, diary, and memoir, and is closely tied to the production of poetry in premodern Japan.[4] While travel writing extends to poems and letters sent home during journeys, fictional tales, war narratives, noh theatre, and many other forms of literature, travel diaries came to be canonised as a genre with set conventions and itineraries and even particular poetic associations with each famous site along the journey.

Carl Thompson characterises travel writing as an 'encounter with difference and otherness' or a 'confrontation with [. . .] alterity'.[5] Citing Paul Fussell, Thompson describes the travel writer's experience of encountering the unfamiliar and claiming validity through actuality. For the noble traveller of premodern Japan, experiences on the road were mediated through the lens of poetic journeys recorded by famous historical and literary figures at set places along travel routes. Although it was not unusual for Japan's early travellers to comment on the strange, peculiar, and unfamiliar sights they met on the road, the conventions of travel writing demanded that writers recall famous poets of the past who had visited the same locations. By citing the images recorded in the poems and prose of previous travellers, these writers of new journeys inscribed themselves into a long history of literary travel. Early Japanese travel writing can thus be seen as an accretionary genre in which diarists and poets referenced the illustrious people, places, and images associated with the famous locations along a travel route while contributing variations on these themes based on set tropes.

Rebecca Steinitz notes that the diary form provides a familiar, identifiable sense of organisation and structure to the reader of travel writing.[6] The recording of daily journals developed in Japan from around the tenth century onward as a means of keeping note of important events and precedents, including proper protocol, by men for male heirs. Such diaries were recorded in a form of classical Chinese used at court, the lingua franca of the bureaucracy and also an important sphere of classical learning for the elite.[7] This style of diurnal writing carried over to the vernacular, and thus came to be associated with poetic writings. The following section will consider the important relationship between diaries and travel writing.

Diaries and travel writing

Japan has a rich history of autobiographical writing, beginning with tenth-century diaries and memoirs and continuing through the 'I-novels' of the early twentieth century. The genre of 'diary literature' (*nikki bungaku*), as it came to be classified in the modern period, is associated with classical court culture and literary production by noblewomen. The early producers of diaries, journals, and memoirs did not envision their writing as belonging to a distinct genre, and their works fluidly traverse the borders of fiction and autobiography and include aspects of poetry, fictional tales, and travel writing.

The tenth to eleventh centuries represent a period traditionally seen as the blossoming of literary diaries in Japan. The particular sociocultural conditions of the court at this time enabled men and women of the highest echelons of society to be highly literate. Accomplished women writers and poets were recruited into the salons of imperial consorts to illuminate their patrons and bring vibrancy and literary acclaim to their circle. The patriarchs behind these consorts and their salons hoped that by better positioning a daughter or sister vis-à-vis the emperor, they might improve the chances of her bearing an heir to the throne, thus contributing to the consolidation of their political power.

During later eras, the vernacular works produced by women of these salons, such as *The Tale of Genji* (Genji monogatari, ca. 1010 CE) by Murasaki Shikibu (ca. 973–ca. 1014 CE), came to be prized as the height of classical literary accomplishment. From a global perspective, literary production during Japan's Heian period (794–1185 CE) can be seen as an anomaly in terms of the wealth of works that were produced, the sociopolitical value placed on literary knowledge, and the important contributions by women that were canonised in later periods. Although the literature of this period spans multiple genres, I shall focus here on works that represent the importance of travel within the diary form, including pilgrimages and journeys undertaken as court assignments.

The history of Japanese 'diaries' and 'journals' is closely tied to the intertwined problems of gender, genre, and script, and to the modern canonisation of a national literary tradition. The development of travel literature can be seen as an extension of diary writing as a form. This is demonstrated by the first literary diary written in the vernacular, which was based on a fifty-five-day journey from Tosa Province (in present Shikoku) to the capital (present Kyoto), narrated through the voice of a woman, but authored by a higher-status man. Examining this diary sheds light on the development of memoir writing and the close relationship between diaries and travel records.

The Tosa Journal

In literary histories of Japan, the *Tosa Journal* (Tosa nikki) is positioned as the first work of diary literature, while also representing one of the earliest examples of a travel diary combining prose and poetry. Composed around the year 935 CE by a famous male poet and scholar, but narrated through the persona of a lower-ranking woman, it presents a peculiar and problematic departure point for studying the genre of diaries (*nikki*) and travel records (*kikō*). The work opens with the following statement:

> I wrote this wondering what it would be like for a woman to try her hand at one of those diaries that men are said to keep. One year, around eight in the evening of the twenty-first day of the Twelfth Month, I embarked on a journey. What follows are notes on some of the things that took place.[8]

The diary then depicts the trip back to the capital across waterways, including periods of waiting for boats to depart. The work combines an underlying theme of lamentation over the death of a daughter with an overarching celebration of the myriad uses and producers of Japanese poetry. The mother composes poems reflecting on her loss as the entourage makes its way towards the capital.

The dead child's mother, who never forgot her for a day or an hour, composed this:

suminoe ni	Please take the boat in
fune sashiyose yo	to the Suminoe shore.
wasuregusa	Before we journey on,
shirushi ari ya to	I will pluck forgetting-grass
tsumite yukubeku	to test the truth of its name.

It is unlikely that she wanted to forget completely. She was probably seeking temporary relief from her longing, hoping to regain the strength to bear it.[9]

The diary contains sixty poems written by a wide range of women and men, adults and children, not all of noble status, who cumulatively provide an introduction to the ways in which poetry may be used along a journey: in farewell missives, at lively banquets, to entertain during transport delays, to hail one's return, and in many other contexts. This can be seen in the expressions of delight when the passengers near their destination, enabling even those with little training to produce passable poems.

In her delight at hearing that it was no longer far to the capital, the seasick old Awaji Grandmother lifted her head from the bilge and recited a poem:

itsu shi ka to	Now the august boat
ibusekaritsuru	comes at last to the inlet,
naniwagata	to long-awaited
ashi kogisokete	Naniwa and with its oars
mifune kinikeri	pushes its way through the reeds.[10]

Seasickness, uncooperative weather, dangerous passages, and stints of boredom are among the trials presented along the journey. More than a month into their trip home, the narrator recounts the passengers' fears:

No rain or wind. We left around midnight, having heard that the pirates were inactive at night, and began to negotiate the Awa Straight whirlpool. It was too dark to tell one direction from another, but we managed to get through, with both sexes praying frantically to the gods and Buddhas.[11]

As an early literary diary, the *Tosa Journal* blurs the boundaries between fact and fiction, between male and female forms of writing, and between the genres of journals and travel writing. The opening statement also sheds light on what a 'diary' or 'journal' (both translations for '*nikki*') might have meant to a tenth-century courtier. Why would a male courtier adopt the script and style associated with a lower-ranking woman and compose a travel record in her voice? To better understand this, we must retrace the role and meaning of diaries in tenth-century Japan and notions of gender and style, while avoiding the urge to apply contemporary notions of 'gender-bending' to premodern Japan.[12]

The *Tosa* author, Ki no Tsurayuki (872?–945 CE), was the preeminent poet of his time, co-editor of the first imperial anthology of poetry, and author of its '*Kana* Preface', one of the most influential explications of the principles of Japanese poetry. Like other men serving at court, he would have been familiar with diurnal records kept by those in the Ministry of Central Affairs who were expected to maintain diaries of the numerous annual ceremonies, court rituals, and official events as records of the activities of the sovereign. By creating a travel diary that was modelled not on pre-existing journals of court life experienced by men but on the vernacular writings of women, he was able to play with poetry and prose to produce a work incorporating multiple voices and poets, which focused on the lament of a mother for her daughter and the many ways in which Japanese poetry could be employed. Journals before the *Tosa Journal* were often recorded in pre-formatted almanacs which included the date, zodiac sign, and an indication of the auspicious or inauspicious nature for each day of the year, followed by a few blank lines for recording content.[13] Writing in the vernacular allowed Ki no Tsurayuki to shift the work away from a rigid record of days on the road and into a more fluid narrative incorporating poignancy and humour.

After safely returning to the capital, Ki no Tsurayuki concludes the work with a summation of the tiresome nature of the journey and the sadness of loss, noting (as was the case in many diaries) the little worth of what he wrote: 'It is hopeless to try to record all the forgettable and painful things that come to mind. After all, I suppose the best thing to do is to tear up these sheets at once.'[14] The next work containing an extensive description of travel which we will examine is the *The Kagerō Diary*. Like the conclusion of the *Tosa Journal*, it begins by discounting the narrative that has been recorded.

The Kagerō Diary

The Kagerō Diary (ca. 974 CE) was written by a noblewoman known as Michitsuna's Mother (ca. 937–995 CE), who was married to one of the court's highest-ranking men, Fujiwara no Kaneie (929–990 CE). Over the course of three books she describes her relationship to her husband, son, and adopted daughter. She includes numerous descriptions of pilgrimages and a lengthy section which describes her travels to a temple and her period of reclusion there. She opens the work by explaining her position and motivation to record her experiences as a memoir:

> Thus the time has passed and there is one in the world who has lived such a vain existence, catching on to neither this nor that. As for her appearance, she can hardly be compared to others, and her intelligence – to say she has some is as good as saying she has none at all – so it is only natural to think she has come to such a useless state she thinks again and again; it is just that in the course of living, lying down, getting up, dawn to dusk, when she looks at the odds and ends of the old tales – of which there are so many, they are just so much fantasy – that she thinks perhaps if she were to make a record of a life like her own, being really nobody, it might actually be novel, and could even serve to answer, should anyone ask, what is it like, the life of a woman married to a highly placed man, yet the events and years gone by are vague; places where I have just left it at that are indeed many.[15]

Despite being positioned for a good marriage, Michitsuna's Mother writes of feeling neglected by a husband whose visits decrease as he fosters other romantic interests, a normal development based on the polygamous marriage practices of tenth-century Japan.

She visits religious sites to pray for children and to seek respite from her daily life. Over the course of her diary she visits shrines and temples at Karasaki, Ishiyama, Narutaki, Hase, and Inari. In Book One, she writes of anticipating her first pilgrimage to Hase, a temple that was a popular travel destination for noblewomen:

Well then, I have had a fervent desire for so many years; I decide that no matter what I must take a pilgrimage to Hase [. . .] I just decide to leave secretly [. . .] Gazing out, I see the surface of the water sparkling in between the trees and find it so moving.[16]

During her other journeys she appears rejuvenated by the new sights she is able to witness. On a trip with her father to Hase she describes stopping at Kasuga Shrine:

Looking around, I could see it was a charming place with trees all around. The garden had a refreshing air; one wanted so much to drink the water from its pure spring that I could appreciate the refrain in the old folk song, 'One would love to stay.'

Later the entourage continues on to the village of Uji, southeast of the capital, where cormorant fishermen gather at the river.

The carriages are drawn up to trestles. When I get down, the cormorant boats are going back and forth right at my feet. As I have never seen live fish before, I stare in fascination. Even though I was tired from the journey, I watched so avidly that I didn't notice the night was growing late.[17]

Although travel was arduous, pilgrimages offered noblewomen like Michitsuna's Mother an opportunity to move out of their lives at court or at home and a chance to pray for benefit in this life while accruing religious merit. For Michitsuna's Mother, pilgrimage served a therapeutic function – she desires to travel most when she perceives being slighted by her husband or is unhappy with her life in the capital. It was clearly an activity she desired and from which she gained pleasure despite the trials of being on the road.

Poetry and travel diaries

Poetry lies at the core of the *Tosa Journal* and the other vernacular works that were canonised as travel literature within the stream of classical literary diaries. Donald Keene writes:

Diaries composed in Japanese usually contain poems, not as embellishments of the texts but as 'facts'. Indeed, the only documents a woman was likely to possess when writing a diary were the poems composed on a given occasion and noted at the time. Diaries sometimes took the form of a collection of poems arranged chronologically and presented with explanatory materials.[18]

Although the autobiographical works written in the vernacular are usually referred to by scholars as 'diaries', most were composed retrospectively and should thus be considered memoirs. The materials for writing about one's life and the journeys one took would have been memories, poetry exchanges that were copied for future reference, letters, and perhaps sketches recorded while travelling. Poetry was a natural resource to employ for writers attempting to produce memoirs and to prove their literary prowess. Among the works that contributed to the development of literary diaries are 'poetry diaries' (*uta nikki*), which are collections of poetry tied together by prose, such as texts like *The Collected Poems of Lady Ise* (Ise shū, 10th c.).[19]

In addition to being a key ingredient in diaries, poetry functioned as a motivation for travel and something one produced during a journey. By the tenth century there was a long and well-established history of poetic travel. Designated sites, particularly those of the eastern provinces that appeared in early collections, formed a network of locations about which literate travellers were expected to write poems.

The first imperial anthology, the *Kokinshū* (Collection of Ancient and Modern Poems, ca. 905 CE) contains one book (Book Nine) dedicated to 'Travel', encompassing a cycle of fifteen poems which take the reader from China to Japan and from the provinces towards the capital. The 1,111 poems in the collection would have been memorised by anyone skilled at poetry, thus enabling them to conjure up the images found within these poems as they visited the same locations. Four of the *Kokinshū* poems draw from an earlier work, *Tales of Ise*, containing the loci classici for many later travel narratives. Episode 9 in *Tales of Ise* came to be particularly influential for poets. It describes the eastward journey of a man, interpreted by later readers to be the famous poet and lover Ariwara no Narihira (825–880 CE), and includes the poems he composed at Yatsuhashi (Eight Bridges), Mount Utsu, Mount Fuji, and the Sumida River. The most famous of these is his response at seeing the eight bridges which cross eight streams in the province of Mikawa (present Aichi Prefecture).

> Under a tree beside the marsh they dismounted and ate some parched rice. The marsh was full of irises in magnificent bloom. The sight moved a companion to say, 'Make a poem about our journey, with each of the five syllables of ka-ki-tsu-ha-ta ["irises"] at the head of each line.' So he did:

KArakoromo	Robe from far Cathay
KItsutsu narenishi	long and comfortably worn,
TSUma shi areba	bound by love to stay
HAru-baru kinuru	I cover these distances
TAbi wo shi zo omofu	shrouded in melancholy.[20]

The images of irises, eight bridges, parched rice, and a group of companions, along with the sentiments of longing for the capital and one's lover there, are cited in innumerable poems by later generations of travel writers.

Poetic toponyms like Yatsuhashi (Eight Bridges), Mount Utsu, Mount Fuji, and Sumida River were known literally as 'poem pillows' (*utamakura*), the places on which a poem would rest. As Herbert Plutschow notes: 'The famous places of poetry (*utamakura*) are perhaps the most important single element that made fictional travel literature possible.'[21] According to Plutschow, the inclusion of Japanese poetry (*waka*) in a travel diary meant that the author's 'vision of the world of travel was restricted by the rhetorical traditions of travel *waka*'.[22] Thus, as the author passed famous places in a journal, he or she was obliged to reference these locations and the famous poetry associated with them. From a literary perspective, novel experiences on the road were of far less significance than the writer's ability to link the journey to this illustrious history of poetic travel. As I have written elsewhere, 'The ground over which one traveled was always already inscribed by an accretion of poetry from the past, which could be tied to new poetic production through references to famous sites and allusions to their multiple layers of associations.'[23]

In his *Newly Compiled Essence of Poetry* (Shinsen zuinō, date unknown), the poet Fujiwara no Kintō (966–1041 CE) explains the process of writing about a poetic site: 'Many of the people of old would place a poem pillow at the upper hemistich and then express their sentiment in the lower hemistich.'[24] A successful poem subtly conveyed that the poet was able to grasp the implications of the literary site and build on the images associated with that location. Travel to the place itself was not essential – one could compose an effective poem based on an understanding of the set images that poets of the past had utilised. Scholarship on Japanese travel literature has often focused on the problem of fictionality, including unrealistic timelines for journeys, borrowed perspectives, and the representation of sites which an author could not have seen or did not exist. These instances of 'fictionality' are better understood in terms of the significance for travel writers of previous representations of a place and the importance of linking one's experience to tropes and conventions associated with set sites along a route.

The idealised, literary version of famous poetic locations was so familiar to readers of the time that many travellers note their disappointment at arriving and seeing for the first time the actual appearance of the place. When Daughter of Takasue (1008–? CE) finally comes to the most famous poetic site of all, the Eight Bridges, or Yatsuhashi, she finds it fails to live up to its name, writing in *The Sarashina Diary* (ca. 1060 CE): 'Only the place-name Yatsuhashi (Eight Bridges) remains; there is not the merest remnant of any bridges, and nothing else to see, either.'[25] Many of the other literary locations on her journey turn out to be similarly unappealing: the beaches lack white sand and the plants famous for growing on the moors elsewhere are obscured by tall reeds. Yet the author still feels compelled to record these literary locations, even if it is simply to 'signal her knowledge of the famous place' by decrying their lack of embodying poetic ideals.[26]

Later writers follow this example at Yatsuhashi, noting their feelings of loss when the location does not live up to its literary representation from *Tales of Ise*. The noblewoman Lady Nijō (1259–? CE), who describes her life as an itinerant nun in the latter half of her memoir, *The Unrequested Tale* (Towazugatari, ca. 1306 CE), writes:

> At the place known as Eight Bridges, finding that the bridges were gone and the rivers dried up, I felt as though I had lost a friend.

> The web of my troubles still
> Streams out in all directions,
> Yet not a trace remains
> Of the Eight Bridges.[27]

Nijō's poem alludes to the *Tales of Ise* episode by referencing the location of Yatsuhashi (or Eight Bridges), the spider-legged rivers, the physical bridges which she anticipates seeing, and the group of friends who made the journey in the tale. Nijō may be disappointed that her experience of visiting the famous site does not match the poetic history of the location, but this theme of disappointment in itself becomes a convention imitated by later writers.

We have examined travel as a vehicle for poetic play in the *Tosa Journal*, pilgrimage as a source of relief in *The Kagerō Diary*, and the trope of poetic disappointment in *The Sarashina Diary* and the *Unrequested Tale*. The final work presents an appeal through poetry, based on a legal dispute for a woman's right to land and documents, and uses travel as a symbol of her sacrifice.

Travel as poetic appeal

Diary of the Sixteenth Night Moon (ca. 1280 CE), written by Nun Abutsu (1225–1283 CE), is structured as an introduction to her circumstances and a description of her departure preparations, a depiction of her journey, and a record of correspondence after arriving at her destination. Some versions include a final lengthy poem (*chōka*). Nun Abutsu's journey is motivated by her desire to secure an inheritance for her sons after the property of her husband, scion of the most influential family of poets, had been usurped by a stepson. Travelling five hundred kilometres over fourteen days, she made her way from the courtier capital (Kyoto) to the new warrior seat of government in Kamakura in order to plead her case. Her prospects were dim, but by writing about her journey she was able to present it as an act of sacrifice carried out by a loyal widow and mother.

Through a series of poems at famous sites, she demonstrates her command over her husband's poetic teachings, often referencing poems composed by those of his lineage. At Fuji River she ties the act of travel to her efforts to protect her children's futures and to uphold the memory of her husband.

> On the eighteenth as we crossed Fuji River at the barrier to Mino Province, the following poem came to mind:

waga kodomo	Were it not
kimi ni tsukaen	for the sake of
tame naraba	my children and my lord,
wataramashi ya wa	would I be crossing you
Seki no Fujikawa	Fuji River by the barrier?[28]

This serves Nun Abutsu well by showcasing her literary skill while integrating an important location where her husband and his father composed a series of poems. It references the arduous nature of travel, crossing rivers and barriers, while asserting the self-sacrifice she is willing to bear.

Other poems exemplify the compositions one would be expected to produce about famous sites encountered on the road; thus some scholars have argued that she was attempting to produce a travel poetry guide for her children. Allusions to *Tales of Ise* appear frequently, such as the famous capital bird at Sumida River. She introduces an image from Episode 9 of the tale again when (as for travellers before her) Yatsuhashi fails to meet her expectations.

> I heard people say, 'We'll spend the night at Yatsuhashi, Eight Bridges'. Darkness hid the bridges from sight.

sasagani no	As night fell
kumode ayauki	I could not cross
Yatsuhashi o	the dangerous
yūgure kakete	eight-legged spider
wateri kanetsuru	bridge at Yatsuhashi.[29]

The poem follows conventions associated with the famous place but also conveys her precarious state, having journeyed away from the security of her family and patron in the capital in order to lay claim to the land estate and literary documents bequeathed by her husband. She underlines this with poems on the pain of travel sent from friends in the capital.

> As I anxiously awaited news from the capital, I received from a trustworthy messenger what appeared to be a reply from the person to whom I had sent a letter via the mountain ascetic I met at Mount Utsu.

tabigoromo	Accompanied by tears
namida o soete	your travel cloak
Utsu no yama	must have been wet by a drizzle
shigurenu hima mo	even as the rain abates
sazo shigure kemu	on Mount Utsu.[30]

Abutsu's travel poems feature pleas to the gods to grant her wishes, demonstrations of the difficulties of a journey, and a series of pointed references to the poetry of her husband's lineage, thus implying that her children will be deserving heirs to the family's poetic teachings. Taken as a whole, her travelogue offers a legal appeal in poetic form, arguing for her rightful place in the family and her access to contested property. Nun Abutsu's use of a poetic travel diary for these purposes shows the extent to which literary conventions of travel had solidified by the late thirteenth century and could be applied in myriad contexts.

Conclusion

We have seen that for the literate elites of premodern Japan, poetic composition was a key motivation for travel, although the journey itself might be necessitated by pilgrimage, accompaniment of a family member or patron, reassignment to a post outside the capital, or simply the desire to remove oneself from day-to-day life. A journey outside the capital was considered onerous, tiring, difficult, and dangerous, but it served as an opportunity to demonstrate literary talent in the form of diaries and poems that linked the author to famous travellers of the past. The earliest example of a travel diary in the Japanese vernacular, the tenth-century *Tosa Journal*, is unusual in showcasing poetry from a range of passengers making their way towards the capital together, implying that travel poetry could be composed by anyone with literary sensibilities. By the thirteenth century, travel conventions determined where one should stop, who and what one might meet, and what sort of response should be produced as a poem. Although genre conventions and readerly expectations might proscribe narratives that strayed far from those of the past, the travel diary could still be crafted to address personal, political, and even legal concerns through skilful composition of poetry and careful contextualisation with prose. If travel writing involves confronting alterity in the case of English-language works, then in the case of premodern Japan it required a reframing of one's own experiences based on the homogeneity of shared sites and the anticipation that one's encounter might echo or at least enable one to engage with representations of famous past visits.

Notes

1 See Imazeki Toshiko, "'Tabi" no hyōgen to kyokō: Chūsei joryū nikki o chūshin ni', *Chūsei bungaku* 39 (1996) and Inada Toshinori, 'Chūsei kikō bungaku no tabi no shosō to sono imi', *Chūsei bungaku* 39 (1996).

2 Mostow responds to Eric Leed's *The Mind of the Traveler* in constructing a framework for Japanese travel outside the European model. Joshua Mostow, 'The Ovular Journey: Women and Travel in Pre-Modern Japan', in *Pacific Encounters: The Production of Self and Others*, ed. Eva-Marie Kröller et al. (Vancouver: Institute of Asian Research, University of British Columbia, 1997), 124.

3 Herbert Eugen Plutschow, 'Japanese Travel Diaries of the Middle Ages', *Oriens Extremus* 29.1/2 (1982): 2.

4 Japanese literary history is commonly divided into the 'premodern' era before 1868 and the 'modern' era after 1868. Some scholars use 'classical', 'traditional', or 'early' as alternative terms to denote this period. Premodern literature is further divided into the 'ancient' (roughly until 1185 CE), 'medieval' (1185–1603 CE), and 'early modern' (1603–1868 CE) periods. This chapter will focus on works of the Heian period (794–1185 CE).

5 Carl Thompson, *Travel Writing* (New York: Routledge, 2011), 9.

6 Rebecca Steinitz, 'Diaries', in *Encyclopedia of the Literature of Travel and Exploration*, ed. Jennifer Speake (New York: Fitzroy Dearborn, 2003), 1:331–34.

7 Today known as *kanbun*, also referred to as Literary Sinitic. For examples of male-authored court journals, see Joan R. Piggott and Yoshida Sanae, eds., *Teishinkōki: Year 939 in the Journal of Regent Fujiwara no Tadahira* (Ithaca, NY: Cornell University Press, 2002) and Christina Laffin, Joan Piggott, and Yoshida Sanae, eds., *Birth and Death in the Royal House: Selections from Fujiwara no Munetada's Journal Chūyūki* (Ithaca, NY: Cornell University Press, forthcoming).

8 Gustav Heldt, trans., 'Tosa Diary', *Traditional Japanese Literature: An Anthology, Beginnings to 1600*, ed. Haruo Shirane (New York: Columbia University Press, 2007), 204.

9 Helen Craig McCullough, trans., 'A Tosa Journal', in *Classical Japanese Prose: An Anthology*, ed. Helen Craig McCullough (Stanford, CA: Stanford University Press, 1990), 95–96.

10 McCullough, trans., 'A Tosa Journal', 96–97.

11 McCullough, trans., 'A Tosa Journal', 92.

12 The term 'gender-bending' is used four times in Lynne K. Miyake, 'The Tosa Diary: In the Interstices of Gender and Criticism', in *The Woman's Hand: Gender and Theory in Japanese Women's Writing*, ed. Paul Gordon Schalow and Janet A. Walker (Stanford, CA: Stanford University Press, 1996), 41–73.

13 Gustav Heldt, 'Writing Like a Man: Poetic Literacy, Textual Property, and Gender in the *Tosa Diary*', *Journal of Asian Studies* 64.1 (2005): 13.

14 McCullough, trans., 'A Tosa Journal', 102.

15 Sonja Arntzen, trans., *The Kagerō Diary: A Woman's Autobiographical Text from Tenth-Century Japan* (Ann Arbor, MI: Center for Japanese Studies, 1997), 57.

16 Arntzen, *Kagerō Diary*, 153.

17 Arntzen, *Kagerō Diary*, 265.

18 Donald Keene, *Seeds in the Heart: Japanese Literature from Earliest Times to the Late Sixteenth Century* (New York: Columbia University Press, 1999), 359.

19 For an examination and translation of the *Ise shū* see Joshua S. Mostow, *At the House of Gathered Leaves: Short Biographical and Autobiographical Narratives from Japanese Court Literature* (Honolulu, HI: University of Hawai'i Press, 2004).

20 Joshua S. Mostow and Royall Tyler, trans., *The Ise Stories: Ise monogatari* (Honolulu, HI: University of Hawai'i Press, 2010), 32–33.

21 Herbert Plutschow, 'Some Characteristics of Premodern Japanese Travel Literature', *Proceedings of the Association for Japanese Literary Studies* 8 (2007): 27.

22 Plutschow, 'Some Characteristics', 28.

23 Christina Laffin, 'Travel as Sacrifice: Abutsu's Poetic Journey in *Diary of the Sixteenth Night Moon*', *Review of Japanese Culture and Society* 19 (2007): 74.

24 Inishie no hito no ōku moto ni utamakura o okite, sue ni omou kokoro o arawasu. Quoted in Nishiki Hitoshi, 'Utamakura to meisho: waka ni tsutsumareta kuni', *Nihonjin was naze, go shichi go shichi shichi no uta o aishite kita no ka* (Tokyo: Kasama Shoin, 2016), 32.

25 Sonja Arntzen and Itō Moriyuki, trans., *The Sarashina Diary: A Woman's Life in Eleventh-Century Japan* (New York: Columbia University Press, 2014), 104.

26 Arntzen and Itō, *The Sarashina Diary*, 95.

27 Karen Brazell, trans., *The Confessions of Lady Nijō* (Stanford, CA: Stanford University Press, 1973), 183.

28 Christina Laffin, *Rewriting Medieval Japanese Women: Politics, Personality, and Literary Production in the Life of Nun Abutsu* (Honolulu, HI: University of Hawai'i Press, 2013), 156.

29 Christina Laffin, trans., 'Diary of the Sixteenth Night', in *Traditional Japanese Literature: An Anthology, Beginnings to 1600*, ed. Haruo Shirane (New York: Columbia University Press, 2007), 784.

30 Laffin, 'Diary of the Sixteenth Night', 786.

10

GUIDANCE AND ADVICE

Alasdair Pettinger

Introduction

Travel guides and travel narratives are easily distinguished, it would seem. They look different, are designed for different purposes and are usually displayed on different shelves. But it has not always been like this. Until the nineteenth century, a clear distinction between books which provided practical advice for travellers and those which provided accounts of the author's own journey barely existed. The travel guide as modern readers might recognise it did not make its entrance until the 1830s, with the first handbooks published by John Murray in London and Karl Baedeker in Koblenz.[1]

Following a brief account of the emergence and development of the modern guidebook, this chapter identifies its key formal features, before going on to discuss the relationship between the guidebook and the narrative travel writing which emerged as a distinctive form alongside it. I then elaborate on this relationship by way of a closer examination of some exemplary texts by authors from early twentieth-century Europe (D. H. Lawrence and Edith Wharton) and late twentieth-century Caribbean (Maryse Condé).

Their guides responded to – and shaped – the needs of a new kind of traveller in Europe, taking advantage of opportunities offered by improvements in public transport, accommodation and other facilities after the end of the Napoleonic Wars. The aristocrats who formed the majority of those undertaking the Grand Tour in the century before were able to rely on the assistance of servants – both their own and of those to whom they carried letters of introduction.[2] The less affluent middle-class travellers who explored the continent in the 1820s did not have the same entourage or personal connections. Instead they faced the somewhat bewildering dependence on commercial transactions with complete strangers.

Baedeker's foreword to his guide to Germany and Austria begins:

> Its principal object is to keep the traveler at as great a distance from the unpleasant, and often wholly invisible tutelage of hired servants and guides (and in part from the aid of coachmen and hotelkeepers), to assist him in standing on his own feet, to render him independent, and to place him in a position from which he may receive his own impressions with clear eyes and lively heart.[3]

This desire to nurture such an 'independent' traveller remains a powerful force in travel guidebook publishing in the early twenty-first century. Both Murray and Baedeker were well-established publishers when their proprietors saw a gap in the market that only they – as authors – felt they could fill. The volumes were instantly successful and were followed by others in quick succession. The two firms borrowed ideas from each other (both adopting the distinctive red covers, for instance), and for a while agreed not to translate a guide into the other's language if the other had got there first. During the 1860s they became more openly competitive; and the rivals frequently accused each other of plagiarism.

Murray's guides were aimed at a wealthier, more educated traveller, suggested by their classical allusions, and tendency only to list the best establishments. Baedeker guides, which were less expensive, catered for a wider range of budgets, and yet were generally regarded as more accurate and more regularly updated, printed on better paper and as including superior maps. If Baedekers were more popular, Murrays enjoyed more prestige, and were widely considered to be of greater literary quality (the guide to Spain written by Richard Ford is often cited as a classic). But the Baedeker style was not without its champions: Bertrand Russell acknowledged that it was one of his early influences, while Paul Fussell admired Baedeker's 'witty, critical tone' and claimed that he was 'a better writer than the bulk of Victorian novelists'.[4]

Despite a rather overdue attempt to address the shortcomings of the series (which had been losing money for forty years), John Murray sold it in 1901 to the London map-maker Edward Stanford.[5] Baedeker continued to dominate the market until 1914, but its international reputation suffered during World War I through the firm's association with German nationalism.[6] In the 1920s and 30s, other guidebook series emerged, including those produced by the tyre manufacturer Michelin and the Touring Club Italiano, reflecting a new wave of tourism made possible by the motor car. Also influential during this period were the Blue Guides published by Muirhead's in association with Hachette's Guides Bleus in France.

After World War II, the increasing possibilities offered in the age of affordable air travel were catered for by the US publisher Fodor (founded 1949), while from the late 1950s, the emerging phenomenon of student backpackers found guides suited to more modest budgets, such as those published by Frommer's (from 1957), Let's Go (1960), Lonely Planet (1972) and the Rough Guides (1982).

The modern guidebook

For the purposes of this study, I follow the useful definition of the mainstream travel guidebook offered by Victoria Peel and Anders Sørensen:

> [A] commercially distributed entity, made for transient non-locals to be used in the field. It contains place representation and is comprehensive as it includes practical information beyond that of a special interest subject. Yet, it is selective, and by evaluating more than just listing it facilitates a selection process. Authority is asserted through sender identity and through the potential to contend [with] 'official' information.[7]

Implicit in such a definition are several formal characteristics, which have remained relatively consistent since Murray and Baedeker dominated the market in the nineteenth century.

Four key features may be identified. Firstly, the guides strive for comprehensiveness: they aim to provide everything a traveller needs in a single, portable volume, which consequently contains a wide range of material, including practical information and advice; essays on history, culture and politics; maps, plans and illustrations; and (where appropriate) a basic phrase-book and dictionary.[8] To save space, the early guidebooks were often printed in small type, on thin paper; and even when they became more generous with their resources, the text continued to employ a characteristically clipped grammar and to make extensive use of abbreviations and symbols, for example:

> 3 M.; road very dusty; carriage in the afternoon 10 fr., or after 5 p.m. 5–7 fr., fee 1 fr.[9]

> It is seven km (no transport) to the park (and ACG) headquarters (Tel 695–5598) [. . .]
> A 4WD trail leads down to the coast, 12 km away.[10]

Secondly, the practical information tends to be presented as imagined possibilities marked by the use of modal verbs ('might', 'should', 'ought') and non-indicative moods (such as the conditional, imperative and subjunctive) – edited in order not to overwhelm the reader with too many choices, sometimes clearly ranked by preference:

> He can either embark on one of the numerous salt-barges which descend the river [. . .] or [. . .] he must hire a boat for himself.[11]

> Those who are not fatigued may now walk towards the Citadel.[12]

> If you're headed for Tamale, try to get a seat on the STC bus, otherwise you'll have to take a dilapidated private bus which leaves very early in the morning and takes all day.[13]

Early guidebooks tended to be structured as a tour, inviting the reader to follow a set route (often determined by the schedules of mail-coaches or passenger trains). Later this was replaced by a less programmatic arrangement that divided the country or countries into discrete regions and then into towns of decreasing order of importance. In earlier guidebooks such as Baedekers recommendations are often expressed in the passive voice: attractions 'are well worth a visit', 'a fine view is obtained' at a particular spot, a journey 'may be easily made' within a specified period of time.

Sometimes they are addressed to reader in the third person (usually as a generic 'the traveller', 'the visitor' or 'the tourist'), occasionally as someone with more specialised interests: 'the ecclesiologist should pay a visit to Barfreston Church'.[14] The first-person plural is common too: 'Keeping the hill Chaboya to the rt., we reach San Juan de Alfarache'.[15] Murray guidebooks, with their more relaxed and less compressed prose, permitted a wider range of personal pronouns, frequently addressing the reader more directly ('After passing Shebrement you follow the edge of the desert') and, on rare occasions, sometimes allowing the author to make an appearance in the first person, not merely as the source of an opinion ('I believe it is the largest species known in Egypt') but also autobiographically ('What appeared most unaccountable in this island was the existence of horned snakes, one of which I killed near the shore').[16]

After World War II, guidebooks tend to consistently address readers more directly as 'you'. And while advice may be qualified in some way ('If you're the least bit worried about safety, avoid both cities') on other occasions, the imperative takes its gloves off ('Ask before you take photographs of people'), sometimes for compelling reasons ('Never, ever touch any rockets, artillery shells, mortars, mines, bombs or other war material you may come across').[17]

While an author or authors are usually identified (if not always on the cover or the title page), the voice is typically impersonal, suggesting the priorities of the brand rather than the idiosyncrasies of an individual. And when a more personal voice intrudes, it is usually in the form of a mission statement signed by the publisher or series founder. This third characteristic suggests that although the guide wants the reader to know that it draws on the first-hand experience and the research of trusted individuals, its authority relies more heavily on a corporate consistency.

It is a consistency that can embrace a range of styles (gazetteer entry, historical survey, practical information, etiquette tip, rhapsodic description) and degrees of enthusiasm: one study of Lonely Planet's *India* noted the way sites are judged using a small pool of adjectives from 'dismal' to 'spectacular'.[18] Historical background (in the past tense) is clearly demarcated from, and subordinate to, description (in the present tense).[19] Items of information are otherwise clearly distinguished and ranked through the use of inset boxes, different fonts and typefaces, bullet points, icons and asterisks. Perhaps the best known of these is 'the Baedeker parenthesis', which interrupts, often bathetically, a descriptive passage in one register with a succinct, practical remark in another:

> The pier affords a pleasant and interesting promenade (donkey 1–2 fr., according to the time), commanding beautiful views of the bay and the mountains enclosing it.[20]

Although a guidebook may be the work of many contributors (including readers, who are invited to notify the publisher of errors and omissions), it is very unusual for conflicting views to be allowed to disrupt the self-confident tone of the institutional 'author' who must avoid any impression of partiality, let alone controversy, in its judgements.[21]

Finally, the guidebook tends to assume a certain kind of reader. While a travelogue represents a journey that has already taken place, the guidebook offers a fantasy that the reader is invited to act out.[22] Baedeker rather than Murray turned out to be the model here, making fewer assumptions about the wealth and education of the person the guide is aimed at, but still targeting those middle-class readers affluent enough to afford overseas travel and able to get time off work to do so, with tastes tending towards the appreciation of nature, art and historical monuments, but not excluding sport or shopping.[23]

A considerable degree of variation is possible. Paul Fussell detected a shift from the 'learning' encouraged by Baedeker to the 'consumption' at the heart of Fodor.[24] And there are clearly differences between the young backpacker targeted by some modern guides and the anglers and amateur botanists, the sick and the convalescent assumed to be among the readers of their Victorian and Edwardian forerunners.[25] One study argues that Lonely Planet's 'alternative' image is 'upheld by establishing affordability, authenticity and tragedy as primary nodal points'.[26] But as the brand began to specifically address, say, women or disabled travellers, and cater for a more affluent audience, this image would be repeatedly redefined.[27] However, what remains relatively constant is the assumption (announced by Baedeker in the 1850s) that the reader is a self-consciously independent traveller, one who feels free to choose from a carefully curated range of destinations and activities that will allow them to enjoy new experiences without falling into danger.[28]

Publishers of guidebooks are understandably nervous about criticisms that might damage their reputation for accuracy and honesty. Many refuse to carry advertising and prohibit their authors from accepting gifts in order to reduce commercial pressures on their editorial, but scandals occasionally surface. In an interview promoting his 'swashbuckling' memoir, *Do Travel Writers Go to Hell?*, Thomas Kohnstamm claimed to have fabricated his contribution to the Lonely Planet guide to Colombia, although the publishers insisted this itself was a fabrication.[29]

If reviews of guidebooks are primarily concerned to identify factual errors, undue favouritism or commercial bias, academic studies tend to demonstrate their ideological presuppositions. In the late 1950s, Roland Barthes took the Blue Guide to Spain to task in his series of essays that explored the workings of what he called bourgeois 'myth': the tendency to reduce history to nature. In the case of the guidebook, this was accomplished by presenting a world where time stood still, populated by ancient monuments, wild landscapes and ethnic stereotypes. From the

1990s this approach has been supplemented by more avowedly post-colonial analyses, with Lonely Planet the subject of many of them.[30] They typically argue that guidebooks consolidate the national identities of readers and shape their attitudes to other cultures, often recycling xenophobic and racist stereotypes, often in accordance with prevailing Western geopolitical priorities. The economic and environmental impact of the activities recommended by the guides is rarely scrutinised by them in depth.

While there may be some truth in such claims, these studies, as Debbie Lisle has argued, often fail to recognise that modern guidebooks are more self-critical than this. In her own essay on Lonely Planet, she shows how an older 'colonial' sensibility has given way to a more self-critical 'humanitarian' outlook that acknowledges global inequalities and the damages as well as the benefits of tourism to developing economies and fragile environments, and proudly donates some of its profits to Greenpeace and various aid projects. The problem, she insists, lies not so much with the publisher's attitudes (which have changed) but with the underlying 'ethical community' established between the brand and the reader, which doesn't just specify what is worth seeing or knowing, but dictates the terms of what counts as the right, responsible, way to travel. Furthermore, it silences those outside this community – the 'irresponsible' travellers, and, more pertinently, the local people who rarely feature in guidebooks, except as helpful intermediaries (such as taxi-drivers or bar-tenders) or picturesque bystanders (especially in the accompanying photographs). It offers no way for the traveller to meaningfully engage with them or appreciate their complex everyday lives.[31] Such arguments long pre-date Lonely Planet. Rudy Koshar, for example, suggested that 'Baedeker descriptions' offered their readers an 'image of a society depopulated by the neutron bomb [. . .] The monuments, churches, and great factories still stood, but most inhabitants had made a mysterious exit, leaving an eerily "post-human" world behind'.[32]

In the early twenty-first century, some guidebook writers, such as Steven K. Bailey, have responded to the scholarly criticisms of the genre by developing 'alternative rhetorical strategies': Bailey acknowledges the choices he makes as author, writes in the first person and takes care to avoid both stereotyping his subjects and making assumptions about the identities and capacities of his readers.[33] Others, working independently, have produced more experimental, light-hearted introductions to the areas in which they live, exploring quotidian details and personal associations normally beyond the scope of conventional guides.[34]

Travel narratives and anti-tourism

Alongside the modern guidebook emerged a new kind of travel narrative, one which eschewed or belittled, rather than embraced, the opportunities made possible by the tourist infrastructure of railways, steamboats, hotels, restaurants and souvenir shops. James Buzard has shown how many nineteenth-century travel books practised an aggressive form of anti-tourism, authored by individuals who sought to wander more spontaneously 'off the beaten track' and produce accounts of unique experiences that record their feelings and impressions rather than describe the people and places they encountered.[35]

In the nineteenth century, travel narratives, or travel sketches, marked their distance from the guidebooks of Murray and Baedeker in various ways. These texts were, like novels and short stories, written in flowing prose, in a relatively consistent style and appearance, broken only occasionally, if at all, by maps or illustrations. Narrated in the first-person past indicative, their primary purpose was to acquaint the reader with the author's subjective response to landscapes and other cultures, not to trace routes or describe places so he or she can follow the same path in the future. In some cases, as Buzard has remarked, the writing would become so impressionistic that it became impossible to extract any practical information from them at all.[36]

Perhaps the most obvious demonstration of this anti-tourism is the travel narrative's frequent derogatory references to guidebooks. In Antwerp, William Makepeace Thackeray claimed to have seen in half an hour more than a hundred British tourists carrying 'the ubiquitous Murray'.[37] Over a century later, Dervla Murphy remarked, of Uganda: 'All these backpackers seem to be coming from or going to the same places and using the same guidebook – the *Lonely Planet*, ironically'.[38] The disparaging image of another traveller 'clutching' a guidebook or with their head (or nose) 'buried' in one remains common currency, despite the evidence that most people use guidebooks selectively and critically, in conjunction with many other sources of knowledge.[39]

Every generation, it seems, must repeat such gestures of territorial demarcation, not least because the line between the two genres is not always clear. In *Abroad*, Paul Fussell asserted confidently that while a guidebook 'is addressed to those who plan to follow the traveler', a travel narrative 'is addressed to those who do not plan to follow the traveler at all, but who require the exotic or comic anomalies, wonders, and scandals of the literary form *romance* which their own place or time cannot entirely supply'.[40] But, as Patrick Holland and Graham Huggan point out, travel narratives are frequently used *as* guidebooks. They refer, for instance, to sightings of travellers in Patagonia consulting Bruce Chatwin's book as a guide; and remind us that even when such books are left at home, they help to create an appetite for travel and certain destinations in the first place.[41]

To complicate matters further, many of the formal devices characteristic of the guidebook are often used in travel narratives too. Sometimes, they are gently subverted for humorous effect. For example, in *Hong Kong* (1990), Jan Morris wryly adapts the impersonal form of address to refer to herself in particular, while simultaneously flattering those readers who would share her heightened sense of curiosity: 'you may be tempted to go to your cabin and sleep, but if you happen to be writing a book, you will prefer to stick it out on deck'.[42]

More commonly, the rhetorical strategies that guidebooks use to help readers imagine themselves *in situ*, are deployed less self-consciously than Morris does. But because they don't form part of the usual repertoire of conventional literary travel writing, they carry a little extra significance. On the one hand, they may remind the reader that the author participates in the rituals of tourism as much as anyone else. In Cuba, notes Martha Gellhorn parenthetically, 'you can hire, with or without driver, a small Russian Lada sedan belonging to INTUR, the Ministry of Tourism', before choosing to do just that.[43] On the other hand, they may, when inserted inappropriately, convey the opposite: that the journey we are following is precisely not a recreational one. 'As you walk through the industrial towns you lose yourself in labyrinths of little brick houses blackened by smoke', writes George Orwell, setting the scene in *The Road to Wigan Pier*.[44] Recounting a difficult passage across mud banks near the Dead Sea, Gertrude Bell momentarily abandons the first-person past indicative to explain that they 'are not high [. . .] but the crests of them are so sharp and the sides so precipitous that the traveller must find his way across and round them with the utmost care'.[45] In both passages, the slip into the language characteristic of guidebooks only serves to mark out how far from a casual tour are the journeys narrated by these books.

When Zora Neale Hurston describes her hometown, Eatonville, Florida, as a 'city of five lakes, three croquet courts, three hundred brown skins, three hundred good swimmers, plenty guavas, two schools, and no jail-house', the clipped, informational prose of the guidebook is converted, with gentle humour, into a poetic celebration of black self-reliance.[46] In other travel books, the guidebook's inelegant catalogue of social facts is adopted without irony. 'Miami is a conservative town, its population composed of refugees from Castro's Cuba, retired Yankees and relatively poor black and white Floridians': this opening sentence from a chapter in Edmund White's *States of Desire* could easily have been lifted from any number of contemporaneous works of non-fiction.[47] Holland and Huggan remark that White's book 'vacillates between the informative mode of the guidebook and the personal, anecdotal style of the travelogue' as if this was unusual.[48]

However, Terry Caesar has suggested that all travel narratives, insofar as they are claiming to be reporting objective facts (describing places rather than the author's subjective response to them), owe a great deal to guidebooks, and that we often underestimate the extent to which 'guidebooks govern the procedures by which any other species of writing on travel is to be considered'.[49]

Going to Italy: D. H. Lawrence and Edith Wharton

'The Baedeker is very nice: I love its plans and maps and panoramas', wrote D. H. Lawrence in November 1916.[50] His enthusiasm might suggest that it was his first encounter with one of the famous guidebooks, but his biographer, John Worthen, believes it 'almost certain' that Lawrence carried a Baedeker on his first trip to Italy with his future wife Frieda, as they travelled from Bavaria to Lake Garda in August 1912.[51] They rented the ground floor of a villa near Gargnano on the western shore of the lake, a few miles over what was then the Austrian border, and stayed until the following April.

The couple would have arrived by steamer, following (in reverse) Route 40 in Baedeker's *Northern Italy*, but no reference to guidebooks appears in the three essays by Lawrence which were published in the *English Review* in 1913 under the title 'By the Lago di Garda'.[52] They disembarked at the most northerly village of the Gardone-Riviera, 'since 1885 a favourite winter-resort for consumptive and nervous invalids, while in the spring and autumn it is frequented by those in search of rest and refreshment', according to the guidebook, which adds: 'The visitors are chiefly Germans'.[53] But the only visitors to appear in these essays are Lawrence himself and (very infrequently) his partner, who, never named, on just two occasions forces the dominant 'I' to become 'we' (59, 69).

Gargnano itself merits only a few lines in Baedeker:

> **Gargnano** (P; *Hôt. Gargnano*, R. 2–3, pens. 6–8 fr., *Cervo*, R. 2–3, B. 1, pens. 7–8 fr., both near the quay, plain but good), an important-looking village (1200 inhab.) amidst lemon and olive plantations, marks the N. limit of the Riviera. The former *Franciscan Monastery* (13th cent.) possesses fine Gothic cloisters.[54]

To write three essays about it would seem to contradict the guidebook's implicit judgement that the place is of little interest. The parenthetical '1200 inhab.' are reduced to a statistical qualifier, like the age of a building. What matters are the two hotels, a former monastery and lemon and olive plantations. As Paul Eggert points out, Baedeker is interested in many things about northern Italy except the northern Italians themselves, who are 'the most notable absence' from the guide.[55] By contrast, Lawrence's essays (which include very few place-names) revolve around detailed encounters and conversations with local people who are usually named.

Lawrence revised these essays and added new material for his book *Twilight in Italy* (1916).[56] This book features long passages of didactic pronouncements of a philosophical character, with capitalised abstract nouns, and is characterised by a more sombre, melancholic mood, the narrator aware of how the war has since changed the world he is describing, thus turning its face more firmly away from the concerns of the guidebook. On the other hand, he seems less concerned to make tourism disappear. More than once Lawrence records being greeted with 'the usual question': asked if he is German or Austrian, alluding to the influx of visitors invisible in the earlier essays (179, 196, 208). And this is balanced by the way he is more attuned also to the movement of Italians leaving, devoting one chapter to encounters with men who have gone abroad to find work (189–204).

In the final chapter, recounting a return visit to Italy he made in September 1913, crossing Switzerland mostly on foot, he notes that '[e]verywhere are the hotels and the foreigners' who seem to 'overshadow' the 'native population' (214). He records several encounters with other travellers, most memorably an exhausted young hiker from South London, packing in the most extensive itinerary his two-week holiday will allow (209, 218–22, 210–12). Asked when he plans to move on, he pulls out 'a guidebook with a timetable' (211). Lawrence cannot understand why he had not taken the train to save his legs. One critic describes him as 'the ever despised tourist on his packaged holiday', but Lawrence's response is not straightforward.[57] He pities him, then decides he hates him for cowardly rushing back to his day job, but cannot resist holding him up as a model of athleticism to shame the overweight, sedentary landlord of the inn (212).

Lawrence's travel writings of 1913–16 tend to mark their difference from guidebooks indirectly, silently departing from their conventions, his occasional allusions to the existence of other travellers not automatically disparaging. By contrast, Edith Wharton's *Italian Backgrounds* (1905) explicitly embraces anti-tourism. Its condemnation of the ubiquitous 'red volumes' might almost be its manifesto.[58] 'One of the rarest and most delicate pleasures of the continental tourist' (85), Wharton writes, is to circumvent the compiler of his guidebook, to seek out the 'parentheses of travel', either by going a different way from the crowds (she makes a point of visiting 'an obscure monastery' that 'many of the people whom we questioned had never even heard of') (86) or by going the same way at different times (she imagines the advantages of visiting Milan at the height of summer: 'think of the empty hotels and railway carriages, the absence of tourists and Baedekers!' [19]).

Thus, while the opening pages invite us to reconstruct a journey that silently corresponds to Routes 96 and 97 in Baedeker's *Switzerland* (1893) (from Thusis into Italy over the pass to Chiavenna and points south), Wharton decides to tarry in Splügen, a small town on the Swiss side of the border where one would normally expect only to change coaches. Like Gargnano, its entry in the guidebook is brief:

> 32½ M. **Splügen** (4757'; pop. 424; *Hôt. Bodenhaus*, R., L. & A. 3½, D. 3, pens. 7–8fr.; *Hôt. Splügen*, R. 2. fr.), the capital of the Rheinwaldthal, enlivened by the traffic on the Splügen and Bernadino routes. A pleasant walk leads to the ruined castle on the old road (pretty view down the valley and of the Piz Tambo).[59]

Lawrence may have privately extolled his choice in passing as 'not a bit touristy',[60] but Wharton publicly justifies hers at great length:

> It is not easy, in the height of the Swiss season, to light on a nook neglected by the tourist; but at Splügen he still sweeps by in a cloud of diligence dust, or pauses only to gulp a flask of Paradiso and a rosy trout from the Suretta lakes. One's enjoyment of the place is thus enhanced by the pleasing spectacle of the misguided hundreds who pass it by, and from the vantage of the solitary meadows above the village one may watch the throngs descending on Thusis or Chiavenna with something of the satisfaction that mediaeval schoolmen believed to be the portion of angels looking down upon the damned.
>
> *(5)*

Terry Caesar wonders if the word 'nook' indicates a specifically female logic – toying with the possibility that women travel writers are more likely to seek alternatives to the paternalistic form of the guidebook than men.[61] Whether this holds or not (and Caesar recommends caution here), Wharton not only condemns the guidebook but resolutely departs from its conventions – making extensive use of narrative devices common in fiction and avoiding its favoured mode, the picturesque (and ensured that illustrations depicting landscape in the initial magazine publication were dropped when the articles were published as a book).[62] And yet, for all the way its prose – with its long sentences, exclamations, questions, strings of subordinate clauses – marks its difference from the style of a guidebook, *Italian Backgrounds* is frequently as prescriptive as Baedeker, if somewhat masked by the use of 'one' rather than 'the traveller' or 'he'.

Furthermore, despite Wharton's attempt to convey the delights of Splügen, it is clear that she soon tires of them. For all its proximity to the frontier, the town, she admits, remained 'stolidly, immovably Swiss' (18). 'We seemed to be living in the landscape of a sanatorium prospectus' (17). And as the Baedeker could have told her, she is anxious to move on. Her decision to stay has yielded nothing special; it is exposed as perverse and bloody-minded. It is as if being an anti-tourist is not a means to an end but an end in itself; her pleasure comes not from avoiding tourists but from observing them superciliously at a distance, 'looking down upon the damned', as she puts it. But in the end, like everyone else, '[w]e took our seats and the driver turned his horses toward the Splügen pass' (20).

'Let's cross Salt River': Maryse Condé on Guadeloupe

The essays by Lawrence and Wharton owe little to the language and structure of guidebooks. Given Lawrence's frequent indifference to other travellers and Wharton's compulsion to look down on them, this is not surprising. But critical reflections on tourism by travel writers can take many forms. One of them is to directly engage with the guidebook by adopting – or rather adapting – some of its distinctive characteristics, in ways that invite readers to question the kinds of choices it usually suggests.

Turning to the other end of the twentieth century, we find several creative writers from the Caribbean who have self-consciously reworked the guidebook from the point of view of locals rather than visitors. The best known is *A Small Place* (1988) by Jamaica Kincaid. Its opening sentence – 'If you go to Antigua as a tourist, this is what you will see' – with its direct address to the reader, the use of the conditional and the certainty with which the narrator promises a certain experience, advertises the recognisable mode in which she will proceed, only to transform it into an excoriation of white privilege.

Here, however, I will focus on a less well-known work, published the same year: *Guadeloupe* by Maryse Condé.[63] Like Kincaid, Condé grew up in the Caribbean and spent much of her adult life abroad, and has produced an equally powerful, unconventional portrait of her homeland that draws heavily on the rhetoric of the guidebook. But while *A Small Place* was published as a slim paperback that announced it unmistakably as a literary essay, *Guadeloupe* looks quite different.

It is a lavishly illustrated coffee-table book, published in a series that includes volumes on (among others) Sierra Leone, Yemen, Senegal and Portugal, and belongs to that sub-category of guidebook that is designed to introduce the tourist to a possible destination rather than provide practical information that one packs in one's luggage. On the front cover, Maryse Condé shares the credit with the photographer Jean du Boisberranger.[64]

Like Kincaid, Condé adopts a number of rhetorical features of the guidebook (addressing the reader as 'you', expertly attuned to the expectations and inclinations of the tourist) while encouraging them to think and act otherwise, even if they are not easily amenable to such persuasion. A recurring tactic is to invoke a guidebook certainty and then immediately qualify it as opinion ('so we are told' ['nous dit-on']) or as one of 'a good number of received ideas' ['un bon nombre d'idées reçues'] that is open to question (10). However, when Condé offers an alternative perspective, she qualifies this, too, as subjective ('I am biased, that's obvious' ['Je suis partiale, c'est evident']) (29), as the product of a personal experience that she is unwilling to endow with unassailable authority; indeed, the text draws on childhood memories and expresses the author's likes and dislikes in a way that *A Small Place* does not, giving the book a much less dogmatic, didactic feel. In fact, while Kincaid attempts to set touristic illusion against a version of reality that appears uncontestable, Condé seems to want to cast doubt on whether Guadeloupe is knowable at all. Even while she hopes to have broken down some preconceptions, she makes it clear that there is much more to discover. The history and social analysis she provides – touching on the economic and political dependence of the islands, and the suppression (and qualified resurgence) of local linguistic and cultural forms – is suggestive rather than programmatic.

In keeping with the demands of the series to which it belongs, *Guadeloupe* is much closer to the organisational conventions of the guidebook than *A Small Place*, at least in the first quarter of the book, in which the author invites the reader to accompany her – 'let's cross Salt River' ['traversons la Riviere Salée'] (12); 'let's rejoin the main highway' ['Retrouvons la route nationale'] (20) – on a tour which can be followed on the stylised, pictorial map which appears at the front, and the final quarter which features visits to the smaller outlying islands. But even here, Condé, a self-confessed 'bad guide' ['mauvaise guide'] (28), departs provocatively from the standard itinerary by ignoring the largest town, Pointe-à-Pitre, and other resorts of Grande Terre (except to acknowledge the tourist's inclination to remain there), and devotes most of her attention to the island of Basse Terre.[65]

> You have already understood as you have followed me that I don't like the sun simply pouring down on the sea and Club Med-style group activities. My Guadeloupe is a little more rainy and more than that, a little sullen, not a bit modern, not laughing with all its teeth showing at the first thing that comes along. [Vous l'avez déjà compris à me suivre, je n'aime pas le soleil versé à pleines mains sur la mer et les plaisirs de groupes, styles Club Méditerranée. Ma Guadeloupe, un peu pluvieuse et même beaucoup, un peu morose, pas moderne pour un sou, ne rit pas de toutes ses dents au premier venu].
>
> *(26)*[66]

Occasionally, despite her detours, she manages to mention some of the brochure highlights – 'Let's not forget that this is where Columbus discovered Guadeloupe' ['C'est, n'oublions pas, le lieu de la découverte de la Guadeloupe par Christophe Colomb'] (20); 'Make sure [. . .] you stop before the plaque commemorating the death of Delgrès and the mulatta Solitude' ['Ne manquez pas [. . .] de vous arrêter devant la plaque commémorant la fin de Delgrès et de la mulâtresse Solitude'] (26) – although one may also read them as if they were interruptions from the Tourist Board of Guadeloupe (thanked for its assistance in small print at the very beginning and end of the book) trying to rein in Condé's errant prose.

And this prose is somewhat dwarfed by the glossy, colour photographs which depict inviting scenery and picturesque locals, images often at odds with the glimpses of 'my Guadeloupe' evoked in the text, although sometimes – serendipitously? – underscoring its point (immediately above the remark about 'not laughing with all its teeth showing' is a picture of a tight-lipped elderly woman looking directly at the camera). As Peter Hitchcock admits, it is 'a gamble, of course, to use the form of tourism for a narrative that deconstructs the exotic imaginary'.[67] Yet the subtle way in which Condé invites her readers to join her in an alternative tour, indulgent enough to allow them to take a speedboat trip while she waits patiently in the harbour (108), arguably has more chance of them boarding their plane home with more understanding (59) than the readers of *A Small Place*, even if it goes no further than recognising how complicated and elusive Caribbean identity is.

Conclusion: the art of travel

Of the three texts chosen for my case studies here, *Guadeloupe* has the closest relation to a long tradition of writing, related to the guidebook, devoted to what might be called 'the art of travel', which aims to cultivate a certain travelling sensibility or heightened awareness when travelling.

Despite its focus on a particular destination, what is distinctive about Condé's unusual guidebook is less its factual content than the strategies it adopts to persuade her readers to break well-established habits. Instead of promising them comprehensiveness, offering everything they need to know or want to hear, she casts doubt on the information she provides or withholds it altogether, asking questions more often than giving answers. By intensifying the visitor's curiosity, rather than satisfying it, and coaxing them towards the unexpected, *Guadeloupe* in the end encourages tourists to take risks, and follow itineraries and pursue activities the author cannot anticipate.

To this extent, its agenda overlaps with those playful self-help books which adapt the imperative mood of the travel guide to issue more open-ended proposals. 'Make a list of all the smells in your neighbourhood', suggests Keri Smith in *How to Be an Explorer of the World* (2008); 'Allow something (or someone) else to choose what direction you head in'.[68] In *Counter-Tourism* (2012) we find injunctions to 'Exchange kisses with a statue' and 'Compare the car parks of different heritage attractions'.[69] They build on the work of Latourex ('*Laboratoire du Tourisme Expérimentale*') established in Strasbourg in 1990, best known to Anglophone readers through the *Lonely Planet Guide to Experimental Travel* (2005).[70] It is with a discussion of this text that Justin D. Edwards and Rune Graulund choose to begin their study of 'innovative travel writing' because it 'does not seek to impose its own new boundaries on travel but to traverse, transform and negotiate conceptions of what contemporary mobility might have to offer us all'.[71] Further investigation of guidebooks could do worse than take off from there.

Notes

1 James Buzard, *The Beaten Track: European Tourism, Literature, and the Ways to 'Culture', 1800–1918* (Oxford: Oxford University Press, 1993), 65–79. For further background on the Baedeker and Murray guides see also Edward Mendelson, 'Baedeker's Universe', *Yale Review of Books* 74.3 (1985); Esther Allen, '"Money and Little Red Books": Romanticism, Tourism, and the Rise of the Guidebook', *LIT: Literature Interpretation Theory* 7.2–3 (1996); Gráinne Goodwin and Gordon Johnston, 'Guidebook Publishing in the Nineteenth Century: John Murray's *Handbooks for Travellers*', *Studies in Travel Writing* 17.1 (2013). For histories of the guidebook which emphasise its pre-modern antecedents, see Nicholas T. Parsons, *Worth the Detour: A History of the Guidebook* (Stroud: The History Press, 2007); and Giles Barber, 'The English–Language Guide Book to Europe up to 1870' in *Journeys through the Market: Travel, Travellers and the Book Trade*, edited by Robin Myers and Michael Harris (New Castle, DE: Oak Knoll Press, 1999).

2 Mendelson, 'Baedeker's Universe', 387.

3 K. Baedeker, *Deutschland und das Österreichische Ober-Italien: Handbuch für Reisende, Vol. 1: Österreich, Süd- und West-Deutschland, Venedig und Lombardei* (Coblenz: Karl Baedeker, 1858), iii, quoted (and translated) in Mendelson, 'Baedeker's Universe', 387–8.

4 Bertrand Russell, 'How I Write' in *The Basic Writings of Bertrand Russell*, ed. Robert E. Egner and Lester E. Denonn (London: Routledge, 1961), 35; Paul Fussell, *Abroad: British Literary Traveling Between the Wars* (New York: Oxford University Press, 1980), 62–3.

5 Goodwin and Johnston, 'Guidebook Publishing', 43–5.

6 Mark D. Larabee, 'Baedekers as Casualty: Great War Nationalism and the Fate of Travel Writing', *Journal of the History of Ideas* 71.3 (2010): 473–7.

7 Victoria Peel and Anders Sørensen, *Exploring the Use and Impact of Travel Guidebooks* (Bristol: Channel View, 2016), 29.

8 Ali Behdad sees a certain obsessiveness here, the accumulation of detail exceeding any conceivable practical purpose, and instead signifying 'completeness': *Belated Travelers: Orientalism in the Age of Colonial Dissolution* (Cork: Cork University Press, 1994), 45–6.

9 K. Baedeker, ed., *Egypt: Handbook for Travellers. Part First: Lower Egypt* (Leipzig: Karl Baedeker, 1878), 219.

10 Nancy Keller et al., *Central America: A Lonely Planet Shoestring Guide*, 2nd edition (Hawthorn, Victoria: Lonely Planet, 1996), 506.

11 *A Handbook for Travellers in Southern Germany* (London: John Murray, 1837), 15.

12 Baedeker, *Egypt*, 284.

13 Alex Newton, *West Africa: A Travel Survival Kit* (South Yarra, Victoria: Lonely Planet, 1988), 184.

14 Karl Baedeker, *Great Britain: Handbook for Travellers* (Leipzig: Karl Baedeker, 1887), 17

15 Richard Ford, *Handbook for Travellers in Spain: Part I*, 3rd edition (London: John Murray, 1855), 214.

16 *A Handbook for Travellers in Egypt* (London: John Murray, 1867), 234–6.

17 Newton, *West Africa*, 46; Ross Velton, *Haiti and the Dominican Republic* (Chalfont St Peter: Bradt, 1999), 23; Chris Taylor, Tony Wheeler and Daniel Robinson, *Cambodia: A Lonely Planet Travel Survival Kit*, 2nd edition (Hawthorn, Victoria: Lonely Planet, 1996), 58.

18 On the adjectival ranking see Deborah P. Bhattacharyya, 'Mediating India: An Analysis of a Guidebook', *Annals of Tourism Research* 24.2 (1997): 381–2.

19 Behdad, *Belated Travelers*, 43–7.

20 Baedeker, *Egypt*, 405. The term 'Baedeker parenthesis' was coined by Mendelson, 'Baedeker's Universe', 387. The device was famously parodied by E. M. Forster – 'The view from Rocca (small gratuity) is finest at sunset' – in *Where Angels Fear to Tread* (1905; repr. London: Penguin, 2007), 13.

21 Bhattacharyya, 'Mediating India', 375–6. Claims to objectivity are challenged in studies of guidebooks to the Philippines, Vietnam and Israel by Scott Laderman, 'Guidebooks', in *The Routledge Companion to Travel Writing*, ed. Carl Thompson (Abingdon: Routledge, 2016), 258–68.

22 Behdad, *Belated Travelers*, 42–3.

23 The enduring alignment of the guidebook with the picturesque – requiring and nurturing a level of refinement previously thought the exclusive property of the upper classes – invites further study. See Inderpal Grewal, *Home and Harem: Nation, Gender, Empire and the Culture of Travel* (Leicester: Leicester University Press, 1996), 97–102; Roland Barthes, 'The Blue Guide', in *Mythologies*, translated by Annette Lavers (1957; repr. St Albans: Granada, 1973), 74.

24 Fussell, *Abroad*, 62.

25 Paul Eggert, 'Discourse versus Authorship: The Baedeker Travel Guide and D. H. Lawrence's *Twilight in Italy*' in *Texts and Textuality: Textual Instability, Theory and Interpretation*, ed. Philip G Cohen (London: Routledge, 1997), 210–11; Jonathan Keates, *The Portable Paradise: Baedeker, Murray, and the Victorian Guidebook* (London: Notting Hill Editions, 2011), 66–85.

26 Matthew Tegelberg, 'Hidden Sights: Tourism, Representation and Lonely Planet Cambodia', *International Journal of Cultural Studies* 13.5 (2010): 498.

27 See especially the study of the various editions of Lonely Planet's *Australia*, from 1977 to 2011 in Peel and Sørensen, *Exploring Travel Guidebooks*, 61–83.

28 Rudy Koshar, *German Travel Cultures* (Oxford: Berg, 2000), 204–12.

29 Thomas B. Kohnstamm, *Do Travel Writers Go to Hell? A Swashbuckling Tale of High Adventure, Questionable Ethics and Professional Hedonism* (Millers Point, NSW: Murdoch Books, 2008). See Haroon Siddique, 'Lonely Planet Writer Plays Down "Fake" Reviews', *Guardian*, 14 April 2008, www.theguardian.com/uk/2008/apr/14/10.

30 Barthes, 'The *Blue Guide*'. For an overview of scholarly treatments of the guidebook, and the overwhelming emphasis on Lonely Planet, see Peel and Sørensen, *Exploring Travel Guidebooks*, 31–69, esp. 58.

31 Debbie Lisle, 'Humanitarian Travels: Ethical Communication in Lonely Planet Guidebooks', *Review of International Studies* 34.S1 (2008): 161–5.

32 Koshar, *Travel Cultures*, 50.

33 Steven K Bailey, 'From 香港 to Hà Nội: Travel Guidebook Writing as a Political Act', in *Politics, Identity, and Mobility in Travel Writing*, ed. Miguel A. Cabañas et al. (New York: Routledge, 2016), 225–37. See also Jenny Walker, 'From "Colour and Flair" to "A Corporate View": Evolutions in Guidebook Writing: An Interview with Jenny Walker', *Studies in Travel Writing* 21.2 (2017): 208–20.

34 See, for example, Stephen Hodge et al., *An Exeter Mis-Guide* ([Exeter]: Wrights & Sites, 2003); Kate Pocrass and Patrick J. Kavanagh, *Mundane Journeys* (San Francisco, CA: Mundane Journeys, 2004).

35 Buzard, *The Beaten Track*, esp. 80–216.

36 Buzard, *The Beaten Track*, 169–72.

37 William Makepeace Thackeray, *Little Travels and Roadside Sketches*, in *The Works of William Makepeace Thackeray* (London: Smith, Elder & Co, 1869), 22:178. See also 179–80, 198, 203.

38 Dervla Murphy, *The Ukimwi Road: From Kenya to Zimbabwe* (London: John Murray, 1993), 78.

39 Peel and Sørensen, *Exploring the Travel Guidebook*, esp. 110–30.

40 Fussell, *Abroad*, 203.

41 Holland and Huggan, *Tourists with Typewriters*, 9, 200.

42 Jan Morris, *Hong Kong: The End of an Empire* (London: Penguin, 1990), 16.

43 Martha Gellhorn, 'Cuba Revisited', *Granta* 10, 'In Trouble Again: A Special Issue of Travel Writing' (1986): 110.

44 George Orwell, *The Road to Wigan Pier* (1937; repr. London: Penguin, 1989), 46.

45 Gertrude Bell, *The Desert and the Sown: Travels in Palestine and Syria* (1907; repr. New York: Dover, 2008), 12.

46 Zora Neale Hurston, *Mules and Men* (1935; repr. Bloomington, IN: Indiana University Press, 1978), 6.

47 Edmund White, *States of Desire: Travels in Gay America* (London: Picador, 1986), 194.

48 Holland and Huggan, *Tourists*, 151.

49 Terry Caesar, *Forgiving the Boundaries: Home as Abroad in American Travel Writing* (Athens, GA: University of Georgia Press, 1995), 96.

50 D. H. Lawrence, *The Letters of D. H. Lawrence, Volume III: 1916–21*, ed. James T. Boulton and Andrew Robertson (Cambridge: Cambridge University Press, 1984), 35.

51 John Worthen, *D. H. Lawrence: The Early Years, 1885–1912* (Cambridge: Cambridge University Press, 1991), 571.

52 D. H. Lawrence, 'By the Lago di Garda' (1913) in *Twilight in Italy and Other Essays*, ed. Paul Eggert (Cambridge: Cambridge University Press, 1994), 51–80. Further references will be included parenthetically in the text.

53 Karl Baedeker, *Northern Italy, including Leghorn, Florence, Ravenna and Routes through France, Switzerland, and Austria: Handbook for Travellers* (Leipzig: Karl Baedeker, 1906), 233.

54 Baedeker, *Northern Italy*, 234.

55 Eggert, 'Discourse versus Authorship', 212.

56 D. H. Lawrence, *Twilight in Italy* (1916) in *Twilight in Italy and Other Essays*, ed. Paul Eggert (Cambridge: Cambridge University Press, 1994), 89–226. Further references will be included parenthetically in the text.

57 Robert Burden, 'Home Thoughts from Abroad: Cultural Difference and the Critique of Modernity in D. H. Lawrence's *Twilight in Italy* (1916) and Other Travel Writing', in *Landscapes and Englishness*, ed. Robert Burden and Stephan Kohl (Amsterdam: Rodopi, 2006), 160.

58 Edith Wharton, *Italian Backgrounds* (New York: Scribner's, 1905), 85. Subsequent references are included parenthetically in the text.

59 Karl Baedeker, *Switzerland, and the Adjacent Portions of Italy, Savoy, and the Tyrol: Handbook for Travellers* (Leipzig: Karl Baedeker, 1893), 375.

60 D. H. Lawrence, *The Letters of D H Lawrence. Volume 1: September 1901–May 1913*, ed. James T. Boulton (Cambridge: Cambridge University Press, 1979), 453.

61 Caesar, *Forgiving the Boundaries*, 53–69. See also Lori Brister, 'The Precise and the Subjective: The Guidebook Industry and Women's Travel Writing in Late Nineteenth-Century Europe and North Africa' in *Women, Travel Writing, and Truth*, ed. Clare Broome Saunders (London: Routledge, 2014), esp. 66–9, 73–4.

62 On Wharton's resistance to the picturesque, see Sarah Bird Wright, *Edith Wharton's Travel Writing: The Making of a Connoisseur* (Basingstoke: Macmillan, 1997), 35–49, esp. 40–2; on her use of fictional devices, see Mary Suzanne Schriber, 'Edith Wharton and Travel Writing as Self-Discovery', *American Literature* 59.2 (May 1987): 261.

63 Another Caribbean text that plays with the conventions of the guidebook is Edwidge Danticat, *After the Dance: A Walk Through Carnival in Jacmel, Haiti* (New York: Crown, 2002), discussed alongside *A Small Place* in Angelique V. Nixon, *Resisting Paradise: Tourism, Diaspora, and Sexuality in Caribbean Culture* (Jackson, MS: University of Mississippi Press, 2015), 33–61; see also Charles Forsdick, 'Traveling, Writing: Danticat's After the Dance' in *Edwidge Danticat: A Reader's Guide*, ed. Martin Munro (Charlottesville, VA: University of Virginia Press, 2010), esp. 106–7.

64 Maryse Condé, *Guadeloupe* (photographs by Jean Du Boisberranger) (Paris: Richer/Hoa–Qui, 1988), 10. Subsequent references appear parenthetically in the text. Translations my own unless indicated otherwise.

65 The Blue Guide to Guadeloupe, for instance, devotes about thirty pages each to Pointe-à-Pitre and Grande Terre, Basse Terre and the smaller islands (in that order): *En Guadeloupe* (Paris: Hachette/Guides Bleues, 1988).

66 I use the translation by Peter Hitchcock, quoting this passage in 'Condé, Crossing, Errancy of Place' in *Imaginary States: Studies in Cultural Transnationalism* (Urbana, IL: University of Illinois Press, 2003), 83.

67 Hitchcock, 'Condé', 83.

68 Keri Smith, *How to Be an Explorer of the World* (New York: Perigree, 2008), 129, 143.

69 Phil Smith, *Counter-Tourism: The Handbook* (Axminster: Triarchy Press, 2012), 23, 96.

70 Rachael Antony and Joël Henry, *The Lonely Planet Guide to Experimental Travel* (Melbourne: Lonely Planet, 2005).

71 Justin D. Edwards and Rune Graulund, *Mobility at Large: Globalization, Textuality and Innovative Travel Writing* (Liverpool: Liverpool University Press, 2012), 3.

11
NARRATIVE

John Culbert

Time, travel, and narrative

Travel accounts, like biographies, are shaped by their subject matter. Just as a life story reflects the timeline of that person's existence, a travelogue follows the journey it relates; in each case, *what* is narrated lends form to *how* it is told. The earliest definition of plot, from Aristotle's *Poetics*, confirms this basic idea: Aristotle says that plot is the imitation (*mimesis*) of an action. To tell a story in this way – mimetically – would be to follow the King's advice in Lewis Carroll's *Alice in Wonderland*: "'Begin at the beginning"', the King tells the White Rabbit, "'and go on till you come to the end: then stop.'"[1] If the narrative instruction to begin at the beginning seems in one sense laughably redundant, like most of Carroll's sallies it also poses a real conceptual riddle. For the King's words in fact provide a succinct example of narrative theory's essential distinction between the tale as recounted and the events to which it refers – *narration* and *story*, respectively, or, in the influential vocabulary of the Russian Formalists, *sjužet* and *fabula* – a distinction whose two parts, the King assumes, make one self-evident harmonious whole. Accordingly, for the ingenuous monarch 'begin' is to narration as 'the beginning' is to story.[2] It is significant that the King gives his directives at a trial where he officiates as judge; a trustworthy account of events is generally expected to be as objective and logical as possible, following the reliable ordering principles of causality and linear chronology. Hence the familiar injunction at trials and interrogations to tell 'just the facts' of the matter.

But of course things are not quite so simple. At the start of one of his travelogues, the French writer Victor Segalen pointedly refuses to abide by the standard pattern of travellers' tales, which he scornfully calls 'acts you swear you accomplished in specific places, during a series of itemized days'.[3] Carroll's own work playfully flouts the King's advice, constantly delighting in riddles, non-sequiturs, pseudo-logic, and puns, as well as journeys so confounding that 'Alice never could quite make out, in thinking it over afterwards, how it was that they began'.[4] And yet, of course, standard narrative order provides a clear frame around Alice's adventures: Alice is bored; she nods off; she sees the White Rabbit and follows him down the rabbit-hole. In the end she wakes up – a supremely conventional narrative device that restores the reign of logic and spatio-temporal order.

The frame-stories that surround Carroll's extravagant fictions suggest that logic and chronology are dominant even where rules of causality and temporal sequence are radically suspended. It should be no surprise, perhaps, that tales recounting human actions should follow time's arrow. And yet, even in a chronicle that stays close to the flow of time, such as the driest of captain's logs, narrative analysis can show that the written record is shaped into *incidents*, *events*, and *episodes*, and therefore into minimal stories, as distinct from mere temporal series. Periods of time are also organised into discrete segments laden with symbolism; departures at dawn differ from those at sunset, days contrast with nights, and seasons are weighted with connotations that reflect the life-cycles of mortal things. The ubiquitous metaphor of life as a journey can expand to an allegorical scale, such that travellers render their experience in the generic forms of a travel *romance* or nar-rative of *ordeal* – each of which has its own distinct treatment of time and history, as Bakhtin has shown.[5] The sequential time of the tale is thus different in kind from that measured by the clock. What holds for the *time* of travel also does for *space*; the word 'journey' (from the French *journée*, or 'day') until recently still meant the distance travelled in the span of a day – an etymological reminder that the space-time of travel is culturally defined. Accordingly, far from being mere descriptive indices, abstract measures of space-time contribute to the traveller's meaningful expe-rience, as we see at the start of Goethe's *Italian Journey* (1816). 'At noon I arrived in Eger', Goethe says, 'and it occurred to me that this place lay on the same latitude as my native town. I felt very happy to be taking my midday meal under a cloudless sky on the fiftieth parallel.'[6] Moreover, narratives tend not to obey strict linearity; they are always more or less *anachronic*. A chronicle as linear as Segalen's 'series of itemized days' will likely include the anachronic techniques of *prolepsis* (prefiguration) or *analepsis* (flashback), if only in asides that mention where the traveller will sleep later that day or his or her regret at not having filled the water jug at a fountain some miles back.

Gérard Genette, the foremost narratologist in the French structuralist tradition, has exhaus-tively catalogued the ways in which a narrated story is organised in relation to the temporal categories of order, duration, and frequency.[7] Drawing like Genette on structuralist linguistics, Seymour Chatman posits that all narratives are shaped along the two poles of 'order and selec-tion', the basic binary matrix out of which time, history, and experience are made meaningful through narrative form.[8] Narrative, then, from its smallest signifying elements to its capacious masterplots, is how mere chronology is shaped into what Paul Ricoeur calls 'human time'.[9] It emerges from these analyses that continuous chronological order can only truly belong to the domain of the *story*, the *discourse* being shot through with alternating speeds, from the temporal jump of an *ellipsis* to the *pause* that freezes time, as well as *repetitions* that revisit scenes which logi-cally occurred only once. Further, the act of reading lends its own anachrones to the process of narrative understanding, for stories imply a reader or listener who lives the tale in their own time.

In the 1970s, narratologists increasingly emphasised the reader's role in the ordering of dis-course, thereby shifting structuralist narratology's focus on the textual artefact to the transac-tional dynamics of 'narrativity'. Writing from a reader-response perspective, Wolfgang Iser argues that however detailed a story's narration may be, its chronology can never be complete, and the inevitable 'gaps' and 'omissions' in a storyline play a vital role in the reader's work of interpreting and making connections.[10] If this is so, however, where does the reader's role end? Patrick O'Neill points out that if we assume the reader is reconstructing a story-world homolo-gous to our own, 'there is no event so simple that it cannot be deconstructed into a potentially infinite series of *constituent* events' (39). Such a conclusion may appear hyperbolic, but it bears significantly on the fundamental distinction between *fabula* and *sjužet* by challenging the norma-tive presumption of a story-world independent of, and prior to, its telling. Accordingly, O'Neill contends that narrative discourse would not simply show in as transparent a way as possible the supposed story, but is a wholly artificial fabrication; further, that verbal fabrication can under-mine the very premise of the story it would be based on. And while these insights might seem most pertinent to *fictional* narratives, where the primary story is of necessity imaginary, O'Neill extends his conclusions to non-fiction as well, whose referents, however factual they may be, are fully mediated by narrative understanding. For readers of travel writing this would call for a thoroughgoing reconsideration of what is often assumed to be the *mimetic* and *representational* nature of the text at hand.

The link between the ostensible *fabula* and its *sjužet* becomes even more problematic when one allows that the things narrated may not constitute simple actions and events but internal psychological experiences: neither journeys nor adventures but purely mental 'transports'. Peter Brooks examines the driving role of desire in the activity of emplotment, arguing that narrative implies a 'dynamic operation' between reader and text.[11] Brooks's Freudian reading of Balzac's *The Wild Ass's Skin*, for instance, shows how a son's transgressive Oedipal desire is reflected in the story's violation of chronology, both in the temporal sequence of the narrated story as well as in its subject, which involves an occult tampering with time itself.[12] Balzac's fantastical premise anticipates the malleability of time among his modernist inheritors. The narrative innovations of much modernist writing reflect the complex temporality of mental life in its relation to the newly discovered realms of the Freudian unconscious and phenomenological time as well as a modern world itself characterised by increasing speed and disjunctive temporalities.

The Futurists' celebration of machinery and modern transportation amidst the technological disruptions of the early twentieth century is echoed in travelogues as different as Edith Wharton's *In Morocco* (1920) and Wyndham Lewis's *Filibusters in Barbary* (1932), while for such writers as Marcel Proust and Virginia Woolf, 'time is not the time of some objective "history,"' writes Peter Nicholls, 'but the rhythm of feeling as it is scrutinized and overlooked by the perceiving mind'.[13] Walter Benjamin provides a more saturnine account of these questions of time, technology, and narrative in his influential essay 'The Storyteller'. Citing a popular German saying that 'when someone goes on a trip, he has something to tell about', Benjamin argues that the traditional pace and rhythm of shared oral narrative contrasts with the violent shocks and ruptures of modern life, most notably the experience of mechanical warfare in the First World War.[14] Benjamin thus insists on the *incommunicability* of modern experience, exemplified by the soldier who returns home unable to speak of what he underwent in battle.[15] Sigmund Freud noted a similar phenomenon and opened up a rich field of inquiry into psychic trauma.[16] Taken up in turn by literary theory, trauma studies have shown how violent stress can warp the experience of time. 'The story of trauma', remarks Cathy Caruth, is 'the narrative of a belated experience.'[17] If, following Caruth's analysis, 'belatedness' is not merely a time-lag in the telling of trauma but an anachrony of experience itself, a reader's ethical response to stories of trauma must allow for breaks, gaps, and silences as aspects of a truth that defies mere logic and objectivity. In Rudolph Wurlitzer's *Hard Travel to Sacred Places* (1995), for example, the reader experiences trauma's enduring aftermath in the author's jolting, fractured account of a harrowing journey undertaken in a state of irremediable grief.[18]

Beginnings, origins, and departures

The relationship between the *how* and the *what* of a narrative is, then, highly complex, and the King's injunction in Carroll's tale blithely skirts over these complications from the very first word, 'Begin'. Beginnings are, moreover, highly arbitrary constructs in narrative. While we might consider a travelogue's starting-point to be a fairly straightforward element of narrative emplotment, a survey of texts quickly shows that such is not the case. A travel account might start proleptically at the end, the arrival at a destination: 'I finish my trek', begins Pierre Clastres's 'The Last Frontier';[19] it might begin *in medias res*, like *The Odyssey*; or it might work backward from the point of arrival, revisiting the previous stops, then go 'further back still', as Robert Dessaix puts it, in an attempt to recover the journey's first impulse.[20] Such a quest for origins might push the story of early inspiration far back into childhood, well before the journey is taken, or even into prehistory, as seen in Chatwin's *In Patagonia*, whose opening pages dwell on the author's child-hood fascination with a 'piece of skin' allegedly deriving from a brontosaurus, a narrative choice strikingly evocative of Balzac's talismanic hide.[21] Chatwin's anecdote alerts us, moreover, to the complex treatment of *causes* in narrative. Whereas scientific discourse is fairly content to assert the linear relationship of causes to effects, narrative analysis reveals the artifice involved in the reconstruction of causes in any given event. A narrated cause can be, for instance, the result of an error of perspective, a witness's lie, or the selection of a single precipitating factor from a host of contributing causes. Further, there is reason to question the assumed linearity of cause and effect, as Jonathan Culler has argued; we often produce causes after the fact, inverting events according to 'the force of meaning'.[22] If, as Culler claims, 'the crucial event is the product of demands of sig-nification', then 'meaning is not the effect of a prior event but its cause' – an insight that calls into question the precedence of the tale over its telling. Chatwin's origin story could be seen, then, as an extreme version of this retroactive impulse in a journey's supposedly forward trajectory.

Edward Said makes a helpful distinction between discursive *beginnings* and *origins*; whereas the former are composed of a mixture of novelty and convention, the product of contin-gent agency within concrete historical circumstances, the latter, he argues, amount to mystified notions of uniqueness and quasi-divine creation.[23] In the light of this analysis, myth is not merely the inherited store of traditional tales of supernatural origins and the innocent template for fan-tastical plot lines in fairy tales, fiction, and entertainment fare; it is, more importantly, the vexing tendency in secular texts of all kinds, including travelogues, to ground their representations in reassuring but ultimately deceitful narrative forms. Travel texts of the age of European explora-tion abound in narrative scenes of 'discovery', of fabulous legends and mythical worlds: 'I felt I was transported to the garden of Eden', writes Bougainville in Tahiti; and as if fatally repeating that biblical origin story, his words are framed by scenes of murder and theft.[24] Spiritual themes of the 'quest' and the 'grail' are more muted but nonetheless present in contemporary travel writing as well. Once we question such metaphysical presuppositions, including that of absolute originality, *beginning*, Said says, 'ultimately implies return and repetition rather than simple linear accomplishment'.[25] If 'to be modern', as Roland Barthes puts it, is 'to know clearly what cannot be started over again',[26] Said's insights provide a useful counter to the notion of modernity as a transgressive break with filiation, lineage, and tradition. Modern writers may well set out to initiate something, to travel somewhere new, but they do so without fully believing in absolute originality or unique departures. The paradigmatic modern instance of what Said calls the 'inter-play between beginning and repetition' is perhaps Joyce's ingenious rewriting of *The Odyssey*'s epic journey as a modern man's experience of wandering introspection.[27] For all its inventive-ness, then, Joyce's *Ulysses* speaks to a general truth of narrative: that stories are composed of borrowed elements and conventions of emplotment. Further, the 'force of meaning', to cite Culler again, can always override the presumed story; as Patrick O'Neill puts it, 'Narrative is arguably predicated entirely on the practice of at least potential deception, on the possibility, in other words, for the story (as discoursed) to move *away* from what really happened.'[28] This last formula suggests another way to consider what it means to *begin* a story or a travelogue; if to begin is to *depart*, that beginning is always a potential departure *from* the verifiable facts. To read travel writing as narrative, then, requires that one always weigh the measure of artifice and indeed *fiction* in even the most documentary of travelling accounts.

Narrative and power

Bronislaw Malinowski, the Polish anthropologist, strikes an epic modernist note similar to Joyce's with the title of his *Argonauts of the Western Pacific*, which was published, like *Ulysses*, in 1922. Moreover, Malinowski's compositional choices at the start of his monograph amply confirm Said's insights on narrative departures. Having briefly described his subject and research methods, the anthropologist shifts abruptly into storytelling mode: 'Imagine yourself', the author says, 'suddenly set down surrounded by all your gear, alone on a tropical beach close to a native village, while the launch or dinghy which has brought you sails away out of sight.'[29] Malinowski's opening scene appeals directly to the reader and solicits an empathetic identification. Accordingly, we share in the author's experience of 'hopelessness and despair', and like him, the reader is cast as 'a beginner [. . .] with nothing to guide you and no one to help you'. The first word, 'imagine', so evocative of children's stories, invites the implied reader to call up a familiar storehouse of popular adventure stories, tales of castaways, survivors, and conquerors. For twenty-first-century readers, Malinowski's opening words are equally evocative of travel and exploration in virtual worlds online, as Tom Boellstorff has shown.[30] To 'imagine yourself' in the scene sketched by Malinowski is to draw immediately upon one's capacity for narrative understanding, a skill so common as to be universal and akin to the innate human capacity for speech, as Roland Barthes famously noted, and yet whose implicit rules and structures have only in fairly recent times been studied by narrative theory.[31] In this light one might see Malinowski's opening scene as reprising the primordial plot structure described by morphological analysis, a kind of grammar of narrative form. According to Jurij Lotman, the most elemental plot line entails a subject (typically a man) who enters or exits a given space (itself associated with femininity), a basic plot that derives from the structural articulation of the binary terms 'boundary' and 'entrance'.[32] As such, the elemental plot structure sketches a journey in miniature. In this way Lotman gives concrete shape to a primordial desire for beginnings intuited by Said: 'there is an imperative connection', Said claims, 'between the idea of a beginning and an aboriginal human need to point to or locate a beginning'.[33] For all that, however, Malinowski's scene is neither natural nor innocent and calls for political scrutiny.

A focus on narrative structure can serve not only to describe the mechanics of composition and reader-response, as we have seen, but also to illuminate their role in larger systems of order and control. Applied to travel writing, narrative analysis provides the means to understand storytelling as an historico-political force, or what Said, speaking of Conrad's fictionalised account of his Congo journey in *Heart of Darkness*, calls 'narrative's sheer historical momentum'. Elaborating on this insight, Said claims that there is a 'far from accidental convergence between the patterns of narrative authority constitutive of the novel on the one hand, and, on the other, a complex ideological configuration underlying the tendency to imperialism'.[34] Accordingly, Said's ground-breaking *Orientalism* shows that travel writing on the Middle East and North Africa participates in a broad historico-cultural function of hegemonising discourse. A travel text such as Nerval's *Voyage en Orient* (1851), for instance, piggy-backed on the 'borrowed authority' of such travelling predecessors as Edward William Lane to compose enduring but deeply flawed representations of the Near East,[35] while the often unfounded and always partisan claims of Orientalist travellers such as Chateaubriand, Richard Burton, Flaubert, and Loti provoked far-reaching geopolitical effects in the region that may still be felt today. Many critics writing in the wake of Said's work have insisted, however, on the subversive potential of travellers' writings, rather than on their role as agents of discursive control; for instance, Kaja Silverman's close reading of T.E. Lawrence's *Seven Pillars of Wisdom* (1926) brings out a queer dimension in the text that, in destabilising gender, also shakes the foundations of masculinity on which the 'dominant fiction' of social reality depends.[36] Similarly, Theresa de Lauretis' essay 'Desire in Narrative' critiques narratology for reifying gender roles in codes of linguistic structure whose universalising claims give cover to masculine pretensions of mastery.[37] Narratology, then, has followed a career like other structuralist methodologies, not merely surpassed by novelty but *deconstructed*, and thereby informing poststructuralist analyses that widen the field of its application, notably in feminist, queer, postcolonial and critical race studies.

Malinowski's lone figure on the beach at the beginning of *Argonauts* can thus be understood as a narrative choice motivated by the politics of race, gender, and empire, and as such the scene is marked by numerous tensions and contradictions. The evocation of a white male interloper in a strange land uses a deeply problematic cliché to claim the reader's attention, and yet the monograph it serves to introduce, based as it is on the new British ethnographic method of intensive local fieldwork, is quite at odds with the conventional figure of the adventurer. To begin as Malinowski does – or as he claims to do – he must dispatch his 'launch or dinghy' while fully erasing from the story the ship that presumably carried him to that part of the world. The beginning, then, is not what it claims to be; it is a narrative construct that strategically omits the apparatuses of transport, domination, and control that allow the anthropologist to appear so innocently on the scene. Moreover, the author's 'hopelessness and despair' induces empathy by drawing on the narrative resources of such earlier explorers as Mungo Park, whose hugely successful *Travels in the Interior Districts of Africa* (1799) dramatised his victimhood to great success, paradoxically inspiring colonial expansion by means of his very weakness and abjection.[38] One could say of Malinowski here what Mary Louise Pratt remarks of Park's narrative: 'He wrote, and wrote himself, not as a man of science, but as a sentimental hero.'[39] Park's decision to foreground his vulnerable sensibilities – 'naked and alone, surrounded by savage animals, and men still more savage' – is a victory of discourse, says Pratt, 'a triumph of the language of sentiment and its protagonist, the individual'.[40] The narrative point of view, or *focalisation*, in Genette's terminology, is highly subjective and trained on the minutest visual detail in the famous scene of Park's near-death experience; Pratt argues that this point of view gives narrative focus to the emerging class of bourgeois subjects, private agents of commerce, and free enterprise in an empire soon destined to span the globe.

Work such as Pratt's contributes to a vital mutation in the field of anthropology, which in the wake of structuralism began to study the role of rhetoric and narrative in what James Clifford provocatively named 'ethnographic fictions'.[41] The contributors to the path-breaking volume *Writing Culture* (1986) demonstrate that narrative, far from being a mere stylistic addition to the science of anthropology, is a constitutive feature of the discipline that is shunted aside in an effort to claim scientific objectivity. Narrative is thus the site of a major contradiction in anthropological discourse. Pointing out that 'opening narratives commonly recount the writer's arrival at the field site', Pratt states that 'personal narrative persists alongside objectifying description in ethnographic writing because it mediates a contradiction within the discipline between personal and scientific authority'.[42] On one side of that contradiction, narrative speaks to the undeniable *point of view* of the ethnographer, of his (usually male) *privilege*, of the *material conditions* of his work, of his *emotions* and *sensations*, and so on. The cost of excluding these narrative elements is what Johannes Fabian calls anthropology's 'denial of coevalness'; that is to say, the negation of the shared time of the encounter between the traveller and his hosts.[43] Modern anthropology, Fabian flatly states, 'bought its scientific respectability at the price of disavowing its literary nature', and one important consequence of this disavowal is a loss of the *temporal* nature of the experience of ethnographic work.[44] This critique leads Fabian to advocate a return to pre-ethnographic travel accounts of the nineteenth century in order to recapture what was lost by anthropology in its shift from narration to scientific discourse. Travel diaries play a particularly important role here and to the extent that a travelogue draws on such material, it 'preserves traces of a learning process, hence of the historicity of knowledge production' (153). It is worth underscoring that this methodological emphasis on time and narration is an explicit challenge to structuralism's rejection of historical analysis for formalist synchronism. Further, Fabian's analysis of the role of the diary in the pre-ethnographic travelogue can be brought to bear on the controversy surrounding the publication of the diary from the period of Malinowski's *Argonauts* field work, *A Diary in the Strict Sense of the Term*. When this text was posthumously released in 1967 it revealed the ethnographer in all his human pettiness and vulgarity, driven to such anger and frustration he could at one point adopt the voice of Conrad's monstrous Kurtz from *Heart of Darkness* – a sobering confirmation that explorers always travelled with 'narrative scripts', as Fabian puts it (143).[45] Malinowski's example shows us that narrative, for a travel writer, is a medium as expansive and enabling as it is partisan and constraining. But anthropology's 'narrative turn' also allows us to see that due to this very complexity, travel writing of the colonial era is a discursive genre no less valuable than ethnography in its problematic staging of travellers' cross-cultural encounters and their invariably political representations of the Other.

Postcolonial journeys

In an influential essay of 1979, Jean-François Lyotard defined the postmodern era by its disbelief in grand narratives. 'The narrative function', Lyotard exclaims, 'is losing its functors, its great hero, its great dangers, its great voyages, its great goal.' Despite the waning of grand narratives, however, storytelling on a smaller scale – local, strategic, and convivial – remains a vital form of knowledge distinct from and opposed to science and instrumental reason, Lyotard argues. The critical reassessment of texts such as Malinowski's *Argonauts* reflects this postmodern context in which myths of progress, liberation, and scientific reason are challenged by a heterogeneous world of 'language games' and competing stories.[46] Likewise, the postmodern revaluation of storytelling may be seen in the flourishing of travel writing that has exploded the Euro-American grand narratives of pilgrimage, discovery, adventure, and conquest, as new travellers, including immigrants and sexual and racial minorities, challenge the traditional figure of the intrepid explorer and privileged tourist.[47] Particularly dramatic contrasts emerge when the ethnographic gaze is reversed, as when postcolonial authors 'write back' to the metropole.[48] Jamaica Kincaid, the Antiguan-born American author, exemplifies this critical reversal of colonial narratives. In *A Small Place* (1988) the author mocks the touristic mentality of wealthy visitors to her native Caribbean island and exposes the neocolonial exploitation fostered by the tourist trade and Antiguan politics. In so doing the author provides an unforgiving picture of a broader globalising world whose travel circuits are still defined by racism and gross inequities of wealth and power. The abiding interest of *A Small Place* lies, however, not only in its bracing portrayal of what vacationers overlook in Antigua but in the ambiguous posture of the author herself who, as returning exile and privileged postcolonial traveller, cannot fully extricate herself from the power and politics she so forcefully critiques. This discordance in Kincaid's narrative voice is evident in the travel account the author penned some seventeen years later. The challenge Kincaid manifestly confronted in authoring *Among Flowers: A Walk in the Himalaya* (2005) was both political and stylistic: to write without committing the sins of the insouciant tourist and to narrate without assuming the role of a latter-day coloniser.

Kincaid's difficulties begin at the very start, and predictably so, as the question of beginnings is a highly fraught one for the author. Like her travelogue, Kincaid's novels and essays demonstrate a near-obsessive concern for beginnings, origins, and departures. This concern is anchored in the retrospection of autobiography and the depiction of her humble origins on Antigua. In the essay 'In History', for instance, the writer evokes herself as one among other 'people who look like me'; in other words, as marked by her black and indigenous heritage.[49] As such, however, Kincaid's identity is also ineluctably bound up with 'the man who started the narrative from which I trace my beginning', namely Columbus, the first European to see her island (160). Kincaid insists on locating 'the beginning of this narrative' (162), all the while troubling herself with the questions, 'When did I begin to ask all this? When did I begin to think of all this and in just this way?' (159). The problem with the question of narrative beginnings is that they are marked by a violent historical rupture, such that Kincaid's postcolonial memory can only uncover origins that are broken, split, and wounded. And so, by a flight of desperate fancy, the author imagines herself as existing *before* the beginning, when she is 'not yet a part of this narrative' (159), in order to claim a self outside of and unknown to the story of European exploration. Ironically, however, that story of discovery and conquest was a boon to the author's beloved field of botany. When, therefore, Kincaid ultimately realises to what extent the collection and taxonomising of plants is linked to the markets and travel circuits of the international slave trade, she is forced to admit she has entered the story. It is as if the author were conscripted into narrative, less subject than object of history's journeys and discoveries. Kincaid thus darkly concedes that 'I have become a part of the narrative of the binomial system of plant nomenclature' (163).

The statement is striking when apposed to *Among Flowers*. Having joined a group of professional plantsmen and botanists on a tour of the Himalayan foothills of Nepal, Kincaid exults in the native flora. 'I felt gloriously happy', she says. 'Everywhere there was something that even I could see was worth collecting. The bounty included: *Hydrangea robusta*, a species of *Lobelia*, *Rhododendron arboreum* subsp. *cinnamomeum* [. . .] *Meconopsis villosa*, *Arisaema propinquum*, *Rhododendron bureavii*, *Acer campbelli*, and the much-desired *Daphne bholua*.'[50] Kincaid's frank acquisitiveness amid this natural 'bounty', dutifully rendered in binomial Linnaean forms, is not unlike the 'Adam-like quality' she deplored in Linnaeus ('In History', 165) or Columbus' relentless naming in the New World: 'he named and he named; he named places, he named people, he named things' (155). With her signature caustic wit, Kincaid's earlier essay 'In History' deflated Columbus' vision of paradise. 'It would not have been paradise for the people living there [. . .] But someone else's ordinary dreariness is another person's epiphany' (155–6). The same insight is proffered in *Among Flowers*, only here it is Kincaid herself, as tourist, who intrudes on the banal life of others: 'while every moment I was experiencing had an exquisite uniqueness and made me feel everything was unforgettable, I was also in the middle of someone else's daily routine, someone captured by the ordinariness of his everyday life' (*Among Flowers*, 166). Kincaid might be faulted for contradicting herself, but this would be to misunderstand a crucial tension in her portrayal of power and privilege. The author's work consistently explores knotted complicities in even the most starkly confrontational contexts. In Kincaid's politics of narrative, to tell a story is never to fully own it, just as each word can only ever be a word stolen back from the coloniser. This ambiguity is compellingly rendered in 'In History': speaking of a rich merchant banker, the embodiment of the heedless opportunism that filled the pockets of slave-traders and botanists alike, Kincaid says, 'He long ago entered my narrative, I now feel I must enter his' ('In History', 164). If 'entering' the master narrative is an act of defiance, a *breaking* and entering, it also implies proximity or even, indeed, complicity with the colonial predecessor.[51] Kincaid thus refers approvingly to William Bartram's *Travels* (1791), an inescapable resource for an American plant-lover, and yet also the narrative of an explorer, forerunner of genocide and colonisation. The reference appears in a passage where Kincaid, speaking of her acquisitive desire, makes the particularly bald statement that 'boundaries [. . .] must be violated' (*Among Flowers*, 115). Similarly, there is a sly contrariness to Kincaid's affection for Frank Smythe's *The Kangchenjunga Adventure* (1930), a colonial-era travelogue that she says 'was like a child's comforter to me' during her trip (31). *Entering* the other's narrative is perhaps to dream and thereby make it one's own, travelling with *and* against it in a double gesture of 'ambivalent narration'.[52]

This ambivalence seems to mark every step of Kincaid's journey. The travelogue is filled with moments of rapture and delight but also pain and discomfort, often in one and the same sentence:

> I complained bitterly to myself, and quarreled with the ground as I trod on it, but even then I knew I was having the very most wonderful time of my life, that I would never forget what I was doing, that I would long to see again every inch of the ground that I was walking on the minute I turned my back on it.
>
> *(101)*

The author's close attention to the space-time of walking lends the text a deceptive naïveté: 'On my journey, there was no coming and going, I was always going somewhere and everything I saw, I saw only from one direction, which was going forward, going toward, and then I was going away' (106). The apparent simplicity of such a notation betrays, however, the painful divisions that make every present moment a moment of passage and loss. Moreover, Kincaid often underscores the time of the writing, adding another level of distance from the journey's moments of presence ('as I am writing this' [29]; 'now as I write this' [118]). This intrusion of the time of narration into the time of the narrated, or what Genette terms *metalepsis*,[53] seems at times to belabour the obvious: 'I only know all of this in retrospect', Kincaid says, 'in sitting at my desk in Vermont and thinking about it, in looking back' (11). But as in narrative fiction, where metalepsis can produce fantastical effects by confusing the distinction between *narration* and *story*, Kincaid's narrative intrusions aim to meld the journey and its telling, as if to heal the division between text and reality. Towards the end of *Among Flowers*, she writes,

> Leaving the pass was like leaving a great book, which has yielded every kind of satisfaction that is to be found in a great book, except that with such a book you can immediately begin on page one again and create the feeling of not having read it before [. . .] How I wanted reaching the pass, going up to it and then leaving it behind, to be something like that, the reading of a great book.
>
> *(138)*

The metaleptic joining of the telling and the told only exacerbates, however, the feeling of lost immediacy. 'To make the experience like a book, here it is in a book I am writing now for myself', Kincaid says. 'But it is very hard to do this, for each word I put in the book is a word I have had to part with, each experience I portray in this book is one I had to part with' (139). The rhythm of this passage, in which words and footsteps are closely joined, is marked by the repetition of the word 'part' and the baffling ambiguity of its separating *and* joining: to *part*, Kincaid insists, is to part *with*. For Kincaid, then, every step and word marks the difference between telling and told, such that the moment of arrival is already the time of departure: 'Our leave-taking', she says, 'perhaps began with our arrival' (153).

To arrive is to begin to leave. The statement flirts with the fantastical, and indeed Kincaid's travelogue often seems to attempt the impossible: to defy reality, to enter her own narrative the way she breaks and enters the master-texts of history, to merge her writing and written self. The metaleptic 'now as I write this' is, then, a *transgression* akin to the boundaries she says she must violate as a plant-lover; and indeed her statement on this point resonates with one critic's definition of metalepsis as a 'transgression of the "sacred boundary" between the world of the telling and the world of the told' – a tampering, in other words, with the fundamental distinction of narrative theory.[54]

In certain respects, moreover, *Among Flowers*'s postmodern reflexivity defies narrative analysis. Towards the beginning of the travelogue Kincaid gives a perplexing account of how her journey started. Though she originally had in mind a trip to China, her friend Dan moves her to change plans. Kincaid writes:

> That first visit he made to Nepal haunted Dan so that he wanted to go there again. It's quite possible that I could hear his longing and the haunting in his voice when he suggested to me that we go looking for seeds in the Himalaya, but I cannot remember it now. And so Nepal it was.
>
> *(4)*

The explanatory 'and so' that closes this decisive passage appears somewhat unwarranted, since the reason for Kincaid's choosing lies in a mere possibility that the author admits she does not even remember. Kincaid's 'and so' is, then, an instance of what Gayatri Spivak calls the author's 'paratactic style',[55] whose disjunctive connections (like parting *with*) splice together while still exposing the break.[56] How, then, to account for Kincaid's response to her friend's 'haunting' and 'longing', from which the entire journey and its telling supposedly derive? How to make sense of this narrative *departure*?

In a bracing critique of the field, Nicholas Royle argues that narratology tries to rationalise and control what are often highly peculiar and even uncanny features of written stories. To explain, for instance, the strange process by which a narrator enters the mind of his character or the way a reader can inhabit the lives of others and see through their eyes, literary critics habitually invoke the terms 'omniscience' and 'point of view'. Royle, in contrast, argues that such phenomena are better described as *telepathy*. For all its paranormal connotations, Royle says that telepathy is a more practical concept than the religiously freighted notion of the god-like 'all-knowing' narrator. Further, 'point of view' or 'focalisation' serves the dubious purpose of rendering perspective as the emanation of a singular, autonomous subject, thereby denying the more uncanny evidence of multiple and contradictory unconscious processes. At the very minimum, the scene of reading entails a strange doubling or sundering of the self. Royle thus concludes that 'The uncanny nature of narrative fiction is indissociable from the strange telepathic reality of being two-to-speak or being two-to-feel.'[57] The passage in which Kincaid is moved by her friend Dan's unspoken longing, or more precisely, in which she is haunted by the possibility of an unspoken longing she may have heard and forgotten, would suggest such a moment of textual telepathy – of feeling at a distance. Moreover, the theme of a haunting voice, combined with the listener's retrospection and forgetting, seems to restage the key features of a scene of primal susceptibility as described by psychoanalyst Jean Laplanche.[58] Judith Butler draws on Laplanche to argue that such perplexing feelings surely affect the resulting story even as they defy an authoritative account. Emphasising the belatedness of a subject's primary influences, given that an infant is always *affected* before he or she has the capacity for self-understanding, Butler suggests that an account of one's origins cannot escape the paradox of constructing after the fact what it intends to merely relate. As a result, Butler says that one must 'accept this belatedness and proceed in a narrative fashion that marks the paradoxical condition of trying to relate something about my own narrative capacity and that, in fact, brings that narrative capacity about'.[59] To tell one's story, then, and especially the story of one's narrative beginnings, is to defeat the claims of that unitary 'one', formed as it is in a temporal interplay of retroactive causality. Likewise, whether Kincaid is feeling her friend's sentiments or unconscious emotions of her own, the passage above stages a scene of being 'two-to-feel', and thus a double causality of desire: '*and* so' (my italics). In this light, one might reconsider all of Kincaid's 'entries' into the narratives of others as instances of telepathy, such as her surprisingly empathetic portrayal of the hated Columbus, a passage in which author, reader, and master text are joined together in an experience of soul-cleaving discovery:

> what the reader (and that is what I have been, a reader of this account of a journey, and the account is by Columbus himself) can feel, can hear, can see, is a great person whose small soul has been sundered by something unexpected.
>
> *('In History', 157)*

These recent innovations in narrative analysis have significant stakes. They provide means to assess the standpoint of the author and the role of *affect* in her postcolonial critique; they revisit theories of 'narrativity' to posit more fundamental dynamics of reader-response; and they place narrative at the centre of basic questions of desire, identity, and subject formation. The range of narrative analysis extends from these fine issues of subjecthood to the broader world stage, from the adventurer's 'small soul' to the 'maps and dreams' of indigenous people.[60] By highlighting the manner in which a traveller's journey is shaped into story, narrative analysis emphasises the constructedness of knowledge and experience, providing tools for the reader to not only appreciate the art of composition but to question the artifice involved in the most seemingly lifelike and ordinary accounts of events. Indeed, it is due to storytelling's very ubiquity and seeming naturalness that its forms of representation can pass for truth, which imposes on the reader of travel writing a critical attention to narrative's role in the propagation of seductive myths and moving fictions.

Notes

1 Lewis Carroll, *Alice's Adventures in Wonderland* (New York: Macmillan, 1920), 182.
2 Victor Shklovsky's *fabula* and *sjužet* have classical predecessors in Aristotle's *logos* and *mythos*; contemporary versions include Todorov's *histoire* and *discours*, Chatman's 'story' and 'discourse', and Cohan and Shires's 'story' and 'narration'. Genette introduced a three-part model of *histoire, récit*, and *narration* of which there are also several subsequent versions by different narratologists. For a list of this terminology and their proponents, see Patrick O'Neill, *Fictions of Discourse* (Toronto: University of Toronto Press, 1994), 21.
3 Quoted in Kimberley J. Healey, *The Modernist Traveler: French Detours, 1900–1930* (Lincoln, NE: University of Nebraska Press, 2003), 8; Victor Segalen, *Equipée*, in *Oeuvres complètes*, ed. Henry Bouillier (Paris: Robert Laffont, 1995), 2:265.
4 Lewis Carroll, *Through the Looking-Glass* (New York: Macmillan, 1875), 39.
5 See M.M. Bakhtin, 'The *Bildungsroman* and Its Significance in the History of Realism (Toward a Historical Typology of the Novel)', in *Speech Genres and Other Late Essays*, ed. Caryl Emerson and Michael Holquist, trans. Vern W. Mc Gee (Austin, TX: University of Texas Press, 1986).
6 Johann Wolfgang von Goethe, *Italian Journey*, trans. W.H. Auden and Elizabeth Mayer (London: Penguin, 1970), 23.
7 See Gérard Genette, *Narrative Discourse: An Essay in Method*, trans. Jane E. Lewin (Ithaca, NY: Cornell University Press, 1980).
8 Chatman, *Story and Discourse* (Ithaca, NY: Cornell University Press, 1978), 28.
9 Paul Ricoeur, *Time and Narrative*, vol. 1, Kathleen McLaughlin and David Pellauer, trans. (Chicago, IL: University of Chicago Press, 1984), 3.
10 Wolfgang Iser, 'The Reading Process: A Phenomenological Approach', *New Literary History* 3.2 (1971): 285.
11 Peter Brooks, *Reading for the Plot: Design and Intention in Narrative* (Cambridge, MA: Harvard University Press, 1992), 47.
12 See Brooks, *Reading for the Plot*, 48–61.
13 Peter Nicholls, *Modernisms: A Literary Guide* (Berkeley, CA: University of California Press, 1995), 264.
14 Walter Benjamin, 'The Storyteller', in *Illuminations*, trans. Harry Zohn (New York: Schocken, 1969), 84.
15 On the effects of mechanisation on the experience of travel, see also Wolfgang Schivelbusch, *The Railway Journey: The Industrialization of Time and Space in the 19th Century* (Berkeley, CA: The University of California Press, 1986).

16 See Sigmund Freud, *Beyond the Pleasure Principle*, James Strachey, trans. (1920; repr. New York: Norton, 1961).

17 Cathy Caruth, *Unclaimed Experience: Trauma, Narrative and History* (Baltimore, MD: Johns Hopkins University Press, 1996), 7.

18 See Rudolph Wurlitzer, *Hard Travel to Sacred Places* (Boston, MA: Shambhala, 1995).

19 See Pierre Clastres, 'The Last Frontier', in *Archeology of Violence*, trans. Jeanine Herman (New York: Semiotext(e), 1994), 9.

20 Robert Dessaix, *Night Letters: A Journey Through Switzerland and Italy* (Sydney: Macmillan, 1996), 5. Interestingly, and further complicating the question of his narrative origins here, Dessaix's 'further back still' echoes Rebecca West, who uses the turn of phrase twice in the opening lines of her Yugoslavian travelogue. See Rebecca West, *Black Lamb and Grey Falcon* (1941; repr. London: Penguin, 1994), 27.

21 Bruce Chatwin, *In Patagonia* (London: Jonathan Cape, 1977), 1.

22 Jonathan Culler, 'Story and Discourse in the Analysis of Narrative', in *The Pursuit of Signs: Semiotics, Literature, Deconstruction* (Ithaca, NY: Cornell University Press, 2001), 174.

23 Edward W. Said, *Beginnings: Intention and Method* (New York: Columbia University Press, 1985).

24 Louis-Antoine de Bougainville, *Voyage autour du monde* (1771; repr. Paris: Presses de l'Université de Paris-Sorbonne, 2001), 213.

25 Said, *Beginnings*, xvii.

26 Roland Barthes, 'From Work to Text', in *Image-Music-Text*, trans. Stephen Heath (New York: Hill and Wang, 1977), 163–4.

27 Said, *Beginnings*, 357.

28 O'Neill, *Fictions of Discourse*, 37.

29 Bronislaw Malinowski, *Argonauts of the Western Pacific* (1922; repr. London: Routledge, 1999), 3.

30 See Tom Boellstorff, *Coming of Age in Second Life: An Anthropologist Explores the Virtually Human* (Princeton, NJ: Princeton University Press, 2008), 3–4.

31 'Narrative', Barthes says, 'is present in every age, in every place, in every society; it begins with the very history of mankind and there nowhere is nor has been a people without narrative. All classes, all human groups, have their narratives [. . .] [N]arrative is international, transhistorical, transcultural: it is simply there, like life itself.' Roland Barthes, 'Introduction to the Structural Analysis of Narrative', in *Image-Music-Text*, 79.

32 See Jurij M. Lotman and Julian Graffy, 'The Origin of Plot in the Light of Typology', *Poetics Today* 1.1/2 (1979): 161–84.

33 Said, *Beginnings*, 5.

34 Edward W. Said, *Culture and Imperialism* (New York: Vintage, 1994), 70.

35 Edward W. Said, *Orientalism* (London: Routledge & Kegan Paul, 1978), 184.

36 Kaja Silverman, 'White Skins, Brown Masks: The Double Mimesis, or With Lawrence in Arabia', in *Male Subjectivity at the Margins* (New York: Routledge, 1992), 15.

37 See Theresa de Lauretis, 'Desire in Narrative', in *Alice Doesn't: Feminism, Semiotics, Cinema* (Bloomington, IN: Indiana University Press, 1984).

38 For a fuller treatment of the themes of misadventure and suffering in travel, including in Park, see Carl Thompson, *The Suffering Traveller and the Romantic Imagination* (Oxford: Clarendon Press, 2007).

39 Mary Louise Pratt, *Imperial Eyes: Travel Writing and Transculturation* (London: Routledge, 1992), 73.

40 Pratt, *Imperial Eyes*, 75, 77.

41 James Clifford, 'Introduction: Partial Truths', in *Writing Culture: The Poetics and Politics of Ethnography*, James Clifford and George E. Marcus, eds. (Berkeley, CA: University of California Press, 1986), 6.

42 Pratt, *Imperial Eyes*, 31, 32.

43 Johannes Fabian, *Time and the Other: How Anthropology Makes Its Object* (New York: Columbia University Press, 2014), 25.

44 Johannes Fabian, *Anthropology with an Attitude: Critical Essays* (Stanford, CA: Stanford University Press, 2001), 146.

45 See Bronislaw Malinowski, *A Diary in the Strict Sense of the Term*, trans. Norbert Guterman (1967; repr. Stanford, CA: Stanford University Press, 1989), 69.

46 Jean-François Lyotard, *The Postmodern Condition: A Report on Knowledge*, trans. Geoff Bennington and Brian Massumi (Minneapolis, MN: University of Minnesota Press, 1984), xxiv.

47 For a survey of the field, see Justin D. Edwards and Rune Graulund, eds., *Postcolonial Travel Writing: Critical Explorations* (London: Palgrave Macmillan, 2011).

48 See Bill Ashcroft, Gareth Griffiths and Helen Tiffin, *The Empire Writes Back: Theory and Practice in Post-Colonial Literature* (London: Routledge, 1989).

49 Jamaica Kincaid, 'In History', in *My Garden (Book)* (New York: Farrar, Straus and Giroux, 1999), 158. Subsequent page references will be provided parenthetically in the text.

50 Jamaica Kincaid, *Among Flowers: A Walk in the Himalaya* (Washington, DC: National Geographic Society, 2005), 121. Subsequent page references will be included parenthetically in the text.

51 On the theme of 'breaking' in Kincaid's discursive politics, see John Culbert, 'Breaking the Truth: Jamaica Kincaid and the Politics of Travel', in *Women, Travel Writing, and Truth*, ed. Clare Broome Saunders (London: Routledge, 2014).

52 Homi K. Bhabha, 'Introduction: Narrating the Nation', in *Nation and Narration* (London: Routledge, 1990), 3.

53 See Genette, *Narrative Discourse*, 234–43.

54 John Pier, 'Metalepsis', in *The Living Handbook of Narratology*, ed. Peter Hühn et al. (Hamburg: Hamburg University Press), accessed 18 March 2018, www.lhn.uni-hamburg.de/article/metalepsis-revised-version-uploaded-13-july-2016.

55 Gayatri Chakravorty Spivak, 'Reading with Stuart Hall in "Pure" Literary Terms', in *An Aesthetic Education in the Era of Globalization* (Cambridge, MA: Harvard University Press, 2012), 355.

56 The 'so' in the previous sentence performs a similar disjunction by means of the rhetorical figure of syllepsis, hovering between a qualifying adverb and explanatory conjunction, which impels a pause and retreading of the passage, if not paralysis: 'That first visit he made to Nepal haunted Dan so . . .'.

57 Nicholas Royle, *The Uncanny* (London: Routledge, 2003), 272.

58 On the theory of 'primal seduction', see Jean Laplanche, *Essays on Otherness*, ed. John Fletcher (London: Routledge, 1999). Generations of critics (cf. Brooks, above) have drawn on Freud's Oedipus complex as the template of a primordial plot of rivalry and tragic desire. Laplanche's notion of primal seduction offers a less normative and masculinist model of early subject formation whose narratological promise still remains to be fully explored.

59 Judith Butler, *Senses of the Subject* (New York: Fordham, 2015), 2.

60 Hugh Brody, *Maps and Dreams: Indians and the British Columbia Frontier* (Vancouver: Douglas & McIntyre, 1981).

12

DESCRIPTION

Benjamin Colbert

In the 5 September 1863 issue of *Punch* appears a short account of the Wye river tour. Signed 'Wye-ator', the Cockney pronunciation of 'viator', the article coaxes fun from the sheer commonplace of the tour and the stock responses it elicits. Since William Gilpin's *Observations on the River Wye* (1782), travel accounts, guidebooks, and illustrated plate books describing the route between Ross and Chepstow had proliferated, as had intertextual references in each new publication to those that came before. In the *Punch* sketch, Wye-ator good-naturedly urges Punch to follow in his footsteps for simple, unadventurous, but no less rewarding pleasures, while deferring to *Taylor's Illustrated Guide to the Banks of the Wye* (1861) for landscape description. However, even Taylor gets the Wye-ator treatment, his view from Windcliff a few miles below Tintern Abbey being peppered with superadded exclamation points, marking flights of 'profanity and snobbishness':

> The spectator stands upon the edge of a precipice, the depth of which is most awful (!), and the river winds at his feet [. . .] The first foreground is to the eye a view from the clouds upon earth (!), and the rich contrast of green meadows to wild forest scenery.[1]

Vincent Crapanzano argues that metaphoric overemphasis (hypotyposis) confirms the narrator as observer even as it renders the accuracy of observation suspect. If excess of emotion inserts the excerpt's narrator into objective description, Wye-ator inserts *himself* by calling attention to this hypotyposis paratextually.[2] Preferring Tintern Abbey by 'cigar-light' and more restrained views, Wye-ator concludes simply that Wye tourism 'sufficiently' stimulates the nerves; its mass appeal lay in its reproducibility, and description that over-emphasises emotional response does not do justice to experiences that cannot and need not measure up.

As in the *Punch* article, description in travel writing raises the problem of how one linguistically negotiates the distance between experience and representation, or how one best represents the truth of experience, both as the verisimilitude of objects seen on tour and of the way in which the traveller sees them. The intertextual depth of works like *Taylor's Illustrated Guide*, itself dependent on previous descriptions of the scenery, calls into question the consequences of repetition and layering of descriptive tropes over time, the hand-me-downs of descriptive technique so humorously invoked in the *Punch* sketch. Is the tourist constrained from acting independently by structures of apperception prepared in advance? And how does one describe scenes that have been described before without surrendering agency and individuality?

This chapter addresses these questions by considering description as *ekphrasis*, a verbal–visual rhetorical mode that prizes the illusion of immediacy. The chapter then discusses specific travel writings that develop these concerns, particularly Thomas Dudley Fosbroke's *Wye Tour, or Gilpin on the Wye* (1818; 6th ed., 1841) – the source in fact of Taylor's Windcliff sketch – as well as Louisa Anne Twamley's *An Autumn Ramble on the Wye* (1838). In part a compendium of Gilpin's *Observations*, Fosbroke's *Wye Tour* and its adjunct *Tourist's Grammar* (1826) transform Gilpin from picturesque theorist to corporate celebrity, ensuring the repetition of textuality and knowledge production in the manner of a commonplace book or album, the cut-and-paste scrapbooking that fused reading practices with composition.[3] By contrast, Twamley's declaration, 'My descriptions are my own', both acknowledges and challenges the overdetermination of description by previous representations of the Wye, including the commercial reproduction of topographical prints, a selection of which help structure her book.[4]

At stake is the question of agency, the extent to which repetitions in description can be seen as 'redescription', a term that Richard Rorty imbues with a communal or shared subjectivity that exceeds the epistemological system within which it seems to be contained. For Rorty, the rejection of 'a privilege attaching to a certain description' is not a recipe for philosophical relativism, but instead asserts human freedom.[5] Considering travel writings on the Wye tour that mediate Gilpinian practice in the early to mid-nineteenth century, this chapter extends Rorty's hermeneutic model to tourism and travel writing. It asks whether redescription can transcend belatedness – the following in the footsteps (physically and rhetorically) of others – and paradoxically express freedom in restraint, expressive agency in excess of rhetorical patterning.[6]

Description, distance, and repetition

In its Latin root, 'describe' (*de-* off, away, aside + *scrībĕre* to write [*OED*]) involves distance, memory, a remove from experience; hence description is fundamental to the crafting of on-the-spot travels into narrative. Field notes might be rough sketches in a pocket journal written in situ or recalled at day's end; marginalia in other travel writings comparing print sources with first-hand observation; or mental notes, associations, and memories. For eighteenth-century continental travellers, as Charles L. Batten observes, notes might themselves be predicated on encyclopaedic manuals for observation such as Bishop Tucker's *Instructions for Travellers* (1757) or Leopold Berchtold's *An Essay to Direct and Extend the Inquiries of Patriotic Travellers* (1789; translated into German, 1791, and French, 1797).[7] Berchtold enjoins travellers 'to commit to paper whatever they find remarkable, hear, or read, and their sensations on examining different objects [. . .] as soon as convenient', then to copy these 'from the pocket-book into the journal before the traveller goes to rest', preserving the immediacy of experience and ensuring a commensurate effect in representation.[8] To direct inexperienced travellers, he provides headings for note-taking and lists of questions to ask under categories pertaining to social utility. For scientific travellers undertaking voyages of exploration, the Royal Society laid down categories for observation in the 1660s that remained influential in the eighteenth and nineteenth centuries.[9] Travels published in the book and periodical marketplace, moreover, are further mediated by publishers, editors, manuscript readers, even typesetters, with layers of textual motivation well beyond on-the-spot description accumulating in the finished work.[10]

James Heffernan's view of *ekphrasis* as 'the verbal representation of visual representation' seems apt as a general definition of description in travel writing, already constructed according to visual and organisational codes.[11] Heffernan's work is guided by the restricted sense of *ekphrasis* as the verbal representation of works of art, but Janice Koelb and Ruth Webb remind us that for classical rhetoric the term applied also to things in nature, and that movement through time as well as static objects might be within its provenance.[12] For Webb, classical *ekphrasis*, translated by the Romans as *descriptio*, is 'a descriptive (*periēgēmatikos*) speech which brings (literally "leads") the thing shown vividly (*enargōs*) before the eyes'.[13] The analogy of the speaker as tour guide, leading auditors on a journey, recurs in this form of rhetorical discourse, but the definition proposes too that the descriptive mode creates through language an illusion of immediacy, empowering auditors/readers as spectators of original sights alongside their speaker/guide.[14] The opposition between narrative and description becomes at best pragmatic, the only distinction sanctioned by classical rhetoric being that description concerns the quality of vividness (*enargeia*) within narrative.

As Koelb remarks, 'two-and-a-half millennia of Western literary criticism have produced very few inquiries into literary description [. . .] Compared with narrative [. . .] which has an "ology" and technical vocabulary of its own, description has not fared well'.[15] Description's demotion and its split from narrative, according to Michel Beaujour, stems from Lessing's influential attack on loco-descriptive poetry in *Laocoön* (1776). Lessing argued that because the linguistic sign bears no integral relation to that which it signifies, only painting and the plastic arts can be truly mimetic.[16] Linguistic description is possible but never entirely successful in creating the illusion that absent things are present, and is suitable only for technical manuals and non-literary genres. The reification of this argument in an ekphrastic theory that favours static works of art, where *ekphrasis* becomes limited to the linguistic imitation of pictures, statues, buildings, and the like, occurred later in the nineteenth century.[17]

Although the term had limited currency in the eighteenth and much of the nineteenth centuries, *ekphrasis* becomes conceptually intertwined in discussions that focus on the transparency of style, be that of scientific travel writing in reproducing the physical world through factual description, or descriptive language's mediation of affective, 'painterly' aesthetic categories: the sublime, the beautiful, and the picturesque. Barbara Stafford's influential *Voyage into Substance* (1984) plots the growth of a Baconian verbal-visual strategy that aims to empower words with the status of things, elevating (contra Lessing) word pictures and travel illustrations into a uniform mechanism for achieving this transparency. However, her argument that scientific travel description winnows out literary *energeia* (forceful writing), relying instead on *enargeia* (vividness), is a distinction blurred if at all present in the texts of classical *ekphrasis*. For Nigel Leask, this underplays a more problematic imbrication of scientific and literary discourses during and beyond the period Stafford covers.[18] Leask places the separation of scientific from more literary travel beyond 1820, when the disciplinary imperatives of science increasingly abstracted its discourse from the travel-related situations in which empirical evidence is often gathered.[19]

Nevertheless, Stafford's denotative descriptive language accords well with aesthetic arguments that elevate organised nature as the object of picturesque discourse. Gilpin, for example, argues: 'Language, like light, is a medium; and the true philosophic stile [. . .] exhibits objects clearly, and distinctly, without soliciting attention to itself'.[20] An anonymous contributor to the *Belfast Monthly Magazine* in 1811 extends Gilpin's analogy, arguing that metaphoric writing too can achieve this effect:

> when the figurative language rivals the vivacity of visual impression, so as to make us think we actually saw, what is only recounted; the description, whether of nature in general, or of human nature, or of the works of art; it may still be properly called *picturesque* [. . .] We see the figures move on the retina of imagination, almost as distinctly as they would appear on the retina of the eye.[21]

Here the contributor coincides with Lessing, who suggests that 'picturesque' [*malerisch*] *enargeia* in language can counterfeit presence:

> every touch [. . .] by means of which the poet brings his subject so vividly before us
> that we are more conscious of the subject than of his words, is picturesque [. . .] it pro-
> duces that degree of illusion which a painted picture is peculiarly qualified to excite.[22]

While Lessing subordinates the descriptive mode in poetry, travel writing escapes such censure and establishes itself popularly as a genre in which a poetics of spatiality – one that relies on visual apprehension and vivid representation – could flourish.

Notwithstanding the theoretical consanguinity between scientific and picturesque travel writing, scientific writers in the period evince discomfort with the linguistic demands placed upon them, often equating the picturesque with a populism which expresses the ends of science (widening understanding) while compromising the means (representing nature accurately). The geologist Samuel Hibbert perceived two readerships for *A Description of the Shetland Islands* (1822), a specialist and a general, rendering his geological descriptions in smaller type so that 'each department of the book may be easily read as a detached work'. John MacCulloch's *A Description of the Western Islands of Scotland* (1819), similarly, admits 'miscellaneous' matter to enliven what otherwise, he writes, would be 'repulsive to a general reader' and 'laborious [. . .] to a geological one'.[23] In one of the few studies to assess travel description across stylistic categories, Paul Smethurst deems the attempt at denotative 'transparency' exemplified in the laconic journals of Captain Cook as 'thin description' that, unlike the 'thick description' proposed by Clifford Geertz, effaces the narrative subject and limits itself to surface phenomena, without gesturing to deeper cultural-semiotic systems of interpretation.[24] However, it still shares with the picturesque a 'search for order in nature' and cannot entirely extract subjectivity from description.[25]

As Leask and Smethurst argue, Romantic-period scientific writers like Forster and Humboldt were reluctant to dismiss the picturesque from scientific description, or to uphold a strict division between the two in travel writing, and, as we have seen, the rhetorical basis for both in ekphrastic thinking follows similar principles to different stylistic ends, be these 'thin' or 'thick', denotative or metaphorical, so long as description functions to bring the object 'before the eye'. In 1835, the secretary to the Royal Geographical Society, Julian Jackson, published an article entitled, 'On Picturesque Description in Books of Travels', which makes the case for an *ekphrasis* of travel writing in all but name. For Jackson, picturesque description plays a crucial role in popularising science by becoming 'the flowery margin [. . .] which [. . .] lures us insensibly on till we arrive at the goal'; a series of 'lively pictures' that establish the moral relations between humans and their surroundings.[26] 'A single picturesque description [. . .] brought, as it were, palpably before our eyes' becomes the call for 'feelings and actions', he writes, echoing the language of classical *ekphrasis* as translated by Webb. Like classical rhetoricians, Jackson emphasises the readers' illusion or delusion that they 'assist as actors, or at least spectators, in such scenes'. *Enargeia* features too: 'It is the business of the text to animate the scene, to warm the landscape, to make the figures move and speak'.[27] This moral affect alone defines the picturesque sufficiently, rather than adherence to rules about what can or cannot please in painting:

> with the traveller picturesque description should have a much wider signification; and
> if he set before our view a dreary desert without a shrub, in all its nudity, its bleak and
> desolate expanse, his description is picturesque. Such scenes, be it observed, are best
> painted by the moral feelings they inspire.[28]

For Jackson, the picturesque and *ekphrasis* are one.

Although ekphrastic readings have seldom featured in travel writing research, such rhetorical approaches as exist have been attuned to the linguistic saturation associated with aesthetic, scientific, and ethnological 'ways of seeing'. The relations between picturesque tourism, eighteenth-century topographical poetry, and the visual arts has been best sketched by Malcolm Andrews's *The Search for the Picturesque* (1989), whose accounts of domestic tours in the Wye Valley, North Wales, the Lake District, and the Scotland Highlands have anticipated specialised studies of those regions.[29] Andrews's influential suggestion that the picturesque forges 'cultural self-definition' through connoisseurship in painting and classical literature – associative filters through which landscape is perceived and described – chimes with Nicola Watson's elaboration of a tourism and travel writing that increasingly casts description in terms of literary touchstones or the former presence of authors.[30] As John Murray writes, setting out his methodology in the first of his influential guidebook series *A Handbook for Travellers on the Continent* (1836),

> Wherever an author of celebrity, such as Byron, Scott, Southey, or Bulwer, has described a place, [the guidebook author] has made a point of extracting the passage, knowing how much the perusal of it on the spot [. . .] will enhance the interest of seeing the objects described.[31]

Among travel theorists, Sara Mills identifies discursive formations that set limits to narration and description in women's travel writing, resulting in formal and conventional repetitions related to Foucault's 'rarefaction of discourse': 'the rather surprising fact that [. . .] texts are [. . .] so repetitive and restricted in the range of their structure, tropes, language choice, tense, statements, events, narrative figure and so on'.[32] David Spurr similarly traces the underlying rhetoric of colonial power in travel writing, journalism, and colonial administration, identifying persistent overlapping tropes which establish the dominance of the narrative 'I/eye' over objects of discourse, yet betray 'a simultaneous avowal and disavowal of its own authority'.[33] Others approach overdetermined travel description via semiotics. For David Scott, 'semiotic tautology', already present in the travel writings of Chateaubriand and Gautier, becomes pronounced in Baudrillard's post-modern simulacrum where signs have been saturated by the media.[34] Equally attuned to writing as motivated discourse, Dean MacCannell describes the paradoxical authenticity of discursive repetition. Reversing Walter Benjamin's notion of 'aura', MacCannell argues that a sense of originality comes about only through, not despite, mass reproduction and the layering of descriptions of culturally significant objects.[35]

For these critics, observation and description are implicated in ideological, value-laden modes of pre-writing that limit the agency of the traveller or writer of travels. Yet, if the subject cannot be emptied out of travel writing even in the most denotative scientific mode, the question remains whether there is a free space behind or within description that liberates the repressed freedom of the subject. In the late eighteenth and early nineteenth centuries, the picturesque becomes the most widespread descriptive strategy in travel writing; accounts of the domestic tour, in particular, were expected to engage in the mode while preserving the freshness of the 'traveller's eye'. The dilemma of modern criticism is played out in this literature: how to write within the 'rules', and compete with the aesthetic directness of painting and engraving, yet produce a sense of textual freedom that might even be true.

Gilpin on the Wye

William Gilpin's theoretical writings on the picturesque and the debates between his contemporaries Uvedale Price and Richard Payne Knight, among others, focused on the question of whether that aesthetic category should be seen as a quality of the object world or rooted in the phenomenology of the percipient.[36] But Gilpin's importance is as much in his practice of picturesque description as its theorisation. The productive tension between the two is articulated in his travel writings, all of which adopted the standardised title, *Observations [. . .] Relative Chiefly to Picturesque Beauty*, in some part of England, Scotland, or Wales. His first book, *Observations on the River Wye, and Several Parts of South Wales [. . .] Made in the Summer of the Year 1770* (1782), circulated in manuscript for nearly a decade before appearing in print. From 1789 to 1800, four more editions indicated his ideas' rising currency. After his death in 1804, his works remained widely available and in 1818 Thomas Dudley Fosbroke described him as 'an oracle; and his work [. . .] a Grammar of the Rules, by which alone the beauties of the Tour, can be properly understood and appreciated'.[37]

In *Observations on the River Wye*, Gilpin states his aim of 'examining the face of a country *by the rules of picturesque beauty*', an aesthetic dependent on the principles of painterly composition expressed by or found in nature rather than in imitation of particular paintings. 'Observations of this kind', he adds, 'through the vehicle of description, have the better chance of being founded in truth; as they are not the offspring of theory; but are taken immediately from the scenes of nature, as they arise'.[38] This emphasises the traveller's presence in nature rather than her or his recollection and representation of it, yet the crucial qualification about 'the vehicle of description' indicates that Gilpin admits a linguistic intermediary between experience and aesthetic framing. Approaching New Weir, 'the second grand scene on the Wye' after Goodrich Castle, Gilpin thus finds himself compromising immediacy with distancing devices, most obviously in the overlay of painterly terminology ('side-screen', 'furniture'), but more subtly through comparisons, aesthetic evaluations, and metaphor:

> The river is wider, than usual, in this part; and takes a sweep round a towering promontory of rock; which forms the side-screen on the left; and is the grand feature of the view. It is not a broad, fractured face of rock; but rather a woody hill, from which large projections, in two or three places, burst out; rudely hung with twisting branches, and shaggy furniture; which, like mane round the lion's head, give a more savage air to these wild exhibitions of nature. Near the top a pointed fragment of solitary rock, rising above the rest, has rather a fantastic appearance: but it is not without it's [sic] effect in marking the scene.[39]

Even the 'fantastic appearance' Gilpin makes a point of *not* describing in any particularised fashion; his prose captures more the indeterminacy that characterises the picturesque rather than the details that might individualise the scene. Immediately after the passage, Gilpin cites from Virgil's *Aeneid* 'an imaginary view with a circumstance exactly similar' and inserts a plate showing the scene as he had sketched it; interart strategies common enough in travel writing, but ones that demonstrate the insufficiency of the particular without superadded reference.

In his *Essay on Picturesque Travel*, Gilpin argues that language as a medium should not 'solicit attention to itself', but in *Observations*, the 'vehicle of description' often proves incommensurate with the task of representation, and descends to repetition. Instead of attempting an account of the scenes below New Weir, Gilpin laments how 'description flags in running over such a monotony of terms. *High, low, steep, woody, rocky* [. . .] are all the colours of language we have, to describe scenes; in which there are infinite gradations; and [. . .] peculiarities'.[40] Tacitly siding with Lessing in comparing linguistic and painterly palettes, Gilpin elsewhere shifts metaphors and considers nature as a foreign language, description as translation: 'Nature's alphabet consists only of four letters; wood – water – rock – and ground: and yet with these four letters she forms such varied compositions; such infinite combinations, as no language with an alphabet of twenty-four can describe'.[41] He at once expands his reader's aesthetic vocabulary, modelling in his own prose descriptive phrasings to be adopted, and at the same time denies its adequacy to the task.

Part of the equivocation results from his ideal of an unmediated experience 'when some grand scene [. . .] rising before the eye, strikes us beyond the power of thought' and 'We rather *feel*, than *survey* it', expressions that invoke the *enargeia* of *ekphrasis* – 'the thing shown vividly (*enargōs*) before the eyes' – without a corresponding trust in description to accomplish the illusion.[42] Although immediacy is Gilpin's ideal, as we have seen, his prose is replete with concessions to distance, the role of imagination, recollection, sketching, and description necessary to the pleasures of landscape appreciation, particularly the process of stocking the tourist's mind with landscape models. (The cumulative imagery of engravings plays a part, too, as when Gilpin deems himself an 'eye-witness' – his phrase – to a landscape park near Hafod which he never visited, but studied through 'a large collection of drawings, and sketches'.[43]) Describing the Vale of Usk near Trecastle, Gilpin writes that

> The whole seemed to consist of one great vale divided into a multiplicity of parts. All together, they wanted unity; but separately, afforded a number of those pleasing passages, which, treasured up in the memory, become the ingredients of future landscapes.[44]

The metaphor of the memory as a commonplace book – linking reading/viewing with writing/viewing – implies a cyclical pattern of aesthetic appreciation. This imaginative act unifies features of memory with those of observation. While Gilpin keeps description at arm's length as a 'vehicle', his manner of thinking about the relationship between the mind's apprehension of picturesque landscape and the phenomenal landscape itself is ekphrastic, couched in figures of speech. Gilpin's practice, and the aims of picturesque tourism more generally, as Koelb suggests, attempts 'a kind of forced merger between place description, the favored form of classical ecphrasis, and art description'.[45]

Fosbroke's *The Wye Tour* and *Tourist's Grammar* literalise the commonplace approach to landscape description. Sold locally at Ross-on-Wye, *The Wye Tour* functioned as a tourist's pocket companion, although subsequent editions diversified its plan. The book became divided between descriptive portions for comparison on the spot, historical matter 'to be read at the Inn', and a journal to the source of the Wye 'for perusal at leisure'.[46] From the first edition, however, *The Wye Tour* was heavily derivative, with passages from Gilpin's *Observations* having pride of place, interspersed with Fosbroke's own remarks and additions from other sources. *The Tourist's Grammar* takes the taxonomies developing in *The Wye Tour* to their logical ends, the full subtitle indicating its scope: *Rules Relating to the Scenery and Antiquities Incident to Travellers: Compiled from the First Authorities, and Including an Epitome of Gilpin's Principles of the Picturesque*. The epitome combines matter from all Gilpin's works (liberally edited and abridged) into a prescriptive and reductive account of 'good' and 'bad' features in landscape, while a second part, the 'Tourist's Grammar' proper, deploys Gilpin's four-letter alphabet of landscape, dividing its material under the headings 'Ground, wood, rock and water', and concludes with an A–Z of specific features. Under each topic in both sections appear edited extracts from 'authorities' (including Archibald Alison, Gilpin, Knight, Price, and Richard Whately) with Fosbroke's linking commentary in square brackets. Both *Wye Tour* and *Tourist's Grammar* form part of Fosbroke's project of popularising the picturesque for tourists and topographical writers alike. His dedicatory letter to John Britton, one of the editors of *The Beauties of England and Wales* (eighteen volumes, 1801–18), fittingly signals his encyclopaedic approach.

Wye Tour takes a less nuanced approach to description than Gilpin, notwithstanding its reliance on him. Fosbroke edits out extraneous matter that Gilpin gleaned second-hand, and dismisses much of Gilpin's description as 'technical discussions'.[47] *Tourist's Grammar* directs itself not only to tourists in pursuit of the picturesque, but to 'topographical writers' to help them 'enliven the heaviness of description'.[48] In both texts, accuracy and vividness are guiding lights, even as the project endeavours to harmonise debates on the picturesque into a single, less theoretically exacting, but not especially cheap form.[49] Although the *Grammar* languished, with no further editions called for, *The Wye Tour* kept pace with Fosbroke's writing career, accruing additions that kept it within the current of Wye tourism.

In fact, the 'small guide-book [. . .] procured at Ross', from which Louisa Twamley quotes a '*glowing* account' of Windcliff in a footnote to her *Autumn Rambles on the Wye* (1838), was most likely the fifth edition of Fosbroke's *Wye Tour* (1837), her addition of a question mark after a flight of rhetoric anticipating *Wye-ator*'s paratextual parody in *Punch* by several decades and to the same effect: a critique of too much exuberance in description.[50] In the original, Fosbroke had just quoted a description by Whately that he deems 'too tame for the subject'; Twamley suggests an aesthetic middle ground with her parry.[51] In denying Fosbroke agency by suppressing his name, however, she may have justly recognised his own scrapbook approach to compiling *Wye Tour*, but, even so, Twamley out-Fosbrokes Fosbroke. The footnote in which she quotes Fosbroke supplements her 'borrowing' of a passage detailing the same scene from Ludwig Heinrich von Pueckler-Muskau's *Tour in England, Ireland, and France, in the Years 1828 & 1829* (1832), the same section that Fosbroke extracted and abridged in his Appendix to *The Wye Tour*. Twamley, too, abridges the text, and goes farther than Fosbroke: she abridges Fosbroke, her real and unacknowledged source.[52]

Twamley's aura

Fosbroke's and Twamley's slippery approach to quotation, paraphrase, and abridgement renders source hunting bewildering even without the possibility of other intertextual debts. Similarly, 'eye-witnessing' of landscape may be synonymous with one's saturation with second-hand engravings, so the mutual reference points between linguistic and painterly aesthetics complicate any linear understanding of the history of picturesque imagery as embodied in writings like those of Gilpin, Fosbroke, Twamley, or the dozens of writers who remarked on or illustrated the Wye Valley during the first half of the nineteenth century. What makes the Birmingham poet, painter, and travel writer, Louisa Anne Twamley, of particular interest is her public avowal of descriptive autonomy:

> My descriptions are my own; I would not add my name to the weighty list of those who have published books of copied paragraphs, each one of which, even a casual observer may detect, and trace up, through all the grades of octavos and quartos, to some traveller of the last century; since whose time, perhaps, the spot is so changed, that the description is not recognizable. This has been so generally the case with the compilers (for I cannot call them authors) of books on the scenery of the River Wye, that I beg to say I am not one of the class.[53]

Although the preface finds Twamley admitting some borrowings from William Coxe's *History of Monmouthshire* and other works, the status of description is not spelled out. Can there be a sense in which she can perform both the editorial sleight-of-hand of the compiler, while still claiming authorial 'ownership' of her descriptions?

Heffernan's notion of *ekphrasis* as the verbal representation of visual representation has an important application to Twamley's descriptive project, since *Autumn Rambles* joins what Rachel Teukolsky calls the 'democratisation of landscape appreciation that defined the 1830s', mani-fested in the many new annuals that combined steel-engraved picturesque views with verbal description.[54] *Autumn Rambles* was the first (and only) number of *The Annual of British Landscape Scenery*, but competitors included *The Landscape Annual* (1830–9), *Heath's Picturesque Annual* (1832–45), and *Turner's Annual Tour* (1833–5). Formally trained, possibly by her relation Sir Thomas Lawrence, Twamley became an accomplished artist who earned her living painting miniatures (she later married a cousin and emigrated to New South Wales, where she wrote the travel books for which she is best known). She exhibited her works at the Birmingham Society of Artists shows and became, according to Vivienne Rae-Ellis, a 'member of the fashionable pic-turesque group of painters and writers of the English Midlands [c. 1829–39]'.[55] Twamley experi-mented through the 1830s with self-illustrated collections of poetry and tales, earning a particular reputation for flower poetry and vibrantly hand-coloured engravings. As the *Monthly Repository* remarked of her first book, *Poems* (which included her sketch of Tintern Abbey and three inter-linked sonnets), 'her poems show that she is a painter, and her paintings that she is a poet'.[56]

With *Autumn Rambles*, Twamley was commissioned to provide 'written descriptions' for engravings by William Radcliffe after drawings by David Cox, Copley Fielding, Charles Radclyffe, and Henry Warren. Besides drawing on Fosbroke and other travel writers, she incorporates extracts from her own poetry and that of others, extending the interart project of her earlier books. Although the plates might have been the book's inception, Twamley's additions are so substantial that at least one early reviewer recognised the annual as a useful guidebook rather than mere keepsake.[57] The balance between plates and written description answers to Jackson's 'Picturesque Description in Books of Travel', where plates present accu-racy in 'a single glance', but work in tandem with written descriptions whose function is 'to animate the scene, to warm the landscape, to make the figures move and speak', and to bring the scenes before the eye and complete the ekphrastic illusion.[58] Twamley gestures to the engravings as supplements ('the annexed plate gives a faithful resemblance [. . .] of the high road which we traversed'), but also inserts herself into scenes, provides dialogue with guides and interactions with passers-by, and establishes emotional colour.[59] Like Gilpin when struck by the scant alphabet of the picturesque, Twamley can be acutely aware of linguistic limita-tions: 'I do not see why I should suppose my readers so dull as not to *know* that all this must be wondrously beautiful, without my ransacking my memory for a squadron of eulogistic adjectives'.[60] Yet she can be equally critical of 'pictorial license', taking to task one of Cox's plates for 'diminishing the exceeding picturesqueness of the place'.[61] At Tintern Abbey, she posits the limitations of both arts in attaining the truth of objects: 'Descriptions may be writ-ten, and pictures painted; but not all the eloquence of the one, nor the excellence of the other, will much avail' to express the character of a place 'that must be *felt* to be understood'.[62] This idealisation of the moment in excess of representation implicates the annual itself as a genre dependent on repetition. 'In lieu of the thousand and one versions of spots, which though we may never have visited them, are now made familiar as household words', Twamley writes, 'let us have something better deserving the name of *original* pictures, in transcripts of the yet unransacked localities, where camp-stools and sandwiches are yet unknown'.[63] 'Words', 'tran-scripts', 'pictures': if Twamley's language oscillates between the painterly and the linguistic, it is only to suggest the impossibility of the 'original' whose 'evanescence' and 'transience' defy the stasis and atemporality of painterly and poetic representation itself.

In her poem, 'November Stroll', first published in *The Romance of Nature* but alluded to and quoted in *Autumn Rambles*, Twamley not only enjoins the reader to seek out 'yet unransacked localities' but also to spot the unfamiliar within familiarity:

> Yet I could find that myriad beauties lay
> E'en in that beaten track: – *beauties* to *me*,
> Though hundreds daily passed along, to whom
> The things I gloried in were all unknown,
> Unseen – unloved.[64]

Description – and the excess of description to which it points – are given value in the poem and travelogue through the figure of the traveller, who stands in for and represents the reader. Twamley quotes 'November Stroll' near the beginning of her chapter describing her boat journey from Ross to Monmouth, a chapter fittingly headed with an epigraph from Wordsworth's 'Tintern Abbey': the concluding exhortation to the speaker's sister, in which she too mediates his experience and the 'lovely forms' of nature in the 'mansion' of her mind/memory. Twamley notes how she herself '[o]ften [. . .] inly repeated those sweet lines, and deeply felt their pure and eloquent truth', before recounting the day of her journey, the opening sentence of which contains ten lines from 'November Stroll' spliced grammatically to her own prose, comparing 'the sun's warm rays' (poem) to 'the picture-like brightness, [of] the fair vale of Monmouth' (prose). Like Wordsworth's 'benediction' to his sister,[65] the excerpt from Twamley's poem begins with a similar social gesture, 'Oh that all Partook the feeling which companioned me / That bright Autumnal morning!', one that exactly mirrors her wish to turn 'the painter's magic power' to social good: 'What would I not have given for the delight of feeling that other eyes would be gratified by Nature's bounty to mine; and that by perpetuating her beauty, though but poorly – I was in some sort acknowledging its blessing'.[66]

Although separated by some fifty pages, the two moments are Wordsworthian, the second a gloss upon the first, and the work as a whole takes seriously Wordsworth's model of the social value of the picturesque underpinning description. Picturesque appreciation *in situ*, she makes clear in her introduction, works like 'inspiration' to interweave the historical and poetical with the visual, all of which are reproduced by 'remembrance pictures'. These in turn colour the manner in which new experiences are perceived aesthetically and emotionally, providing what Twamley calls an 'after-enjoyment'. Unlike Gilpin, Twamley reconnects this experiential *enargeia* to travel description, the verbal representation of these 'memory pictures'. If the 'power at will of re-producing a past scene before the mind's eye' becomes the mark of an *ekphrasis* within the self, it falls to description and illustration working in tandem to produce those scenes for others.[67] Tourism emerges from Twamley's writings not as a single solipsistic pleasure, but as a communal activity; its value lies in its self- and social-integration through memory and memory's public face: description.

In her interpretation of Wordsworthian *ekphrasis*, Twamley seems to escape from what Richard Rorty refers to as the 'glassy essence' of post-Cartesian thought, the idea that mind 'mirrors' nature unproblematically, and that description aims for accuracy and commensurability between language and reality. Her programme for description in her paintings, poetry, prose poems, and travel writing depends on *enargeia*, the charging of language with emotion and imagination in order to bring past touristic experiences 'before the eye' ('the romantic notion of man as self-creative' for Rorty).[68] Although Wordsworth distrusted Gilpinian rules of the picturesque as well as the popular forms of tourism that emerged from them, Twamley remotivates Wordsworth so that descriptive *enargeia* might take place within rather than against the communal social space of the *Annual*, the Wye Tour, and popular reading and tourism more generally. Rorty's notion of a philosophy that dispenses with epistemology for hermeneutics, trading 'glassy essence' for 'new, better, more interesting, more fruitful ways of speaking', or, as he more commonly puts it, 'edification', thus resembles the picture of tourism emerging from Twamley's pages, where the self and the social are linked and perpetuated under the sign of picturesque description in travel writing.[69]

Further research

Twamley's 'ownership' of descriptive agency within an overdetermined Wye tourist discourse, her attention to the pictorial exigencies of the landscape annual genre, and the circumspection expected of women writers within a commercialised public sphere all have implications for travel research beyond her own particular case and her own era. If descriptive strategy might be seen as a methodology for recovering agency or, at least, resisting the larger discourses that threaten to engulf travel writers, description can be an important focus for analysing the works of writers, especially women, operating under discursive restraints more generally. We might also ask (and attempt to answer) the question of what happens to travel writing research when we stop privileging narrative, or when we consider narrative and description in the classical ekphrastic sense as interlocking modes. Ekphrastic readings of travel writing at the very least open up new possibilities for interart projects that study the complex relationships between verbal and visual travel representation only hinted at in this chapter. Research on annuals, letterpress-plate books, and travel illustration need not, and should not, privilege one of the constituent art forms. Above all, travel writing research might heed the advice of the clergyman and writer George Gregory (1754–1808) to his son: 'Description is the rock on which most narrators of travels suffer shipwreck, especially when they attempt to be picturesque'.[70] For Gregory, the more one attempts to describe a landscape, the farther one gets from it, so incommensurate is language to the task; the artistry of the descriptive writer resides in selection of detail. Following from this, among the challenges to travel writing research raised by this chapter is the question of whether we can discover new ways of evaluating the effectiveness of descriptive technique as well as its imbrication in social, historical, political, and intellectual contexts.

Notes

1 'Wye-ator' [pseud.], 'Wye and Wayfare', *Punch* 45 (5 September 1863), 96.
2 Crapanzano argues that metaphoric overemphasis or hypotyposis confirms the narrator as observer even as it renders the accuracy of observation suspect. See his 'Hermes' Dilemma: The Masking of Subversion in Ethnographic Description', in *Writing Culture: The Poetics and Politics of Ethnography*, ed. James Clifford and George F. Marcus (Berkeley, CA: University of California Press, 1986), 58.
3 For the Romantic commonplace book, see Jillian M. Hess, 'Coleridge's Fly-Catchers: Adapting Commonplace-Book Form', *Journal of the History of Ideas* 73.3 (July 2012): 463–83.
4 Louisa Anne Twamley, *An Autumn Ramble on the Wye* (London: W. S. Orr and Co., [1838]), 11. After marrying her cousin in 1839, Twamley published as 'Mrs. Charles Meredith'.
5 Richard Rorty, *Philosophy and the Mirror of Nature* (Princeton, NJ: Princeton University Press, 2009), 375.
6 For 'belatedness', see James Buzard, *The Beaten Track: European Tourism, Literature, and the Ways to 'Culture' 1800–1918* (Oxford: Clarendon Press, 1993), 110–14.
7 Charles L. Batten, Jr., *Pleasurable Instruction: Form and Convention in Eighteenth-Century Travel Literature* (Berkeley, CA: University of California Press, 1978), 84–91. For the circulation of Berchtold's *Essay* in Heinrich August Reichard's *Guide des voyageurs en Europe* (1793), see also Silvia Collini and Antonella Vannoni, eds., *Les instructions scientifiques pour les voyageurs: XVIIe–XVIIIe siècle* (Paris: L'Harmattan, 2005), 21.
8 Leopold Berchtold, *An Essay to Direct and Extend the Inquiries of Patriotic Travellers*, 2 vols (London: Printed for the Author, 1789), 1: 43.
9 See Robert Boyle, 'General Heads for a Natural History of a Countrey, Great or Small', in Royal Society, *Philosophical Transactions* (London, 1665–6), discussed in Paul Smethurst, *Travel Writing and the Natural World, 1768–1840* (New York: Palgrave Macmillan, 2013), 25–6.

10 See Innes M. Keighren et al., *Travels into Print: Exploration, Writing, and Publishing with John Murray, 1773–1859* (Chicago, IL: University of Chicago Press, 2015).

11 James A. W. Heffernan, *Museum of Words: The Poetics of Ekphrasis from Homer to Ashbery* (Chicago, IL: University of Chicago Press, 1993), 3 (original emphasis).

12 Janice Koelb, *The Poetics of Description: Imagined Places in European Literature* (New York: Palgrave Macmillan, 2006); Ruth Webb, *Ekphrasis, Imagination and Persuasion in Ancient Rhetorical Theory and Practice* (Aldershot: Ashgate, 2009).

13 Webb, *Ekphrasis*, 51.

14 Webb, *Ekphrasis*, 52. The *Commentarium in Aphthonii Progymnasmata* compares *ekphrasis* to tourism: 'just as if someone took a recent arrival in Athens and guided him around the city, showing him the gymnasia, the Peiraeus and each of the rest [of the sights]; metaphorically, therefore, the speech which relates (*aphēgeomai*) everything in order, relating to both the action and the person and showing [it] in detail is called *periēgēmatikos*' (qtd. in and trans. by Webb, 205).

15 Koelb, *Poetics of Description*, 4.

16 See Michel Beaujour, 'Some Paradoxes of Description', *Yale French Studies* 61 (1981): 27–59, esp. 37–41.

17 Webb, *Ekphrasis*, 5–6.

18 Barbara Maria Stafford, *Voyage into Substance: Art, Science, Nature, and the Illustrated Travel Account, 1760–1840* (Cambridge, MA: MIT Press, 1984), 48; Nigel Leask, *Curiosity and the Aesthetics of Travel Writing 1770–1840* (Oxford: Oxford University Press, 2002), 5–8.

19 Leask, *Curiosity*, 7.

20 William Gilpin, 'On Picturesque Beauty', *Three Essays* (London: R. Blamire, 1792), 18n.

21 'On the Word Picturesque' [signed 'A. P.'], *Belfast Monthly Magazine* 31 (February 1811): 117–18.

22 Gotthold Ephraim Lessing, *Laocoon: An Essay upon the Limits of Painting and Poetry*, trans. Ellen Frothingham (New York: Noonday Press, 1957), 88.

23 Samuel Hibbert, *A Description of the Shetland Islands, Comprising an Account of Their Geology, Scenery, Antiquities and Superstitions* (Edinburgh: Archibald Constable, 1822), v; John MacCulloch, *A Description of the Western Islands of Scotland, Including the Isle of Man*, 3 vols (London: Archibald Constable, 1819), 1: ix. See also Benjamin Colbert, 'Travel Narrative', in *The Encyclopedia of Romantic Literature*, ed. Frederick Burwick (Chichester: Wiley-Blackwell, 2012), 3: 1452–3.

24 Smethurst, *Travel Writing*, 40. See also Clifford Geertz, 'Thick Description: Toward an Interpretive Theory of Culture', in *The Interpretation of Cultures: Selected Essays* (New York: Basic Books, 1973), 3–30.

25 Smethurst, *Travel Writing*, 54–6; 17.

26 Julian R. Jackson, 'On Picturesque Description in Books of Travels', *Journal of the Royal Geographical Society* 5 (1835): 381.

27 Jackson, 'Picturesque Description', 383; 382; 383; 383.

28 Jackson, 'Picturesque Description', 385.

29 See Benjamin Colbert, 'Introduction: Home Tourism', in *Travel Writing and Tourism in Britain and Ireland*, ed. Benjamin Colbert (Basingstoke: Palgrave Macmillan, 2012), 1–12.

30 See Malcolm Andrews, *The Search for the Picturesque: Landscape Aesthetics and Tourism in Britain, 1760–1800* (Aldershot: Scolar Press, 1989); Nicola J. Watson, *The Literary Tourist: Readers and Places in Romantic and Victorian Britain* (New York: Palgrave Macmillan, 2006).

31 John Murray, *A Handbook for Travellers on the Continent* (London: John Murray and Son, 1836), iii.

32 Sara Mills, *Discourse of Difference: An Analysis of Women's Travel Writing and Colonialism* (London: Routledge, 1991), 69.

33 David Spurr, *The Rhetoric of Empire: Colonial Discourse in Journalism, Travel Writing, and Imperial Administration* (Durham, NC: Duke University Press, 1993), 7.

34 David Scott, *Semiologies of Travel from Gautier to Baudrillard* (Cambridge: Cambridge University Press, 2004), 165; 160; 25.

35 Dean MacCannell, *The Tourist: A New Theory of the Leisure Class* (Berkeley, CA: University of California Press, 1999), 43–8.

36 See Andrews, *Search for the Picturesque*, 39–66.

37 Thomas Dudley Fosbroke, *The Wye Tour, or Gilpin on the Wye, with Historical and Archaeological Additions . . . &c &c.* (Ross: W. Farror, 1818), vii.

38 William Gilpin, *Observations on the River Wye, and Several Parts of South Wales, &c. Relative Chiefly to Picturesque Beauty; Made in the Summer of the Year 1770*, 2nd ed. (London: R. Blamire, 1789), 2.

39 Gilpin, *Observations*, 38.

40 Gilpin, *Observations*, 41.

41 Gilpin, *Observations*, 85.

42 Gilpin, *Observations*, 49–50 (emphasis in original); Webb, *Ekphrasis*, 51. Gilpin goes on to suggest that painting, and by extension descriptive writing, forms a 'secondary pleasure' that may equal and even exceed immediacy in the kind of its pleasure but not its intensity: 'There may be more pleasure in recollecting, and recording, from a few transient lines, the scenes we have admired, than in the present enjoyment of them', *Three Essays*, 49–50.

43 Gilpin, *Observations*, 79. Gilpin ventriloquises the writer of a journal to parts of Wales he had not yet visited, so it is never entirely clear whether such comments are superimpositions of Gilpin's or in the 'found' MS.

44 Gilpin, *Observations*, 93–4.

45 Koelb, *Poetics of Description*, 111.

46 See Preface to Thomas Dudley Fosbroke, *The Wye Tour*, new ed. (Ross: W. Farror, 1822). Fosbroke siphoned off material into additional companion volumes. See *Companion to the Wye Tour. Ariconensia; or Archæological Sketches of Ross, and Archenfield* (Ross, 1821) and *Outlines of Monmouthshire and South Wales* (listed as in the press in *Airconensia*, although no copy survives).

47 Fosbroke, *Wye Tour* (1818), vii. Fosbroke edited out these criticisms of Gilpin in subsequent editions of the book.

48 Thomas Dudley Fosbroke, *The Tourist's Grammar; or Rules Relating to the Scenery and Antiquities Incident to Travellers: Compiled from the First Authorities, and Including an Epitome of Gilpin's Principles of the Picturesque* (London: John Nichols and Son, 1826), iii.

49 The guides were sold at 7s., approximately £15 in current spending power.

50 Twamley, *Autumn Ramble*, 46.

51 Thomas Dudley Fosbroke, *The Wye Tour, or Gilpin on 'The Wye,' with Picturesque Illustrations: to Which Is Added an Appendix [. . .]*, 5th ed. (Ross: W. Farror, 1837), 118. The Appendix was published separately as *The Wye Tour [. . .] Forming an Appendix [. . .]*, new ed. (Ross: W. Farror, 1837).

52 In his *Tour in England, Ireland, and France,* translated by Sarah Austin, 2 vols (London: Effingham Wilson, 1832), Pueckler-Muskau writes: 'Over this ridge you again discern water – the Severn, five miles broad [. . .] on either shore of which you see blue ridges' (2: 192); Fosbroke alters punctuation and mistranscribes the word 'shore' as 'side': 'Over this ridge you again discern water, the Severn five mile broad [. . .] on either side of which you see blue ridges' (*Appendix*, 47). Twamley follows Fosbroke's punctuation and wording exactly (*Autumn Ramble*, 45).

53 Twamley, *Autumn Ramble*, 6.

54 Rachel Teukolsky, *The Literate Eye: Victorian Art Writing and Modernist Aesthetics* (Oxford: Oxford University Press, 2009), 32. My list of Annuals in this paragraph is also drawn from Teukolsky.

55 Vivienne Rae-Ellis, *Louisa Anne Meredith: A Tigress in Exile* (Hobart: St. David's Park, 1990), 38.

56 [Leigh Hunt?], review of *Poems, with Illustrations*, by Louisa Anne Twamley, *Monthly Repository* 9.100 (April 1835): 289.

57 See 'Review of *Annual of British Landscape Scenery*', *Tait's Edinburgh Magazine* 5.60 (December 1838): 799–800.

58 Jackson, 'Picturesque Description', 383.

59 Twamley, *Autumn Ramble*, 62.

60 Twamley, *Autumn Ramble*, 37.

61 Twamley, *Autumn Ramble*, 88; 89.

62 Twamley, *Autumn Ramble*, 51 (original emphasis).

63 Twamley, *Autumn Ramble*, 141.

64 Louisa Anne Twamley, 'A November Stroll', *The Romance of Nature; or, the Flower-Seasons Illustrated* (London: Charles Tilt, 1836), 215, ll. 5–8. Twamley's introduction to *Autumn Rambles* alludes to the poem: 'but there is another track to which I would guide all who are yet unacquainted with its myriad beauties [. . .] which adorn and enrich the varied scenery on the banks of our fair WYE' (10).

65 Twamley, *Autumn Ramble*, 99–100. Twamley follows her friend William Howitt's popular *The Book of the Seasons; or the Calendar of Nature* (London: Henry Colburn and Richard Bentley, 1831) in reproducing the passage from Tintern Abbey, including Howitt's substitution of the 'benedictions' for 'exhortations': 'with what healing thoughts / Of tender joy wilt thou remember me, / And these my benedictions' (xxiii).

66 Twamley, *Autumn Ramble*, 100; 141.

67 Twamley, *Autumn Ramble*, 11.

68 Rorty, *Philosophy*, 358.

69 Rorty, *Philosophy*, 360; see also 357–65.

70 George Gregory, *Letters on Literature, Taste, and Composition, Addressed to His Son* (Philadelphia, PA: Bradford and Inskeep, 1809), Letter XXIII [Voyages and Travels], 208.

13

LECTURES

Tom F. Wright

Travel lectures 1830–1900

Travelling, and speaking about one's travels, have always been interdependent acts. It is no surprise, therefore, that one of the most historically popular means of communicating the experience of travel has been oral delivery before a live audience. There is something timeless about the dynamic involved: travellers, often returning home from experiences overseas, invite a community to listen to an account of what they have seen. Such an act was understood as a desirable civic good as far back as Plato, who argued of the homecoming wanderer, 'if he have himself made any observations, let him communicate his discoveries to the whole assembly'.[1] Presentations of this type have provided a parallel tradition to the written history of travel discourse ever since.

As I explore in this chapter, however, it was in the nineteenth century that this form exerted its most powerful cultural influence, in the brief historical moment between the emergence of a mass performance culture and the rise of cinema. As increasingly formalised circuits for public speaking developed in Europe and North America, lectures by travellers became an established idiom of an emerging transatlantic show culture, with audiences from Glasgow to San Francisco sitting transfixed before the first-hand accounts of distant lands and exotic peoples. At its height the travel lecture reached audiences as wide as, if not wider than, those for written accounts, and attending such talks became one of the scarce means by which many people acquired an insight into world geographies and global cultures.

Thinking about the history of travel lectures also forces us to think about the relationship of all travel writing to the world of performance. As this chapter explores, lectures on travels were often part of a multimedia spectacle, with a live narrator frequently embedded within a continuum of technologies intended to simulate the pleasures and sensations of travel. In what follows, I provide a broad sketch of some of the characteristics and scope of the travel lecture phenomenon as it was experienced in Britain and the United States from 1830 until the birth of cinema. I do so through the examples of three of its more prominent but largely forgotten figures – Albert Smith (1816–1860), Bayard Taylor (1825–1878) and Esther Lyons (1864–1938) – showing how their talks helped create a popular culture of cosmopolitanism and shape one of the primary aesthetic modes of early motion pictures. By focusing on this nineteenth-century moment, I argue for the travel lecture phenomenon as one of the more under-appreciated and idiosyncratic cultural practices in travel studies.

Definitions

For the purposes of this discussion, the 'travel lecture' can be broadly defined as an oral rendition of first-hand experience, imparting esoteric knowledge about distant places or peoples to a live audience. They were oratorical performances that fused description and comparison to communicate the realities of unfamiliar geographic and social conditions, often with the cardinal aim of allowing audiences to travel vicariously. As such, the term covers presentations and styles as diverse as any of the modes of writing discussed in this collection, occupying a discursive overlap with several other modes of lecture hall fascination and inquiry – natural history, popular anthropology, comparative politics, autobiography, landscape description. Approaches and registers ranged from the urbane to the demotic, from the scientific to the touristic. In providing this broad platform for cross-cultural reflection, the eyewitness travel report offered a significant degree of freedom to orators. Performers could and did exploit their remit and their data to advance all manner of arguments. Travel talks were perhaps above all performances of interpretation, or dramas of appraisal, and as with the wider genre of nineteenth-century travel writing, they came to centre on a rhetoric of nationhood and otherness, themes amplified through performance.

Though often based on a lone figure standing to speak before a crowd, travel lectures were also embedded in a multimedia ecology of visual technologies. The physical contexts in which they were performed were various, ranging from the austere lecture halls of small-town America or provincial Britain to much grander spaces in London, Philadelphia or Boston that were essentially working theatres. The latter settings were often relevant to the medium, since the more successful lectures were supported by visual aids and theatrical flair. Travel presentations became particularly associated with magic lantern shows or stereopticon presentations, with the commentary of the speaker supported by photographs projected on glass.[2] But the most notable media interface for travel lectures was the phenomenon of the panorama, giant landscape paintings on slow-moving pulleys that guided audiences through an often grand natural scene or terrain. They were similar to the more established form of the diorama, or fixed circular 360-degree painting, but were mobile, allowing performers to tour with them. The most notable exponents of the form were US showmen such as John Banvard (1815–1891), whose panorama of the Mississippi played at the Egyptian Hall in London with enormous success between 1848 and 1850.[3] Others took viewers on journeys along the Hudson, Mersey or Rhine, simulated train journeys from Pittsburgh or Manchester, or led them through the skylines of Rome and Paris.[4] Specialised panoramas also served more specific purposes. Not least was their use as ways to communicate a reform message, as in the case of those employed by the fugitive William Wells Brown (c.1814–1884) to illustrate 'Views of the Scenes in the Life of an American Slave' during his late 1840s lecture tours in Europe.[5]

In one sense panorama shows were art exhibits, and relied for their appeal on the quality of the illustrations. However, the presence of the commentator-lecturer meant that these were closer to live theatrical shows than to exhibitions, and were customarily promoted in terms of the narrative skills of the impresario, who talked audiences through the scenes. At the heart of even the most elaborate travel lecture presentation, therefore, was the narrative voice, recounting and interpreting esoteric personal experiences. As John Plunkett has argued, 'in contrast with the grand history paintings of the early panoramas, the showman acted as a democratic interlocutor between picture and audience'.[6] Oral renditions of travel material allowed for emotions and drama to be experienced communally. Even amidst visual stimulation, it was always language that made this happen. Speakers' resources of description and evocation were called upon to bring alive the meanings of what audiences saw as images flashed before them.

Thanks to a culture of reportage in the popular press, these oral events were frequently recorded in print through stenography and shorthand, and broadcast to readers in their newspaper in the days following the performance.

Scholarship

The travel lecture's place at a disciplinary crossroads has contributed to its surprising scholarly neglect. In recent years, however, the genre has received increased attention from social, cultural and media historians, and from those studying the pre-history of film. From the US perspective, the growth and development of the lecture circuit upon which most such lectures were delivered has been explored by Donald Scott and Angela Ray.[7] As Scott maintains, 'the travel lecture was less a travelogue than a kind of comparative ethnography', and a key genre in a form through which far-flung communities 'created a sense of belonging to a national public'.[8] The essays collected in *The Cosmopolitan Lyceum: Lecture Culture and the Globe in Nineteenth-Century America* (2013) considered the travel lecture as one form through which ideals of popular cosmopolitanism were developed and sustained.[9] My own work, particularly in *Lecturing the Atlantic: Print, Speech and an Anglo-American Commons 1830–1870* (2017), has shown how travel was a key lecture hall mode of cultural mediation and diplomacy.[10] British lecturing has attracted far less scholarship to date, though the rise of public science in Mechanics' Institutes and organisations such as the Royal Geographic Society has been well explored by Diarmid Finnegan and Jon Klancher.[11]

Another strand of thinking about travel lectures to date has placed them within broader contexts of show culture and early cinema. Richard Altick's classic study *Shows of London* (1978) categorised travel lectures as one of many types of cultural form that emerged in a nineteenth-century 'moment when faith in the redemptive powers of education for the adult masses was nearing its peak'.[12] David Chapin's *Exploring Other Worlds: Margaret Fox, Elisha Kent Kane, and the Antebellum Culture of Curiosity* (2004) placed travel discourse within one such broader context.[13] Erkki Huhtamo sketched the relationship of lectures to the panorama in *Illusions in Motion: Media Archaeology of the Moving Panorama and Related Spectacles* (2013).[14]

The most common discussion of travel lectures has come from media and film historians. Charles Musser's *High-Class Moving Pictures* (1991) used the late nineteenth-century travel lecturer-narrator Lyman Howe as an exemplar of the transition from the culture of itinerant lecturer-showmen to the modern motion picture exhibitors.[15] In *Atlas of Emotion: Journeys in Art, Architecture and Film* (2002) Giuliana Bruno traced the genealogies between the travel lecture and early film aesthetics, an argument developed in Lynn Peterson's *Education in the School of Dreams: Travelogues and Early Nonfiction Film* (2013).[16]

Albert Smith's 'Mont Blanc'

Perhaps the most prominent of all British travel lecturers was the explorer and showman Albert Smith. A former medic, published novelist and contributor to *Punch* and *Bentley's*, like many writers of his generation he used his literary fame to turn his hand to the lucrative mode of travel writing. After returning from an excursion to the Ottoman Empire in 1849, he published *A Month at Constantinople* (1850) and, surprised by its positive reception, opted to capitalise on the public appetite for his experiences by translating his material into a form suitable for the stage. Smith hired Willis's Rooms in London's West End, and circulated advertisements for an illustrated lecture entitled 'The Overland Mail'. Marketed as a grand 'Literary, Pictorial, and Musical Entertainment', the show premiered on 28 May 1850.[17]

During the summer of 1851, Smith undertook a new expedition to the Alps, resulting in another popular published account of his travels, *The Story of Mont Blanc* (1853).[18] Building upon the success of his previous show, he planned and conceived an even more elaborate stage event to communicate his Alpine experiences in a striking new manner. In March 1852 his performance of 'Mont Blanc' opened at the Egyptian Hall, and went on to become one of the defining entertainments of the mid-Victorian London stage.[19] By the end of his second season in 1853, Smith had given 471 performances and performed to an astonishing 193,754 people, including a special performance for Queen Victoria and at Osborne House.[20] By the time 'Mont Blanc' closed in 1858 it had been performed over 2,000 times, and the cultural frenzy around it led to a host of spin-off products, including engravings, dances, stereoscopic pictures, plates decorated with Smith's portrait and even a 'Mont Blanc' game. When the craze for his Alpine lectures eventually reached its selling point in the late 1850s, Smith travelled to Hong Kong and incorporated his new book *To China and Back* (1859) into a new hybrid travel lecture entertainment, called 'Mont Blanc to China'.

'Mont Blanc' was a strikingly immersive multimedia presentation, with the Egyptian Hall transformed into an imagined *mise-en-scène* of Switzerland, complete with simulations of a flower-rimmed Alpine lake. Smith himself emerged from an elaborately painted chalet to face his audience. The painter William Beverly had accompanied him on his journey to Chamonix, and his illustrations formed the backdrop of the show. The painted scenes of the journey depicted in other lantern slides were shown in the window behind Smith on stage, offering a dioramic journey of Smith's own mountain ascent. During the second season in 1853, the scenography was to become even more flamboyant, augmented with living fish in the lake, with characteristic Swiss objects dotted throughout the auditorium.[21]

Nonetheless, Smith still provided the centre of the drama himself. As he recognised, 'the diffusion of knowledge, instead of entertainment, was getting rather tiresome; in fact, there was great danger of instruction becoming a bogie to frighten people away rather than attract them'.[22] His narrative met this problem by navigating multiple rhetorical and discursive levels. Costumed in full evening dress, he proceeded to introduce these scenes, and provide a narrative accompaniment consisting of anecdotes, literary description, impersonations of Swiss characters and patter songs. The presentation mixed geographical and cultural information with satirical asides of questionable taste, and on occasion Smith broke into songs that offered comic commentary on his material. Just as the *Illustrated London News* had trailed the performance by presenting reproductions of Beverley's panoramic images, the London *Morning Advertiser* struggled to capture for its readers the mixed mode of presentation:

> viewed as a whole – as a diorama, musical, comic, and sentimental mélange – an 'at home' – a lecture, or a combined literary and imitative production, the 'Ascent of Mont Blanc' need not fear comparison with any two hours and a half of intellectual and social enjoyment ever offered to an appreciating public.[23]

Having attended one of the same shows, the young Henry James recalled the reckless levity of 'big, bearded, rattling, chattering, mimicking Albert Smith':

> [T]he brief stop and re-departure of the train at Épernay, with the ringing of bells, the bawling of guards, the cries of travellers, the slamming of doors and the tremendous pop as of a colossal champagne-cork, made all simultaneous and vivid by Mr. Smith's mere personal resources and graces.[24]

In these ways, Smith embodied the travel lecturer as both narrator and impersonator. This was the sense captured in the *Morning Advertiser*'s reference to an 'at home', an allusion to Charles Mathew, pioneer of the monopolylogue with his one-man show *At Home* (1818), in which he circled through a series of characters. This mode was particularly well suited to the mode of the travel lecture, with its reliance upon a sense of sequential observations and encounters with local inhabitants. 'Mr. Albert Smith', noted the *Times*, 'unites two distinct classes of entertainment – the instructive diorama [. . .] which has of late, become so much the rage, and the humorous song and character sketch.'[25] As another commentator put it, whereas the majority of the speeches of typical panorama narrators were purely information and nothing more than 'a page of a dictionary read aloud', Smith's lectures were more far more reliant on his charisma to hold the piece together.[26]

Thanks to Smith, the travel lecture had become a viable commercial form and a prominent feature on the London stage. J. S. Bratton's history of the London stage situates him as 'another manifestation of the Victorian modernity so astoundingly expressed in the Crystal Palace', but also in terms of his peculiarly performed social position, offering the 'spectacle of the real [. . .] a presentation of reality itself, authentic, non-fictional and taken possession of by an ordinary man, an entirely unmade-up, unfictionalised man, a gentleman in no way different from the paying customers; one of ourselves'.[27] As Erkki Huhtamo has argued, the Mont Blanc phenomenon 'was the culmination of the moving panorama as a medium' but the focus on his own lecturing and narration also places him squarely within the tradition of the travel lecture.[28] After all, as Huhtamo continues, 'while for most showmen, the primary attraction was the panorama, for Smith his own name was more important than the title of his entertainment. The spectators came to see him tell his stories, impersonate characters, sing songs', and translate his travels into an oral form, drawing the mysteries of travel back to the realm of performance.[29]

Bayard Taylor: 'the great American traveller'

While the travel lecture was a growing feature of 1850s British show culture, it had already become a major force in the lecture circuit on the other side of the Atlantic. Alongside self-improvement topics, travel was among the most popular topics on the circuit of venues known as 'lyceums'. Perennially popular subjects were locations such as the Holy Land, Western Europe and the developing American West; most attractive of all were the even more exotic locations of Africa, the Far East and the Arctic. To be sure, the ostensible emphasis of these events was frequently on entertainment and escapism. Yet other categories of lecturer offered more sub-stantively educational experiences to audiences, such as explaining Westward expansion and the plight of Native Americans or discussing political revolutions in Europe, or even using reports of travel as a vehicle for the anti-slavery cause.[30] The versatility of travel lectures attracted a host of well-known writers to attempt the genre, including Ralph Waldo Emerson (1803–1882), Herman Melville (1819–1891) and Frederick Douglass (1818–1895). But the emblematic travel lecturer of the period was Bayard Taylor (1825–1877), the travel writer, poet and diplomat whose lectures dominated the platform in the 1850s, and whose complex stance embodied some of the tensions between reform and entertainment.

Taylor had risen to fame as the author of *Views Afoot: Europe Seen with a Knapsack and Staff* (1846), whose tale of the rise of a resourceful self-made Pennsylvania boy's adventures in the Old World offered a generation of middle-class Americans an innovatory guide to enjoying the Old World 'on the cheap'. Fluent in several languages and possessed of considerable per-sonal charm, he found himself a natural traveller, and his combined voyages were on a vaster scale than those of any author or performer, covering more ground than most of his American contemporaries. Having travelled through California and Mexico, sailed down the Nile, accompanied the commercial 'opening' of Japan in 1853 and published newspaper and book-length accounts of his experiences, he had become a literary hero and patriotic icon in the United States. Upon his return from Japan in 1854, he observed to his publisher that 'curiosity is alive to see "The Great American Traveller." It provokes me and humiliates me, but I suppose it is natural, and I must submit to it'.[31]

Taylor duly embarked upon the lecture circuit, satisfying the curiosity of audiences across the nation who, as one memorialist put it, 'longed to look upon this friend who had been with them such a pleasant companion in so many strange lands'.[32] He proved an immediate success, and though he soon grew to resent the time-consuming pressures of lecturing, he could not resist its rewards and repeatedly undertook full winter tours.[33] His was a self-consciously exotic lecture hall act. His repertoire consisted of a nucleus of five main lectures on far-flung locations – 'The Arabs' (toured from 1853), 'Japan and Loo Choo' (1853), 'India' (1854), 'Life in the North' (1858) and 'Moscow' (1858) – alongside which he frequently delivered a more abstract piece entitled 'The Philosophy of Travel' (1856).[34] Taylor also periodically appeared in the costume of the region about which he was speaking, adopting Oriental robes while performing 'The Arabs' or an oversized Cossack cap for touring 'Moscow'.[35]

This theatrical element of his act was central to Taylor's appeal. However, unlike fellow performers such as Smith who became increasingly reliant upon visual aids, Taylor's art was a primarily literary phenomenon. Much of Taylor's approach involved informational accounts filtered through familiar mid-century racial theory, codifying and classifying the peoples he had met in relation to putative American progress. Taylor's colonial vision clearly represents the most challenging aspect of his work for modern readers, and his lectures were filled with repeated claims along the lines that 'every important triumph which man has achieved since his creation belongs to the Caucasian race. Our mental and moral superiority is self-evident'.[36]

But Taylor's style also developed from an early reductive emphasis on racial stratification towards vivid geographic sketches that served as dramatic highlights. It was this latter quality that was clearly most admired by audiences. 'Japan and Loo Choo' was praised in New York in 1854 for its 'extremely graphic [. . .] descriptions of the island scenes' that generated 'the strongest expressions of pleasure from the audience'; an 1855 Ohio report recorded that 'his listeners can see clearly in their mind's eye the things of which he speaks'.[37] Having attended 'Moscow' in 1858, *The Philadelphia Press* deemed him 'a true, faithful word-painter of scenes that come within the range of his perceptive intellect. Taylor's powers are certainly extraordinary'.[38]

Taylor's status as an everyman contributed to his popularity, but elite culture was sceptical about him. Fellow poet and editor Park Benjamin coined the notorious, widely circulated witticism that Taylor had 'travelled more and seen less than any man living'.[39] Melville, perhaps harbouring a degree of resentment at his rival's lyceum success, is believed by some to have used Taylor as the basis for 'The Cosmopolitan', the worldly but naive dilettante in *The Confidence Man* (1856).[40] A contemporary coolly remarked of his lecturing that 'reports of his latest trip are always well-received by the large class who (as Goethe says in his analysis of playgoers) do not care to think, but only to see that something is going on'.[41] Modern critical opinion of his lecturing has generally concurred, considering him at best as a minor heir to the Genteel Tradition of such derided figures as Henry Wadsworth Longfellow, at worst as a mere shill of colonialism, a disseminator of the racial prejudices of his day.[42] David Mead concluded of his platform career that 'his appeal was conscious and calculated; he had no share in the ideal of spreading culture'.[43]

However, others saw the political potential in Taylor's act. Having attended the lecture at Willard's Hall on 23 December 1863, Abraham Lincoln wrote to Taylor, with whom he had a passing personal acquaintance, requesting the commission of a lecture on the realities of Russian serfdom, as an instructive parallel to Confederate slavery.[44] Though evidently deeply flattered, Taylor, due to time constraints, was forced to decline, but declared himself eager to 'contribute, though so indirectly, to the growth of truer and more enlightened views among the people'.[45] In his mind, he did so through offering hymns to these benefits of breadth of experience, and the cultivation of an attitude of cultural openness and cosmopolitanism. As a lecture hall celebrity, he personified for many the newly obtainable goal of foreign travel, its potential for social mobility and personal growth, by offering audiences a form of 'performed cosmopolitanism'. Attending his performances, Taylor's admirers gained exposure to an aspirational way of life via a persona that was literary, itinerant and amicable, an apparent representative of broadminded republican masculinity.

One sign of the maturity of Taylor's chosen form was that by the 1850s, the travel lecture had become a popular target for satire. Humorists such as Artemus Ward began to tour the lecture circuit offering comic talks billed as straightforward eyewitness travel accounts, with talks billed as 'Sixty Minutes in Africa' that made much fun of the genteel pomposity of the art that Taylor and Smith specialised in.[46] The most prominent parody of this type was 'A Lecture on the Sandwich Islands', or sometimes 'Our Fellow Savages of the Sandwich Islands', the performance that helped introduce obscure journalist Mark Twain to national consciousness.[47] In this piece and in others, Twain parodied the lofty tone of Pacific missionaries and the gullibility of audiences willing to be easily impressed by the performing traveller. By taking aim at the conventions and assumptions of the travel lecture, burlesques such as these mocked the high-minded sobriety of the lecture hall, debunked the prestige surrounding the activities of orators such as Taylor and exposed travel lecturing as merely another confidence trick.[48]

Esther Lyons, 'the Klondike girl'

One final figure who helps illustrate the final pre-cinematic flowering of the travel lecture is the American journalist and sometime explorer who published under the stage name Esther Lyons. Marketing herself as the first white woman known to have crossed the famous and perilous Chilkoot pass, Lyons was one of the most notable of many writers who capitalised on public fascination with the 1897–1898 Gold Rush in the Yukon area of north-western Canada. After publishing an illustrated volume, *Esther Lyons's Glimpses of Alaska* (1897), she chose to translate these impressions to the lecture platform. She became a star on the circuit for a few short seasons, and remains a mysterious and poorly understood figure, often confused with a famous actress of the day whose name she shared. Yet as Guiliana Bruno has shown, this self-made businesswoman and traveller was not only a peculiarly resourceful entertainer, but one of the last figures to successfully capitalise on the Anglo-American public's thirst for live voice and visuals before the entire genre was transformed by the motion picture industry.[49]

In the years between Taylor and Lyons, the American lecture circuit had changed in several ways. Having previously been centred on the major cities of the North East, lecture venues had proliferated across the nation, and now incorporated a new type of outdoor tent network known as Chautauqua, after the upstate New York lake on whose banks these events were first held. Lecture culture had also evolved from a rather austere focus upon self-improvement towards a broader theatrical emphasis upon livelier forms of entertainment. The travel lecture was an evergreen draw in this new context, versatile enough both to meet both shifting tastes and to incorporate new technological forms of presentation.

When Lyons took her 'Klondike' act to the great halls of the East Coast cities, she spoke accompanied by nearly 200 images of the region and of life among the prospectors, 'thrown upon the canvas by a colored stereopticon'.[50] But it was also still a physical performance, in which Lyons brought to life the realities of prospecting. An advertisement for her Boston show promised that after the lecture Miss Lyons will appear in her Klondike costume in the midst of a mine in full operation. She will show the sluice-boxes at work, give a practical demonstration of panning and exhibit to the audience the largest nugget (value $589.11) ever taken out of the Klondike.[51]

Reports from that lecture recall how 'Miss Lyons in her simply, yet eloquent manner, carried the audience, as it were, into the land of hidden wealth'.[52] Some commentators stressed how, through the combination of visual and verbal stimulation, 'the series of photographs and the lecturer's vivid description carries the listener away and he can almost imagine he is making the dangerous trip himself'.[53]

It is arguable that by this point in the evolution of the travel lecture, people were coming to these events more for the images than for the lecturer. Ostensibly, they were both informational, offering descriptions of the landscape and native peoples of the Klondike, and aspirational, dispensing advice for those who might seek their fortune there. But clearly the chief draw was the combination of thrilling subject and uniquely dynamic performer. As Charles Musser observes, though, the retinue of those offering travel presentations in these years included a 'large fraternity [. . .] Stereopticon lecturers (as well as photographers) were overwhelmingly men and represented the world as they saw and understood it'.[54] Lyons was not the only famous woman travel lecturer of the day; other female performers included Delia Akeley, Mary Jobe Akeley and Osa Johnson.[55] However, Lyons's exploits carried with them a unique frisson given the picturesque danger of her experiences in what promotional materials called 'that hazardous gorge from which has come such stirring tales of hardship and death [. . .] Miss Lyons bears the distinction of being the first of her sex to explore the Yukon'.[56]

Lyons certainly presented her experiences as physically daring. 'The horrors of the Chilkoot pass', she informed an audience at New York's Carnegie Hall in March 1898, were that of 'a wall of rock on one hand and a wall of ice on the other [. . .] [and] crevasses to slip through.'[57] In Boston the next month, reporters had duly been impressed at how she had survived the landscape:

> Many have perished there from starvation, others have been buried in the mountainous drifts of snow, and only a few days since dispatches told of 30 men or more being crushed to death beneath a mighty avalanche. And yet she passed it safely.[58]

Lyons went even further to de-feminise her performances, cultivating the persona of a harddrinking resourceful prospector, boasting to her New York audience that 'we found it convenient to travel in zigzag fashion, and as one of our Indian guides had somehow got hold of a bottle of whisky, we had all the zig-zagging we wanted'.[59] Dressed in striking fashion, 'with sluice and pan, appearing in her Chilkoot costume', she struck quite a figure, both on the East Coast, and throughout the country.[60] Reporters for Indiana's Terre Haute *Saturday Evening Mail* found it hard to square the 'retiring, refined, quiet woman of medium height' with having braved the Chilkoot as early as the spring of 1894 and 'the perils and terrors of the interior of Alaska when strong men shrank from the trip'.[61]

As Karen Mahoney has shown, this image of the female prospector offered up a powerful political symbol of independence and determination. 'For those travelling to the Klondike', she notes, women like Lyons 'became key players in an event which captured the world's attention, and became sought-after speakers not only on the subjects of fashion and women's domestic interests, but also on their opinions of government and economic possibilities.'[62] Lyons played up to the image of the independent female traveller in unapologetic fashion. Asked in Indiana whether she preferred domestic or public life, she answered, 'Domestic, but unfortunately I am one of the army of breadwinners, and my desires are of course stifled by my necessities.'

In the years following her 1898–1899 performances, however, Lyons's lectures became embroiled in controversy as some questioned the truthfulness of her accounts. To some, it was questionable whether she had made the journeys about which she spoke, or engaged in the difficulties she made money from speaking about. By 1902 the *New York Times* was reporting in sceptical fashion about the 'enterprising' Miss Lyons, and her willingness 'to fairly coin money with an illustrated lecture' of uncertain value.[63] In fact, the authenticity of the photographs featuring her remains in doubt today. The Library of Congress official notes accompanying them add that

> [a]lthough Lyons wrote a series of articles about the expedition she claimed to have taken, and lectured about it for the rest of her life, later research indicated there is no evidence of her participation in the expedition and that, in fact, she could not have been on the expedition at that time.[64]

Modern scholars therefore encounter the inescapable and timeless problem of both performance and travel: the association with the confidence trickster. The boundaries between the vocations of traveller, actress and travel lecturer were as porous as ever, and this was a slippage that would be exploited even more fully in the age of cinema. Whether or not she conquered the Klondike, she turned audience after audience into converts to her particular performed vision of womanhood. Lyons thus represents not only an intriguing transitional figure between the waning of the nineteenth-century travel lecture and its incorporation into cinema, but an emblem of the ambivalent regard and overly critical fixation on questioning the actual truth of exploits that has always been attached to feminist self-fashioning.

Conclusion: the transition to early cinema

As Bruno notes, 'in a strict historical sense, film and travel met physically at the turn of the century on the set of the travel lecture'. As the moving image became a reality in the 1880s, the parallel between it and travel was one of the most forceful in early cinema. By offering the pleasures of travel whilst sitting motionless in a chair, Bruno continues, film 'incorporated the representational drive and the spatial unconscious of travel culture, with its visible dislocations'.[65] This revolutionary new technology propelled and then absorbed the travel genre just as traveller-lecturers later incorporated motion pictures into their display. Among the most prominent of such transitional figures were Lyman Howe (1856–1923), John Stoddard (1850–1931) and Burton Holmes (1870–1958). Holmes coined the term 'travelogue' in 1903 for his new breed of entertainment, and in his performances such as 'Through Europe with a Kodak' (1901) was one of the first to put all of these elements of the travel lecture together.[66]

Travel lectures represent a dynamic and still largely underexplored archive of cultural activity. More than simply part of nineteenth-century spectacle culture, popular renditions of travel experiences were influential 'rational amusements', showing mass culture at its most straightforwardly moral. If, as Judith Adler and others have argued, all processes of travel represent modes of performance, the travel lecture phenomenon proposes a suggestive way in which aspects of this performance might be said to occur upon travellers' return.[67] It offered a literary and oratorical mode through which issues of nationhood and social identity could be thought through in communal performative context. It was a space whose creative potential was exploited by the figures discussed in this chapter, and by many more besides, as a unique vehicle for cultural expression.

The hybrid nature of this oral and visual form reminds us of the specific material histories that lay beneath an often over-arching and static notion of travel writing. Scholarship on the history of travel and its dissemination is growing increasingly attuned to the modalities of the different forms of text, media and platforms through which the globe has been understood. Opening up the definitional scope of travel writing to incorporate travel oratory, presentations and lectures allows travel to become once again a mobile concept in both its origins and its output. A great deal still remains to be discovered about this idiosyncratic mode, and about the cultures of listening and performing that connect our own fixation with on-screen monologues of David Attenborough, Rick Steves or Michael Palin back to the solemnity of the nineteenth-century lecture hall.

Notes

1 Plato, 'Laws' XII, in *Plato: Complete Works*, trans. Trevor J. Saunders, ed. John M. Cooper (Indianapolis, IN: Hackett, 1997), 1320.
2 See Theodore X. Barber, 'The Roots of Travel Cinema: John L. Stoddard, E. Burton Holmes and the Nineteenth-century Illustrated Travel Lecture', *Film History* 5.1 (1993): 68.
3 See Susan Tenneriello, *Spectacle Culture and American Identity, 1815–1940* (New York: Palgrave Macmillan, 2013).
4 Wolfgang Schivelbusch, 'Panoramic Travel', in *The Nineteenth-Century Visual Culture Reader*, ed. Vanessa R. Schwartz and Jeannene M. Przyblysi (New York: Routledge, 2004), 93. See also Bernard Comment, *The Panorama* (London: Reaktion, 2002), 63–4.
5 See Junius P. Rodriguez, ed., *Slavery in the United States: A Social, Political, and Historical Encyclopedia* (Santa Barbara, CA: ABC-CLIO, 2007), 209.
6 John Plunkett, 'Screen Practice Before Film', accessed 19 May 2016. www.bftv.ac.uk/projects/exeter.htm.
7 Donald Scott, 'The Popular Lecture and the Creation of a Public in the Mid-Nineteenth-Century United States', *Journal of American History* 66.4 (1980): 791–809; Angela Ray, *The Lyceum and Public Culture in the Nineteenth-Century United States* (East Lansing, MI: Michigan State University Press, 2005).
8 Scott, 'The Popular Lecture', 803.
9 Tom F. Wright, ed., *The Cosmopolitan Lyceum: Lecture Culture and the Globe in Nineteenth-Century America* (Amherst, MA: University of Massachusetts Press, 2013).
10 Tom F. Wright, 'The Results of Locomotion: Bayard Taylor and the Travel Lecture in the Mid-Nineteenth-Century United States', *Studies in Travel Writing* 14.2 (2010): 111–34; Wright, *The Cosmopolitan Lyceum*; Tom F. Wright, *Lecturing the Atlantic: Speech, Print and an Anglo-American Commons 1830–1870* (Oxford: Oxford University Press, 2017).
11 See Diarmid Finnegan, 'Geographies of Scientific Speech in Mid-Victorian Edinburgh', in *Geographies of Nineteenth-Century Science*, ed. David N. Livingstone and Charles W. J. Withers (Chicago, IL: University of Chicago Press, 2011), 153–77; Jon Klancher, *Transfiguring the Arts and Sciences: Knowledge and Cultural Institutions in the Romantic Age* (Cambridge: Cambridge University Press, 2013).
12 Richard Altick, *The Shows of London* (Cambridge, MA: The Belknap Press of Harvard University Press, 1978), 197.
13 David Chapin, *Exploring Other Worlds: Margaret Fox, Elisha Kent Kane, and the Antebellum Culture of Curiosity* (Amherst, MA: University of Massachusetts Press, 2004).
14 Erkki Huhtamo, *Illusions in Motion: Media Archaeology of the Moving Panorama and Related Spectacles* (Cambridge, MA: MIT Press, 2013).
15 Charles Musser, *High-Class Moving Pictures: Lyman H. Howe and the Forgotten Era of Traveling Exhibition, 1880–1920* (Princeton, NJ: Princeton University Press, 1991).
16 Giuliana Bruno, *Atlas of Emotion: Journeys in Art, Architecture and Film* (London: Verso, 2002); Jennifer L. Peterson, *Education in the School of Dreams: Travelogues and Early Nonfiction Film* (Durham, NC: Duke University Press, 2013), 3.
17 Altick, *Shows of London*, 200.
18 Albert Smith, *The Story of Mont Blanc* (London: David Bogue, 1853).
19 Altick, *Shows of London*, 200–10.

20 See Alan McNee, *The Cockney Who Sold the Alps: Albert Smith and the Ascent of Mont Blanc* (Brighton: Victorian Secrets, 2015), 145.

21 See Huhtamo, *Illusions in Motion*, 23.

22 Quoted in Altick, *Shows of London*, 197.

23 Quoted in Huhtamo, *Illusions in Motion*, 22.

24 See Christopher Hibbert, *Queen Victoria: A Personal History* (New York: Basic Books, 2000), 191; Henry James, *A Small Boy and Others* (New York: C. Scribner's Sons, 1913), 247.

25 Quoted in Huhtamo, *Illusions in Motion*, 22.

26 Quoted in Huhtamo, *Illusions in Motion*, 129.

27 J. S. Bratton, *The Making of the West End Stage: Marriage, Management and the Mapping of Gender in London, 1830–1870* (Cambridge: Cambridge University Press, 2011), 121.

28 Huhtamo, *Illusions in Motion*, 205.

29 Huhtamo, *Illusions in Motion*, 205.

30 I discuss a range of such uses in Wright, 'The Results of Locomotion'.

31 Bayard Taylor to James. T. Fields, 17 February 1854, in *Life and Letters of Bayard Taylor*, ed. Marie Hansen-Taylor and Horace E. Scudder (Boston, MA: Houghton, Mifflin, 1884), 269.

32 Isaac Edwards Clarke, *A Tribute to Bayard Taylor: Read before the Literary Society of Washington, March 8, 1879* (Washington, DC: Mohun Bros., 1879).

33 See Larzer Ziff, *Return Passages: Great American Travel Writing* (New Haven, CT: Yale University Press, 2001), 156–8.

34 For this essay, the following lecture manuscripts have been examined: 'Japan and Loo Choo', 'The American People', 'Moscow', 'The Philosophy of Travel', 'American Life', 'The Animal Man'. All manuscripts held at Chester County Historical Society, Pennsylvania.

35 'Bayard Taylor', *Putnam's Monthly* 4.4 (August 1854). See also Peter G. Buckley, 'Paratheatricals and Popular Stage Entertainment', in *The Cambridge History of American Theatre, Vol. 1: Beginnings to 1870*, eds. Don Wilmeth and Christopher Bigsby (Cambridge: Cambridge University Press, 2008), 475.

36 Quoted in Richmond Croom Beatty, *Bayard Taylor: Laureate of the Gilded Age* (Oklahoma City, OK: University of Oklahoma Press, 1936), 153.

37 'Bayard Taylor's Lecture', *New York Evening Post*, 21 January 1854; 'Bayard Taylor Lecture', *Daily Toledo Blade*, 15 January 1855.

38 'Bayard Taylor', *Philadelphia Press*, 6 November 1858.

39 Hansen-Taylor, *Life and Letters of Bayard Taylor*, 523.

40 See Hans-Joachim Lang and Benjamin Lease, 'Melville's Cosmopolitan: Bayard Taylor in The Confidence-Man', *Amerikastudien* 22 (1977): 289.

41 Higginson, 'The American Lecture System', 363.

42 Richard Cary, *The Genteel Circle: Bayard Taylor and His New York Friends* (Ithaca, NY: Cornell University Press, 1952). For recent postcolonial readings, see Ziff, *Return Passages*, 118–69.

43 Mead, *Yankee Eloquence in the Middle-West*, 118.

44 Lincoln to Taylor, 25 December 1863, in *Abraham Lincoln: Speeches and Writings 1859–1865*, ed. Don E. Ferhenbacher (New York: Library of America, 1989), 93.

45 Taylor to Lincoln, 28 December 1863, in *Abraham Lincoln: Speeches and Writings 1859–1865*, 93.

46 'Sixty Minutes in Africa', *Cincinnati Inquirer*, 5 March 1863.

47 'The Sandwich Islands' stenographed lecture report, Cooper Union, New York City. For details on this lecture and its reception see Sid Fleischman, *The Trouble Begins at 8: A Life of Mark Twain in the Wild, Wild West* (New York: Greenwillow Books, 2008), 124–6.

48 'Criticism on Mark Twain's Lecture for Adult Readers – Not to be read by People with weak stomachs', *Jamestown Journal*, 28 January 1870.

49 Bruno, *Atlas of Emotion*, 111.

50 'Lecture on the Klondike', *Boston Evening Transcript*, 9 April 1898.

51 'Popular Lectures', *Boston Evening Transcript*, 8 April 1898.

52 'Lecture on the Klondike', *Boston Evening Transcript*, 9 April 1898.

53 'Esther Lyons Lectures on the Klondike', *New York Inquirer*, 2 March 1898.

54 Quoted in Bruno, *Atlas of Emotion*, 111.

55 For Delia and Mary Jobe Akeley see Edward P. Alexander, *The Museum in America: Innovators and Pioneers* (Walnut Creek, CA: AltaMira Press, 1997), 43–5. Further examples are provided in Fatimah T. Rony, *The Third Eye: Race, Cinema, and Ethnographic Spectacle* (Durham, NC: Duke University Press, 1996), 120.

56 'Lecture on the Klondike', *Boston Evening Transcript*, 9 April 1898.

57 'Klondike in Carnegie Hall', *New York Times*, 2 March 1898.

58 'Miss Lyon's Lecture', *Boston Evening Journal*, 12 April 1898.

59 'Klondike in Carnegie Hall', *New York Times*, 2 March 1898.

60 'Klondike in Carnegie Hall', *New York Times*, 2 March 1898.

61 'Heroine of Alaska', *Terre Haute Saturday Evening Mail*, 19 February 1898.

62 Karen Mahoney, 'Bloomers and Pluck: The Intersection of Journalism and Femininity in the Reporting of the Klondike Gold Rush of 1898', Unpublished Dissertation, Athabasca University, January 2012.

63 'Mistaken Identity', *New York Times*, 13 April 1902.

64 'Klondike Girl Photographs', LOT 13810 (F) [P&P], Library of Congress.

65 Bruno, *Atlas of Emotion*, 111.

66 Rick Altman, *Silent Film Sound* (New York: Columbia University Press, 2004), 58.

67 Judith Adler, 'Travel as Performed Art', *American Journal of Sociology* 94.6 (1989): 1366–91. See also Helen Gilbert and Anna Johnson, eds., *In Transit: Travel, Text, Empire* (New York: Peter Lang, 2002).

PART III

Sensuous geographies

14

SEEING

Margaret Topping

Seeing and being seen are the conventional indicators of cultural capital for the traveller, but the presumption that value is guaranteed by vision and visibility is disrupted by travellers who are 'deprived' of sight: their journeys will inevitably be narrated differently and, as such, will trigger a new and potentially troubling form of learning on the part of the sighted armchair-traveller reading their narratives. These reflections, which form the basis of the first sections of this chapter, give way to a more complex ethical dilemma when armchair-travellers leave the comfort of home to travel physically in the company of blind or partially sighted people. When grounded in philanthropic endeavour, and specifically in so-called charity or gap-year tourism, the link between cultural capital and being seen (in the performance of good works) is muddied by the competing impulses of voyeurism and empathy in the act of looking: as discussed further below, however benevolent their intentions, such travellers are increasingly subject to criticism as neo-colonialists and/or as consumers of 'poverty porn'. The final sections of the chapter thus explore how an analysis of charity or gap-year tourism has the potential to destabilise the common association between travel and spectatorship: the ethics of seeing and being seen, and associated positions of power, are subjected to uneasy scrutiny when sight is displaced as the primary means of experiencing the world. Conversely, and parenthetically, a reflection on charity tourism via the lens of seeing and being seen also offers new perspectives on what is now a multi-million-pound industry.

Being seen (i): the selfie

In response to the rise of both popular and scholarly debate on the global selfie phenomenon – a phenomenon itself authenticated by the term's inclusion in the *Oxford English Dictionary* for the first time in 2013 – journalist Megan Garber ponders its ambivalent reception:

> Are you sick of reading about selfies? Are you tired of hearing about how those pictures you took of yourself on vacation last year are evidence of narcissism, but also maybe of empowerment, but also probably of the click-by-click erosion of Culture at Large?[1]

As both material evidence of 'having been there',[2] and as supposed proof of the kind of cultural capital that marks out the cosmopolitan traveller, the selfie offers both a physical and a psychological image of the photographer/photographee, albeit one that the 'authentic' traveller may interpret as a failure to *look* on the part of the selfie-taker; a failure to look, moreover, which risks trivialising culture, people and emblems. For the selfie is the ultimate multi-directional commodification of travel, not only framing a partial and often stereotyped vision of the culture visited, but also seeking to confirm the value of the traveller through the composition of the image and its synecdochic associations: thus, for example, if France = Paris = capital of culture = Louvre = Mona Lisa, then a selfie in front of da Vinci's painting represents proof of cultural and economic capital. The phenomenon provides a fresh twist on the 'world-as-exhibition' proposed by John Urry in which, in his discussion of Haussman's Paris, spectacular views 'come to be signifiers of the entity "Paris"'.[3]

Selfies of this kind are also increasingly a marker of social capital, given the instantaneous sharing of images allowed by social media and almost simultaneous validation through likes and retweets. But within this lies an interpretative uncertainty, as Garber notes: does the practice of taking selfies denote narcissism or is it an empowering marker of self-esteem? Is the person represented an 'authentic' cultural devotee or a superficial, high-speed consumer of stereotyped cultural emblems?[4] And beyond the context of cultural markers, we are equally uncertain as to how to read the increasing use of the selfie as an outlet for the danger- and adventure-seekers traditionally associated with the figure dubbed the 'agoraphile' traveller by French sociologist Jean-Didier Urbain, that is the thrill-seeking individual who 'yearns for wide open expanses' and has a 'tyrannical obsession with vastness'.[5] The democratisation of travel and the ease of smartphone photography allow death-defying feats to be within the reach of even those travelling in the familiar. More people were reported to have been killed while taking selfies in 2015 than died in shark attacks (twelve versus eight),[6] while a dedicated *Wikipedia* page provides a full list of all known selfie-related deaths and injuries.[7]

The privileging of vision as the most reliable (and, as the selfie example suggests, socially valuable) sense by which to mediate the encounter between the traveller and the world is a familiar trope of travel writing, while the relationship of sight to discourses of power and appropriation has been well established since the publication in 1992 of Mary Louise Pratt's *Imperial Eyes*.[8] This cultural privileging of sight – or ocularcentrism, to use Martin Jay's term[9] – has implications for both visual and textual modes of recounting the experience of travel. The visual representation of travel in photography is, as suggested by the brief discussion of the selfie, implicated in discourses of power, capture and commodification, which themselves have their origins in the early use of photography as a literal tool of colonial expansion.[10] But writers too grapple with the challenges, possibilities and limitations of a textual visualisation of the experience of travel. At one end of the spectrum, Western (colonial) travellers commonly fail, in their descriptions of the cultures visited, to avoid the position of privileged spectator viewing a preordained spectacle. At the other end of the spectrum are travel writers seeking to textualise travel as a multi-sensorial experience based on physical discomfort as much as pleasure, rather than presenting a carefully contrived 'vision'. Such writers seek to evoke or replicate touch, hearing, smell and taste – both through their chosen focal points and through the stylistic textures of their narratives. Francophone Swiss traveller-writer, Nicolas Bouvier, for instance, demonstrates his attentiveness not only to the ethical minefield of looking – primarily as mediated by the camera lens – but also to the discomfort of not controlling one's own image when the object of another's gaze. Most strikingly, too, he not only recreates textually his experience of sounds, tastes, smells, touch, but he also articulates our mode of apprehending the world with reference to a phenomenological plenitude, as here, when he draws on both our sense of hearing and of taste without reference to sight:

We lend a distracted, deceitful, jaded, and above all monophonic ear to the polyphony of the world, and this way of reading the world on a single stave separates us from all that is succulent, desirable, liberating. [A la polyphonie du monde, nous prêtons une oreille distraite, fourbue, blasée et surtout monodique et cette lecture sur une portée nous sépare de tout ce qui est succulent, souhaitable, libératoire.][11]

Notwithstanding the quest of writers such as Bouvier for a renewal of the senses in travel writing, the dominance of vision in the account of travel survives in the dominance of sighted travel writers. Charles Forsdick has described the 'discursive normativity' that associates moving with seeing within travel writing as a genre.[12] A focus, therefore, on the works of blind or visually impaired travellers opens up the possibility of destabilising that discursive normativity.

Travelling without seeing

Textual images associated with sight commonly persist in the work of blind or partially sighted travellers. The travel journalism of Ryan Knighton, for example, makes marked use of visual metaphor: in a 2012 article on his journey to Egypt in the immediate aftermath of the Arab Spring, he describes being 'one of only four *gawkers*' at the Pyramids; the experience of being ferried around to touristic sites in a taxi is 'like [being at] a drive-in *movie*'; he describes how, on arriving at the site of the Sphinx, he '*stared* at nothing', while the 'absence of tourists' at these locations was, he noted, his 'only *glimpse* of the revolution' (all italics are my own).[13] The prevalence of images of seeing in Knighton's journalism highlights the dominance of sight as the conventional guarantor of 'truth' in the travel experience, an idea underlined by the unsettling effect his status as a blind traveller has on the representatives of Egypt's tourist infrastructure: from the pilot of his flight, to the taxi driver who ferries Knighton to his hotel and the hotel staff, the primary reaction is one of shock and horror at the idea of a blind man travelling alone and, indeed, walking through the streets of Cairo: 'I asked about a restaurant within walking distance. Both clerks puzzled a moment. "Walk? You cannot walk." "It's OK. I'm Canadian."' Yet it also marks the blind traveller's ironic consciousness of the multisensory deprivation on which much travel writing is based, at the same time as it foregrounds the richness of his experience of Egypt via a reliance on other senses, notably taste and smell:

Around me, all I could hear were skidding tyres and honks. There was a complementary smell, too, as though you were huffing on a tailpipe. Cairo is a car, I thought [. . .] A glass of juice appeared in my hand and brightened my senses, the cold and the tart of lemons cutting away the drive.

Knighton's ultimate conclusion that his is 'a privileged Western blindness' in comparison to that of the blind Egyptian women to whom, even in their own culture, movement is denied creates a new matrix linking disability studies, post-colonialism, gender and mobility studies which further disrupts the discourses of power and appropriation created by the privileged overlaying of mobility and sight. When he visits a school and residence for blind girls and women, he notes the absence of any sound of canes to guide the residents, and asks how the residents manage to walk around Cairo without them. '"Blind men use canes," Amal [his host] said, "but the girls do not. The shame is too much. So they walk feeling with their hands. Mostly they stay inside."' Knighton is haunted by the image of these women groping their way along walls in the open streets; as such, he challenges his readers not to associate blindness *per se* with impotence, but rather to recognise the reality of multiple, overlapping inequalities which have more to do with a culture that disables (further) on gender grounds than with a specific physical disability.

Beyond the field of travel journalism, Jean-Christophe Perrot's and Diego Audemard's co-authored *Tandems africains* [*Africa on Tandems*] recounts the two Frenchmen's 13,500-kilometre journey across sub-Saharan Africa throughout which the two sighted Western travellers rely on a total of twenty-seven blind or partially sighted local guides riding as tandem passengers on their bikes.[14] The seeing writers' 'outsider' experience of the cultures visited is thus mediated by the non-seeing insider knowledge of the guide. In addition to the disruption to the supremacy of vision as the primary means of acquiring cultural knowledge that this implies, it also highlights a relationship of democratic co-dependence between sighted and unsighted that challenges the structures of ocularcentrism more generally. The rest of this discussion focuses on Perrot and Audemard's journey from a number of perspectives which develop in new ways the preceding observations on vision, power and self-representation: examining the journey's links with charity tourism, and exploding the unequal relationship between bestower and receiver of good works which that tends to imply, allows for this challenge to occur. Ultimately, the two French travellers must metaphorically lose their sight in order to see; they relinquish, with some hesitation, the impulse to see and be seen, to which (charity) tourists may succumb, in favour of being led by their blind and partially sighted guides.

Notre boucle est bouclée[15]

This is a refrain which is repeated throughout the early sections of the text of *Tandems africains* – a refrain in its musical sense, for not only are shared rhythms necessary to the synchronicity of the travellers' physical movement forward on the tandems, but music is also a common means by which linguistic and/or cultural barriers are traversed. 'Le contact est noué: c'est magique' (36) [we've made contact; it's magical]: this in response to one of the French travellers, Diego Audemard's, improvised performance on his violin with one of the co-pilots, Azzeddine, who plays the oud. Diego's VTT – violon-tout-terrain [all-terrain violin], a play on the French 'vélo-tout-terrain' [all-terrain bike], is present throughout the text as a means of facilitating contact by sensory means other than vision. Indeed, many of their co-pilots are musicians; thus music is, in a sense, played on a loop (one of the meanings of 'boucle') throughout the succession of journeys that make up the narrative. Yet each individual journey, of which there are twelve in twelve different African countries, also takes the form of a geographical loop that returns their two native co-pilots (who change with each country) to their starting point after two weeks accompanying Audemard and Perrot. A basic map showing the circuit followed on each stage of the journey prefaces each new section of the book. The overarching journey on which Diego and Jean-Christophe, and their anthropomorphised tandem bikes, Noisette and Cyrano, are the constant parties is also a circular one which takes them from Lyon's Place des Terreaux and returns them to the same spot exactly a year later (or at least only ten minutes late, as Diego's girlfriend playfully reminds him). The circular itinerary and mini-itineraries reflect the metal rings (another definition of 'boucle') that characterise their mode of transport, just as the disrupted scopic regimes in which the narrative is grounded – sighted travellers are guided by sightless natives – at once draws attention to, and underplays, the importance of both the eyes as the key mediator for making contact with the world, and their prosthetic for capturing and preserving that contact, the camera lens.

These circles within circles appear to denote a journey which consciously eschews a linear teleology and which, as such, prioritises the experience of travelling over that of reaching one's destination, notwithstanding the emphasis in the text on individual achievement and overcoming difficulties, noted by Forsdick in the discussion referenced above. The textual narrative also provides us with access to multiple narratives, in which the 'non-voyants' are not spoken *for*, not passive agents, and in which, as a result, the traditional power dynamics associated with traveller and travellee (especially in developing countries) are disrupted precisely through the act of dismantling the binary relationship of agency and passivity that characterises the relationship between seeing and non-seeing people – at least as it may be constructed in the eyes of the former. This reflects an aspiration articulated by Lehbours ould el-Id, president of a Mauritanian charitable association, that could, in a sense, be used to summarise the text as a whole; he explains how through his own work: 'I wish to break down the barriers between countries, regions, able-bodied and disabled' ['Je souhaite briser les frontières entre les régions, les pays, les hommes et les handicapés'] (46).

Yet such a reading, I would argue, is enabled only through the retrospective reflection of the two travellers, as elaborated in the account of the return home and, above all, the epilogue (i.e. the last two sections of the text). It is in these sections that they articulate their unanticipated need to write their journey again and to do so differently from the contemporaneous blog published on their website. It is this that positions *Tandems africains*, the published narrative, at the end of an ethical – and in parallel a representational – journey. For it is, I would argue, significant that this shift from a contemporaneous blog (2002–3), navigable in bite-sized snapshots of any segment of their journey, to a substantial (345-page) text, published in 2007, which demands to be read in sequence (despite appearances to the contrary), is also a shift from the visual to the non-visual, from image to text. The marginalisation of the photographic narrative in this evolution signals a progression from 'gap-year' charity tourism to a more troubled – and for both travellers and readers, troubling – ethical journey. If, as one of their blind co-pilots, Théophile, remarks, 'in this third millennium, the blind man is not the one who cannot see, but the one who does not know that he can see without seeing' ['En ce troisième millénaire, est aveugle non celui qui ne voit pas, mais celui qui ne sait pas qu'il peut voir sans voir'] (216), then the sighted travellers, Jean-Christophe and Diego, have to 'lose their sight' in order to see 'properly'. The representational correlative of this loss of sight is a shift from the spatiality of the image (as reflected in the dominance of photographs in their contemporaneous blog) to the temporality of text in the published (2007) narrative. A hint at this increasingly troubled perspective is arguably present in the gradual fading of the refrain, 'notre boucle est bouclée', after its initial prominence in the early part of the book. The circle is broken both physically and metaphorically, for not only are the travellers frequently required to stop to repair or replace parts of the wheels of their bikes, but the neat circularity of micro and macro departures and returns is disrupted by a more jagged journey of (self-) discovery.

Being seen (ii): charity tourism

Judith Brodie, the UK Director of the charitable organisation VSO (Voluntary Services Overseas), prompted a certain outrage in a 2006 article in which she likened gap-year students seeking to undertake good works abroad to 'neo-colonialists'.[16] That a travel industry has developed in recent years to support the organisation of gap years and charity tourism more generally is for another discussion of the ethical tension between charitable endeavour and the commodification of disadvantage, but how valid an approach is this to take to the year-long experience of Jean-Christophe and Diego in sub-Saharan Africa? They are both twenty-two years old at the time of travelling; they take a year out of their university study to complete this journey; and they are financed through savings and sponsorship, notably by the city of Lyons which pays for one of the tandems, and by the Lyons-based bookshop, 'Raconte-moi la terre', which gives its name to their expedition. Their motivation for undertaking this adventure is set out in the published narrative as being born of both 'the call of wide open spaces' and 'always the same desire to construct one's own image of the world, to seek out wide open spaces, and, above all, to share with others the challenge that one has set for oneself ['Toujours cette même envie de construire sa propre image du monde, de rechercher les grands espaces, et surtout de partager avec d'autres les défis que l'on s'est lancés'] (9). While this shared experience ultimately becomes one of communion with the blind and visually impaired co-pilots, the implied emphasis at this stage is that the others with whom the journey will be shared are friends and family at home. Only with this primary motivation in place – one absolutely reminiscent of the agoraphile traveller and his association with danger, conquest, the unknown, the passage to manhood – does the precise nature of the expedition evolve:

> Week after week [. . .] the dream becomes reality. First of all, the idea is a round-the-world tour, then a round-the-world tour on bike, followed by a journey on tandems; then on tandems with blind people, and finally: a year on tandems with local blind people travelling across the continent of Africa. [Semaine après semaine, au fils des discussions et des réflexions personnelles, le rêve prend réalité, il se métamorphose en idée, qui s'affine en concept. C'est d'abord l'idée d'un tour du monde, puis celle d'un tour du monde à vélo, suivie de celle d'un périple à tandem, puis un tandem avec des non-voyants, et enfin: un an à tandem avec des non-voyants locaux sur le continent africain.]
>
> *(9–10)*

First impressions of these opening pages suggest a child-like escalation, an excited one-upmanship to aggrandise the adventurers. And indeed, the myth of their journey is pre-emptively crafted as text in their minds from the outset:

> *Just imagine it . . .*
> *Two tandem pilots, two blind passengers . . .*
> *The pilots guide, the passengers explain the customs of their country . . .*
> *All four pedal and narrate the world together.*
> *[Imaginez . . .*
> *Deux pilotes de tandem, deux passagers non-voyants . . .*
> *Les uns guident, les autres expliquent les coutumes de leur pays . . .*
> *Tous quatre pédalent et se racontent la terre.]*
>
> *(10)*

Italicised, set apart and indented as above, this worthy image already has the ring of soundbite publicity for a documentary or a book. That the two young men's knowledge and experience of Africa, of 'the "world of disability"' ['le "monde du handicap"'], and of riding a tandem (presented in that order), is rudimentary is no cause for hesitation, they freely admit (10–11). Undertaking the necessary research on each of the areas where they admit their knowledge is limited, and securing the finance for their journey, are merely the first of many 'trials' ['épreuves'] that will test 'our fighting spirit, our aggressiveness' ['notre combativité, notre hargne'] (11). The scene is thus set for an adventure and a journey of self-discovery, but also for the performance of both. At this stage, the immediately foreseen consumers of this performance are, as previously noted, the family and friends of Jean-Christophe and Diego for whom they create the multi-media website pre-departure and which they augment throughout the journey as the key means of representing themselves and the travellee. The website, by their own admission, is the primary vehicle for documenting their travel for those with whom they otherwise have very limited contact (one phone home call per month). They therefore carry with them a laptop (courtesy of Hewlett Packard) and a camera (courtesy of Kodak). Both companies are acknowledged on the website and in the subsequent book.

At the time of writing this chapter, the website is still live,[17] and notwithstanding my broader discussion here and elsewhere of the possibilities and limitations of various media in the representation of travel, it does provide a fascinating record of their journey, and of the lives and perspectives of their co-pilots. It also showcases the work of organisations in all of the countries visited that support the integration into the mainstream of people with disabilities, primarily, but not exclusively, with visual impairments. It thus acts as a tool of 'sensitisation' ['sensibilisation'] (53), a primary motivation that emerges in the course of the journey, but first articulated by the co-pilots rather than by the French travellers whose initial emphasis, as detailed above, is on adventure and exploration. The website has multiple access points from which to search the resource, some created prior to the journey (About Us; Our Project), some clearly added much later: the latter include the audio book version of *Tandems africains* and the constructed soundscapes which include contemporaneous recordings of ambient noise as well as conversations, songs and other audio artefacts retrospectively superimposed with excerpts from the published narrative.

Of particular significance to the proposed shift from charity tourism to ethical travel discussed here is the website's blog. This includes entries for every stage of the journey (which map onto the main chapters of the published narrative), and within each longer stage, one can click on individual episodes (catalogued with reference to locations and individuals). Drop-down menus for each stage thus allow the web viewer to drop in and out of the journey at any point and to access a standalone vignette of a day or a place. Some of these are descriptions of local organisations supporting blind and visually impaired people, and a common pattern here is to reproduce the organisation's mission statement, key officers and other data, as the basis of the entry. The specificity of the visit of Jean-Christophe and Diego is present only through photographic images that show them at meetings or at the venue. Others are diaristic accounts of what the two travellers (and their co-pilots) did on a given day, in which case the largely present-tense (first-person singular or plural) accounts are noticeably factual rather than analytical, descriptive – and even then minimally so – not reflective. Once again, photographs, which show Jean-Christophe and Diego (and very often their co-pilots) in situ, 'performing' the tasks that underpin their adventure, do much of the 'work' of narration and representation. As noted previously, these photographs are the visual record of 'having been there' and, given the charitable context, of 'having done that'. They are the markers of capital, albeit in the sense of the travellers' liberal, socially responsible credentials, rather than the purportedly cosmopolitan socio-cultural capital highlighted at the beginning of this discussion in relation to the selfie. As much about being seen as seeing, photographs such as these acquire a very different status in the retrospectively published book where choice and positioning render them at once more marginal and more potent. Indeed, one of the realisations reached by the authors – which is crystallised in and, given its position in the epilogue, arguably led to, the writing of the published text – is that 'we too often travel thanks to photos alone' ['on voyage trop souvent seulement grâce aux photos'] (334). Thus, while photographs do appear in the retrospectively published account, they are collected together as sixteen pages at the centre of, and distinctive from, the text: there is one page with images of all of their co-pilots, one page for each of the twelve countries visited, and one page each for: 'Return to France' ['Retour en France']; 'Shared passions: photos and music' ['Passions partagées: photos et musique']; 'Hand play' ['Jeu de main']; and 'Life on a tandem' ['Une vie de tandem']. Of these, 'Hand play' is most arresting for its focus on the tactile and on mutual physical contact. One image stands out, showing a white hand guiding the finger of a black hand to a location on a map, in an action that is, in one sense, as unexplained as it is poignant in another. Crucially, though, while these images are affective, they are not the avatars of the textual narrative.

From charity tourism to ethical travel: beyond being seen

The transition from charity tourism to ethical travel is, of course, neither as binary nor as definitive as the subtitle above may imply. Nevertheless, the evidence of a disruption to the primacy of vision has clear ideological implications. The shift away from the photographic emphasis in the contemporaneous website on 'being seen', and from the attendant emphasis on apprehending place through sight, challenges the carefully maintained distance of ocularcentrism, and the spectacle of so-called 'poverty porn'.[18] Key moments of challenge on the journey stimulate this reflection, troubling the charitable vision of the travellers, the most striking being when one of the proposed co-pilots, Sinayako, asks how much he will be paid to take part in the expedition. Jean-Christophe and Diego are taken aback at the suggestion ('surprised, taken unawares' ['surpris, pris au dépourvu']) (117), not having considered that others would seek to be remunerated when they themselves are not:

> I can't possibly accept this idea: pay them! We're neither a business nor a charity. We're not living off this project. The fact that this is all done without payment may dictate its limits, but it's also its strength [. . .] Money cannot corrupt what we have set out to do. [Je n'arrive pas à accepter cette idée: les payer! Nous ne sommes ni une entreprise ni une ONG. Nous ne vivons pas de ce projet. Sa dimension gratuite peut en être la limite, mais constitue aussi sa force [. . .] L'argent ne doit pas corrompre ce que nous sommes venus faire.]
>
> *(118–19)*

Admittedly, such instances are rare, and the vast majority of co-pilots request no payment. However, Jean-Christophe and Diego's surprise is indicative of an ironic blend of selfing and othering: on the one hand, they elide the differences between self and other by assuming that the basis of Western charitable interventions is normative. As such, they fail to take account of socio-economic inequality at a global level, assuming perhaps, instead, a celebratory globalism of the kind proposed by Arjun Appadurai.[19] What they initially fail to recognise is that even 'poor [Western] students' on a year out of their study will appear to be in a position of privilege to the materially disadvantaged African co-pilots and other travellees. With a certain naivety, Diego describes how 'when we were in France we thought the tandem would create the possibility of meeting people, or moments of spontaneous sharing' ['En France, nous pensions que le tandem permettrait des rencontres, des moments de partage spontanés'] (117) which would provide a 'reward which isn't always financial' ['récompense qui n'est pas toujours financière'] (118). The charitable gift of an opportunity for which gratitude, not payment, is expected, echoes curiously – and doubtless unconsciously – the post-abolition discourse of 'the gift' ['le don'], and those few co-pilots who turn down the offer of the trip in the absence of payment are othered by the French travellers, precisely because the latter seem reluctant to accept the validity of this position as fitting within an acceptable moral compass.

These instances also demonstrate the different rates of the two travellers' own ideological journeys: as with their physical journey, they overtake each other, then slip behind in turn. Here, while Jean-Christophe is ultimately pragmatic in his response ('It's a cultural issue. We have the luxury of knowing the difference between work and holidays. That's not the case for them' ['C'est une question culturelle. Nous avons le luxe de connaître la différence entre travail et vacances. Ce n'est pas leur cas'] [118]), Diego's concern is that to pay their co-pilots would corrupt their journey. The 'purity' of their intentions risks taint through monetisation, and yet this too reveals a naivety which could so easily become a position of moral superiority: on being asked again for financial recompense on a later stage of their journey, this time by Klé and Dramane, Diego writes:

> These words are like stab wounds. They forget that we are in the same state of fatigue as they are. We've cycled together. We have to overcome our moral fatigue. We have to motivate them again. The experience we've had since Bamako that's immortalised in the blog we co-wrote with them is already a very precious reward. [Ces paroles sont comme des coups de poignard. Ils oublient que nous sommes dans le même état de fatigue qu'eux. Nous avons pédalé ensemble. Nous devons surmonter notre fatigue morale. Il faut les remotiver. L'expérience vécue depuis Bamako, immortalisée par le journal de bord coécrit avec eux, est déjà une très belle récompense.]
>
> *(140)*

The frequent occasions when the stereotypical preconception of 'Whites' ['les Blancs'] as 'rich gits' ['des richards'] (50) who are open for exploitation puncture painfully the image of benevolent travellers bestowing their favour on innocent natives. The fact that some of the native people they encounter assume that the blind co-pilots are receiving substantial remuneration from the Frenchmen and encourage them to greater 'exploitation' in which they can share is both an affront to the Frenchmen and generally untrue of the co-pilots.[20] Yet, it also highlights the realities of agency on the part of the blind or visually impaired guides in contrast to an implied coupling, in Diego's mind, of sightlessness and powerlessness or presumed passive gratitude. These instances thus represent another key trigger for a lessening emphasis on seeing and being seen, and an increasing shift from a position of responsibility and leadership to one of co-dependency. Just as the proposed shift from charity tourism to ethical travel with which this section began requires a recognition of nuance and permeability, so too do the French travellers come to understand that no single ethical alignment characterises their own position, or that of the co-pilots, or that of the local people they encounter. Increasingly, all of the protagonists struggle with too easy, too clearly delineated perspectives. Thus, borders become porous, producing a narrative characterised not by an inversion of the conventional power dynamic between self and other, but an equalising cross-fertilisation which decentres the primacy of vision.

From responsibility to co-dependency

From the outset of the published account of their journey, semantic shifts trouble the discursive normativity that associates the Western traveller with agency and the culture visited with passivity. The common trope of the landscape-as-spectacle present in the works of earlier travel writers gives way to a grammatical shift into agency, as 'Morocco gradually reveals itself to us' ['Le Maroc se découvre à nous progressivement'] (22). While still playing on the trope of the exotic culture as feminised, eroticised and available for possession, the formulation instead places control of her image with the 'seductress'. In parallel, the blind and partially sighted 'passengers' ['passagers'] who are originally characterised (in the preface to the book) as being 'our responsibility' ['notre responsabilité'] (11) emerge from the first circuit undertaken in Diego and Jean-Christophe's journey as being far from passive, and indeed not only active, but activist: the first organisation working with blind and partially sighted people which they come across (in Morocco) is currently occupied by protestors:

201

Since the State hadn't honoured its promise of jobs for blind and partially sighted graduates, they have been striking for the past year and occupying the headquarters of the organisation by way of protest. [L'État n'ayant pas honoré des promesses d'emplois pour les diplômés non voyants et malvoyants, ces derniers font grève depuis un an et occupent de force le siège de l'organisation pour protester.]

(23)

These early challenges to the Frenchmen's preconceptions of passivity on the part of their co-pilots pave the way for a subtle and sometimes uneasy negotiation of the shifting positions of master and apprentice, 'parent' and 'child'. A questioning as to who is in the position of power – 'it's getting difficult to know who is the guide, between Issa who opens the gates of the town, Azzeddine and Khalid who translate and explain, and us, who are helping our friends find their way, hand in hand' ['Il devient difficile de savoir qui est le guide, entre Issa qui ouvre les portes de sa ville, Azzeddine et Khalid qui traduisent et commentent, et nous-mêmes, qui aidons nos amis à se diriger, main dans la main'] (27) – progresses to an acceptance by Diego and Jean-Christophe of their identity as 'young pupils' ['de jeunes élèves'] (47); and ultimately to a position of physical and phenomenological co-dependency: they need to find a rhythm that allows them to progress physically on the tandem, and this gradually broadens to an apprehension of the world around them that is conditional on a synaesthetic sharing of sense, as discussed further below.

It is tempting to read this shift to co-dependency as a metaphor for cultural relativism, and for a rethinking of the (power) relationship between self and other. The focus of this discussion is, indeed, theoretical in its quest to displace binaries in favour of porosity, complexity and multiplicity and to challenge some of the bases of charity tourism, but the text is also a form of activism against marginalisation that sits at the confluence of race, gender, class and disability. It places front and centre an engagement with the socio-cultural realities of economically marginalised, blind African men, whose own fundamental contention is quite simply that 'people with disabilities are capable of much more than others think' ['un aveugle et toute personne handicapée en général sont capables de beaucoup plus de choses qu'on ne le pense'] (54). Diego and Jean-Christophe develop their own sense of empathy with the blind people they encounter, articulating their own early sense of disorientation and enforced reliance on others for local knowledge with reference to blind people who are obliged to put themselves in others' hands (71). More literally, too, they try to experience the physical reality of sightlessness (as when Diego is blindfolded to equalise the field between himself and some blind children with whom he plays football [182]); and all of this underpins the increasing valorisation of the other senses as a pathway to phenomenological 'truth'.

Etre aveugle ce n'est pas la fin du monde[21]

This understated refrain belies the emphasis on sensory richness that increasingly characterises the text, and while this plenitude is retrospectively expressed in or as a textual narrative, an implied reflection on the inadequacy of the word also characterises the contemporaneous experience. While their pre-journey research is drawn unquestioningly from textual sources, first-hand experience soon makes clear the reality of multilingualism for the two French travellers, and not only in the sense of a language barrier. They do, of course, need to learn 'our first words of Arabic' ['nos premiers mots d'arabe'] (21), but increasingly, they are immersed in a polyphony of sounds of which verbal communication is but one example, the bedfellow of the sound of the violin, the oud and the rhythmic hum of the bikes:

The couplets interlace in French and in Arabic, accompanied by Toubkal, the oud, and VTT the violin. Guided by this melody, Khalid gets us back to Djama'a el-Fna square. [Les couplets s'enchaînent en français et en arabe, accompagnés par Toubkal, le luth, et VTT, le violon. Guidé par cette mélodie, Khalid nous retrouve sur la place Djama'a el-Fna.]

(34)

Music becomes a privileged mode of communication between Diego the violinist (and by proxy Jean-Christophe), the many co-pilots who are also musicians and the local people the foursome encounter. The auditory becomes a communicative bridge between the members of this 'veritable tandem orchestra' ['véritable tandem orchestre'] (25), but it is also the trigger for enhancing Diego's and Jean-Christophe's sense of hearing. The musician, Diego, becomes an apprentice to sound in new ways. In Mali, for instance, his co-pilot Klé's heightened sense of hearing

makes me discover certain elements in the landscape that I'm unable to see. It's then my turn to explain to him what I've been able to see thanks to him. Between me and him, who is the blind one? The one who can see without being able to see or the one who can't see what he can see? [me fait découvrir certains éléments du paysage que je suis incapable de voir. C'est ensuite mon tour de lui préciser ce que j'ai pu voir grâce à lui. Entre lui et moi, qui est l'aveugle? Celui qui peut voir sans voir ou celui qui ne voit pas ce qu'il peut voir?]

(127)

The physically blind lead the symbolically blind who increasingly recognise that a normative privileging of sight risks dimming not only the other senses, but the acuity of visual perception itself. Sight becomes arrogant, lazy: an intellectual construction of what one expects to see replaces the unmediated apprehension of truth through sensation. However, this new, acute attention to bodily sensation owes something to physical collapse as much as to the enriched and enriching sensory openness to the world facilitated by the co-pilots. The celebrated philosopher of perception, Merleau-Ponty, emphasises the 'porosity' of self and outside world. Counter-intuitive from a point of view of Cartesian agency, Merleau-Ponty reminds us that we are susceptible to the world because we are not separable from it: 'Nothing determines us from outside, not because nothing acts upon us, but on the contrary, because I am from the start outside myself and open to the world'.[22] Susceptibility gives way to an acceptance of vulnerability for Diego: contracting a parasitic infection while in Benin (197–205), his body refuses to yield to the power of the mind, evacuating itself, physically and metaphorically, of contamination. He realises that it is a 'thing among things', to paraphrase Merleau-Ponty, part of the fabric of the world, and this 'thingness' is experienced through bodily pain that challenges both physical wellbeing and ideological certainty. Profoundly democratising, physical collapse renders the body a site of ethical encounter; yet the full implications of this are realised only in the subsequent rewriting of the experience as text at which point thought and perception can ultimately align: 'The body is our general medium for having a world', writes Merleau-Ponty, while 'truth does not inhabit only the inner man, or more accurately, there is no inner man, man is in the world, and only in the world does he know himself' (xii).

The ultimate outworking of this egalitarian partnership between self and world, body and intellect, sighted and blind is present in images of perception suggestive of synaesthetic fusion, as Diego sees through Klé's sense of hearing and smell:

I scrutinise the horizon and finally notice on the left some smoke rising in the distance above the trees. A few crackling sounds, a few smells are enough for Klé to expand my field of vision. [Je scrute l'horizon et finis par apercevoir sur la gauche une fumée qui s'échappe des arbres au loin. Quelques crépitements, quelques odeurs suffisent à Klé pour élargir mon champ de vision.]

(128)

What next for seeing and being seen?

We come full circle then to the realisation of co-dependency between French traveller and blind co-pilot with which this chapter opened, but what are the implications of the discussion that has brought us here for the ethics and politics of vision in charity or gap-year tourism? Certainly, the purpose of the chapter is not to condemn Perrot, Audemard or any other travellers embarking on journeys of this kind; it is to recognise, however, that charity tourism inevitably has an ambiguous relationship to the selfless altruism in which it is theoretically grounded. Diego and Jean-Christophe are not neo-colonialists, but the early – and perhaps inevitable – naivety of these gap-year travellers shares something of the discourses of discovery and domination associated with seeing and thus knowing.[23] It is the experience of the journey itself that challenges these assumptions. Moreover, alongside this journey of self-discovery is a genuine and potentially lasting impact on the travellees: not only does the project draw the attention of local media to the capacities of those deemed incapable of undertaking such feats, but profits from the subsequent book are also donated to the organisations represented by those who participated in the journey. Jean-Christophe and Diego undergo a process of realisation, but it is not an epiphany with its implications of instantaneity as in a photographic image, for it is only in writing the experience as textual narrative with a distance of three years – rather than through the promise of knowing through the immediacy of sight – that its full ethical implications can be articulated, albeit crucially not resolved. The impulse to re-write emerges out of the difficulty of their return and reintegration into life in France. As we read in the epilogue:

It's by becoming aware of a page to be turned, page to be written, to be critiqued and recounted, that J.-C. and I decided to create this book. Three years after our return, we are just beginning to digest the richness of the experience we lived. [C'est en prenant conscience d'une page à tourner, d'une page à écrire, à decrier et raconter, que J.-C. et moi avons decide de faire ce livre. Trois ans après notre retour, nous commençons tout juste à digérer la richesse de l'expérience vécue.]

(343)

The ongoing impact of the journey for Diego is clear: 'I've never come home!' ['Je ne suis jamais revenu!'] (334), he is tempted to reply when asked how he has found his return to France.

Seemingly paradoxically, it is in the transition from the contemporaneous documenting of their journey on their website (largely through photographs and immediate reactions) to a crafted, retrospective narrative in which, as noted above, text predominates, that the bodily experience of travel can be 'digested'– that is, through an evocation of aural, haptic, gustatory phenomena, rather than a reliance on the visual. To echo again the terms of Merleau-Ponty, a realisation of the body in its permeability to the world, in its position as thing in the fabric of things, is the condition for the realignment of thought and perception by which to know the world. Key to that is a displacement of the dominance of seeing and being seen.

Seeing and being seen: a final perspective through the lens of voluntourism

One of the essays in Marina Novelli's 2005 edited book, *Niche Tourism: Contemporary Issues, Trends and Cases*, sets out to catalogue some of the different forms of 'volunteer tourism'/'voluntourism', of which gap years are a key example.[24] The essay, written by Michelle Callanan and Sarah Thomas, provides a largely quantitative analysis of a total of 698 projects advertised on the GoAbroad.com website. By way of introduction, the essay usefully highlights the altruistic bases of these endeavours, while also recognising that gap-year tourism is equally centred on self-development and CV enhancement. The authors chart the evolution in this market from its creation in the 1980s and 1990s as an alternative to mass tourism, to a situation where it is now, ironically, becoming a form of mass tourism in itself. According to a 2003 study quoted in the essay, approximately 250,000 people aged between eighteen and twenty-five reportedly left the UK for gap-year voluntourism in that same year. One can only assume the number has increased, not least because of celebrity gap-year phenomena, such as the high-profile experiences of Princes William and Harry. The authors' discussion ends with a series of questions for the industry:

> Are there any official codes of conduct/guidance for such projects? Should such codes be defined along the same lines as The Ecotourism Society's code of conduct for ecotour operators? These codes could be developed along the same lines as Tourism Concern's Himalayas Tourist Code on cultural and environmental good practice (Tourism Concern, 1995) and 'Danger tourists', Survival International's cultural guidelines for tourists (Survival International, 1996). As these projects are linked to charities/social development activities, should they be regulated? Should explicit criteria for skills and experience be used more extensively by such organisations? Is there a need for organisations to actively screen and select candidates to participate in projects that match their skill profile?[25]

A number of 'ethical tour operators', including those offering gap-year opportunities, do indeed provide advice on how to travel and volunteer in ways that not only respect the host culture, but avoid doing actual harm despite motivations to the contrary. They also commonly provide discussion forums where questions such as 'Should I take photographs?' or 'Should I participate in spiritual ceremonies?' are asked, but even in their formulation, such questions imply the possibility of definitive answers. In fairness to the representatives of the tour operators who reply online to user questions, they tend not to offer easy answers but rather reflective responses that at the very least raise awareness of the ethical thorniness of the question. The possibility of developing codes of practice is problematic as these are inevitably disembodied. They are generic, rather than being grounded in individual challenges and dilemmas; they are based on intellectual knowledge, not phenomenological plenitude, or indeed emptiness as Diego experiences. Moreover, to focus on quantifiable skills, not qualitative experience, as the essay writers suggest may be necessary, is to reduce the experience of gap-year voluntourism to a selection of utilitarian capacities. While this may be to some extent essential for a project that requires specific skills, such as in building, to rely on projections of likely fit takes no account of the necessity to adapt, to reevaluate and to reposition oneself – in short, to recognise the reality of oneself as one thing among others in the fabric of a world one does not yet know. Moreover, in light of the focus of this chapter, a sneaking unease emerges when viewing websites promoting ethical travel opportunities on which organisations may pay to appear, their projects advertised like holiday destinations via photographs displaying sun-drenched vistas, majestic elephants and smiling children. We are back in the realms of seeing and being seen, and the visual 'place-myths' created by Urry's 'desiring bodies'.[26]

Perhaps most striking is that existing scholarly discussions of voluntourism rely on the expertise of sociologists, legal and governance specialists, and so on, and not on the work of the humanities, or, specifically, of travel writing scholars. If the humanities offer us a means of interrogating the narratives by which we understand ourselves in relation to the world, then a multidisciplinary approach to voluntourism provides a way of thinking beyond it as commodity or statistic, and instead as an embodied experience that transcends the controlled image of oneself and the controlling spectacle of the 'other'. As Perrot and Audemard finally realise:

> That is surely the lesson we've learnt from the journey: we need one another. A tandem with only one pilot won't let us achieve what we have done as two. It's difficult to separate yourself from the other half of the team. Each of us was blind in our own way.
>
> *(338)*

Notes

1 Megan Garber, 'The End of the Selfie Hype Cycle', *The Atlantic* (October 2014), accessed 15 March 2017, www.theatlantic.com/technology/archive/2014/10/selfies-are-boring-nowand-thats-why-theyre-finally-interesting/381001.

2 Roland Barthes, 'Rhetoric of the Image' [1964], in *Image – Music – Text*, trans. Stephen Heath (New York: Hill and Wang, 1977), 44.

3 John Urry and Jonas Larsen, *The Tourist Gaze 3.0*, 3rd edn (Thousand Oaks, CA: Sage, 2011), 166 and 160. The chapter on 'Vision and Photography' offers further illuminating insights into the questions of photography, longing and desire evoked here (155–88).

4 The opening scene of Agnès Varda's 2000 film *Les Glaneurs et la glaneuse* provides an ironic visual representation of this idea of high-speed tourist consumerism. Albeit from the pre-selfie era, it includes a sequence, which moves between normal and high speed, featuring a succession of tourists photographing, and/or having their photographs taken in front of, Millet's painting *Les Glaneuses* in the Musée d'Orsay. The film is available with English subtitles from Artificial Eye, entitled *The Gleaners and I*. The opening sequence can also be viewed on YouTube: www.youtube.com/watch?v=aKgjjEJvMbM (accessed 17 March 2017).

5 Jean-Didier Urbain, 'I Travel Therefore I Am: The "Nomad Mind" and the Spirit of Travel', trans. Charles Forsdick, *Studies in Travel Writing*, 4 (2000): 145, 149.

6 Helena Horton, 'More People Have Died by Taking Selfies This Year than by Shark Attacks', *Daily Telegraph*, 22 September 2015, accessed 17 March 2017, www.telegraph.co.uk/technology/11881900/More-people-have-died-by-taking-selfies-this-year-than-by-shark-attacks.html.

7 'List of Self-Related Injuries and Deaths', *Wikipedia*, accessed 17 March 2017, https://en.wikipedia.org/wiki/List_of_selfie-related_injuries_and_deaths.

8 Mary Louise Pratt, *Imperial Eyes: Travel Writing and Transculturation* (London: Routledge, 1992).

9 Martin Jay, *Downcast Eyes: The Denigration of Vision in Twentieth-Century French Thought* (Berkeley, CA: University of California Press, 1994).

10 For further analysis of the role of photography in colonialism, see: Eleanor. M. Hight and Gary. D. Sampson, 'Introduction: Photography, "Race", and Post-Colonial Theory', in *Colonialist Photography: Imag(in)ing Race and Place*, ed. Eleanor M. Hight and Gary D. Sampson, 1–19 (London: Routledge, 2004).

11 Nicolas Bouvier and Hervé Guyader, *L'Oreille du voyageur: Nicolas Bouvier de Genève à Tokyo* (Geneva: Éditions Zoë, 2008), 116; my translation. Subsequent page references are included parenthetically in the text.

12 Charles Forsdick, 'Travel, Disability, Blindness: Venturing beyond Visual Geographies', in *New Directions in Travel Writing Studies*, ed. Julia Kuehn and Paul Smethurst (London: Palgrave, 2015), 114.

13 Ryan Knighton, 'Sightless in Cairo', *The Guardian*, 1 April 2012, accessed 15 March 2017, www.theguardian.com/travel/2012/apr/01/blind-in-egypt-travel-cairo. These references to seeing are part ironic, part regretful, for while, as noted above, Knighton experiences Egypt through other senses, he also notes his sense of deprivation. He describes a compulsive desire to overeat because '[m]issing out on the sights can make a blind guy feel empty. Any more monuments, I'd develop an eating disorder'.

14 Jean-Christophe Perrot and Diego Audemard, *Tandems africains: du Sahara au Kilimandjaro guides par des non-voyants* (Paris: Presses de la Renaissance, 2007), 338. There is no published translation into English of the text. All translations are therefore my own, and the page references are to the French original. The book is made up of a preamble, ten main chapters written alternately by Perrot and Audemard, a conclusion and an epilogue.

15 The phrase comes to mean 'we've completed the cycle' or 'we've come full circle'. Literally, though, 'une boucle' is a buckle, loop or hoop and, as such, it has a variety of physical, geographical and metaphorical resonances for this journey.

16 Patrick Barkham, 'Are These the New Colonialists?', *Guardian*, 18 August 2006, accessed 15 March 2017, www.theguardian.com/society/2006/aug/18/internationalaidanddevelopment.education; and Lucy Ward, 'You're Better Off Backpacking – VSO Warns About Perils of "Voiluntourism"', *Guardian*, 14 August 2007, accessed 15 March 2017, www.theguardian.com/uk/2007/aug/14/students.charitablegiving. For an overview of scholarly discussion of this phenomenon, see Nancy Gard McGehee, 'Volunteer Tourism: Evolution, Issues, Futures', *Journal of Sustainable Tourism*, 22 (2014): 847–54.

17 *Tandems africains*, accessed 10 September 2017, www.lessenspartages.com.

18 For a critical engagement with the tensions between philanthropy and voyeurism in 'poverty tourism', see, for example: Evan Selinger and Kevin Outterson, 'The Ethics of Poverty Tourism', *Environmental Philosophy*, 7.2 (2010): 93–114. The term 'poverty porn' has become increasingly popularised, but first appears in Fabian Frenzel et al., *Slum Tourism, Power and Ethics* (London: Routledge, 2012), 69.

19 See Arjun Appadurai, 'Disjuncture and Difference in the Global Cultural Economy', in *The Cultural Studies Reader*, ed. Simon During (London: Routledge, 2004), 220–30.

20 'Sometimes, we are confronted directly in these terms: "You have money, help me [. . .]". Dramane and Klé take it upon themselves to reply in these cases, because of the risk of being insulted by passers-by saying: "You're profiting from the Whites and not sharing. You're wicked!"' ['Parfois, nous sommes abordés directement dans ces termes: "Vous avez de l'argent, aidez-moi [. . .]". Dramane et Klé se chargent alors de répondre, au risque de se faire insulter par les passants: "Vouz pouvez profiter des Blancs et vous ne voulez pas partager. Vous etes méchants!"'] (126).

21 'Being blind isn't the end of the world'.

22 Maurice Merleau-Ponty, *Phenomenology of Perception*, trans. Colin Smith (1945; repr. London: Routledge, 2002).

23 I am thinking here of the intersection of knowledge, representation and power as articulated in Edward Said's *Orientalism* (London: Routledge & Kegan Paul, 1978).

24 Michelle Callanan and Sarah Thomas, 'Volunteer Tourism: Deconstructing Volunteer Activities within a Dynamic Environment', in *Niche Tourism: Contemporary Issues, Trends and Cases*, ed. Marini Novelli, (Oxford: Elsevier, 2005), 183–200.

25 Callanan and Thomas, 'Volunteer Tourism', 199.

26 Urry and Larsen, *The Tourist Gaze*, 173–4.

15

HEARING

Tim Youngs

Recovering sound

Many critics and students of travel writing focus on its manifestation of the 'imperial eye', to use the term popularised by Mary Louise Pratt.[1] That phrase punningly conjoins the power of the Western gaze and the self (the eye/I). Yet, as other contributors to the present volume remark, the prominence of the visual in readings of travel writing causes the roles of the other senses to be overlooked.[2]

Hearing, the subject of this chapter, would seem to be the most objective of all the senses. Smell, taste and touch more obviously involve personal sensations and can evoke individual memories, while sound, even when it recalls what has been heard before, retains an external presence. (Sight does so, too, but visual perception when travelling seems more intimate than does the aural.) Nonetheless, how sounds are produced and heard may be markers of gender, ethnicity, age, culture and of nature, or what one regards as natural. Perceptions of and attitudes towards these factors are socially constructed and subjective.

In the discussion that follows, I hope to show that noticing the variety of sounds in travel writing, and how they are picked up, will further our appreciation of how the genre works and of how multilayered it is. In particular, I shall examine the possibility of a sonic objectivity as against sonic subjectivities. That is to say, given the argument mounted by many critics that travel writing is never truly objective, I shall consider whether this holds true of the presence of sound in travel writing also. Another main concern of this chapter is the interplay of what I call sonic tenses: the production or detection of sounds that effect movements between the ancient, the near-past, the immediate present and the future.[3] These seem especially to occur at moments of individual, social or cultural crisis.

Sounds add texture to places and to their description. Yet scholarly attention to what is heard has been scant in comparison with critical scrutiny of the sights the traveller sees.[4] Vanessa Agnew is among those critics who aim to rectify this imbalance, in the case of her essay, 'Hearing Things', by encouraging us to recognise 'the centrality of sound to the grand tour – little remarked on in the scholarly literature'. Agnew argues that

> [s]ince sound and music were central to the eighteenth-century traveller's experience [. . .] there is something to be learned by examining the types of auditory experience sought out by the traveller, as well as from the auditory experiences elaborated, imagined or elided in travellers' accounts of their journeys.[5]

She notes that 'Charles Burney (1726–1814) [. . .] pioneered a new concept: the eyewitness was transformed into an earwitness, one who testified to the subjective aural experience of travel'.[6] Two of Agnew's statements are particularly pertinent here. The first is that travellers may have 'made things up and heard things that were not there in order to conform to readers' expectations',[7] so, just as is the case with descriptions of sights, we should be wary of accepting descriptions of sounds at face value. Second, the grand tour 'provided an ever-changing sonic backdrop that ran parallel to the more regulated, professionalised appraisal of serious music', and it is there that Agnew believes 'we can recuperate something of the lost auditory world of the eighteenth century – one that recovers both its music and its sounds; here that we find an echo of the musical past awaiting its reconstruction'.[8]

Another academic effort at that sonic reconstruction is Tanya Merchant's essay on the 'Ichkari Soundscape'.[9] Merchant observes that previous accounts and recordings of music from Uzbekistan were produced by male travellers who lacked access to the spaces in which women made their music and who thus present a limited and misleading impression while purporting to be authoritative. Considering work from the first four decades of the twentieth century by British anthropologist, geographer and writer Annette B. Meakin, US journalist and activist Anna Louise Strong and Swiss travel writer Ella Maillart, as well as drawing on her own field-work, Merchant aims to situate European women's accounts of the *ichkari* soundscape in dialogue with those of male travellers, and to 'contextualize these accounts within the stories and remembrances of that [colonial and early Soviet] era told by Uzbek women musicians in the post-independence era'.[10] Merchant concludes that the women travellers' works 'provide important details of women's roles in Central Asia and differ significantly from works by men who traveled through Central Asia in the late nineteenth and early twentieth centuries'.[11] Despite the women's versions displaying the 'arrogance and misunderstanding' characteristic of most contemporary Western accounts, 'the reader may gain [from them] a broader sense of the bustling soundscape of the *ichkari*'. Moreover, the three women's narratives, notwithstanding the 'bias and disdain' they exhibit, 'confirm the oral histories that women in the region continue to tell about themselves'.[12] Through such accounts and appropriately attuned readings of them, sound can be reconstructed and awareness increased of how its production, perception and transmission are gendered. Thus Agnew and Merchant underline the importance of noticing sound, they indicate the difference made by the identity of the auditor-traveller and they offer some reasons why descriptions of sound may be selective and depend upon the auditor's position.[13]

Touching sounds

Noting that '[t]ouch is the most personal of the senses. Hearing and touch meet where the lower frequencies of audible sound pass over to tactile vibrations (at about 20 hertz)', R. Murray Schafer proclaims that '[h]earing is a way of touching at a distance'.[14] Sounds travel to us. When we journey, they do so in ways that may make us feel immersed or alienated. Either way, our distance from them is apparent, for immersion means we move within from a starting point that is outside. As Emily Thompson remarks, '[l]ike a landscape, a soundscape is simultaneously a physical environment and a way of perceiving that environment'.[15] Hearing thus signals our presence and apartness.

In travel writing a key distinction in the treatment of sounds, and an important element in determining our relationship to them, is whether they are identified as emanating from nature or are culturally generated. Here, especially, the question of whether sound can be objectively heard and described is most pronounced. The reception of sounds as markers of nature or culture is particularly resonant after the Industrial Revolution and in the Machine Age. Often sounds are represented as symbolic of conflict between the natural and mechanical worlds, a depiction that carries powerful cultural attitudes and values. A crunching example is audible in Barbara Joans' report of a conversation with fellow motorbike rider Debby Lindblom, who recalls her first experience of roadkill:

> 'This chipmunk was in its own world. I was the intruder. The critter was just using its own paths, enjoying its own life, not aware of me at all and I killed it.
>
> 'There I was, riding in the natural world, in the middle of Mother Nature and feeling very lucky to be there and lucky to have the ability to reach that world, and I killed an animal in its own home. I am a murderer. I killed somebody in its own home. After that I felt haunted [. . .] It would have been justice if I'd died too. So I am going to stay off the bike for a while.'[16]

This haunting, self-recriminatory anecdote is made stronger by the revelation that: '"I heard the sound of its death. Both wheels bumped over it. I had a hard time making it home. I was the intruder, the invader"'.[17] By contrast, to walk alone outside of built-up areas is, according to one philosopher of walking, to be 'perpetually distract[ed]' by being 'buried in Nature':[18]

> Everything talks to you, greets you, demands your attention: trees, flowers, the colour of the roads. The sigh of the wind, the buzzing of insects, the babble of streams, the impact of your feet on the ground: a whole rustling murmur that responds to your presence. Rain, too. A light and gentle rain is a steady accompaniment, a murmur you listen to, with its intonations, outbursts, pauses: the distinct plopping of drops splashing on stone, the long melodious weave of sheets of rain falling steadily.[19]

The contrast between Joans' destructive mechanical invasion and Gros's harmonious, attentive stepping into nature illustrates how the sonic becomes emblematic. Sounds are never simply 'out there'. They are filtered through our consciousness and they chime or clash with our cultural values. As we heard in Joans' story and shall hear again, the discordant can haunt.

The remainder of this chapter will examine the representation of sounds in selected travel texts of the twentieth and twenty-first century in order to investigate their connotations and the contribution they make to other facets of the narrative, such as plot, theme and character. It will compare the treatment of non-mechanical sounds with artificial ones and investigate what happens when the two meet. It will consider the handling of sonic tenses – in particular the use of sounds to evoke the past in the present – and analyse their function.

Wildfowl and hammers

H.V. Morton's *In Search of England* (1927), a book that remains in print, listens to the early twentieth century and listens out for echoes of the past. It is largely concerned with the effects upon the author's home country of industry, empire and new transport technologies. An early instance of sound used symbolically in it comes when the author watches people prepare for the departure of an Atlantic liner from Southampton. He observes in particular the parting of a young woman (a 'girl'), who is off to New York, and a man. As the latter walks down the gangway, Morton knows, 'remembering ancient agonies', that the man 'felt the ship to be an inhuman monster dragging her away from him; that every blast of the siren was like a burst of devil's laughter'.[20] As Morton feels sorry for the pair, the 'siren laughed again with fiendish hoots; and slowly – so slowly – the ship moved with two tugs beneath her great bows' (28). Here a vessel that offers an improvement in the pace and comfort of travel is viewed as a monstrous, infernal thing that separates loved ones from each other. In what becomes a common theme in modern writing, innovations meant to improve our lives have a negative impact. There is a sonic rupturing of what we hope to be the continued, natural state of affairs. This happens in personal relationships and in social ones, too.

In Morton's book and in other interwar condition-of-England travelogues, a prevalent motif is the disappearance of traditional ways of life as they become displaced by modernity. Ghosts are often summoned in order to suggest that although the past has departed it may leave a trace behind. The lingering presence might be benign, disruptive or even malevolent. In an example of the first of these, Morton remarks: 'On a sunny afternoon there is no place known to me in which you would be more likely to see a ghost in daylight than the ruins of Beaulieu Abbey', though it 'would not be a horrid spectre' but a 'pleasant lay brother' (33). The setting seems tranquil: 'Tall trees lean from soft grass, and little blue flowers in clumps grow from the ruined cloisters. There is a colony of primroses over the walls of the chapter house'. Sound plays a role here: in what we might call the sonic pastoral, the pleasantness of the surroundings is made audible as 'the air becomes lazy with the drone of bees' (33).

Very soon after this bucolic scene, Morton employs a haunting noise to indicate lost industry. Walking along the Beaulieu River, he comes to Buckler's Hard, 'a dead village under grass', where '[g]reat timbers go down into the water, rotting and covered with weed. In the field are gigantic dips and hollows full of lush grass and flowers' (36). This visual demonstration of nature growing over the impressions of human activity is given an audible equivalent as Morton describes how 'the wildfowl cries where once the caulking hammer sounded' (37). Here, Morton writes:

> In those dips and on those rotting slipways once rested the stout oak-built ships which helped to found the British Empire. This unknown, forgotten village in Hampshire was once loud with the sound of forge hammers, here thousands of great oak trees were formed into ships of the line.
>
> *(36)*

Similarly, he recalls that 'Henry Adams, the veteran shipbuilder, settled here, and soon the country was loud with hammers knocking against the wooden walls [i.e. the ships] of England' (36). Mechanisation puts an end to shipbuilding at Buckler's Hard and human labour is replaced by the return of nature.

This is, Morton exclaims: 'A ghostly place!' He hopes that when the remains of the last slipway fall into the river, 'some old native will see, faint as if spun in mist [. . .] a gallant ship [. . .] come creeping home [. . .] to fade like a night fog into the English grass which gave her birth' (37). Morton uses sound (hammers, wildfowl) to convey the past and present of this place, conveying the changes that have happened to it and signalling what these stand for. As he sums it up: 'The history of Buckler's Hard is, apart from its interest as a dead village which played its part in Empire, well worth telling; for it shows how swiftly time and fate can alter a place' (36).

Cultural geographer David Matless claims that '[c]onsidering the sonic landscape of a particular region shows how the contested valuation of that landscape works in significant part through sonic judgement, with the aesthetic, ecological and social enfolded through sonic geography'.[21] We can substitute history for geography here, though of course the two are linked. And although Morton does not give the changes such heavily moral treatment as some commentators do similar scenes, there is a wistfulness to his writing about Buckler's Hard from which we infer regret at the passing of individual, hand-laboured craft, no matter how inevitable its replacement by machinery is seen to be. Morton communicates this sense of diminution through the invocation of sound in print. He does not report it; he creates it through sonic symbolism. And although he does not directly make a moral point, he tells us what to draw from it: how places are subject to rapid change. The changes might not be for the better but the return of nature may serve as a soothing consolation.

There is a sadness to Morton's encounter with the signs of the past. Sound frequently plays a part in the creation of this mood. In the Cornwall village of St Anthony-in Roseland, where he spends a night in a cottage, the children 'have left the nest, and the old people stay on among the flowers' (67). The woman whose cottage he stays in recalls how the schoolroom, in what Morton sees as 'a tumble-down shack', was 'full every morning' and there was 'noise and [. . .] chatter' (67). The narrator employs pathetic fallacy to have the loneliness and melancholy reflected in the sounds of nature:

> One by one the sounds of day are stilled, until the robin is left alone to sing in his high-pitched elegy.
>
> I know no sadder little song. Nature's Angelus bell. It has no beginning and no end. It ceases suddenly in the middle of a phrase as if waiting for an answer that never comes, or is perhaps inaudible to the ear of man. The light is drawn out of the sky minute by minute, and the little throatful of heartache goes on and on in the gathering darkness.
>
> *(67)*

When Morton's host tells him that she has lit the lamp and that his supper is ready, he replies that he will be there in a second and '[d]own the darkening lane I hear the slow tramp of boots. An immense stillness seems to have closed its hand on the earth, and the words fade from this paper' (67).

By contrast, in Bath,

> Noises [. . .] are louder than anywhere else on earth. A motorcycle coming up Stall Street sounds like a giant rattling Cleopatra's Needle [. . .] Bath was made for chairs. Sedan and the other kind. Anything else on wheels is a rude invasion.
>
> *(112)*

(In a visual companion to this conjunction of sonic tenses, Romans are invoked later when Morton is at the Newport Arch in Lincoln, 'the only Roman town gate still in use in England', where he watches 'motor-cars run in under the arch which has admitted the spears of the legions into Lindum' [178].) In Bath he again has a vision of ghosts, this time of contemporaries at the Roman bath wearing togas (113).

Morton's detection of the sounds of the past allows him to make connections even as they seem in danger of being lost. So, in the small town of Brandon in Suffolk, where '[t]he lost art of chipping flint has been kept alive [. . .] for tens of thousands of years', he watches a man speedily making a succession of flawless gun-flints:

> the glassy hard tinkle of his little metal hammer on the flint was one of the most fascinating sounds I have heard – a sound, I thought, to which the human race won its battle for mastery over the beasts thousands of centuries ago.
>
> *(207)*

But that man, Mr Edwards, cannot make an arrow-head, and the man who can, Mr Spalding, to whom Morton is directed by Edwards, is unable to make gun-flints. Between the two men there is a balance but it is one that is in jeopardy as there are only half a dozen flint-knappers left in the town (Spalding himself is not regarded by them as one) and most of them regard it as a part-time job. Morton thus gathers that 'the flint-knapping trade, like so many ancient trades, may die out with this generation' (207). This threatened extinction is an instance of what Morton refers to as 'the sad, modern tendency towards standardization' (97), but he has heard and been thrilled by the sound that has endured through history and that marks the ascendancy of humanity.

Urban haunts

Nearly a century later, spectres still haunt the British landscape. Writing about his own two-month, coast-to-coast walk from Hornsea to Crosby following the M62, John Davies senses the ghosts of past villages displaced or destroyed by the motorway. Under the Ouse Bridge, the 'M62 makes spectral sounds': 'in the sudden stillness the senses open to the booming, cracking, clanking noises above'.[22] He 'reimagin[es] Roman Legions moving across the landscape of the North' (24) and then envisions a day

> when the motorways will become dead roads, mossed over, and people will walk them, fantasising about the violent roaring vehicle convoys which once used them. After the oil runs out, or some inevitable catastrophe hits our dying civilisation, future people will look back on us that way. We will be ghosts to them.
>
> *(24)*

The tenses in evidence in this passage are typical of a common attempt to position oneself historically when the urge to do so arises from a discomfort with the technology of modernity. The summoning of the Romans, done so often in Morton's day also, serves to provide a bridge to the past, even if that bridge is crumbling, while the figuring of ourselves as ghosts to later generations acts as a reassurance that the current noise will one day quieten. We see, or rather hear, this when Davies meets a farmer, Brian, who stands

> north west of Scammonden Reservoir, by a fence bordering the eastbound edge of the motorway [. . .] rais[ing] his voice above the roaring traffic to tell me that the scattered stones by which we stood were, until the coming of the M62, a hamlet called Han Head.
>
> *(20)*

The tension between the road and nature is articulated in the competition between the motorway sounds and Brian's need to be louder.

In contrast, Iain Sinclair's book of walking around London's orbital road, the M25, seems reconciled to the urban, even sometimes to welcome it. Sinclair aims to explore the road, whose 'noise is explained away as part of the general acoustic interference that assaults our ears'.[23] Many of Sinclair's descriptions show mechanical and organic sound in competition against each other, but he refuses to indulge in a hackneyed rejection of the modern in favour of the natural. Instead, he shows them in a curious coexistence. He will not look backward. For example, early on in his narrative, he tells of hearing 'a howling that was to be one of the defining characteristics of my motorway walk: the chorus of the boarding kennels'. Pets are left there, 'out on the fringes, where their din will cause least offence' and their 'yelps and snarls, the prolonged baying, would be muffled in traffic' (15).

Sinclair refers to his hearing on Bull's Cross bridge, one of the 264 bridges on the M25, what he calls 'acoustic layering': the sound of car tyres, of the caged dogs and cats, riders emerging from the woods around Theobalds Park and an overheard fragment of dog-walkers' conversation (15). Later, he writes of how he and Renchi (Laurence Bicknell), with whom he shares some of the walks, and who has borrowed a pocket recorder, 'talked a lot about sound but never cracked it' (216). Following the River Colne to Uxbridge, Sinclair exclaims: 'Sound is elusive. No slap of tide, no river romance of clicks and creaks. Our own muted footfalls on worn turf, on trampled mud, splashing through spring puddles' (216–17).

There may be no 'river romance' here, but there is something elemental about the soft footsteps on the grass, the mud and the water. The impression is heightened by the revelation that Sinclair is unable accurately to recall Renchi's speech, either from his own notes or from the recorder, which was not used: 'Sound is an element. Like the canal, the motorway' (217). Sinclair laments that he and Renchi lack 'the skill, the eavesdropping genius of composer/ guitarist Bruce Gilbert (once of Wire)', who, on site at 'obscure locations', 'gather[s] material to construct a sound field'. Sinclair suggests that: 'From units of sound you can make a world, re-edit the past. Put it on a loop. Bruce long ago cracked the thing we were still struggling with: he learnt how to "play the gaps"' (217).

The paradox is that Sinclair plays for us the sounds that he says are elusive. He edits the past, shutting out some sounds and tuning in to others. And in doing so he fashions his own character as one who embraces, rather than flees, the urban. He is attuned to the noise of the city.

Sinclair acknowledges the modern and its mixed soundscapes without rejecting what others would disfavour as discordant. He finds '[t]he sounds of the road, as the M25 approached the tangled interchange with the M4 [. . .] compulsive [. . .] complex and [. . .] many-voiced' (227). It is a symphony of the post-industrial world. Where the natural and mechanical coexist, Sinclair not only refuses to find solace in the former but gently pokes fun at those who do. Thus, 'recover[ing] a taste of what was lost when Heathrow (the village) turned into landfill', they come across '[a] run of deep-England gardens, thatched wishing wells, early season blooms, determined to ignore the incursions of an international airport' (238). The 'rustic fantasy thrives' despite the fact that '[y]ou can't hear yourself speak, the flow of traffic is continuous and agitated' (238). That 'rustic fantasy' is, one assumes, part of what Sinclair earlier calls 'the fiction that is England' (15).

Whereas many travel writers, especially in the age of the so-called new nature writing, desire to get away from the urban and to have audible proof, such as bird sound, of their retreat from it, Sinclair revels in urban cacophony. Writing of how 'we hit one of those passages where the Green Way is swallowed and overridden by furiously competing narratives', he describes runway approach lights in fields along the road and the vibrations from the planes coming into land 'shak[ing] our skeletons'. But he does not retreat from this assault. Rather, '[t]he madness of this pilgrimage through a landscape that challenges or defies walkers' gives him 'a pure adrenalin rush'. Resting on the verge at the large roundabout where the sign for the M25 'is a holy relic on our Milky Way', Renchi 'contemplates the vortex: planes, vans, airport buses. Tremendous discriminations of noise' (239). What to others would be an undifferentiated, barely tolerable cacophony is to Sinclair a blend of distinguishable, busy, exciting sounds.

We find an even more positive response to modern transport (this time on the M1) in a poem by Andrew Taylor. One of several of Taylor's Twitter poems, it reads, in its entirety, 'Watford Gap grass verge through coffee steam, reassurance of / traffic noise, knowing we are an hour away – the beauty of the / service station'.²⁴ Here the volume of sound emitted by motorised vehicles is welcome, even calming, as it indicates progress and direction. In another work, 'M58 poem: Right Snow Wrong Quantities', Taylor writes:

> we seek the north
>
> and recreation
>
> the hills a white tint legacy
> of location   spots of time
> the nourishment   of minds
>
> repaired invisibly
>
> such sound   landscape matched
> sonic cathedrals   made out of ice[.]²⁵

Those 'sonic cathedrals' refer to 'the combination of noises that one would hear in that landscape', though they are also whatever we want the line to be.²⁶ There is a celebration here of natural and artificial sounds pitched together.

Where Sinclair seems not to welcome sounds is in the supermarket – in this case the Cobham branch of Sainsbury's, where he has breakfast, but since 'Sainsbury's is universal (like America)', it might be anywhere. The store's 'acoustic environment keeps trippers in a trance state'. Sinclair's dismay here is not at the modern but at a soulless capitalism in which 'Supermarkets are the [. . .] brothels of the senses' (317), and of which the Millennium Dome is the carbuncle.

Immersion and distance

Sounds are heard not only on land but under the water, too. In an article in *American Ethnologist*, Stefan Helmreich offers a 'first-person anthropological report on a dive to the seafloor' in the three-person submersible, *Alvin*, of the Woods Hole Oceanographic Institution in Massachusetts.²⁷ He is conducting 'ethnographic research into how oceanographers imagine and encounter such abyssal ecologies as hydrothermal vents' (623). He tells us that as his party begins their hour-long descent on a dive that will last about eight hours in Canadian waters, he is

> fascinated by the sounds that accompany and enable [it]. The snug seven-foot-diameter interior of our titanium sphere is awash in the metallic and muffled pings of distant sonar devices, the echoes of telephone voices from the *Atlantis*, and the quiet pop music that percolates from Alvin's stereo sound system. These bleep-blooping, burbling, and babbling sounds do, in fact, contribute, I find, to a feeling of immersion. Submerging into the ocean almost seamlessly merges with a sense of submerging into sound – and into a distinctively watery soundscape. The easy image comes to me of *Alvin* as a ball of culture submerged in the domain of nature.
>
> *(621)*

Helmreich posits a fusion of the natural and cultural. He even asserts that the combination of the submersible and its scientists is a cyborg, 'kept in tune and on track through the self-correcting dynamics of visual, audio, and tactile feedback' (622). Helmreich's anthropological essay is specialised and probably not what most readers would consider to be a typical travel text. In it, he pays 'special attention to the role of sound in constituting the experience of cybernetic and cultural immersion' and informs us that his inquiry is 'animated by an auditorily inspired attention to the modulating relations that produce insides and outsides, subjects and objects, sensation and sense data' (622). In essence, though, he is replacing the primacy of sight with an awareness of sound: of how we hear it and of how we position ourselves in relation to it. (This is so literally as well as metaphorically, since the dive he is on is using 'a high-resolution imaging sonar system [. . .] to map portions of the Mothra Hydrothermal Vent Field' [622].) Helmreich explains that '[r]ather than seeing from a point of view, then, I suggest tuning in to surroundings and to circumstances that allow resonance, reverberation, echo – senses, in brief, of presence and distance, at scales ranging from individual to collective' (622). Thus '[u]sing my dive in *Alvin* as a narrative vehicle, I meditate less on what I saw [. . .] and more on what we [. . .] heard and listened to' (622). Helmreich also reminds us that new technologies alter our perception of sound. He wonders about the technical work that allows us to hear what Jacques Cousteau 'once named "the silent world"' and which has now 'bec[o]me so sonorous', and about the cultural effects, for example on people aboard submarines (623).

Immersion, or the attempt to achieve it, happens in cultural as well as natural elements. Migrant and diasporic travel writing furnishes several examples, with the protagonist feeling both a connection with and a distance from a culture or landscape overseas. Here, sound conveys temporal distance but it signals a cultural remove, too. Several instances in Amryl Johnson's *Sequins for a Ragged Hem* (1988) exemplify this. Johnson, who was born in Trinidad and moved to England at the age of eleven, presents a dream-like passage of herself while visiting Tobago and looking for a conch as a souvenir for her mother in the place 'where fishermen discarded the shells of their catch'.[28] She writes: 'The third time I blew the conch, they came down from the mountains, machete in hand. The cry which stung their lips was one of freedom. Rebellion was in the wind, seeking out the eye of the hurricane' (149).

We are not told any more about these machete-wielding, freedom-seeking men, but must assume they are the slaves. Her envisioning of them (in response to her blowing of the shell) suggests a link but one that cannot physically be realised. These are hauntings. As with Morton's hammers, they are echoes of the past that enter the present. Sounds, then, are used by both writers to add texture to the historical landscape. But what they signify speaks also of each travel-narrator's position. For Morton, they are a way of coming to terms with modernity by replaying what has been lost. For Johnson, they speak of both her cultural origins or inheritance and her distance from them. The acoustic thus performs a temporal function, bringing past and present together, if fleetingly, as the protagonists attempt to make sense of their identity in relation to each.

Silence, the absence of sound, may be used similarly. Johnson's book has a striking example of this in her description of Carnival in Trinidad. She relates how she was 'hooked' by the appearance of 'Washerwoman, the queen of the band River'. When Washerwoman

> came on stage, there was no music for her. She danced dressed in white, pure, stark against the silence [. . .] she played havoc with my senses [. . .] I had a strange feeling as if she and I had been removed from that environment to a different setting. There were just the two of us on a dirt road which had canefields on either side [. . .] The heat waves cut, fragmenting the clothes line, her body, the basket under her arm. And yet she kept coming. Slowly advancing against the steamy heat which fractured her image.
>
> *(37)*

But then '[t]he experience was shattered by a voice announcing the next contestant' (37). The dancer's silent presence has transmuted her into an emblematic figure of the past, whose personal and cultural significance for Johnson has the author stepping magically, trance-like, out of the moment. The spell does not last, however; it is broken by the carnival announcement. Although the narrator tells us she would meet with the woman 'again soon', it will be a more mundane encounter: 'A woman in white cotton simple and plain, her washing blowing in a Caribbean breeze' (37).

Sequins for a Ragged Hem includes scenes that remind us that in print we are made aware of speech *as* speech when it sounds different. In travel writing the sound of the spoken word is commented on when travellers hear voices (languages, dialects or accents) that are foreign to them, or when auditors make visitors realise their own foreignness to the context. This often occurs in travel writing when the narrator's identity is being emphasised, usually as an individual in an unfamiliar situation. For example, at Vigie airport in St Lucia and walking to immigration, Johnson senses: 'Something was very wrong. A strangeness I had not met before. Something warding me off, not to an alarming degree, but distancing me, nevertheless'. In the queue, she listens 'and recognized it for what it was. French patois'. She hears several people talking excitedly but 'much to my annoyance, I never did find out what was going on' (173). Although she has heard French patois spoken before, in Trinidad and in Grenada, the occasions were infrequent. She tells us:

> To hear it being spoken all around me was like a giant step out of the darkness. I already knew it was the language the people spoke among themselves. I listened, hoping to understand a little. I couldn't make head nor tail of anything being said.
>
> *(173)*

A double alienation is in effect here. Not only does Johnson have trouble feeling that she belongs in her childhood home of Trinidad, but she is further distanced by the French patois she hears spoken, especially in St Lucia. She feels '[i]solated by words I could not understand' (177). She concludes that '[t]he alienation [. . .] was nothing to do with environment and everything to do with language, which fused history and people to an anchor of place and fate' (178). Her individual predicament as an outsider who cannot adequately reconnect with her juvenile and ancestral home is reinforced. Sound, local sound, serves as a sonic barrier. A little later, still in St Lucia, the 'constant patois' is one of the things to which she attributes her feeling of '[o]verwhelming loneliness' (186).

Of course, a factor that has the potential to break one's isolation is the sound of one's own language or accent. Again in St Lucia that happens when a 'strange sensation' rushes through the narrator as she hears an accent 'which clearly defined the speaker's country of abode [and] made me realise how far we both were from the adopted country' (179). Instead of resulting in the reassuring presence of a fellow national and common identity, however, the proximity of another Briton only furthers Johnson's existential solitariness. This is reflected in her oblique reference to Britain, which she does not name here but to which she refers in a detached way as 'the speaker's country of abode'. This suggests she does not regard it as home. Far from finding a companion, then, the encounter constitutes 'one of those times' that Johnson is 'reminded I was in exile' (179). That exile refers to Johnson's situation in the Caribbean but it signifies also that she does not feel fully at home in Britain. This is underlined when, informing us that the accent belongs to a British-born girl who is with her St Lucian-born mother and aunt who have long been resident in London, Johnson writes of the unsettling irony that '[w]e were all holiday-making in an exotic setting' (183). Thus the region of her upbringing has become remote, exotic, and she is a tourist in it.

Johnson's voice is distinct from the islanders' but there is not much sense of kinship or any other bond with the girl with the English accent either. Her situation between nations is a result of the emigration that has resulted from a colonial relationship. This nuanced, complex postcolonial condition is very different from the crude binaries of certain colonial travel texts in which the Other is not even granted the facility of speech, as is exemplified by Henry Morton Stanley's description (misjudged, as it turns out) of the notorious Bumbireh massacre. In the run-up to his account of shooting the advancing Africans, Stanley writes: 'The natives were quick-eyed. They saw the boat moving, and with one accord they swept down the hill uttering the most fearful cries'.[29] Such animalistic depictions led to Chinua Achebe's statement, in his denunciation of Joseph Conrad as a bloody racist, that he could not identify his fellow Africans in colonial literature. Achebe writes of Conrad's Africans that '[i]n place of speech they made "a violent babble of uncouth sounds [. . .]"' and '"exchanged short grunting sounds even among themselves"'.[30] When Conrad does grant them speech, Achebe claims, it is to damn them even more, through their own mouths, thus serving more explicitly Conrad's purpose of 'letting the European glimpse the unspeakable craving in their hearts'.[31]

Conclusion

This chapter has shown that attention to sound in travel writing reveals its use as far more than descriptive detail. Sounds are not merely heard; they are processed and interpreted by the auditor. They are then transmitted, through the medium of print, to the reader. During these stages of processing, interpretation and transmission, they are invested with meaning and cultural value. Less examined by critics than is the eye, hearing is of course only one of the senses on which most travel writing depends. One is mindful of David Matless's caveat that 'to mark out the sonic is not to argue that it can be granted autonomy, or that it provides some privileged arena for social and cultural enquiry'.[32] Travel writers, like other kinds of writer, are often advised to call on all the senses. *Lonely Planet's Guide to Travel Writing* observes: 'Most travel articles include good visual descriptions of the places where the stories are set, but writers far too frequently ignore their other senses in their depiction'.[33] The *Guide* urges aspirant writers: 'Let your ears and nose and taste buds and fingers do as much work as your eyes'.[34] Yet isolating sound lets us hear it better and allows us more fully to appreciate its role in the multi-sensual arena.

Sounds may be external but, as this chapter has shown, they also function in travel texts in profoundly symbolic ways. They reinforce our sense of the identity and character of the protagonist-narrator, of the traveller's relationship with the surroundings and with other people, and they vibrate with cultural significance. However, as Agnew states, 'aural phenomena are often regarded as transparent forms of historical evidence'.[35] Academic emphasis on the 'tourist gaze' (to use John Urry's phrase), illuminating and valuable as it is, has come at the cost of the traveller's ear, though we should be cautious when we attempt to rectify the imbalance. There are three main reasons for this caution. First, as has been said above, so that we avoid privileging one sense over another; second, and relatedly, to prevent imposing an ableist discourse that excludes the experiences of D/deaf travellers; and third, to be wary of imposing our own mood on sound, especially when that might make for a romantic tone. That last risk is evident in the following commentary. Helmreich notes of the term 'soundscape' that '[e]cologically minded musician R. Murray Schafer advanced the term in 1977 to call attention to his worry that natural sonic environments were being polluted by industrial noise'.[36] This might not seem so different from the nostalgia for pre-industrial sounds that we encounter in many travel texts in the mechanical age. And one might ask whether some of those scholarly books and chapters that seek to recover the sounds of the past are motivated by the same wish of the traveller to hear them. Veit Erlmann opines:

> Clearly, postcolonial and poststructuralist critiques of modernity at times appear to be couched in nostalgic terms, wishing for the living voice, the cry, and guerrilla tactics. Which is why it is crucial to emphasize that it is not enough to denounce vision and replace it with a new sensibility based on the ear.[37]

Perhaps the urge to capture or recapture sound is felt more strongly, too, because in reading we do no not hear the sounds directly ourselves; we only encounter written representations of them. On the other hand, just as new technologies may be responsible for the erasure of some of those sounds, so they can preserve and disseminate them. For example, James Kari's collection of Alaska Athabascan travel narratives presents five speakers' narratives with, in alternate lines, transcriptions of the Ahtna with English translation and the Ahtna spoken on a CD.[38] The narratives are 'a set of walking tours of traditional Ahtna lands by [. . .] experts'.[39] According to Kari,

> [t]he details and facts in these narratives certainly must place this collection among the most detailed examples of foot travel ever published in the language of a hunter-gatherer culture. In the five chapters, in just over 102 minutes of speech nearly 1,200 miles of trails and routes are described.[40]

One can read in Ahtna and English, and hear in Ahtna, Jim McKinley, speaking of a place '"where songs extend across"' the Copper River and telling us: 'Now the white man has taken this place from us, you know'.[41] Sounds in travel narratives come from all directions.

Notes

1 Mary Louise Pratt, *Imperial Eyes: Travel Writing and Transculturation* (London: Routledge, 1992).

2 Not only in travel writing studies. Introducing a collection of essays on *Hearing History*, Mark M. Smith states his hope that '[i]deally, we will begin to contextualize the past within the larger rubric of all the senses and thus free mainstream historical writing from the powerful but blinding focus on vision alone'. Mark M. Smith, 'Introduction: Onward to Audible Pasts', in *Hearing History: A Reader*, ed. Mark M. Smith (Athens, GA: The University of Georgia Press, 2004), xxi.

3 For discussion of sonic temporalities in the modern technological age see Wolfgang Ernst, *Sonic Time Machines: Explicit Sound, Sirenic Voices, and Implicit Sonicity* (Amsterdam: Amsterdam University Press, 2016).

4 For some exceptions that deal with music in contact zones see: Dwight F. Reynolds, 'Music in Medieval Iberia: Contact, Influence and Hybridization', *Medieval Encounters* 15.2–4 (2009): 236–55; D.R.M. Irving, *Colonial Counterpoint: Music in Early Modern Manila* (New York: Oxford University Press, 2010); John Koegel, 'Spanish and French Mission Music in Colonial North America', *Journal of the Royal Musical Association* 126.1 (2001): 1–53; Robert Stevenson, 'Written Sources for Indian Music until 1882', *Ethnomusicology* 17 (1973): 1–40; Alfred E. Lemmon, 'Jesuit Chroniclers and Historians of Colonial Spanish America: Sources for the Ethno-Musicologist', *Inter-American Music Review* 10 (1989): 119–29.

5 Vanessa Agnew, 'Hearing Things: Music and Sounds the Traveller Heard and Didn't Hear on the Grand Tour', *Cultural Studies Review* 18.3 (December 2012): 68.

6 Agnew, 'Hearing Things', 70.

7 Agnew, 'Hearing Things', 77.

8 Agnew, 'Hearing Things', 78.

9 Tanya Merchant, 'Narrating the Ichkari Soundscape: European and American Travelers on Central Asian Women's Lives and Music', in *Writing Travel in Central Asian History*, ed. Nile Green (Bloomington, IN: Indiana University Press, 2014), 193–212. Merchant explains that the 'ichkari' refers to the 'inside', the 'home and hearth' that was traditionally regarded as the domain for respectable women in contrast to the 'tashkari', the 'outside/public' realm, 'which was the purview of men (or less respectable women) until the forced unveiling campaigns of the 1920s' sponsored by the Soviet government which saw women 'push[ed] into the public sphere and into the workplace' (194).

10 Merchant, 'Narrating the Ichkari', 195.

11 Merchant, 'Narrating the Ichkari', 205.

12 Merchant, 'Narrating the Ichkari', 210.

13 For discussion of an attempt to 'use the page to convey the soundscapes of the Kathmandu Valley, and make room for both visitors' and residents' perspectives', see David Henderson, 'Traffic Patterns', in *Theorizing Sound Writing*, ed. Deborah A. Kapchan (Middletown, CT: Wesleyan University Press, 2017), 42. Concerned to 'communicate a jangly hubbub' (142), Henderson explains how '[i]n these experimental inscriptions of the soundscapes of the Kathmandu Valley in Nepal, I merge the ethnographic and the phonographic, the humanistic representation (straddling the artistic and the scientific), and the sonic representation (linking the textual and the pictorial) [. . .] Each has, as its starting point, a recording I made' (152).

14 R. Murray Schafer, 'The Soundscape', in *The Sound Studies Reader*, ed. Jonathan Sterne (London: Routledge, 2012), 62.

15 Emily Thompson, 'Sound, Modernity and History', in *The Sound Studies Reader*, ed. Jonathan Sterne (London: Routledge, 2012), 117.

16 Barbara Joans, *Bike Lust: Harleys, Women, and American Society* (Madison, WI: University of Wisconsin Press, 2001), 125–6.

17 Joans, *Bike Lust*, 126.

18 Frédéric Gros, *A Philosophy of Walking*, trans. John Howe (2014; repr. London: Verso, 2015), 54.

19 Gros, *A Philosophy of Walking*, 54–5.

20 H.V. Morton, *In Search of England* (London: Methuen, 1927), 27–8. Further page references will be given parenthetically.

21 David Matless, 'Sonic Geography in a Nature Region', *Social & Cultural Geography* 6.5 (2005): 763.

22 John Davies, 'M62: In the Company of Ghosts', in *In the Company of Ghosts: The Poetics of the Motorway*, ed. Alan Corkish et al. (Liverpool: erbacce-press, 2012), 20. Further page references will be given parenthetically.

23 Iain Sinclair, *London Orbital: A Walk around the M25* (2002; repr. London: Penguin, 2003), 11. Further page references will be given parenthetically.

24 Andrew Taylor, 'Twitter Poem', in *In the Company of Ghosts: The Poetics of the Motorway*, ed. Alan Corkish et al. (Liverpool: erbacce-press, 2012), 162. The poem also appears in *In Transit*, ed. Sarah Jackson and Tim Youngs (Birmingham: The Emma Press, 2018), 29.

25 Andrew Taylor, 'M58 Poem: Right Snow, Wrong Quantities', in *In the Company of Ghosts: The Poetics of the Motorway*, ed. Alan Corkish et al. (Liverpool: erbacce-press, 2012), 27.

26 Personal communication, 21 May 2017.

27 Stefan Helmreich, 'An Anthropologist Underwater: Immersive Soundscapes, Submarine Cyborgs, and Transductive Ethnography', *American Ethnologist* 34.4 (2007): 621. Further page references will be given parenthetically.

28 Amryl Johnson, *Sequins for a Ragged Hem* (London: Virago, 1988), 148. Further page references will be given parenthetically. Johnson claims that *Sequins* is 'not a travelogue' (2), but it manifestly combines travel and memoir.

29 Henry M. Stanley, *Through the Dark Continent* . . . [1878] (London: Sampson Low, Marston, Searle, & Rivington, 1890), 151.

30 Chinua Achebe, 'An Image of Africa: Racism in Conrad's *Heart of Darkness*', in *Joseph Conrad: Heart of Darkness: An Authoritative Text, Backgrounds and Sources, Criticism*, ed. Robert Kimbrough (New York: W. W. Norton 1988), 255.

31 Achebe, 'An Image of Africa', 255–6.

32 Matless, 'Sonic Geography', 746.

33   Don George, *Lonely Planet's Guide to Travel Writing* (Footscray, Vic.: Lonely Planet, 2009), 47.

34   George, *Lonely Planet's Guide*, 47.

35   Agnew, 'Hearing Things', 77.

36   Helmreich, 'An Anthropologist Underwater', 623.

37   Veit Erlmann, 'But What of the Ethnographic Ear? Anthropology, Sound, and the Senses', in *Hearing Cultures: Essays on Sound, Listening, and Modernity*, ed. Veit Erlmann (Oxford: Berg, 2004), 5.

38   James Kari, ed., *Ahtna Travel Narratives: A Demonstration of Shared Geographical Knowledge among Alaska Athabascans*, told by Jim McKinley, Frank Stickwan, Jake Tansy, Katie John and Adam Sanford; transcribed and edited by James Kari (Fairbanks, AK: Alaska Native Language Center, University of Alaska, 2010).

39   James Kari, 'Introduction', in *Ahtna Travel Narratives*, ix.

40   Kari, 'Introduction', xiii.

41   Jim McKinley, '"Atna" K'et Kayax "eł Tl'atina" Ngge': Ahtna Villages on the Copper River and in the Klutina River Drainage', in *Ahtna Travel Narratives*, 18, 19.

16

TOUCHING

Sarah Jackson

In *Black Lamb and Grey Falcon: A Journey Through Yugoslavia* (1941), Rebecca West recounts her travels through Macedonia with her husband and their guide Constantine. Visiting a monastery near Ochrid, they meet a young priest described by West as 'sensitive and a little sad'.[1] He is clearly keen for them to stay, bringing them wine, sheep's cheese and eggs, although they have already eaten, and asking questions about life outside Macedonia. West remarks: 'He spoke with something that was not quite curiosity, that was more tactile; the effect was as if a very gentle blind person were running his finger-tips over one's features'.[2] In these few tender words, West's description of the priest brings together a number of key ideas that are addressed in the present chapter: travel, touch, blindness and the tactile properties of language.

Despite West's specific attention to the sensation of touch at this moment in her travelogue, accounts of the tactile remain largely overlooked by both authors and critics of travel writing. In light of such neglect, this chapter investigates the representation of touch in a region where multisensory perception is central to both navigation and survival: the Antarctic. It considers how travellers narrate their experiences of temperature and texture in seemingly un*touchable* territories, thinking about the ways that the extreme environment might mediate the perception and expression of contact. Rather than overlooking touch, Apsley Cherry-Garrard's *The Worst Journey in the World* (1922) and Sara Wheeler's *Terra Incognita* (1996), I propose, show us the significance of tact in the world's most inhospitable regions. These works are characterised not only by accounts of physical strength, but also by a sensitivity to the texture of the ice. Considering the ways that the glacial features of the Antarctic ask us to confront the limits of tactile experience, this chapter asks whether and how a preoccupation with touch – and the threat of its loss – is explored through a poetics of tact.

The multisensory dimensions of travel

Before embarking on a discussion of tactile experience in the Antarctic, this chapter offers a brief survey of the representation of touch in travel writing. Addressing the impact of visual impairment on multisensory perception, it draws on research by Paul Rodaway, Eitan Bar-Yosef and Charles Forsdick in order to stress the importance of developing an aesthetic of touch. Indeed, as Carl Thompson notes, travellers have long been driven by 'a Romantic desire to visit sites of unspoilt natural beauty, and/or cultures seemingly untouched by modernity'.[3] And yet despite the desire to access destinations that remain hitherto untouched, tactile experience – cited by Santanu Das as the most 'intimate' and yet 'elusive' sense – is most often relegated to the background in literary representations of travel.[4] In *Sensuous Geographies*, for instance, Paul Rodaway argues that 'haptic geographies are often overlooked, since the tactile experience is such a continuous and taken-for-granted part of everyday encounter with the environment'.[5] The subordination of touch is evident in many aspects of Western culture and runs parallel to the ocularcentrism that has dominated since Aristotle set out the individuation of the five senses. The sense of touch, in particular, is traditionally associated with a proximity to the body and has thus been conceptualised as opposed to order and cognition. Vision, on the other hand, is linked to knowledge and enlightenment, and remains privileged in Western culture. Michel Serres, for example, points out that 'many philosophies refer to sight; few to hearing; fewer still place their trust in the tactile, or olfactory. Abstraction divides up the sentient body, eliminates taste, smell and touch, retains only sight and hearing, intuition and understanding'.[6] This is notwithstanding the fact that contemporary critics recognise that the senses are co-implicated in a complex system and that, as Serres says, the skin itself can be understood as a '*sensorium commune*: a sense common to all the senses, forming a link, bridge and passage between them'.[7]

It comes as little surprise that this ocularcentrism pervades Western travel writing. Charles Forsdick, for instance, notes:

> Travel literature provides a telling illustration of the ways in which the visual has been progressively policed, framed, normalized, and also, particularly since the eighteenth century, increasingly privileged (beginning with the picturesque and scientific empiricism, and continuing via phenomena such as the imperial and tourist gaze).[8]

The relationship between vision and travel is neatly captured in the phrase 'sightseeing'. The *Oxford English Dictionary* dates the term as early as 1824, but it endures in present society's assumption that even if we have different modes of looking, we travel to 'see' the world. In her study of the origin of sightseeing, Judith Adler observes the pre-eminence of the eye as a detached and judicious measure of experience in the seventeenth and eighteenth centuries.[9] The Romantics, too, emphasised the importance of vision, even if, as Adler argues, there was an attempt to close one's eyes to external reality in order to see otherwise. Following Adler, Eitan Bar-Yosef remarks that this privileging of the eye was fortified by 'the rise of mass-tourism in the mid-nineteenth century'; he goes on to state that the 'growing democratization of travel reinforced the prominence of sight, encapsulated in the "tourist gaze"'.[10] However, in *The Tourist Gaze*, the text to which Bar-Yosef refers, John Urry points out that 'the concept of the gaze highlights that looking is a learned ability and that the pure and innocent eye is a myth'.[11] If the visualisation of the journey is a cultural construction, it is one that we can challenge by re-reading the multi-sensorial dimensions of travel. In fact, as Adler points out, in the early sixteenth century the 'aristocratic traveler [. . .] went abroad for *discourse* rather than for picturesque views or scenes'.[12] She goes on to illustrate other examples of travel writing that are packed with descriptions of smells, tastes and touch too, making specific reference to the 'many thermalists seeking tactile contact with waters of varying mineral composition' in the eighteenth century.[13] Challenging the ocularcentrism of much travel writing, she thus draws attention to a need to develop our understanding of tactile experience.

Bringing together studies in disability and travel writing, Charles Forsdick considers narratives by visually impaired travellers. He notes that despite a 'residual discursive normativity' in which texts are 'saturated with the vocabulary, tropes and devices of sightedness', their accounts '*illuminate* the ways in which differing configurations of sensory engagement lead to differing constructions of space and place in the journey narrative'.[14] This, he argues, encourages a move from the monosensory to the multisensory, considering the equally important roles that hearing, smell, touch and taste have to play in the ways that journeys are narrated. Forsdick also draws on the work of Bar-Yosef, who considers the ways that different disabilities 'affect the journey and its textual construction'.[15] The subjects of Bar-Yosef's study include James Holman, often known as the 'Blind Traveller'. Holman, Bar-Yosef points out, normalises his disability by suggesting that all travellers are in some ways 'disabled': they are 'either deaf (to the local language) or blind (to the reality around them) or both'.[16] There are, this seems to suggest, other ways of 'seeing' the world. In *A Voyage Around the World*, Holman insists that although the 'picturesque' is denied to him, his circumstances afford

> a stronger zest to curiosity, which is thus impelled to a more close and searching examination of details than would be considered necessary to a traveller who might satisfy himself by the superficial view, and rest content with the first impressions conveyed through the eye.[17]

Stressing the need for a 'more close and searching examination', Holman suggests that his blindness offers him a certain insight. Ascending Vesuvius during its eruption in June 1821, for instance, he is reported to have insisted, 'I see things better with my feet'.[18] The irony of this is recounted by biographer Jason Roberts, who explains: 'The air was scarcely breathable, the ground audibly unstable. They were shifting in their stances, almost hopping. Too much contact with the fuming ground could burn their feet through their shoes.'[19] The notion of seeing with one's feet is something to which this chapter will return, but while his work retains a discursive normativity involving vision, Holman's narrative also demonstrates the particular significance of the intimacy of touch in a 'close and searching examination'.[20]

Bar-Yosef is concerned with the narrative strategies used by Holman to narrate his journey and cites his account of reaching the summit of Adam's Peak in Sri Lanka:

> We reached the summit just before the sun began to break, and a splendid scene opened upon us. The insulated mountain rising up into a peaked cone of 7420 feet above the level of the sea, flanked on one side by lofty ranges, and on the other, by a champagne country, stretching to the shore, that formed the margin of an immense expanse of ocean; I could not see this glorious sight with the *visual* orbs, but I turned towards it with indescribable enthusiasm; I stood upon the summit of the Peak, and *felt* all its beauties rushing into my very heart of hearts.[21]

Substituting feeling for seeing in his unfailingly accurate prose, Holman's narrative achieves an impressionistic quality. His sensory impairment actually enables him to acquire, he suggests elsewhere, 'so great a delicacy, as to afford degrees of information, which under ordinary states it is incapable of'.[22] But not only do references to touch form a rich component of his travel writing, his emphasis on feelings also opens up questions about the ways that language itself is textured by its attempts to communicate an experience of contact – to touch the reader.

Developing a haptic aesthetic

Adler, Bar-Yosef and Forsdick's challenges to Western ocularcentrism are characteristic of a recent turn towards multisensory perception in criticism and theory. Santanu Das, for instance, notes that 'there has been a sudden swell of interest in the senses', accompanied by a 'move towards a more physical understanding of past literatures and cultures'.[23] Touch in particular, he says, is the subject of recent critical attention. Rather than taking it for granted, critics are stressing its rich aesthetic and affective potential. This is central to Rodaway's aim to explore the emotional geographies that sensuous experience of the world arouses. In his discussion of touch, Rodaway considers the ways that our tactile encounters help us to 'make sense' of a place and its people. His examination of the tactile clearly extends beyond the reach of the hand. He uses the term 'haptic', which comes from the Greek 'to touch' or 'to lay hold of', in order to emphasise a more complex relationship with the environment that includes touch, kinaesthesis (the sense by which the voluntary motion of the body is perceived), proprioception (the relative sense of the position and movement of different parts of the body) and the vestibular sense (the sense of balance or orientation). Drawing on James J. Gibson's 'haptic system', which defines touch as 'a system involving the coordination of receptor cells and the muscles of the body', Rodaway argues:

> Touch geographies are the sensuous geographies arising out of the tactile receptivity of the body, specifically the skin, and are closely linked to the ability of the body to move through the environment and pick up and manipulate objects. Touch can be passive and active, a juxtaposition of body and world and a careful exploration of the size, shape, weight, texture and temperature of features in the environment.[24]

Not simply referring to direct contact with the skin but to our position within and movement through our environment, the haptic enables us to consider the multisensory quality of geographical experience. Integral to this is an awareness of the body's perception of its own locomotion or movement through unfamiliar environments.

Considering this turn to movement, recent critics have drawn attention to the kind of travel that demands physical strength or perceptive subtlety. Examining the Victorian tactile imagination, for instance, Alan McNee observes the development of a philosophy of mountaineering in which 'the human subject's physical contact with the material reality of mountain landscapes was regarded as validating and supplementing visual evidence'.[25] Emphasising the 'connection between physicality and perception', McNee explains that the steepness of a mountain slope in the distance is not restricted to purely visual dimensions; its impact lies in the physical effort and haptic sensibility that encountering it induces.[26] He points out that 'sight alone was insufficient to fully understand and appreciate mountains. It had to be supplemented by evidence gleaned from the physical experience'.[27] Rather than being reduced to a supporting sense–perception, the haptic is essential to the literary representation of movement. Moreover, the role of the haptic for Victorian mountain–climbers, McNee writes, introduces a 'new form of the sublime', which gives rise to 'a new prose style which increasingly emphasized the embodied experience of the climber, and the physical sensations that climbing involves, just as much as the things climbers see on their expeditions'.[28] Although he does not on this occasion go on to specify in detail the form that this prose style takes, he stresses its significance for communicating the haptic aesthetic. And while he does not consider polar exploration in particular, his account of the haptic sublime brings new light to such narratives, where the extreme conditions demand an acute sensitivity to textures and surfaces, temperatures and tact.

Frostbitten fingers

In 1910, Apsley Cherry-Garrard joined Captain Robert Falcon Scott's final expedition to the Antarctic aboard the *Terra Nova*, describing his experiences as well as citing fragments from his diary, letters and the records of the other explorers on the trip, in *The Worst Journey in the World* (1922).[29] Cherry-Garrard recalls in his diary: 'Before I left England people were always telling me the Antarctic must be dull without much life', but on arrival, he admits, 'the whole place teems with life'.[30] This is echoed more than eighty years later by another British traveller and writer, Sara Wheeler, who describes her experiences with the National Science Foundation's Antarctic Artists and Writers Program in 1994–95 in *Terra Incognita* (1996). She recalls her discussions with the 'Seismic Man': '"People call this a sterile landscape, because nothing grows or lives. But I think it's *pulsating* with energy – as if it's about to explode"', she tells him.[31] Similarly, Diane Ackerman, who travelled to the Antarctic Peninsula as a tourist and recorded her experiences in 'White Lanterns' (1991), notes: 'Before coming to the Antarctic, I had thought that penguins lived in a world of extreme sensory deprivation'.[32] She insists, however: 'I had found just the opposite – a landscape of the greatest sensuality. For one thing, there was so much life'. She even claims to have been unable to eat during the trip because she was 'being fed so thoroughly through [her] senses' (197). Time and again, visitors to the Antarctic are faced with the richness of sensory experience. Both Ackerman and Wheeler pay credit to Cherry-Garrard's epic in their own work; its title, Ackerman points out, became 'synonymous with trekking to Antarctica' (197). It is interesting to note that Ackerman also describes Cherry-Garrard's classic as 'sensitive' (197), and it is this sensitivity – or at least its attention to the affective resonances of tactile experience – that reinforces the need to closely examine the haptic in accounts of polar exploration. Cherry-Garrard, like Wheeler and Ackerman, demands a heightened attention to the connections between physicality and perception; his writing exposes the relationship between text and tact.

The Antarctic is, as Francis Spufford explains in the introduction to *The Antarctic: An Anthology*, a place of 'sensory extremes': 'In the winter dark, or in the strange depthless glow of a white-out', he writes, 'it shut down your senses with tormenting thoroughness, but at other times it overloaded them with colour and dazzle'.[33] Particularly noteworthy are the 'visual delight[s]' described by early explorers, who, Spufford notes, 'learned to see beauty in the fractal, unplanned complexity of stone, of snow, of water, of ice'.[34] But these visual delights are frequently marked by an unreliability of optical information; the fact that vision is not always to be trusted in these conditions leads to an increased reliance on multisensory perception. In fact, these works tend to exhibit a curious attention to the *loss* of vision experienced while travelling through the region. Cherry-Garrard, for instance, who is already acutely short-sighted, describes 'curious optical delusion[s]' (246) during their journey. Moreover, during the long harsh winter months, he says, 'it was too dark to do anything but feel our way' (277). The frequent blizzards ensure that 'you cannot see your stretched-out hand, especially on a dark winter day' (462), but the most common complaint arises as a result of snow-glare. He records: 'Our difficulties during the next four days were increased by the snow-blindness of half the men' (366). His companion, Henry 'Birdie' Bowers, describes the symptoms: 'My right eye has gone bung, and my left one is pretty dicky [. . .]. It is painful to look at this paper, and my eyes are fairly burning as if someone had thrown sand into them' (366). These visual impairments contribute to a multisensory approach that is particularly relevant to polar exploration precisely because the conditions in the Antarctic place demands on different perceptive skills. Cherry-Garrard makes this clear when he says: 'We began to realize, now that our eyes were more or less out of action, how much we could do with our feet and ears' (293), and recalls Wilson's acknowledgement that 'eventually we travelled on by the ear, and by the feel of the snow under our feet, for both the sound and the touch told one much of the chances of crevasses or of safe going' (258). *The Worst Journey in the World* is thus imbued with a multi-sensorial language. Rather than navigate by sight, the explorers are forced to 'feel' their way south; they are, as Cherry-Garrard admits, quite literally 'groping [their] way' (360).

In his definition of the haptic, Rodaway refers to thermoreception – our sensitivity to heat and cold. A preoccupation with thermoreception in polar travel writing may come as little surprise, but also notable are the ways that the extreme temperatures are bound up with a traveller's emotional regulation; as Francis Spufford notes in *I May Be Some Time*, 'heat and cold probably provide the oldest metaphors for emotion that exist'.[35] Sara Wheeler describes one man she meets as 'taciturn, as cold as the ice in which he buried his explosives' (167). Often, however, it is not so much the temperature that affects her moods; the degree of visibility is attuned to a sense of emotional enlightenment. She writes:

> On clear days, when I walked around the new Wooville or looked out from the long window by my desk, the landscape spoke to me so directly that it no longer seemed to be made of corporeal ice. It had become a kind of cosmic symbol of harmony and of a peaceful freedom beyond poverty, gas bills and unrequited love.
>
> *(283)*

Wheeler, like other polar explorers, becomes particularly attuned to thermoreception. She notes: 'We came to know what temperature it was even before we looked at the thermometer hanging on the antenna, and we noticed every degree of change' (270). As a result, *Terra Incognita* is filled with detailed accounts of the relative temperatures of different stations:

> At McMurdo the mean temperature in January is minus three degrees Celsius, whereas at Rothera it is a sweaty two degrees above zero. At the Pole, the January mean is minus twenty-eight. It can reach minus fifty at McMurdo in the winter, but the lowest temperature ever recorded at Rothera is minus thirty-nine.
>
> *(194)*

To put this into context, Wheeler explains that 'our eyes froze shut if we blinked for too long' (264) and describes the effects of the temperature on her manual handling of objects, recalling a visit to Robert Falcon Scott's hut when she found herself struggling with the door: 'To free up my hands', she writes,

> without thinking I had put the key in my mouth, where it had instantly frozen to my lips. Lucia had been obliged to exhale energetically over my face to unstick the key without the loss of too much of the skin on my lips.
>
> *(291)*

But also prevalent are her descriptions of the wind: 'When the wind whipped up it sliced through any number of layers like a pneumatically driven carving knife' (100). 'No one ever quite gets used to [. . .] the brutalizing effect of the wind' (17), she writes, and on first walking down to Scott's hut on McMurdo Sound, she finds 'the exposed flesh between my goggles and balaclava immediately began to feel as if it were burning' (21–2). The primary sensory experience, it seems, is one of pain, and Spufford points out that 'almost all travellers seem to insist, in what they wrote afterwards, on the physical misery of Antarctic living'.[36] He continues: 'Sensations to look forward to included having the pus in your blisters turn to ice and expand, having wounds ten years old reopen, and having the soles of your feet fall off'.[37] This forms part of what Thompson describes as the 'curious logic' of travel: 'The dangers and hardships that travel can throw', he writes, 'seem actually to be part of the pleasure and purpose of travel'.[38] But in testing the limits of physical endurance, these writers also confront the possibilities and the limits of the haptic.

Cherry-Garrard and Wheeler are faced with these limits precisely because survival in the region is bound up with sensation's loss. For conditions in the Antarctic are at their most critical when they result in the cessation of sensory perception – when frostbite threatens.[39] Cherry-Garrard cites Captain Scott – 'Our fingers [are] constantly numbed' (128–9) – and goes on to explain, 'The difficulty was to know whether our feet were frozen or not, for the only thing we knew for certain was that we had lost all feeling in them' (144). He also notes that when they wore their mittens, they could 'scarcely feel anything – especially since the tips of our fingers were already very callous' (251). Wheeler points out that while frostbite is not in itself 'a highly dangerous injury', it is one 'that can soon become fatal if untreated' (17). As a result, travellers must insulate the very limbs that enable them to perceive at all. In *The Home of the Blizzard* (1915), the Australian explorer Douglas Mawson records the condition of his feet:

> [T]he thickened skin of the soles had separated in each case as a complete layer, and abundant watery fluid had escaped saturating the sock. The new skin beneath was very much abraded and raw. Several of my toes had commenced to blacken and fester near the tips and the nails were puffed and loose.[40]

With the aid of bandages, he binds the old skin back in place, and 'over the bandages', he writes, 'were slipped six pairs of thick woollen socks, then fur boots and finally crampon over-shoes. The latter, having large stiff soles, spread the weight nicely and saved my feet from the jagged ice encountered shortly afterwards'.[41] Mawson thus offers an example of the repeated efforts made to insulate the body from the environment. As much as the explorers might desire to make contact with uncharted territory, they also learn that this contact must always be mediated by its withdrawal. Expressing the desire to conquer a territory whose very appeal lies in its inaccessible, unreachable and untouchable qualities, these writers offer us an account of a region that simultaneously invites *and* withdraws from close contact. In other words, the haptic aesthetic has an antithetical resonance: touch tends towards its own extremes, where one is always at risk of touching (or being touched) too much.

Texture and texturisation

Clearly, travellers to the South Pole endure extreme physical hardship. But to focus on this would be to deny what Spufford refers to as Antarctica's 'treasures for the senses', and readers might be struck by the repeated references to sensory pleasure in many accounts.[42] Mawson, for instance, recalls:

> So glorious was it to feel the sun on one's skin after being without it for so long that I next removed most of my clothing and bathed my body in the rays until my flesh fairly tingled – a wonderful sensation which spread throughout my whole person, and made me feel stronger and happier.[43]

Nevertheless, the majority of references to comfort in Cherry-Garrard's work (and there are many) highlight the benefits of bundling up rather than stripping off. He describes their 'comfortable warm roomy home' (192) at Cape Evans and notes that his 'personal impression of [. . .] early summer sledging on the Barrier was one of constant wonder at its comfort' (333). He and his companions gain particular pleasure from the texture and warmth provided by different furs and fabrics. On the ship, Bowers clings to his dressing gown, which he describes as 'my great comfort, as it was not very wet, and it is a lovely warm thing' (53), and Cherry-Garrard refers to the 'delicate dog-skin linings' of Wilson's gloves – 'beautiful things to look at and to feel when new' (298). These skins and furs mediate between the explorers and their environment, without limiting their sense of touch too much:

> The effect of walking in finnesko is much the same as walking in gloves, and you get a sense of touch which nothing else except bare feet could give you. Thus we could feel every small variation in surface, every crust through which our feet broke, every hardened patch below the soft snow. And soon we began to rely more and more upon the sound of our footsteps to tell us whether we were on crevasses or solid ground.
>
> *(258)*

As both Cherry-Garrard and Holman observe, seeing with one's feet is crucial to survival.

References to texture are rife in works by Cherry-Garrard, Ackerman and Wheeler. The most striking accounts, however, are related to the surfaces of the snow and ice – textures that are discerned via 'haptic visuality': when, as Laura Marks puts it, 'the eyes themselves function like organs of touch'.[44] Drawing on and adapting Gilles Deleuze and Félix Guattari's account of smooth and striated space, Marks distinguishes haptic from optic visuality by explaining:

> Haptic looking tends to move over the surface of its object rather than to plunge into illusionistic depth, not to distinguish form so much as to discern texture. It is more inclined to move than to focus, more inclined to graze than to gaze.[45]

In this manner, as her eyes graze the scene, Ackerman explains that icebergs are 'not always smooth':

> Many had textures, waffle patterns, pockmarks, and some looked pounded by Persian metalsmiths. A newly calved iceberg lay like a chunk of glass honeycomb, spongy from being underwater [. . .]. Another had beautiful blue ridges like muscles running along one side.
>
> *(230)*

Cherry-Garrard stresses, however, that these textures are not simply of aesthetic concern, but are central to his survival. He describes surfaces that are 'appallingly soft' (113), 'very heavy' (126) and 'beastly, slippery, sloping' (239). In particular, the men loathe the 'hardest and smallest snow crystals', pulling a sledge through which 'was just like pulling through sand' (245), or for Bowers, 'pulling a sledge over treacle instead of ice' (174). In fact, these difficult surfaces ultimately prove fatal for Captain Scott's team. Discovering their frozen bodies eight months after Scott's last diary entry, eleven miles from the nearest depot on their return from the Pole, Cherry-Garrard discerns, 'The immediate trouble was bad surfaces' (517). Haptic perception, then, moves beyond aesthetic experience to a matter of life and death.

Antarctic travel narratives are packed with descriptions of texture, thus providing a new and apt context for McNee's account of the 'haptic aesthetic'. But it also becomes clear that literary representations of the region are themselves 'textured' by expressions of touch and feeling; in a sense, the embodied surface of the prose, what we might call – after Renu Bora and Jenny Chamarette – its 'texturality', is characterised by an acute sensitivity to changes in our contact with other people, as well as with the landscape that surrounds us.[46] Wheeler's prose, for instance, is frequently terse, but not without lyricism. Discussing her preparations for the journey and the texture of her new clothes, she writes:

When we had satisfied ourselves that no part of our extensive new wardrobe would chafe or pinch or expose our soft flesh to the rigours of frostbite, we packed up our bags and the scowler despatched us into the sunshine.

(12)

Direct and incisive, her prose is also textured by a sensitivity to the affective resonance of the landscape: 'The sun moved steadily, always at the same elevation, and the ice glinted secretively, shimmering in the distance like heat. The surface was creased with tiny ridges and embossed with minuscule bumps' (105). Cherry-Garrard's prose also provides evidence of this texturality. For instance, describing his depot journey of January 1911, he writes: 'Only where the stream presses against the Bluff, White Island and, most important of all, Cape Crozier, and rubs itself against the nearly stationary ice upon which we were travelling, pressures and rendings take place, forming some nasty crevasses' (114). Here, verbs such as 'pressing', 'rubbing' and 'rending' convey a sense of the physicality of the environment, and the relative roughness or smoothness of the language contributes to its texturisation. Shifting away from the detached scientific prose that characterises much of *The Worst Journey in the World*, Cherry-Garrard also incorporates passages rich with intimacy; recalling Alice Fulton's account of the 'materiality' of words and their 'sensual, and especially tactile presence',[47] the reader observes the full range of linguistic registers employed as he describes a summer blizzard:

You may sleep dreamlessly nearly all the time, rousing out for meals, or waking occasionally to hear from the soft warmth of your reindeer bag the deep boom of the tent flapping in the wind, or drowsily you may visit other parts of the world, while the drifting snow purrs against the green tent at your head.
But outside there is raging chaos. It is blowing a full gale: the air is full of falling snow.

(115–16)

The purring, drowsy warmth of this passage jars with its raging chaos, and as a result, the haptic aesthetic of Cherry-Garrard's narrative is simultaneously hypnotic and terrifying. This texturisation is heightened by the fragments of letters, diary excerpts and other accounts that he incorporates into his own; a narrative collage in which texts rub up against one another to generate their own comforts and frictions. This texturality communicates something of the 'feel' of Antarctica. While Spufford insists that Antarctica teaches us that 'words [. . .] are not what the world is made of', what is in fact increasingly clear is the way that the texture of Antarctic experience writes itself into literary language.[48]

The human touch

But there are other ways of touching, and a sensitivity to texture extends itself to accounts of human contact; after all, haptic experience involves not only an encounter with the natural landscape and its extremes, but also one's contact – or lack thereof – with other people. In *Terra Incognita*, Wheeler stresses that despite the isolation, close relationships are formed. Her companion Pete explains:

'Well, relationships here are especially close', he said eventually. 'It's obvious, isn't it – you can't share it with anyone else. I hardly ever talk about Antarctica at home. No one would understand. There's no place like this, and because of that it becomes emotional.'

(148)

This closeness often translates into physical touch experiences, and Wheeler frequently refers to 'hugging' (178), 'kissing' (45) and even 'a flurry of awkward embraces' (237) as she and her colleagues arrive and leave the ice. She recounts her experience of being on nightwatch: 'This involved creeping into pitrooms and shaking slumbering male bodies by the tautly-muscled shoulder' (237). In fact, this physical intimacy also tends towards discomfort. Finding the hut where Cherry-Garrard, Bowers and Wilson camped during their winter journey to collect the Emperor penguin eggs, she lies down in its ruins:

> The crewman and pilot leapt over the low wall and landed on top of me.
> 'Bit cramped in here, with three', the crewman shouted over the wind. Indeed.
> Cherry's party had bulky reindeer sleeping bags to contend with, too, and the stove.
>
> *(139–40)*

Wheeler's narrative indicates the difficulties of finding a balance between distance and proximity, between touching and not-touching, even in a place where human contact appears so remote.

Like Wheeler, Cherry-Garrard observes the contradictory conditions of human contact in the Antarctic. He says that 'both sexually and socially the polar explorer must make up his mind to be starved' and at the same time admits, 'life in such surroundings is both mentally and physically cramped' (596). For the most part, descriptions of physical contact are markedly restrained. Continually emphasising the companionship between the men, he acknowledges only that 'to be absolutely accurate I must admit to having seen a man in a very "prickly" state on one occasion. That was all' (230). Notwithstanding this restraint, his narrative, like Wheeler's, is rich with intimacy. Perhaps most interesting is the way that his companions are frequently characterised in terms of their capacity to touch, despite their withdrawal from contact. He emphasises Wilson's 'great gift of tact' (2) on several occasions, for instance, and Oates is often admired for having 'capable hands' (183). He also reports Scott's suggestion: '"I should like to have Bill to hold my hand when we get to the Pole"' (514).[49] Thus, while accounts of physical human contact in *The Worst Journey in the World* are relatively sparse, the experience is nevertheless represented using a vocabulary of tact.

Nobody knows, of course, if or how the polar party comforted each other in their final days. What is remarkable, however, is the reference to touch that lies at the heart of Francis Spufford's retelling of Scott's journey. In *I May Be Some Time*, as he imagines Scott's death alongside Wilson and Bowers, Spufford introduces a compelling desire to touch: 'Scott has a terrible desire that he must keep quelling, to reach and shake them, to try and summon again their company'.[50] Yet, he suggests, Scott knows that 'he must not touch them at all. He is entirely alone, beyond all hope'.[51] Eventually, however, having written his famous final words – 'For God's sake look after our people' – Scott (according to Spufford) reasserts this need for human contact:

> Scott kicks out suddenly, like an insomniac angry with the bedclothes. Yes, alright, but *quickly* then, without thinking. He pulls open the sleeping bag as far down as he can reach, wrenches his coat right open too, lays his arm deliberately around the cold lump of the body of his friend Edward Wilson (who is not sleeping, no, but dead) and holds tight.[52]

This passage expresses not only the contradictory injunctions surrounding touch, but also indicates our desire for human contact in extreme isolation. While Rodaway argues that haptic geographies are overlooked because tactile experience is so taken for granted, when such experience is threatened, our need to dispel isolation through the tactile is clearly paramount, even if it can only take place in the imagination.[53]

There are, of course, many different ways of making human contact, but it is the recurrence of the handshake that is most remarkable. In *The Worst Journey*, Cherry-Garrard includes Lashley's description of the moment they leave Scott and the polar party: 'the time came for the last handshake and good-bye. I think we all felt it very much' (399). This British trait recalls Henry Stanley's famous meeting with Dr Livingstone. Stanley, a Welshman, admits that he 'would have embraced' Livingstone, but 'he being an Englishman, I did not know how he would receive me'.[54] The greeting is instead accompanied by a firm handshake: 'I replace my hat on my head and he puts on his cap, and we both grasp hands, and I then say aloud, "I thank God, Doctor, I have been permitted to see you."'[55] But the handshake is far from restricted to the British in accounts of polar travel. In *The South Pole* (1912), when Roald Amundsen reaches his destination, the Norwegian notes: 'We all shook hands, with mutual congratulations; we had won our way far by holding together, and we would go farther yet – to the end'.[56] And in *Terra Incognita*, Wheeler also describes the triumph of a Japanese explorer named Susumu Nakamura: 'After handshakes all round (anyone would think they were English), the party began unfurling corporate flags for the inevitable sponsorship photographs' (118). Her own encounters, likewise, are dominated by experiences of the hand – she describes shaking the 'bearpaw extended by the hapless wing-commander' (2), and meeting a 'tall loose-limbed Alaskan': '"They call me Too-Tall Dave", he said as he pumped my hand, crushing a few unimportant bones' (154). Most acutely, however, she notices the absence of the handshake when she arrives at Rothera, the British base. In fact, she warms only to Ian, 'one of the few who came up to shake hands when I arrived' (214). Ironically, it is the British who seem less inclined to shake her hand.

A welcome or greeting, a gesture of friendship or the confirmation of a contract, the handshake – and its gendered connotations – of course means different things in different places and at different times. Geoffrey Bennington explains that 'a handshake is of course not a simple thing, either historically or phenomenologically'.[57] He describes it as 'somewhere between the "blow" and the "caress"'; 'supposedly a gesture of trust and confidence [. . .] originally it would appear as proof that [the hand] is not holding a weapon'.[58] Considering the imperial accounts of polar exploration, the significance of the handshake in the Antarctic multiplies: if imperial eyes, why not imperial hands?[59] Signalling triumph at the South Pole as well as mediating ongoing battles over territories rich in natural resources, the handshake perhaps signifies the tact that surrounds touch: when is touching too much?

The law of tact

Antarctica, it seems, provides us with a rich tactile geography, but it is one that veers between sensation and its loss: our ability to write about travel in the region demands that we touch, but not too much. Touch, then, must be mediated by tact, which Steven Connor explains means 'subtlety, refinement and so on'; in other words, a 'particular kind of lightness of touch'.[60] Tact, he says, is a touch that 'retracts itself, but not fully'; like the Antarctic handshake, it plays at the border between not-touching and touching too much.[61] In his study, Connor draws on the work of Jacques Derrida, who writes in *On Touching – Jean-Luc Nancy* that tact warns against the excess of touch, it is a 'moderation of touch', where 'some kind of reserve holds it on the brink of exaggeration'.[62] Touch, it seems, is inhabited by a '*law of tact*', as Derrida calls it, a law that means 'do not touch or tamper with the thing itself, do not touch on what there is to touch'.[63] Referring to the effects of tampering, Derrida also alludes to an unlawful or unethical touch – a tact that takes on a particular resonance in terms of the imperial legacies of exploration. By the end of the nineteenth century, Antarctica was considered to be the last 'untouched' territory on earth. In the early twentieth century, nations including Britain, Norway, France, Japan and Germany were all involved in competition to reach the South Pole under the name of scientific advancement and the claim to new territory. Following the race to the South Pole and subsequent scientific research in the area, the Antarctic Treaty established in 1961 aimed to 'demilitarise Antarctica', to 'promote international scientific cooperation' and to 'set aside disputes over territorial sovereignty'.[64] Polar exploration is thus mediated by its own law of tact: do touch, but not too much. Derrida's two contradictory orders – 'do do and do not do' – are inscribed in efforts to leave one's mark on unexplored territories – to make it one's own *and* to leave it looking pristine, virginal, intact.[65] Literary representations of Antarctica are thus bound up in this law of tact: touch, but do not appropriate; touch, then withdraw.

An exploration of the haptic aesthetic suggests that these travelogues – in different ways – each confront a law of tact: a law issuing from the extreme conditions of the landscape, from social expectations as well as from international politics. Despite this, works by Cherry-Garrard and Wheeler, among others, show us that touch lies at the heart of Antarctic exploration. Representing the texture of their travels in their own texturised prose, these tactile geographies are always poised at the extremes of haptic experience – where attempts to touch new places and peoples are marked by a withdrawal of contact. This law of tact – and the mediation of contact with remote territories and untouched lands – has significant implications for how we read the haptic aesthetic in travel writing; while the conditions of the Antarctic might present us with an extreme case, I propose that tactile geographies are nevertheless always already mediated by Derrida's law of tact: 'touch *without* touching, without touching *too much*, where touching is already too much'.[66]

Notes

1 Rebecca West, *Black Lamb and Grey Falcon* (1941; repr. Edinburgh: Canongate, 2006), 726; with particular thanks to Tim Youngs for alerting me to this passage.
2 West, *Black Lamb and Grey Falcon*, 727.
3 Carl Thompson, *Travel Writing* (London: Routledge, 2011), 54.
4 Santanu Das, *Touch and Intimacy in First World War Literature* (Cambridge: Cambridge University Press, 2005), 20.
5 Paul Rodaway, *Sensuous Geographies: Body, Sense and Place* (London: Routledge, 1994), 42.
6 Michel Serres, *The Five Senses: A Philosophy of Mingled Bodies* (I), trans. Margaret Sankey and Peter Cowley (London: Continuum, 2008), 26.
7 Serres, *The Five Senses*, 70.
8 Charles Forsdick, 'Travel Writing, Disability, Blindness: Venturing Beyond Visual Geographies', in *New Directions in Travel Writing Studies*, eds Julia Kuehn and Paul Smethurst (London: Palgrave, 2015), 115.
9 Judith Adler, 'Origins of Sightseeing', *Annals of Tourism Research* 16.1 (1989): 7–29.
10 Eitan Bar-Yosef, 'The "Deaf Traveller," the "Blind Traveller," and Constructions of Disability in Nineteenth-Century Travel Writing', *Victorian Review* 35.2 (2009): 140.
11 John Urry and Jonas Larsen, *The Tourist Gaze 3.0*, 3rd edition (London: Sage, 2011), 1.
12 Adler, 'Origins of Sightseeing', 9.
13 Adler, 'Origins of Sightseeing', 24.
14 Forsdick, 'Travel Writing', 122, 116–17; my emphasis.
15 Bar-Yosef, 'The "Deaf Traveller"', 134.
16 Bar-Yosef, 'The "Deaf Traveller"', 139.
17 James Holman, *A Voyage Round the World* (London: Smith, Elder & Co., 1834), 1:5.

18 Cited in Jason Roberts, *A Sense of the World* (London: Simon & Schuster, 2006), 2.

19 Roberts, *A Sense of the World*, 3.

20 It is worth noting that Roberts and Holman also stress the importance of sound and smell for Holman's navigation.

21 James Holman, *A Voyage Round the World* (London: Smith, Elder & Co., 1835), 3:227–8, cited in Bar-Yosef, 'The "Deaf Traveller"', 145.

22 James Holman, *The Narrative of a Journey* (London: Rivington, 1822), vii, cited in Bar-Yosef, 'The "Deaf Traveller"', 144.

23 Das, *Touch and Intimacy*, 12.

24 Rodaway, *Sensuous Geographies*, 41–2, 41; James J. Gibson, *The Senses Considered as Perceptual Systems* (Boston, MA: Houghton Mifflin, 1966).

25 Alan McNee, 'The Haptic Sublime and the "Cold Stony Reality" of Mountaineering', *19: Interdisciplinary Studies in the Long Nineteenth Century* 19 (2014): 4. See also Alan McNee, *The New Mountaineer in Late Victorian Britain: Materiality, Modernity and the Haptic Sublime* (London: Palgrave Macmillan, 2016).

26 McNee, 'The Haptic Sublime', 3.

27 McNee, 'The Haptic Sublime', 4–5.

28 McNee, 'The Haptic Sublime', 14, 8. The relationship between travel writing and the sublime has been discussed at length elsewhere. Thompson, for instance, notes that in the Romantic era, 'a growing interest in the Sublime made mountains objects of aesthetic pleasure': Carl Thompson, *The Suffering Traveller and the Romantic Imagination* (Oxford: Clarendon, 2007), 29. McNee, however, points out that in contrast to Edmund Burke's argument that the sublime gives delight only when viewed at a distance, the haptic sublime 'involves the presence of real physical danger, rather than the potential or imagined threat that had previously been associated with the sublime' (15). His account of the haptic sublime thus depends on close physical contact between the mountain and the climber.

29 For a history of Antarctic exploration prior to Apsley Cherry-Garrard's *The Worst Journey in the World*, see: *Travels, Explorations and Empires: Writings from the Era of Imperial Expansion 1770–1835*, volume 3 'North and South Poles', ed. Peter J. Kitson (London: Pickering and Chatto, 2001); *Nineteenth-Century Travels, Explorations and Empires: Writings from the Era of Imperial Consolidation, 1835–1910*, volume 1 'North and South Poles', ed. Peter J. Kitson (London: Routledge, 2003).

30 Apsley Cherry-Garrard, *The Worst Journey in the World* (1922; repr. London: Vintage, 2010), 98. Further references are included parenthetically in the text.

31 Sara Wheeler, *Terra Incognita: Travels in Antarctica* (London: Vintage, 1997), 161. Further references are included parenthetically in the text.

32 Diane Ackerman, 'White Lanterns', in *The Moon by Whale Light* (New York: Vintage, 1992), 197. Further references are included parenthetically in the text.

33 Francis Spufford, 'Introduction', in *The Antarctic: An Anthology*, ed. Francis Spufford (London: Granta, 2007), 7.

34 Spufford, 'Introduction', in *The Antarctic*, 6.

35 Francis Spufford, *I May Be Some Time: Ice and the English Imagination* (London: Faber, 1996), 13.

36 Spufford, 'Introduction', in *The Antarctic*, 2.

37 Spufford, 'Introduction', in *The Antarctic*, 2.

38 Thompson, *The Suffering Traveller*, 4, 2.

39 Roberts also highlights Holman's fear of frostbite during his fated journey in Siberia, noting that 'As touch was the primary sense by which he comprehended the world, numbness was a sort of second blindness. The threat of frostbite held special terrors' (Roberts, *A Sense of the World*, 203).

40 Douglas Mawson, *The Home of the Blizzard* (1915; repr. Edinburgh: Birlinn, 2000), 187.

41 Mawson, *The Home of the Blizzard*, 187–8.

42 Spufford, 'Introduction', in *The Antarctic*, 6.

43 Mawson, *The Home of the Blizzard*, 188.

44 Laura Marks, *The Skin of the Film: Intercultural Cinema, Embodiment, and the Senses* (Durham, NC: Duke University Press, 2000), 162.

45 Marks, *The Skin of the Film*, 162. See also Gilles Deleuze and Félix Guattari, '1440: The Smooth and the Striated', in *A Thousand Plateaus: Capitalism and Schizophrenia*, trans. Brian Massumi (Minneapolis, MN: University of Minnesota Press, 2004), 523–51.

46 Renu Bora, 'Outing Texture', in *Novel Gazing: Queer Readings in Fiction*, ed. Eve Kosofsky Sedgwick (Durham, NC: Duke University Press, 1997), 94–127; Jenny Chamarette, 'Flesh, Folds and Texturality:

Thinking Visual Ellipsis via Merleau-Ponty, Hélène Cixous and Robert Frank', *Paragraph* 30.2 (2007): 34–49.

47 Alice Fulton, *Feeling as a Foreign Language: The Good Strangeness of Poetry* (Saint Paul, MN: Graywolf Press, 1999), 77.

48 Spufford, 'Introduction', in *The Antarctic*, 15.

49 Wheeler also employs such metaphors; she describes Wilson as Scott's 'right-hand man' and notes that Shackleton 'always has his finger on the pulse of his men' (*Terra Incognita*, 53, 35).

50 Spufford, *I May Be Some Time*, 332.

51 Spufford, *I May Be Some Time*, 332.

52 Spufford, *I May Be Some Time*, 336.

53 Although it is beyond the scope of the present study, this also raises questions regarding our efforts to keep 'in touch' with other people and the role of communication technologies in travel writing. The sending of correspondence and the use of the radio, telephone and email recur throughout accounts of polar exploration. Rodaway notes: '"Keeping in touch" is most often, it seems, referring to letter writing or, nowadays, the ubiquitous phone call, rather than a literal connectedness with other people and places' (Rodaway, *Sensuous Geographies*, 54).

54 Henry Morton Stanley, *How I Found Livingstone: Travels, Adventures and Discoveries in Central Africa, Including Four Months Residence with Dr. Livingstone* (London: Sampson Low, Marston, Low, and Searle, 1872), 411.

55 Stanley, *How I Found Livingstone*, 439.

56 Roald Amundsen, *The South Pole: An Account of the Norwegian Expedition in the Fram, 1910–12*, volumes 1–2, trans. Thorvald Nilsen, Kristian Prestrud and A. G. Chater (1912; repr. London: C. Hurst, 1976), cited in Spufford, *The Antarctic*, 110.

57 Geoffrey Bennington, 'Handshake', *Derrida Today* 1.2 (2009): 168.

58 Bennington, 'Handshake', 168.

59 Mary Louise Pratt, *Imperial Eyes: Travel Writing and Transculturation* (London: Routledge, 1992).

60 Steven Connor, *The Book of Skin* (London: Reaktion Books, 2004), 259.

61 Connor, *The Book of Skin*, 262.

62 Jacques Derrida, *On Touching – Jean-Luc Nancy*, trans. Christine Irizarry (Stanford, CA: Stanford University Press, 2005), 47.

63 Derrida, *On Touching*, 66.

64 See 'The Antarctic Treaty', British Antarctic Survey, accessed 28 April 2015, www.bas.ac.uk/about/antarctica/the-antarctic-treaty.

65 Derrida, *On Touching*, 68, 47.

66 Derrida, *On Touching*, 67.

17

TASTING

Heidi Oberholtzer Lee

A hermeneutic of appetite in Early American travel writing

The field of Early American literary studies, focusing on texts from the mid-seventeenth century through the mid-nineteenth century, provides a rich library of materials for those specialising in the study of travel writing. Extensive exploration and travel by European sailors, missionaries, merchants, and immigrants, as well as the Middle Passage voyages of the slaves that they imported, and the voluntary migration or forced relocation of native peoples, profoundly shaped this period in the Americas. Early American literary history thus encompasses a vast archive of texts of mobility that record travellers' journeys of pain and suffering, economic profit, pilgrimage, and a sense of adventure and discovery.

Historians have drawn on this archive of travel writing to produce a wide array of commodity studies – on sugar, cod, pecans, and chocolate, to name just a few. Historical monographs, such as those by James E. McWilliams or Trudy Eden, examine what Early Americans ate, why, how they prepared it, and whom this affected, though the relationship between travel and taste remains unexplored in these analyses. Early American literary scholars, too, have mined works of travel writing for material for food studies, cannibalism studies, body studies, and postcolonial scholarship. Among the best known of these literary scholars are David S. Shields, writing on American foodways broadly, sometimes rice and wine specifically, and Etta M. Madden, along with her religious studies co-editor Martha L. Finch, who together marshal scholarship on food in utopian communities. Their primary interests lie outside of travel writing, however.[1]

Travel writing typically contains descriptions of food and eating, taste and orality, production and consumption, and these can be read for their discourses of embodiment, incorporation, appetite, and desire. Early Americans read and understood their environments, themselves, and others through what I call a 'hermeneutic of appetite'. Through their tongues and stomachs, they encountered their worlds and the people in them. They ate the plants they found; they tasted the foods of native peoples and immigrant neighbours. They cooked, canned, smoked, preserved, and thereby dominated wild environments new and intimidating to them, sometimes controlling or even decimating the peoples inhabiting those environments as well. Of most concern here is not what Early American travellers actually ate, but rather what they *reported* they ate or did not eat. Why did they emphasise their tasting of certain foods, labelling them civilised and endowing them with particular political or cultural importance, while neglecting to mention the tasting of other foods, or naming these foods only to malign them as dirty, disgusting, inferior, or savage? The insights of anthropologists and sociologists help us to identify how Early American writers used a rhetoric of food to distinguish themselves from some peoples and cultures, while aligning themselves with others – sometimes building alliances through a language of foodways, other times making clear the boundaries that they were not willing to cross.

In this chapter, I shall provide close readings and analysis of two texts: the *Travels* of William Bartram (1739–1823), scientist, botanist, explorer, and friend of America's Founding Fathers, whose work is now nearly canonical among Early Americanists; and the even better-known journals of Meriwether Lewis (1774–1809) and William Clark (1770–1838), the subject of deep, sustained, and serious treatment by historians, but whom literary scholars have largely neglected. I analyse both of these texts through an interdisciplinary American Studies theoretical framework that draws upon gender studies, ecocriticism, consumption studies, and postcolonialism, a framework informed by the insights of anthropology, sociology, and history, in addition to my own field of literary studies.

Bartram, I argue, locates his definition of heroism in his gut, literally in the way that his narrator hunts, cooks, eats, or refrains from eating his environment. He thereby advances his understanding of a male hero as someone capable of exhibiting a necessary, and often carnivorous, aggressiveness but who more often manifests empathy, self-restraint, and pacific tendencies to help maintain balance within what Bartram describes as the 'human economy' and the 'economy of nature'. This delicate balance between aggression and gentleness that I identify in Bartram's conception of heroism provides a helpful way for scholars to address the puzzling relationship between Bartram's Quaker identity and his seeming celebration of violence and images of war in *Travels*. It also establishes a basis for understanding the gastronomical heroism and masculinity that characterise the work of later American authors such as Lewis and Clark, James Fenimore Cooper, Henry David Thoreau (who we know read and promoted Bartram's text[2]), and Herman Melville. More generally, Bartram's descriptions of his gustatory predilections serve as a clear example of how a travel writer's notations of personal taste and alimentary adventures may reveal both individual and cultural assumptions about gender roles, national identity, and the relationship between humans and the environment.

My second case study, the journals of Lewis and Clark, reflects a hermeneutic of appetite as well, and, like Bartram's work, advances the idea that heroic masculinity can be established and demonstrated through appropriately assertive, even aggressive, but still civilised and disciplined interaction with the natural environment. There are differences between how these texts understand their relationship to or within the anthropocene, however, and descriptors of taste serve as important markers of these. Bartram, as a botanist and naturalist, focuses on the complex interplay between humans, flora, and fauna. His documentation of taste helps to tease out the interconnectedness between human and natural economies, here 'economies' loosely meaning 'systems of living exchange'. United States President Thomas Jefferson tasked Lewis and Clark, on the other hand, with a military project designed not only to document and explore the contours of the American West not yet well known by the fledging American nation, but also, explicitly, to understand its possibilities for economic profit and the promotion of national interests and identity. Taste, for them, is linked more concretely to money and commerce, not the broader 'exchanges' upon which Bartram meditates, and they mark their heroic masculinity by documenting how they secure the *power* to taste. Lewis and Clark employ their synecdochic appetites as markers of and justifications for a national and imperial appetite that will, justifiably they think, spread across and consume the continent.

Indeed, Lewis and Clark participate in a widespread Early American literary conversation that positions proper and manly consumption at the very heart of American imperialist expansionism, or what literary critic Frederick Kaufman wryly labels 'manifest dinner'.[3] The two captains base much of the legitimacy of their own and their nation's claims to western lands on their ability to eat moderately, to consume cooked rather than raw foods, and, in particular, to eat meat in addition to plant matter. These habits of consumption, they insist, qualify them as the most manly of men, as the most civilised of men, to explore, cultivate, and dominate the West. They encode their heroism in strongly gendered terms and connect their aggressive masculinity to the potential for successful American domination of native peoples and indigenous plants and animals.

In both Lewis and Clark's journals and in Bartram's text, we see how the sense of taste can be used to demarcate both gender and culture. Bartram highlights the relationship between taste and environment, and Lewis and Clark between taste and nation-building. They serve as examples of how travel writing deploys taste as a category to demarcate differences, as well as similarities, between peoples, their cultural practices, their values, and their dreams for themselves and their futures.

William Bartram as gastronomical alligator warrior and snake bird connoisseur

William Bartram's *Travels*, published in 1791, recounts the naturalist's journey through the Carolinas, Georgia, Florida, and 'the Cherokee Country' from 1773 to 1778 under the patronage of Dr John Fothergill of London. Literary scholars and historians have read *Travels* as an early eco-text and work of environmentalism, as well as a fascinating study of how botany and politics can converge in a work of naturalism.[4] In this chapter, I am interested in the graphic descriptions of the alimentary violence of the natural world that memorably pervade Bartram's work and in how this taste-based rhetoric of violence reveals Bartram's understanding of what defines a post-revolutionary, American male hero. Bartram, I argue, defines his heroism gastronomically, by reporting what his travelling narrator can hunt or track, kill, cook, consume, or even intelligently avoid consuming. This reflects his understanding of masculine heroism as primarily exhibiting empathy, self-restraint, and pacifism, yet still maintaining the capacity for a sometimes aggressive physicality. He thought both aspects of this manliness necessary for an appropriate relationship between humanity and nature. Anthropologist Jon Holtzman notes that through 'potent' and 'sensuous' descriptions of food and taste a culture may reveal inherent contradictions in how it constructs and determines what constitutes masculinity.[5] We see such tensions, though not necessarily contradictions, revealed in Bartram's work. He envisions ideal American masculinity as self-controlled, but potentially savage; as peaceful, but with the capacity for war. Detailing the scope, variety, and objects of his taste allows him to test, explore, justify, and promote a portrait of heroic masculinity that influences how Americans view themselves in relation to their environment. Description of taste often links the body with the places and spaces it inhabits.

Bartram details his own tastes, as well as those he observes in flora and fauna, particularly the tastes in nature that he sees reflected and esteems in himself. For example, he effusively praises an insect-devouring plant, a 'carnivorous vegetable'.[6] He recalls its 'motion and volition' and admires its assertive self-gratification (15), qualities that he subsequently demonstrates to be similar to his own. He follows his vivid descriptions of aggressive *plant* appetite with equally if not more striking anecdotes about fierce *animal* appetite. For example, he casts himself as an epic hero who wields a club to battle large numbers of attacking and 'greedy' alligators (115).

A quest for dinner – both on the part of the alligators and of Bartram – occasions the fight. He wins the battle, after which he celebrates his victory not with a ravenously eaten meal of raw or hurriedly cooked food, but with a multi-step, laborious preparation of broiled fish and rice, seasoned with oil, pepper, salt, and oranges, the latter substituting for vinegar. 'I sat down and regaled myself cheerfully' (119), he remembers, invoking the savouring of his food, its carefully considered preparation and taste, as the reward for his heroism. A hero eats well, cooks wisely, and enjoys the taste of fine cuisine. The ability to savour these tastes is itself the spoils of his battle, and its civilised and restrained expression evidences that his gastronomical heroism did not require descent into savagery (114–24).

Furthermore, these tastes help to secure in Bartram's memory the emblematic alligator battle that he fought nearly a decade before and to reinforce his understanding and memory of having proved his manliness. As anthropologist David E. Sutton points out, taste and memory are intricately and powerfully intertwined. As transitory as eating may seem, taste is actually an evocative sensory experience that helps the brain to store and cue memories permanently.[7] Though many years have passed since Bartram fought the alligators, the memory of the feast that followed the battle helps bring into focus the details of the events that preceded it, as well as the joy and relief of the battle's alimentary denouement.

Bartram's assertion of his own heroic physicality extends beyond the forcefulness of his limbs to also underscore the gastronomical heroism of his adventurous stomach and risk-taking tongue. Indeed, he often aggressively eats nature, asserting his dominance over the natural world by ingesting it, and, perhaps most importantly, by *recording* how he subsumes the environment into his own body. Bartram ascribes to his tongue an almost patriotic fervour in its successful conquest of the 'virgin' lands, a gustatory colonisation of the environment that recurs in significantly more pronounced ways in the journals of Lewis and Clark as well as other nineteenth-century American texts.[8] A dominating masculinity clearly and repeatedly surfaces in Bartram's narrative. Not entirely unlike the 'butcher[ing] [. . .] devouring spider' that Bartram admires early in his text as it cunningly attacks and then 'feasts' on a 'large fat bomble bee', Bartram asserts his predatory role as he boldly embarks on a taste journey, sampling nature as he travels, and tasting foods unfamiliar to the Anglo-American palate (20).[9] He expresses his fascination with a trout that is 'remarkably ravenous; nothing living that he can seize upon escapes his jaws' (108). A few lines later, Bartram exhibits this same ravenous behaviour, ironically eating the trout whose ravenousness he had noted and remarking on the deliciousness of that same fish (109). He admires the power of predators and celebrates that power in himself.

Bartram similarly documents other taste experiments that suggest a bold and adventurous palate. For instance, he extols the virtues of young raccoons, which he assures his readers 'are excellent meat' (75), but cautions against the meat of what he calls 'Snake Birds' (125), which he believes subsist 'intirely on fish' and thus their 'flesh smells and tastes intolerably strong of it' (126).[10] Snake bird meat 'is scarcely to be eaten' unless one is 'constrained by insufferable hunger' (126). The desperate voraciousness that apparently entices Bartram to sample snake bird thus elides into gastronomical advice for the civil gourmand. Bartram also commends the pericarpium and berries of the *Laurel magnolias* as having 'an agreeable spicy scent, and an aromatic bitter taste' (91), evoking the much-sought-after New World flavours of West Indian 'spice' as well as 'bitter' chocolate or coffee that drew some of the earliest adventurers to the Americas. He notes that the 'beautiful spreading tree' *Zanthoxylum clava-herculis* produces an 'aromatic berry [that] is delicious food for the little turtle dove; and epicures say [. . .] gives their flesh a fine flavour' (93). He subsequently warns travellers, however, against dining on the mud fish, whose meat is 'white and tender, but soft and tastes of the mud, and is not much esteemed', or the soft-shelled tortoise of East Florida, which is 'extremely fat and delicious', but whose meat is 'apt to purge people not accustomed' to it and who eat it in 'excess' (157–8).[11] As with the snake bird, Bartram here again points out that he has eaten foul-tasting or potentially risky food to impress upon his readers his ability to manage nature through eating it or cooking it. We do not know whether Bartram truthfully reports his diet here or whether he represents as his own the knowledge that he gained from his native American hosts, but, either way, he tells readers of his appetite and his ability to analyse the taste of food to advance his reputation as a heroic, discerning man of the American wilderness and wildlife.

While Bartram recommends 'studying and contemplating the works and power of the Creator' and 'learn[ing] wisdom and understanding in the economy of nature', tending to 'our duties to each other, and all creatures and concerns that are submitted to our care and controul', his economic philosophy ultimately centres more on humans than the environment (70). He samples the aforementioned 'excess' of tortoise meat (158) and during his travels catches more trout than he can use or preserve before they go bad, a wasteful act for which he never evidences any regret (117). Bartram associates the abundance of food with hospitable or civil human practice or with restoring mental and physical well-being. He expresses no qualms about the concept of plenty, as opposed to scarcity or simple necessity. He envisions human and natural economies as flowing, living exchange. Natural cycles of seasonal growth and then death allow for and even promote feasting, as well as fasting. Humans in nature, as well as the alligators Bartram earlier observed, are part of this cyclical gastronomy. Coupling his manly, aggressive appetite with the balance of what he describes as 'civility and hospitality', Bartram happily enjoys his peaceful time with the 'White King of Talahasocht', who offers him a 'repast [. . .] consisting of bear ribs, venison, varieties of fish, roasted turkies (which they call the white man's dish), hot corn cakes, and a very agreeable cooling sort of jelly, which they call conte: this is prepared from the root of the China briar' which is made in a manner that when 'sweetened with honey [and cooled] becomes a beautiful, delicious jelly, very nourishing and wholesome' (203–4). Throughout the text, Bartram regularly mentions dining with native Americans of various tribes. His meals with them seem to help him bridge some cultural difference and further foster his appreciation for peoples with whom he believes he shares an appropriate love of nature. These meals encourage peace and civility. The vocabulary he uses to describe the tastes featured at these meals – 'agreeable' (203) and 'nourishing and wholesome' (204) – applies to practices of sociability, not exclusively to food. Bartram selects gastronomical terminology sufficiently malleable and flexible not only to detail flavour, but also to gesture towards the admirable qualities of his hosts.

When Bartram hunts for turkey and encounters a lynx which seeks the same prey, one anticipates from having read other of his chapters that an epic battle between two closely matched foes will ensue. However, this encounter with a 'cunning fellow-hunter' concludes in civility, with neither the turkeys nor the lynx meeting death (109). Bartram instead concludes his day still enjoying a 'delicious meal' and 'wholesome repast' that satisfies 'hungry stomachs' with 'plenty of delicious and healthful food' (109). '[O]ur stomachs keen, with contented minds; under no control, but what reason and ordinate passions dictated', he and his peers were 'far removed from the seats of strife' (110). The contented food critic also here enfolds in his modelling of masculine, heroic appetite an impulse towards moderation and balanced passions, sometimes indulging in feasting for the sake of civility and hospitality more than for sheer rapaciousness. Voracious eating and tasting serve his manly characterisation only when he seeks to communicate his dominance over his environment and over the other species in it that compete with humankind. Excessiveness, violent appetite for its own sake, has little place in Bartram's representation of ideal humanity. Wolves, trout, and alligators are instinctively rapacious, while men are not (145, 108, 115). Humans only exhibit immoderate appetite and tasting when engaged in an epic struggle against the environment, not when sharing food with their fellows. Again, the sensuousness of this taste experience secures the permanence of a memory – here not just an individual memory, but a communal memory – of a peaceful, civilised experience shared between native and Anglo-American peoples. Taste, in contrast to just 'vision or words', writes Sutton, is 'useful for encoding' such a memory 'of context pasts'.[12] Bartram retrieves this meal from his memory to document for posterity how two disparately tasting communities, with himself a central heroic ambassador here, came together successfully in a moment of honourable, noble gourmandise.

If Bartram could simply have focused on the success and sophistication of his heroic ambassadorial tastes, why then did he expend so much ink in describing his violent tastes as well? Manly heroism reflected both the balances and extremes that he saw and respected in the 'economy of nature' that he studied. Sometimes overtly identifying as a member of the pacifist Society of Friends, Bartram promoted peace, but he was also a spy for the American cause during the Revolutionary War and dedicated his book to war heroes (first George Washington, then Thomas Mifflin).[13] He saw in himself and humanity at large the same kinds of cycles and patterns that he discerned in the environment – a 'natural' interplay of feast and fast, plenty and scarcity, savagery and gentleness, violence and placidity. He advocated moderation as a marker of civilisation, but portrayed himself and humankind as not completely divorced from the polarities and seeming contradictions of the nature in which they lived. The violence in which he engaged was 'natural', as well as a path towards civilisation that did not efface or abuse nature, but that brought nature under the protective auspices of humanity. His self-assertion and aggressiveness were necessary, worthy of praise, just as his sociability and participation in hospitality were. Heroic, masculine appetite, he argued, could be measured in the diversity of its strengths, the multiplicity of its expressions, not in a singular, narrow, over-indulged appetite. The remembered flavours of his meals functioned to draw from his past those moments when his tastes marked his heroic victories of physical strength in battle, his accomplished and educated palate, and his ambassadorial acumen and sociability. Bartram's work serves as a fine example of how the sensuousness of taste in travel writing can signal physical, intellectual, cultural, and social comment and self-definition. By detailing flavour through vocabulary not exclusively gustatory, Bartram helps to make taste as a category more easily convey broader social and cultural experiences.

Meriwether Lewis and William Clark as captains of consumption

We have seen how William Bartram's gastronomical heroism centres on how he ingests, manages, or resists the environment through which he travels and the creatures that are a part of it. Captains Meriwether Lewis and William Clark's journals (1803–1806), which document their exploratory expedition from the American Eastern states and mid-West to the Pacific Ocean and back, similarly work out a definition of masculine heroism that entails aggressive, carnivorous eating. Their tasting, however, is rooted in a broader understanding of what constitutes appropriate American economic consumption in an increasingly imperialist context. As postcolonial scholars point out, nineteenth-century Americans' travel to the West and to the Mexican South often included not only exploration and delighted reports of the animal, plant, or mineral resources found there, but also explicit argument for the appropriation of these resources and lands. Travel writers additionally suggested how these resources might best be used and consumed, usually in contrast to the practices of the native peoples already using (or *underutilising*, so wrote the explorers) these resources.[14] Many Americans hoped to settle the western part of the United States and to use the land and resources there to displace Great Britain as the economic hub of the Atlantic.[15] With Thomas Jefferson's presidency and the Louisiana Purchase of 1803, Americans expanded their national boundaries significantly. Jefferson hoped this would further farmers' prospects and bolster the American economy without leading to industrialisation.[16] Early nineteenth-century literatures gathered vocabularies of consumption to reveal a remarkable confluence in the languages of gastronomy, economy, and imperialism. As Frederick Kaufman notes, for most nineteenth-century Americans, 'Yankee America' was a 'vast, engulfing power, a grand, nationalist stomach' that hungered for expansion across the continent.[17] Anne Norton, too, explains, 'Eating offered a descriptive paradigm for two of the most important features of Western culture: conquest and commerce'.[18] We thus find that early nineteenth-century Americans like Lewis and Clark view their world through a hermeneutic of appetite, and they argue that their means of conspicuous consumption, moments of publicly displayed eating linked to their economic values, can mark their status. Their tasting habits, they believe, distinguish them from the native peoples in their midst and at the nation's new borders, and reinforce their individual and national right to dominate.

Almost every other page of the Lewis and Clark journals details some moment of exchange – whether economic, gastronomic, or sexual – between the men of the Corps of Discovery and the members of the native American tribes they encountered as they travelled.[19] In contrast to Bartram's descriptions of moderate and civil native Americans, Lewis and Clark regularly portray them as consuming savagely, which entailed trading unwisely and eating immoderately, femininely, and bloodily. They viewed most of the tribes as having little to teach them about the moderation of appetites, and they complained that the natives' poor economy of body debilitated the Corps. Clark commented in March of 1805, for example, that his men were '[g]enerally healthy except venerials complains which is verry Commion amongst the natives and the men Catch it from them'.[20] Rampant disease, Clark implies, resides in the 'immoderate' native body, not in the promiscuous behaviour of the Corps of Discovery. Both Lewis and Clark, in fact, openly comment on how their men 'gratify the passions' (6:75), and the pair vacillate between complaining of a native population that 'view[s] Sensuality as a Necessary evel' (6:75) and looking askance at another tribe that does 'not hold the virtue of their women in high estimation, and will even prostitute their wives and daughters for a fishinghook or a stran [sic] of beads' (6:168). The captains scorn the natives not for commodifying sexuality, but rather for assigning it a market value above or below what the captains think it worth.[21] They respect moderation and business acumen when they admit to finding it in indigenous peoples, but the two explorers more often write derisively of those who are too 'extravigent' (3:163), 'craveing' (6:61), 'never Satisfied' (6:60), or 'verry Selfish and Stingey of what they have to eate or ware' (5:259). Lewis and Clark look for a human economy that values equity and temperance but seem unwilling to recognise that what they call selfishness on the part of the natives may sometimes reflect more on the captains' inappropriately excessive requests. The captains see in the natives an excessiveness that they generally ignore in themselves, even when they provide counter-evidence of its existence.[22]

Though Lewis and Clark condemn native immoderation, they praise excessiveness in terms of their own attitude towards the land, its produce, and the desire it inspires in their own bodies. Lewis, who writes often of cooking and medical care, remarks in June of 1805, 'my fare is really sumptuous this evening; buffaloe's humps, tongues and marrowbones, fine trout parched meal pepper and salt, and a good appetite; the last is not considered the least of the luxuries' (4:287). He praises the bounty of the land and notes the hearty delight with which he responds to it. His 'good appetite' is itself part of the sumptuousness of this feast, an unexpected and praiseworthy 'luxury', as he calls it. The pleasures of tasting are here not to be taken for granted, and they are in themselves a reward for the hard work of exploration and travelling.

The two men attempt to adjust their tastes to the flavours they can access, learning to eat 'of the small guts of the buffaloe cooked over a blazing fire in the Indian stile without any preperation of washing or other clensing' and finding 'them very good' (4:386). Lewis claims that 'if any Indians can subsist in the form of a nation in these mountains with the means they have of acquiring food we can also subsist' (4:437). He has no qualms about his men adopting the 'Indian stile' of cooking, and he will not, he insists, be proven too weak to survive when the natives can do so. He and his men will learn to appreciate the good tastes that nature offers them, and they will experience the luxury of bounty that might not be readily discernible to effeminate or less adaptable tongues.

In fact, much of the Corps of Discovery's detailed reports of its hunting and frequent meat-eating may be interpreted as their desire to establish themselves for posterity as strong, truly masculine, economically empowered Americans, in contrast to feminised and immoderate native Americans. We need not read their accounts as a fully accurate record of what foods were most available along the journey. Both hunting and meat-eating have historically been associated with power, particularly masculine power, for traditionally men have hunted and women have transformed the raw results of the hunt into cooked meat for them.[23] Meat itself 'was a valuable economic commodity; those who controlled this commodity achieved power. If men were the hunters, then the control of this economic resource was in their hands'.[24] Crèvecoeur may have argued that American hunting and the subsequent eating of 'wild meat' developed 'ferocious, gloomy, and unsocial' habits in its practitioners, but most American men celebrated their hunting skills as having been a significant factor in their winning the Revolutionary War.[25] They continued to think of hunting as an important representation of military strength. Lewis and Clark could therefore draw on this positive understanding of American hunting to establish their own reputations as influential and powerful men.

Of course, without many women among them, the Corps must cook their meat themselves, and they demonstrate concern not only with the meticulous tallying of how much game they kill, but also with the taste and preparation of their food, whether meat or plant. Clark mentions his 'Sumptious brackfast of venison' (6:69). Lewis brags of 'a kind of pudding with [. . .] burries' that he instructs McNeal how to make, and he boasts that a local Chief 'declared it the best thing he had taisted for a long time' (5:95). Elsewhere Lewis describes how he and Clark kill a number of buck and buffalo for the preparation of another pudding that Lewis praises as 'one of the greatest delacies of the forrest'. Arguing that the excellence of this dish merits 'a place' in his journal, Lewis offers a detailed recipe that begins:

> About 6 feet of the lower extremity of the large gut of the Buffaloe is the first mosel that the cook makes love to, this he holds fast at one end with the right hand, while with the forefinger and thumb of the left he gently compresses it, and discharges what he says *is not good to eat*.

After a rigorous kneading of this meat, twice seizing it, tying it fast, stuffing it, compressing it, distending it, and filling it, the intestine is finally ready to be 'baptised in the missouri with two dips and a flirt, and bobbed into the kettle'. '[A]fter it be well boiled', Lewis concludes, 'it is taken and fryed with bears oil untill it becomes brown, when it is ready to esswage the pangs of a keen appetite or such as travelers in the wilderness are seldom at a loss for' (4:131). Clearly Lewis and Clark convey a pride in their culinary acumen, and Lewis, here especially, portrays himself as both chef and gourmand, transforming heretofore unfamiliar buffalo meat into a 'delicacy' recognisable to coastal American palates. Its flavour he gestures to quite broadly, defining it, by contrast, as 'good to eat'. The sensuousness of taste he couples with the sensuousness of food preparation. He amorously, even sexually, woos and conquers the meat, dominating it as he does the landscape from which it comes.

The 'keen appetite' that Lewis suggests most male travellers experience cannot be satisfied exclusively with vegetarian fare, he insists. The two captains at one point admit to having maintained a vegetarian diet for themselves for a time, and Lewis confesses that he 'was always much attatched' to 'vegitable food' (5:143). Yet, he and Clark are quick to emphasise that plants do not satisfy them as the natives would have been satisfied. Some men may never admit to being full, pertinently notes anthropologist Jon Holtzman, lest food be thought to have 'defeated' them. Gluttony 'indexes healthy manly vigor', he remarks, even though, contradictorily, 'masculinity is also constructed by an ability to control one's appetite'.[26] Evidencing such conflicting definitions of masculinity, Lewis remarks in 1805, 'I had eat nothing yesterday except one scant meal of the flour and berries except the dryed cakes of berries which did not appear to satisfy my appetite as they appeared to do those of my Indian friends' (5:95). Lewis distinguishes here between his own carnivorous, voracious appetite, and the feeble, herbivorous appetite of the natives. Their tastes are too easily satisfied, he suggests. A civilised but ravenous appetite like his, and the imperial American appetite that it emblematises, deserves satisfaction, he implies.

While Lewis disparages native appetites as feeble and docile, he also presents native tastes and patterns of consumption as too wild and crude to qualify natives to own this environment. They present two problematic extremes, he believes – too tame at some moments, while too violent at others. In one particularly graphic episode of his journal, he describes the native inhabitants as eating like animals. He recounts how they approached a meal of deer 'like a parcel of famished dogs each seizing and tearing away a part of the intestens'. He claims,

> [H]ad I not [. . .] had a pretty keen appetite myself I am confident I should not have taisted any part of the venison shortly. [E]ach one had a peice of some discription and all eating most ravenously. [S]ome were eating the kidneys [. . .] the blood runing from the corners of their mouths.
>
> *(5:103)*

He expressed disgust that humans could take a 'shape so nearly allyed to the brute creation' (5:103).[27] Lewis here focuses primarily on the equation of native American to animal, significantly native American to dog, the animal by which he and a Nez Perce man would later debate the definition of food and insult each other (7:212). To Lewis, this scene of frenzied, savage meat-eating contrasts with his gourmet recipes and his thoughtful, slow preparation of meat.[28] At the same time, however, Lewis, without providing any details of his own involvement, admits that his own appetite demanded assuagement, and he himself tasted the same meat torn apart by the natives. He obliquely references here the fine line that he and his men sometimes walk between sufficiently modifying their tastes to survive in the wild and allowing their tastes to be modified to the extent that they become wild themselves. In this passage, Lewis additionally may be displacing onto the native Americans the bloodiness and wildness that he senses in his own imperialist culture. He reveals the significant challenge posed to the Corps of preserving the distinction between wild appetites and wild men, between being civilised American providers and barbaric animal consumers. His text uncovers the tension between the appropriately ravenous, carnivorous masculinity that he praises and the unbridled, immoderate savagery that he eschews.

Ultimately, though, through their detailed recipes and reportage of new flavours in gourmet form, Lewis and Clark conclude that they, their men, and Americans more broadly have proved the sophistication and heroic, manly strength of their consumption, which they use to justify continued expansion to satisfy imperial appetites. Whereas William Bartram focused on living and 'natural' systems of exchange and on the remembered flavours of his meals to mark his physical heroism and ambassadorial sociability, Lewis and Clark explore through taste primarily American habits of consumption and the economic implications of continued trans-continental expansion. In both works of travel writing, we see taste used to distinguish animal from human, one human from another, and one people from another. While these authors recommend the pleasures of taste and we note its sensuous power to cue important and treasured memories, we see also some of its less benign uses in travel writing – to justify the unbridled domination of environment and other people. These eighteenth- and nineteenth-century American texts show both the delight and weapon that the category of taste may deploy, a particular sensuous power that emerges in many other works of travel writing in other times and places as well.[29]

Avenues for future scholarship on taste and travel writing

Through reading these Early American travel texts, we see how postcolonial scholars' work on theorising and explaining the forms and techniques of imperialism draws out from descriptions of taste and foodways larger arguments about who should have power and why. We further learn from consumption studies how to tease out and articulate the explorers' debates about economic exchange, as well as the meaning and status implied by specific commodities, in this case alimentary exchange and food itself. Ecocriticism and gender studies help us to see how taste may mark individual travellers' understanding of the relationship between themselves and their environment, between humanity and nature in general, and the role of humanity in serving nature or being served by it. Taste may reveal one individual's understanding of what it means to be gendered male, for example, or to perform that expression of masculinity in the broader culture and in relation to a specific environment. Here the environment is a 'natural' one, though taste could similarly be used to explore the relationship between gender and urban environment. Such relationships will likely emerge in food description, which often offers writers opportunities to explain their bold forays into the new, their hesitation at what seems uncertain, their resistance to what defies a familiar label, and their journey back and forth between literal but likewise metaphorical home and unexplored terrain.

While trans-Atlantic and hemispheric studies have contributed new and exciting interpretive paradigms for our readings of quite a few Early American travel accounts, what might trans-Pacific or globalisation studies do to recontextualise Bartram, Lewis, and Clark, and other travel writers, as part of an even larger community of transnational scientists, collectors, and explorers, whose journeys under the sponsorship and for the interests of entirely different nations and governments nevertheless document these travels in vocabularies that often bear striking resemblance to one another? Vocabularies of taste are sufficiently malleable and flexible that writers can employ them in a wide variety of contexts to detail flavours in tandem with the patterns of sociability and hospitality that curate those flavours. A 'sweet' time with friends might centre on 'sweet' desserts. Taste, unlike the other four senses, can serve as a powerful mode of archiving specific memories in the brain and then subsequently on paper. Travel writing nearly always includes passages about food, foodways, and taste, and scholarly attention to this alimentary and appetitive description clearly holds great promise for those interested in researching how we remember and record the flavours of our bodily experiences, our exchanges with other people, and our relationship to our environments.

Notes

1   I should like to acknowledge the helpfulness of the library staff at Eastern University as I completed research for this chapter. Those in attendance at the Bermuda and Alexandria biennial conferences of the Society of Early Americanists also provided excellent feedback on my conference papers that contributed to this chapter, as did Sandra Gustafson, Glenn Hendler, Javier Rodriguez, Thomas Slaughter, Sara Crosby, Margaret Abruzzo, and Jacqueline DenHartog. My own work focuses specifically on food in early American travel writing. See, for example, Heidi Oberholtzer Lee, 'Appetite and Desire in Early American Travel Narratives' (PhD diss., University of Notre Dame, 2005); 'Turtle Tears and Captive Appetites: The Problem of White Desire in the Caribbean', in *Travel and the Body*, ed. Marguerite Helmers and Tilar J. Mazzeo, Special issue of *Journal of Narrative Theory* 35 (2005): 307–25; and '"The Hungry Soul": Sacramental Appetite and the Transformation of Taste in Early American Travel Writing', *Early American Studies* 3.1 (2005): 65–93. Outside my subfield of early American literature, scholarship that *focuses* on food in travel writing has been only slightly more visible, though still minimal. *Passing mention* of food in scholarship about travel writing is, of course, ubiquitous. Few travel accounts are without at least a brief mention of an encounter with new foods or habits of dining. The topic of food in travel writing clearly remains wide open for innovative and original scholarship.

2   Pamela Regis, *Describing Early America: Bartram, Jefferson, Crèvecoeur, and the Influence of Natural History* (Philadelphia, PA: University of Pennsylvania Press, 1992), 43.

3   Frederick Kaufman, 'Gut Reaction: The Enteric Terrors of Washington Irving', *Gastronomica: The Journal of Food and Culture* 3: 2 (2003): 41–2, 49.

4   For environmental and ecocritical analyses, see Thomas Hallock, 'On the Borders of a New World: William Bartram's Travels', in *From the Fallen Tree: Frontier Narratives, Environmental Politics, and the Roots of a National Pastoral, 1749–1826* (Chapel Hill, NC: University of North Carolina Press, 2003), 149–73; Timothy Conley, 'Ante-Americanisms: Friendly Critiques of the Emerging Nation', in *(Anti)-Americanisms*, ed. Michael Draxlbauer, Astrid M. Fellner, and Thomas Fröschl (Vienna: Lit Verlag, 2004), 33–58; M. Allewaert, 'Swamp Sublime: Ecologies of Resistance in the American Plantation Zone', *PMLA* 123.2 (2008): 340–57, 534; Charles H. Adams, 'Reading Ecologically: Language and Play in Bartram's *Travels*', *Southern Quarterly* 32.4 (1994): 65–74; and Matthew Wynn Sivils, *American Environmental Fiction, 1782–1847* (Burlington, VT: Ashgate, 2014), esp. 15–28. For ecopolitical readings, see John D. Cox, *Traveling South: Travel Narratives and the Construction of American Identity* (Athens, GA: University of Georgia Press, 2005); Douglas Anderson, 'Bartram's *Travels* and the Politics of Nature', *Early American Literature* 25.1 (1990): 3–17; Thomas Hallock, '"On the Borders of a New World": Ecology, Frontier Plots, and Imperial Elegy in William Bartram's *Travels*', *South Atlantic Review* 66.4 (2001): 109–33; and Christopher Looby, 'The Constitution of Nature: Taxonomy as Politics in Jefferson, Peale, and Bartram', *Early American Literature* 22.3 (1987): 252–73.

5   Jon Holtzman, *Uncertain Tastes: Memory, Ambivalence, and the Politics of Eating in Samburu, Northern Kenya* (Berkeley, CA: University of California Press, 2009), 57, 63, 65, 86.

6   William Bartram, *Travels*, ed. James Dickey (New York: Penguin, 1988), 15. Subsequent references to Bartram's *Travels* will be indicated with page numbers in parentheses in the body of the text.

7   David E. Sutton, *Remembrance of Repasts: An Anthropology of Food and Memory* (Oxford: Berg, 2001), esp. ix, 2, 73, 86, 88, 97–8, 101–2.

8   Here we see a connection with what scholars such as John Cox have commented on as a nationalist, political argument in Bartram, and with what Christopher Iannini notes to be the 'desire for mastery' and expression of 'colonialist desire' embedded in the text. Cox, *Traveling South*; Christopher Iannini, 'The Vertigo of Circum-Caribbean Empire: William Bartram's Florida', *Mississippi Quarterly: The Journal of Southern Cultures* 57.1 (Winter 2003–2004): 147–55.

9   For comment particularly on Bartram's 'rapt stud[ies] of predatory scene[s]', see Philip G. Terrie, 'Tempests and Alligators: The Ambiguous Wilderness of William Bartram', *North Dakota Quarterly* 59.2 (1991): 25.

10 Snake birds are a species of cormorant or loon. See *The Travels of William Bartram: Naturalist's Edition*, ed. Francis Harper (Athens, GA: University of Georgia Press, 1958), 629.

11 Bartram's 'mud fish' refers to the bowfin. Kathryn E. Holland Braund, 'William Bartram's Gustatory Tour', in *Fields of Vision: Essays on the Travels of William Bartram*, ed. Kathryn E. Holland Braund and Charlotte M. Porter (Tuscaloosa, AL: University of Alabama Press, 2010), 33–53. See page 40 on the bowfin and the article as a whole for historical work on food and foodways in Bartram's text.

12 Sutton, *Remembrance of Repasts*, 102.

13 Thomas P. Slaughter, *The Natures of John and William Bartram* (New York: Alfred A. Knopf, 1996), 196.

14 See, for example, the work of Amy Kaplan and Donald E. Pease, eds., *Cultures of United States Imperialism* (Durham, NC: Duke University Press, 1993); Amy Kaplan, *The Anarchy of Empire in the Making of U.S. Culture* (Cambridge, MA: Harvard University Press, 2002); John Carlos Rowe, *Literary Culture and U.S. Imperialism: From the Revolution to World War II* (New York: Oxford University Press, 2000); Malini Johar Schueller and Edward Watts, *Messy Beginnings: Postcoloniality and Early American Studies* (New Brunswick, NJ: Rutgers University Press, 2003); and Anne Norton, 'Eater and Eaten in the Primordial West', in *Alternative Americas: A Reading of Antebellum Political Culture* (Chicago, IL: University of Chicago Press, 1986), 203–18.

15 Cary Carson, Ronald Hoffman, and Peter J. Albert, eds., *Of Consuming Interests: The Style of Life in the Eighteenth Century* (Charlottesville, VA: University Press of Virginia, 1994); T. H. Breen, *The Marketplace of Revolution: How Consumer Politics Shaped American Independence* (Oxford: Oxford University Press, 2004); Gordon S. Wood, *The Radicalism of the American Revolution* (New York: Knopf, 1992); Jon Butler, *Becoming America: The Revolution Before 1776* (Cambridge, MA: Harvard University Press, 2000); John Brewer and Roy Porter, eds., *Consumption and the World of Goods* (New York: Routledge, 1993); Allan Kulikoff, *From British Peasants to Colonial American Farmers* (Chapel Hill, NC: University of North Carolina Press, 2000); and John Lauritz Larson, *Internal Improvement: National Public Works and the Promise of Popular Government in the Early United States* (Chapel Hill, NC: University of North Carolina Press, 2001).

16 Charles Sellers, *The Market Revolution: Jacksonian America, 1815–1846* (New York: Oxford University Press, 1991), esp. 39.

17 Kaufman, 'Gut Reaction', 41–2, 49.

18 Anne Norton, 'Eater and Eaten in the Primordial West', in *Alternative Americas: A Reading of Antebellum Political Culture* (Chicago, IL: University of Chicago Press, 1986), 212.

19 David Murray, in Chapter 20 of this volume, titled 'Foreign exchange', notes that '[t]ravels of any duration inevitably involve the traveller in exchanges of various sorts' (280) and that these exchanges negotiate both power and understanding of value. Certainly we see in Lewis and Clark's journals such power dynamics and differing systems of value.

20 Meriwether Lewis and William Clark et al., *The Journals of the Lewis and Clark Expedition*, ed. Gary E. Moulton, 13 vols (Lincoln, NE: University of Nebraska Press, 1983–2001), 3:324. Subsequent references to *The Journals* in this section will be indicated with page numbers in parentheses in the body of the text. For an easily searchable, online edition of the journals of Lewis and Clark, as well as other excellent, related secondary sources, see *The Journals of the Lewis and Clark Expedition*, University of Nebraska Press/University of Nebraska-Lincoln Libraries-Electronic Text Center, http://lewisandclarkjournals.unl.edu.

21 For an analysis of literary descriptions of the economic value of female chastity, see Karen A. Weyler, *Intricate Relations: Sexual and Economic Desire in American Fiction, 1789–1814* (Iowa City, IA: University of Iowa Press, 2004).

22 See Thomas P. Slaughter, *Exploring Lewis and Clark: Reflections on Men and Wilderness* (New York: Alfred A. Knopf, 2003), esp. 136–9, for a related discussion of waste and excess in Lewis and Clark's hunting practices.

23 Matt Cartmill, *A View to a Death in the Morning: Hunting and Nature through History* (Cambridge, MA: Harvard University Press, 1993), 233; David J. Silverman, '"We chuse to be bounded": Native American Animal Husbandry in Colonial New England', *William and Mary Quarterly* 60.3 (July 2003): 511–48, esp. 518. Most twenty-first-century palates would categorise early American cooked meats as completely undercooked or rare. Kay Moss and Kathryn Hoffman, *The Backcountry Housewife* (Gastonia, NC: Schiele Museum of Natural History, 2001), 42. While the distinction between the raw and the cooked is almost universal, what constitutes the raw and the cooked is relative to time, place, and culture. See especially Chapter 1, 'The Invention of Cooking', of Felipe Fernández-Armesto, *Food: A History* (London: Pan Books, 2001), and Claude Lévi-Strauss, *The Raw and the Cooked*, Introduction to a Science of Mythology: I, trans. John and Doreen Weightman (New York: Harper and Row, 1969). See Jon Holtzman, too, for comment on how 'in many societies, meat is disproportionately masculine': Holtzman, *Uncertain Tastes*, 97, and Daniel Justin Herman, *Hunting and the American Imagination* (Washington, DC: Smithsonian Institution Press, 2001), 18.

24 Carol J. Adams, *The Sexual Politics of Meat: A Feminist-Vegetarian Critical Theory* (New York: Continuum, 2000), 45.

25 J. Hector St. John de Crèvecoeur, *Letters from an American Farmer and Sketches of Eighteenth-Century America* (1782; New York: Penguin, 1986), 76–7; Herman, *Hunting*, 5.

26 Holtzman, *Uncertain Tastes*, 86.

27 For a discussion of the shift in British literature from the positive, 'romantic view of the savage', and his 'freedom from restraint', to the mid- to late nineteenth century's portrayal of the same as quite 'undesirable', see Tim Youngs, 'Digesting Africa: Representations of Eating by Nineteenth-Century British Travellers to Africa', in *Food for Thought ou les Avatars de la Nourriture,* ed. Marie-Claire Rouyer (Bordeaux: Université Michel de Montaigne-Bordeaux III, 1998), 96.

28 Tim Youngs points out that white travellers' 'elaboration in culinary practice', as well as 'politeness in eating consist[ing] of social and cultural intervention through the use of implements and ceremony', can be used to justify colonial practice as well as imply immorality on the part of native peoples. Tim Youngs, *Travellers in Africa: British Travelogues, 1850–1900* (New York: Manchester University Press, 1994), 58, 62.

29 See Youngs, *Travellers in Africa,* esp. Chapter 2, 'Victorian Writing; African Eating: Digesting Africa', for references to later works of travel writing emerging from East and Central Africa, as well as Youngs's and his sources' postcolonial theorising of the relationship between power and foodways.

18

SMELLING

Clare Brant

An introduction to smell studies

Most historical reviews of olfactory studies take Alain Corbin as a progenitor. His book *Le Miasme et la Jonquille* (1982) was translated into English in 1986 as *The Foul and the Fragrant*, providing an enduring binary. Corbin's discussion of bad odours triggering public health improvements throughout the late eighteenth and early nineteenth centuries in France helped create a grand narrative in the history of smell.[1] This was developed further by Constance Classen, David Howes and Anthony Synott in *Aroma* (1994). They proposed a grand narrative of de-odourisation in the developed West, in which increasingly unacceptable bodily smells are displaced by a preference for no smell. As the authors put it, smell has been 'silenced' in modernity.[2] Since *Aroma*'s publication, at least three main arguments have been pursued: first, people in periods earlier than the eighteenth century were concerned about sanitation smells, and had complex cultures of olfactory meanings; second, de-odourisation can be accompanied by re-odourisation and is not a simple practice of removing smell; third, though de-odourisation is important, the history of hygiene is but one note in olfactory culture.

Jonathan Reinarz's book *Past Scents* (2014) addresses key themes of religion, the perfume trade, race, gender and urban environments. He sees cities as catalysts for reduced tolerance of smell, whether in New Zealand, the Philippines or Brazil. He thinks 'there is evidence that some towns and cities are actually losing their smells'.[3] This seems to be confirmed by Jonathan Drobknik's analysis of what he calls 'the olfactory nowhereness' of the white cube in modern architecture as an aesthetic and ideological paradigm.[4]

On the other hand, there is plentiful evidence that smells help define contemporary urban life. Writing about his travels as a cycle courier in London, Jon Day proposes:

> You learn the secret smells of the city: summer's burnt metallic tang, the sweetness of petrol; the earthy comfort of fresh laid tarmac. Some parts of London have their own smells, like olfactory postcodes. The shisha bars on Edgware Road fill the area with a sweet smoky haze; the mineral tang of Billingsgate fish market wafts over the Isle of Dogs.[5]

What one might call civic olfactory tourism has been developed by the tourist board of York, England, in a scratch and sniff guide to the city featuring smells of antiquities, railways and wild heather. York also houses a museum, the Jorvik Viking Centre, where historical smells are explicitly included in its visitor experience. There are also smell maps for specific cities: a growing genre with digital reach. Kate McLean's map of Edinburgh, Auld Reekie, inscribes local aromas including brewing trade smells, boys' toilets, penguins at the zoo and cut grass from golf courses.[6]

In what he calls an 'olfactory inventory of multiculture', Alex Rhys-Taylor argues for the importance of smell in the formation of culture as he walks around an East London market where immigrants and locals mingle and stay distinct like odours. In doing so he teases out a layered history through street food, and a sensuous geography through attention to movements in air which are also movements of time: 'Before I had been passing aromas, now an aroma passed me'.[7] Movement in air, temporality and seasonality are also part of my own smell log featuring a deerhound, a railway station and a park, another inventory where life writing invokes smell to explore experiences both personal and collective and, like Rhys-Taylor's findings, related to a politics of time and space.[8]

The politics of space are important in cultural studies, and *The Smell Culture Reader* explores numerous olfactory environments. What its editor Jim Drobnik regards as 'smell's elusiveness and imponderability' is also 'a remarkable diversity of olfactory phenomenon'. Themes he outlines are the strange semiotics of smell; prominent odours that are ignored while subtle ones are fixated on; imaginary smells projected onto others; smells variously interpreted as nostalgic or traumatic; fragrant experiences translated into metaphors, and vice-versa; olfactory evocations in texts; visual embodiment of smells; ambient scents with psychophysical effects; spiritual olfactory phenomena; space-and-identity transforming fragrances; odours that can be variously abject, narcissistic or obsessive.[9] All of these can helpfully be considered in relation to travel writing.

The home-and-away rhythm of travel writing provides entry points into dialectical patterns of social movement. J. Martin Corbett, writing under the flag of organisational studies, cites Mary Douglas's view that the social body constrains how we perceive the physical body. Corbett suggests that in eighteenth-century Europe, the most pressing demands for the control of olfactory space came from staff employed within total institutions: notably, the ship, the prison, the mortuary and the hospital.[10] One could consider that in different periods other spaces might have been the site of similar conflict – the temple or church, for example. Corbett suggests fresh directions through a nexus of class, subjectivity and self: 'Social groups who continue to be targeted via the processes of olfactory discrimination, location, and regulation are many and varied' – including manual workers, the elderly, women, ethnic groups and tobacco smokers (all of whom have been the subjects of olfactory studies) –

> Yet the history of deodorisation suggests that whilst such out-groups are often assigned an odour, they are rarely allowed a voice. What is notable is the absence of research on the ways in which these groups perceive their own smell, and the role this plays in the construction of subjectivities and identity.[11]

The paradigm of scent as medium between self-other relations is less interesting to Corbett than the ways in which scent constructs – and deconstructs, in the full Derridean sense – the self as unified subject. For travel writing studies, this approach invites us to consider what olfactory hybridity would smell like.

Many smells now inherently part of Western olfaction are themselves hybridised – thus imperial commodities like coffee and chocolate; whereas most spices retain more exotic potential. Domestic travel writing is a good source for exploring when, where and how olfactory imports come to seem native. There are many instances of olfactory racism among colonials, like Edward Long's view in his *History of Jamaica* (1774) that a supposedly fetid smell correlated with African stupidity.[12] It would, however, be wrong to adduce a Whig version of olfactory history in which we evolve from a benighted past to a progressive present. One of the first Jesuits in Japan was commissioned to report on cultural differences, including sensory ones.[13] Luis Frois S.J. thought the Japanese, unlike Europeans, did not delight in the scent of flowers, preferring their sight; even if he misunderstood the attraction of plum blossom or chrysanthemum, amongst others, he was being attentive to particularities in smell cultures.[14] Robin Gill asks why Frois drew such strong contrasts between European and Japanese preferences: 'One guess would be that the Jesuits, forbidden to engage in carnal pursuits, sublimated their libido into their probiscus'.[15] Gill also suggests smell preferences were shaped, as in the Middle East, by different aesthetics of gardens. Relativity here can be explained in various ways: my point is that Frois seeks more to understand than to judge alternative aromas. Hybridity can involve exchanging, translating or mixing smell cultures.

In a stink

Malodours are most commonly linked to the human body – sweat, bad breath, farts and, above all, excrement. Here psychoanalysis is as useful as history in accounting for repugnance (etymologically, fighting back) and disgust. Tobias Smollett, dubbed 'the learned SMELFUNGUS' by his rival Laurence Sterne,[16] may productively be read both historically and psychoanalytically. He represents situations of filth in ways that fit a grand narrative of de-odourisation, reinforced by a medical training which perceived foul air as a trigger for disease. Despite its many fountains, Rome is filthy, thinks Smollett: 'The corridors, arcades and even stair-cases of their most elegant palaces, are depositories of nastiness, and indeed in summer smell as strong as spirit of hartshorn'.[17] He has a historical narrative about smell, proposing that Ancient Rome was also filthy, with cloacal dirt and dead bodies clogging the streets, whilst houses were filthy from sweat, vomits and incessant spitting. His sources come from classical literature and the evidence of ruins: 'we must naturally conclude they were strangely crouded together, and that in general they were a very frowzy generation'.[18] 'Frowzy' was a late seventeenth-century coinage; in 1766 it indicated ill-smelling. But in his focus on corpses and bodily exudations Smollett produces the primary objects of repulsion which Julia Kristeva orchestrates into a theory of the abject: that in expelling substances we stigmatise as loathsome, we remind ourselves we are alive.[19]

These *poetics* of excrement are redolent of uses for travel writing. Dominique Laporte's provocative *History of Shit* argues that the management of human waste is central to our identities.[20] Excreting involves travel, even in just *going* to the bathroom.

Working on 'shiterature', Peter Smith proposes an aesthetic he calls 'fecopoetics'.[21] In travel writing simple practices of defecation – outdoor or exposed – are commonly stigmatised as disgusting by writers accustomed to hidden sewage systems. For V.S. Naipaul, 'Cairo revealed the meaning of the bazaar: narrow streets encrusted with filth, stinking even on this winter's day'.[22] Journeying on to India, Naipaul returns repeatedly to the subject of defecation. 'Indians defecate everywhere. They defecate, mostly, beside the railway tracks. But they also defecate on the beaches; they defecate on the hills; they defecate on the riverbank; they defecate on the streets; they never look for cover'.[23] Naipaul does not invoke stink as a trigger in part because Churchillian rhetoric conveys the subject's power. 'Many critics claim that Naipaul is obsessed with the subject', says Casey Blanton.[24] But fecopoetics here are interestingly odourless: Naipaul relates shit to sight rather than smell, contending that Indians refuse to see dirt, out of fear of pollution. It is a subtly different argument from the usual First World condemnation of outdoor excretion as primitivism.

Shit carries a lexicon of repression; smell warns of its presence. In *Sea and Sardinia* (1923), D.H. Lawrence explores what he hopes is a land of old Europe. Arriving at a filthy inn, he and his companion, the 'queen bee' or 'q-b', try to escape by going on a walk. 'We went up a little side turning past a bunch of poor houses towards a steep little lane between banks. And before we knew where we were, we were in the thick of the public lavatory'.[25]

'And before we knew where we were': unusually, there's no malodour alerting Lawrence to the nearness of excrement, an absence as disturbing as the presence of warning stink to Smollett. Smell indicates how experience is *sequenced* through the senses. Lawrence and the 'queen bee' walk till dusk, then 'we had to get back. And run the gauntlet of that stinking, stinking lane? Never'.[26] Lawrence marches the q-b a very long way round. By the end of the day he is in a complete black rage, and includes in his curses 'the sordid villagers who had the baseness to squat their beastly human nastiness in this upland valley'.[27] He doesn't need to load up the description: 'stinking' is redolent enough. Tropes of lowness and animality – baseness, beastly – threaten the psyche with abject matter, unmanageable by reason.

It may sound perverse to suggest that smell doesn't have to be written to be present; it goes against literary criticism's well-founded insistence on sticking to the text. But the sense of smell diffuses through a sensorium which may or may not be particularised. Consider this, again by D.H. Lawrence. He has arrived at Sorghono, tetchy after his long journey. There is only one hotel and it is not promising. As they go to inspect the available bedroom, Lawrence's senses are on the qui vive, firstly through touch and hearing:

> [the landlord] led the way down the passage, just as dirty as the road outside, up the hollow, wooden stairs also just as clean as the passage, along a hollow, drum-rearing dirty corridor, and into a bedroom. Well, it contained a large bed, thin and flat with a grey-white counterpane, like a large, poor, marble-slabbed tomb in the room's sordid emptiness; one dilapidated chair on which stood the miserablest weed of a candle I have ever seen: a broken wash-saucer in a wire ring: and for the rest, an expanse of wooden floor as dirty-grey-black as it could be, and an expanse of wall charted with the bloody deaths of mosquitoes. The window was about two feet above the level of a sort of stable yard outside, with a fowl-house just by the sash. There, at the window flew lousy feathers and dirty straw, the ground was thick with chicken droppings. An ass and two oxen comfortably chewed hay in an open shed just across. And plump in the middle of the yard lay a bristly black pig taking the last of the sun. Smells of course were varied.[28]

As this description travels between bedroom and barn it defies the separation of indoor and outdoor that is often a frontier for awareness of smells. It is not until the last sentence that Lawrence draws attention to smell, and yet in doing so he asserts its presence all the time. Sensuous geographies include smell, *of course*.

Lawrence makes an interesting comparison with Tobias Smollett, who is also full of enquiries and rage, so much so that one contemporary of Smollett's said his *Travels* should properly be titled QUARRELS through France and Italy.[29] Again, psychoanalysis helps explicate rage, as a primal response to the thwarting of primary needs. Emotional explosions are often set off by deprivation or disappointment over the basic comforts of travel. Clean sheets, a decent meal, a reasonable bill, civil exchange and personal safety constitute a long-running ideal of Western travel, at least until going unwashed came to suggest a desirably deeper contact with nature. Leaving Sestri di Levante, Smollett complains,

> In short, we had a very bad supper, miserably dressed, passed a very disagreeable night and payed a very extravagant bill in the morning, without being thanked for our custom. I was very glad to get out of the house with my throat uncut.[30]

Lawrence is similarly judgemental on a boat to Trapani. On board is an Italian family recovering from sea-sickness who are managing to eat tea. Watching the children's messy table manners sends Lawrence into a fury:

> They look at one another, the elder ones, and laugh and comment, while the two young ones mix themselves and the table into a lemon–milk–orange–tea–sugar–biscuit–cake–chocolate mess. This inordinately Italian amiable patience with their young monkeys is astonishing. It makes the monkeys more monkey-like, and self-conscious incredibly, so that a baby has all the tricks of a Babylonian harlot, making eyes and trying new pranks. Till at last one sees the southern Holy Family as an unholy triad of imbecility.[31]

Smell and taste contribute distinctly to this moment of heightened senses and without having to be articulated. They help curdle knowledge produced by the senses – here, that the sacred is profaned. One can also read it as a psychoanalytically charged scene: Lawrence is watching the children make a faeces-like substance and play with it. Pleasure in excrement characterises the anal stage, according to Freud.[32] Lawrence's enraged response to mucky eating shows unconscious motives are acted out through sensuous topography.

Rage is quite common in travel writing. Heightened senses are a cause, a product and an outlet of it. Angry travellers tend to favour a lexicon for things they dislike: dirty, filthy, beastly, disgusting. Smollett nearly always had an argument about the bill and on several occasions tried to beat his host with a cane: this is violent stuff. Lawrence was violent with words. A vocabulary of disgust has associations with abject aromas – stinking, foul, noisome, reeking. We talk of assaulting the senses: anger is a way to fight back. It is also part of the traveller's defences, managing fear, shame, loss of control. Innkeepers are gatekeepers to the beyond, the foreign, the unknown; innkeepers are also gatekeepers of prejudices, particularly of nation or region. Through a long history of hospitality and business, they give and they charge: hostelry is socially complex.[33] The traveller is often vulnerable – tired, hungry, just ahead of nightfall – and not in command of language or customs. Fears for safety and luggage attend. Yet lodgings are the necessary punctuation of travels, when the traveller must stop, eat and sleep. Smell is well placed to protect not only the body with the sniff of investigation but also the psyche with the sniff of contempt.

Plants, animals and identity

Both Smollett and Lawrence are alert to plant smells, about which they are often positive: Smollett writes of herbs in the background and Lawrence of trees – cedar, mimosa, citrus. Here writers' preferences relate to cultural options that include gender, class and nation as shaping forces. Noting the popularity of fern fragrances for Victorian men in England, Catherine Maxwell is punctilious about geographical particularity: 'France was itself divided in opinion about perfume at this time. The period of the Second Empire (1852–1870) saw a revival of ani-malics and the use of stronger exotic scents such as vetivert and patchouli'.[34] But not everyone shares this attention to detail. As Frances Trollope recorded in 1835:

> I remember being much amused last year, when landing at Calais, at the answer made by an old traveller to a novice [. . .] making his first voyage. 'What a dreadful smell!' said the uninitiated stranger [. . .] 'it is the smell of the continent, sir!' replied the man of experience. And so it was.[35]

During the Victorian period and exemplified by the entry under *Osmologia* in R.G. Mayne's *Expository Lexicon of the Terms, Ancient and Modern, in Medical and General Science* (1860), 'the word *osmology* indicated simply "a treatise on smells"'. Anthropologists now use the term to identify how people 'from Africa to the Amazon and from China to New Guinea' use olfactory perceptions 'to order the world', says Janice Carlisle, arguing that 'in this sense it is applicable to the no-less-exotic realm of Victorian fiction'.[36] If the past is a foreign country, osmologies of smell in literature can have historically specific meanings. A rose may smell differently sweet.

Nonetheless, in much travel writing, plant and animal smells provide an expansive way of entering a place and assuming a concomitant altered identity. In *Wild* (2008), Jay Griffiths' first walk in the Amazon begins with attention to touch, then smell:

> Amazon stinging, itching and stroking you with velvet; Amazon biting, scratching and softly feathering you; the whole forest winks at you, rubs your warm thighs and grins. A tree bark smells of nutmeg; certain plants smell of rotting flesh; there were flowers sweet as honey and a fungus smelling of old and thoughtful mould. I could smell a fine mist of rain and a sour smell from a plant here, a fetid smell from a plant there, the consoling smell of moss, the zinging smell of sap. I could almost smell the sunlight, heavy and lovely as hops.[37]

Here the smells are translated from a familiar world – an experientially English world, honey and hops, and also translated into a metaphysical world, thoughtful and consoling. Familiar knowl-edges engage with unfamiliarity through smell. For Griffiths smell also articulates the limits of cultural identity. In the Australian desert, the Gikwe Bushmen are able to read tracks as the newspapers of the desert. Griffiths copies their skill in an imaginative projection:

> Tracks need not be visible and there is a whole world of tracks written in the intimate signature of scent. English has no word for being deaf-of-the-nose, because we don't even know what we miss by not being able to sniff out the tales and tracks of smells. Maybe here rabbit's urine twangs near a saltbush, or there a mouse has emitted a puff of fear by the spinifex. Maybe a scent-hint still hangs near a thorn, dusky musk linger-ing, furry with desire, spicing a low branch with gamy loin-smell of kangaroo. Maybe the gall of a rejected male kangaroo still sulks by the acacia, and a lizard's ant-breath oils the air around its favourite siesta rock. And the ants secrete their own squeaking smells, faint pheromones by which they communicate. Water-scent, too, lilting lightly in the still dry air, trickles a tiny track to those able to follow it.[38]

Smells release stories, dramas and moods. Griffiths delicately avoids anthropomorphising; invis-ible creatures populate the landscape on their own terms, like ant-breath. Past and present merge in the lingering narrative of scent, not in a clichéd Proustian trigger of memory but in a dynamic of species exchange which explicates unfamiliar places and defamiliarised identity.

Smell and power

The traveller is typically in transit and temporary, vulnerable to insecurity. In *The Happy Isles of Oceania* (1992), Paul Theroux stays in Easter Island – 'Always there was the smell of damp or dusty roads and the stink of dog fur'[39] – and camps on a beach. After a troubling dream,

> I woke up in my tent under the palms at Anakena thinking: A traveller has no power, no influence, no known identity. That is why a traveller needs optimism and heart, because without confidence travel is misery. Generally, the traveller is anonymous, ignorant, easy to deceive, at the mercy of the people he or she travels among.[40]

We talk of smells being powerful: engaging with smell is a way to escape burdens of powerlessness. Theroux associates the traveller's lack of power with lack of control over naming: 'The traveller might be known as "The American" or "The Foreigner" – the *palangi*; the *popaa*, as they said here in Rapa Nui. But there was no power in that'.[41] Being able to name a smell – damp roads, dog fur – confers compensatory power. While smell in travel literature conventionally conveys something of place, it can also empower the figure who changes place, the traveller.

Recasting identity through odour is key to a passage in Griffiths' *Wild* in which in the company of shamans she takes hallucinogens and shape-shifts, a potentially powerless process. Griffiths defines herself against high-cultural Oxford, where she becomes a magnificent angry jaguar in the middle of the High Street:

> I smelled everything; noticed, watched and heard everything. People had fled. The High Street was deserted. I was stalking something by scent: not the scent of a creature, rather it was the scent of anger, the trail of an injustice, and I was prowling with a fury far older than me, far larger than my individual concerns. I could smell myself. I plunged my nostrils deep towards the fur of my groin and I sniffed up the satisfying, heady musk of wild female jaguar, and I roared, a ferocious roar of wild and perfect contempt.[42]

Smell here provides knowledge to the traveller of where-you-are and who-you-are, especially powerful at night when sight is restricted. The next night, Griffiths completes the process of mothering her jaguar self into being: 'When, with one last effort, the process was complete, the first thing I did was sniff myself. I smelled of meat and musk and damp hot fur. Jaguar, in groin, pelt and whisker, panting and alert'.[43] This traveller now has power, influence and identity.

Ontologies of smell map boundaries. Travelling through foreign or alien places can evoke powerful emotions associated with identity, especially fear and desire. Odour marks group threats which can be problematic to express, given the usually voluntary undertaking of travel and the need to trust strangers. George Orwell addressed head-on some social constructions of smell. In *The Road to Wigan Pier* (1937), he describes in detail the cramped housing of the working class. Squalor is expressed through stink. But where D.H. Lawrence turns to primal rage to contain threat, Orwell attempts to analyse the origins of smell-inflected class prejudice:

> It is summed up in four frightful words which people nowadays are chary of uttering, but which were bandied about quite freely in my childhood. The words were: *The lower classes smell.*

That was what we were taught – *the lower classes smell*. And here, obviously, you are at an impassable barrier. For no feeling of like or dislike is quite so fundamental as a physical feeling.[44]

Alok Rai suggests Orwell was impelled to seek out situations which confirmed his adversarial cast of mind.[45] Physical revulsion through smell becomes in this light a Jungian struggle to reconcile mental contradictions in the psyche of the traveller. Orwell's olfactory confession, too easily read as crude prejudice, is instead an effort to show how prejudice is constructed. In part two of his text, smell becomes explicitly a carrier of ideology:

> Socialism, at least in this island, does not smell any longer of revolution and the overthrow of tyrants; it smells of crankishness, machine-worship and the stupid cult of Russia. Unless you remove that smell, and very rapidly, Fascism may win.[46]

Although Eastern-bloc Communism has been widely associated with the smell of cabbage, it is often emotion which gives a visceral charge to that aroma, rather than the other way around.[47] Describing the Soviet Union, Christoph Niedhart claims,

> Socialism had its particular stench and a characteristic dust. The houses smelled of cabbage, of wet socks and sweat; the backyards reeked of diesel and trash, and sometimes of coal. Even the vastness of Siberia's far north, the tundra, smelled of oil. And nobody seemed to care.[48]

Cabbage offends not as a vegetable smell but as a moralised smell, the reek of stupidity and carelessness. Normally the physicality of olfaction guarantees experiential truth. Using smell to construct ideological landscapes as much as physical ones, travel writers co-construct identity and power. It is a difficult combination for readers to resist.

Blind travellers

Traditionally smell takes a lowly place in Western hierarchies of the senses, and to attend to it invites closing off traditionally higher senses, especially sight. There is a subgenre of travel writing where smell takes centre stage: writings by blind travellers. Blindness is commonly construed by the sighted as a state of helplessness; these travellers prove otherwise. The most astonishing instance is Robert Holman, who in the early nineteenth century travelled around Europe, then to Siberia and finally around the world, using the roughest means of transport.[49] For most of these travels he was alone and on the tightest budget. Holman wrote using a Noctograph, a wooden frame with guide wires and carbon paper which received impressions made by a stylus.[50] Holman's 'impressions' were highly particularised, especially of sound and smell – for instance, a Tartar postilion smelled of horses, fermented rye and Russian leather.[51]

It is important to stress we should not assume blind people have heightened senses. Some may, some may not, just as among sighted people. But there is something instructive for literary critics in literally screening out vision, about shedding the distractions of sightseeing and the picturesque. As one blind writer, Nicola Naylor, puts it, 'I too am often dumbfounded by the way non-sighted sight, my "third eye" perception or a sixth sense can enrich my experiences of the world'.[52] Although a discourse of sight lingers in 'third eye', this rearrangement of the senses and sense hierarchies is exploratory, itself a kind of travel. Blind travel writers question how we use different senses and what we count as sense organs. Blogger Tony Giles, for example, cited the 'atmosphere' of a place, saying, 'I can feel it through my skin'.[53] Their writings are attentive to the language of these transactions. This provides a useful analogy for smell, a process which also struggles with expression. In Naylor's *Jasmine and Arnica* (2001), disability becomes a conduit for possibility. Fiercely independent, she combines the conventionally vulnerable categories of woman and lone traveller with being blind. She doesn't tell people she can't see; she rarely uses a cane; she resists all attempts, including kind ones, to help her. All she wants is someone to make sure she gets the right bus. Naylor visits India with the aim of learning about ayurvedic understandings of smell to develop her practice as an aromatherapist. The jasmine of her title is ironically not an orientalist signifier: it is what she takes with her, along with arnica, as a Western medicament for anxiety. In gardens, in scent production businesses, in strings threaded through women's hair, Naylor recognises jasmine's power to mediate immediacy, particularity and universality. Jasmine also becomes a sign of resolve: in Mysore, exhausted by travel, she reflects: 'The world had become a phantasmagoric picture show in which I acted and spectated, but which I could no longer direct. As I sat, dazzled by the glow from the palace, I smelt the stirring power of jasmine'.[54]

The reorganisation of perception attendant on blindness has even led to the suggestion that travellers could pretend to be blind to enhance other senses.[55] Actual or feigned blindness thus generates 'the aromatic equivalent of a *flâneur* or *voyeur* – maybe a *dégustateur* or *flaireur*, a connoisseur who, like a wine taster savouring a bouquet, can discover and nose-talgically possess aromas before they evaporate'.[56]

Future directions?

Despite globalisation, there are plenty of places travellers have yet to reach. In the deep ocean, many creatures have a highly attuned sense of smell of which we understand little.[57] Initial forays into space have captured new smells: moon-dust smells of gunpowder, according to astronauts; another space traveller describes the smell of space as 'pleasant sweet smelling welding fumes'.[58] Besides new places, there are forms of travel in development, like dark tourism, whose destinations are places of death and destruction. The emotional disturbances of dark tourism call affect into question, unsettling subjectivity in ways that refocus senses. Bodies, mass graves, concentration camps, slave castles and the like manifest odours of mute remains and ghosts.[59] Spectators make an effort to 'hear' the dead; smell often conveys their presence. Here smell acts as an ethical essence, paradoxically eloquent of life's residues rather than its fleetingness. We could think more about such reversals of sensual norms.

Digital technology promises new developments relevant to smell in travel writing. California Digiscents, a now-defunct company with the tagline 'Savour the World', promised 'with iScent technology, you can travel anywhere in the world or to any time period in the past'.[60] Its device coded smells digitally and translated them to a chemical-storing cartridge which diffused selected aromas into the user's space. Any excitement about snortals, scent-enabled web portals or smell tracks to accompany travel writing is premature: as Simon Niedenthal observes, 'The track record of scented media is largely one of abject failure'.[61] Smell, taste and touch are variously excluded from digital sense impressions, or rather they are reconfigured through prosthetics.[62] The future may bring us cameras that can capture smell and apps that release it;[63] meanwhile digital travel writers are urged to reference smells as authentifications of places and themselves, and bloggers are advised to use smell as a kind of return ticket. 'That is the big difference between photographs and smells: One reminds you of where you've been, the other returns you there'.[64] A Facebook discussion about 'What smell most says "travel" to you?' featured aviation fuel, diesel, suitcases, tents, 'the cologne of adventure travellers – insect repellent', rain on tarmac – industrial-world smells that nonetheless are perceived as romantic.[65]

Recent developments in tourism indicate the future of smell may be increasingly constructed through categories of authentic and inauthentic. Surveying a large sample of travel accounts old and new, Dann and Jacobsen argue,

> Although the olfactory was established as a sense of the modern, it is post-modernism that fully brings out its potential – smells are eclectic, random and individual [. . .] Experiences of smell thus fit neatly with the search by Western tourists for idiosyncratic experiences.[66]

Yet mass-market paradigms organise olfactory values so that, crudely, 'nice places smell good, nasty places smell bad'.[67] In the absence of unpleasant odours from pre-modern practices, suitably banished to rural hinterlands, postmodernists hollow out urban places to fill 'with aromas that answer specific cultural needs – with elements of cooked nature [. . .] that correspond to the playful and capricious tastes of the citizenry'.[68] Hence the popularity of sensual markets and aromas of street food, olfactory indicators of a harmonising of that binary – the raw and the cooked – which Lévi-Strauss proposed as a basis for understanding myth through structural anthropology.[69] Amanda Anderson argues that cosmopolitanism is often the consequence of a tension between elitism and egalitarianism; it resists localism and insists on 'worldliness'.[70] Inevitably there are overlapping allegiances, which can be analysed through travel writing's olfactory geographies.

The anthropology of odour provides valuable directions for literary criticism by investigating scent tribes and communities, with beliefs and meanings using categories different from Western societies. The Suya people of Brazil, for instance, classify animals in an ontology in which smells have meaning (rather than the simpler good/bad valuation of Western thought).[71] Foul and fragrant have become something of an imprisoning vocabulary: beyond the binary, there are richer lexicons.

Smells are constituents of concepts and practices of the personal, familial, tribal, social and global (in digital travel writings especially); also of concepts and practices of the somatic, linguistic, socio-economic, aesthetic and theistic. They are also a *medium* of all these constructions (and others). Smells often travel to us – thus an eighteenth-century diagram of the path of scent from a rose depicts a burst of outward-travelling lines.[72] Scents are closely tied to place, and scent studies are often place-specific. There are benefits in this localism, but for companions of travel writing it raises the question of how scents and languages of smell are situated in space – and time, an important vector in travel. 'Smells serve to corroborate, rarely to bear, the whole burden of evidence of a political, socio-cultural, or other inquiry'.[73] Grand narratives of de-odourisation and hedonistic re-odourisation need handling with care lest they mask counternarratives. 'Civilisation evidently despises odor', laments Jonathan Reinarz, though travellers and readers may disagree. He concludes that 'in the fields of the humanities and social sciences it [smell] has only begun to show its potential to open vast new territories of exploration'.[74] His choice of metaphor suggests that travel writing is a great place to start.

Notes

1 Alain Corbin, *The Foul and the Fragrant: Odor and the French Imagination*, trans. Miriam L. Kochan et al. (Cambridge, MA: Harvard University Press, 1988).

2 Constance Classen et al., *Aroma: The Cultural History of Smell* (London: Routledge, 1994).

3 Jonathan Reinarz, *Past Scents: Historical Perspectives on Smell* (Urbana, IL: University of Illinois Press 2014), 179, 203.

4   Jim Drobnick, 'Volatile Effects: Olfactory Dimensions of Art and Architecture', in *The Empire of the Senses: The Sensual Culture Reader* ed. David Howes (Oxford: Berg 2005), 267.

5   Jon Day, *Cyclogeography: Journeys of a London Bicycle Courier* (London: Notting Hill Editions, 2015), 32.

6   'Smellmap: Edinburgh', Sensory Maps, accessed 24 January 2016, http://sensorymaps.com/portfolio/smell-map-edinburgh.

7   Alex Rhys-Taylor, 'The Essences of Multiculture: A Sensory Exploration of an Inner-City Street Market', *Identities: Global Studies in Culture and Power* 20.4 (2013): 395, 397. On cities, see also Kelvin E. Low, 'The Sensuous City: Sensory Methodologies in Urban Ethnographic Research', *Ethnography* 16.3 (2015): 295–312.

8   Clare Brant, 'Scenting a Subject: Odour Poetics and the Politics of Space', *Ethnos: Journal of Anthropology* 73.4 (2008): 544–63.

9   Jim Drobnick, 'Introduction: Olfactocentrism', in *The Smell Culture Reader*, ed. Jim Drobnick (Oxford: Berg 2006), 5.

10 Quoted in J. Martin Corbett, 'Scents of Identity: Organisation Studies and the Cultural Conundrum of the Nose', *Culture and Organization* 12.3 (2006): 225.

11 Corbett, 'Scents of Identity', 225.

12 Simon Gikandi, *Slavery and the Culture of Taste* (Princeton, NJ: Princeton University Press, 2012), 227.

13 Luis Frois, S.J., *The First European Description of Japan, 1585: A Critical English-Language Edition of Striking Contrasts in the Customs of Europe and Japan*, eds Daniel T. Reff et al. (London: Routledge, 2014).

14 Robin Gill, *Topsy-Turvy 1585: The Short Version: A Translation and Popular Introduction of the Famous Treatise by Luis Frois SJ Listing 611 Ways Europeans & Japanese are Contrary* (Key Biscayne: Paraverse Press, 2005), 577–9.

15 Gill, *Topsy-Turvy*, 579.

16 Laurence Sterne, *A Sentimental Journey*, ed. Gradner D. Stout, Jr. (1768; repr. Berkeley, CA: University of California Press, 1967), 116.

17 Tobias Smollett, *Travels through France and Italy*, ed. Frank Felsenstein (1776; repr. Oxford: Oxford University Press, 1981), 243.

18 Smollett, *Travels*, 243.

19 Julia Kristeva, *Powers of Horror: An Essay on Abjection*, trans. Leon S. Roudiez (New York: Columbia University Press, 1982).

20 Dominique Laporte, *History of Shit*, trans. Nadia Benabid and Rodolphe el-Khoury (Cambridge, MA: MIT Press, 2002).

21 Peter J. Smith, *Between Two Stools: Scatology and its Representation in English Literature, Chaucer to Swift* (Manchester: Manchester University Press, 2012), 11, 18.

22 V.S. Naipaul, *An Area of Darkness: An Experience of India* (London: André Deutsch 1964), 13–14.

23 Naipaul, *Area of Darkness*, 70.

24 Casey Blanton, *Travel Writing: The Self and the World* (1995; repr. London: Routledge 2002), 89.

25 D.H. Lawrence, *Sea and Sardinia* (1921; repr. Harmondsworth: Penguin, 1996), 105.

26 Lawrence, *Sea and Sardinia*, 106.

27 Lawrence, *Sea and Sardinia*, 107.

28 Lawrence, *Sea and Sardinia*, 104.

29 Philip Thicknesse, quoted by Frank Felsenstein, Introduction to *Travels through France and Italy by Tobias Smollett* (Oxford: Oxford University Press, 1981), xii.

30 Smollett, *Travels*, 211.

31 Lawrence, *Sea and Sardinia*, 47.

32 Sigmund Freud, *Three Essays on the Theory of Sexuality* [1905] in *On Sexuality*, ed. Angela Richards (Harmondsworth: Penguin, 1977), 103.

33 See, for example, Kevin J. James, 'The Irishness of the Irish Inn: Narratives of Travel Accommodation in Ireland from Union to Home Rule', *Studies in Travel Writing* 17.1 (2013): 22–42.

34 Catherine Maxwell, 'Scents and Sensibilities: The Fragrance of Decadence' (inaugural lecture, Queen Mary, University of London, 29 May 2012).

35 Frances Trollope, *Paris and the Parisians*, quoted in James Munson and Richard Mullen, *The Smell of the Continent: The British Discover Europe* (London: Macmillan, 2009), ix.

36 Janice Carlyle, *Common Scents: Comparative Encounters in High-Victorian Fiction* (Oxford: Oxford University Press 2004), 9.

37 Jay Griffiths, *Wild: An Elemental Journey* (Harmondsworth: Penguin, 2008), 11.

38 Griffiths, *Wild*, 292.

39 Paul Theroux, *The Happy Isles of Oceania: Paddling the Pacific* (Harmondsworth: Penguin, 1992), 615.

40 Theroux, *Happy Isles*, 616.

41 Theroux, *Happy Isles*, 616.

42 Griffiths, *Wild*, 97.

43 Griffiths, *Wild*, 97.

44 George Orwell, *The Road to Wigan Pier* (1937; repr. London: Penguin, 1989), 119.

45 Alok Rai, *George Orwell and the Politics of Despair: A Critical Study of the Writings of George Orwell* (Cambridge: Cambridge University Press, 1998), 73.

46 Orwell, *Wigan Pier*, 201.

47 This association has a longer history than I have space for here. Eugene Lyons uses it in his account of Stalinist Russia, *Assignment in Utopia* (London: Transaction Publishers, 1938): he says the Hotel Lux, which housed many communist exiles from Germany, has a prison aura and cabbage odours (16).

48 Christoph Neidhart, *Russia's Carnival: The Smells, Sights, and Sounds of Transition* (Lanham, MD: Rowman and Littlefield, 2003), 1.

49 Jason Roberts, *A Sense of the World: How a Blind Man Became History's Greatest Traveller* (London: Pocket, 2006), who draws on James Holman, *Narrative of a Journey, Undertaken in the Years 1819, 1820, 1821* (London: F.C. and J. Rivington, 1822); *Travels through Russia, Siberia, Poland Austria, Saxon, Prussia, Hanover, &c, &c*, 2 vols (London: G.B. Whittaker, 1825); *A Voyage Round the World, Including Travels in Africa, Asia, Australasia, America, Etc. Etc*, 4 vols (London: Smith, Elder, & Co., 1834–35).

50 Roberts, *Sense of the World*, 78.

51 Roberts, *Sense of the World*, 184.

52 Nicola Naylor, *Jasmine and Arnica* (London: Eye Books, 2001), 17.

53 Lance Richardson, 'Come to Your Senses', *Traveller*, 1 March 2014, accessed 2 February 2016, www.traveller.com.au/come-to-your-senses-33h4z#ixzz2vYauI8VB.

54 Naylor, *Jasmine*, 220–1.

55 William H. Whyte, *City: Rediscovering the Center* (New York: Doubleday 1988), 79.

56 Graham Dann and Kristian Steen Jacobsen, 'Tourism Smellscapes', *Tourism Geographies* 5.1 (2003): 20.

57 'The Deep Sea', MarineBio, accessed 2 February 2016, http://marinebio.org/oceans/deep.

58 Gene Cernan quoted in 'The Mysterious Smell of Moondust', NASA Science, accessed 2 February 2016, http://science.nasa.gov/science-news/science-at-nasa/2006/30jan_smellofmoondust; Don Pettit, 'The Smell of Space', accessed 2 February 2016, http://spaceflight.nasa.gov/station/crew/exp6/spacechronicles4.html.

59 John Lennon and Malcolm Foley, *Dark Tourism: The Attraction of Death and Disaster* (London: Thompson Learning, 2004); Emma Willis, *Theatricality, Dark Tourism and Ethical Spectatorship: Absent Others* (Basingstoke: Palgrave Macmillan, 2014), 206–10.

60 On scentography, see Charles Platt, 'You've Got Smell', *Wired*, 11 January 1999, accessed 2 February 2016, www.wired.com/1999/11/digiscent.

61 Vijayalaxmi N. Patil, 'A Seminar Report on Digital Smell', accessed 2 February 2016, http://sdmcse2006.pbworks.com/f/print1.pdf; Simon Niedenthal, 'Beyond the Snortal: Scented Media and Games', University of Copenhagen, 30 November 2010, accessed 2 February 2016, http://game.itu.dk/index.php/Game_Lecture:_Beyond_the_Snortal:_Scented_media_and_games.

62 Dan Rosenbaum, 'MWC Day 2: Wearables to Gain a Sense of Smell', *Wearable Tech Insider*, 3 March 2015, accessed 2 February 2016, http://wearablesinsider.com/2015/03/03/mwc-day-2-wearables-to-gain-a-sense-of-smell.

63 Oliver Wainwright, 'Scentography: The Camera that Records Your Favourite Smells', *Guardian*, 28 June 2013, accessed 2 February 2016, www.theguardian.com/artanddesign/architecture-design-blog/2013/jun/28/scentography-camera-records-smells-memory; 'Share Touch, Smell and Taste via the Internet', *Euronews*, 2 February 2015, accessed 2 February 2016, www.euronews.com/2015/02/02/share-touch-smell-and-taste-via-the-internet.

64 Daisann McLane, 'Want Memories? Follow Your Nose', *National Geographic Traveler*, accessed 2 February 2016, http://travel.nationalgeographic.com/travel/traveler-magazine/real-travel/smells.

65 Devlin Nightingale, 'What Does Travel Smell Like?', *Getaway*, 14 May 2012, accessed 2 February 2016, http://blog.getaway.co.za/travel-news/travel-smell-like/#sthash.iwdXvPxN.dpuf.

66 Dann and Jacobsen, 'Tourism Smellscapes', 20.

67 Dann and Jacobsen, 'Tourism Smellscapes', 5.

68 Dann and Jacobsen, 'Tourism Smellscapes', 15.

69 Claude Lévi-Strauss, *The Raw and the Cooked*, Introduction to a Science of Mythology: I, trans. John and Doreen Weightman (New York: Harper and Row, 1969).

70 Amanda Anderson, *The Way We Argue Now: A Study in the Cultures of Theory* (Princeton, NJ: Princeton University Press, 2005), 69–92, 73.

71 David Howes et al., 'Anthropology of Odor', accessed 2 February 2016, www.david-howes.com/senses/Consert-Odor.htm.

72 *Diagram of a Rose emitting odoriferous particles, decreasing in strength from A through B to C*, reproduced and discussed by William Tullett, 'The Macaroni's "Ambrosial Essences": Perfume, Identity and Public Space in Eighteenth-Century England', *Journal for Eighteenth-Century Studies* 38.2 (2015): 163–80. I am very grateful to the author for this reference.

73 Hans J. Rindisbacher, 'Smells of Switzerland', in *From Multiculturalism to Hybridity: New Approaches to Teaching Modern Switzerland*, eds Karin Baumgartner and Margitt Zinggeler (Newcastle-upon-Tyne: Cambridge Scholars Press, 2010), 231.

74 Reinarz, *Past Scents*, 218.

PART IV

Interactions

19

HOSPITALITY

Kevin J. James

Hospitality and civilisation in travel writing

It seems in travel writing that virtuous hospitality is attributed to those cultures that inhabited a distant, nobler age, or to those that persist in putatively unchanging and primitive form. When Victorians waxed about the generous hospitality of the 'Ancients', for instance, it was tempting to use it as a foil for its modern commercialised forms. In contrast with the unmeasured and spontaneous provision of shelter, protection and fare across cultures that was said to constitute genuine, traditional hospitality, precise strictures governed the business of hospitality in their own age. The Canadian barrister Robert Vashon Rogers expounded on this intricate legal framework. *The Law of Hotel Life: Or, The Wrongs and Rights of Host and Guest* was published in 1879 as a companion to an earlier volume exploring transport law.[1] It introduced its discussion with light-hearted banter between a husband-narrator leaving the fictitious village of 'Blank' with his new bride, playfully dubbed 'Mrs Lawyer', bound for the city of 'Nowhere'. *En route* to their hostelry, the bride asked her husband why villages boasted 'inns' and cities 'hotels'. He responded with a casualness that was belied by extensive case law foot-noted throughout the book:

> 'There is no real difference', I replied, glad to have the subject changed from the one Mrs. Lawyer had first started. 'The distinction is but one of name, for a hotel is but a common inn on a grander scale. Inn, tavern, and hotel are synonymous terms'.

In response to his wife's question – 'What do the words really mean?' – the lawyer entered into extended discourse on the origins of the word 'hotel' and 'inn'.[2] Mixing an exposition on law and history, as well as obscure etymology, with the conventions of the travelogue, Rogers supplied a readable account of the evolution of the hotel and laws of commercial hospitality. The narrative persona admitted of many playful digressions, allowing Rogers to introduce flamboyant characters as he crafted an amusing discourse on legal principles and the history of the modern hostelry and hospitality. Reflecting on its long pedigree, the narrator recounted that through

> many gradations, the primeval well has become the well-stocked bar-room of to-day; the antique hovel is now the luxurious Windsor, the resplendent Palace, the Grand Hotel du Louvre; the uncouth barbarian, who showed to each comer his own proper

corner to lie in, has blossomed into the smiling and gentlemanly proprietor or clerk, who greets you as a man and a brother; the simple charge of a piece of iron or brass for bed and board (then synonymous) has grown into an elaborate bill, which requires ducats, or sovereigns, or eagles to liquidate.[3]

The narrator's party, however, was to enjoy none of the opulence of 'the luxurious Windsor' on this auspicious night. Struck by the sparseness and Spartanness of the newlywed couple's hostelry, the lawyer evaluated its basic provisions to lie strictly within the compass of the inn-keeper's minimal obligations to supply 'reasonable and proper accommodation'.[4]

At its core, hospitality involves relations of power acted out in spaces that are claimed as 'belonging' in some way to 'hosts', who in turn extend their access and use to 'strangers' (often as 'guests'), as well as to 'familiar people'.[5] It can be undertaken as a duty, in which case its obligations are often religiously or culturally sanctioned, or as pleasure. The premise under-girding hospitality as an abstract principle has often collided with its practice, especially in the marketplace. Travel writing offers opportunities to explore these conflicts – to foreshadow and guide readers through unfamiliar social codes, and also entertain them with accounts of transgressions and violations as hosts and guests struggle to find common ground across cultures. Hospitality is central to travel because it can involve encounters with unfamiliar people, institutions, cultures and codes. As an idea it engages sociologists, anthropologists, political scientists and philosophers, now more than ever as a subject for critical scholarly agendas that focus on intensified migration and mobility – of tourists, refugees and others – throughout global networks.[6] Yet great cultural or physical distances are not required to detect shifts in the character of hospitality, though often it is explored and expressed within an exoticising, Orientalist idiom – dating back to accounts of eastern journeys of Marco Polo and others. Writers might narrate striking differences in the cultures of hospitality within a short compass of their own 'homes' – between urban and rural milieux, across regions and socio-economic strata. And they often express ambivalence towards institutions of modern hospitality, and the motivations behind their operation.

Rogers's account, taking in matters ranging from the weighty to the comparatively curi-ous and trivial, underscored how western hospitality had become deeply embedded within legal codes in an age when, as one reviewer remarked, 'the immensely increased facilities for travel, the variety and complexity of business affairs, and the increase of wealth, have com-bined to make "mine host" and "mine inn" far more important elements than before in the life of men'.[7] Medieval and early modern hospitality had developed highly elaborate codes that guided interactions in a variety of sites, from homes to inns, and ordered communal life.[8] The modern era introduced new institutions of travel, supplying travel writers with opportunities to test new geographic and generic frontiers. Usually, travel writers foreswore Rogers's inter-weaving of footnote and fictional persona in favour of the authority of personal experience alone. Authors ruminated on the history of travel, often in wide-ranging expositions on the distinctive accommodations, people and food encountered in the ancient caravanserais of the eastern Silk Road, the monasteries of medieval Europe, the great houses of the European aris-tocracy and gentry, the continental *pensione* and *auberge*, and the posting inn. They were some-times grafted onto meta-narratives charting the extinction of traditional hospitality cultures, grounded in customs forged in isolation and before the age of commerce. This positioned the social codes of the primitive in an ambiguous light. Oft-cited was James Bruce of Kinnaird's pithy observation that '[h]ospitality is the virtue of barbarians, who are hospitable in the ratio that they are barbarous'.[9] The modern age had displaced the altruistic motivation behind hospitality – its intrinsic moral imperatives – and subsumed it within the commercial system, with crass commercial incentives. Rogers, for his part, cheekily suggested that the hotel clerk was the modern barbarian who had once motioned to the corner in which guests could lie.[10] But now, of course, there were bills to settle at the end of the stay. Travel writers seeking to locate genuine, uncorrupted hospitality, following cultural precept or Biblical exhortation, for instance, rather than the dictates of commerce and the logic of the profit motive, seldom found it in their own time. It yet burnt bright amongst some primitive tribes of the New World and in the caravanserais of the East, and flickered in those reaches of Europe where the full force of modern life had not yet penetrated. As one writer opined, charting hospitality's decline with civilisation's rise:

> Hospitality originally imported kindness and attention towards the stranger and sojourner. At present it has, however, a more extensive signification. In its primitive and genuine sense, it is rarely found amidst the seats of luxury and wealth; like other rude virtues, it seems banished in a great measure from populous and polished societies to remote and lonely retreats. It is still found dwelling among the savage tribes, and is cherished by the uncouth and untutored rustic. As civilization and commerce, with their attendant luxuries and refinements, make advances, simple and primitive hospitality disappears, and, in its place, ostentatious profusion and excess preside at the boards of the wealthy, the vain, and the voluptuous.[11]

This perspective on primitive hospitality encoded a critique of its elaborate, stratified, market-driven western manifestations. The extinction of primeval forms was a corollary of economic, social and legal development – and of an almost mechanistic systematisation of the relations of hospitality that reached its apotheosis in the service culture of the American 'palace' hotel. It created new tensions as it collided with ideals and historically grounded ideas of hospitality, even as it manifested new modern forms and precepts of commercial hospitality that many people lauded.[12] Few were the travellers who wholeheartedly reiterated Chateaubriand's unambiguous claim that Europeans brought with them calamities: after the French discovery of the Mississippi, '[q]uarrels and jealousies subsequently ensanguined the land of hospitality'.[13] Yet many offered ambivalent appraisals of how hospitality was subsumed within the dictates of industrial capitalism.

Hospitality: precepts and practice, past and present

Implicit in Rogers's writing were two questions that lay at the heart of accounts of travel and hospitality: how grounded were social relations of hospitality within specific cultures and periods, rather than being universal and transhistorical? Could hospitality and advanced industrial capitalist civilisation coexist? Hospitality, as a set of protocols and practices regulating social interactions that are predicated on supplying strangers with the trifecta of shelter, protection and nourishment, implicates people and space in a variety of roles. As the nineteenth century progressed and the extent of travel infrastructure grew (and with it the tourist 'sector'), travel writers explored emerging forms of hospitality. They were particularly fascinated by the ways in which a comparatively new institution – the hotel – was becoming a defined space (and architectural form, in which there was no evident private/domestic function to its spaces, as was the case in private homes or inns that welcomed guests), and hospitality a 'service' with large retinues of labour. If hospitality ranked 'among the first of the barbaric virtues', in the teleology of hospitality's progression from the huts and tents of hunter-gatherers to the modern grand hotel, it became a trope to state that conventions of mutuality were now relinquished to the cash nexus.[14] Describing exotic rituals of hospitality allowed them to tantalise readers and qualify, if not rebuke, narratives of western triumphalism, building on Enlightenment and Romantic preoccupations with putatively primitive societies. Often their accounts yielded remarkably critical self-examinations, as well as highly embellished and ossified representations of the Other: mobilised in support of abolitionism, the hospitable savage held a mirror to the face of 'civilised' society which tortured its own in Inquisitions, and incarcerated some who wielded the pen as a weapon of truth.[15] If the African, Arab and New World Indian, as well as the Gael, furnished examples of uncorrupted hospitality, Judeo-Christian civilisation furnished its own touchstones, too. Indeed, accounts of hospitality and inhospitality lay at the core of Christian narratives and didactics: the preeminent case was the Virgin Birth, which had occurred in the insalubrious confines of a manger, Mary and Joseph having been turned away from inns that were full. Mindful of Christian obligations articulated by St Benedict,[16] medieval religious orders supplied travellers with rest and repasts – and in the process developed conventions that endured for centuries. Yet, however boundless they professed their intentions to be, their resources – food and space – circumscribed institutions' capacity to extend limitless hospitality. Hence they restricted hospitality to certain travellers (often men, in the case of monasteries), to those travelling for a certain purpose (such as pilgrimage), and even then for specific durations, after which guests were obliged to depart. The spatial regimes of the monastery, like those of the inn, were also critical to the performance of hospitality and sociability, organised around the separation of hosting from other operations, and demarcating public, shared spaces that were open to guests from other spaces that were not.[17] This delicate choreography required implicit acceptance of the limits of hospitality, and even its informal transactional dimensions: guests would 'offer' gratitude in the form of compensation for shelter and nourishment, while many 'rules of the house' relied on unspoken mutual adherence. As the infrastructure of western travel expanded in the medieval and early modern periods, leading to the development of a wider network of coaching inns and, in the nineteenth century, large-scale hotels, the commercial moorings of the hospitality sector became much more formalised – generating a corpus of 'inn literature' that extolled the vestiges of a purportedly unique site of authentically English hospitality: the hotel visitors' book, for instance, became a canvas for manuscript textual experimentation.[18] It also exposed contemporary places of hospitality to increasing scrutiny – as the microspaces of the inn's modest rooms, its dining table, inglenook and parlour, were displaced by a hospitality culture on a more ambitious scale, but with ambiguous cultural moorings.

The legal opinion of Rogers's narrator notwithstanding, for many commentators, the inn and the hotel were markedly different institutions, though then, as now, there was a plethora of types and sub-types, from *pensiones* to commercial hotels to 'floating palaces' that plied the Atlantic to repurposed buildings such as country houses and barracks to, more recently, modern motels, bed and breakfasts and Airbnb accommodation. As the urban hotel came to signify a new scale and form of commercial hospitality, travel writers scoured rural districts for more authentic, deeply rooted forms of travel accommodation.[19] Their eyes settled on the village inn.

To the prolific late Victorian and Edwardian travel writer James John Hissey, a motorcar was no obstruction to traditional travel. If anything, it allowed him to embrace the open road, map in hand, on his own terms.[20] Penetrating the rural areas of his home country, Hissey delighted in glimpsing traditional realms – and practices – of English commercial hospitality, most notably at its most venerable and venerated site: the inn. 'I infinitely prefer a country hostelry to a town hotel', Hissey wrote in *The Charm of the Road*.[21] Joining legions of writers who invoked the verses of William Shenstone, Hissey also imputed simplicity, cordiality and intrinsic authenticity to the institution – all qualities that eluded guests in the opulent grand hotel:

> I have always a keen eye for an inn with a garden, and the more homely the inn the better it pleases me, so long as it be clean and mine host obliging. Luxury I do not crave; simple, wholesome fare, civility, and comfort, are the things I seek, and seldom seek in vain. 'Shall not I take mine ease at mine inn?' Now, at a modern luxurious hotel I never feel quite at mine ease – the stony-eyed manager and head waiter repel me; to the latter I only represent so much in tips, and I resent losing my individuality in a mere number. When I sit down to table in such establishments, the first thing the waiter generally demands of me is my number; my name I can remember, but my number I always forget; it changes with every hotel.[22]

Hissey nostalgically cast the inn as a site that stubbornly resisted systems of technology and labour regimes associated with the hotel.

The door to the house where refuge was offered, the entrance to the monastery where pilgrims laid their heads for the night, the gates of the caravanserai where traders found respite along long routes, and the lintel above the inn's door – all demarcated physical boundaries beyond which distinctive social codes prevailed. The concept of the threshold, epitomised in travel writing by the hostelry's doorstep dividing host and guest, the familiar and the unfamiliar, has figured prominently in travel writing from Antiquity onwards: in the context of hospitality, it gives travellers pause for thought as they cross it: does it mark their initiation into the domestic realm of the unfamiliar? What codes govern hospitality beyond it?[23] In recounting travel experiences, narrators have often assumed an ethnographic stance: Marco Polo was flummoxed by what he regarded as the peculiar practice of men abandoning their homes and their own wives, sisters and daughters in acts of hospitality to strangers in Kamul, in the district of Tanguth. The practice persisted even after Mangu Khan issued an edict requiring guests to lodge in places of public resort or caravanserais.[24] The study of how material and symbolic thresholds have been handled in travel writing before, during and after Polo's travels, has become a central concern in literary and cultural theory.[25] Even when some social roles seem as well defined as the physical entrance to the caravanserai, house, inn and hotel, boundaries can be shifting and ambiguous: consider, for instance, the role family members play as guests of, and hosts to, each other. Moreover, many hostelry operators can be viewed as cultural and commercial 'brokers'. Consider the unique position of the Jamaican-born nurse and travel writer Mary Seacole, whose wide-ranging nineteenth-century travels from the Americas to the Crimea to Singapore offer a unique perspective on the cultures that she encountered.[26] Seacole was the daughter of a Scottish soldier and a Creole boarding-house keeper, sister of a keeper of a hotel in Chagres, California and a restaurant hostess in her own right. She, like many others, from the Greek innkeepers of Istanbul and Jerusalem to the Armenian Sarkis brothers who founded the fabled Raffles Hotel in Singapore, was a cultural intermediary, ambiguously placed between host and guest.

In his paean to the inn, James John Hissey was not alone in portraying the rural hostelry as a vessel of cultural persistence – of immersion in as near a form of authentic sociability as could be achieved in his commercial age. Prior to the nineteenth century, many English travellers narrated continental places of accommodation either as familiar 'English' outposts in foreign realms, catering specifically to their tastes and comforts, or as decidedly alien and inferior places. Mariana Starke, like many others, navigated prospective travellers through the geography and quality of commercial accommodation, warning, for instance, that one good hotel in Naples nonetheless suffered from a 'bleak situation' and 'is liable to a stench from the drains'.[27] As the European tourist infrastructure developed, and as the tourist embraced the rural hostelry as a site of cultural immersion, writers began to express appreciation for foreign hospitality – materialised in food and accommodation and enveloped in cultural rituals that were as distinctive as the landscapes through which they travelled. There were antecedents to this travel writing grounded in appraisals of English historical institutions, such as 'Mine Inn', published in Charles Dickens's *Household Words* in 1853. Dickens's article was not so much a travelogue as a rumination on the special place of the inn in the literary, political and social history of Britain. 'To the contemplative man, and to the lover of social antiquities', the author contended, 'the subject of inns is associated with the pleasantest, the kindliest, the most genial, and the most elevated humanities'.[28] Reminding readers that Chaucer's pilgrims had set forth from the Tabard Inn in Southwark, the author noted that Shakespeare had privileged the inn as a site for his great works, and that Walter Scott, too, had favoured them in his literary enterprises.[29] Tellingly, the piece ended with an exposition on the extinction of an English institution:

> 'Mine inn' is rapidly becoming an institution of the past; it will soon be numbered among the things departed. The roadside inn, and the coaching inn, should have disappeared with post-chaises and fast stage coaches. They still linger on; but they are daily being pushed from their stools by Railway Hotels, Terminus Taverns, and Locomotive Coffeehouses. They will soon have to say with the Latin Accidence, *eramus* – we were.[30]

The writer of this elegiac reflection contended that a unique set of social and cultural practices and spaces were in eclipse. The hotel was advancing with the speed of another transformative travel and social technology – the railway. With the profusion of grand hotels in the United Kingdom, European countries and their colonies and territories, inns emerged in a remarkable wave of cultural nostalgia as touchstones of English culture, as central to the nation's soul as the village church and green, and as sites of cordiality, comfort and simple and satisfying fare. The inn was also an institution signifying English commercial vitality – especially in Elizabethan and Georgian times. A burgeoning library of early twentieth-century titles written in a sentimental tone, intertwining building histories, comments on celebrated visitors and evocative illustrations, grew in the inter-war period.[31]

What gave rise to this particular sub-genre of writing? Partly it was bound with an explicitly documentary enterprise – to record for posterity iconic English inns immortalised by poets and authors. But underpinning this project was anxiety about England's own faltering economic dominance, expressed in critiques of the industrialisation of hospitality, and the nomadism of modern life.[32] Reflecting on the inn's displacement, Charles G. Harper wrote:

> For although the Vandal – identified here with the brewer and the landlord – has been busy in the great centres of population, destroying many of those famous old hostelries our grandfathers knew and appreciated, and building in their stead 'hotels' of the most grandiose and palatial kind, there are happily still remaining to us a large number of the genuine and cosy haunts where the traveller, stained with the marks of travel, may enter and take his ease without being ashamed of his travel-stains or put out of the countenance by the modish visitors of this complicated age, who dress usually as if going to a ball, and whose patronage has rung the death-knell of many an inn once quaint and curious, but now merely 'replete with every modern convenience'.[33]

The physical destruction of the inn and the erection of the hotel was paralleled by the extinction of time-honoured customs and this narrative. Interlaced spatial and social ordering limited meaningful interaction in the interest of efficiency. In hotels, Harper related, 'every trace of local colour is effaced', and

> [a] barrier is raised between yourself and the place. You are in it, but not of it or among
> it; but something alien, like the German or Swiss waiters themselves, the manager, and
> the very directors and shareholders of the big concern.[34]

Many travel writers repeated the assertion that the hotel guest's individuality was effaced by a mechanistic hospitality that also ordered 'hosting' along an elaborate division of labour.[35]

The hotel's ancestors (indeed its etymological origins) were in the grand and exclusive domiciles of the elite, who extended their own hospitality on highly selective terms. The hotel was grounded in a culture of exclusiveness and its social regimes still required a high degree of cultural capital to navigate. Moreover, the American hotel signified cosmopolitanism and modernity: technology, differentiation of labour and scientific management. It became an emblem of America's dynamic capitalism. But it also institutionalised and patterned exclusion and segregation – along racial, class and gender lines. The prolific writer Abba Good Wollson lamented the many 'petty discomforts' which women endured at travelling hotels. Men were supplied with the hotel register and newspapers, for instance, while women, confined to the ladies' parlour, flipped through advertising albums or stared at empty walls. The character of hotel hospitality, it seemed, depended very much on who was being served.[36]

As an exemplar of the application of technology on a scale that was as great as the heights of New York's grand hotels, the hotel provoked wonder, envy and disquiet. Even Charles G. Harper admitted the superior amenities of the ideal hotel type in this new age: thick carpets and electric light, billiard-room, tennis-ground and golf-links.[37] Its revolving door bore no resemblance to the old threshold of the inn and private home, and enabled rapid circulation in and out of the institution: 'it has not one single strain of Home in it. Home is where the out-of-date lingers, and modern conveniences that add to the complexity and the worry of life have no corner'.[38] Home, it seemed, offered the template for authentic hospitality. In charting the inn's eclipse, Harper offered a parabolic account of a cycling traveller who had thirty years ago enjoyed the hospitality of landlady – 'a smiling, simple, motherly woman'.[39] When he arrived unheralded at her door, she welcomed him to enjoy a hearty dinner with her family, after which he offered ten pence in compensation. The next year the cyclist took the same path – now more worn – and found subtle changes at the inn. The landlady's manner, and the interior spaces, had changed ('the parlour had now lost something of its sacramental detachedness, and had become a sort of dining room',[40] and the inn now boasted a bar). The roast beef of the year before was now served cold. The whortleberry tart boasted fewer berries and thicker crust. The cheese was now cut ahead of time for guests, and glass had replaced pewter. Most blatantly, the charge had risen to 1s 6d. Only a year or so later, he discovered that the surrounding village had been transformed, and the landlady now greeted guests in formal attire. Her inn was more lavishly furnished, but an indifferent lunch was charged at half a crown.[41] The veneers of the hotel were unmistakable, but the pretensions of hotel management, the landlady's miserly portions of cheese and her crustier pies betrayed her mercenary motive.

Other travel writers offered more favourable evaluations of the hotel system in the United States, where it appeared to evolve organically, and manifest a unique dynamism that suited the young nation's peculiar social and commercial patterns of development. At one point in his conversations with a well-travelled 'Mr. L. Inthelaw', the narrator of Robert Vashon Rogers's travelogue is told emphatically that 'as good as are some of the hotels of Europe, the American ones surpass them all both in size and in general fitness of purpose'.[42] Many travellers concurred with the narrator: the vastness of the American territory, and its expansive railway network, as well as the 'natural disposition of our people to travel' made the 'hotel system [. . .] without parallel in the world'.[43] American hotels were as ambitious as the republic's bold political experiment, their food as bountiful as the farms that supplied them and their service culture, like the system of hereditary ranks that it proclaimed to throw off in revolution, a singular departure from the hierarchies and hide-bound practices of even the most modern European hotel. The *table d'hôte* of the European hotel – with its limited menu and its set-times – conspired against conviviality and the flexibility that were the hallmarks of American hospitality, while even the 'grand hotels' of Europe's capitals were dwarfed by those of the great American urban centres, where hotels became cities within cities. The novelty of this peculiar American institution, and its role in ordering American social life, attracted considerable debate as commentators ranging from the Alpinist and writer Albert Smith to the writer George Augustus Henry Sala questioned the functions and form of this hospitality 'machine'.[44] They also discussed the role of the hotel as a public institution in the United States: a centre of restless movement, of intense sociality and of bustling commerce.[45] Remarking on the distinctive character of the hotels in the USA, Frederick Maryatt found the fluidity and sociability evident in the country's inns and eating regimes:

> There are no neat, quiet little inns, as in England. It is all the 'rough and tumble' system, and when you stop at humble inns you must expect to eat peas with a two-pronged fork, and to sit down to meals with people whose exterior is anything but agreeable, to attend upon yourself, and to sleep in a room in which there are three or four other beds (I have slept in one with nearly twenty), most of them carrying double, even if you do not have a companion in your own.[46]

If travellers to America found its inns a contrast to their own hostelries, Americans in Britain and in Europe noted the deficiencies and peculiarities of 'hotels' there. Offering a perspective on *England from a Back-Window; with Views of Scotland and Ireland*, the American journalist James Montgomery Bailey asserted, as so many of his contemporaries did, that 'the European hotel system is much different from the American hotel system', and derided the 'British-American' hotel's woeful efforts to emulate its American counterpart.[47] Bailey found the 'European' meal plan curious, served in Britain, unlike in America, without the complements of bread and butter, and without a commensurately generous choice of dishes.[48] Yet, however much Bailey evinced preference in his account for the American hotel system and American fare, he reserved great affection for the same hospitable English institution – the inn – that so many English travel writers revered for its quaintness and domestic virtues.[49] England's rustic charm, its early prosperity and its cultural vibrancy: all these touchstones of a peculiar, historical, pastoral Englishness were materialised under its thatched roof and timber beams. It was not an entirely modern place, and because of that its hospitality was less subsumed within the logic of modern capitalism. This position generated anxiety – and it was partly reflected in nostalgic discourses of the English inn's 'golden age'. The English inn, which once epitomised the country's precocious development, was now an ossified signifier of the age of Shenstone, Addison and other luminaries. At early English inns, their proponents contended, 'purchased hospitality' came at a reasonable charge: the obligations of guests were commensurate with the provisions made by the host for their comfort. Moreover, the quality of accommodations compared favourably with the gut barracks, the dirty auberges, the bare barns, which did duty for inns in Germany, France, and Italy. It contrasted especially with the flea-haunted Spanish posadas, where the muleteers and their beasts slept on the same straw, and where he who did not bring his dinner with him was likely to go to bed fasting.[50]

Yet these continental rural places, such as the French *auberge*, like the Silk Road caravanserai and the medieval monastery, could also be romanticised – and offer a device through which strictures and structures of modern hospitality could be appraised. Colouring these comparisons was the observation that many hostelries in places such as Switzerland went out of their way to accommodate the customary eating times and religious practices of their English guests.[51] But the English traveller did not have to cross the ocean or English Channel to find evidence that hospitality, its spaces and its codes, were culturally grounded. Evaluations of Welsh, Scottish and Irish inns also revealed the extent to which the English traveller located primitive and unfamiliar protocols and institutions close to home, and used evaluations of the hostelry for wider cultural appraisal. Irish, Welsh and Scottish hospitality cultures often figured within a primitivist narrative, as *Chambers's Journal* suggested in this account of the era that preceded commercial tourism:

> It was necessary in wild countries and among small communities, that those who were compelled to travel should find food and shelter wherever the welcome smoke announced a human abode. Logan in his Wigwam, deep in the gloomy shade of the forest, gave as kind a welcome to the wayfarer as an Arab sheik could have done; and, half a century ago, even the mountain districts of our own isles, Connaught and Kerry, Wales and the Highlands, were famous for the patriarchal fashion in which a stranger was received and feasted, and in due course passed on from castle to hall, and from grange to abbey, among swarms of new friends, to whom his very name was before unknown.[52]

If the hostelries of the UK's geographic primitive, patriarchal 'peripheries' offered foils for England's advanced commercial inns, their efforts to adapt to the strictures of commercial hospitality in the age of recreational travel were sometimes treated as risible, and became devices for comical description, satire, sharp critique and occasional ruminations on the nature of the cultures of the 'home' country or region of the traveller. Even so-called improved hostelries were still deficient when compared to the venerable English institution; indeed, if anything, they revealed the gulf in sensibilities between a culture disciplined in the structures of industrial capitalism, and others struggling to adapt to it. The *Thorough Guide*'s reflections on the quality of the landladies in North Wales, for instance, remarked that

> [t]he Welsh housewife, though not perhaps quite a paragon of neatness in her domestic arrangements, is, generally speaking, a liberal and sedulous caterer for the requirements of her visitors and takes a personal pride in their comfort, which one often misses in more sophisticated places.[53]

This landlady embodied the ambiguities and ambivalences of travel writing: she failed to satisfy the highest expectations of her guests, but also personified the efforts of Welsh innkeepers to raise their hostelries to English standards of comfort. This was generous praise in comparison to other districts where landlords also embodied some foreign cultural quintessence. In his evaluation of accommodation in the Highlands of Scotland, the *Thorough Guide*'s M.J.B. Baddeley found the innkeeper's occasional flintiness colliding with the requirements of the modern tourist, undermining the reputation of all who plied the trade in Scotland.[54] These evaluations of the comparatively inferior character of hostelries extended to Ireland, where despite the presence of some establishments that met with the writer's approval, Baddeley lamented that indigenous habits endured. In rural Ireland, the figure who attracted great attention was the 'Boots' – a Jack-of-all-Trades who was rendered as an obtuse caricature in many accounts of travel:

> [t]he fair and at the same time faithful writer on Irish Hotels is awkwardly placed. He joyfully acknowledges the anxiety of everybody in the establishment, notably 'Boots', to contribute to his comfort, but patience is apt to be sorely tried by the general laxity of management, which often entirely upsets the day's programme, showing itself at one time in orders for an early 'call' being quite forgotten, at another in breakfast being served two minutes before train or mail-car is timed to start, and generally in unpunctuality and untidiness. The most suicidal habit, however, to which the Irish hotelkeeper is prone is carelessness about those sanitary arrangements which are now-a-days essential to the success of any place professing to accommodate tourists.[55]

In contrast to these appraisals, Baddeley wrote glowingly of the hotels and inns of the Lake District, where he remarked that

> [t]here is a welcome absence – of that grasping spirit and extortionate charging for small items which make the very mention of many Scotch hotels a 'bugbear' to the Southerner, and the result is a much more agreeable and friendly feeling between 'mine host' and his guest for the time being.[56]

The inns and hotels of the eastern counties of England won similar approval from the *Thorough Guide*'s C.S. Ward,[57] signalling how inns became microspaces in which wider cultures were evaluated.

As these narratives suggest, space was inextricably bound with sociability: indeed the microspaces of the commercial hostelry, from the grand lobbies and corridors of the hotel to cosy inglenook near the roaring fire of the inn, shaped narratives of social encounters, often centred on food and drink. At the threshold of the inn door, guests entered not only a distinctive physical world, but also one of intense sociability, in which the pivotal figure was the landlord or the landlady – the 'host' or 'hostess' who superintended the regime of hospitality as once hostellers had done in the old monasteries. Landladies featured prominently in narratives of hospitality – as did maids and staff of small and large establishments. They were amongst the suite of rural characters that constituted the modest and often quirky realm of the inn, which offered a striking contrast with the retinue of multilingual, international staff in the cosmopolitan hotel.

To James John Hissey, the people who superintended the inn were amongst its greatest attractions. They forged strong personal bonds with guests:

> the landlord himself welcomes you and takes a personal interest in your welfare as long as you are under his roof, where a motherly landlady busies herself to look after your comforts, and a be-ribboned maid waits quietly upon you. It is all so restful, and there you feel really at home away from home.[58]

This depiction of the inn as the traveller's 'home away from home' was a trope in travel writing, and partly reflected the prevalence of family labour at the inn. Hissey dramatised this point (and simultaneously softened the commercial nature of his transaction with the innkeeper) by underscoring the maternal qualities of the landlady. In his travelogue *The Road and the Inn* he reflected on the old landlords of coaching inns of yore, 'usually men of substance, with much knowledge of the world besides, and with also, it is said, "the manners of an archbishop"'.[59] 'Alas!' he declared, 'that race is extinct'.[60] Not for Hissey, nor indeed for the legions of writers who joined him in extolling the inn, did the landlord supply, as Charles G. Harper wrote, 'the mark for satire and invective' – a figure 'licensed, sweated, regulated, and generally put on the chain'.[61] If Harper was perhaps contemplating figures such as 'Boniface', from George Farquhar's early seventeenth-century comedy *The Beaux' Stratagem*, the travel writer professing a keen eye for local detail personified native eccentricity in the Scottish, Welsh, Irish, French and Swiss Boniface, as well as those in more far-flung inns. As the traveller ventured north to Scotland, for instance, the Highland innkeeper became the embodiment of unflinching miserliness. In Wales the novelty of the majority language, the frequent presence of a harpist and the predominance of female waiters struck the traveller as singular,[62] as the principality's mountains became a site of recreation from the mid-Victorian period.

In contrast, the grand hotel furnished a retinue of figures that travel writers discussed to dramatise the institution's vast and impersonal character – a regime of hospitality that was certainly professional, but guided by the profit motive. In observing the multitudes who milled in its lobbies, the travel writer also had the opportunity to reflect on his or her own identity and individuality – an individuality that the institution itself suppressed. The hotel system effaced all but the most cursory of social interactions, and ordered them minutely by task. *Chambers's Journal*, remarking on the comparative intimacy that prevailed at the continental inn, noted the unremitting advance of the hotel, 'reared by joint-stock companies, and managed with methodical regularity'. While acknowledging the merits of their amenities, the writer joined legions of others who bemoaned the anonymity of guests, who were now identified by room number:

> His number weighs on him with a crushing weight. Somehow, he experiences sensations a good deal like those of a captive in the mines of Siberia, who is told that he is dead to the world, save as 7790. Yet he must carry the hideous arithmetical shadow about with him from coffee-room to bar, from chamber to smoking-room, and cannot get so much as a draught of bitter beer without signing a cheque for it as Sixty-six, B.[63]

This reduction of the guest to a mere number reflected persistent anxiety that the scale of these institutions made hosts and guests alike nameless participants in a service factory that subjected them to systemised surveillance and corporeal 'management', as guests were shepherded through registration by clerks, up elevators to their rooms by bellboys, and fed sumptuous fare in ornate restaurants by an elaborate staff. As Charles G. Harper lamented in his survey of the English inn:

> Most of the old inns are gone, too, and in their place, only too frequently, the traveller finds the modern, company-owned hotel, with a foreign manager who naturally takes no interest in the guests he, as a matter of fact, rarely sees, and with whom no guest could possible foregather. In the modern barrack hotel the guest must necessarily be impersonal – one of a number going to swell the returns. No one quite willingly resigns himself to being a mere number; it is, indeed, one of the greatest of the convict's trials that he has lost his name and become identified by a letter and a row of figures.[64]

The inn's landlord and landlady welcomed guests into a cultural micro-space governed by indigenous social regimes, where the charges were fair, and where none of the elite hotel's barriers of class and gender filtered out 'undesirable' guests. Wasn't a cardinal principle of hospitality its extension to all who required it? The hotel offered an eclectic retinue of practised German waiters, French chefs and Swiss managers, and a menu heavily inflected by fashion and foreign influence.

As many examples here have suggested, meals offered writers occasion to expound on the peculiarities of native dining rituals while physically digesting the products of their kitchen. Food was a central dimension of sociability, and was bound with the spaces of hospitality. At the inn, food and drink were often described, in Hissey's pithy and approving declaration, as 'simple, wholesome fare'.[65] The flavours of the region infused the roasted beef, which was often prepared in view of guests, and even shared with them at the family table. When the British inn adopted the pretences of the hotel – worse still, the utterly foreign *table d'hôte* – it lost its cultural co-ordinates. Charles G. Harper asserted that the spaces of eating were different at the inn (there was no 'general coffee-room then, save for commercial travellers and such social gentlemen as preferred even inferior company to solitude' – with no *table d'hôte* save that for coaching parties[66]). His reverence for the inn extended to spaces of consumption, the social contexts of ingestion and the food itself, which was as pure as the soil from which it was drawn. The country inn, 'with its honeysuckled porch and scrambling profusion of climbing roses up to the bedroom windows, had an even more home-like character in its methods of dealing with its guests'.[67] Here the 'eggs and the milk and butter were all sweet and new. Generous jugs of cream softened the tartness of the black-currant pudding or the green-gooseberry tart'. Fowl was well fed, mutton and beef were home-grown and 'knew nothing of the anti-septic preparations or frozen chambers', while the fresh vegetables came straight from the garden, 'neither tinned nor carted in for miles in huge waggon loads, well rammed down and tightly compressed'.[68] Inn fare distilled the essential pureness of the soil, and permitted the guest to partake of the countryside and consume culture in a tangible way, from the kitchen of his host. Commensality, often a feature of dining at small-scale inns, stressed the intimate social context in which native food and drink were shared, and valorised the inn as a site of a peculiar rituals of familial sociability – far removed from the strictures and unfamiliar social dynamics of the hotel, whose menus were elaborate and eclectic, responding to the dictates of fashion by adopting cuisines from around the globe.

The extent to which places of accommodation, their staff and their food and drink constituted 'authentic' markers of the toured culture was a subject of particular concern in travel writing. The search for regimes of intimate and indigenous hospitality became a more acute incentive as recreational travel accelerated and hotel culture advanced. Despite the range of hostelry types that complicates the inn–hotel binary, these generic markers tended to mark a claim to specific forms and traditions of hospitality: the inn a place of quaintness and tradition whose genealogy stretched back centuries, the hotel a creature of capitalist modernity, both deracinated and deracinating.

Conclusion

Spaces and social regimes of hospitality were often placed within an ambiguous binary of familiarity and otherness, and barbarism and civilisation that reveals the complex positioning of space, people, food and beverage as authenticating features of travel writing. Paeans to the American hotel heaped praise on its innovations, but also expressed anxiety over its alienating hotel culture, while wistful narratives of traditional English hospitality expressed ambivalence about an age in which commerce and industry seemed outsized for the English inn. 'Primitive' civilisations offered caricature figures for the light-hearted travelogue, but also sources for serious reflection on the absence of a cultural and moral imperative in the 'business' of modern hospitality.

These political and cultural incentives for shaping a particular narrative of the inn were not lost on travel writers: 'We travellers are unwilling to be thought of merely as numbers identical with those of our own bedrooms', Charles G. Harper insisted, before adding knowingly,

> and we like to believe, against our own better judgement, that the old-fashioned hosts and hostesses were pleased to see *us*; which of course, in that special sense, was not the case. But a little make-believe sometimes goes a great way, and we need never, unless we have a mind to distress ourselves, seek the tongue of humbug in the cheek of courtesy.[69]

An ambivalent stance towards 'modern hospitality' lies at the heart of many travel accounts, old and new. Travellers may be able to grasp the system of signification that lends weight and meaning to various food and accommodation 'brands', and to such acts as proffering a warm cookie at check-in, but they are aware that management has made careful calculations of return on profit before the plate has been offered. As many travellers seek a more intimate, 'local' experience, and fulminate against deficiencies or lavish compliments on much more public, virtual platforms compared to the hotel visitors' books of their forebears, their expectations are guided by a dynamic culture of travel and repose with deep historical roots. That history figured into narratives of the condition of modern travel codes and amenities, but also supplied a source for reflection on what compromises and corruptions were inherent in the commercialisation of hospitality. Writers often grapple with an underlying tension that proceeds from the fundamental motivation behind acts and offerings associated with hospitality, however crude or elaborate, and the mutual obligations attached to them. We may not travel with modern-day versions of Robert Vashon Roger's treatise at hand, and we may not wish to imagine ourselves as 'customers' instead of 'guests', or of hospitality as a commodity. Yet, should we desire to be reminded of the extensive legal underpinnings of the sector, whether breakfast is included, the limits of the innkeepers' liability, whether we may smoke or welcome pets into our rooms, when we must vacate them, and the maximum allowable charge, we can usually find it, in abridged form, discreetly affixed to the back of hotel-room doors.

Notes

1 Robert Vashon Rogers, Jr., *The Law of Hotel Life, or the Wrongs and Rights of Host and Guest* (San Francisco, CA: Sumer Whitney and Company, 1879), 2–3; Robert Vashon Rogers, Jr., *Wrongs and Rights of a Traveller. By Boat – By Stage – By Rail* (Toronto: R. Carswell, 1875).

2 Rogers, *Law of Hotel Life*, 3.

3 Rogers, *Law of Hotel Life*, 5.

4 Rogers, *Law of Hotel Life*, 7.

5 Kevin D. O'Gorman, *The Origins of Hospitality and Tourism* (Woodeaton, Oxfordshire: Goodfellows Publishers Limited, 2010), 11–24.

6 Notions of 'conditional' and 'unconditional' hospitality are critical areas of scholarly analysis. See, for instance, Jacques Derrida and Anne Dufourmantelle, *Of Hospitality: Anne Dufourmantelle Invites Jacques Derrida to Respond*, trans. Rachel Bowlby (Stanford, CA: Stanford University Press, 2000); Conrad Lashley, Paul Lynch and Alison Morrison, *Hospitality: A Social Lens* (Kidlington, Oxfordshire and Amsterdam: Elsevier Ltd., 2007); Mustafa Dikeç, Nigel Clark and Clive Barnett, 'Extending Hospitality: Giving Space, Taking Time', *Paragraph* 32 (2009): 1–14 (this is an introduction to issue 1 of the volume, which explores issues related to the critical study of hospitality in a variety of contexts).

7 Unsigned review of *Hotel Life, or the Wrongs and Rights of Hotel Guest: by R.Vashon Rogers, Jr., Canadian Law Journal* 15 (December 1879): 326.

8 See, for example, Felicity Heal, *Hospitality in Early Modern England* (Oxford: Oxford University Press, 1990).

9 James Bruce, *Travels to Discover the Source of the Nile*, 2nd edition (Edinburgh: James Ballantyne, 1804), 1:73.

10 Rogers, *Law of Hotel Life*, 5.

11 *The Reveries of a Recluse; or, Sketches of Characters, Parties, Events, Writings, Opinions, &c.* (Edinburgh: Oliver & Boyd, 1824), 159.

12 For a superb discussion of the American hotel analysed through the lens of hospitality, see A.K. Sandoval-Strausz, *Hotel: An American History* (New Haven, CT: Yale University Press, 2007). See also Molly W. Berger, *Hotel Dreams: Luxury, Technology, and Urban Ambition in America, 1829–1929* (Baltimore, MD: Johns Hopkins University Press, 2011).

13 James Spence Harry, *Atala. By Chateaubriand* (Chicago, IL: Belford-Clarke Co. 1891), 3.

14 'Hotels', *Chambers's Journal of Popular Literature, Science and Art* 19.491 (30 May 1863): 345.

15 Thomas Branagan, *The Guardian Genius of the Federal Union; or, Patriotic Admonitions on the Signs of the Times, in relation to the Evil Spirit of Party, Arising from the Root of all our Evils, Human Slavery, being the first part of the Beauties of Philanthropy* (New York: 'Published for the Author', nd), 68–9.

16 See Bruce L. Vernarde, ed. and trans., *The Rule of Saint Benedict* (Cambridge, MA: Harvard University Press, 2011).

17 Julie Kerr, *Monastic Hospitality: The Benedictines in England, c. 1070–c. 1200* (Woodbridge: The Boydell Press, 2007).

18 Rita Singer, 'Leisure, Refuge and Solidarity: Messages in Visitors' Books as Microforms of Travel Writing', *Studies in Travel Writing* 20.4 (2016): 392–408; Kevin James, '"[A] British Social Institution": The Visitors' Book and Hotel Culture in Victorian Britain and Ireland', *Journeys: The International Journal of Travel and Travel Writing* 13.1 (2012): 42–69.

19 James John Hissey, *Through Ten English Counties* (London: Richard Bentley & Son, 1894).

20 See Esme Coulbert, '"The Romance of the Road": Narratives of Motoring in England, 1896–1930', in *Travel Writing and Tourism in Britain and Ireland*, ed. Benjamin Colbert (Houndmills: Palgrave Macmillan, 2012), 201–18.

21 James John Hissey, *The Charm of the Road. England and Wales* (London: Macmillan and Co., Limited, 1910), 53.

22 Hissey, *Charm of the Road*, 53.

23 For a good overview of this subject, see O'Gorman, *Origins of Hospitality*.

24 Thomas Wright, *The Travels of Marco Polo, The Venetian. The Translation of Marsden Revised, with a Selection of his Notes* (London: Henry G. Bohn, 1854), 109–13.

25 The journal *Hospitality & Society* has played a central role in the advancement of the critical study of hospitality; on the topic of thresholds, see a short editorial by Jennie Germann Molz and Alison McIntosh, 'Hospitality at the Threshold', *Hospitality & Society* 3.2 (2013): 87–91.

26 Mary Seacole, *The Wonderful Adventures of Mrs Seacole in Many Lands*, edited by W.J.S. (London: James Blackwood, 1857).

27 Mariana Starke, *Letters from Italy, between the Years 1792 and 1798* (London: T. Gillet, 1800), 2:330.

28 'Mine Inn', *Household Words* 8.189 (5 November 1853): 238.

29 'Mine Inn', 239–40.

30 'Mine Inn', 240.

31 A wave of early twentieth-century publications included Josephine Tozier, *Among English Inns. The Story of a Pilgrimage to Characteristic Spots of Rural England* (Boston, MA: L.C. Page & Company, 1904); Charles G. Harper, *The Old Inns of Old England. A Picturesque Account of the Ancient and Storied Hostelries of our Own Country* (London: Chapman & Hall, 1906); George Thomas Burrows, *Some Old English Inns* (London: T. Werner Laurie, [1907]); Henry P. Maskell and Edward W. Gregory, *Old Country Inns of England* (London: I. Pitman, 1910). In the interwar period, the burgeoning number of publications included Cecil Aldin, *Old Inns* (London: William Heinemann, 1921); William Monckton Keesey, *Tales of Old Inns. The History, Legend and Romance of Some of our Older Hostelries* (London: Trust Houses, 1927); A.E. Richardson, *The Old Inns of England* (London: B.T. Batsford Ltd., 1934); George Long, *English Inns and Road-Houses* (London: T. Werner Laurie, 1937).

32 Charlotte Bates, 'Hotel Histories: Modern Tourists, Modern Nomads and the Culture of Hotel-Consciousness', *Literature & History* 12.2 (2003): 62–75.

33 Harper, *Old Inns of Old England*, 1:1–2.

34 Harper, *Old Inns of Old England*, 1:2.

35 [George Augustus Sala], 'American Hotels and American Food', *Temple Bar: A London Magazine for Town and Country Readers* 2 (July 1861), 345–56. See also 'F.A.', 'English Hotel Life', *London Society* 22.129 (September 1872), 256–61.

36 Abba Good Woolson, *Women in American Society* (Boston, MA: Roberts Brothers, 1873), 122–3.

37 Harper, *Old Inns of Old England*, 1:69.

38 Harper, *Old Inns of Old England*, 1:70.

39 Harper, *Old Inns of Old England*, 1:256.

40 Harper, *Old Inns of Old England*, 1:257.

41 Harper, *Old Inns of Old England*, 1:258.

42 Rogers, *Law of Hotel Life*, 54.

43 Rogers, *Law of Hotel Life*, 54.

44 See, for instance, Albert Smith, *The English Hotel Nuisance* (London: David Bryce, 1855); Sala, 'American Hotels and American Food', 345–56.

45 See Berger, *Hotel Dreams* and Sandoval-Strausz, *Hotel*.

46 Frederick Marryat, *Second Series of a Diary in America, with Remarks on Its Institutions* (Philadelphia, PA: T.K. & P.G. Collins, 1840), 104.

47 J.M. Bailey, 'The Dansbury-News Man', *England from a Back-Window; with Views of Scotland and Ireland* (Boston, MA: Lee and Shepard, 1879), 59.

48 Bailey, *England from a Back-Window*, 61.

49 Bailey, *England from a Back-Window*, 60.

50 'Hotels', 346.

51 See *Hand-book for travellers in Switzerland and the Alps of Savoy and Piedmont . . . New ed.* (London: John Murray, 1811), xxxiii.

52 'Hotels', 345.

53 M.J.B. Baddeley and C.S. Ward, *North Wales (Part II.)* (London: Dulao & Co., 1885), xi.

54 M.J.B. Baddeley, *The Highlands of Scotland (As Far As Stornoway, Lochinver, and Lairg)* (London: Dulau & Co., 1881), xv.

55 M.J.B. Baddeley, *Ireland (Part I.). Northern Counties including Dublin and Neighbourhood*, 2nd ed. (London: Dulau & Co., 1890), xii.

56 M.J.B. Baddeley, *The Thorough Guide to the English Lake District* (London: Dulau & Co., 1880), xxi.

57 C.S. Ward, *The Eastern Counties* (London: Dulau & Co., 1883), ix.

58 Hissey, *Charm of the Road*, 53.

59 Hissey, *Road and the Inn*, 99.

60 Hissey, *Road and the Inn*, 99.

61 Harper, *Old Inns of Old England*, vol. 1, 36.

62 Richard Warner, *A Walk through Wales in August 1797* (Bath: R. Cruttell, 1798), 147.

63 'Hotels', 347–8.

64 Harper, *Old Inns of Old England*, 1:59.

65 Hissey, *Charm of the Road*, 53.

66 Harper, *Old Inns of Old England*, 1:68.

67 Harper, *Old Inns of Old England*, 1:68.

68 Harper, *Old Inns of Old England*, 1:68.

69 Harper, *Old Inns of Old England*, 1:59.

20

FOREIGN EXCHANGE

David Murray

Questions of value

Travels of any duration inevitably involve the traveller in exchanges of various sorts with the people encountered along the way. These exchanges may involve looks, gestures, words, germs, bodily fluids, and objects of all kinds but it is the exchange of material objects, and the representations of these exchanges, which is the focus of this chapter. In accounts of early travel and contact with other cultures, one of the most fascinating things is the way that these many-faceted exchanges of objects involve radical challenges to the ideas of value on which each side is operating. Objects can have value because of their utility (food, tools, weapons), their attractiveness as ornament, because they partake of the sacred or divine, or because they have special resonance in the memory of their owners. (In the case of the exchange of people, the value is more complex, including their ability to work, or give sexual pleasure, but this raises other questions outside my remit here.) When cultures foreign to each other meet and exchange objects, the slipperiness of these categories often becomes apparent, and can even prompt a relativisation of the whole idea of value. One of the purposes of this chapter is to explore these questions of value, and to try to tease out just what each side had in mind, but another purpose is to look at the ways in which these exchanges have been represented and misrepresented, at the time and later, and try to understand the obfuscation and effacement of what actually happens in exchanges, particularly in early accounts of European exploration. The obfuscation is largely because of Eurocentric assumptions about what is valuable, but it is also because of a broader set of tropes to be found in early accounts that justify European conquests under a language of amity and benevolence. It is worth considering these larger rhetorical patterns before looking at the exchanges and the objects themselves.

A common pattern in early European accounts is the almost simultaneous assertion of the otherness and opacity of other languages and cultures and the assertion of transparent communication across these languages and cultures. Stephen Greenblatt has shown the ways in which the assumption of cultural transparency is linked to linguistic transparency and the denial of any problems of communication. He finds

> a recurrent failure to comprehend the resistant otherness of New World peoples. On the one hand there is a tendency to imagine the Indians as virtual blanks – wild unformed creatures, as naked in culture as they are in body. On the other hand, there

is a tendency to imagine the Indians as virtual doubles, fully conversant with the language and culture of the Europeans [. . .] One minute the Indians have no culture; the next moment they have ours.[1]

This vacillation is also present in describing the processes of exchange and trade, where we find wildly differing assessments of the people encountered: they are by turns innocent, unworldly, and generous, or greedy, calculating, and treacherous; understandable and tradeworthy or frustratingly perverse in how they value things.

The effacement of the problems of difference serves the purpose of obscuring the actual processes of conquest and the operations of power. Perhaps the most obvious instance of this was the sixteenth-century Requerimiento, a formal written pronouncement of God-given Spanish sovereignty over the newly discovered land and peoples, which was read out to the mystified locals. As part of this legal fiction, the absence of any linguistic objection to the formal claim on behalf of the Spanish crown was taken as assent. Eric Cheyfitz has described the more general process of obfuscation in travel narratives, where, he says, 'what were necessarily the difficulties, discords, indeed absences of translation are displaced into fictive accords of communication'.[2] He is referring here to the assumptions about linguistic transparency, but his description applies equally well to the processes of effacement and misrecognition in operation in all sorts of material exchanges.

In early narratives of European travel and conquest the language vacillates, often dramatically, between expressions of wonder at the strangeness of the new and ethnocentric assumptions that all is understandable, and between an aristocratic stance of benevolence and generosity, in which the travellers are bestowing religious and cultural favours on the natives, and a stance of narrow economic calculation about what the new place and people can yield. The main impetus, after all, was economic. Thomas Churchyard's verses in 1578 on Humphrey Gilbert's Newfoundland enterprise refer to the boldness needed when 'you seeke to traffike there, / where never yet was trade'.[3] This statement could of course mean a place the English have yet to reach, so that they could then establish trade and economic exchanges, but it could also mean establishing a market, a set of new needs and demands among people who do not understand the conventions of trade – something to be explored later in this chapter. While it would be a mistake, as I will show, to see the stance of benevolence as simply a cover for the more calculating approach, it certainly allowed the travellers to present themselves as givers, and not as takers and conquerors. The assumption of cultural and religious superiority meant that what was being imposed on those they conquered could be seen as a gift and not an imposition. This was an important element in the effacement of the operations of power involved in the many exchanges taking place.

While this chapter will focus mainly on early examples of imperial and colonial exploration, where it may now be easy in retrospect to see the inequalities of power and how these were concealed in contemporary accounts, my broader argument will be that the predisposition to see exchange as straightforward and not to consider the mediations of power is in fact a constant in travel and travel writing. This may be seen in the reluctance in many anthropological encounters to make explicit the full dimensions of the exchanges and to acknowledge what is being given and exchanged. In the case of anthropology, for example, the need is not for gold or commodities but for knowledge or cultural objects. Yet there is often no mention that these are frequently paid for with money or with material goods such as food. The tendency, certainly in earlier ethnographies, was to subsume these exchanges within a larger narrative in which friendship and trust gave the key to unmediated communication and cultural access. As Frank Cushing said of the Zuni Indians he stayed with, 'they love me and I learn'.[4] Only in glimpses do we get a sense of the harder realities, as in Bronislaw Malinowski's posthumously published *A Diary in the Strict Sense of the Term* (1967). Malinowski's most famous or infamous statement ('On the whole my feelings toward the natives are decidedly tending to "Exterminate the brutes"'[5]) needs to be contextualised, but it is significant that in the sentence immediately before it he is talking about a material exchange designed to provide him with knowledge: 'At moments I was furious with them [the people of Mailu, New Guinea], particularly because after I gave them their portions of tobacco they all went away.'[6] Even today we can find echoes of this attitude in the average holiday traveller's investment in seeing their particular place as unspoiled and the locals as pleased to see them. It still comes as something of a shock to come across the honesty and unsentimentality of Paul Bowles, who is refreshingly clear about the power relations behind his relations with Moroccans, freely acknowledging that he paid for everything, ranging from sex to information.[7]

Early North American encounters

I shall now look at material exchanges themselves, and will draw on a growing awareness among scholars of the processes by which objects change meaning through their circulation, which has been especially fruitful in thinking about cross-cultural encounters. In particular the work of Arjun Appadurai and Igor Kopytoff, in tracing the journeys of objects and giving them the equivalent of biographies, has allowed us to see the ways that objects can move in and out of their role as commodities. As they are exchanged they take on a multiplicity of personal, emotional, and cultural meanings, to the extent that seeing them only in terms of market and economy is reductive. For Kopytoff, 'The only time when the commodity status of a thing is beyond question is the moment of actual exchange.'[8] He sees a 'perennial and universal tug-of-war between the tendency of all economies to expand the jurisdiction of commoditization and of all cultures to restrict it'.[9] This sort of approach may be useful in supplementing the more narrowly economic application of Marxist ideas on commodity (though it has to be said that Peter Stallybrass's brilliant essay 'Marx's Coat' did something similar some years before).[10] Ethnographers and cultural historians have offered more detailed examples of ways in which, in Nicholas Thomas's words, 'Objects are not what they were made to be but what they have become', namely what he calls 'entangled objects'.[11]

As well as using these theorisations of the object, I want to draw on discussions of the gift and of giving, which were themselves originally stimulated by ethnographic encounters, and theorisations prompted by them. An awareness of the different dynamics of gift-giving, and its relation to power and prestige within and across cultures, can supplement our sense of what is actually happening in travel encounters as well as the rhetorical strategies involved in describing them. Before pursuing this, though, it is worth looking at some early European travel accounts to illustrate some of the patterns I intend to discuss.

One recurrent image that has become a cliché is that of the first encounter, in which the indigenous people are fascinated by worthless trifles or baubles, and will give in exchange for them objects of 'real' value like gold or provisions. Because of their certainty about what is valuable and what is not, Europeans assume that Indians are gullible and the exchange is an unequal one. As Greenblatt puts it,

> [w]here they might have imagined mutual gift-giving, or, alternatively, a mutually satisfactory economic transaction, the Europeans instead tended to imagine an exchange of empty signs, of alluring counterfeits, for overwhelming abundance. Objects of little value provide access to objects of immense value.[12]

We might note here the difference between Christopher Columbus encountering people in the Caribbean and the already-established European trading relations with West Africa, for instance, where there were precedents and patterns for knowing what each side valued and wanted. It is interesting that the experience of African tastes had influenced Columbus's choice of cargo, so that he already had at hand the trinkets and shiny objects with which he hoped to attract the interest of the Indians.

We can get some sense of the complications from the accounts in Columbus's journals of his iconic first encounters in the West Indies. When the Spanish sailors land, taking their royal standard, Columbus,

> that we might form great friendship, for I knew that they were a people who could be more easily freed and converted to our holy faith by love than by force, gave to some of them red caps, and glass beads to put round their necks, and many other things of little value, which gave them great pleasure and made them so much our friends that it was a marvel to see.[13]

The Indians swim to the ships, bringing parrots, cotton thread, and darts and they get glass beads and small bells in exchange. 'In fine, they took all, and gave what they had with good will.'[14] Here the exchanges are presented not as trade or self-interested barter but as the free exchange of gifts. The next group they meet, as they sail on, seem 'more domestic and tractable people, yet also more subtle. For I observed that those who brought cotton and other trifles to the ship knew better than the others how to make a bargain.'[15] Columbus soon starts to see problems because of the mismatch of expectations.

> As the Indians are so simple and the Spaniards are so avaricious and grasping, it does not suffice that the Indians should give them all they want in exchange for a bead or a bit of glass, but the Spaniards would take everything without any return at all. The Admiral always prohibits this.[16]

The three statements present different scenarios which are incompatible (free gifts and mutual hospitality, sophisticated trade between people with similar economic understandings, and innocent gift-givers being exploited for self-interested material gain). The constant vacillation between these interpretations is due to more than the incoherence or unreliability of the Columbus texts, as it is also widespread in many other accounts. It reflects not only the genuine confusion, as each side tries to work out the other's agendas and how to read their actions, but also the need in these accounts to portray the Europeans as motivated by Christian benevolence. At the same time it wants to justify the voyage in both imaginative and material terms, as reflected in Greenblatt's phrase, 'marvelous possessions'.

One object that exemplified these contradictions was gold, the search for which is an integral part of many accounts of early European travel and exploration. These accounts move across the categories of the exotic and marvellous, but the sense of the exorbitant and excessive is always underpinned with hard economic calculation. We see this in an extravagant sentence from Columbus's account of a later voyage: 'Gold is most excellent. Gold constitutes treasure, and he who possesses it may do what he will in the world, and may so attain as to bring souls to paradise.'[17] Gold here is taking on mystical powers, and Marx later referred to this statement in a discussion of the belief in the magical or fetishistic power of money.[18] It is worth noting that the term fetish is itself the product of cultural and economic exchange, and reflects the entanglement of disparate registers of value. Stemming from the Portuguese *feitiço*, it was used in early trading exchanges on the Coast of West Africa to mean something of value or special attraction, and then also came to be applied by the Europeans to the objects of African worship. To the visitors, these objects were just dirty and worthless, and the idea developed that Africans worshipped base objects rather than anything higher or spiritual. This confirmed for Christian Europeans the primitive level of African development, characterised by brute materiality, without any spiritual dimensions. Marx was later brilliantly to turn the tables on such hierarchical and ethnocentric thinking by using the term to describe the way that modern Western societies invest objects with powers they do not possess, coining the term commodity fetishism.[19]

This fetishistic fascination with gold co-exists, ironically, with the recurrent trope of the gullible savage, who is enchanted by the worthless shiny trifle – an idea that reaffirms European superiority, while refusing to acknowledge that objects acquire value in circulation, rather than having an absolute value that is known only by Europeans. It also ignores the fact (which must have puzzled many of the indigenous people) that these adventurers had come halfway across the world precisely in search of an object with no usefulness or intrinsic value – gold. Scattered throughout Columbus's description of native people are comments on the small gold ornaments they wear, which are hints for him of an abundance that is constantly elusive. 'This day little gold was got by barter, but the Admiral heard from an old man that there were many neighbouring islands [. . .] in which much gold is found; and there is even one island that was all gold.'[20] Elvira Riches has shown how this is rhetorically handled in the accounts: 'The absence of gold – the real means of reserve – is filled by an accumulation of representations that keep renewing the promise of impossible Dorados.'[21] She sees in the accounts of the first two voyages 'a register of exchange through which the wealth of the Indies is conveyed by a syntax of the wonderful that encompasses both texts and physical displays'.[22] She argues that for Columbus gold was not so much a natural resource to be located and exploited but a holy gift, a parallel to the gift of Christianity that the Europeans were bringing, thus justifying what Greenblatt calls Christian imperialism. Amplifying Greenblatt, Riches shows how Columbus's writings operate within an 'economy of the marvelous', in a 'process of supplanting gold with the erotic and the exotic'.[23] As she notes, Peter Hulme has also shown how gold operates in Columbus's account at the intersection of different discourses that were available to him to frame the new encounters – on the one hand that of the Orient and trade, and on the other that of savagery and otherness, and Hulme demonstrates how the language shifts from one to the other.[24]

There are interesting parallels between Columbus's text and Walter Raleigh's account of his voyage to Guiana a century later, in that Raleigh's account is an often desperate attempt to mask the failure to actually find gold by producing glowing promises and prospects. Whereas Columbus invokes the infinite gift of God's grace, of which the finding of small amounts of gold is a token, indicating more to come, Raleigh invokes the grace and generosity of Queen Elizabeth, whose favour is crucial to his enterprise. An obsession with finding gold runs through the book, and Raleigh even complains about having to give out gold coins in order to get information about sources of gold.[25] One of the effects of this obsession was to distract voyagers and settlers from the urgent and practical need to establish material trade and exchanges and a workable economic base for the new colonies if they were not to starve. We can see this in John Smith's bitter complaints about the struggles to establish a colony in Virginia:

> But the worst mischiefe was, our gilded refiners with their golden promises, made all men their slaves in hope of recompence, there was no talke, no hope, no worke, but dig gold, wash gold, refine gold, load gold, such a brute of gold.[26]

If gold embodied the heady mix of the exotic, the marvellous and the materially profitable, the reality was much more often the desperate need to establish material exchanges and trade, initially to ensure survival after long voyages and then to set up trading networks. It is here that we see most interestingly the different registers of language involving giving and trading, and the concealments of the operations of power. In North America the development of the fur trade eventually involved fixed rates of exchange, and a European model of trade and economic value, but this was not before a range of conflicting ideas of exchange and value had to be negotiated. Strings of shell beads known as wampum, for instance, which had complex spiritual and cultural values, became seen increasingly as a medium of currency under the impact of increasing trade. It has also been argued that the beaver itself, and its pelt, changed its meaning and value for Native Americans as it became exchangeable for all sorts of commodities, and the trappers become involved in a market economy.[27]

The Enlightenment and the Pacific

This process can be told as part of a larger self-critical European narrative of a fall from innocence and reciprocity into selfish mercantilism. If we now look beyond America at some British and French eighteenth-century travel accounts, we can see more clearly the influence of the ideas of the Enlightenment, and how accounts of other apparently simpler and more innocent societies, like those of the South Pacific, were used to critique the corruptions of European society. By the eighteenth century many of the larger voyages embodied the Enlightenment aim of the advancement of knowledge, as well as having the usual economic and political motives, so that while earlier accounts influenced Enlightenment thinking about society, later accounts were themselves already shaped by such values, which partly informed the expeditions. Since these voyages were explicitly scientific as well as imperial enterprises, objects were now being acquired specifically to expand and store knowledge of new species and ways of life. They were bound not for Wunderkammer, or cabinets of curiosities, but for museums, though sometimes the categories may have been blurred, as when Cook's surgeon William Monkhouse acquires the body of 'a child which was in a dried state' from his father, who 'readily bartered it for a trifle', or when Joseph Banks acquires a human head by the threat of a musket when his offer of 'a pair of old Drawers of very white linen' was rejected.[28] In his journal Cook complains that his crew, while visiting a Maori community, were giving 'the clothes from of [sic] their backs for the merest trifles, things that were neither usefull nor curious, such was the prevailing passion for curiosities'[29] – an interesting reversal of the trope of trifles and innocent natives. But just a page later Cook records that he himself obtained 'an Ear ornament made of glass very well form'd and polished'.[30] This must have been made from something traded earlier from one of Cook's ships, so perhaps interested him as a curiosity, an 'entangled object', or as something offering insight into Maori art or craftsmanship.

The accounts of the famous expeditions of James Cook and Louis-Antoine de Bougainville are infused by scientific curiosity, and the ships carried their full complement of scientists. Descriptions of what they found are interlaced with Enlightenment speculation about the nature of the peoples encountered and what this says about human nature in general. Cook, for instance, as a corrective to earlier derogatory characterisations of Australian Aborigines, asserts that

> they are far more happier than we Europeans; being wholly unacquainted not only with the superfluous but the necessary Conveniences so much sought after in Europe, they are happy in not knowing the use of them. They live in a Tranquillity which is not disturb'd by the Inequality of Condition: The Earth and sea of their own accord

furnishes them with all things necessary for life, they covet not Magnificent Houses, Houshold-stuff &cᵃ, they live in a warm and fine Climate and enjoy a very whole-some Air, so that they have very little need of Clothing and this they seem to be fully sencible of, for many to whome we gave Cloth &cᵃ to, left it carelessly upon the Sea beach and in the woods as a thing they had no manner of use for. In short they seem'd to set no Value upon any thing we gave them, nor would they ever part with any thing of their own for any one article we could offer them; this in my opinion argues that they think themselves provided with all the necessarys of Life and that they have no superfluities.[31]

Such texts allow us to see the interactions as involving a mixture of friendship and exploitation, reciprocity and theft, genuine communication and misrepresentation on both sides. As with earlier expeditions, the relation between the attitudinising and self-justification of the pub-lished accounts and the realities of the exchanges is hard to pin down, but we do get occasional glimpses. Bougainville's published account of a Tahitian girl, for instance, is couched in classical allusions and influenced by ideas of noble savages:

In spite of all our precautions, a young girl came on board, and placed herself upon the quarter-deck [. . .] The girl carelessly dropt a cloth, which covered her, and appeared to the eyes of all beholders, such as Venus shewed herself to the Phrygian shepherd, having, indeed, the celestial form of that goddess.[32]

What we find in his journal of the time, though, is rather different, and it occurs in the context of a material exchange:

A great deal of bartering with the Savages who do not seem to be surprised to see us [he was not aware of Samuel Wallis's earlier visit], and are skilful traders but display good faith. A young and fine-looking young girl came in one of the canoes, almost naked, who showed her vulva in exchange for small nails.[33]

He describes the Tahitians as 'great thieves, though honest in trade', and later, describing happy family groups, he muses:

They do not seem to rob each other, nothing can be locked in their huts [. . .] Being curious for novelties leads a few of them to steal, anyhow there are scoundrels every-where, and the chiefs tell us to fire on thieves.[34]

This sort of tentative on-the-spot musing is likely to become systematised in published accounts into portraits of idealised behaviour and societies, but a crosslight on such expeditions can be thrown by looking at a less well-known but significant voyage by Jean-François de Galaup, comte de Lapérouse, whose round-the-world expedition came to a tragic end with the loss of both ships, *Astrolabe* and *Boussole*, and their crews in the South Seas. The published account is based on his journals, which survived, but it also includes a statement outlining the purpose of the trip, explicitly laid down in the reprinted decree of the national assembly and the King's Memoir, and includes 'Operations relating to Astronomy, to Geography, to Navigation, to Natural Philosophy and to the different branches of Natural History'.[35] To this end there were ten scientists with their equipment on board, but what is of interest for my purposes can be found in the detailed inventory of goods taken on board that are set aside specifically 'for making presents and exchange'.[36] Here we find a fascinating array of objects. As well as raw materials – iron in bar, copper in sheets – there are tools in great numbers (2,000 hatchets, 700 hammers, a million 'pins assorted'), but also 600 looking glasses and 2,600 combs. Interesting too is the cheaper and gaudier end of the spectrum – 700 medals 'with the king's effigy', and 5,000 livres worth of 'fine jewellery, consisting of rows of beads, white, coloured, striped changeable and reflecting', 900 livres worth of 'toys and common jewellery consisting of magic lanterns, flint-glass bottles [. . .] whistles in bone and wood etc', and no less than 2,800 livres' worth of 'Tinsel, consisting of galloons, network in Spanish points, Brandenburghs etc in gold, in silver and in coloured foil'. There are 1,200 livres of 'silk ribands' and innumerable sorts of cloth. Altogether these items for presents and exchange are costed at 58,365 livres, more than three times the cost of supplying 'instruments of astronomy, navigation, natural philosophy etc and of books bought in France'.[37] This is for two ships on a long circumpolar trip, but such extensive provision for presents is still striking.

La Pérouse was aware that he was following partly in Cook's footsteps, and that his relations with the natives were affected by his previous contacts. In his one-day visit to Easter Island, for example, he explicitly comments in his *Journal* that he has a less negative view of the inhabitants because he is not as desperate for provisions as Cook was when he arrived there, and wants nothing from them. He is in fact remarkably indulgent of what he sees as their thieving ways, but is clear that if this were more than a brief visit he would have to assert his authority. As it is, the description of the inhabitants refusing nails but stealing everyone's hats is quite comic, and his tone is ironic. Returning to his men after a short trip inland he 'found almost everyone hatless and with no handkerchiefs'. When his own is snatched he accepts it as 'I did not want to claim the exclusive right to be protected by the sun since almost no one else now had a hat'.[38] While accepting that the local people have a different idea of what constitutes theft, he also tries to account for it in terms of a fall from innocence. No-one, he says,

> who has read the accounts of the most recent travellers could take the South Sea natives for savages; on the contrary, they have made great advances towards civilisation and I believe that they are as corrupted as they can be, given their circumstances. My opinion on this is not based on their various thefts, but on the way they went about it; the cheekiest scoundrels in Europe are less hypocritical than these islanders. All their displays of friendship were a pretence and their features did not display a single feeling that was genuine.[39]

The sign of corruption here is not greed but the ability to conceal, which is seen as a fall from innocence, but there is still the idea of an original unsullied state.

In general, we might note a change in these Enlightenment accounts from the overt claims for imperial and Christian benevolence found earlier, to implicit assumptions of the superiority, if not of civilisation, then of science, and while there is less masking of theft or the motives for trade by the language of giving, and ceremony than we find elsewhere, the accounts still overlook the significance of objects that are taken and of the power relations in taking them. This looks forward to the later claims made in the name of science for the expropriation and retention of ritual objects or parts of bodies by anthropologists and scientists now being challenged by indigenous peoples.

Mauss and the power relations of giving

In examining these accounts, I have tried to illustrate how the dynamics of the actual exchanges, in which the indigenous people are learning how to deal with the Europeans, are ignored in favour of essentialising summaries of primitive character, and how this idea of a wholly different form of society and economic behaviour became an attractive tool in political thinking. It was not until the work of Marcel Mauss, though, that there was a sustained attempt to understand the full implications of the puzzling forms of gift exchange found in some so-called primitive societies, and to generalise from them to the social and economic behaviour found in developed Western economies. In *The Gift: The Form and Reason for Exchange in Archaic Societies*, published in 1924, Mauss explained the operation of gift exchange in societies in the Pacific Northwest of America, Melanesia and Polynesia, and focused not on the gifts themselves, but on the structures of exchange and reciprocity which bind these societies in mutual obligations. A gift, he argued, always implies an obligation of some sort, so in one sense there is simply no such thing as a free gift. Rather, there is a 'prestation' a 'total social fact'. The importance of Mauss was not just that he offered a way of understanding a puzzling and alien system, and in anthropological terms fleshed out Émile Durkheim in demonstrating the importance of seeing individual actions as part of a social whole.[40] As a socialist he also wanted to show a working alternative to the market economy and to challenge narrow utilitarian and mercantile assumptions, by demonstrating that even market societies have always operated a gift economy in many spheres, and in fact need to do so. In other words, although he deals with exotic practices such as the kula ring and potlatch, it is the universality of the gift-giving relation which has the effect of undermining any binary contrasts of reciprocal communities versus self-interested traders. This clearly chimes with my argument here about the complexity of cross-cultural exchanges, and allows us to see that both sides are in varying degrees using and operating within the obligations of the gift.[41] In European societies this can be seen most clearly where the language of trade and aristocratic gentility intersect, and I want to take another look at an early account to show this in operation, and then to show the persistence of these ideas in later trade.

In many early European accounts the tension between the stance of benevolent giver and the reality of calculating trade was often couched in class terms, that is between the role of gentleman and trader, but this is a distinction that keeps breaking down as mercantile concerns become increasingly evident as the real drivers of the enterprise, and it is reflected in the way that exchanges are represented. A sense of the complexity of some of the negotiations can be seen in John Smith's account of trading with the Algonquian leader Powhatan in Virginia. The reliability of Smith's various accounts of his travels is open to serious doubt, and his encounters with Powhatan have been subjected to some rich analyses.[42] What I want to bring into relief is the way they typify many early accounts in the complicated combination of aristocratic and mercantile registers of language, in which trading exchanges are presented on both sides as acts of friendship sealed with gifts. In any society one of the real expressions of power and sovereignty is the ability to present yourself as the giver and not the taker. This is the act of the sovereign, which is why he or she is often compared to the sun, which endlessly gives and does not take. (It is also the prerogative of God, of course.)

The difference between a nobleman or gentleman and a tradesman was that the nobleman supposedly was not motivated by greed or profit, but by higher motives. Of course, the rich and powerful were supported by those below them, in the form of tributes and other extortions, but it was ideologically presented as all theirs to distribute to the lower orders. In John Smith's accounts, we can see clearly how the power to give or trade is being negotiated within a language of aristocratic values. Smith first describes how Captain Newport, the leader of the

English settlement, had tried to negotiate with Powhatan. The English were actually desperate for corn and food in general, so Newport tried a straight trade, to which, according to Smith, Powhatan responded:

> Captain Newport it is not agreeable with my greatnes, in this pedling manner to trade for trifles, and I esteeme you a great werowans [leader]. Therefore lay me down all your commodities togither, what I like I will take, and in recompence give you that I thinke fitting their value.[43]

So Powhatan here is taking the high ground, and insisting that as the sovereign leader he will choose what to give, as opposed to trade. Newport mistrusts this, but goes along with it and lays out his goods, only to get a very small amount of corn in return:

> Captain *Newport* thinking to out brave this Salvage in ostentation of greatnes, & so to bewitch him with his bounty, as to have what he listed, but so it chanced *Powhatan* having his desire, valued his corne at such a rate, as I thinke it better cheape in Spaine, for we had not 4. bushels for that we expected 20. hogsheads.[44]

This time, adopting another tactic, Smith,

> smothering his distast (to avoide the Salvages suspition) glaunced in the eies of Powhatan many Trifles, who fixed his humour upon a few blew beads; A long time he importunatly desired them, but Smith seemed so much the more to affect them, so that ere we departed, for a pound or two of blew beads, he brought over my king for 2 or 300 bushels of corn, yet parted good friends.[45]

At the end of another such exchange, Powhatan, 'remembering himselfe to congratulate their kindnesse, he gave his old shoes and mantle to Captain Newport'.[46] Are the old shoes an insult, or is it the gesture that is significant? Then again, if, improbably, the mantle was the beautiful object now displayed in the Ashmolean, then it is a very considerable gift.[47]

In other words, each side is trying to get what it can, but trying to gain the moral high ground through presenting what they are doing as generous, dictated by nobility not greed, using the language of gifts and benevolence, but for their own ends. Evidence that this tension between giving and trading was present not just in encounters with primitive gift-giving cultures, but was more widespread, is offered in Cynthia Klekar's incisive account of British trading voyages to China and Japan. Here we have Europeans encountering cultures with at least as much sense of their own cultural superiority as Europeans have of their own and she shows how the negotiations were focused not only on the exchange of gifts but on the status of these gifts. The challenge for the Europeans was to move the relation beyond the rhetoric of gift-giving and mutual obligation to that of trade, which was difficult in dealing with a Chinese emperor who saw all gifts as tribute from inferiors, and Klekar describes the problems of Lord George Macartney's embassy in Jehol, China, in 1793, in trying to establish the right relation. 'In the case of gifts – the emperor consistently referred to them as tribute while Macartney corrected the interpreter, identifying them as presents'.[48]

Klekar usefully challenges the opposition between mercantile and gift-giving economies in most studies of the gift and points out that European conceptions of trade implicitly, and sometimes explicitly, assume a basis of mutual trust against which the trade operates. This trust is established by diplomacy and gift-giving, and Klekar shows how because of this 'the language of the gift underwrites economic negotiations and relations of power and domination'.[49] She follows Derrida and Bourdieu in recognising the importance of misrecognition in the process of trade, and argues that it supports a collective fantasy of equal exchange.[50] Her study incisively illustrates how

> despite the capitalist nature of trade, its success depended on suppressing the differences between a restricted economy of profit and a general economy of the gift. Beyond the language of mutual civility, the actual portrayal of gifts attempts to present trade in the conceptual framework of civilized cooperation, as a means to establish friendly ties rather than competing markets.[51]

In reality, though, '[e]mbodied in the gifts that each culture considers valuable is an attempt to display through benevolence a cultural dominance'.[52]

This is precisely what I think we can see between Smith and Powhatan, and elsewhere in accounts of cross-cultural exchange, where at least one side, and sometimes both, while claiming the mutuality and equality of trade, actually wanted it to operate unequally to their advantage. The language of gifts and obligations informs the rhetoric and does the work of obscuring and allowing misrecognitions to exist. In showing a pattern in which the workings of self-interest and material realities are effaced by the rhetoric and stances of amity and benevolence, it is important not to use this approach reductively. This means trying to steer between a purely material approach in which economic self-interest is always the 'real' motivation, which would be to see all societies on the European model of *homo economicus*, and alternatively giving too much weight or credence to the various justifications and rationalisations involved in exchanges. Attention to the exchanges and objects themselves, and how value is created and sustained in each culture and then across the cultures in exchange, has, I hope, helped to show how complex these cross-cultural encounters often are.

The experience of being a traveller has often involved privation, fear, and powerlessness, especially in the many cases of forced travel and flight from danger or hunger that have been a constant in our history. In such cases, we might argue, the operations of power and material need or greed seem far from the ideological stances and obfuscations of the narratives I have been using, which portray Europeans in positions of material power, possessed of a sense of cultural superiority. But while such narratives may be untypical of most travellers' experiences, they are not so untypical of travel writing in general, dependent as it has largely been on literacy, and shaped as it has been by literary models and conventions. My aim has been to show that attention to what is being exchanged, and what this has meant to those on each side of the exchange, often reveals submerged ideological and cultural agendas, and power relations. In this sense all items of exchange are 'entangled objects', and though this chapter has focused on accounts of early contacts, it has also attempted to show that this approach is equally relevant to later travel writing.

Notes

1 Stephen Greenblatt, *Marvelous Possessions: The Wonder of the New World* (Oxford: Clarendon Press, 1991), 95.

2 Eric Cheyfitz, '*Tarzan of the Apes*: US Foreign Policy in the Twentieth Century', *American Literary History* 1.2 (1989): 352.

3 Thomas Churchyard, *A Discourse of the Queenes Maiesties Entertainement . . .* (London, 1578; STC 5226), sig. H4v.

4   Frank Hamilton Cushing, *Zuni: Selected Writings of Frank Hamilton Cushing*, ed. Jesse Green (Lincoln, NE: Nebraska University Press, 1979), 137.

5   Bronislaw Malinowski, *A Diary in the Strict Sense of the Term*, trans. Norbert Guterman (New York: Harcourt, Brace and World, 1967), 69.

6   Malinowski, *A Diary*, 69.

7   Simon Bischoff, ed., *Paul Bowles Photographs: 'How Could I Send a Picture into the Desert?'* (Zurich: Scalo Publishers, 1994), 227.

8   Igor Kopytoff, 'The Cultural Biography of Things: Commoditization as Process', in *The Social Life of Things: Commodities in Cultural Perspective*, ed. Arjun Appadurai (Cambridge: Cambridge University Press, 1986), 83. See also the other essays in Appadurai's collection.

9   Kopytoff, 'The Cultural Biography of Things', 17.

10 Peter Stallybrass, 'Marx's Coat', in *Border Fetishisms: Material Objects in Unstable Spaces*, ed. Patricia Spyer (London: Routledge, 1998), 183–207.

11 Nicholas Thomas, *Entangled Objects: Exchange, Material Culture, and Colonialism in the Pacific* (Cambridge, MA: Harvard University Press 1991), 4. See also Annette Weiner, *Inalienable Possessions: The Paradox of Keeping-While-Giving* (Berkeley, CA: University of California Press, 1992); Christopher L. Miller and George R. Hamell, 'A New Perspective on Indian–White Contact: Cultural Symbols and Colonial Trade', *Journal of American History* 73.2 (1986): 311–28; and Mary W. Helms, 'Essay on Objects: Interpretations of Distance Made Tangible', in *Implicit Understandings*, ed. Stuart B. Schwartz (Cambridge: Cambridge University Press, 1994), 355–76.

12 Greenblatt, *Marvelous Possessions*, 110.

13 Christopher Columbus, *The Journal of Christopher Columbus (During his First Voyage, 1492–93) and documents relating the voyages of John Cabot and Gaspar Corte Real*, translated with notes and an introduction by Clements R. Markham (London: Hakluyt Society, 1893), 37. The reliability of all accounts of these encounters is dubious, in that they are second-hand summaries. Peter Hulme describes what we have as 'a transcription of an abstract of a copy of a lost original'. *Colonial Encounters: Europe and the Native Caribbean, 1492–1797* (London: Routledge, 1986), 17. Amongst a wealth of criticism, see Margarita Zamora, *Reading Columbus* (Berkeley, CA: University of California Press, 1993), and Stephen Greenblatt, ed., *New World Encounters* (Berkeley, CA: University of California Press, 1993).

14 Columbus, *Journal*, 37.

15 Columbus, *Journal*, 46. The original is 'referay el pagamento'. The Las Casas version has 'regatear sobre los precios y paga'.

16 Columbus, *Journal*, 127.

17 Quoted in Urs Bitterli, *Cultures in Conflict: Encounters Between European and Non-European Cultures, 1492–1800* (Stanford, CA: Stanford University Press, 1986), 75.

18 Karl Marx, *Capital: A Critique of Political Economy*, vol. 1, trans. Ben Fowkes (1867; repr. London: Penguin, 1990), 1:229.

19 On the history of the fetish, William Pietz has produced a string of remarkable essays. See especially 'The Problem of the Fetish. I', *Res: Anthropology and Aesthetics* 9.1 (1985): 5–17; 'The Problem of the Fetish, II: The Origin of the Fetish', *Res: Anthropology and Aesthetics* 13.1 (1987): 23–45; 'The Problem of the Fetish, IIIa: Bosman's Guinea and the Enlightenment Theory of Fetishism', *Res: Anthropology and Aesthetics* 16.1 (1988): 105–24; 'The Fetish of Civilisation: Sacrificial Blood and Monetary Debt', in *Colonial Subjects: Essays on the Practical History of Anthropology*, eds. Peter Pels and Oscar Salemink (Ann Arbor, MI: Michigan University Press, 1999), 53–81; 'Death of the Deodand: Accursed Objects and the Money Value of Human Life', *Res: Anthropology and Aesthetics* 31.1 (1993): 97–108. See also my discussion in *Matter, Magic, and Spirit: Representing Indian and African American Belief* (Philadelphia, PA: University of Pennsylvania Press, 2007), 10–21.

20 Columbus, *Journal*, 119.

21 Elvira Vilches, 'Columbus's Gift: Representations of Grace and Wealth and the Enterprise of the Indies', *MLN* 119.2 (2004): 221.

22 Vilches, 'Columbus's Gift', 215.

23 Vilches, 'Columbus's Gift', 212.

24 Hulme, *Colonial Encounters*, 32–40.

25 Walter Raleigh, *The Discovery of the Large, Rich, and Beautiful Empire of Guiana, with a relation of the great and golden city of Manoa (which the Spaniards call El Dorado) of 1596*, ed. Robert H. Schomburgk (London: Hakluyt Society, 1848). See also Mary C. Fuller, *Voyages in Print: English Travel to America, 1576–1624* (Cambridge: Cambridge University Press, 1995).

26 Philip L. Barbour, ed., *The Jamestown Voyages Under the First Charter, 1606–1609* (London: Cambridge University Press, for the Hakluyt Society, 1969), 2:393–4.

27 For an overview of the many discussions of the nature of the exchanges involved in the fur trade, including the role of wampum, see my *Indian Giving: Economies of Power in Indian-White Exchanges* (Amherst, MA: Massachusetts University Press, 2000).

28 Nicholas Thomas, *Cook: The Extraordinary Voyages of James Cook* (New York: Walker and Company, 2003), 98, 108.

29 J.C. Beaglehole, ed., *The Journals of Captain James Cook on his Voyages of Discovery: Volume II, The Voyage of the Resolution and Adventure, 1772–1775* (Cambridge: Cambridge University Press, 1961), 171.

30 Beaglehole, *Journals of James Cook*, 172.

31 J.C. Beaglehole, ed., *The Journals of Captain Cook on His Voyages of Discovery, Volume I, The Voyage of the Endeavour, 1768–1771* (Cambridge: Cambridge University Press for the Hakluyt Society, 1955), 399. For an excellent account of Cook, which also discusses this passage, see Pauline T. Strong, 'Fathoming the Primitive: Australian Aborigines in Four Explorers' Journals, 1697–1845', *Ethnohistory* 3.2 (1986): 175–94. Thomas also points out that this sort of generalisation is more typical of Banks than Cook, who is more empirical. Thomas, *Cook*, 129.

32 Louis-Antoine de Bougainville, *Voyage Round the World Performed by Order of his most Christian Majesty in the Years 1766, 1767, 1768, 1769* (London, 1772), 218–19.

33 Louis-Antoine de Bougainville, *The Pacific Journal of Louis-Antoine de Bougainville, 1767–1768*, trans. and ed. John Dunmore (London: The Hakluyt Society, 2002), 60.

34 Bougainville, *Pacific Journal*, 64, 67. For some context on the interaction of travel accounts and enlightenment thinking, see Judith Still, *Enlightenment Hospitality: Cannibals, Harems and Adoption* (University of Oxford: Voltaire Foundation, 2011), 50–1. See also John Patrick Greene, 'French Encounters with Material Culture of the South Pacific', *Eighteenth-Century Life* 26.3 (2002): 225–45. Greene makes the point that the absence of clear communication leads to a simplifying of what Europeans think 'natives' want, or how they value things. The value of an article for them may be what they can trade it for – not to Europeans but to neighbours, because they are also within a trade network if they are part of a string of islands, for instance.

35 J.F.G. de la Pérouse, *A Voyage Round the World, in the Years 1785, 1786, 1787, and 1788*, ed. M.L.A. Milet-Mureau (London: 1798), 1:59–63, 95–104.

36 La Pérouse, *A Voyage Round the World*, 1:315.

37 La Pérouse, *A Voyage Round the World*, 1:315–20.

38 J.F.G. de la Pérouse, *The Journal of Jean-François de Galaup de la Pérouse, 1758–1788*, trans. and ed. John Dunmore (London: The Hakluyt Society, 1994), 1:65.

39 La Pérouse, *Journal*, 1:67.

40 Durkheim elaborated his concept of 'social fact' in *The Rules of Sociological Method*, tr. W.D. Halls, ed. Steven Lukes (1895; repr. Houndmills: Palgrave Macmillan, 2013).

41 Marcel Mauss, *The Gift: The Form and Reason for Exchange in Archaic Societies*, trans. Ian Cunnison (1924; repr. London: Routledge, 2002). See also Christopher Gregory, *Gifts and Commodities* (London: Academic Press, 1982); Maurice Godelier, *The Enigma of the Gift*, trans. Nora Scott (Chicago, IL: Chicago University Press, 1999); Caroline Humphrey and Stephen Hugh-Jones, eds., *Barter, Exchange and Value: An Anthropological Approach* (Cambridge: Cambridge University Press, 1992) and Gadi Algazi, ed., *Negotiating the Gift: Pre-Modern Figurations of Exchange* (Göttingen: Vandenhoeck & Ruprecht, 2003). More broadly, see David Graeber, *Toward an Anthropological Theory of Value: The False Coin of Our Own Dreams* (New York: Palgrave, 2001).

42 See Eric Cheyfitz, *The Poetics of Imperialism: Translation and Colonization from* The Tempest *to* Tarzan (Philadelphia, PA: University of Philadelphia Press, 1997); William Boelhower, 'Mapping the Gift Path: Exchange and Rivalry in John Smith's "A True Relation"', *American Literary History* 15.4 (2003): 655–82; and Martin H. Quitt, 'Trade and Acculturation at Jamestown, 1607–1609: The Limits of Understanding', *William and Mary Quarterly* 52.2 (1995): 227–58.

43 Barbour, *Jamestown Voyages*, 2:392.

44 Barbour, *Jamestown Voyages*, 2:392.

45 Barbour, *Jamestown Voyages*, 2:392.

46 Barbour, *Jamestown Voyages*, 2:414.

47 See Christian Feest, 'The Collecting of American Indian Artifacts in Europe, 1493–1750', in *America in European Consciousness, 1493–1750*, ed. Karen Ordahl Kupperman (Chapel Hill, NC: University of North Carolina Press, 1995).

48 Cynthia Klekar, '"Prisoners in Silken Bonds": Obligation, Trade, and Diplomacy in English Voyages to Japan and China', *Journal for Early Modern Cultural Studies* 6.1 (2006): 100.

49 Klekar, '"Prisoners in Silken Bonds"', 88.

50 Derrida's influential essay 'From Restricted to General Economy: A Hegelianism without Reserve', *Writing and Difference*, trans. Alan Bass (1967; repr. London: Routledge, 2003) took up the implications of George Bataille's work on sacrifice and excess, best represented in his *Visions of Excess: Selected Writings, 1927–1939* (Minneapolis, MN: University of Minnesota Press, 1985). For the development of Derrida's thinking see his *Given Time: Counterfeit Money*, trans. Peggy Kamuf (1991; repr. Chicago, IL: University of Chicago Press, 1992), and *The Gift of Death*, trans. David Wills (1992; repr. Chicago, IL: University of Chicago Press, 1995). For a very useful account of Bourdieu's thinking on the gift, see Ilana F. Silber, 'Bourdieu's Gift to Gift Theory: An Unacknowledged Trajectory', *Sociological Theory* 27.2 (2009): 173–90.

51 Klekar, '"Prisoners in Silken Bonds"', 91.

52 Klekar, '"Prisoners in Silken Bonds"', 91, 103.

21

BETWEEN LANGUAGES

Michael Cronin

A salient feature of modernity is the major growth in travel and the movement of people around the globe. One of the world's most important items of trade is tourism.[1] Globalisation emerged from the late 1980s onwards as a significant focus of academic and popular interest as commentators examined the impact of the accelerated circulation of goods, signs and people on the self-reflexivity and the social, economic and cultural praxis of human beings. In appraisals of the evolution of modernity, theories of travel have been increasingly to the fore.[2] These movements, both individual and collective, are taking place between speaking subjects on a planet that is currently host to around 7,000 languages.[3] Critical literature on travel writing, has, however, until very recently largely ignored this fundamental dimension to travel, namely the relationship of travellers to other languages and how this relationship has affected, in turn, their relationship to their mother tongue. The absence of reflection on language difference in travel writing criticism is all the more puzzling in that one of the more common experiences of travellers is to find themselves literally at a loss for words or to experience the humiliations or frustrations of language incomprehension or inadequacy. A failure to consider questions of language and translation can lead to both a misrepresentation of what is purportedly experienced by the writer and a neglect of a crucial element in determining how a travel narrative is to be constructed. In considering the question of language difference in travel narratives, key questions revolve around the myth of language transparency, how language relates to power and the notion of commensurability or the possibility of representation on the basis of universals.

Travel in a world of languages is beset by difficulty. There are the multiple difficulties of translation: the ever-present possibility of mistranslation; the loss of meaning; the pitfalls of approximation; the fraught political economy of translation in the Eurocentric capture of other peoples and places through the use of former colonial languages; the tendentious myth of transparent, non-refractory translation. When considering travellers moving between languages we can view the traveller as a translator just as we might on the other hand view the translator as traveller, the translation an 'account' of the journey from one culture and language to another. Travellers in many instances, like translators, find themselves straddling borderlines between languages and cultures.

A useful framework for assessing the consequences of language difference in travel writing is Roman Jakobson's tripartite division of the operations of translation. Intralingual translation or translation within a language is the interpretation of verbal signs by means of other signs belonging to the same language. Interlingual translation or translation between languages is the interpretation of verbal signs by means of verbal signs from another language. Lastly, intersemiotic translation or translation into or from something other than language is the interpretation of verbal signs by means of signs belonging to non-verbal sign systems.[4]

Intralingual travel

In the case of intralingual travel, the focus is on differences within a language shared by travellers with their travellees. They may be speaking the same language, but are they saying the same thing? What appears in the beginning to be a liberation from the perceived burden of language difference soon turns out to be much more problematic as the return of the translation repressed appears in the guise of fraught negotiations with the use of language in different cultural contexts. Accent variety, variations in lexical usage, different modes of intentionality, the large range of sublanguages of any language of territorial extension, and code switching with other minoritised languages in different settings, bring to the fore the unsettling complexity of a common language whose commonality the traveller can no longer take for granted. One consequence of the exploration of the knotted detail of intralingual detail is that it gives the lie to a commonplace rhetoric of exhaustion with respect to travel. Intralingual travel writing makes manifest not the restricted repetitiveness of travel encounters but the potentially infinite series of finer discriminations as travellers track or experience the social, regional, national and international metamorphoses of the mother tongue.

Interlingual travel

Interlingual travel involves travellers finding themselves in another language and culture where they have a greater or lesser knowledge of the language. In spite of the fact that interlingual travel is a common feature of many travel texts, it is notable that the fact of language difference or translation can be concealed to create an illusion of language transparency. Questions that can be asked in investigating interlingual travel concern how travellers situate themselves with respect to language difference. Do they make this difference manifest? Do they say anything about their levels of competence? Do they hide or reveal the presence of translators or mediators? What are the social, political and cultural consequences of language difference in the strategies of narrative representation of self and other? In interlingual travel, there is a recurring problematic around the desire to understand the world through language and the limits of travellers' ability to learn, speak or understand other languages. Lexical exoticism (the insertion of foreign words, translated or untranslated into the text) or the invocation of translation as intertextual presence in the form of phrase books, dictionaries and foreign-language tourist literature are strategies for highlighting the interlingual dimension to travel. If travel and language difference are predicated (at least potentially) on relationship and reciprocity, then gender is a recurrent feature of interlingual travel with notions of desire and representation bound up with the gendering of languages or the speakers of those languages. At a basic level, studies of interlingual travel can be divided along the diachronic and synchronic axes.

Synchronic analyses are to be found in Michael Cronin, *Across the Lines: Travel, Language and Translation* (2000), Loredana Polezzi, *Translating Travel: Contemporary Italian Travel Writing in English Translation* (2001) and Charles Forsdick, *Travel in Twentieth-Century French and Francophone Cultures* (2005) which are all studies that largely focus on interlingual travelling in twentieth-century settings.[5] A recurrent concern in all three of these works is the manner in which notions of language difference feed into narrative strategy and, in the case of Polezzi, how ideas of Italian identity are shaped by the reception of different travel narratives in translation. In other words, the aim is not only to look at the travel writer between languages but to look at the fortunes of the travel accounts themselves between languages. One consequence of this perspective is to argue that travel writing between languages or travel writing in translation can occupy an important place in the shaping of emerging national and cultural identities. Jacobus Naude, for example, examines the formative role of travel accounts written in a language that had a peripheral status in a specific colonial setting, while Jane Conroy and Eoin Burke have investigated how the translation of travel accounts from foreign languages can be used to mobilise support or sympathy for a particular ethnic grouping.[6]

A diachronic perspective on interlingual travelling is provided by Carmine G. Di Biase's edited collection, *Travel and Translation in the Early Modern Period* (2006), where the translation practices and travel encounters with language difference of, among others, Luther, Erasmus and Milton are investigated and set in the broader context of the centrality of language alterity and translation to the transformative world views of the early modern period.[7] One country that features prominently in this period and later is Italy. Mirella Agorni in *Translating Italy for the Eighteenth Century: British Women, Translation and Travel Writing (1739–1797)*, which was published in 2002, and Paola Daniela Smecca in *Representational Tactics in Travel Writing and Translation* (2005), mainly focus on how translation functions with travel writing to elaborate particular constructions of Italian and Sicilian life and identities.[8] This functionality is present at two levels. Firstly, the way that language difference is selectively presented in travel accounts to reinforce pre-existing patterns or cultural stereotypes, and secondly, the manner in which the translations of the travel accounts themselves were instrumentalised for precise cultural or political purposes by travellers who also operated as language brokers or translators.

Intersemiotic travel

The more countries travellers visit, the fewer of the languages they are likely to know. Intersemiotic travel covers situations where the traveller has no knowledge of the foreign language. The absence of a shared or an understood language can be perceived in two radically different ways. On the one hand, it can be seen as deeply incapacitating – the traveller adrift in a world of impenetrable and/or threatening signs. On the other, the release from language meaning can usher in a kind of sensory rebirth where all the other forms of communication – taste, smell, sight, (phonic) sound, touch (see Part III of the present volume) – which are habitually overshadowed by the semantic hegemony of meaningful speech are now brought to the fore. These other forms of communication between humans take on a renewed significance for the traveller. It is arguable that the premium placed on the visual, which is a feature of different forms of travel writing, is bound up with the alternative communication strategies of intersemiotic travel. Of course, where there is no common language, the travel writers can have an interpreter to translate for them into a language that they understand. In many instances, indeed, the indigenous status of the interpreter as informant would seem to add credibility to the travel account. The question that needs to be asked of these language brokers or mediators is: to what extent are their views representative of the communities whose language they speak? What is the particular social standing of these interpreters in their societies? Does familiarity with foreign, often dominant or former imperial languages tell us something about the positioning of the interpreters in networks of power, empire or economic privilege? The history of empire is repeatedly characterised by a nervousness around the potential for translators/interpreters to function as double agents.[9] The emergence of the guidebook can be seen at one level as the attempt to create an autonomous, monolingual space where the traveller is no longer dependent on the linguistic ministrations of doubtful others.[10] These questions and topics are explored at length in Paula G. Rubel and Abraham Rosman, *Translating Cultures: Perspectives on Translation and Anthropology* (2003), and in the contributions, notably by James St. André and Elena Filonova, to the special issue of *The Translator* edited by Loredana Polezzi and dedicated to the theme of 'Translation, Travel, Migration' (2006).[11] Power differentials in language brokerage, whether disguised or made visible, are an enduring feature of travel writing from the ethnographer on the road to the travelogue camera crew on location.

Endotic travel and language

In any discussion of travel writing and language difference, it is useful to pay heed to the distinction set up by the French travel theorist Jean-Didier Urbain between exotic travel and endotic travel.[12] Exotic travel is defined as the more conventional mode of thinking about travel where travel is seen to involve leaving the prosaic world of the everyday for a distant place, even if the notion of 'distance' can vary through time. Exotic travel implies leaving familiar surroundings for a place which is generally situated at some remove from the routine world of the traveller. From the perspective of macro-modernity, where far becomes ever nearer through improvements in forms of transportation, it becomes all the more commonplace to equate travel with going far. Endotic travel, on the other hand, is an exercise in staying close by, not leaving the familiar and travelling interstitially through a world we thought we knew. Michael Cronin, for his part, makes a distinction between 'horizontal travel' and 'vertical travel'.[13] Horizontal travel involves the linear passage from place to place and corresponds more closely to what is normally thought of as travel. The term 'horizontal travel' is preferred by Cronin as 'exotic' is heavily loaded with regard to both historical usage and perceived choice of destination. 'Vertical travel', on the other hand, involves temporary dwelling in a particular place for a period of time where travellers begin to explore their surroundings in great detail. The difference between endotic travel and vertical travel is that whereas endotic travel implies exploration of a familiar world or landscape, 'vertical travel' can potentially occur anywhere that the traveller remains stationary for prolonged periods of time.

It is in the context of the endotic/vertical that it is possible to situate two forms of travelling practice that involve language difference. The first is drawn from the New Nature Writing where travelling through local places involves a close attention to the intense investment of place by dialectical varieties of a dominant language or traces of languages of invasion, conquest or migration. A notable example is Robert Macfarlane's *Landmarks* (2015) where he argues that his work is 'a book about the power of language − strong style, single word − to shape our sense of place'.[14] He sets about compiling a 'Counter-Desecration Phrasebook' with glossaries grouped under the headings of Flatlands, Uplands, Waterlands, Coastlands, Underlands, Northlands, Edgelands, Earthlands, Woodlands and a glossary left blank for the reader's own use. These glossaries in their coverage of the British landscape draw on 'Norn and Old English, Anglo-Romani, Cornish, Welsh, Irish, Gaelic, the Orcadian, Shetlandic and Doric dialects of Scots, and numerous regional versions of English, through to the last vestiges of living Norman still spoken on the Channel Islands' (1). Each glossary follows a discussion of a nature writer who has travelled through a particular area and where explicitness of naming is synonymous with accuracy of description. Nan Shepherd, Roger Deakin, John Alex Baker, Richard Skelton, Richard Jeffries, Jacquetta Hawkes, John Muir and Barry Lopez are among the writers discussed, their travels through landscape a pilgrimage of poetically precise perception.

The second form of endotic travelling practice informed by language experience is inspired by the multilingual cities of late modernity, which are increasingly described as sites of linguistic 'superdiversity'.[15] Sherry Simon in *Translating Montreal: Episodes in the Life of a Divided City* (2006) and *Cities in Translation: Intersections of Language and Memory* (2011) tracks the evidence of language difference both diachronically and synchronically in a variety of urban sites from Kolkata to Barcelona.[16] What is repeatedly emphasised in both studies is the manner in which practices of travel through the city become the primary mode of revealing the diverse and frequently contested space of language difference. How one travels, who travels, and where one comes from and goes to in the city become an integral part of the narratives of urban life, the travel stories of migration, displacement and settlement.

In a multilingual world, therefore, language and language difference are an inevitable feature of travel. How travellers deal with the fact of languages other than their own, or radically distinct varieties of their own language, has clear implications for their capacity to engage with or interpret the realities they encounter. From the point of view of language difference, there are two clear impacts. The representational impact relates to the ability of the travel writer to represent in the language of the writer the thoughts, values and experiences of others who do not speak his or her language. Pronouncements about the lives and habitats of others, however strong or tenuous the truth claims, do suppose an access to knowing that must, however, take account of a multilingual world. The instrumental impact relates to the translation pressures generated by travel itself on language communities. In other words, if the travel writers are the practitioners of a major world language, to what extent are these travellers complicit in global linguicide that may see up to 90 per cent of the more than 7,000 languages in the world disappear by the end of the century?[17] This raises the question of what it means to travel linguistically in a minor key. In other words, are there ways in which minor-language travelling practices differ from major-language travelling practices? Does the dominant narrative language of the travel account impinge on the sensitivity of the travel writer to particular aspects of culture and identity?[18] In order to explore these questions and others arising from the presence of language difference in travel writing, I want to consider two travel accounts, both published in the same year, 1977: one, Patrick Leigh Fermor's *A Time of Gifts: On Foot to Constantinople – From the Hook of Holland to the Middle Danube*, in a major language; the other, Pádraig Ó Fiannachta's *Ó Mháigh go Fásach* [From Plain to Desert], in a minor language, Irish Gaelic.[19]

Minority

Ó Fiannachta's account covers a three-week journey from Nairobi to the Turkana district in north-west Kenya. As a native speaker of Irish from the south-west of Ireland, Professor of Irish in St Patrick's College, Maynooth and the person most closely identified with the translation of the Catholic bible into modern Irish, it is less than surprising that language should loom large in his travels. Before starting on his journey, he describes his preliminary engagement with *Teach Yourself Swahili* but soon admits that 'bhíos an-mhíshasta leis an salacharáil bheag Swahili a bhí foghlamtha agam' [I was very unhappy with the little smattering of Swahili that I learnt] (6). He picks up a few phrases from Boniface, a Kenyan student, in the college, but this belated apprenticeship serves only to underline the limits to language growth. In a sense, Ó Fiannachta's dilemma is a cogent illustration from the point of view of language difference of what might be termed temporal asymmetry in travel. That is to say, there is often a striking difference between the time required to acquire even a passable mastery of a foreign language and the time that is generally given over to the travel itself (in this case, three weeks) or indeed the preparations for it. The language deficit in Ó Fiannachta's case is all the more palpable in that he frames it in terms of colonial and post-colonial relationships. In the pre-travel narrative he describes a conversation with an ex-Irish army officer, Colonel O'Neill, who is organising a visit by Scots Gaelic poets and musicians to Ireland. O'Neill had served as part of the UN peacekeeping force in the Belgian Congo in the early 1960s and he describes a scene where he had to give a speech. O'Neill asked that his speech be translated into Swahili and proceeded to address the mixed gathering of Congolese and Belgians in Swahili and Irish. The Congolese greeted the speech in Swahili with enthusiasm which was not matched by a warm reception on the part of the Belgian colonial officials. In recounting this story, Ó Fiannachta clearly situates the practice of language in a colonial history of language encounter, a history that is all the more fraught in that he spends most of his time with Irish Catholic missionaries. In the colonial histories of Africa, missionaries often occupied a dual role of being, in certain instances, fluent in and supportive of the retention of local languages and, in others, complicit in forced assimilation to the dominant imperial languages.[20]

Given the dual sensitivities around minoritised language use and former colonial subjection, it is notable that throughout the account there is the repeated use of lexical exoticism. Words and phrases in different Kenyan languages, Swahili, Turkana, Kikuyu, are scattered throughout the text. Ó Fiannachta spends much of his time with two Irish missionaries, Caoimhín and Pádraig, who are fluent in Turkana and Swahili, respectively. When Ó Fiannachta is in the Turkana district, he writes a poem in English for a religious service which is then translated into Turkana, and he recites the poem in both languages at the service. If temporal asymmetry is a problem ghosting language acquisition it might also be said to extend to the tension between travel and dwelling in the travel narrative. While in Kenya, Ó Fiannachta is eager to involve himself in the missionary activities of his colleagues from religious instruction in the schools to officiating at religious services. He seeks to dwell among the local people but his limited language competence in Swahili and Turkana means that from giving sermons to hearing confessions he is constantly thrown back on English as a lingua franca. He is unavoidably associated with a language whose status or influence he finds problematic. In his forays into a simulacrum of a more permanent form of settlement, language difference constantly reminds him of his essentially mobile or transient presence.

Ó Mháigh go Fásach problematises conventional notions of language distribution – the ready association between language and territory – by showing how travel encounters bear testimony to the travels of languages themselves. On more than one occasion, he meets fellow missionaries who are Irish speakers and much is made of these shared moments around a common language outside of Ireland. In a mission station in Turkana, Ó Fiannachta celebrates a sung mass in Irish for two Irish expatriates. This sense of a diasporic language presence for the minority language extends to other branches of the Celtic family. In Thika outside Nairobi he meets a nurse from Blaenau Ffestiniog (Ó Fiannachta, tellingly, leaves the name untranslated) in Wales, a native speaker of Welsh. Ó Fiannachta, who had lived in Wales for a number of years and had earlier written an account of Irish-Welsh links, *An Chomharsa Choimhthíoch* [The Foreign Neighbour] (1957), relishes the opportunity to speak the language and the end of the evening is spent in the company of others singing Welsh songs whose titles are left untranslated.[21] Thus, one function of travel narratives is often to destabilise the geographical fixity of language and demonstrate that languages like their speakers undertake journeys and can often be present in the most unlikely settings. Travel, in this respect, is not just the prerogative of major languages or lingua francas.

Language difference, the presence of language otherness, in colonial or former colonial settings, potentially raises for the travel writer the question of language rights or, more broadly, cultural rights. Ó Fiannachta notes that in the Turkana district the medium of instruction in the state schools was to be English, not Turkana. Earlier in his account, he meets a group of young native clerical students in Kaiboi, in the Rift Valley. At the heart of the discussion is 'ceist an dá chultúr' [the two cultures question] (31). The debate centres on the respective merits of western, Christian culture and native cultures and to what extent certain practices such as polygamy or spitting as a sign of respect or friendship should be tolerated or repressed. Ó Fiannachta is not immune to the cultural condescension he castigates elsewhere and at one point when he sees a group of young Turkana warriors readying themselves for battle he feels that he is witnessing a scene straight from the ancient Irish epic, the *Táin Bó Cuailnge*. He is constantly reminded by those he meets, however, that indigenous cultures and languages are under intense pressure. One Ugandan nurse, Betty, tells him that she saw the 'seanchóras á smiotadh ós cómhair a súl' [the old system shattered before her eyes] (33). The fate of cultures and the fate of languages are indissociable for the traveller. As he prepares to return to Ireland he wonders about the purpose or the meaningfulness of much of the missionary activity in Africa, an activity which has shadowed travel writing at various stages in its evolution. His conclusion points forward to contemporary concerns in the emerging discipline of ecolinguistics which Aran Stibbe has defined as 'critiquing forms of language that contribute to ecological destruction, and aiding in the search for new forms of language that inspire people to protect the natural world'.[22] Ó Fiannachta wonders whether the Irish missionaries will be able to come up with 'córas éigin nua, córas a bheidh préamhaithe in ithir thirim an fhásaigh féin, córas nach mbeidh Béarla briste mar shlat tómhais ar a fheabhas, ach tuiscint ar an timpeallacht agus comhar an fhásaigh mar bhlátha ar a chraobh' [some new system, a system which is located in the dry land of the desert, a system whose excellence is not judged by broken English but whose flowering would be seen in an understanding of the environment and of the community of the desert] (92). Here the travel through language difference in a minority language becomes not surprisingly the reaffirmation of the importance of language difference even if the journey itself points up the recurring tension between aspiration, competence and understanding in the fractured worlds of language contact.

Majority

It is precisely the absence of linguistic understanding that appears, at first, to attract the young Patrick Leigh Fermor to a life on the road. Among the charms of travel were the capacity to 'gaze at things with a changed eye and listen to new tongues that were untainted by a single familiar word' (18). His initial passage through the Low Countries does indeed seem to deliver on this promise. In a tavern he orders 'by signs' (28) and in Gorinchem a police constable shows him 'without a word' (32) to a cell where he finds accommodation for the night. In summing up his experience of travelling through the Netherlands, he confesses that '[a]lthough we were reciprocally tongue-tied' (38), the contact that he had with the Dutch led to enduring feelings of affection and admiration. Leigh Fermor's ignorance of Dutch brings him into the realm of intersemiotic travel and it is notable that one effect is to heighten the importance of the visual as a channel of communication for the travel writer. He speaks of the 'three-dimensional Holland' (35) that had been springing up all around him ever since he had arrived in Rotterdam. For the English traveller, 'a hundred mornings and afternoons in museums and picture galleries and country houses' (35) had provided a ready template for viewing Dutch cities and landscape. However, it is arguable that what Leigh Fermor describes as the gratifying compliance of the Dutch landscape to initial expectation is less to do with the pump priming of an artistic education and more to do with the necessary languages of interpretation in the absence of the shared medium of spoken language. That is to say, as Leigh Fermor has no Dutch to speak of, he must draw on a different frame of understanding to capture what he is experiencing on his journey. Unable to understand what is being said, he can try to make sense of what he sees in another way, namely through seeing itself.

That there is a pre-existing visual grammar to capture the nuances of Dutch architecture and landscape is convenient but not adequate to explain the pre-eminence of the visual that results from the intersemiotic framing of the travel. Leigh Fermor notes further on in his account that 'the link between journeys and painting, especially this sort of journey, is very close' (175). The tutelary figure he mentions as he moves through Dutch-speaking lands is the Flemish painter, Peter Breughel. Breughel, as the metonymic reminder of the Low Countries experience, points to that reaching out in travel writing for forms of communication or analysis that might ordinarily be conveyed through shared language but that seek other avenues of expression (even if paradoxically, the 'painting' in the travel narrative is always, ultimately, a matter of words).

When Leigh Fermor crosses the border from Holland into Germany, readers know they are linguistically in a different territory because, very quickly, German words and phrases, lines from German drinking songs, begin to find their way into the narrative. It is clear that for the writer one is no longer in a land where speech is 'untainted by a single familiar word'. Leigh Fermor soon feels compelled to explain parenthetically this sudden change in linguistic key:

> (I still remembered a few German phrases I had picked up on winter holidays in Switzerland, so I was never as completely tongue-tied in Germany as I had been in Holland. As I spoke nothing but German during the coming months, these remnants blossomed, quite fast, into an ungrammatical fluency, and it is almost impossible to strike, at any given moment in these pages, the exact degree of my dwindling inarticulacy.)
>
> *(45)*

Though he continues to refer to his shortcomings in German, the extent of reported speech, the transcription of verses of drinking songs and mottoes on tavern walls, and his learned recitation of passages from the German translation of Shakespeare display an increasing ease with the language which clearly situates the German and Austrian section of the journey in the interlingual. Though the concern with visual representation remains, there is in contrast to the Dutch passages a vivid evocation of people encountered, from the young women in Stuttgart to the garrulous widow of Chief-Postmaster Hübner in Mitter Arnsdorf, Austria. History, literature and politics begin to feed their way into the account. Indeed, as Leigh Fermor becomes more and more immersed in the German-speaking world, the focus gradually begins to shift from the interlingual to the intralingual, his journey becoming as much a form of travelling within a language as an odyssey between languages. In Cologne, he hits upon the idea of travelling up the Rhine in a barge, and in a bar he befriends two bargees, Peter and Uli. He is urged to address them using the informal *du* rather than the formal *Sie*, a recurring linguistic leitmotif on his trip. But another lesson awaits him in the form of initiation into the varieties of German itself, the bargees' 'Low German speech, even sober, would have been blurred beyond the most expert linguist's grasp' (53). As he moves further south, he claims that the habit of 'grasping and speaking German' had been 'outpaced by another change of accent and idiom' (81). By the time he gets to Munich, the 'accent had changed again' and he begins to detail the changes:

> Many words were docked of their final consonants; Bursch – 'a chap' – for instance, became 'bua'; 'A' was rolled over into 'O', 'Ö' became 'E', and every O and U seemed to have a final A appended, turning it into a disyllable.
>
> *(119)*

Even if Bavarian dialect continues to present difficulties for the traveller, he begins to view their language not from the outside in but the inside out. In one passage, he speaks of traditional Bavarian antipathy to the Prussians. A frequent butt of humorous stories was:

> a hypothetical Prussian visitor to the province. Disciplined, blinkered, pig-headed and sharp-spoken, with thin vowels and stripped consonants – every 'sch' turning into 's' and every hard 'g' into 'y' – this ridiculous figure was an unfailing prey for the easy-going but shrewd Bavarians.
>
> *(136)*

The shift to the intralingual here is almost as if Leigh Fermor were situating himself in terms of language difference on the terrain of the endotic rather than the exotic, as if he were a language native of the place rather than a foreign-language observer. The language of the other shifts from being instrumental, a means of eliciting help or information, to evaluative, a way of revealing or exposing underlying tensions in the host society.

In a sense, right from the outset, *A Time of Gifts* is caught up in the fallout of language difference. Leigh Fermor in his 'Introductory Letter to Xan Fielding' notes that it was language that was responsible for his being sent to Crete to participate in guerrilla activities against the German occupiers of the island, 'unexpectedly in a modern war, it was the obsolete choice of Greek at school which had really deposited us on the limestone' (1). It was study of the classical languages that later proves to be a bond between Leigh Fermor and a captured German general. Leigh Fermor completes a poem by Horace the general begins to recite when the dawn sun breaks over Mount Ida on the island. Implicit, of course, in this scene of language commonality is a sense of classical languages and class uniting these two officers across the military divide.

In the account, language difference is situated between the two poles of élite multilingualism and vernacular multilingualism or, in the case of the latter, what Alastair Pennycook and Emi Otsuji have called 'multilingualism from below'.[23] Staying outside Munich with the family of Baron Rheinhard von Liphart-Ratshoff, Leigh Fermor finds himself in a house 'full of books in half a dozen languages' (125). The evenings were spent in 'conversation and books' (126) and in one scene the Baron reads out Mark Antony's speech from Julius Caesar in Russian, French, German and Italian. In the house of another Baron, Baron Schey or 'Pips' in Slovakia, there is another equally well-stocked library whose 'books, in German and French and English, had overflowed in neat piles on the floor' (318). The well-read Baron discusses with the young Leigh Fermor the work of, among others, Hölderlin, Rilke, Stefan Georg, Hofmannsthal, Christian Morgenstern and Proust. The Barons capture a particular cosmopolitan culture of élite multilingualism that is frequently associated with the upper echelons of Germanophone Mitteleuropa.[24] Indeed, the ability to speak a number of 'prestige' languages was seen as the mark of properly educated people and would dictate their choice of travel destination from the French capital to the German spa.

Vernacular multilingualism, on the other hand, becomes much more of a pressing reality for Leigh Fermor when he crosses over into Slovakia. In the city of Bratislava, Leigh Fermor claims something had changed. There was a new feeling in the air, hard to define. He then clarifies this feeling by adding, '[p]erhaps it had something to do with the three names of the city and the tri-lingual public notices and street names: the juxtaposition of tongues made me feel I had crossed more than a political frontier' (270). In Bratislava, multilingualism is quotidian and omnipresent but Slovak and Hungarian are not part of the standard repertoire of élite multilingualism so the travel writer finds himself having to rely on German and scraps of Slovak and Hungarian to make his way through Slovakia and the Marches of Hungary. As he shifts from the interlingual to the intersemiotic the account begins to dwell more extensively on physical dress or the phonic as opposed to the semantic properties of language. Thus, we read of 'the muffled vowels of the Slovaks and the traffic-jams of consonants and the explosive spurts of dentals and sibilants' (272) and 'the astonishing sound of Magyar – a dactylic canter where the ictus of every initial syllable set off a troop of identical vowels with their accents all swerving one way like wheat-ears in the wind' (273). The travel writer moving between the worlds of élite and vernacular multilingualism plays out in a sense that shifts from the travel literature of privilege to the 'travel stories' of migration described by James Clifford, with Bratislava as a metonym of the teeming, metrolingual metropolises of late modernity.[25]

Baron Pips spoke excellent English and, just like the Irish traveller in Kenya, the English travel writer picks out those who speak his native language. The difference is that for most of Leigh Fermor's interlocutors, English is not their native or national language, so the lingua franca becomes not only a channel of information but an object of observation in its own right. The most notable example is Konrad, a native speaker of Frisian whom Leigh Fermor meets in Vienna and who has learnt his English from reading Shakespeare's plays. Konrad's unselfconscious use of archaisms, 'there is no lack of base ones, footpads and knaves who never shrink from purloining', is a more exaggerated form of Baron Pips' occasional weakness as an accomplished non-native speaker of English for 'an Edwardian turn of phrase' (318). The language difference here is between native and non-native usage and the narrative representation of non-native usage in a major global lingua franca such as English has of course become a stock comic opportunity for a host of English-language writers, whatever their genre.

As migration leads to the continuing increase in the linguistic diversity of cities and countries, the question of language difference will be an inescapable dimension to writing about travel and places. Just as travel writing gives mobility a language, mobility gives travel writing the complex gift of not one language but many.

Notes

1 Statista, 'Global Travel and Tourism Industry – Statistics and Facts', accessed 29 August 2017, www.statista.com/topics/962/global-tourism.

2 See for example John Urry, *Mobilities* (Oxford: Polity, 2007).

3 Ethnologue, 'How Many Languages Are There in the World?', accessed 29 August 2017, www.ethnologue.com/guides/how-many-languages.

4 Roman Jakobson, 'On Linguistic Aspects of Translation', in *Theories of Translation: An Anthology of Essays from Dryden to Derrida*, ed. Rainer Schulte and John Biguenet (Chicago, IL: University of Chicago Press), 144–51.

5 Michael Cronin, *Across the Lines: Travel, Language and Translation* (Cork: Cork University Press, 2000); Loredana Polezzi, *Translating Travel: Contemporary Italian Travel Writing in English Translation* (London: Ashgate, 2001); Charles Forsdick, *Travel in Twentieth-Century French and Francophone Cultures* (Oxford: Oxford University Press, 2005).

6 Jacobus Naude, 'The Role of Pseudo-Translations in Early Afrikaans Travel Writing: A Corpus-Based Translation Analysis', *Southern African Linguistics and Applied Language Studies* 26.1 (2008): 97–106. Jane Conroy, 'Changing Perspectives: French Travellers in Ireland, 1785–1835', in *CrossCultural Travel*, ed. Jane Conroy (Oxford: Peter Lang, 2003), 131–42; Eoin Bourke, ed. and trans., '*Poor Green Erin': German Travel Writers' Narratives on Ireland from Before the 1798 Rising to After the Great Famine* (Oxford: Peter Lang, 2012).

7 Carmine G. Di Biase, ed., *Travel and Translation in the Early Modern Period* (Amsterdam: Rodopi, 2006).

8 Mirella Agorni, *Translating Italy for the Eighteenth Century: British Women, Translation and Travel Writing (1739–1797)* (Manchester: St. Jerome, 2002); Paola Daniela Smecca, *Representational Tactics in Travel Writing and Translation* (Rome: Carocci, 2005).

9 Douglas Robinson, *Translation and Empire: Postcolonial Theories Explained* (Manchester: St. Jerome, 1997).

10 Michael Cronin, 'The Empire Talks Back: Orality, Heteronomy and the Cultural Turn in Interpreting Studies', *Translation and Power*, ed. Edwin Gentzler and Maria Tymoczko (Boston, MA: University of Massachusetts Press, 2002), 45–62.

11 Paula G. Rubel and Abraham Rosman, *Translating Cultures: Perspectives on Translation and Anthropology* (Oxford: Berg, 2003); Elena Filonova, 'Between Literacy and Non-Literacy: Interpreters in the Exploration and Colonization of Nineteenth-Century Alaska', *The Translator* 12.2 (2006): 211–31; Loredana Polezzi, 'Translation, Travel, Migration', *The Translator* 12.2 (2006): 169–88; James St. André, 'Travelling towards True Translation: The First Generation of Sino-English Translators', *The Translator* 12.2 (2006): 189–210.

12 Jean-Didier Urbain, *Secrets de voyage: menteurs, imposteurs et autres voyageurs immédiats* (Paris: Payot, 1998), 217–32.

13 Cronin, *Across the Lines*, 19.

14 Robert Macfarlane, *Landmarks* (London: Hamish Hamilton, 2015), 1. All subsequent references are to this edition, incorporated in the text with pagination in parentheses.

15 Jan Blommaert, *Ethnography, Superdiversity and Linguistic Landscapes: Chronicles of Complexity* (Bristol: Multilingual Matters, 2013).

16 Sherry Simon, *Cities in Translation: Intersections of Language and Memory* (London: Routledge, 2011); Sherry Simon, *Translating Montreal: Episodes in the Life of a Divided City* (Montreal: McGill-Queen's University Press, 2006).

17 Daniel Nettle and Suzanne Romaine, *Vanishing Voices: The Extinction of the World's Languages* (Oxford: Oxford University Press, 2002).

18 Heather Williams, Kathryn Jones and Carol Tully, 'Introduction: Wales and Travel Writing', *Studies in Travel Writing* 18.2 (2014): 101–6.

19 Patrick Leigh Fermor, *A Time of Gifts: On Foot to Constantinople – From the Hook of Holland to the Middle Danube* (London: John Murray, 2013); Pádraig Ó Fiannachta, *Ó Mháigh go Fásach* (Má Nuad: An Sagart, 1977). All subsequent references are to these editions, incorporated in the text with pagination in parentheses.

20 Vicente L. Rafael, *Contracting Colonialism: Translation and Christian Conversion in Tagalog Society under Early Spanish Rule* (Durham, NC: Duke University Press, 1993); Sara Pugach, *Africa in Translation: A History of Colonial Linguistics in Africa and Beyond 1814–1945* (Ann Arbor, MI: University of Michigan Press, 2012).

21 Pádraig Ó Fiannachta, *An Chomharsa Choimhthíoch* (Baile Átha Cliath: FÁS, 1957).

22 Arran Stibbe, *Ecolinguistics: Language, Ecology and the Stories We Live By* (London: Routledge, 2015), 1.

23 Alastair Pennycook and Emi Otsuji, *Metrolingualism: Language in the City* (London: Routledge, 2015), 49.

24 Claudio Magris, *Danube*, trans. Patrick Creagh (London: Harvill Secker, 1989).

25 James, Clifford, 'Travelling Cultures', in *Cultural Studies*, ed. Lawrence. Grossberg, Cary. Nelson and Paula, A. Treichler (London: Routledge, 1992), 96–111.

22

ANIMALS

Elizabeth Leane

Nonhuman travellers and travellees: interspecies relations in travel writing

It is difficult to imagine a travel narrative that does not include some mention of encounters with nonhuman beings. There are very few places to which humans can travel that are not already inhabited and traversed by other species. The Antarctic plateau and outer space might qualify, but even then, animals trail-blazed – or, more accurately, were forced to trail-blaze – the routes.[1] The first humans to reach the South Pole – a Norwegian team led by Roald Amundsen in 1911 – used sledges pulled by Greenland huskies, and one of the first human acts at the so-called 'last of all places' was the slaughter of a dog named Helge, who was 'portioned out on the spot' to provide food for his companions.[2] Monkeys, mice, rats, rabbits and dogs reached space before humans, many of them dying as a result.[3] In more mundane locations, animals have been and are ubiquitous, transporting, accompanying, assisting, intriguing, ignoring, pestering, threatening and occasionally eating human travellers, and themselves in turn being ridden, harnessed, transported, mistreated, befriended, photographed, pursued, classified, hunted, killed and frequently consumed. It is no surprise, then, that almost any travel narrative read with attentiveness to the presence of animals will yield incidents of some kind every few pages, some trivial, some highly revealing.

More surprising is the relative paucity of criticism focusing on animals in travel writing – both individual animals and particular species. To the extent that travel writing studies is a branch of literary studies, this neglect reflects prevailing approaches (until recently) within this larger field. Literary critics have not entirely ignored animals in the texts they study, but rather have tended to consider them interesting only where they can be read as figures for human qualities.[4] This tendency to look *through* rather than *at* the textual animal can also be found in analyses of animals in travel texts.[5] While figurative uses of animals can of course be relevant to actual animals, readings such as these put their emphasis on what the animal imagery says about intra-human relationships, rather than human–animal relationships.

Human–animal relationships are, by contrast, the key concern of the burgeoning interdisciplinary field of 'animal studies',[6] the study of 'the cultural, philosophical, economic and social means by which humans and animals interact'.[7] While this new field has triggered an 'animal turn' within the mainstream of many other humanities and social science disciplines including literary studies, travel writing studies has been slow to draw on its insights. There are, of course, exceptions: canonical texts in which animals play an obviously large role, including foundational medieval travel narratives, early modern exploration narratives and hunting narratives, have all received attention from implicit or explicit animal studies perspectives.[8] However, these efforts comprise a small body of tightly focused scholarship when compared to travel writing studies as a whole.

This comparative lack of engagement between animal studies and travel writing studies may have an explanation in the close ties between the latter and postcolonial criticism. In *Postcolonial Ecocriticism: Literature, Animals, Environment* (2010) Graham Huggan and Helen Tiffin note that while '[p]ostcolonialism's major theoretical concerns [. . .] offer immediate entry points for a re-theorising of the place of animals in relation to human societies', several factors – most prominently, 'the metaphorisation and deployment of "animal" as a derogatory term in genocidal and marginalising discourses' – make it hard 'even to discuss animals without generating a profound unease, even a rancorous antagonism, in many postcolonial contexts today'.[9] Particularly fraught are intersectional approaches that draw parallels between the structures of oppression operating through race and species categorisation, such as between the historical enslavement of African people and the contemporary treatment of animals. Huggan and Tiffin, drawing on a growing body of criticism, argue that it is because genocide, slavery and other forms of injustice are 'predicated on the categorisation of people *as* animals' – that is, the strategic shifting of a culturally determined species boundary between beings classed as 'human' and those classed as 'nonhuman' – that interrogation of these and all other categories of othering and oppression must 'proceed together'.[10] In the period since Huggan and Tiffin made these observations, their arguments have been borne out by an increasing engagement of postcolonial critics with the nonhuman.[11] Because animals often function in travel writing both as symbols of racialised human others and as others in their own right, this realisation of structural parallels in the construction of difference must underlie analyses of the representation of nonhuman travellers and 'travelees'.[12]

Categorising human–animal relations in travel narratives

Any analysis of human–animal relations in travel writing faces a large and diverse group of texts, of which only a small subset can be dealt with here. Like Philip Armstrong in his animal-centric analysis of modern fiction, I am interested in texts that share 'the inclusion of human–animal relations as significant components of their representational structures'.[13] While drawing on a range of examples, I focus below on a few prominent texts from the late nineteenth and twentieth centuries, in order to illustrate a possible typology of the roles animals are allocated in travel narratives: the animal as *quest-object*; the animal as *instrument of travel*; and the animal as *companion*.

The first category refers to any journey in which an animal encounter, violent or peaceful, is framed in the narrative as the primary motivation for travel. The prospect of a meeting with an animal, or species of animal, gets the narrator moving. These narratives, whether they deal with hunting, specimen collection or photography, can be considered quests and examined through the narrative conventions of that genre. The second category covers narratives in which animals are included in a journey and its narrative(s) in a primarily instrumental role, as a means to ensure human survival, comfort and/or movement. The obvious reason is transport, but animals also frequently appear as sources of food (meat or milk) and clothing, as fuel (particularly in polar environments), and as guards and protectors. The final category includes those narratives in which an animal travels with a human largely for companionship, a situation that, although usually arranged by the human for his or her purposes, tends to be represented as one of comparative mutuality.

These categories are not intended to be exhaustive or exclusive. They produce their own problems – such as a focus on charismatic megafauna – and exclude other kinds of important encounter (for example, narratives in which animals function primarily as pest or threat). Moreover, they obviously overlap. An animal included in a journey for practical purposes may become a mascot or beloved companion (the explorer Matthew Flinders wrote a biography of his well-travelled ship's cat, Trim[14]). Conversely, a companion may be reduced to a material resource: Helge, the 'useful and good-natured' sledge dog killed for food at the South Pole when he was no longer able to work effectively, was also the 'best friend' of the explorer who was required to slaughter him with a 'blow to the skull'.[15] Broadly speaking, however, each category can be associated with a particular category of animal: wild animals in quests; 'beasts of burden' such as horses, donkeys, mules, camels and elephants in the second; and domestic animals in the last.

The three categories are chosen not only according to the role animals play in journeys, but also to their function in the corresponding narratives. A journey motivated by an animal encounter draws its narrative frame from this aim, usually beginning with its description and ending with its achievement (or failure). Transport animals, to the extent that they interrupt the human narrator's intended journey through (most often) refusal, determine the structure of the narrative flow, becoming co-authors of a sort. A companion animal may act as a silent auditor of the narrator's opinions and reflections – voiced aloud in a one-sided dialogue or simply understood – and in this sense become a version of the ideal reader.

Animals as quest-objects: Cherry-Garrard's *Worst Journey*

Probably the largest category of travel narratives substantially concerned with animals comprises those in which an encounter with another species provides the primary motivation for the journey. This covers a generically, historically and politically diverse group of texts, including accounts of hunting trips, scientific specimen gathering, expeditions to capture animals for zoological collections, journeys to photograph rarely seen creatures, environmentally focused searches for disappearing species and 'last-chance tourism'. These seemingly disparate activities are often historically and discursively intertwined.[16]

In terms of narrative structure, journeys of this nature can be classified as quests. As Tim Youngs observes, 'most journeys are quests of some kind [. . .] [The quest] is probably the single most important organising principle of travel writing'.[17] The distinction in my classification is that an animal is the object of the quest. Thus, although John Steinbeck's *Travels with Charley* (1962) announces itself as a quest ('in search of America') and Robyn Davidson's *Tracks* (1980) can be read as a quest for self-transformation, I have classed these texts under other categories, as in each case animal encounters are not the primary reason for travel.

The most studied kinds of travel texts in which an animal encounter is the prime motivator are hunting and safari narratives, especially the more self-consciously literary contributions to the genre, such as Ernest Hemingway's *Green Hills of Africa*.[18] However, I want to move away from this relatively well-explored territory to examine a text set in a region in which the established conventions of the hunting narrative fail: Apsley Cherry-Garrard's *The Worst Journey in the World: The Story of Scott's Last Expedition to the South Pole* (1922).

Although the 'last continent' began to be explored in the late nineteenth and early twentieth centuries, when the imperial 'hunting mentality' was in full swing, the complete lack of large land-based species in Antarctica (where the largest terrestrial species is a midge) made its traditional tropes unviable.[19] As Brigid Hains writes, penguins and seals 'disappointed the would-be hunter [. . .] Antarctic animals were comic rather than worthy adversaries [. . .] grotesquely

cumbersome on land, and defenceless against dogs and guns'.[20] At the same time, the continent's lack of indigenous human inhabitants put human–animal relations into stark relief. In
the absence of humans, wild animals structurally took the place of colonised human subjects,
becoming the 'other' that explorers displaced, exploited and scientifically classified as part of
the process of territorial occupation. However, the continent's isolation meant that the humans
based there for years at a time attached a strong sense of companionship to the animals around
them. Expeditions also brought domestic animals who acted as companions, but these inevitably doubled as working animals, and (as in the case of Helge and her fellows) sometimes food
sources. The roles that animals (particularly dogs) were made to play in this unfamiliar environment were confused and overlapping.

All of these complex relations are evident in Cherry-Garrard's account of the British
Antarctic Expedition, led by Robert F. Scott, who famously died in early 1912 along with
four companions on a return journey from the Pole. *The Worst Journey* is frequently cited as
a classic of travel and exploration writing. The founding volume of the 1990s *Picador Travel
Classics* series, Cherry-Garrard's text (according to the *New York Review of Books*) is 'to travel
writing what *War and Peace* is to the novel [. . .] the book by which all the rest are measured'.[21]
Humanities-educated and paying a thousand pounds to join the expedition, Cherry-Garrard
was designated the expedition's 'assistant zoologist', his superior being the artist, physician and
naturalist Edward Wilson. The 'worst journey' of his book's title is not, however, the journey
to the South Pole which took the lives of Wilson, Scott and others, but an earlier midwinter
journey to an Emperor penguin colony. The narrative of this expedition, told in a seventy-page
chapter that gives the book its structural core, can be read in terms of the animal-motivated
imperial quest.

The imperial quest narrative, according to Robert Fraser, has its origins in transcultural myths
of 'male protagonists who [. . .] set out with a team of picked companions' to reach a desired
object, such as 'a golden fleece, or the skin of some fabulous animal'.[22] Key elements include
'an onerous journey across uncharted regions, the reaching of the goal, the conquest, a withdrawal'.[23] This generic description fits Cherry-Garrard's narrative very nicely. Cherry-Garrard
is part of a selected male team that also includes Wilson and a third expeditioner, Henry 'Birdie'
Bowers. Their five-week journey is conducted entirely in darkness with temperatures drop-
ping below 70 degrees Fahrenheit. The 'fabulous animal' they are in search of is the Emperor
penguin, in early embryonic form inside an egg (a factor that determined the timing of their
journey). Cherry-Garrard explains that the embryo was thought to be a key evolutionary link
between birds and mammals and hence 'might be of the utmost importance to science'.[24]

Because the moment of actual encounter with the 'longed-for or dreaded object' of the quest
risks anti-climax, 'quest-narratives traditionally protect these moments by disguising them and
making them into absent centres'.[25] The object may go initially unrecognised or (as in Peter
Matthiessen's *The Snow Leopard* [1978]) fail to appear at all.[26] Ostensibly, Cherry-Garrard refuses
this convention, highlighting the moment of first encounter with the penguins (which happens mid-narrative) with the one-word paragraph, 'And then we heard the Emperors calling'.[27]
Soon after, the men manage to climb down to the colony, collect five eggs (two of which they
accidentally smash), kill three birds for fuel and head home. However, Cherry-Garrard retrospectively empties the quest-object of meaning by reporting with heavy irony at the end of the
chapter the indifferent reception given to the eggs by the London Natural History Museum
after the expedition's return.[28]

While it later became clear that that the eggs were of little relevance to evolutionary history, Cherry-Garrard could be confident that the journey's quest-object would have automatic
appeal to his post-war readers. King penguins (subantarctic birds with golden markings similar

Figure 22.1 Charles Paine, 'For the Zoo book to Regent's Park,' 1921. © TfL from the London Transport Museum collection

to Emperors, but 85–95cm tall, compared to 100–130cm for Emperors[29]) had first arrived in Regent's Park Zoological Gardens in 1865. Initially considered rather odd, they became increasingly popular with visitors over the following decades, during which several other penguin species were added to the collection.[30] By the 1920s, penguins were the 'poster children' for the zoo in a very literal sense, featuring on advertisements in the London underground (Fig. 22.1).

Antarctic exploration films, including those of Herbert Ponting and Frank Hurley, foregrounded wildlife, particularly penguins, framed in highly anthropomorphic ways as comical and endearing (Ponting used a soft-toy penguin when he spoke at his film screenings).[31] Readers were kindly disposed, then, towards penguins, but the Emperor, a species that had not at this point been successfully transported to zoos, still held considerable mystique. Cherry-Garrard points out that his team was the first ever to see an Emperor colony during the birds' breeding season.[32]

Despite – or perhaps because of – the charismatic nature of the penguin, Cherry-Garrard spends surprisingly little time reflecting on or describing the animal that motivates his journey. This then is another mechanism through which he decentres the quest-object. His description of the actual encounter with the birds occupies a small fraction of the chapter. Most of the narrative focuses on the human journey rather than on its animal object – particularly the hardships the men endured and the unfailingly good-natured companionship they managed to maintain. Reflecting on the expedition fifty years later, Nancy Mitford wryly comments that the Emperors' living conditions seem to be such that 'the R.S.P.C.A. ought to do something'.[33] Cherry-Garrard's anthropocentrism encourages such a response: he devotes so much space to the dreadful experiences of the men in conditions very hostile to their bodies that it is hard to accept that the Emperors – themselves readily anthropomorphised birds – are well adapted to that environment.

Cherry-Garrard's is not the only example of a travel narrative in which the animal identified as the object of desire and *raison d'être* of the journey is in the end peripheral to the narrative. Bruce Chatwin's later classic, *In Patagonia* (1977), relates a journey ostensibly taken to obtain a piece of skin from a brontosaurus (actually, mylodon or giant sloth). While he does accomplish 'the object of this ridiculous journey' by its conclusion, the narrative is far more engaged with human characters, incidents and histories.[34] The quest for an animal often collapses into another quest: in Matthiessen's *The Snow Leopard*, for example, the search for a rare animal is also a search for inner solace. When the second quest is automatically read as the 'real' one, however, the animal itself is yet again reduced to mere metaphor.

Whether they involve hunting, photographing, collecting or merely seeing a particular species, journeys in search of animals are frequently objectifying. The animals they describe, Richard Kerridge suggests, 'seem to allow the observer to look intimately at them from a position of self-contained subjectivity'.[35] While the agency of a sought-after animal may be evident in its elusive behaviour, the nature of the quest narrative means that the human–animal encounter is inevitably fleeting, precluding the sustained interaction needed to narrow the interspecies distance and open the possibility of mutuality.

This is not true of all travel writing dealing with animals, however. The following sections examine narratives of journeys to which human–animal intersubjectivity is central, although not always welcome.

Animals as instruments of travel: Stevenson's *Travels with a Donkey*, Shand's *Travels on My Elephant* and Davidson's *Tracks*

One of the more prominent of literary nonhuman travellers is Modestine, a donkey purchased by Robert Louis Stevenson to facilitate his foot-travels through a mountainous region in the south of France in 1878. Having acquired a kind of improvised bed-roll that allowed him to sleep in the open air occasionally, Stevenson was unable to carry his equipment on his own, 'merely human', shoulders, instead relying on a 'beast of burden'.[36] His journey was explicitly undertaken with a resultant narrative in mind, and the title he chose when the book was published the following year – *Travels with a Donkey in the Cévennes* – encapsulates the ambiguity of his relationship with Modestine. In the sense that she travels *with* Stevenson (the name used as shorthand here for the author's carefully constructed persona), Modestine is a companion, a seemingly equal partner in the journey, at least as important discursively as the destination itself. However, as an unnamed, indefinite animal – 'a donkey' – she is reduced to generic status and denied subjectivity.

The oscillation between these two versions of Modestine is manifested in the text in, on the one hand, her constant frustration of Stevenson's aims (presented largely comically), which reveal her agency and character; and, on the other, the author's continual disregard for the suffering he imposes on her. To address her recalcitrance and avoid the constant ridicule of the local people, Stevenson strikes her first with a cane, then (on advice) a switch, and finally a 'goad' (a stick with a small metal pin attached), before discovering that her forelegs are 'no better than raw beef on the inside', and blood streams from under her tail (69). Refusing to believe the locals' prediction that she would become a companion animal, beloved 'like a dog', he nonetheless becomes mawkish about his loss after he sells her, with the text's final sentence describing his weeping at her absence (69). Their complex developing relationship is as central to the text as the description of the landscape and reflections on local traditions, people, politics and religion.

As a key character in a canonical text by a prominent novelist, Modestine has received more critical attention than perhaps any other animal in travel writing. Oliver Buckton gives a nuanced and detailed analysis of her representation, but reads from animal to human, interpreting the donkey as a figure for Stevenson's troubled relationship with his own body and with femininity.[37] Morgan Holmes, adopting an animal studies perspective, argues that Stevenson constructs his treatment of Modestine as 'a matter of a stranger conforming to the customs of the foreign land through which he travelled'.[38] He argues that 'Instead of positing essential species otherness, Stevenson helps us see the roles that nationally-inflected custom and prejudice play in shaping humans' attitudes and relationships towards other animals over which they claim authority'.[39] In contrast to Buckton's analysis, Holmes's animal-centric reading moves from nationalism to speciesism: Modestine is no longer understood as a vehicle through which to understand human relations; rather, humans' attitudes towards other humans sheds light on their treatment of animals.

While Holmes reads both Stevenson's final realisation of Modestine's importance to him and his maudlin mourning for her loss straightforwardly, the text's concluding passage can be interpreted as highly ironic. The donkey initially described by Stevenson as a 'diminutive she-ass, not much bigger than a dog, the colour of a mouse' (39) becomes upon his loss of her 'the colour of an ideal mouse, and inimitably small' (126). The two of them have, he explains, by this time become 'fast companions' (126). As the narrative progresses, Stevenson does indeed reach a kind of harmony with Modestine, as when, for example, the two travellers enjoy a moonlit scene late in the journey (121–122). However, there has been no suggestion of the intimate bond he finally claims, nothing to justify his invocation of one of Wordsworth's 'Lucy' poems – 'And oh! / The difference to me!' – and his public tears (126). The passage deliberately echoes Stevenson's first purchase of Modestine from a weeping priest, whose protestations of affections for his donkey are belied by his reputation: 'He had a name in the village for brutally misusing the ass' (40). Stevenson's motivation for adopting an ironic tone to describe Modestine's farewell, however, is ambiguous. His irony could indicate an acknowledgement of the hypocritical and self-indulgent nature of his emotion, given his previous treatment of her. Equally, it could indicate that his bond with the donkey was indeed closer than he admitted, and by seriously acknowledging it he would open himself to more ridicule, this time from his readers.

Similarly, the hyperbole of Stevenson's initial reduction of Modestine to a mechanical object, a 'self-acting bedstead on four castors', can be read both as a form of self-mockery and a means of distancing – an ironic admission of his overly Cartesian attitude towards the animal that also serves as an excuse for his behaviour (40). The issue then is how to read Stevenson's detailed description of his violent use of Modestine: as simply a reinforcement of long-standing views of the donkey as resilient to 'harsh treatment' or as a prompt to rethink this stereotype.[40] While Stevenson adopts his increasingly cruel methods to avoid the knowing smiles of the locals he meets, it is not until he decides to 'spare the donkey' (by taking the advice of an ex-muleteer to redistribute the load) that the ridicule lessens (72). And, arguably, Stevenson brings the cruel treatment of a transport animal into question simply by making it – and her – a central subject of his narrative. The whipping of donkeys, horses and many other animals to facilitate human mobility goes entirely unmentioned in many travel accounts.

Stevenson's constant emphasis on Modestine's gender also contains elements of irony, relying on the reader to recognise the distance between stereotypical perceptions of donkeys as ugly, stubborn and slightly ridiculous and the self-effacing 'lady-friend' that Stevenson constructs through his naming and addressing of her (62).[41] 'I am worthy of the name of an Englishman', writes the author (a Scot) after first mentioning his use of his staff on the donkey, 'and it goes against my conscience to lay my hand rudely on a female' (43). Being a 'lady' bestows on Modestine aspects of human (classed) subjectivity, but also makes her vulnerable to the same objectification and mistreatment to which female humans are often subject. Buckton notes that 'the charge of misogyny may be levelled at Stevenson in those passages in which he details the abuse of the donkey while also emphasizing her femininity'.[42] But these passages can be read in both directions, highlighting the parallels between the process of othering enacted through species and through gender.

A comparison of the gender politics of *Travels with a Donkey* with a more recent text involving a transport animal, Mark Shand's *Travels on My Elephant* (1991), reveals a similar metaphorical process by which an animal is simultaneously awarded the subjectivity of a human then relegated, as a female, to being the object of male desire or conquest. Shand's narrative describes a trek through north-east India, supported by a heavy-drinking all-male retinue, with (and sometimes on) an elephant he names Tara. Here, the typical journey of transformation is attached to Tara as much as to Shand: purchased from an organised group of travelling beggars, she gradually improves her health and 'manners' so that by the text's conclusion she is a 'princess' destined for a peaceful life in a private British-owned park.[43] Despite Shand's belated realisation that Tara is always 'in control', the narrative is constructed as a male rescue fantasy of an attractive female in distressed circumstances.[44] The gender politics of Shand's report of his first encounter with Tara are inescapable:

> Then I saw her. My mouth went dry. I felt giddy, breathless [. . .] With one hind leg crossed over the other, she was leaning nonchalantly against a tree, the charms of her perfectly rounded posterior in full view, like a prostitute on a street corner. I knew then that I had to have her.[45]

Where Modestine's 'mouse-coloured wedge-like rump' (55) is constantly flagellated, Tara's 'big fat bottom' is frequently the object of the male narrator's gaze (as well as of pats, injections and prods from spears).[46] Both animals are awarded human subjectivity of a sort only to be re-objectified. It seems that in these texts any attempt to overcome one category of difference must be achieved at the expense of another.

At the same time, Shand succeeds in bringing a nonhuman being to the fore of his travel narrative. Tara – and elephants more generally – are the obsessive topic of his book; he constantly describes her behaviour and character, and cites numerous anecdotes and cultural histories to contextualise it. As he describes in an Afterword, Shand went on to devote himself to the cause of elephant conservation.

Structurally similar to both *Travels with a Donkey* and *Travels on My Elephant* is Robyn Davidson's well-known travel narrative *Tracks* (1980). Davidson, however, frames her relationship with her camels – a mixed group of four – very differently from the way the male writers examined here fashion their corresponding situations. Stevenson and Shand both give their books titles that emphasise an animal's relationship to themselves – suggesting, respectively, distant companionship and possessive conquest; Davidson's title, by contrast, refers not just to the many paths (human and nonhuman) she and her camels follow, but to the traces they leave behind. Herself the subject of unwanted male attention, propositions, and occasional threats, and determined to escape conventional Western ideals of femininity, Davidson knows what it is to be relegated to an object. Where Stevenson constructs Modestine as a 'lady-friend' and Shand presents Tara's journey as one from prostitute to princess, Davidson rails against her *own* popular designation as the 'camel lady', with its patronising connotations.

Davidson's representation of human–animal encounters is not, however, entirely unproblematic. Her declarations of affection for her camels, who seem 'virtually human', sit uncomfortably with her use of violence to make them achieve her ends, something she (like Stevenson and Shand) considers a necessary but disturbing part of using transport animals.[47] And ultimately, Davidson's story is not *about* camels to the extent that Shand's is about elephants; the narrative emphasis is rather on her personal transformation. As Youngs writes, 'even texts that appear radical in their politics are at risk of using the Other exploitatively to the advantage of the self', and this is as true of nonhuman beings as other categories of difference.[48] Like any travel text, those discussed here neither can nor should be read as entirely 'for' or 'against' animals, but rather as part of a complex ongoing negotiation of species relationships.

Animals as travel companions: Steinbeck's *Travels with Charley*

While animals frequently feature as companions in narratives of human travel, they often remain in the background, mentioned every so often but rarely well delineated. The title of Jerome K. Jerome's late nineteenth-century novel-cum-travelogue *Three Men in a Boat (To Say Nothing of the Dog)* ironically highlights the common status of the companion animal as a parenthetical extra.[49] The opening sentence of *Tracks* has Davidson arriving 'in the Alice at five a.m. with a dog', and it is Diggity's accidental death, rather than any particular destination, that signals the end of her journey.[50] However, Diggity takes a discursive back seat to the more exotic (and refractory) camels for much of the narrative.

Charley, the French standard poodle who accompanies John Steinbeck in his tour across the United States, takes a front seat, both in the custom-built camper truck that transports them and as a character in the narrative. Steinbeck's title – *Travels with Charley: In Search of America* – immediately signals a different relationship from those evoked by Stevenson's or Shand's. Charley is designated by name rather than species, and the new reader is encouraged to presume this appellation refers to a human companion – a buddy in a road journey. Steinbeck generates humour from his implicit assumption that readers will judge Charley by the same standards they would judge a human: 'It is my experience that in some areas Charley is more intelligent than I am, but in others he is abysmally ignorant. He can't read, can't drive a car, and has no grasp of mathematics'.[51]

Published late in Steinbeck's career, *Travels with Charley* was considered 'likeable and amusing' but 'lightweight' by the *New York Times*' reviewer, perhaps partly because it devoted so much textual space to a dog.[52] Douglas Dowland, in a recent attempt at recuperating the text within the Steinbeck corpus, barely even mentions the 'pet poodle' who gives the book its title.[53] However, as Małgorzata Rutkowska shows in an analysis of dogs in contemporary American travel writing, Steinbeck's work catalysed a subgenre of companion animal travel narratives. Rutkowska provides a detailed analysis of the relationship that Steinbeck constructs between himself and Charley, and the multiple roles in which he casts the poodle: a substitute for family; an 'ambassador with strangers'; a guard and watchdog; a 'displaced partner in conversation'; a naïve observer whose perspective allows Steinbeck to defamiliarise and criticise aspects of his own society (particularly the treatment of African Americans); and an alter-ego for the author.[54] In one of several meta-textual moments, Steinbeck himself points to one of Charley's literary functions when he meets a travelling actor whose own dog 'keeps the performance simple' and 'picks it up when it goes stale' (867).

From an animal studies perspective, one of the most interesting aspects of *Travels with Charley* is the way in which Charley's position with respect to the species boundary shifts discursively and strategically for different (human) purposes. Although Steinbeck insists that 'Charley is not human; he's a dog, and he likes it that way', ambiguity lingers over the circumstances in which Charley is designated 'animal', and hence over the logic of this designation itself (886).

The first of many American 'customs' Steinbeck discusses is hunting. Although critical of incompetent hunters, he has 'nothing against the killing of animals. Something has to kill them, I suppose' (803). Although he is no longer interested in the activity, Steinbeck has decked his truck out in hunting gear to give the impression of being a typical American man on a typical trip, not a famous writer hoping to glean new insights into his nation (770). However, when he and Charley encounter hunting season in Maine, it becomes vital that the large poodle – who from a distance resembles a deer – is not mistaken for the kind of animal that can be unproblematically killed. Steinbeck therefore ties a red handkerchief around Charley's tail, noting 'this is not meant to be funny' (804). Later in the narrative, Steinbeck's double standard is put to the test when he considers shooting a coyote, a wild animal deemed a pest to farmers. He describes how he had his rifle's cross hairs centred on the coyote when it 'sat down like a dog'. Instead of shooting, he leaves two cans of dog food (907–908). Steinbeck's relationship with Charley has led him to question the 'non-criminal putting to death' of other animals.[55]

Much later, when Steinbeck drives apprehensively into Texas, Charley (whose fur is blue-grey) becomes a means through which white Texans affirm racial otherness, their temporary (and supposedly inadvertent) promotion of the poodle to the category of 'human' working simultaneously to dehumanise African Americans:

> The blue-fingered man at my gas tank looked in at Charley and said, 'Hey, it's a dog! I thought you had a nigger in there.' And he laughed delightedly. It was the first of many repetitions. At least twenty times I heard it.
>
> *(932)*

Later, during a conversation with another Texan, Steinbeck is told how difficult it is to let black Americans 'be people': 'suppose [Charley] could talk and stand on his hind legs. Maybe he could do very well in every way. Perhaps you could invite him to dinner, but could you think of him as people?' (941) However, when the same man goes on to reflect on evenings he spends with 'an old Negro couple' – 'we are just three pleasant [. . .] things living together' – Steinbeck picks up on his unusually neutral choice of noun: '"Things," I repeated. "That's interesting – not man and beast, not black and white, but pleasant things"' (942).

This vision of radical dissolving of difference recalls an earlier passage in which Steinbeck reflects on two lengthy periods he spent alone as a winter caretaker at Lake Tahoe. Remembering how he lost all 'subtleties of feeling' as time went on, he speculates that 'the delicate shades of feeling, of reaction, are the result of communication, and without such communication they tend to disappear' (858). Considering cases of children who have been brought up by wolves and who may have eventually come to think like them, Steinbeck turns to the reverse case of Charley, who 'has always associated with the learned, the gentle, the literate, and the reasonable both in France and in America' (858). Contradicting his earlier statement, he declares that 'Charley is no more like a dog than he is like a cat' (858). Here, Charley's attitude to the world has less to do with his identity as a dog than with his upbringing and his companions: cultural context, rather than biology, produces subjectivity.

The reflections on the nature of difference that Steinbeck is afforded in his travels are in large part the product of his ongoing and developing relationship with Charley. Where the animal quest structurally requires only a fleeting encounter, and the transport animal narrative often focuses on a troubling battle between nonhuman and human will, the companion animal narrative creates space for a more positive sustained examination of interspecies interaction.[56]

Conclusion

I have offered here a preliminary typology of the representation of animals in travel texts based on the functions animals perform for humans in these narratives. This is not because animal agency is not evident in travel writing – on the contrary, it is frequently present and often exploited for comic purposes (as in Modestine's refusals) – but rather because travel writing is, by definition, written by humans, and even the most sympathetic representation of nonhumans must be instrumental, if only in the function the latter play in the narrative.[57] Animal-authored travel narratives are not, however, impossible to imagine: they can be found, for example, in the material tracks and traces (such as the hoofprints of Davidson's camels) that nonhumans leave behind them. Neither is it impossible to read these tracks as texts, taking into account the various ways in which humans interact with and interpret them.[58] For now, however, my threefold categorisation – animal as quest-object, instrument of travel, and companion – offers one pragmatic way of organising what is potentially a very rich field. Working within these categories, my analyses show how an animal studies approach can produce new insights into well-known and well-studied travel texts, and these texts, conversely, can enrich our understanding of human–animal encounters.

Notes

1 The term 'animal' is itself considered problematic within the field of animal studies, as it elides the biological categorisation of humans as animals, and discursively lumps all nonhuman species together in one category as 'other', perpetuating rather than interrogating the grounds on which this binary division occurs.

2 Roald Amundsen, *The South Pole: An Account of the Norwegian Antarctic Expedition in the 'Fram', 1910–1912* (London: Hurst, 2001), 2:122.

3 'A Brief History of Animals in Space'. NASA, accessed 21 October 2015, http://history.nasa.gov/animals.html.

4 Graham Huggan and Helen Tiffin, *Postcolonial Ecocriticism: Literature, Animals, Environment* (London: Routledge, 2010), 149–150.

5 Jean-Yves Le Disez, for example, reads 'animal imagery' for what it says about human travellers' negotiation of a culture considered more 'primitive': 'Animals as Figures of Otherness in Travel Narratives of Brittany, 1840–1895', in *Perspectives on Travel Writing*, ed. Glenn Hooper and Tim Youngs (Aldershot: Ashgate, 2004), 72, 76.

6 Again, this terminology is considered problematic; there are several competing terms, including 'human-animal studies', 'critical animal studies', 'animality studies' and 'zoocriticism', all with different political and theoretical emphases.

7 Philip Armstrong and Laurence Simmons, 'Bestiary: An Introduction', in *Knowing Animals*, ed. Philip Armstrong and Laurence Simmons (Leiden: Brill, 2007), 1.

8 See, for example, Jean-Claude Faucon, 'La Représentation de l'animal par Marco Polo', *Médiévales* 32 (1997), and Sophia Magnone, 'Bien Manger, Bien Mangé: Edible Reciprocity in Jean de Léry's *Histoire d'un voyage faict en la terre du Brésil*', *Journal for Early Modern Cultural Studies* 14.3 (Summer 2014): 107. Other examples are given later in the present chapter.

9 Huggan and Tiffin, *Postcolonial Ecocriticism*, 135.

10 Huggan and Tiffin, *Postcolonial Ecocriticism*, 135, 138.

11 See, for example, Shefali Rajamannar, *Reading the Animal in the Literature of the British Raj* (New York: Palgrave Macmillan, 2012); and the special section on 'Nonhuman Empires' in *Comparative Studies of South Asia, Africa and the Middle East* 25.1 (2015).

12 Like other critics, I find Mary Louise Pratt's term 'travelee' – to refer to those 'persons [in this case, animals] traveled to (or on) by a traveler, receptors of travel' – a useful categorisation: Mary Louise Pratt, *Imperial Eyes: Travel Writing and Transculturation* (London: Routledge, 1992), 242.

13 Philip Armstrong, *What Animals Mean in the Fiction of Modernity* (Abingdon: Routledge, 2008), 4.

14 Matthew Flinders, *Trim: The Story of a Brave, Seafaring Cat* (London: Collins, 1977).

15 Amundsen, *South Pole*, 2:123.

16 See, for example, John Mackenzie, *Empire of Nature: Hunting, Conservation and British Imperialism* (Manchester: Manchester University Press, 1998); Finis Dunaway, 'Hunting with the Camera: Nature Photography, Manliness, and Modern Memory, 1890–1930', *Journal of American Studies* 34.2 (2000): 207–330.

17 Tim Youngs, *The Cambridge Introduction to Travel Writing* (Cambridge: Cambridge University Press, 2013), 87, 101.

18 See, for example, Huggan and Tiffin, *Postcolonial Ecocriticism*, 145–147; Rajamannar, *Reading the Animal*, 108–116; Jopi Nyman, 'Ethical Encounters with Animal Others in Travel Writing', in *Travel and Ethics: Theory and Practice*, ed. Corinne Fowler, Charles Forsdick and Ludmilla Kostova (New York: Routledge, 2014), 108–127.

19 For 'hunting mentality' see Mackenzie, *Empire of Nature*, 171.

20 Brigid Hains, *The Ice and the Inland: Mawson, Flynn and the Myth of the Frontier* (Carlton South: Melbourne University Press, 2002), 62–63.

21 Al Alvarez, 'A Magnificent Failure', *New York Review of Books* 44.11 (1997), accessed 21 October 2015, www.nybooks.com/articles/archives/1997/jun/26/a-magnificent-failure.

22 Robert Fraser, *Victorian Quest Romance: Stevenson, Haggard, Kipling, and Conan Doyle* (Plymouth: Northcote House, 1998), 5.

23 Fraser, *Victorian Quest Romance*, 5–6.

24 Apsley Cherry-Garrard, *The Worst Journey in the World* (London: Picador, 1994), 239–240, 274.

25 Kerridge, 'Ecologies of Desire', 170.

26 Kerridge, 'Ecologies of Desire', 175.

27 Cherry-Garrard, *Worst Journey in the World*, 270.

28 Cherry-Garrard, *Worst Journey in the World*, 304–306.

29 Hadoram Shirihai. *A Complete Guide to Antarctic Wildlife: The Birds and Marine Mammals of the Antarctic Continent and Southern Ocean*, 2nd ed. (London: A. & C. Black, 2007), 47, 51.

30 Steven Martin, *Penguin* (London: Reaktion, 2009), 78.

31 For more detail see Elizabeth Leane and Steve Nicol, 'Filming the Frozen South: Animals in Early Antarctic Exploration Films', in *Screening Nature: Cinema Beyond the Human*, ed. Anat Pick and Guinevere Narraway (Oxford: Berghahn, 2013), 127–142.

32 Cherry-Garrard, *Worst Journey in the World*, 274.

33 Nancy Mitford, 'A Bad Time', in *The Water Beetle* (London: Hamish Hamilton, 1962), 27.

34 Bruce Chatwin, *In Patagonia* (1977; repr. London: Vintage-Random House, 2005), 249.

35 Kerridge, 'Ecologies of Desire', 173.

36 Robert Louis Stevenson, *Travels with a Donkey in the Cévennes* (London: Chatto & Windus, 1986), 39. Subsequent references are included parenthetically in the text.

37 Oliver Buckton, *Cruising with Robert Louis Stevenson: Travel, Narrative, and the Colonial Body* (Athens, OH: Ohio University Press, 2007), 67–93.

38 Morgan Holmes, 'Donkeys, Englishmen and Other Animals: The Precarious Distinctions of Victorian Interspecies Morality', in *European Stevenson*, ed. Richard Ambrosini and Richard Dury (Newcastle-upon-Tyne: Cambridge Scholars, 2009), 116.

39 Holmes, 'Donkeys', 111.

40 Jill Bough, *Donkey* (London: Reaktion, 2011), 129.

41 Bough, *Donkey*, 129–133.

42 Buckton, *Cruising*, 77.

43 Mark Shand, *Travels on My Elephant* (London: Eland, 2012), 182.

44 Shand, *Travels*, 167.

45 Shand, *Travels*, 21.

46 Shand, *Travels*, 44.

47 Robyn Davidson, *Tracks* (1980; repr. London: Picador-PanMacmillan, 1998), 241.

48 Youngs, *Cambridge Introduction to Travel Writing*, 93–94.

49 Jerome K. Jerome, *Three Men in a Boat (To Say Nothing of the Dog)* (Bristol: J. W. Arrowsmith, 1889).

50 Davidson, *Tracks*, 3.

51 John Steinbeck, *Travels with Charley: In Search of America* in *Travels with Charley and Later Novels 1947–1962* (New York: Library of America, 2007), 781. Subsequent references are included parenthetically in the text.

52 Oliver Prescott, 'Books of the Times', *The New York Times*, 27 July 1962, 23, accessed 10 August 2014, http://query.nytimes.com/gst/abstract.html?res=9D07E5D8153DE63BBC4F51DFB1668389679 EDE.

53 Douglas Dowland, '"Macrocosm of Microcosm Me": Steinbeck's *Travels with Charley*', *Literature Interpretation Theory* 16 (2005): 311.

54 Małgorzata Rutkowska, 'Travellers and Their Faithful Companions: Dogs in Contemporary American Travel Writing', in *Animal Magic: Essays on Animals in the American Imagination*, ed. Jopi Nyman and Carol Smith (Joensuu: University of Joensuu, 2004), 125, 129, 131, 134.

55 Jacques Derrida, '"Eating Well" or the Calculation of the Subject' in *Points . . . : Interviews 1974–1994*, trans. Peggy Kamuf et al., ed. Elisabeth Weber (Stanford, CA: Stanford University Press, 1995), 278.

56 Other examples of this genre include Bruce Fogle, *Travels with Macy: One Man and His Dog Take a Journey through North America in Search of Home* (London: Ebury, 2005) and Clare de Vries, *I & Claudius: Travels with My Cat* (New York: Bloomsbury, 1999).

57 I am employing here Youngs's 'guiding principle' that 'travel writing consists of predominantly factual, first-person prose accounts of travel that have been undertaken by the author-narrator'. *Cambridge Introduction to Travel Writing*, 3.

58 The final chapter of Robert Macfarlane *The Old Ways: A Journey on Foot* (London: Penguin, 2013), for example, gestures in this direction. See also Etienne Benson's 'Animal Writes: Historiography, Disciplinarity, and the Animal Trace', in *Making Animal Meaning*, ed. Linda Kalof and Georgina Montgomery (East Lansing, MI: Michigan State University Press, 2011), 3, for an academic discussion of 'the relationship that is established in the course of writing, where "writing" is understood as a form of tracking and leaving tracks that is less specific to the human species than is usually assumed'.

PART V

Paratexts

23

EDITORIAL MATTERS

Michael G. Brennan

Editorial challenges

Travel writings are now central to many areas of humanities and social sciences and treated as significant primary sources for a wide range of literary, historical, geographical, anthropological and ethnographic concerns. But unlike well-established textual conventions for handling prose, poetry and drama, editorial standards for the vast corpus of international travel writings are still very much under debate. The challenges facing a modern editor of travel writing may initially be defined within four broad categories: genre, authorship, textual history and readership (both contemporary and modern). The treatment and balancing of these categories often play a significant part in determining the overall design of a modern edition with respect to how its introductory materials should be presented, what kinds of critical apparatus (including footnotes, annotations and textual collations) are required and what other supplementary materials (such as maps, glossaries, illustrations, bibliographies, appendices and indices) should be supplied to support the intended readership.[1]

In relation to genre, the term 'travel writing' has only recently replaced the multi-purpose categorisation of 'writings about travel' or the vague terminology of the pre-1980 Modern Language Association Bibliography, 'travel, treatment of'.[2] Travel writing is now recognised as a diverse and ever-shifting genre, central to most literary cultures, but one which has never settled (and is unlikely to do so) into a unifying paradigm. From the sixteenth century onwards travel narratives emerged in England as an engaging and flexible form of writing. They were aimed, variously, at memorialising an author's achievements, instructing fellow travellers, entertaining unknown readers, inspiring nationalistic and imperial ambitions, stimulating commercial investments and supporting military or naval campaigns. Hence, the modern editor frequently needs to determine from (often incomplete or elusive) contemporaneous documentary and textual evidence how the composition of a travel text might have once related to a specific set of social, political, economic, scientific, imperialist or religious perspectives. In some cases it will also be necessary to assess how later circulations of the text in either manuscript or print related to sustained or new political, commercial, imperialist or other causes.[3]

Secondly, the fluidity of early-modern concepts of authorship may further complicate the editor's initial assessment of a travel text. The original author or collaborative authors may be unknown or, at best, biographically hazy, leading to challenging or even insurmountable problems in contextualising the original purpose of a travel account. Sometimes, the fact that an author is now remembered primarily as a courtier, diplomat, merchant, explorer, adventurer, privateer, cleric, religious exile, servant, student or scholar can prove either central or misleading to an understanding of the intended purpose and scope of a travel text. Indeed, some compilers of travel accounts – such as Richard Hakluyt – never or rarely travelled outside their own country and brought only scholarly and editorial expertise rather than geographical knowledge to their collections.

Modern concepts of distinctions between subjectivity and objectivity and the assumed integrity of single authorship can also prove inapplicable to writings about travel. The concept of sequential multiple authorship – with one compiler of a travel account silently drawing descriptions, factual information and the first-hand observations of others into his or her own narrative – is a familiar one in this field.[4] Modern standards of improper use of sources or plagiarism cannot be applied to a form of writing in which authors (especially in guidebooks and formal travel reports) were expected to compile detailed and up-to-date narratives by drawing together an accretion of valuable knowledge and observations from other sources which would only rarely be acknowledged. The modern editor may also sometimes encounter additional handwritten annotations and descriptions made by contemporary readers in their personal copies of travel documents – an editorial challenge which often raises important but notoriously elusive issues of early provenance and ownership.

Thirdly, accurately establishing the textual descent and integrity of a particular travel account through manuscript or printed versions (or both) may prove complex for the modern editor since the author's original versions (including rough jottings, notebooks, ships' logs, personal correspondence, working copies and private fair copies or presentation manuscripts) may have long since been lost or sometimes have remained previously unrecognised (as with Richard Hakluyt's account of the Spanish Armada, discussed below). Either known or unidentified transcribers of surviving manuscript copies of travel accounts may have silently made substantive emendations to surviving copies which can no longer be identified – or only spotted if the modern editor can also access the original author's version (as with Hakluyt's account of the Cadiz Expedition, see below). Furthermore, many works of travel disseminated in English were originally written in another language (as was Hakluyt's Spanish Armada account) and the modern editor must try to assess both the accuracy of the translation and the specifics of how the translator may have adjusted the foreign language source in either factual substance or linguistic inflexion for ulterior nationalistic, political, religious or other purposes. Furthermore, as the editing of travel accounts continues to proliferate, it is becoming increasingly common for the appearance in print of a modern edition to flush out either earlier or later versions of the text or foreign translations which were previously unknown or merely suspected.[5]

The fourth category, relating to the editor's assessment of past, present and potential readerships of both the original work and the modern edition, can prove especially complex. While it might be assumed that a modern edition should be accessible to all kinds of interested readers, the editor's presentation of the possible original reasons for the writing, manuscript circulation and any contemporaneous or later printings of travel texts often requires careful handling in both introductory materials and annotations. For example, early sixteenth-century narratives about the discovery and exploitation of the New World can at first be regarded as exciting accounts of heroic and marvel-filled explorations, even though the original narratives may have been initially drafted and circulated primarily to confirm the global ascendancy of the Spanish Empire. Consequently, later English translations were carefully edited and published as an implicit means of challenging and appropriating the reputation of Spanish imperialism for the commercial purposes of English naval exploration and colonisation.[6] Finally, as in the case (below) of Charles Lord Howard of Effingham (1536–1624), the commander of the English fleet against the Armada, identifying the original owner of a manuscript can sometimes provide crucial contextual perspectives on its circumstances of composition or transcription which may not have been otherwise realised by the modern editor.

Modern editors must always give careful consideration to the amount and scope of annotations and other supporting materials provided for their readers, including historical, biographical, geographical and other cultural, political or religious notes, as well as maps, glossaries, illustrations and bibliographies of relevant primary and secondary materials. For example, during the Jacobean period two of the most informative printed accounts of travels within continental Europe were compiled by Thomas Coryate (1577?–1617) and Fynes Moryson (1565/6–1630). *Coryat's Crudities* (1611) contains a wealth of historical, geographical, sociological and cultural information but it is still only available to modern readers through either rare book libraries possessing the original 1611 edition, or (now more commonly) via websites such as Early English Books Online, archive.org website, Google books (1776 edition) or in an unannotated two-volume reprint of 1905 by the Glasgow publisher, MacLehose.[7] Similarly, Moryson's *An Itinerary* (1617) remains one of the most detailed works of travel writing printed during the Jacobean period, documenting his perspectives on much of Western Europe, as well as Turkey and the British Isles. Modern readers, however, still struggle to utilise this text productively since it has only been reprinted, again by MacLehose, in an unannotated four-volume edition of 1907–8. Current web resources tend to reproduce merely the original 1617 edition or the MacLehose reprint without additional annotations identifying its detailed references to people, places and other items of literary or historical interest.[8]

The annotations in any future editions of Coryate and Moryson would need to strike a reasonable balance between providing enough information to facilitate a clear understanding of a text and the risk of overwhelming its readers with historical, geographical, cultural or other details. Such a balance is far from easy to achieve since travel writings are now readily incorporated into so many different academic disciplines and perused by a wide range of both general and specialist readers, including those interested, for example, in domestic politics, international affairs, architecture, garden design, mercantile trade, ecclesiastical and theological matters, pilgrimage routes and military and naval affairs. Prospective editors of Coryate and Moryson would also need to treat historiographical evidence derived from their narratives with caution or, in David Henige's memorable phrase, 'systematic doubt', since the blending of factual observations with imaginative or embellished recreations is far from uncommon during this period of travel writings.[9]

Richard Hakluyt's *The Principal Navigations*

This chapter will now explore some of these editorial challenges within the context of two well-known and often quoted accounts of Anglo-Spanish relations during the late-Elizabethan period. *The Principal Navigations* of Richard Hakluyt (1552?–1616) was first published as a single volume in 1589 and then significantly expanded into three volumes between 1598 and 1600. His accounts of the Spanish Armada (1588) and the Cadiz Expedition (1596) appeared at the end of the first volume of the second edition and offer an intriguing range of editorial problems common to many forms of travel writing from this period. Both of these edited texts form part of Oxford University Press's 'The Hakluyt Edition Project', comprising a fourteen-volume critical and annotated edition of almost 600 accounts of travel, exploration and related documents, totalling some 1.76 million words.

Hakluyt's editorial work remains of central importance to the history of the textual editing of travel writings in that he sought to blend the methodologies of both English and continental predecessors in collecting together informative and geographically diverse narratives for publication. In response to earlier English publishing practice, he followed the example of Richard Eden (c.1520–76) and Richard Willes (1546–79?) who had translated and edited, respectively, the 1555 and 1577 editions of Peter Martyr's *De orbe novo decades* or *Decades of the New World*. This landmark publication provided a series of early sixteenth-century reports of New World explorations.[10] Hakluyt was also mindful of well-established continental models of editing, exemplified by the German cartographer Sebastian Münster (1488–1552) in his *Novus orbis* (1532), the first Northern-European collection of global voyages, and the Venetian civil servant Giovanni Battista Ramusio (1485–1557), who had advocated the humanist ideal of meticulous transcription from the 'best' manuscript and printed sources available in his *Navigationi et Viaggi* (1555–9). In this respect, Hakluyt's publications mark in England a decisive cultural and bibliographical moment in the emergence, as Joan-Pau Rubiés explains, 'of travel writing as a distinctive genre central to the late Renaissance system of knowledge'. He sought in *The Principal Navigations* to build on, rather than replace, the major contribution of these earlier collections, 'both in English (by Eden and Willes, which he freely ransacked) and in other languages of the learned (in particular Ramusio's magnificent collection, which was never translated from Italian to English in full)'.[11]

If it is assumed that Hakluyt wished to provide his contemporary readers with the 'best' available text of a travel narrative, it is crucial for the modern editor to determine how the term 'best' should be interpreted within the context of Hakluyt's own time. It should not be confused with current standards of textual editing, usually based upon a carefully selected copy-text in conjunction with readings from other related manuscript and printed versions, thereby providing modern readers with what is assumed to be a reliable rendering of the author's concluding draft of (or final intentions for) a work. *The Hakluyt Handbook*, edited by D.B. Quinn, details all known sources for items included in both the 1589 and 1598–1600 editions of *The Principal Navigations*. It confirms Hakluyt's eclectic use of identifiable printed and manuscript sources (although not necessarily the specific printed editions or manuscript versions utilised) as well as a substantial number of unidentifiable sources which are assumed to have been drawn primarily from now lost manuscript accounts.[12] But considerable uncertainty still remains over various key aspects of the publication process for *The Principal Navigations*. It is not known, for example, whether Hakluyt sent marked-up manuscript and/or printed copies to the printers of his 1589 and 1598–1600 editions, or if he employed scribes to transcribe some of these printers' texts, or if he copied out in his own hand large sections of these manuscript drafts since no printers' authorial or scribal manuscripts or marked-up proofs are known to have survived.

Modern readers of Hakluyt's volumes have usually envisaged him selecting and editing his numerous travel narratives not only for literary and commercial reasons but also for the purposes of English national propaganda. In making these choices, he was guided by both geographical and cosmographical reasons (as well as by the essentially random availability and survival of informative accounts) and by a network of influence and court patronage which included Sir Philip Sidney and Sir Walter Ralegh and, most significantly for *The Principal Navigations*, two successive Secretaries of State, Sir Francis Walsingham and Sir Robert Cecil, and the Lord High Admiral Charles Lord Howard of Effingham.[13]

Hakluyt's choice of copy-text for his account of the Spanish Armada in *The Principal Navigations* (1:591–607) has only recently been established by the present author. It was previously supposed that it had been derived from either the Cologne (1597?) or Antwerp (n.d.) editions of *Historia Belgica* by the Flemish historian Emanuel van Meteren (1535–1612) – whom

Hakluyt knew personally – or perhaps from one of its earlier German editions (1596, 1597, 1598). Alternatively, it was suggested that van Meteren may have personally supplied a manuscript text 'directly to Hakluyt, in advance of the Latin edition, for him to translate'.[14] But it now seems that Hakluyt did not directly access his account of the Armada expedition from either a manuscript or printed version of *Historia Belgica*. Instead, during the mid-1590s the London scribe and commercial hack writer Richard Robinson (1544/5–1603) compiled a series of manuscripts relating to the Dutch revolt and the allied English war effort, including in 1595 Latin transcriptions from van Meteren's as yet unpublished *Historia Belgica*. He continued this scribal work in 1596 with accounts of both the Armada campaign and the Cadiz Expedition. Robinson's transcription of the Armada narrative states that it was derived from a Cologne text of van Meteren's account of the Spanish Armada (contained in the fifteenth book of his *Historia Belgica*). It was completed by Robinson on 9 July 1596 and then presented to Howard of Effingham who had given Robinson on 18 July 1595 another manuscript account from which he had transcribed this carefully written copy.[15]

Robinson's Latin manuscript transcription, rather than a printed edition of *Historia Belgica*, became the primary source for Hakluyt's English account in the 1598 edition of *The Principal Navigations*. Its lavish dedication (fol. 1v) to Howard also directly prefigures Hakluyt's dedication to him of this entire volume of *The Principal Navigations*. It would seem, then, that the inclusion of both the Spanish Armada and Cadiz narratives at the end of this volume was probably occasioned at a relatively late stage in the pre-production process (or even when printing of the earlier sections of the volume had already begun) as much by Charles Howard, as by Hakluyt himself. Since Robinson had in 1596 completed for Howard his transcription (derived from van Meteren) of the Armada engagement, it was probably opportune and personally useful for Hakluyt to utilise this particular text. After all, the volume in which it appeared was to be dedicated to Howard and his achievements in leading the English fleets during the Spanish Armada and at the Cadiz Expedition were proclaimed on its title-page. Hakluyt, thereby, could pay gracious tribute to Howard through both the preliminary and concluding matter offered by this volume. Even though these two accounts in no way fitted with its broader geographical or mercantile remit, it may be that Howard not only suggested or requested their inclusion but also personally supplied a copy of Robinson's Latin manuscript transcription from which Hakluyt could make his English translation.

Hakluyt's account of the Cadiz Expedition (1596)

During 1598 Charles Howard, by then Earl of Nottingham, collaborated with Robert Devereux, Earl of Essex, in preparing the country against an anticipated (if exaggerated) threat of a Spanish invasion and in 1599 he alone was appointed to 'an unprecedentedly powerful commission' as 'Lord Lieutenant-General of all England' in overall charge of all military defences.[16] This pointed absence of the more youthful and militarily experienced Earl of Essex from such a commission may be fed back into the curious circumstances surrounding the inclusion – and then sudden excision – of an account of the triumphant 1596 Cadiz Expedition which immediately followed that of the Spanish Armada at the end of the first volume of the 1598 edition of *The Principal Navigations*. This latter voyage had been jointly led by Howard as sea-commander and Devereux as land-commander, and in his 'Epistle Dedicatorie' Hakluyt enthusiastically praised Howard's role in this 'late renowned expedition and honorable voyage unto Cadiz'. He also noted that he had derived his text largely from an account by 'a very grave and learned Gentleman, which was an eye witness in all that action'.[17] Given that this individual was Dr Roger Marbeck (1536–1605), Howard's personal physician on the Cadiz voyage, it seems likely that Hakluyt's use of his manuscript as the sole source for his account of the expedition was, as already seems the case for the Spanish Armada, personally approved by Howard himself.[18]

If Hakluyt did source both his Armada and Cadiz accounts from Howard's private library, it remains far from clear as to what then occasioned a radical, post-publication excision of the Cadiz (but not the Armada) account – literally by cutting out the relevant leaves – from some 1598 volumes (probably those still remaining in the hands of stationers and booksellers). Hakluyt's Cadiz voyage account was unexpectedly and rapidly suppressed, resulting in various (but by no means all) copies of the 1598 volume being thus crudely emended in about October 1599, with the title-page of the volume reprinted (omitting any mention of Cadiz) and the publication date revised from 1598 to 1599. However, brief passing references to the expedition in the 'Epistle Dedicatorie' (sig. *2v), preface (sig. **2v) and contents list (sig. **4v) remained untouched in this 1599 reissued edition. Anthony Payne has calculated that of 110 examined copies with the 1598 title-page, sixty copies retain the Cadiz leaves and of 130 examined copies with the 1599 title-page, fifty-five copies still include them. He concludes: 'The implication of this is that, if there was censorship it was not especially effective as the Cadiz leaves survive in so many copies and [. . .] that it was short-lived and confined to a particular time and set of political circumstances.'[19]

The most likely reason for this censorship lies in Queen Elizabeth's and Sir Robert Cecil's deep annoyance at the Earl of Essex's failed Irish expedition between April and late September 1599, leading to his unauthorised truce with the Earl of Tyrone. Essex's erratic behaviour immediately following this debacle instigated his temporary house-arrest and forced withdrawal from court, ultimately leading to his ill-fated rebellion and execution for treason in February 1601. Alternatively, this censorship may have also been prompted by lingering resentment over the political controversy occasioned by the Cadiz venture itself. Elizabeth considered that Essex had tried to hijack the expedition for his own purposes to establish an English garrison and naval base in the city, a strategy which she had specifically vetoed. It had also been rumoured that Essex was secretly planning to publish a 'True relation' of the expedition, glorifying his own leadership and heroism. To prevent such partisan propaganda, William Cecil, Lord Burghley, had ensured that the Council, via the licensing authority over stationers of John Whitgift, Archbishop of Canterbury, imposed a blanket ban on all publications about Cadiz immediately after the expedition's triumphant return to England.

Perhaps most significantly, Hakluyt wished to dedicate the second and third volumes of *The Principal Navigations* to Burghley's son, Sir Robert Cecil, then Secretary of State (1596–1608) and the most influential opponent of Essex in advocating a negotiating peace with Spain. It may be that Sir Robert was the prime instigator of the excision of the Cadiz leaves since in 1599 he was keen to secure his own still uncertain position at the royal court, following the death of his father, Lord Burghley, on 4 August 1598. Hakluyt's personal cultivation of the younger Cecil was notably successful. Appointed in 1599 as Sir Robert's personal chaplain, he was promised (at Cecil's request) the next reversion to a chaplaincy at the Hospital of the Savoy, in London.[20] Finally, through Cecil's influence he was installed as a prebendary (4 May 1602) and archdeacon (3 December 1603) of Westminster Abbey. He duly dedicated to Cecil the second (1599) and third volumes of *The Principal Navigations* (dedication dated 1 December 1600), as well as his edition of António Galvão's *Discoveries* (1601). From the Armada and Cadiz narratives it is clear that modern editors of travel writings at this period must take into account not only which surviving manuscript and/or printed sources should be utilised as copy-texts but also the often complex historical and personal circumstances determining the processes by which editors of early-modern travel texts obtained the requisite primary literary materials for their intended publications.

Later texts and editors of Hakluyt's Spanish Armada and Cadiz Expedition accounts

It seems that this censorship of Hakluyt's account of the Cadiz Expedition was short-lived since the 1600 edition of John Stowe's *Annales of England*, dedicated on 24 November to Archbishop Whitgift, still an official licenser for the press, included an account of the Spanish Armada (1244–61) and – apparently without any problems – 'The Abstract of the expedition to Cadiz 1596' (1282–93), both utilising (but without acknowledgement) Hakluyt's accounts and supplementary information.[21] Hakluyt's narratives of the Spanish Armada and the Cadiz Expedition were also reprinted, primarily for propaganda purposes, in a four-volume folio collection edited by Samuel Purchas (1575–1626), *Hakluytus Posthumus or, Purchas his Pilgrimes* (1624/5), the year in which George Villiers (1592–1628), Duke of Buckingham, led another attack on Cadiz, inspired by both Sir Francis Drake's 1587 raid and the 1596 joint expedition of Charles Howard, Earl of Nottingham, and the Earl of Essex. The title-page of this work also bore a small inset illustration of the defeat of the Armada. The clergyman and compiler of travel accounts, Purchas knew Hakluyt personally and had borrowed from him various manuscript and printed sources for the second edition of his own earlier compilation of travel literature, *Purchas, his Pilgrimage* (1613; rev. and repr. 1614). Purchas, who envisaged a 'militantly theological' purpose for his publications, viewed himself as Hakluyt's rightful literary successor and acquired in about 1620 a range of the latter's manuscripts which he extensively used in his *Pilgrimes* collection.[22]

During the nineteenth century two major editions of *The Principal Navigations* were published. The first was printed in five volumes as *Hakluyt's Collection of the Early Voyages, Travels, and Discoveries of the English Nation*, edited by R.H. Evans, J. Mackinlay and R. Priestley of London (1809–12). It reproduced *verbatim* Hakluyt's accounts of the Armada (2:1–18) and Cadiz Expedition (2:19–33). Over seventy years later, a sixteen-volume edition of *The Principal Navigations* was edited by Edmund Goldsmid, who extensively reordered Hakluyt's materials, and published in Edinburgh by E. and G. Goldsmid (1885–90). Volume seven, *England's Naval Exploits Against Spain*, included Hakluyt's Armada and Cadiz Expedition accounts taken from the 1598–1600 edition with perhaps also reference to the Purchas and Evans, Mackinlay and Priestley editions.[23] Between 1903 and 1905 the Glasgow firm J. MacLehose and Sons published, in conjunction with The Hakluyt Society, a twelve-volume edition of *The Principal Navigations* (1598–1600), with only slight modifications in spelling and the addition of illustrations of contemporary maps, plans, charts and portraits. The fourth volume contained the accounts of the Armada and the Cadiz Expedition.[24] A new essay was also added and, for the first time, a comprehensive index of the volumes was supplied by Marie Minchon and Elizabeth Carmont.[25] Since 1905 this edition has remained the standard point of reference for the majority of readers of *The Principal Navigations* who lack ready access to the original 1598–1600 edition, along with a cheaper eight-volume Everyman's Library edition, excluding all Latin texts, published by J.M. Dent in 1907.

During the last three decades there has been a significant escalation of interest in Hakluyt's *The Principal Navigations* from various historical, literary, geographical and cultural perspectives and a comprehensive new edition is patently needed. The Oxford University Press edition selected as its copy-text the Huntington Library's copy of Hakluyt's original 1598–1600 edition. However, the Cadiz leaves are missing from this volume and so the copy-text for this account has been taken from the Bodleian Library, Oxford, copy (Savile X 12) once owned by the scholar and politician Sir Henry Savile (1549–1622). This copy has been chosen because it is an original 1598 printing and the Cadiz leaves are clearly original to this volume with no attempt having been made to remove them. This new fourteen-volume edition (produced by twenty-three volume editors) retains old spelling (with some standard modernisations, such as 'i' for 'j' and 'u' for 'v', etc.) but does not seek to create a facsimile of typographical effects (such as the use in 1598–1600 of black letter) and standardises roman and italic type to modern usage. Most importantly, this edition of *The Principal Navigations* provides via its footnotes comprehensive annotations of all persons, places, vessels, obscure or complex military and naval terminologies, dates, routes and other factual details and via its endnotes additional textual and editorial information.

Such rigorous editorial standards offer a major step forward in understanding the nature and importance of Hakluyt's choice of texts for his accounts of the Armada and the Cadiz Expedition. Of all the previous editions, none attempted any textual collations or tried to identify Hakluyt's original sources. Only Goldsmid's 1885–90 edition provided selected explanatory annotations. Even so, he felt it necessary to apologise for the paucity of these glosses, lamenting: 'I can assure any who may be disposed to cavil at their brevity that many a *line* has cost me hours of research' (1:vii). In contrast, 'The Hakluyt Project' provides readers with a stable and authoritative text of the 1598–1600 edition of *The Principal Navigations*.

Finally, this new edition of *The Principal Navigations* seeks to stimulate current and subsequent generations of scholars to conduct further research into Hakluyt's accounts of the Armada and Cadiz Expedition, not least with a view to noting both the contemporary authority of these texts and their significant omissions. The Armada account was compiled, indirectly, from a Dutch original and the Cadiz account from the private record of the Lord Admiral's personal physician who had no prior experience of seamanship or naval engagements. Hence, it is inevitable that these two narratives offer partisan and incomplete accounts. Roger Marbeck's narrative of the Cadiz Expedition is, predictably, highly subjective and in its manuscript draft he reveals his naïve fascination with various standard naval practices. He describes in detail how naval vessels traditionally encountered and saluted one another at sea and such spectacular sights as passing shoals of flying fish. However, Hakluyt systematically excised such incidental details from his printed account in *The Principal Navigations* as extraneous to his primarily nationalist and propagandist purposes. Similarly, this account offers substantial listings of over eighty English participants since Marbeck was clearly at pains to provide as detailed a record as possible of the naval and court personnel involved in the expedition. No previous attempt had ever been made to identify all of these individuals or to assess their roles in the expedition. But, in contrast, the Armada account is much more selective – as is to be expected from a continental text – in its naming of commanders, officers, crews, volunteers and chaplains among the English fleet. Its references to English vessels are no more than perfunctory and it lacks throughout the detailed knowledge of the organisation and day-to-day running of the fleet which is so apparent in Marbeck's informative, albeit amateur, account of the Cadiz Expedition.

To take only one historically significant omission, no mention is made in Hakluyt's Armada narrative (i.e., via Robinson's transcription from van Meteren's Latin text) of the presence and conspicuous feats of bravery of the retired sea-commander, military officer and Member of Parliament, Sir George Beeston (c.1520–1601). Beeston, probably in his late sixties at the time of the Armada crisis, had participated in the Battle of Musselburgh (1547) and the Siege of Boulogne (1548). During Queen Mary's reign he was a Gentleman Pensioner and served at sea during the 1570s in command of a new warship, the *Dreadnought* (launched 1573). By 1576, as befitted his age, he was primarily occupied on land supervising the shore defences at Gravesend but during the Armada conflict he took to the sea for one final adventure, again commanding the *Dreadnought*, and was knighted for bravery on the deck of Howard of Effingham's flag-ship, the *Ark Royal*.

Hakluyt's Armada account does at least make brief reference to several other English naval notables, such as Sir Francis Drake (1540–96), George Clifford (1558–1605), Earl of Cumberland, Lord Henry Seymour (b.1540) and Thomas Fleming (fl.1580s), whose pinnace, the *Golden Hind*, first sighted the Spanish fleet as it approached The Lizard.[26] It is also especially informative in its referencing of the Spanish commanders and sea captains, such as the commander of their fleet, Alonso Pérez de Guzmán, Duke of Medina Sidonia (1550–1615) and its two deputy commanders, Juan Martínez de Recalde (d.1588) and Miguel de Oquendo y Segura (d.1588), since van Meteren had a detailed knowledge of the Spanish hierarchy. Indeed, modern readers need to recognise that the overall balance of the naval information in van Meteren's account is sometimes weighted (especially at the beginning of the account) far more towards the Spanish than English fleet. But numerous other examples of English individuals and vessels known from other contemporary sources to have been involved in the repulse of the Spanish fleet could be readily added to those included in this account, even though Hakluyt's third-hand (i.e., via Robinson and van Meteren), continental account makes no specific mention of them.

In conclusion, the modern editor needs to make clear how van Meteren (via Robinson's transcription) tends to view the significance of the Armada Fleet from the perspective of its potential impact on the Low Countries and Spanish Netherlands as much as England. Hakluyt reproduces without qualification van Meteren's statement that the Spaniards considered conquering England to be 'lesse difficult then the conquest of Holland and Zeland' and also cites his usage of the Spanish printed pamphlet, *La Felicissima Armada*, published at Lisbon on 9 May 1588. Similarly, he sometimes accepts without question errors incorporated into van Meteren's original text. For example, he describes Juán de Escobedo (1530–78) as secretary to Philip II rather than, as was the case, to his brother, Don John of Austria. The Oxford University Press edition of Hakluyt's *The Principal Navigations* implicitly underlines, therefore, an editorial need for the collecting together (ideally in digital form) and thorough reassessment of all surviving contemporary manuscript and printed accounts (in various languages) of the Spanish Armada engagement of 1588 and the Cadiz Expedition of 1596.

Future directions for travel writing

The Oxford edition of Hakluyt's *The Principal Navigations* was intended from its earliest planning stages to be published in both hardback (aimed primarily at the library market and select bibliophiles) and digital form as part of the 'Oxford Scholarly Editions Online' series. The rapid technological developments in electronic texts over recent years offer to all genres of literary editing the most important advances in textual scholarship since they provide not only facilities for online searching but also unlimited possibilities for the future emendation and expansion of the edition. For example, the seven volumes of *The Cambridge Edition of the Works of Ben Jonson*, edited by David Bevington, Martin Butler and Ian Donaldson, were published in paper form in 2012 but this project also offers a comprehensive online edition which is regularly updated with new and revised materials. This process enables editors (and their contributing readers) to continue to respond to developments in editorial thinking as well as to newly discovered materials and fresh interpretations of Jonson's works. The digital texts also provide a fully searchable version of the printed edition, including all introductory materials, textual collations and commentaries.

Digital technology, however, can offer much more than a mere online reflection of a printed edition. In the case of the Cambridge Jonson project, the electronic edition also provides 'hundreds of digital images and dozens of searchable old-spelling transcriptions of the early printed versions of Jonson's texts and some of the major manuscripts' which can be viewed either independently or in comparison with the modern-spelling version or other relevant documents reproduced on the project's website. Print editions, in the words of Martha Nell Smith, have in the past been 'necessarily faith-based, for readers cannot adequately see the documentary evidence that determines everything from genre to suitability for inclusion in a scholarly edition'.[27] In contrast, the Ben Jonson digital edition also provides in support of its primary textual materials a wide range of essays and archival documents relevant to Jonson's life, performance history and afterlife, including about '80 old-spelling texts, 550 contextual documents, 88 essays, several hundred high-quality images, and 100 music scores' as well as details of 'more than 1300 stage performances' and a 'cross-linked bibliography of over 7000 items'.[28]

When this kind of electronic technology is applied to the editing of travel texts, a range of important new possibilities readily become apparent. Since so many early modern travel accounts were originally written in languages other than English and often translated into other languages both before and after the English translation(s), reproducing texts of all such multilingual versions becomes prohibitively expensive in print. But in digital form, there is no limit to the number of texts and editions of a work which can be made simultaneously available to both editors and readers – a process which will surely enrich both the editorial process and the reader's engagement with specific travel narratives. In this respect, digital technology also significantly enhances the possibilities for collaborative editing since materials can be posted and revised by several hands as the project progresses.

Electronic processes are now offering new ways of readily retrieving information from damaged or apparently illegible documents. For example, the 'David Livingstone Spectral Imaging Project' utilises 'spectral imaging technology and digital publishing to make available a series of faded, illegible texts produced by the famous Victorian explorer when stranded without ink or writing paper in Central Africa'.[29] With the possibilities of electronic searching and the open-ended collation of large amounts of data from a growing collection of related texts and images, the concept of a constantly updatable electronic edition is now becoming an intrinsic (and increasingly essential) element in the textual editing of travel writings. These new perspectives, however, offer major challenges to currently active academic editors who have only been trained in the compilation and dissemination of travel texts through paper publications. Clearly, this rapidly evolving age of digital textual editing will require the development of a range of new editorial skills and the increasing collaboration of editors of travel writings with technologically adept digital practitioners as well as with the compilers of online editions of other works from the written and visual arts, humanities and sciences.

Notes

1 See Germaine Warkentin, ed., *Critical Issues in Editing Exploration Texts* (Toronto: University of Toronto Press, 1995), and Pierre-Esprit Radison, *The Collected Writings, vol. 1, The Voyages*, ed. Germaine Warkentin (Toronto: The Champlain Society, 2012) for further discussion of these issues.

2 Mary Baine Campbell, 'Travel Writing and Its Theory', in *The Cambridge Companion to Travel Writing*, ed. Peter Hulme and Tim Youngs (Cambridge: Cambridge University Press, 2002), 261.

3 See, for example, Michael G. Brennan, ed., *The Origins of the Grand Tour* (London: The Hakluyt Society, 2004), for the diverse travel records (1649–54) of the youthful Robert Montagu (partly drafted by his tutor Mr Hainhofer), witty letters home from the continent (1655–8) from William Hammond and a panegyric account of Banaster Maynard's travels (1660–3) by his servant Robert Moody.

4 The detailed travel narratives in the diary of John Evelyn (1620–1706) contain a wealth of apparently first-hand topographical, political and cultural details. However, his description of Paris was written not at the time of his main visit to the city in 1643 but during his retirement in the 1670s. Evelyn was also heavily dependent upon a popular guidebook, *Le voyage de France* (Paris, 1643) by Claude de

Varennes, for much of his specific detail. Like many of his contemporaries, Evelyn regarded travel narratives not as original commentaries but as informed amalgamations of first-hand and authoritative secondary information. John Evelyn, *The Diary of John Evelyn*, ed. E.S. de Beer (Oxford: Clarendon Press, 1955).

5 This writer's edition of *The Travel Diary of Robert Bargrave* noted that printed extracts (published in 1836–7) had probably been drawn from a then lost transcription: Robert Bargrave, *The Travel Diary of Robert Bargrave, Levant Merchant (1647–1656)*, ed. Michael G. Brennan (London: The Hakluyt Society, 1999), 48–51. In 2014 Anthony Payne discovered this later version (c.1700) of Bargrave's account in the stock room of the London antiquarian booksellers Maggs Bros where it had probably been stored since the 1930s (private correspondence).

6 See my essay, 'The Texts of Peter Martyr's *De orbe novo decades* (1504–1628)', *Connotations* 6.2 (1996/7): 227–43. It traces the varying nationalistic and expansionist purposes of the numerous Latin, Italian, Spanish, German, Dutch and English editions of Martyr's narratives in relation first to Spanish and Portuguese (Catholic) imperialism and then to English (Protestant) global expansionism and colonisation through its 1555 (ed. Richard Eden), 1577 (ed. Richard Willes), 1587 (ed. Richard Hakluyt) and 1612, 1625 and 1628 (ed. Michael Lok) editions.

7 Since 2011 a print-on-order copy of this Glasgow edition has also been available from the Nabu Press.

8 Unpublished chapters from Moryson's *Itinerary* were included in *Shakespeare's Europe*, ed. Charles Hughes (New York: Blom, 1967); and the MacLehose edition is available on the archive.org website. The 1617 edition is also accessible via Early English Books Online and the University College, London, Digital Collections website.

9 See David Henige, *Historical Evidence and Argument* (Madison, WI: University of Wisconsin Press, 2005), 39.

10 See note 6.

11 Joan-Pau Rubiés, 'From the "History of Travayle" to the History of Travel Collections: The Rise of an Early Modern Genre', in *Richard Hakluyt and Travel Writing in Early Modern Europe*, ed. Daniel Carey and Claire Jowitt (London: The Hakluyt Society, 2013), 26, 31.

12 D.B. Quinn, ed., *The Hakluyt Handbook* (London: The Hakluyt Society, 1974), [1589 edition] 2:341–77, [1598–1600 edition], 2:378–460.

13 George Bruner Parks, *Richard Hakluyt and the English Voyages* (1928; repr. New York: F. Ungar, 1961), 123–32, 173–86; Peter C. Mancall, *Hakluyt's Promise: An Elizabethan's Obsession for an English America* (New Haven, CT: Yale University Press, 2007), 183–94, 221–34.

14 Quinn, ed., *Hakluyt Handbook*, 2:382; John Parker, *Van Meteren's Virginia, 1607–12* (Minneapolis, MN: University of Minnesota Press, 1961), 12–17. For Hakluyt's contacts with van Meteren, see *Hakluyt Handbook*, 1:300, 307, 311; Mancall, *Hakluyt's Promise*, 210–13.

15 Bodleian Library, Oxford, MS Tanner 255. Robinson's title-page (fol. 1r) notes that the account was first written in German in 1594, translated from German into Latin and also printed in German in 1595 and then transcribed by him in Latin in 1596.

16 James McDermott, 'Charles Howard, Second Baron Howard of Effingham and First Earl of Nottingham (1536–1624)', in *Oxford Dictionary of National Biography*, ed. H.C.G. Matthew and Brian Harrison (Oxford: Oxford University Press, 2004, online edition).

17 Richard Hakluyt, *The Principal Navigations, Voyages and Discoveries of the English Nation* (London, 1598), sig.*2v.

18 Hakluyt's account was edited from a copy of Marbeck's (possibly autograph) manuscript narrative, 'A Breefe and a true Discourse of the late honorable voyage unto Spaine, and of the wynning, sacking and burning of the famous Towne of Cadiz there'. See BL Sloane MS 226 and Bodleian Library, Oxford, Rawlinson D 124. Howard may have also loaned to Hakluyt another manuscript account of the Cadiz expedition, 'An English quip for a Spanish quo' (Bodleian Library, Oxford, MS Rawl B 259), which Richard Robinson had transcribed and presented him with in October 1596.

19 Anthony Payne, 'Richard Hakluyt and the Earl of Essex: The Censorship of the Voyage to Cadiz in the Principal Navigations', *Publishing History*, 72 (2012) [2014]: 7–52, 7–8. To circumvent this censorship, the excised leaves may have been made available at the time of sale by the bookseller for reinsertion at the purchaser's discretion. Semi-facsimile copies of the Cadiz leaves were also printed in about 1720 and 1795 and various copies of the original 1598–1600 edition contain these later additions.

20 Quinn, ed., *Hakluyt Handbook*, 1:313, 316–19.

21 Anthony Payne, *Richard Hakluyt: A Guide to His Books and to Those Associated with Him 1580–1625* (London: Quaritch, 2008), 16–19, 64–5; Payne, 'Richard Hakluyt', 24–7.

22 Repr. *Hakluytus Posthumus or Purchas His Pilgrimes*, 20 vols (Glasgow: James MacLehose and Sons [in collaboration with The Hakluyt Society], 1905–7), 19:510 [Spanish Armada] and 20:23 [Cadiz Expedition], both mainly from Hakluyt with additional material from van Meteren's *Historia Belgica*. See L.E. Pennington, ed., *The Purchas Handbook: Studies of the Life, Times and Writings of Samuel Purchas, 1577–1626*, 2 vols (London: The Hakluyt Society, 1997), 1:353–4, 2:463; and James P. Helfers, 'The Explorer and the Pilgrim? Modern Critical Opinion and the Editorial Methods of Richard Hakluyt and Samuel Purchas', *Studies in Philology*, 94 (1997).

23 *England's Naval Exploits Against Spain*, 7.132–64 (Armada account) and 165–86 (Cadiz account). In 2006 the University of Adelaide created an electronic edition of the Goldsmid edition under Creative Commons (http://ebooks.adelaide.edu.au/h/hakluyt/voyages). The 1589 and 1598–1600 editions, as well as those by Evans (1809–12) and Goldsmid (1885–90), are accessible via http://onlinebooks. library.upenn.edu/webbin/book/lookupname?key=Hakluyt. However, the MacLehose edition (1903–5) is only available to US readers on this site.

24 *The Principal Navigations* (1905–7), 4.197–236 (Armada account) and 236–68 (Cadiz account).

25 *Compassing the Vaste Globe of the Earth. Studies in the History of the Hakluyt Society 1846–1996*, ed. R.C. Bridges and P.E.H. Hair (London: The Hakluyt Society, 1996), 296.

26 Hakluyt had probably also consulted an English propaganda pamphlet by J.[ames?] L.[eigh?], *An Answer to the Untruths* (London, 1589), supposedly a translation of a Spanish tract but really written and printed in England (by Arnold Hatfield for the London stationer Thomas Cadman). He may have also accessed other manuscript accounts, including one written personally by Lord Burghley. See Denis B. Woodfield, *Surreptitious Printing in England 1550–1640* (New York: Bibliographical Society of America, 1973), 27–9.

27 Martha Nell Smith, 'Electronic Scholarly Editing', in *A Companion to Digital Humanities*, ed. Susan Schreibman, Ray Siemens and John Unsworth (Oxford: Blackwell, 2004), 311. See also Marilyn Deegan and Kathryn Sutherland, eds., *Text Editing, Print and the Digital World* (Farnham: Ashgate, 2009); and Tim Youngs, *The Cambridge Introduction to Travel Writing*, Chapter 12, 'The Way Ahead: Travel Writing in the Twenty-First Century' (Cambridge: Cambridge University Press), 177–89.

28 http://universitypublishingonline.org/cambridge/benjonson/ accessed 8 June 2019.

29 'The David Livingstone Spectral Imaging Project, Livingstone Online and the UCLA Digital Library Program', accessed 9 April 2017, http://livingstone.library.ucla.edu/about.htm; Adrian S. Wisnicki, 'Journey into Digital Humanities: One Victorianist's Tale', *Journal of Victorian Culture*, 18.2 (2013).

24

MAPS

James R. Akerman

Literary scholars since the 1980s have embraced the cartographic and the spatial as critical categories. A number of these scholars have discussed the influence of map literacy and cartographic sensibility in Renaissance literature in particular, prompting the editors of the grand *History of Cartography* project to devote an entire section of the Renaissance volume to cartography and literature.[1] The metaphorical use of mapping as a category of analysis has also been popular in literary and cultural studies; and while I am generally in favour of the widening meaning of 'map' in scholarship, this historian of cartography clings to the notion that actual *maps* – that is, graphic representations of space and spatial relationships – are still underserved by literary criticism, and surprisingly so in the field of travel literature. In their study of John Murray and his travel publications, Innes Keighren, Charles Withers, and Bill Bell observe that the preoccupation of map scholars with the 'mimetic authority and content and meaning of maps' and of literary scholars with text tends to pull them in opposite directions.[2] The present work is a modest attempt to address this gap, offered in the hope of suggesting topics for further inquiry.

The task is problematised from the start by the admission that most travel texts do not include maps. Only guidebooks and exploratory accounts, with their goal of delineating new territory previously unknown or poorly understood by their authors or readers, consistently include maps. The choice to map the territories described and visited in other travel accounts and in fictional narratives, seems mostly to be just that – a matter of choice. But this perhaps in itself argues for considering why or when their presence or absence is warranted.

From a purely physical perspective, the map–text relationship in works of travel is one of juxtaposition and correlation – the placement of maps and texts meant to be read together in close proximity to each other. This has been far easier for a publisher to achieve since the introduction of lithography, electromechanical, and now digital methods of composition; all of which reduced the cost of printing images and text seamlessly on the same page.[3] The possibilities are illustrated by *The Cape Ann Trails* promotional travel brochure published in Gloucester, Massachusetts in the 1930s. On one side is a map drawn by a commercial artist we know only as 'Mons'; on the other a complementary narrative by Edward Vassar Ambler (Figures 24.1 and 24.2).

The generously annotated map delineates, describes, and illustrates a circuit around the historic and picturesque peninsula. Twenty-eight points of interest along the route are identified

Figure 24.1 Recto, Mons, *The Cape Ann Trail* (Gloucester, MA: City of Gloucester and Gloucester Chamber of Commerce, 1930). Courtesy of the Newberry Library

by number, each of which is briefly described in textual vignettes and small illustrations along the margin of the map. On the back Ambler amplifies these descriptions and weaves them into a narrated tour, seamlessly weaving navigational language into contemplations of the Cape's landscape and history, including its literary history:

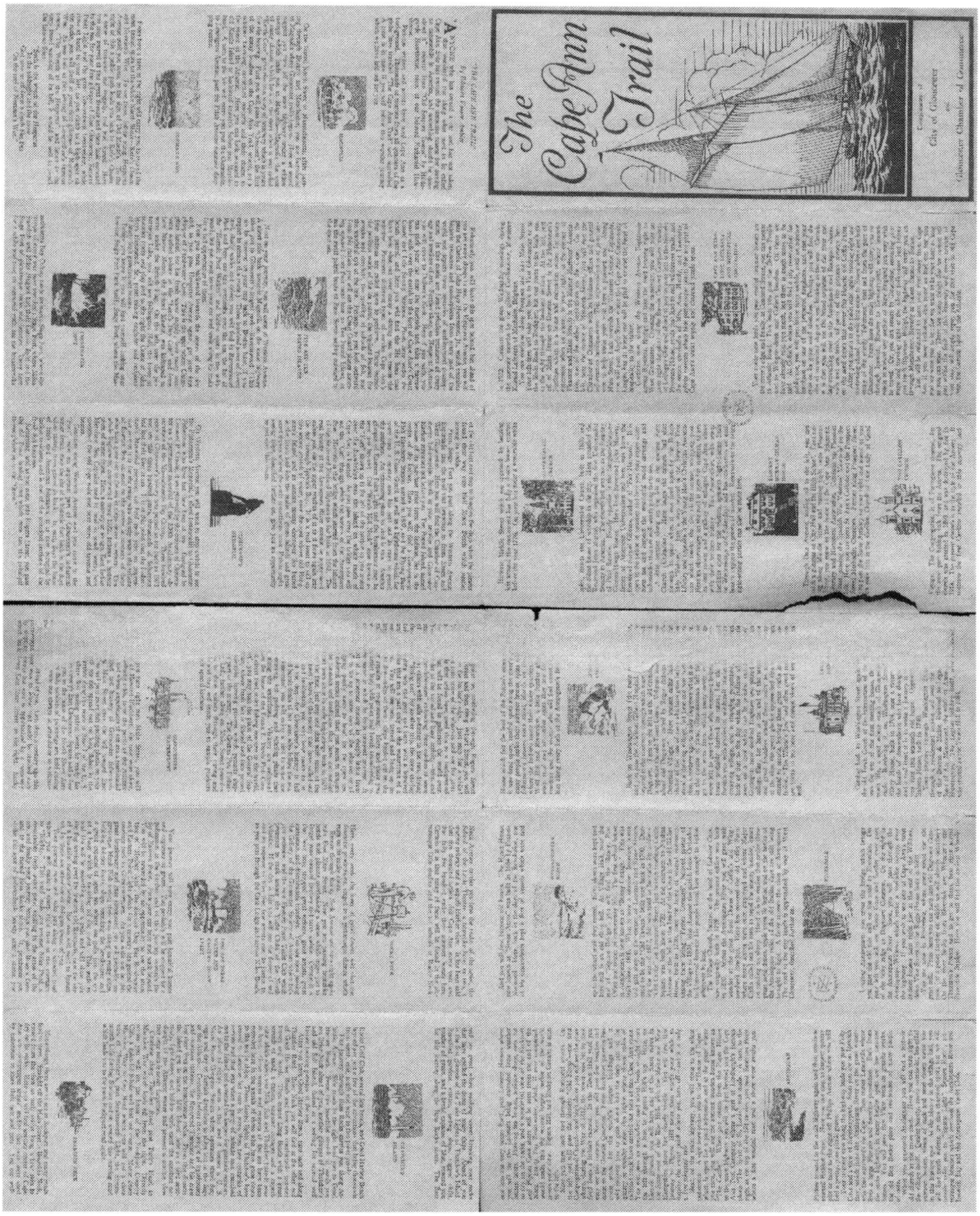

Figure 24.2   Verso, Mons, *The Cape Ann Trail* (Gloucester, MA: City of Gloucester and Gloucester Chamber of Commerce, 1930). Courtesy of the Newberry Library

From here a turn to the right will carry you to two of the most famed spots on the whole North Shore – Rafe's Chasm and Norman's Woe. To see these follow along Hesperus Avenue until you come to the sign of Del Monte's. To the right of this a public path leads back to Rafe's Chasm, a scene of romance and tragedy, real and filmed. Here you may marvel at this great fissure and then outward to the sea for your first glimpse of East Gloucester, Easton, Point Light and the great Government breakwater, while close at hand to your left, as you climb to a high spot on the rocks, you will thrill to your first glimpse of Norman's Woe. As you look at this setting of Longfellow's famous poem, 'The Wreck of the Hesperus', and listen to the deep toned warning of its bell, it would be good to recall the famous lines:

> Such is the wreck of the Hesperus
>
> In the midnight and the snow
>
> God save us all from a death like this
>
> On the reef of Norman's Woe.[4]

The connection between narration and navigation and the coordination of map and text is rarely so explicit as in this example; neither is it always so instrumental or pragmatic. But wherever maps are found in travel texts, they appear because the play between the cartographic and the verbal adds to the imagination of the spaces in which the work is set.

Itineraries, navigation, narrative

Many types of maps can and have been used to support travel or comprehension of a travel narrative. Those that do so most plainly are itinerary or route maps, 'which are primarily concerned with the representation of a single route or corridor of movement'.[5] There are two main types. One is the strip map, so-called because the geographical coverage of the map is narrowed so that only a narrow strip of territory is depicted, focusing the eye and the mind on the route itself.[6] The second type is the route-enhancing map, in which a track or journey is traced across a general map that places the route within a larger geographical context (such as England, the Pacific Ocean, or the Sahara Desert), so that the viewer 'follows a trajectory over or across a plotted space in a visual narrative composed of points or episodic places reached and traversed'.[7]

The strip map traces its descent from ancient and medieval textual forms such as itineraries and sailing directions. In their leanest forms these were sequential lists of places along the course of a specific route or journey. Frequently these lists were, however, embellished by wayfinding instructions, descriptive and historical, and could be read as travel narratives. In the fifteenth and sixteenth centuries sailing directions began to incorporate coastal profiles and maps to support comprehension of the accompanying wayfinding text, and these evolved into the first maritime atlases, in which a series of connected charts plot a route described by accompanying text. The first printed maritime atlas, *De Spieghel der Zeevaerdt*, compiled by Lucas Janszoon Waghenaer and published in 1584–85, maps two routes in a series of connected charts, heading south and north from the Netherlands.[8]

On land, John Ogilby's *Britannia*, published in 1675, was the first printed work to effectively combine strip road maps and itinerary text. The distinctive maps, rendered on each page to create the illusion that they form a single continuous strip, were the model for all subsequent road maps of this type published in the West. Most of the text is concerned with road navigation: the choice of forks and crossroads, the quality of road surfaces, gradients, distances, and orienting landmarks. But here and there Ogilby remarked on markets and other economic activities, the histories of larger towns, and the occasional roadside novelty. Leaving Chippenham, along the road from London to Bath, for example:

you omit the Road on the Right to Bristol, and bearing to the Left, take your Way by Cosham Church and Hall, and at 98'3. [i.e., 98 miles, 3 furlongs from London] enter Pickwith a Village of 2 Furlongs Extent; then ascending an Hill of 3 Furlongs, Hastebury House on the Right, and Chapel of Plaister on the Left, cross a Vale and leave Box Church on the Right, descend an Hill of 4 Furlongs, and enter Somersetshire at 104'0. Thence you pass through Bathford a small Village, and cross the Avon over a Stone-Bridg, and come to Boneaston alias Baneston at 105'4. A small Village, where you leave Bathampton Church on the Left.

Hence at 107'4. through Wallcot a small Village, you 3 Furlongs farther come to the City of BATH, which is seated on the River Avon, and in a Vale begirt with high Hills; a City of great Antiquity, call'd by Ptolomy, Udata Therma; by Antonine, Aqua Solis; by the Britains, Caer-Badon; and by the Saxons, Bathanceaster: The City is not large, containing but one Parish-Church besides the Cathedral or Abby, yet it is well built and well inhabited, which is occasion'd by it's Medicinal Baths; It gives Title to the Right Honorable John Earl of Bath; is Govern'd by a Mayor, Recorder, Common-Councel, &c. and hath 2 Markets weekly, on Wednsdays [sic] and Saturdays.[9]

The correlation between this passage and the map on the accompanying plate is very strong (Figure 24.3).

Reading (and travelling) upwards from 'Chipenham' at lower left, we do indeed encounter 'Cosham Church' and its hall, 'Pickwick', ascend a hill, find 'Haselbury house' on our right, the 'Chappell of Plaister' on our left, the church at Box to the right, then descend a hill and cross the boundary of Somersetshire at Bathford, cross the Avon over a stone bridge, and so on to Bath. This may not make for engaging travel reading, but the lavish in-folio format of the book was nevertheless likely meant more to support vicarious travel 'within doors' than actual travel.[10] Portable versions, or 'epitomes' of Ogilby's road book appeared as early as 1676. However, to reduce costs and retain portability, their publishers had to sacrifice either the navigational text or the maps.

In the first part of the nineteenth century, the most durable of guidebook genres for American travellers was the river guide, also composed of strip maps and accompanying text. These began as navigational tools for the pilots of flatboats and other small craft, but slowly took on the textual elements and imagery that would appeal to passengers on steamboats, with little change in the maps that accompanied them. The first of these, *The Ohio Navigator*,[11] was published in 1801 by a Pittsburgh bookseller and entrepreneur, Zadok Cramer. Its core text was a navigational instruction for the route, recommending the safest channels on fickle currents and alerting the navigator to hazards, obstructions, islands, and landing places. Maps were added to the volume in the fifth edition. Though crude in execution, the simple woodcuts worked closely with accompanying navigational text. The *Navigator* underwent many revisions and expansions over more than two decades, adding historical and descriptive material more typical of a guidebook or travelogue. During the infancy of passenger railroads in the 1830s and 1840s, enterprising British and American publishers issued small guides to rail routes, pairing strip maps and descriptive text of passing scenery keyed to text on the accompanying map.[12] Similar formats were popular in the first decades of automobile travel, and airlines of the 1920s, 1930s, and 1940s produced illustrated brochures and maps that combined photographs and other images, detailed strip maps, and text describing points of interest below, in an era when aircraft still flew low enough to the ground to make such

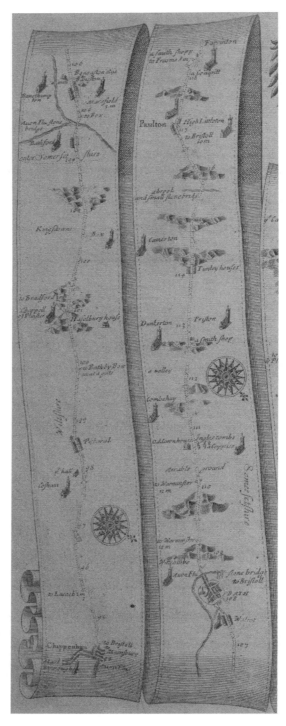

Figure 24.3 Detail, 'The roads from London to Bath & Wells', in John Ogilby, *Britannia* (London, 1675). Courtesy of the Newberry Library

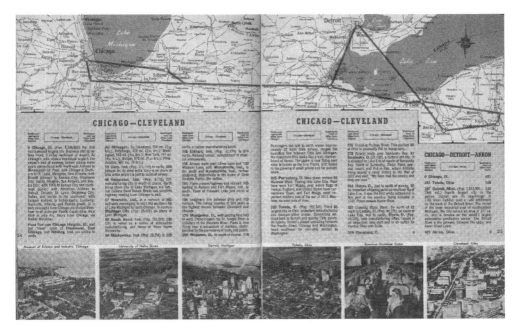

Figure 24.4　United Air Lines, 'Chicago–Cleveland,' in *United Air Lines Maps of the Main Line Airway* (Chicago, IL: Rand McNally for United Air Lines, 1945). Courtesy of the Newberry Library

detail meaningful. One (Figure 24.4) published by United Air Lines in 1945, lays out thirty-two pages of strip maps of the 'main line' connecting the eastern and western coasts of the United States via Chicago, accompanied by descriptions of cities and landmarks visible from either side of the aircraft. Near Wauseon, Ohio, '[p]assengers can look north, to where, approximately twenty miles from [the] airway, ranges the boundary line between Indiana and Michigan. Northwestern Ohio looks like a vast checkerboard of farms'.[13]

Route-enhanced maps record a course of travel within a larger geographical context than is typical of strip maps. They are widely used today to prescribe the routes of walking or driving tours, as in modern Dorling Kindersley or Michelin guidebooks. They originated, however, as synopses of European voyages of discovery. Among the most famous is that which appeared in the atlas accompanying the account of James Cook's third voyage published in 1785 (Figures 24.5 and 24.6).[14]

The cartographer, Lieut. Henry Roberts, had served with Cook on both the *Discovery* and the *Resolution*. On a world chart Roberts traced the course of each of Cook's three voyages to the Pacific made between 1768 and 1780 (the last of which was completed after Cook's death in Hawaii in February 1779). The technique mirrors that of track charts, traces of ships' logs that were routinely drawn on printed charts to record the daily positions, courses, and significant events of a voyage, to be filed with appropriate naval authorities upon completion of the voyage.[15] Logs and track charts also narrated the incidents and findings of a voyage, and as such provided the basis for many expeditionary accounts that made their way into print for official or popular consumption. Here, distinctive solid, dashed, or dotted lines distinguish the track of each voyage. Dates and annotations along each route highlight and summarise events of geographical and historical significance described in accompanying published accounts.[16] At intervals along each track are the dates at which specific points were crossed, often at places where

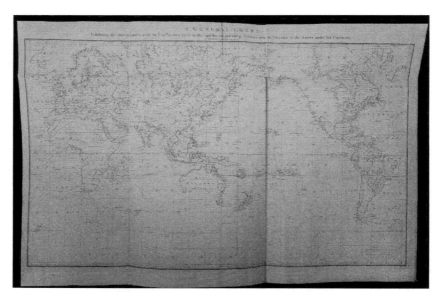

Figure 24.5   Henry Roberts, 'A General Chart: Exhibiting the Discoveries, Made by Captn. James Cook in This and Two Preceding Voyages; with the Tracks of the Ships under His Command,' in James Cook, *A Voyage to the Pacific Ocean . . . in the Years 1776, 1777, 1778, 1779, and 1780* (London: H. Hughs, G. Nicol, and T. Cadell, 1785), Atlas. Courtesy of the Newberry Library

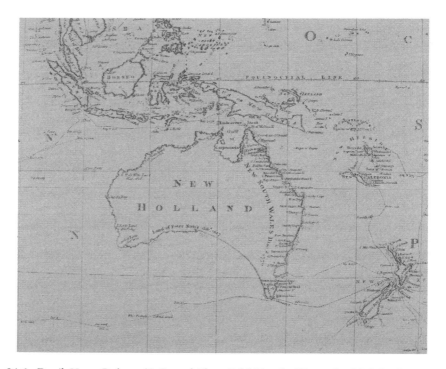

Figure 24.6   Detail, Henry Roberts, 'A General Chart: Exhibiting the Discoveries, Made by Capt.n James Cook in This and Two Preceding Voyages; with the Tracks of the Ships under His Command,' in James Cook, *A Voyage to the Pacific Ocean . . . in the Years 1776, 1777, 1778, 1779, and 1780* (London: H. Hughs, G. Nicol, and T. Cadell, 1785), Atlas. Courtesy of the Newberry Library

major changes of course occurred. Notes document sightings of flotsam and jetsam [. . .] turtle, and sea gulls, recorded either out of boredom or because they promise the proximity of land. At lower left, the track follows the discovery and exploration of the coast of New South Wales (eastern Australia) made by the Endeavour from April to August 1770. This reconnaissance is described in the account of Cook's first voyage:

> April the 18th [1770], towards the evening, judging ourselves near the land, we handed topsails; and at night lying-to we sounded with one hundred thirty fathoms of line, but found no ground [. . .] On Saturday we saw smoke on shore, and afterwards a high hill, which we named Cape Dromedary, from its likeness to the back of that animal [. . .] On Monday the 21st of August we passed several flats, and observed several openings in the main land, which appeared like islands, some of them at a great distance; and at half past two in the afternoon, we stood towards a passage, which seemed to extend through the country, and the same evening anchored about the middle of it [. . .] Immediately after a party landed from the ship, to examine the country; and from a small eminence discovered the Indian sea; upon which they fired several vollies, and were answered by a general discharge from the ship. We then took possession of the country [. . .] in the name of his Britannic Majesty.[17]

Another annotation indicates where Cook's second voyage reached its most southern point, testing summer navigation in the Antarctic, and reached 71° south in January 1774 where a 'firm field and vast Mountains of ice' blocked further poleward progress:

> [Jan.] 29. The islands of ice began to multiply, and the loose ice to incorporate; but the weather continued moderate, and generally clear [. . .] Came in sight of a fog bank, which had a great appearance of land, and many who were thought the best judges asserted that it was land; however it proved upon trial a deception, as well as the former [. . .] Taking a view from the mast-head nothing was to be seen but a dreary prospect of ice and sea. Of the former might be seen a whole country as far as the eye could carry one, diversified with hills and dales, and fields, of imaginary plantations, that has all the appearance of cultivation; yet was nothing more than the sports of chance in the formation of those immense bodies of congregated ice. This second attempt at discovery of land in this dreary region being attended with no better success than the first, the captain thought it adviseable to give over the pursuit for the present, and once more to direct the ship's course to the northward.[18]

The cartoonish 'Map of John Steinbeck's Travels with Charley' incorporated in the endpapers of early editions of John Steinbeck's *Travels with Charley in Search of America* illustrates the durability and flexibility of the route-enhanced map as complement to modern travel narratives. The map shows the circuit around the United States that Steinbeck took in 1960.[19] Much like the book itself, the map is a collection of anecdotal images of the country, tied together by free-drawn line. The artist, Don Freeman, an illustrator and author of children's books, included nearly thirty pictorial vignettes, each of which corresponds to a passage in the text. Some of these are merely scenic images, typical of those one might find in a contemporary guidebook: Niagara Falls, Chicago's skyscrapers, the big trees of the Pacific Northwest, and the deserts of the Southwest. Across the Midwest are three images showing the passage of time from fall to winter: ripe ears of corn and pumpkins, strutting turkeys, and a snow-covered sign for Fargo, North Dakota, a little to the west of which is a man, leaning on a barbed wire fence, whom Steinbeck encountered west of Bismarck. In New Mexico there is a stack of pancakes surmounted by a candle – a birthday supper for Charley. In the southeast, the map recalls Steinbeck's encounter in New Orleans with a crowd harassing an African American child attempting to integrate a white public school.

Roberts' and Freeman's maps are strikingly different in design and inspiration: one emulates the reportage and precision of the track chart; the other draws inspiration from popular illustration. By these different means, however, both achieve a spatial synopsis of entire journeys, conveying as well, each in their own way, their epic proportions.

Exploration

We look to the Mediterranean to find the first Western travel accounts richly illustrated with maps. Copies of Cristoforo Buondelmonti's 'Liber insularum arcipelagi' circulated in manuscript during the fifteenth century. The work drew heavily on Buondelmonti's own travel experiences in the Aegean in the service of the Medicis, and there can be little doubt that the simple maps of the islands he visited, as many as seventy-nine in some copies, were based on his own observations. A printed edition, with sonnets replacing prose, was published by the Venetian sailor Bartolomeo da li Sonetti in 1485. Benedetto Bordone updated and expanded the concept in 1528, and for two centuries thereafter the *isolario* became a popular encyclopaedic work illustrating and describing islands around the world.[20] Bernhard von Breydenbach's *Peregrinatio in Terram Sanctam* (Mainz, 1486) recounts a pilgrimage made by the author with the painter Erhard Reuwich from Mainz to Jerusalem in 1483–84. The work was subsequently published in several languages until 1522, usually accompanied by woodcut views of six ports they visited along the way and a magnificent panoramic map of the entire Holy Land centred on an outsized image of Jerusalem, all drawn from life by Reuwich. Reuwich's Holy Land map is generously annotated with notable shrines and landmarks of interest to pilgrims, including many that the author did not himself visit but which are indicated for the interest of others who might follow them.[21]

Accounts of European explorations in America, Africa, and Asia followed closely upon the Columbian Encounter, but included few maps at first. The 1494 Basel edition of the so-called *Columbus Letter* included the first printed images of the New World, including three that are geographical in character though they are the fantastic creations of some unknown artist.[22] As exploratory accounts proliferated, they were gathered (and often put into print for the first time) by editors and commentators for wider distribution. Until the end of the sixteenth century, however, the cartographic content of collections was somewhat indifferent. The first volume of the *Decades* compiled and published serially by Pietro Martire d'Anghiera includes a map of the Caribbean and the Terra Firma coast, but maps appeared rarely in subsequent instalments and editions. By the middle of the sixteenth century, the trade in printed maps was on a more secure footing, particularly in Venice and Rome. The Venetian cartographer Giacomo Gastaldi contributed nine maps to *Delle Navigationi et Viaggi,* compiled by his friend Giovanni Battista Ramusio between 1554 and 1559.[23] The first collection published in London by Richard Hakluyt, *Divers Voyages* (1582), incorporated only a copy of Richard Thorne's world map of 1537 and Michael Lok's map of the North Atlantic. The first two editions of the larger *Principal Navigations* (1589 and 1598) included only world maps, though the latter, the famous Wright-Molyneux world chart based on Mercator's project, was among the most important world maps published in its century.[24]

Working on the continent, Theodore de Bry had greater access than Hakluyt to the skilled engravers and resources needed to bring exploratory accounts and illustrations, and cartography together. The thirteen volumes of the *India Occidentalis*, dealing with explorations of the Americas, included forty-nine separate accounts and 590 engravings. Much of this ground was already covered by Ramusio and Hakluyt, but the De Bry *Collectiones peregrinationum* (which included a second series dealing with Asia and Africa) marked a turn towards a more commercially oriented publication of exploratory accounts, one in which imagery was increasingly sought by readers.[25] The first two volumes, devoted to Thomas Hariot's account of the exploration and attempts to establish a colony in Virginia (i.e. North Carolina) in 1585–87, and Le Moyne's account of the Ribualt-Laudonnière expedition to Florida in 1564–65, were the most impressive in their integration of map and text. Hariot's account features his own general map of Virginia and twenty-three further images mostly by John White. The map, 'Americae pars, nunc Virginia dicta', hews closely to the narrative. In fact, it could be said that many of White's views both map and narrate White and Hariot's explorations of the North Carolina coast (Figure 24.7). The narrative relationship between map and text is still more fully developed by De Bry's 1591 publication of Jacob Le Moyne's account, featuring forty-three illustrations.[26]

Published accounts of single or related expeditions became the norm during the seventeenth century. Among early examples, the collected *Voyages* of Samuel de Champlain is remarkable in its narrative use of maps. Written by the explorer himself, *Les voyages du sieur de Champlain Xaintongeois* recounts his travels in New France made between 1603 and 1611.[27] The two large folding maps in the volume depicting the St Lawrence gulf and valley and whole of northeastern North America receive the most attention from historians of cartography. But the twenty-four smaller maps and views are more notable in this context because of their close working relationship with the narrative. Champlain's maps combine symbolic elements typical of the navigational charts of his day that reflect his training and skill as hydrographer (precisely indicated

Figure 24.7   John White, Map of barrier islands, Secotan, and Weapemeoc, in Thomas Hariot, *Admiranda narratio fida tamen, de commodis et incolarum ritibus Virginiae* (Frankfurt-am-Main: Theodor de Bry, 1590). Courtesy of the Newberry Library

scales, soundings, markings for shoals, coastal features in semi-profile) with features that reflect his talent as a narrator: depictions of structures, ships, and landmarks and alphabetically keyed annotations referring to events and places that figure in the accompanying narrative. The first plate appears early in the account of Champlain's voyage of 1604–7, under the command of Pierre Du Gua de Monts, with the goal of finding suitable places for anchorage and settlement in Acadia (Nova Scotia). Titled 'Port de la heve', it describes a portion of the coast of Nova Scotia near what is now LaHave that was the site of the first landfall of Champlain and de Monts in Acadia in May 1604 (Figure 24.8, left).

The publisher has inserted the plate directly into the printed text block, a feat requiring some skill, since the metal type and the engraved plate had to be printed separately on entirely different presses. Below the plate is a key to the map with nine entries (A–I) referring to specific geographical features. Two Indian villages are visible on the shore, as well as two forests. On the facing page (Figure 24.8, right), a map titled 'Por du Rossÿnol' refers to an encounter with a certain Rossignol, a fur poacher (that is, operating without authorisation from the king) with whom they had a confrontation, apparently depicted by the armed men ashore at left. A later and larger plate 'pour la page 119' relates events at the great harbour of 'Le Beau port' (Gloucester, Massachusetts) visited in September 1606 and seriously considered as a place for a major settlement, but rejected after a violent encounter with the local Indians. These culminate in an attempted Indian ambush of a small party led by 'Le sieur de Poitrincourt' (at 'T' in the bottom centre, that Champlain himself (at 'V') was able to prevent).

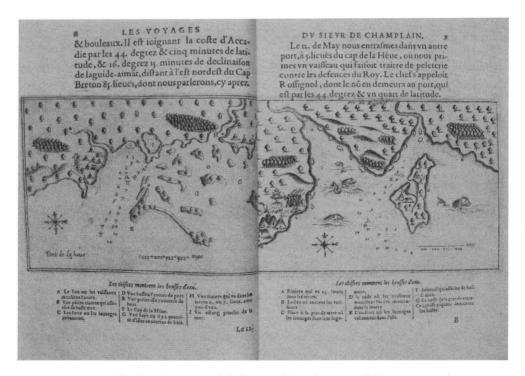

Figure 24.8 Samuel de Champlain, 'Port de la heve' and 'Por du Rossÿnol,' in *Les voyages du sieur de Champlain Xaintongeois, Capitaine ordinaire pour le Roy, en la marine* (Paris: Iean Berjon, 1613). Courtesy of the Newberry Library

Mapping imaginary travel

The influence of the exploratory travel account and rising cartographic literacy on early modern writing has been widely acknowledged by literary scholars.[28] Yet, despite the broadly geographic, even cartographic, sensibilities of early modern fiction, the incorporation of maps in works of fictive travel was optional at best. Simone Pinet, writing of *Don Quixote*, explains that Cervantes's clear knowledge of, and interest in, mapping underpinned his scepticism about the ability of maps to represent truth on the ground. In Don Quixote's words,

> [C]ourtiers, without leaving their chambers or the thresholds of the court, walk the whole world looking at a map, without spending a penny, or suffering heat or cold, hunger or thirst; but we, the true knights errant, exposed to the sun, the cold, the air, the merciless weather night and day, on foot and on horseback, we measure the whole earth with our own feet, and we do not know the enemies merely in painting, but in their very being.[29]

Don Quixote's 'denial' of maps, as Pinet characterises it, explains why no map of his mysterious journey appeared in editions of *Don Quixote* until the eighteenth century.[30] In contrast, Theodore Cachey relates Lodovico Ariosto's praise of virtual travel enabled by map reading:

> Let him wander who desires to wander. Let him see England, Hungary, France, and Spain. I am content to live in my native land. I have seen Tuscany, Lombardy, and the Romagna, and the mountain range that divides Italy [. . .] And that is quite enough for me. Without ever paying an innkeeper, I will go exploring the rest of the earth with Ptolemy, whether world be at peace or war. Without ever making vows when the heavens flash with lightning, I will go bounding over all the seas, more secure aboard my maps than aboard ships.[31]

The first editions of Ariosto's travel fantasy *Orlando Furioso* (published in parts, 1516–32) have no maps, but a mid-century edition by Vincenzo Valgrisi includes illustrations of narrative scenes, most of which have cartographical elements, many explicitly quoting maps in the Ptolemaic tradition.[32]

Since the time of the *isolario* the geographical characteristics of islands as small self-contained worlds have made them durably attractive to writers of fiction and social commentary, from the *Utopia* of Thomas More to the dystopian Westeros of George R. R. Martin's *Song of Ice and Fire* fantasy series.[33] The separation of the island, its *isolation*, allows authors to create worlds and societies in which geographical reality cannot or does not intrude or contaminate; and this allows writers to maintain the purity of the histories and societies in which they situate their stories – never mind that the narratives are most often parables addressing the cares and follies of actual human societies. As scenes for morality plays, political or religious commentary, or pure fantasy, islands passed the test of geographical plausibility. They could serve as allegories for the real world, because known geography did not refute their existence. By extension, the island world can represent, satirise, and distort the outside world and its history to suit the needs of a narrative without the interference of actual societies or histories.[34]

The list of novels and fantasies, teen fiction, and children's stories that utilise islands, or which create worlds or continents apart from the familiar human world, is almost endless, once one ponders on it. In many cases, the incorporation of maps in editions of such works was little more than a device intended to stimulate and situate the fantasy narrative. In the case of Tolkien's

Middle Earth mapping out an alternative world was critical to the author's creative process; the maps, in effect preceded and shaped the narratives he created.[35]

It was plausible for Daniel Defoe and Jonathan Swift to set the action of *Robinson Crusoe* (1719) and *Gulliver's Travels* (1726) on uncharted islands because Western explorers discovered new islands with regularity well into the nineteenth century. And of course, these works specifically parodied the travel accounts that were the talk of the political and literary circles in which the authors conversed. Defoe and Swift even had a cartographic muse, their friend Hermon Moll, a German or Dutch emigrant who was London's most successful commercial cartographer of the early eighteenth century. Moll's various geographical works were influenced by the mercantilist imperialism that flavoured the exploratory literature of the day, which Defoe embraced and Swift lampooned. Moll made the maps for Defoe's *Tour thro' the Whole Island of Great Britain* (1724–7) and these directly influenced the artists who created the maps incorporated in *Robinson Crusoe* and *Gulliver's Travels*.[36]

Though Moll was a friend of Swift's, the maps in *Gulliver's Travels* were supplied by the publisher, and perhaps without the author's permission. Bracher was able to establish nevertheless that the book's cartographer used the world map attached to Moll's *The World Described* in 1719 as the basis for the coastlines of real places proximal to the fantastic places described in the narrative. Hence, Lilliput ('Discovered A.D. 1699') appears to the Southwest of Sumatra, Balnabarbi ('Discovered A.D. 1701') east of Japan, and Brobdingnag ('Discovered A.D. 1703') appears as a peninsula north of California (Drake's 'New Albion'). In this way the credibility of the geography revealed by the false explorer is explicitly tied to actual geography, deepening the parody of the exploration project, and to the way in which new discoveries are announced in maps in publications.

A century and a half later, in *Treasure Island* (1883) Robert Louis Stevenson drew heavily on his interest in the exploration of the Pacific Ocean, imperial themes, and the tropes of travel writing. *Treasure Island* was Stevenson's first novel, coming midstream in a career that had focused on travel essays and books.[37] Like the maps in *Robinson Crusoe* and *Gulliver's Travels*, Stevenson's map emulates contemporary exploratory and commercial cartography, specifically charts of newly encountered islands and explored coasts. But it departs from these earlier examples in its level of topographical detail and engagement with the narrative itself.

Pragmatics and memory: mapping in guidebooks and later travelogues

The presence of maps in the early guidebooks and popular travelogues before the nineteenth century was relatively limited; the decision of publishers and authors to include them was affected more by pragmatic matters – the cost of acquiring and printing the maps weighed against the price and market. Over the course of the nineteenth century the rise of leisure time, together with the reduction of the cost of travel over longer distances enabled by the industrial technologies, encouraged the publication of travel guidebooks and popular travelogues. The parallel decline in the cost of reproducing images in printed texts supported the proliferation of maps and other images in guidebooks and other travel publications, and in turn helped to make them more appealing to the general public.

With increasing frequency, travelogues incorporated maps to illustrate especially notable localities visited by the authors (Figure 24.9) as well as route-enhanced maps showing their itineraries.[38]

Government-sponsored exploratory expeditions also flourished and their published reports were often deeply invested in cartography, and enjoyed wide circulation in both official and popular forms. This was especially true in the United States, where the century-long conquest of

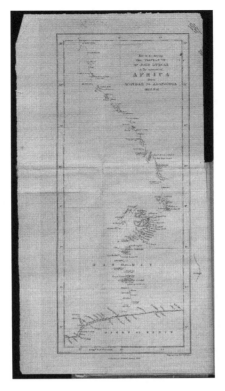

Figure 24.9 'Map to Accompany the Travels of Mr. John Duncan in the Interior of Africa from Whydah to Adafoodia 1845 & 1846,' in John Duncan, *Travels in Western Africa, in 1845 & 1846* (London: Richard Bentley, 1847). Courtesy of the Newberry Library

a broad swath of the North American continent was documented by a host of exhaustive survey maps, geologic sections, and topographic views (Figure 24.10). In places like the Yellowstone Plateau, home of the world's first National Park, accounts of ostensibly scientific expeditions were both narratively and visually attractive and were easily translated into popular guidebooks.[39]

In Europe, early guidebook series, such as Murray's, began as collections of distinctive travel narratives. Over time they adopted the more encyclopaedic and pragmatic structure that is familiar to us today.[40] During the nineteenth century, guidebook series expanded in every measurable way: the number of publishers engaged in the trade, the geographical scope and number of publications in each series, the number of pages in each guidebook, and most especially the number and types of maps and illustrations they included. The 1846 (2nd) edition of Murray's guidebook to Northern Italy included a large folding map of the territory (inserted into a pocket at the back of the volume) and plans of Venice, Milan, and Florence. The 1863 (9th) edition included fifteen city plans and seven plans of significant buildings and art galleries. By the late nineteenth century, Murray's *Northern Italy* had added several district maps to the still growing number of city and architectural plans. The addition of regional maps reflected the greater mobility of travellers, the increasing density of the railroads, and improvement of roads and rural transportation. Indeed, the growth of the size of guidebook volumes was partially accounted for by the greater attention paid to smaller towns, natural attractions, and rural districts. While supporting a profusion of maps, the encyclopedism of later nineteenth- and early twentieth-century

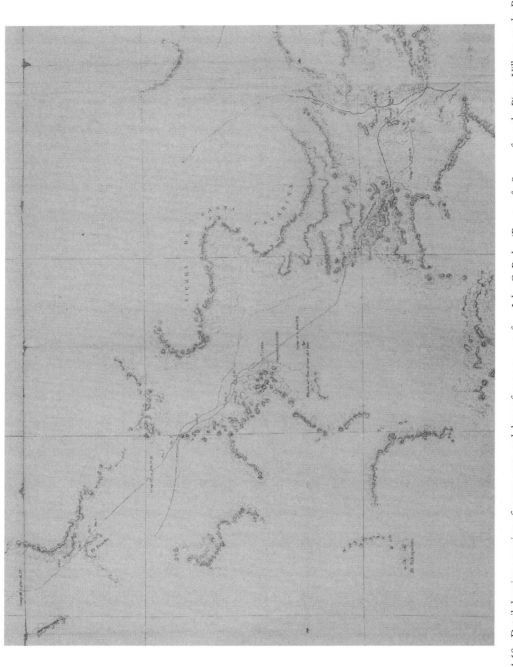

Figure 24.10 Detail showing a portion of survey route and dates of encampment, from John G. Parke, 'Route of a Survey from the Pimas Villages on the Rio–Gila to Mesilla on the Rio–Bravo-del-Norte with a View to Determine the Practicability of a Railroad from the Mississippi to the Pacific Ocean through that Region,' in *[Report of the Secretary of War Communicating the Several Pacific Railroad Explorations]*, Atlas, 33d Cong., 1st sess. House. Ex. doc. no. 129 (Washington, DC, 1855). Courtesy of the Newberry Library

guidebooks diminished the narrative aspect of the text. There were variations in house style of course, and some subjects, such as a tour along the Rhine, fairly demanded a narrative approach to map and text alike.

Battlefield tourism, as well, was almost by definition concerned with the narration of the events that bring tourists to these places. While the memorialisation of fields of battle is an ancient practice, these became common elements of travel accounts and guides only during the nineteenth century. The American Civil War was a watershed in the publication of maps and guides for battlefield tourists. The millions of soldiers and their families who survived the conflict provided a large supply of potential visitors. The railroad and the proximity of the major population centres of the northeastern and mid-Atlantic states to the eastern theatre of war put Gettysburg, Fredericksburg, and Antietam within easy reach of an expanding middle class. Gettysburg, the turning point in the war, was singled out for particular attention in guidebooks, including several devoted specifically to it. Of these, John Bachelder's *Gettysburg: What to See, and How to See It* (1872) is among the more innovative. The book includes only a single panoramic map of the battlefield, annotated with the locales and units that prominently featured in the three days of battle (July 1–3, 1863). The panorama is laid out in squares, indexed by letters and numbers on the margins of the map, so that readers can readily find locations mentioned in the narrative. Most ingeniously, reader-travellers are instructed to pause at several points where it is possible to survey the nearby battlefield. A compass is inserted in the text at this point with radiating place names indicating the direction to landscape features that figured prominently in the battle (Figure 24.11).[41]

This guided onsite tour of battlefields reached its apogee with those published in the service of memorial tourism after World War I. The unprecedented brutality of the Great War and the sheer number of combatants and war dead produced a wave of visitations by aggrieved families and the merely curious that lasted roughly a decade after the close of the conflict, particularly

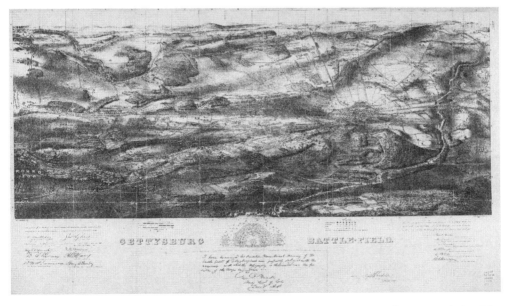

Figure 24.11 John B. Bachelder, 'Gettysburg Battle-field: Battle Fought at Gettysburg, Pa. July 1st, 2d & 3d 1863 by the Federal and Confederate Armies,' in *Gettysburg: What to See, and How to See It* (Boston, MA: Bachelder, 1873). Courtesy of the Newberry Library

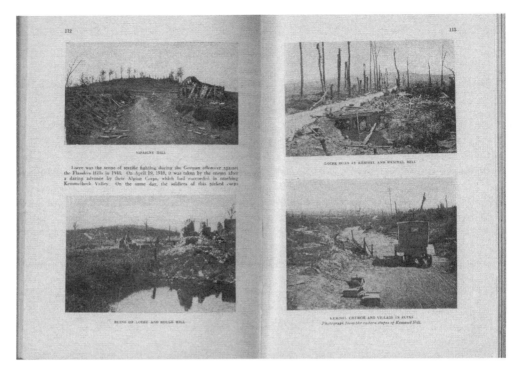

Figure 24.12 Tour map, photographs, and narrative of battlefield in the vicinity of Scherpenberg, Belgium, April 1918 (Battle of the Lys), in *Ypres and the Battles of Ypres* (Clermont-Ferrand, France: Michelin & cie, 1920). Courtesy of the Newberry Library

along the former Western Front. Most of these visitors were primarily interested in finding the graves of loved ones, but guidebooks also outlined itineraries that traced the course of battle along broad stretches of the front. War tourism along the Western Front was especially well suited for visitation by automobile, which allowed tourists to range along an expanse of battlefield crossing from one side of the front line to another, and witness the destruction of nearby villages and towns by bombardment. No guidebooks did this more effectively than Michelin's extensive series of guides to the Western Front, published from 1917 to the late 1920s targeted at both Francophone and Anglophone audiences. Combining photography and specially designed route maps with narrative and navigational instructions, each guide consisted of a series of itineraries that narrated the course of each campaign or battle as they guided travellers across the terrain (Figure 24.12).[42]

Coda

Michael Blanding's 2014 book, *The Map Thief*, tells the story of E. Forbes Smiley III, an

> esteemed and respectable antiquarian map dealer, [who] spent years doubling as a map thief until he was finally arrested while delicately tearing maps out of books in the Yale University Library in 2005. He would later confess to the theft of 97 maps valued at over $3 million total, and serve 3 years in prison for his crimes.[43]

The majority of Smiley's thefts were from books and atlases held by research libraries in the United States and Britain, including my home institution, the Newberry Library. He exploited a weakness in the security of rare book libraries, which do not always catalogue individual maps in textual works; and he capitalised on the interest of map collectors in maps as artefacts that tends to disregard the context in which they were originally placed. Antiquarian map and print dealers routinely and *legally* have removed maps from books they own since the antiquarian map trade emerged in the nineteenth century. They have done so, of course, because the market supports it. Historically, map collectors have been more interested in their ability to display their maps, or in the pleasure they derive from bringing together maps of a particular place or by a particular cartographer, than they are in the map's relationship to the text it once accompanied. The pendulum of map connoisseurship and map scholarship is now swinging towards a greater appreciation of the need to integrate map and text.

Notes

1 'Literature and Maps', in David Woodward, ed., *The History of Cartography*, vol. 3, *Cartography in the European Renaissance* (Chicago, IL: University of Chicago Press, 2007), 401–76. A number of scholars have worked in this field. I am especially indebted to Jordana Dym, who has been studying the broad dimensions of this topic for many years, and with whom I have had many profitable conversations.

2 Innes M. Keighren, Charles W. J. Withers, and Bill Bell, *Travels into Print: Exploration, Writing, and Publishing with John Murray, 1773–1859* (Chicago, IL: University of Chicago Press, 2015), 155.

3 See David Woodward, ed., *Five Centuries of Map Printing* (Chicago, IL: University of Chicago Press, 1975).

4 *The Cape Ann Trail* (Gloucester, MA: City of Gloucester and Gloucester Chamber of Commerce, 1930).

5 James R. Akerman, 'Finding Our Way', in James R. Akerman and Robert W. Karrow, Jr., *Maps: Finding Our Place in the World* (Chicago, IL: University of Chicago Press, 2007), 19–63.

6 For an overview of the format, see Alan M. MacEachren, 'A Linear View of the World: Strip Maps as a Unique Form of Cartographic Representation', *American Cartographer* 13 (1986): 7–25; and Alan M. MacEachren and Gregory B. Johnson, 'The Evolution, Application and Implications of Strip Format Travel Maps', *Cartographic Journal* 24.2 (1987): 147–58.

7 David Woodward, 'Roger Bacon's Terrestrial Coordinate System', *Annals of the Association of American Geographers* 80.1 (1990): 109–22. Cited in Tom Conley, 'Early Modern Literature and Cartography: An Overview', in David Woodward, ed., *The History of Cartography*, vol. 3, *Cartography in the European Renaissance* (Chicago, IL: University of Chicago Press, 2007), 406, fn. 15.

8 Lucas Janszoon Waghenaer, *De Spieghel der Zeevaerdt* (Leyden: Christoffel Plantijn, 1584–85).

9 John Ogilby, *Britannia. London, 1675* (Amsterdam: Theatrum Orbis Terrarum, 1970), 69.

10 This critique was made by Thomas Gardner in his *Pocket-Guide to the English Traveller* (London, 1719); cited by Catherine Delano-Smith, 'Milieus of Mobility: Itineraries, Route Maps, and Road Maps', in James R. Akerman, ed., *Cartographies of Travel and Navigation* (Chicago, IL: University of Chicago Press, 2006), 54, n. 150. This point as well was made by Garrett Sullivan, 'The Atlas as a Literary Genre: Reading the Inutility of John Ogilby's *Britannia*', presented at the Thirteenth Kenneth Nebenzahl, Jr., Lectures in the History of Cartography, The Newberry Library, 1999; also J. B. Harley, introduction to *John Ogilby. Britannia, London 1675* (Amsterdam: Theatrum Orbis Terrarum, 1970).

11 The first edition covered navigation on the Ohio River only. Subsequent editions, titled *The Navigator*, added the navigation of the lower Mississippi from its junction with the Ohio to New Orleans. For an introduction to this work and bibliography of editions, see Karl Yost, ed., *The Ohio and Mississippi Navigator of Zadok Cramer: Third and Fourth Editions* (Morrison, IL: K. Yost, 1987).

12 *A Chart and Description of the Boston and Worcester and Western Railroads* (Boston, MA: Bradbury & Guild, 1847). See Gerald A. Danzer and James R. Akerman, 'American Railroad Maps, 1828–1876', in *Mapping Movement in American History and Culture*, James R. Akerman and Peter Nekola, eds. (web resource, The Newberry Library, 2016). http://mappingmovement.newberry.org/essay/american-railroad-maps-1828-1876.

13 United Air Lines, *United Air Lines Maps of the Main Line Airway* (Chicago, IL: Rand McNally for United Air Lines, 1945), 24–25.

14 'A General Chart: Exhibiting the Discoveries, Made by Capt.n James Cook in This and Two Preceding Voyages; with the Tracks of the Ships under His Command', in James Cook, *A Voyage to the Pacific Ocean . . . in the Years 1776, 1777, 1778, 1779, and 1780* (London: H. Hughs, G. Nicol, and T. Cadell, 1785), vol. 10, pl. 1.

15 Andrew S. Cook, 'Surveying the Seas: Establishing the Sea Routes to the East Indies', in James R. Akerman, ed., *Cartographies of Travel and Navigation* (Chicago, IL: University of Chicago Press, 2006), 69–96.

16 The accounts of the first two voyages were initially published separately shortly after they occurred: James Cook, *A Journal of a Voyage Round the World, in His Majesty's Ship Endeavour, in the years 1768, 1769, 1770, and 1771* (London: T. Becket and P. A. DeHondt, 1771); and James Cook, *Journal of the Resolution's Voyage, in 1772, 1773, 1774, and 1775* (London: F. Newbery, 1775).

17 Cook, *A Journal of a Voyage Round the World, in His Majesty's Ship Endeavour, in the years 1768, 1769, 1770, and 1771*, 109, 126–27.

18 Cook, *Journal of the Resolution's Voyage, in 1772, 1773, 1774, and 1775*, 124–26.

19 John Steinbeck, *Travels with Charley in Search of America* (New York: Viking, 1962). It should be noted that, while Steinbeck did make such a journey, it is now considered likely that the account is at least partially fictional. A Pittsburgh-based journalist, Bill Steigenwald, published an essay disputing the book's veracity based on his own attempt to reconstruct Steinbeck's itinerary. See Bill Steigenwald, 'Sorry, Charley: Was John Steinbeck's *Travels with Charley* a Fraud?', *Reason*, April 2011, accessed August 15, 2017, http://reason.com/archives/2011/04/04/sorry-charley. At least some literary scholars have accepted that the narrative of events and dialogue is not to be taken too literally, notably Jay Parini, 'Introduction', in *John Steinbeck, Travels with Charley, 50th Anniversary Edition* (New York: Penguin, 2012).

20 George Tolias, 'Isolarii', in David Woodward, ed., in *The History of Cartography*, vol. 3, *Cartography in the European Renaissance* (Chicago, IL: University of Chicago Press, 2007), 263–84.

21 Hugh William Davies, *Bernhard von Breydenbach and His Journey to the Holy Land, 1483–4: A Bibliography* (London: J. &. J. Leighton, 1911); Kenneth Nebenzahl, *Maps of the Holy Land: Images of Terra Sancta through Two Milliennia* (New York: Abbeville, 1986), 63–66; Peter Meurer, 'Cartography in the German Lands', in David Woodward, ed., *The History of Cartography*, vol. 3, *Cartography in the European Renaissance* (Chicago, IL: University of Chicago Press, 2007), 1181.

22 See 'The Basle 1494 Columbus Letter', Osher Map Library, Smith Center for Cartographic Education', University of Southern Maine, www.oshermaps.org/special-map-exhibits/columbus-letter. Viewed June 5, 2016.

23 Robert W. Karrow, Jr., *Mapmakers of the Sixteenth Century and Their Maps* (Chicago, IL: Speculum Orbis, 1993), 226–30.

24 Anthony Payne, *Richard Hakluyt: A Guide to His Books and to Those Associated with Him, 1580–1625* (London: Bernard Quaritch, 2008), 29–39; R. A. Skelton, 'Hakluyt's Maps', in *The Hakluyt Handbook*, D. B. Quinn, ed. (London: The Hakluyt Society, 1974), vol. 1, 48–73; Peter C. Mancall, *Hakluyt's Promise: An Elizabethan's Obsession for an English America* (New Haven, CT: Yale University Press, 2007), 174–79.

25 Michiel van Groesen, *The Representations of the Overseas World in the De Bry Collection of Voyages (1590–1634)* (Leiden: Brill, 2008), 35–49.

26 Stefan Lorant, ed., *The New World: The First Pictures of America, Made by John White and Jacques Le Moyne and Engraved by Theodore de Bry*, rev. ed. (New York: Duell, Sloan and Pearce, 1965).

27 Samuel de Champlain, *Les voyages du sieur de Champlain Xaintongeois, Capitaine ordinaire pour le Roy, en la marine. Divisez en deux livres. Ou, journal tres-fidele des observations faites és de descouvertures de la Nouvelle France: tant en la description des terres [. . .]* (Paris: Iean Berjon, 1613).

28 See especially Tom Conley, *The Self-Made Map: Cartographic Writing in Early Modern France* (Minneapolis, MN: University of Minnesota Press, 1996); John Gillies, *Shakespeare and the Geography of Difference* (Cambridge: Cambridge University Press, 1994); Richard Helgerson, *Forms of Nationhood: The Elizabethan Writing of England* (Chicago, IL: University of Chicago Press, 1992); Ricardo Padron, *The Spacious Word: Cartography, Literature, and Empire in Early Modern Spain* (Chicago, IL: University of Chicago Press, 2004); and Jeffrey N. Peters, *Mapping Discord: Allegorical Cartography in Early Modern French Writing* (Newark, DE: University of Delaware Press, 2004).

29 Miguel de Cervantes, *Don Quixote de la Mancha*, 2 vols., ed. Francisco Rico (Madrid: Critica, 1998), vol. 1, 673, quoted in Simone Pinet, 'Literature and Cartography in Early Modern Spain: Etymologies and Conjectures', in David Woodward, ed., *The History of Cartography*, vol. 3, *Cartography in the European Renaissance* (Chicago, IL: University of Chicago Press, 2007), 469.

30 'Mapa de una porcion del Reyno de España que comprehendre los parages por donde anduvo Don Quixote', in Miguel de Cervantes Saavedra, *El ingenioso hidalgo Don Quixote de la Mancha* (Madrid: Don Joaquin Ibarra, 1780).

31 Lodovico Ariosto, *The Satires of Ludovico Ariosto: A Renaissance Autobiography*, trans. Peter DeSa Wiggins (Athens, OH: Ohio University Press, 1976), Satire 3.55–66 (61), quoted in Theodore J. Cachey, Jr., 'Maps and Literature in Renaissance Italy', in David Woodward, ed., *The History of Cartography*, vol. 3, *Cartography in the European Renaissance* (Chicago, IL: University of Chicago Press, 2007), 450.

32 Lodovico Ariosto, *Orlando Furioso de m. Lodovico Ariosto tutto ricoretto* (Venice: Vincenzo Valgrisim 1565). Copy referenced, the Newberry Library, Case Y 712.A70565. See Cachey, 'Maps and Literature in Renaissance Italy', 456–58.

33 Its television version, *The Game of Thrones*, is notably and famously introduced by an award-winning credit sequence that travels over an animated map of Westeros and the adjacent continent of Essos. Each presentation is customised to include only places that figure in the narrative of the episode following.

34 See Simon Pinet, *Archipelagoes: Insular Fictions from Chivalric Romance to the Novel* (Minneapolis, MN: University of Minnesota Press, 2011), and Ricardo Padron, 'Mapping Imaginary Worlds', in James R. Akerman and Robert W. Karrow, Jr., eds., *Maps: Finding Our Place in the World* (Chicago, IL: University of Chicago Press, 2007), 265–71.

35 Wayne G. Hammond and Cristina Scull, eds., *J.R.R. Tolkien, Artist and Illustrator* (Boston, MA: Houghton Mifflin, 1995); *The Invented Worlds of J.R.R. Tolkien: Drawings and Original Manuscripts from the Marquette University Collection, October 21, 2004–January 30, 2005, Patrick and Beatrice Haggerty Museum of Art, Marquette University, Milwaukee, Wisconsin* (Milwaukee, WI: Haggerty Museum of Art, Marquette University, 2004); J. R. R. Tolkien, *The Art of the Hobbit*, Wayne G. Hammond and Cristina Scull, eds. (London: HarperCollins, 2012); and J. R. R. Tolkien, *The Art of the Lord of the Rings*, Wayne G. Hammond and Cristina Scull, eds. (London: HarperCollins, 2015).

36 See Dennis Reinhartz, *The Cartographer and the Literati* (Lewiston, NY: Edwin Mellen Press, 1997); Glyndwyr Williams, *The Great South Sea: English Voyages and Encounters 1570–1750* (New Haven, CT: Yale University Press, 1997), 165–70, 206–13; Srinivas Aravamudan, 'Defoe, Commerce, and Empire', in John Richetti, ed., *The Cambridge Companion to Daniel Defoe* (Cambridge: Cambridge University Press, 2009), 45–63; Burton J. Fishman, 'Defoe, Herman Moll and the Geography of South America', *Huntington Library Quarterly* 36.3 (April 1973): 227–38; and Frederick Bracher, 'The Maps in "Gulliver's Travels"'. *Huntington Library Quarterly* 8.1 (November 1944): 59–74.

37 Oliver S. Buckton, *Cruising with Robert Louis Stevenson: Travel, Narrative, and the Colonial Body* (Athens, OH: Ohio University Press, 2007).

38 See Jordana Dym, 'More Calculated to Mislead than Inform: The Cartography of Travel Writers in Central America, 1821–1950', *Journal of Historical Geography* 30.2 (2004): 340–63.

39 See, for example, Ferdinand Vandeveer Hayden, *Preliminary Report of the United States Geological Survey of Montana and Portions of Adjacent Territories; being a Fifth Annual Report of Progress* (Washington, DC: Government Printing Office, 1872), 42nd Congress, 2nd Sess., House Ex. Doc. 326 (Serial Set 1520); and James Richardson, *Wonders of the Yellowstone Region in the Rocky Mountains* (London: Blackie & Son, 1874).

40 Keighren, Withers, and Bell, *Travels into Print*.

41 John B. Bachelder, *Gettysburg: What to See, and How to See It* (Boston, MA: Bachelder, 1873).

42 James R. Akerman, 'Mapping, Battlefield Tourbooks, and Remembering the Great War', in *History of Military Cartography*, ed. Elri Liebenberg, Imre Demhardt, and Soetkin Vervust (Heidelberg: Springer-Verlag, 2015), 159–77.

43 Quoted from Michael Blanding author site, www.michaelblanding.com/mapthief, viewed April 4, 2016; Michael Blanding, *The Map Thief* (New York: Gotham Books, 2014).

25

BOOK AND PRINT TECHNOLOGY

Innes M. Keighren

Introduction: from script to print and reprint – crafting Basil Hall's *Account of a Voyage of Discovery to the West Coast of Corea* (1818)

Reflecting upon the composition of his bestselling *Missionary Travels and Researches in South Africa* (1857), David Livingstone reckoned the task of writing more 'irksome and laborious' than that of travelling itself: 'I think I would rather cross the African continent again', he noted somewhat hyperbolically, 'than undertake to write another book. It is far easier to travel than to write about it.'[1] Although Livingstone's confession was largely rhetorical – intended to demonstrate his diffidence at assuming the role of author – it nevertheless highlights the very real labour that was expended in turning travel-in-the-field into travel-on-the-page. This transformational effort (what Marie-Noëlle Bourguet has called the 'voyage into narration'[2]) has been the subject of considerable scholarly attention in, among other fields, literary studies, book history and the history of science.[3] Understanding the means by which travellers' *en route* writing in journals and field notebooks became more-or-less polished print has encouraged an examination of, among much else, inscriptive practice, authorial performance and conventions of genre.[4]

The historian of travel literature Ian MacLaren has been particularly attentive to the multistage process connecting the acts of travel and in-the-field inscription to subsequent practices of transcription, editing and publication.[5] MacLaren has shown that the metaphorical journey from field to page was rarely smooth and that travellers' words typically underwent a variety of transformations – both voluntary and imposed – in becoming print. Close scrutiny of the various states and stages of travel writing is necessary, MacLaren has argued, to understand not only how the world was represented in words, but also how those words were refined, elaborated, amended and omitted (by the traveller and others) to serve particular social, political, economic, aesthetic or intellectual agendas. One of the consequences of MacLaren's call – and, more generally, of interdisciplinary dialogue between historians of the book and scholars of travel literature – has been a greater consideration in recent years of what Adriana Craciun has called the 'manifold social agents and contingencies involved in bringing exploration writings into public circulation'.[6]

One expression of this enquiry has been a critical reappraisal of the nature of authorship *vis-à-vis* travel writing. Although it has long been understood that a travel text is rarely (if ever) defined by its generic qualities alone – as a 'factual, first-person account of a journey undertaken by the author' – a number of studies have revealed the authorship of texts to be, at turns, contested, contingent and collaborative.[7] Building upon work in literary criticism concerned with the historical role of editors and literary advisors in the making and shaping of prose and poetry, the authorship of travel texts has been shown to be, more often than not, multiple – bearing the imprint of ghost writers and editors, patrons and publishers.[8] The changes wrought to the form, content and purpose of travel writing in its convoluted journey from pencil or pen to print were many and varied, and historians of the genre have become increasingly interested in the role played by publishers and printers in the making and meaning of texts.[9] Although a concern with author-publisher relations, and with the material production and circulation of travel texts, has often been implicit in studies of the genre, a number of recent investigations have taken as their explicit focus the publication process and the role of publishers and of the economies and technologies of print in determining – as MacLaren has it – 'the changes that could occur when a travel journal metamorphosed into a published commodity'.[10]

This chapter – in examining the changes that occurred during the authorship, publication and reprinting of one nineteenth-century narrative of travel in subtropical latitudes, Basil Hall's *Account of a Voyage of Discovery to the West Coast of Corea, and the Great Loo-Choo Island* (1818) – describes how the perspectives of book history can be applied to the study of travel writing. In showing how (between manuscript and print, and across four editions between 1818 and 1840) Hall's text changed stylistically and materially, I signal the importance of attending to the practices of authorship and publishing in understanding the form, content and purpose of nineteenth-century travel texts. Before turning to consider the production of Hall's narrative in detail, however, I offer here a brief summary of the craft – material, economic and social – of bookmaking in the nineteenth century and its influence on the making of books of travel.

Bookmaking and the technologies of print

For historians of the book, the personal and professional relationships between authors and their publishers have long been rich veins of study.[11] Book historians have interrogated authors' and publishers' archives in seeking to understand how decisions were made concerning the form and content, format and price of texts. Publishers' ledgers – recording the practical and financial details of book production – have afforded scholars important insights into the economics of the publishing industry.[12] Historians of the book have been attentive, also, to the practices and equipment of book production and have shown how advances in print technology, particularly in the nineteenth century, lowered the cost of book manufacturing and brought texts to wider audiences.[13]

The commonplace changes in meaning and material form that attended the publication of written accounts of travel had more than simply an isolated effect on the individual book in question; the systematic emendation, editorial tinkering and stylistic polishing imposed on texts by their publishers (with or without the approval of their authors) had wider-reaching consequences for questions of genre in travel writing and for popular understandings of specific geographical regions. The historian Janice Cavell has, for example, examined this process in relation to nineteenth-century accounts of British exploration in the Arctic and has shown how a 'coherent metanarrative of Arctic exploration' – which positioned the high latitudes as a site of heroic, masculine endeavour – emerged from a 'welter of [literary] voices'.[14] Much of the responsibility for the popular construction of the Arctic as a theatre of courageous effort in the face of sublime nature has been attributed to John Barrow, Second Secretary to the Admiralty and principal promoter of Arctic exploration in the first half of the nineteenth century. Barrow was, as Cavell has it, the 'epitome of the behind-the-scenes manipulator' and exerted a particular influence on published accounts of Arctic exploration by dint of his being a literary advisor to the house of John Murray.[15] Murray was official publisher to the Admiralty and was responsible for issuing the majority of narratives of Admiralty-sponsored expeditions. In almost all cases, these accounts passed across Barrow's desk – in his dual capacity as Second Secretary and literary advisor to Murray – and were altered in various ways as a consequence.[16]

Beyond questions of editorial intervention intended to ensure that Admiralty expedition narratives satisfied official and popular expectations in regard to procedural rigour and bodily fortitude, decisions over the format of these books were influenced by financial considerations and concerns over authority. For Murray and Barrow, issuing Admiralty narratives in lavish and expensive quarto volumes made sense for two reasons: first, despite their high price (which typically exceeded £3), the appetite of well-to-do bibliophiles was sufficiently strong that Murray could typically expect to clear a 'stunning profit'; second, the imposing physical form of the quarto – particularly when supplemented by fine, hand-coloured illustrations and maps – befitted its status as official narrative and satisfied Barrow's desire for an object of prestige.[17] The decision to publish books in expensive quarto format was, however, frequently subject to rebuke by a periodical press that considered this mode of publication – what it termed 'book-making' (as distinct from the making of books) – as nothing other than self-aggrandisement and profiteering.[18] The critical success of a printed work of Arctic travel depended, then, on its assuming an appropriate physical form; its textual content was often insufficient alone to ensure its positive reception.

Nineteenth-century publishers' decisions as to the format and illustration of a book of travels were often informed by the financial implications which different modes of printing and of image making presented. Recent scholarship on the approach taken by John Murray to the publication of its travel texts between the late eighteenth and mid-nineteenth century has shown that judgements were daily made as to the likely impact on the profitability of a text of the technologies employed to produce its maps and images (and, indeed, as to whether such material should be included at all).[19] Copperplate engraving typically allowed for greater precision and complexity than did woodcut illustrations, but was more expensive as a consequence; hand-coloured engravings were more expensive still. The transition in the nineteenth century to lithography and steel engraving allowed for the creation of cheaper, more durable and more easily printed illustrations.[20] Where a book was printed from stereotype plates, as was increasingly the case as the nineteenth century progressed, later editions could be issued (often at the hands of a different printer) without the expense of recomposing the text.[21]

As a text of travels made the transition from finalised manuscript to typeset page, it passed into the hands (and the control) of a compositor who assembled the author's words in upside-down metal type on a wooden composing stick. The compositor's job was, however, more than simply manual; it extended to making small, but crucial, corrections to punctuation, grammar and syntax.[22] In this sense, the author's text remained in a state of flux until the type had been committed to the galley – the tray in which composed type was assembled to create the final page – and printed. From the galleys, page proofs were run off to be checked and corrected by the printer; thereafter revised proofs were sent to the author for approval. The itinerant habits of many traveller-authors meant, of course, that they often had 'little time to correct proofs before they were off again on another long expedition'.[23] In such instances, it has been shown that responsibility was often devolved to their publisher or a nominated proxy; again, the relinquishing of authorial oversight created a further opportunity for the text-as-printed to diverge from the text-as-written. At the same time, however, the various stages of verification and correction that proofing offered attentive authors allowed them to address errors and omissions before their words finally reached sharp-eyed readers and critics.

In what follows, I examine the influence of Craciun's 'manifold social agents' on the authorship, publication and edition history of Basil Hall's *Account of a Voyage of Discovery to the West Coast of Corea*. Hall's text is notable in being both one of the first British accounts of Korea and a bestseller (a contemporary of Hall described it as 'one of the most interesting and valuable books of naval adventure which has made its appearance since the voyages of Cook and Byron'), but its selection here reflects its rather more generic qualities; it is but one (or four, if we consider its editions separately) of hundreds of travel texts published in Britain during a century increasingly obsessed with writing and reading about the world.[24]

The nineteenth-century reading public's preoccupation with travel writing reflected not only the entertainment and diversion that such work offered but also the national strategic significance that knowledge of the wider world was assumed to afford. Writing in 1832, an anonymous contributor to the *Penny Magazine* argued that travel writing was nothing less than a vital economic and political resource:

> To a nation like England, whose greatness and prosperity depend so immediately on navigation and intercourse with foreign lands, books of voyages and travels will always be particularly interesting. The people of other countries, distant from the sea, or cut off from foreign commerce, may peruse them from motives of mere curiosity; but to ourselves and other maritime people, they offer information essential to our pursuits, and of real and most important use as instructors and guides.[25]

Irrespective of the validity of the *Penny Magazine*'s characterisation of Britain's exceptionalism in respect to its interest in travel writing, it is evident that throughout the nineteenth century accounts of travel and geographical exploration 'captivated public audiences and journalist commentators alike'.[26] For his part, Hall did as much as he could to satisfy that interest.

Following the publication of his *Account of a Voyage of Discovery*, Hall went on to write a number of successful books based upon his global travels, becoming one of the most popular authors of the first half of the nineteenth century. Hall's texts – which were 'variously excerpted, serialized, pirated, anthologized, and reprinted in both high-end and the cheap periodical press' – circulated widely; they were, as Clare Pettitt has noted, 'passed around artisans' reading circles in pubs and taverns, and on the shelves of Mechanics' Institute libraries and provincial circulating libraries across the land'.[27] Hall's efforts to keep pace with the popular appetite for travel writing proved ultimately unsustainable and led to what one of his contemporaries described as 'mental alienation' – his 'constant literary exertion weakened his brain, and he lost his reason'.[28] Whilst many nineteenth-century travel writers were maddened by the field, Hall was driven to distraction by his role as author.

The production, publication, reception and republication of Hall's *Account of a Voyage of Discovery* speak to a number of concerns which have emerged in recent years to do with travellers' inscriptive practices and with the role of publishers in the editing and mediation of printed accounts. Attention to Hall's book shows how a publisher's archive can be used to understand the decisions (whether literary, financial or personal) that shaped the form and content of a text of travel.

Assembling Hall's *Account of a Voyage of Discovery to the West Coast of Corea* (1818)

Basil Hall's *Account of a Voyage of Discovery* described his 1816 oceanic travels in the East China Sea as captain of HMS *Lyra* – a Royal Navy vessel sent to support William Amherst in his efforts to establish diplomatic and commercial links with the Qing imperial court. Hall's narrative has been described as 'especially precious' for what it reveals about British travel in East Asia before the 'advent of full-blown Victorian industrial and imperial expansion'.[29] More than its anecdotal significance, however, Hall's book communicated important geographical and anthropological information concerning East Asia to British audiences. As one of Hall's biographers has noted, *Account of a Voyage of Discovery* can be considered significant for a number of reasons:

> it contains the earliest Western hydrological description of parts of the west coast of Korea, it provides the earliest Western description of the geology of Korea, it contains a description of ordinary life in rural Korea just before the impact of European imperial and commercial expansion, and it provides a graphic first-hand account of the political conditions of Korea at the close of the Chosŏn dynasty.[30]

Whilst the value of its textual content has been recognised, little scholarly attention has been paid to the production and publication of the book itself.[31]

In searching for an appropriate and willing publisher for his narrative, Hall was presented with an obvious choice: John Murray. This was not simply a consequence of that firm's reputation as an authoritative publisher of travel texts, but because Murray had already issued two related accounts – John McLeod's *Narrative of a Voyage, in His Majesty's Late Ship* Alceste, *to the Yellow Sea* (1817) and Henry Ellis's *Journal of the Proceedings of the Late Embassy to China* (1817) – and remained keen to capitalise on popular interest in the political and geographical novelties which the voyage and embassy presented.[32] Given that South East Asia was 'virtually unknown to western audiences', Murray was keenly aware that 'anything written from first-hand encounter was both novel and informative' and likely to sell well as a consequence.[33] For his part, Hall saw publication as a financial opportunity as well as a chance to satisfy popular curiosity. Writing to Murray over the terms of his contract, Hall confessed 'I do want some ready money, certainly, to pay off a plaguey debt – but I [also] have a strong desire to keep up some kind of interest in this "cruize" [sic]'.[34]

Although *Account of a Voyage of Discovery* was Hall's first book, he had maintained a personal journal since joining the Royal Navy in 1802. Reflecting several years later on the style and content of his first maritime journal, Hall found it wanting – it was, by his own assessment, 'a record of insignificant facts which lead to nothing, useless as memorandums at the time, and of course not more useful at the distance of eight-and-twenty years'.[35] With the benefit of hindsight, Hall recognised that what his early journal writing lacked was an emotional and subjective register. For Hall, the journal writer's 'opinions and his feelings' were fundamental to a compelling journal, serving as the 'lights and shades and colours of a painting, which, while they contribute fully as much to the accuracy of a representation as the correctness of the mere outline, impress the mind of the spectator with a still more vivid image of the object intended to be described'.[36] Information alone did not, in Hall's opinion, make for a persuasive journal – impression was equally significant. Without their subjective and emotional components, journals were, Hall argued, 'like Chinese paintings, without shading or relief [. . .] drawn with such a barbarous perspective, that every thing [sic] appears to lie in one plane'.[37] In the same way that art that did not follow Western conventions of linear perspective offended Hall's aesthetic sensibilities, so a journal that lacked personal depth was, by definition, incomplete and difficult to interpret. Notwithstanding Hall's desire for emotional resonance in his writing, he was nevertheless committed to the chronological integrity of the journal form, believing it vital to preserve 'the exact order' in which events were 'known to have happened'.[38] This anxiety for periodicity doubtless reflected the formal constraints of log-book writing which governed Hall's formal inscriptive and observational practices at sea.

As was the case with many nineteenth-century works of travel, *Account of a Voyage of Discovery* represented the effort of more than one author. Whilst Hall's narrative did not make explicit the editorial input of Murray and of the firm's literary advisors (in this sense Hall's text is not atypical), it did offer proper credit to those who contributed to its paratextual elements: its charts, tables and other appendices. Hall acknowledged in the book's preface that his own journals and recollections had been supplemented by those of Herbert Clifford – a lieutenant aboard the *Lyra* – who had been given permission by the Admiralty to accompany Hall on half pay and without an allocated duty.[39] As Hall noted, Clifford was thus

> enabled to devote himself entirely to the acquisition of knowledge; and had it in his power to record many interesting occurrences of the voyage, which the numerous duties of my station left me but little leisure to observe or describe.[40]

The book's chart of the Yellow Sea was, Hall noted, 'taken from a Chart by Captain Daniel Ross', a 'scientific and able surveyor' of the East India Company.[41] Finally, Hall credited the assistance of the artist William Havell who had worked up – 'from sketches taken on the spot' by Hall and by a midshipman on the Lyra's sister ship, *Alceste* – detailed 'drawings of scenery and costume'.[42] All told, *Account of a Voyage of Discovery* represented the collective efforts of at least half-a-dozen contributors to its text and images.

New Year's Day 1818 found Hall at work on the book's galley proofs. He was, he told Murray, 'glad to observe the progress of the Printer' and confirmed that he was working 'tooth & nail' to correct the sheets in a timely fashion.[43] In an effort to render distinct the voyage's narrative from its scientific and nautical contributions, the decision had been taken – we may assume by Murray – to place these latter components in an appendix 'in order to avoid the interruption which such details are apt to occasion when inserted in a journal'.[44] The separation of narrative and data was, in this respect, a means of catering to the distinctive requirements and expectations of the popular and professional audiences to whom the book was addressed. This choice as to the book's physical arrangement attracted the praise of the critical press when the book was published (in quarto format at £2 2s). The Murray-owned (but independently edited) *Quarterly Review* noted, for example, that 'the objectionable manner in which scientific travellers usually communicate the results of their observations' – 'interweaving the details of science with the general narrative' – had happily been 'judiciously obviated' in Hall's book.[45]

Despite the book's relatively high price, *Account of a Voyage of Discovery* sold well and earned, in its first year, almost £200 for Hall and £100 for Clifford.[46] The success of the quarto edition gave Hall and Murray impetus to pursue a second edition, targeted at 'the General reader' and 'brought down below a guinea' in price.[47] The surviving correspondence between Hall and Murray shows that the production of the cheaper second edition – published as a 7s 6d duodecimo volume in 1820 – required significant negotiation in relation to the book's content and particularly its scientific appendices. Hall was especially anxious, for example, that the charts which accompanied the first edition would be retained in the second, and offered to 'bear all the expense' of including them.[48] Ultimately, however, the second edition – issued under the slightly altered title of *Voyage to Corea, and the Island of Loo-Choo* – was 'confined to the narrative alone, to the exclusion of all technical and other details, not cal-culated to interest the general reader'.[49] Only one chart, intended to allow readers to 'know where abouts [*sic*] they were', was reproduced in the second edition.[50] The elimination of Clifford's vocabulary also meant that this edition of the text was, superficially at least, the work of Hall alone. In compressing his quarto volume into a duodecimo format, it was also necessary for Hall – in concert with the Murray firm – to abridge the text significantly, elimi-nating any extraneous descriptive material. The nine plates that had illustrated the quarto edi-tion were reduced to just four in the duodecimo text, all of which were retitled and redrawn (by an anonymous hand) for reproduction in the smaller format.

Also evident in Hall's correspondence with Murray over the second edition is his concern for precision and nuance in the text, notwithstanding the expunging which its reduced size necessi-tated. Hall provided Murray with a list of errata and proposed alterations: 'profusion of cloth' was now to read 'profusion of drapery'; 'genteel' to read 'polite'; 'took' to read 'carried'.[51] Although much can be made of the textual alterations between the book's first and second editions – which included changes to tense, among other things – it is sufficient to note that even as a printed artefact, Hall's narrative was not fixed and immutable; his in-the-field experiences were ripe for more nuanced recasting with the benefit of yet further temporal distance.

Hall's text appeared in a yet further guise in 1826 as the first number of the Edinburgh publisher Archibald Constable's new experiment in cheap print: the *Miscellany*. The ambition of the series was – in responding to rapidly increasing literacy rates – to make 'Standard Works [. . .] accessible to the great mass of the Public'.[52] Issued under the revised title *Voyage to Loo-Choo, and Other Places in the Eastern Seas, in the Year 1816*, this was an 'enlarged and improved edition' of the 1818 text but, at 3s 6d, was only one fourteenth the cost.[53] The original text was supplemented by two new additions: an account of Captain Murray Maxwell's celebrated 1816 attack on Chinese defensive batteries at Canton and notes based upon an interview between Hall and Napoleon Bonaparte at St Helena in 1817. The latter of these additions had been originally intended for inclusion in the 1818 edition of Hall's book, but had briefly been lost. At the time of the book's original publication, Hall wrote to Murray to complain 'it is a seri-ous annoyance to lose such a document, and I am half tempted to advertise it'.[54] Happily for Hall, the notes were recovered at some point after 1818 (they are now in the collections of the National Army Museum).[55]

The advertised improvements to the 1826 text were largely stylistic. Evidently dissatisfied with certain descriptive elements of the original text, Hall 'raised into higher relief' certain descriptions of 'scenery and character'.[56] For at least one contemporary critic of the revised book, Hall's tinkering was illustrative of an improvement in his literary and analytical approach: 'such emendations [. . .] exhibit the history of a mind matured to a more perfect power of obser-vation and expression, by a more extended commerce with nature and mankind'.[57] Distance from the field – geographical and temporal – could, in concert with retrospective editing, thus render a travel text of greater value. Whilst Hall did not substantially alter his text after 1826, the whole was rarely fixed and immutable. In 1840, in an effort to tap a growing popular and political interest in China, the book was reissued by the London publisher Edward Moxon under the revised title *Narrative of a Voyage to Java, China, and the Great Loo-Choo Island* and at the knock-down price of 2s 6d. Repositioned as a cheap text which might 'help to throw some light on [. . .] the great Chinese question, and the probability of our [Britain] being obliged, in self-defence, to occupy some insular position in those seas', Hall's book was provided, twenty-two years following its initial publication, with renewed topical relevance.[58]

As attention to the 1818, 1820, 1826 and 1840 editions of Hall's book shows, nineteenth-century texts of travel were often dynamic entities, being subject to textual emendation (during and after their publication) and periodic repositioning within an expanding and fast-changing literary marketplace. In the more than two decades which separated the first and final editions of Hall's narrative, the composition and expectations of the British reading public had changed: where once publishers had sought to satisfy the appetite of a small number of bibliophiles with expensive quarto volumes, now an increasingly literate population constituted a mass market for publishers and demanded from them cheap print.[59] The edition history of Hall's text serves to illustrate that changing and expanding literary marketplace; packaged first for an elite, Hall's book eventually became 'accessible to nearly all classes'.[60]

Conclusion

What the example of Hall's travel text shows is quite how complex the processes were by which lived experience was rendered as written narrative and by which the acts and facts of travel became material, saleable commodities. The changes to form and content that accompanied the publication of travel texts point to the significance of various professional actors – publishers, editors, compositors, artists, engravers and mapmakers, among many others – who worked with (occasionally in opposition to) authors in bringing their words to book. Whilst these actors were occasionally motivated by different practical imperatives, they were typically united by a desire to demonstrate authenticity and to present the text as a faithful and reliable record of the events it described.

Existing scholarship on the publication of travel writing has provided important insights into the collaborative and contested nature of authorship, into the dual concerns of authority and profitability which influenced the form and content of printed books and into the different ways in which texts (and their paratexts) sought to communicate truth and authenticity to readers. As a consequence of the geographical and temporal focus of these studies, they have tended to address only certain kinds of travel writing: that which emerged from expeditionary, missionary or scientific travel; much less that which came later from experiential or pleasurable travel. Whilst the relationship between professional twentieth-century travel writers and their publishers – such as that between Bruce Chatwin and the firm of Jonathan Cape – have been mined for biographical and anecdotal grist, they have tended not to constitute a primary focus of scholarly attention (not least because issues of copyright and the protective tendencies of the executors of literary estates often preclude such work).[61] Likewise, book historians' examinations of twentieth-century publishing have been relatively inattentive to travel writing as a genre.[62]

Given these particular lacunae, there is considerable potential for historians of travel writing concerned with issues of authorship and publication to trace these concepts through the twentieth century and to examine how they were influenced by the emergence of travel writing as a profession and by publishing innovations such as the mass-market paperback. Among the many publishers of travel narratives ripe for further investigation is the London firm of Mills and Boon which – before it established itself as a leading producer of romantic fiction – issued the work of several twentieth-century women travellers (including Edith Butcher, Maria Czaplicka, Frances Gostling, Charmian London and Bessie Pullen-Burry). All such studies are, of course, contingent on the existence of appropriate repositories of primary source material, such as the National Library of Scotland's John Murray Archive and the University of Reading's Archive of British Publishing and Printing.[63] Irrespective of chronological focus, however, it is clear that scholars of travel writing must take seriously the production processes by which their objects of study were crafted by asking a series of related questions: why and in what ways did authors write in the field; how and why were their words amended by their editors and publishers; which factors influenced the printed form their travel texts assumed; how and why did these texts vary in subsequent reprints, editions and translations? By more carefully examining the making of travel texts, it is possible to more fully appreciate the apparent aspirations of their authors and publishers, their status as economic and epistemological objects, their contemporary reading and reception and their varied and multifaceted afterlives.

Notes

1 David Livingstone, *Missionary Travels and Researches in South Africa* (London: John Murray, 1857), 8.
2 Marie-Noëlle Bourguet, 'The Explorer', in *Enlightenment Portraits*, ed. Michel Vovelle, trans. Lydia G. Cochrane (Chicago, IL: University of Chicago Press, 1997), 296.
3 The relationship between travellers and their publishers and editors has been a longstanding and implicit concern in travel writing studies. Tim Youngs has, for example, examined the roles variously of William Blackwood and John Murray in the production of nineteenth-century texts of African exploration. See Tim Youngs, *Travellers in Africa: British Travelogues, 1850–1900* (Manchester: Manchester University Press, 1994).
4 Such work is exemplified by scholarship on David Livingstone's *Missionary Travels* (1857). See, for example, Felix Driver, '*Missionary Travels*: Livingstone, Africa and the Book', *Scottish Geographical Journal* 129.3–4 (2013); Louise C. Henderson, 'David Livingstone's *Missionary Travels* in Britain and America: Exploring the Wider Circulation of a Victorian Travel Narrative', *Scottish Geographical Journal* 129.3–4 (2013); Leila Koivunen, 'Africa on the Spot and from the Distance: David Livingstone's *Missionary Travels* and Nineteenth–Century Practices of Illustration', *Scottish Geographical Journal* 129.3–4 (2013); and Justin Livingstone, 'The Meaning and Making of *Missionary Travels*: The Sedentary and Itinerant Discourses of a Victorian Bestseller', *Studies in Travel Writing* 15.3 (2011).
5 Ian S. MacLaren, 'Exploration/Travel Literature and the Evolution of the Author', *International Journal of Canadian Studies* 5 (Spring 1992); Ian S. MacLaren, 'In Consideration of the Evolution of Explorers and Travellers into Authors: A Model', *Studies in Travel Writing* 15.3 (2011).
6 Adriana Craciun, 'Oceanic Voyages, Maritime Books, and Eccentric Inscriptions', *Atlantic Studies* 10.2 (2013): 172.
7 Glenn Hooper and Tim Youngs, 'Introduction', in *Perspectives on Travel Writing*, ed. Glenn Hooper and Tim Youngs (Aldershot: Ashgate, 2004), 2; Charles W. J. Withers and Innes M. Keighren, 'Travels into Print: Authoring, Editing and Narratives of Travel and Exploration, c.1815–c.1857', *Transactions of the Institute of British Geographers* 36.4 (2011).
8 Jack Stillinger, *Multiple Authorship and the Myth of Solitary Genius* (New York: Oxford University Press, 1991).
9 Innes M. Keighren, Charles W. J. Withers and Bill Bell, *Travels into Print: Exploration, Writing, and Publishing with John Murray, 1773–1859* (Chicago, IL: University of Chicago Press, 2015).
10 Ian S. MacLaren, 'Creating Travel Literature: The Case of Paul Kane', *Papers of the Bibliographical Society of Canada* 27.1 (1988): 81.
11 Important contributions include David Finkelstein, *The House of Blackwood: Author-Publisher Relations in the Victorian Era* (University Park, PA: Pennsylvania State University Press, 2002); Robert L. Patten, *Charles Dickens and His Publishers* (Oxford: Clarendon Press, 1978); Richard B. Sher, *The Enlightenment and the Book: Scottish Authors and Their Publishers in Eighteenth-Century Britain, Ireland, and America* (Chicago, IL: University of Chicago Press, 2007); and J. A. Sutherland, *Victorian Novelists and Publishers* (London: Athlone Press, 1976).
12 Alexis Weedon, *Victorian Publishing: The Economics of Book Production for a Mass Market, 1836–1916* (Aldershot: Ashgate, 2009).
13 Alan C. Dooley, *Author and Printer in Victorian England* (Charlottesville, VA: University Press of Virginia, 1992); Aileen Fyfe, *Steam-Powered Knowledge: William Chambers and the Business of Publishing, 1820–1860* (Chicago, IL: University of Chicago Press, 2012).
14 Janice Cavell, *Tracing the Connected Narrative: Arctic Exploration in British Print Culture, 1818–1860* (Toronto: University of Toronto Press, 2008), 9.
15 Cavell, *Tracing the Connected Narrative*, 55.
16 Fergus Fleming, *Barrow's Boys: A Stirring Story of Daring, Fortitude and Outright Lunacy* (London: Granta Books, 1998); Keighren et al., *Travels into Print*.
17 Janice Cavell, 'Making Books for Mr Murray: The Case of Edward Parry's Third Arctic Narrative', *The Library: Transactions of the Bibliographical Society* 14.1 (2013): 52.

18 Cavell, 'Making Books for Mr Murray', 45.

19 Bill Bell, 'Authors in an Industrial Economy: The Case of John Murray's Travel Writers', *Romantic Textualities: Literature and Print Culture, 1780–1840* 21 (Winter 2013); Keighren et al., *Travels into Print*.

20 Frances Robertson, *Print Culture: From Steam Press to Ebook* (Abingdon: Routledge, 2013).

21 Fyfe, *Steam-Powered Knowledge*.

22 Sarah Wadsworth, 'Charles Knight and Sir Francis Bond Head: Two Early Victorian Perspectives on Printing and the Allied Trades', *Victorian Periodicals Review* 31.4 (1998).

23 Bell, 'Authors in an Industrial Economy', 17.

24 Anonymous, 'Popular Literature', *Mechanics' Magazine* 176 (6 January 1827): 30.

25 Anonymous review of *Fragments of Voyages and Travels*, by Basil Hall, *Monthly Supplement of The Penny Magazine* (30 April 1832): 45.

26 Keighren et al., *Travels into Print*, 1.

27 Clare Pettitt, 'Exploration in Print: From the Miscellany to the Newspaper', in *Reinterpreting Exploration: The West in the World*, ed. Dane Kennedy (New York: Oxford University Press, 2014), 91.

28 Anonymous, 'Hall, Basil', in *The Supplement to the Penny Cyclopaedia of the Society for the Diffusion of Useful Knowledge* (London: Charles Knight, 1846), 2:9; Anonymous, preface to *Voyages and Travels of Captain Basil Hall, R.N.* (London: Thomas Nelson and Sons, 1895), 6.

29 James H. Grayson, 'Basil Hall's *Account of a Voyage of Discovery*: The Value of a British Naval Officer's Account of Travels in the Seas of Eastern Asia in 1816', *Sungkyun Journal of East Asian Studies* 7.1 (2007), 2, 1.

30 Grayson, *Basil Hall's Account*, 9.

31 Grace Koh, 'British Perceptions of Joseon Korea as Reflected in Travel Literature of the Late Eighteenth and Early Nineteenth Century', *Review of Korean Studies* 9.4 (2006); James McCarthy, *That Curious Fellow: Captain Basil Hall, R.N.* (Dunbeath: Whittles Publishing, 2011).

32 Gao Hao, 'The Amherst Embassy and British Discoveries in China', *History* 99.337 (2014).

33 Keighren et al., *Travels into Print*, 54.

34 Hall to Murray II, 16 November 1817. John Murray Archive, MS.40504, National Library of Scotland.

35 Basil Hall, *Fragments of Voyages and Travels, Including Anecdotes of a Naval Life* (Edinburgh: Robert Cadell, 1831), 1:37.

36 Hall, *Fragments of Voyages*, 1:38–39.

37 Hall, *Fragments of Voyages*, 1:211.

38 Basil Hall, *Account of a Voyage of Discovery to the West Coast of Corea, and the Great Loo-Choo Island* (London: John Murray, 1818), 203.

39 William R. O'Byrne, *A Naval Biographical Dictionary* (London: John Murray, 1849).

40 Hall, *Account of a Voyage*, vii–viii.

41 Hall, *Account of a Voyage of Discovery*, ix.

42 Hall, *Account of a Voyage of Discovery*, ix. Havell's work is examined more fully in Luciana Martins, 'The Art of Tropical Travel, 1768–1830', in *Georgian Geographies: Essays on Space, Place and Landscape in the Eighteenth Century*, ed. Miles Ogborn and Charles W. J. Withers (Manchester: Manchester University Press, 2004).

43 Hall to Murray II, 1 January 1818. John Murray Archive, MS.40504.

44 Hall, *Account of a Voyage of Discovery*, viii.

45 Anonymous review of *Account of a Voyage of Discovery to the West Coast of Corea*, by Basil Hall, *Quarterly Review* 18.36 (January 1818), 308.

46 Hall to Murray II, 2 March 1819. John Murray Archive, MS.40504.

47 Hall to Murray II, 2 March 1819. John Murray Archive, MS.40504.

48 Hall to Murray II, 7 March 1819. John Murray Archive, MS.40504.

49 Basil Hall, *Voyage to Corea, and the Island of Loo-Choo* (London: John Murray, 1820), vii.

50 Hall to Murray II, 27 June 1819. John Murray Archive, MS.40504.

51 Hall to Murray II, 2 March 1819. John Murray Archive, MS.40504.

52 Anonymous, preface to Basil Hall, *Voyage to Loo-Choo, and Other Places in the Eastern Seas, in the Year 1816* (Edinburgh: Archibald Constable, 1826), ii.

53 Anonymous, 'Popular Literature', 30. The first number of Constable's Miscellany comprised three volumes under the title *Hall's Voyages*. *Voyage to Loo-Choo* occupied volume 1 and *Extracts from a Journal, Written on the Coasts of Chili, Peru, and Mexico, in the Years 1820, 1821, 1822* (1826–27) occupied volumes 2 and 3.

54 Samuel Smiles, *A Publisher and His Friends: Memoir and Correspondence of the Late John Murray* (London: John Murray, 1891), 2:62.

55 'Notes of an Interview with Bonaparte, at St. Helena, on the 13th August 1817', National Army Museum, NAM. 1968–07-391-1.

56 Anonymous, review of Basil Hall, *Voyage to Loo-Choo, Monthly Review* 1.2 (February 1826), 126.

57 Anonymous, review of *Voyage to Loo-Choo*, 127.

58 Anonymous, preface to Basil Hall, *Narrative of a Voyage to Java, China, and the Great Loo-Choo Island* (London: Edward Moxon, 1840), n.p.

59 In his study of the publication and reception of the anonymously issued *Vestiges of the Natural History of Creation* (1844), James Secord has neatly illustrated how nineteenth-century books were repurposed and repackaged to appeal to different audiences. See James A. Secord, *Victorian Sensation: The Extraordinary Publication, Reception, and Secret Authorship of Vestiges of the Natural History of Creation* (Chicago, IL: University of Chicago Press, 2000).

60 Anonymous, review of *Narrative of a Voyage to Java*, 554.

61 Susannah Clapp, *With Chatwin: Portrait of a Writer* (London: Jonathan Cape, 1997); Alasdair McCleery, 'Dead Hands Keep a Closed Book', *Times Higher Education*, 5 June 2008, accessed 3 March, 2015, www. timeshighereducation.co.uk/features/dead-hands-keep-a-closed-book/402227.article.

62 See, for example, Eric de Bellaigue, *British Book Publishing as a Business since the 1960s: Selected Essays* (London: British Library, 2004) and Iain Stevenson, *Book Makers: British Publishing in the Twentieth Century* (London: British Library, 2010).

63 Alexis Weedon and Michael Bott, *British Book Trade Archives, 1830–1939: A Location Register* (Bristol: Simon Eliot and Michael Turner, 1996).

BIBLIOGRAPHY

Abderrezak, Hakim. 'Burning the Sea: Clandestine Migration and the Strait of Gibraltar in Francophone Moroccan "Illiterature".' *Contemporary French and Francophone Studies* 13.4 (2009): 461–9.

Abir-Am, Pnina G. and Dorinda Outram, eds. *Uneasy Careers and Intimate Lives: Women in Science, 1789–1979.* New Brunswick, NJ: Rutgers University Press, 1989.

Achebe, Chinua. 'An Image of Africa: Racism in Conrad's *Heart of Darkness.*' In *Joseph Conrad: Heart of Darkness: An Authoritative Text, Backgrounds and Sources, Criticism,* edited by Robert Kimbrough, 251–62. New York: W. W. Norton, 1988.

Ackerman, Diane. 'White Lanterns.' In *The Moon by Whale Light,* 181–240. New York: Vintage, 1992.

Adams, Carol J. *The Sexual Politics of Meat: A Feminist-Vegetarian Critical Theory.* New York: Continuum, 2000.

Adams, Charles H. 'Reading Ecologically: Language and Play in Bartram's *Travels.*' *Southern Quarterly* 32.4 (1994): 65–74.

Adams, Percy G. *Travelers and Travel Liars 1660–1800.* Originally published 1962. New York: Dover, 1980.

Adler, Judith. 'Origins of Sightseeing.' *Annals of Tourism Research* 16.1 (1989): 7–29.

Adorno, T. W. 'The Essay as Form,' translated by Bob Hullot-Kentor and Frederic Will. Originally published 1958. *New German Critique* 32 (1984): 151–71.

Agnew, Vanessa. 'Hearing Things: Music and Sounds the Traveller Heard and Didn't Hear on the Grand Tour.' *Cultural Studies Review* 18.3 (2012): 67–84.

Agorni, Mirella. *Translating Italy for the Eighteenth Century: British Women, Translation and Travel Writing (1739–1797).* Manchester: St. Jerome, 2002.

Akerman, James R., ed. *Cartographies of Travel and Navigation.* Chicago, IL: University of Chicago Press, 2006.

Akerman, James R. 'Finding Our Way in the World.' In *Maps: Finding Our Place in the World,* edited by James R. Akerman and Robert W. Karrow, Jr., 19–63. Chicago, IL: University of Chicago Press, 2007.

Akerman, James R. 'Mapping, Battlefield Tourbooks, and Remembering the Great War.' In *History of Military Cartography,* edited by Elri Liebenberg, Imre Demhardt and Soetkin Vervust, 159–77. Heidelberg: Springer-Verlag, 2015.

Aldin, Cecil. *Old Inns.* London: William Heinemann, 1921.

Alexander, Caroline. *One Dry Season: In the Footsteps of Mary Kingsley.* London: Bloomsbury, 1989.

Alexander, Edward P. *The Museum in America: Innovators and Pioneers.* Walnut Creek, CA: AltaMira Press, 1997.

Algazi, Gadi, ed. *Negotiating the Gift: Pre-Modern Figurations of Exchange.* Göttingen: Vandenhoeck & Ruprecht, 2003.

Allen, Deborah. 'Acquiring "Knowledge of Our Own Continent": Geopolitics, Science, and Jeffersonian Geography, 1783–1803.' *Journal of American Studies* 40.2 (2006): 205–32.

Allen, Esther. '"Money and Little Red Books": Romanticism, Tourism, and the Rise of the Guidebook.' *LIT: Literature Interpretation Theory* 7.2–3 (1996): 213–26.

Allen, John Logan, ed. *North American Exploration.* 3 vols. Lincoln, NE: University of Nebraska Press, 1997.

Allewaert, M. 'Swamp Sublime: Ecologies of Resistance in the American Plantation Zone.' *PMLA* 123.2 (2008): 340–57.

Altick, Richard. *The Shows of London.* Cambridge, MA: The Belknap Press of Harvard University Press, 1978.

Altman, Rick. *Silent Film Sound.* New York: Columbia University Press, 2004.

Amit, Vered. 'Circumscribed Cosmopolitanism: Travel Aspirations and Experiences.' *Identities: Global Studies in Culture and Power* 22.5 (2015): 551–68.

Amundsen, Roald. *The South Pole: An Account of the Norwegian Expedition in the 'Fram', 1910–12,* translated by Thorvald Nilsen, Kristian Prestrud and A. G. Chater. 2 vols. Originally published 1912. London: C. Hurst, 1976.

Amundsen, Roald. *The South Pole: An Account of the Norwegian Antarctic Expedition in the Fram, 1910–1912,* translated by A. G. Chater. 2 vols. Originally published 1912. London: Hurst, 2001.

Anderson, Amanda. *The Way We Argue Now: A Study in the Cultures of Theory.* Princeton, NJ: Princeton University Press, 2005.

Anderson, Douglas. 'Bartram's *Travels* and the Politics of Nature.' *Early American Literature* 25.1 (1990): 3–17.

André, James St. 'Travelling Toward True Translation: The First Generation of Sino-English Translators.' *The Translator* 12.2 (2006): 189–210.

Andrée, Salomon August, Knut Frænkel and Nils Strindberg. *Andrée's Story: The Complete Record of His Polar Flight, 1897,* translated by Edward Adams-Ray. New York: Viking Press, 1930.

Andrews, Malcolm. *The Search for the Picturesque: Landscape Aesthetics and Tourism in Britain, 1760–1800.* Aldershot: Scolar Press, 1989.

Anon. Preface to *Narrative of a Voyage to Java, China, and the Great Loo-Choo Island,* by Basil Hall. London: Edward Moxon, 1840.

Anon. Preface to *Voyage to Loo-Choo, and Other Places in the Eastern Seas, in the Year 1816,* by Basil Hall. Edinburgh: Archibald Constable, 1826.

Anon. Preface to *Voyages and Travels of Captain Basil Hall, R.N.* London: Thomas Nelsons and Sons, 1895.

Antony, Rachael and Joël Henry. *The Lonely Planet Guide to Experimental Travel.* Melbourne: Lonely Planet, 2005.

Appadurai, Arjun. 'Disjuncture and Difference in the Global Cultural Economy.' In *The Cultural Studies Reader,* edited by Simon During, 220–30. London: Routledge, 2004.

Appiah, K. Anthony. 'Identity, Authenticity, Survival: Multicultural Societies and Social Reproduction.' In *Multiculturalism: Examining 'The Politics of Recognition,'* edited by Amy Gutmann, 149–64. Princeton, NJ: Princeton University Press, 1994.

Aravamudan, Srinivas. 'Defoe, Commerce, and Empire.' In *The Cambridge Companion to Daniel Defoe,* edited by John Richetti, 45–63. Cambridge: Cambridge University Press, 2009.

Archer, Caroline, with Alexandre Parré. *Paris Underground.* New York: Mark Batty, 2005.

Ariosto, Lodovico. *The Satires of Ludovico Ariosto: A Renaissance Autobiography,* translated by Peter DeSa Wiggins. Athens, OH: Ohio University Press, 1976.

Ariosto, Lodovico. *Orlando Furioso de m. Lodovico Ariosto tutto ricoretto.* Venice: Vincenzo Valgrisi, 1565.

Aristotle. *De Anima (On the Soul),* translated by Hugh Lawson-Tancred. London: Penguin, 1986.

Armitage, Simon and Glyn Maxwell. *Moon Country: Further Reports from Iceland.* London: Faber and Faber, 1996.

Armstrong, Joshua. 'Empiritexts: Mapping Attention and Invention in Post-1980 French Literature.' *French Forum* 40.1 (2015): 93–108.

Armstrong, Philip. *What Animals Mean in the Fiction of Modernity.* Abingdon: Routledge, 2008.

Armstrong, Philip and Laurence Simmons. 'Bestiary: An Introduction.' In *Knowing Animals,* edited by Philip Armstrong and Laurence Simmons, 1–24. Leiden: Brill, 2007.

Arntzen, Sonja. *The Kagerō Diary: A Woman's Autobiographical Text from Tenth-Century Japan.* Ann Arbor, MI: Center for Japanese Studies, The University of Michigan, 1997.

Arntzen, Sonja and Itō Moriyuki, trans. *The Sarashina Diary: A Woman's Life in Eleventh-Century Japan.* New York: Columbia University Press, 2014.

Ashcroft, Bill. 'Afterword: Travel and Power.' In *Travel Writing, Form and Empire: The Poetics and Politics of Mobility,* edited by Julia Kuehn and Paul Smethurst, 229–41. New York: Routledge, 2009.

Ashcroft, Bill, Gareth Griffiths and Helen Tiffin. *The Empire Writes Back: Theory and Practice in Post-Colonial Literature*. London: Routledge, 1989.

Auden, W.H. and Christopher Isherwood, *Journey to a War*. London: Faber and Faber, 1939.

Auden, W. H. and Louis MacNeice. *Letters from Iceland*. London: Faber and Faber, 1937.

Augé, Marc. *Un ethnologue dans le métro*. Paris: Hachette, 1986.

Ba, Omar. *Je suis venu, j'ai vu, je n'y crois plus*. Paris: Max Milo editions, 2009.

Ba, Omar. *N'émigrez pas! L'Europe est un mythe*. Paris: J.C. Gawsewitch, 2010.

Ba, Omar. *Soif d'Europe: Témoignage d'un clandestin*. Paris: Editions du Cygne, 2008.

Bachelder, John B. *Gettysburg: What to See, and How to See It*. Boston, MA: Bachelder, 1873.

Baddeley, M. J. B. *Ireland (Part I)*. 2nd ed. London: Dulau & Co., 1890.

Baddeley, M. J. B. *The Highlands of Scotland (As Far as Stornoway, Lochinver, and Lairg)*. London: Dulau & Co., 1881.

Baddeley, M. J. B. *The Thorough Guide to the English Lake District*. London: Dulau & Co., 1880.

Baddeley, M. J. B. and C. S. Ward. *North Wales (Part II)*. London: Dulao & Co., 1885.

Bailey, Elisabeth Tova. *The Sound of a Wild Snail Eating*. Dartington: Green Books, 2010.

Bailey, J. M. 'The Dansbury-News Man.' In *England from a Back-Window; with Views of Scotland and Ireland*. Boston, MA: Lee and Shepard, 1879.

Bailey, Steven. 'From 香港 to Hà Nội: Travel Guidebook Writing as a Political Act.' In *Politics, Identity, and Mobility in Travel Writing*, edited by Miguel A. Cabañas, Jeanne Dubino, Veronica Salles-Reese and Gary Totten, 225–37. New York: Routledge, 2016.

Bakhtin, M. M. 'The *Bildungsroman* and Its Significance in the History of Realism (Toward a Historical Typology of the Novel).' In *Speech Genres and Other Late Essays*, edited by Caryl Emerson and Michael Holquist, translated by Vern W. McGee, 10–59. Originally written between 1936 and 1938. Austin, TX: University of Texas Press, 1986.

Balm, Roger. 'Expeditionary Art: An Appraisal.' *Geographical Review* 90.4 (2000): 585–602.

Bannet, Eve Tavor. *Empire of Letters: Letter Manuals and Transatlantic Correspondence, 1688–1820*. Cambridge: Cambridge University Press, 2005.

Bannet, Eve Tavor. *Transatlantic Stories and the History of Reading: Migrant Fictions 1720–1820*. Cambridge: Cambridge University Press, 2012.

Barber, Giles. 'The English-Language Guide Book to Europe Up to 1870.' In *Journeys through the Market: Travel, Travellers and the Book Trade*, edited by Robin Myers and Michael Harris, 93–106. New Castle, DE: Oak Knoll Press, 1999.

Barber, Theodore X. 'The Roots of Travel Cinema: John L. Stoddard, E. Burton Holmes and the Nineteenth-Century Illustrated Travel Lecture.' *Film History* 5.1 (1993): 66–85.

Barbour, Philip L., ed. *The Jamestown Voyages Under the First Charter, 1606–1609*. 2 vols. London: Cambridge University Press, for the Hakluyt Society, 1969.

Barnes, Trevor J. and James S. Duncan, eds. *Writing Worlds; Discourse, Text and Metaphor in the Representation of Landscapes*. London: Routledge, 1993.

Barthes, Roland. 'The *Blue Guide*.' In *Mythologies*, translated by Annette Lavers 74–7. Originally published 1957. London: Granada, 1973.

Barthes, Roland. 'From Work to Text.' In *Image-Music-Text*, translated by Stephen Heath, 155–64. Originally published 1971. New York: Hill and Wang, 1977.

Barthes, Roland. 'Introduction to the Structural Analysis of Narrative.' In *Image-Music-Text*, translated by Stephen Heath, 79–124. Originally published 1966. New York: Hill and Wang, 1977.

Barthes, Roland. 'Rhetoric of the Image.' In *Image-Music-Text*, translated by Stephen Heath, 32–51. Originally published 1964. New York: Hill and Wang, 1977.

Barton, Ruth. '"Huxley, Lubbock, and Half a Dozen Others": Professionals and Gentlemen in the Formation of the X Club, 1851–1864.' *Isis* 89.3 (1998): 410–44.

Barton, Ruth. '"Men of Science": Language, Identity and Professionalization in the Mid-Victorian Scientific Community.' *History of Science* 41.1 (2003): 73–119.

Bartram, William. *Travels*, edited by James Dickey. New York: Penguin, 1988.

Bar-Yosef, Eitan. 'The "Deaf Traveller," the "Blind Traveller," and Constructions of Disability in Nineteenth-Century Travel Writing.' *Victorian Review* 35.2 (2009): 133–54.

Bataille, Georges. *Visions of Excess: Selected Writings, 1927–1939*. Minneapolis, MN: University of Minnesota Press, 1985.

Bate, Jonathan. *Romantic Ecology*. London: Routledge, 1991.

Bate, Jonathan. *The Song of the Earth*. London: Picador, 2000.

Bates, Charlotte. 'Hotel Histories: Modern Tourists, Modern Nomads and the Culture of Hotel-Consciousness.' *Literature & History* 12.2 (2003): 62–75.

Batten, Charles L. *Pleasurable Instruction: Form and Convention in Eighteenth-Century Travel Literature*. Berkeley, CA: University of California Press, 1978.

Baudrillard, Jean. *Amérique*. Paris: Editions Grasset & Fasquelle, 1986.

Beaglehole, J. C. *The Life of Captain James Cook*. Stanford, CA: Stanford University Press, 1974.

Beaglehole, J. C., ed. *The Journals of Captain James Cook on His Voyages of Discovery: Volume I, The Voyage of the Endeavour, 1768–1771*. Cambridge: Cambridge University Press for the Hakluyt Society, 1955.

Beaglehole, J. C., ed. *The Journals of Captain James Cook on His Voyages of Discovery: Volume II, The Voyage of the Resolution and Adventure, 1772–1775*. Cambridge: Cambridge University Press, 1961.

Beatty, Richmond Croom. *Bayard Taylor: Laureate of the Gilded Age*. Oklahoma City, OK: University of Oklahoma Press, 1936.

Beaujour, Michel. 'Some Paradoxes of Description.' *Yale French Studies* 61 (1981): 27–59.

Beck, Ulrich. 'Cosmopolitan Realism: On the Distinction between Cosmopolitanism in Philosophy and the Social Sciences.' *Global Networks* 4.2 (2004): 131–56.

Beck, Ulrich. 'The Cosmopolitan Society and Its Enemies.' *Theory, Culture and Society* 19.1–2 (2002): 17–44.

Behdad, Ali. *Belated Travelers: Orientalism in the Age of Colonial Dissolution*. Cork: Cork University Press, 1994.

Beinart, William. 'Men, Science, Travel and Nature in the Eighteenth and Nineteenth-Century Cape.' *Journal of Southern African Studies* 24.4 (1998): 775–99.

Belknap, Robert E. *The List: The Uses and Pleasures of Cataloguing*. New Haven: Yale University Press, 2004.

Bell, Bill. 'Authors in an Industrial Economy: The Case of John Murray's Travel Writers.' *Romantic Textualities: Literature and Print Culture, 1780–1840* 21 (Winter 2013): 9–29.

Bell, Gertrude. *The Desert and the Sown: Travels in Palestine and Syria*. Originally published 1907. New York: Dover, 2008.

Bendixen, Alfred and Judith Hamera, eds. *The Cambridge Companion to American Travel Writing*. Cambridge: Cambridge University Press, 2009.

Benjamin, Walter. 'The Storyteller.' In *Illuminations*, translated by Harry Zohn, 83–109. Originally published 1936. New York: Schocken, 1969.

Bennett, Jane. *The Enchantment of Modern Life*. Princeton, NJ: Princeton University Press, 2001.

Bennington, Geoffrey. 'Handshake.' *Derrida Today* 1.2 (2009): 167–89.

Benson, Etienne. 'Animal Writes: Historiography, Disciplinarity, and the Animal Trace.' In *Making Animal Meaning*, edited by Linda Kalof and Georgina Montgomery, 3–16. East Lansing, MI: Michigan State University Press, 2011.

Berchtold, Leopold. *An Essay to Direct and Extend the Inquiries of Patriotic Travellers*. 2 vols. London: Printed for the Author, 1789.

Berger, Molly W. *Hotel Dreams: Luxury, Technology, and Urban Ambition in America, 1829–1929*. Baltimore, MD: Johns Hopkins University Press, 2011.

Bernard, Andreas. *Lifted: A Cultural History of the Elevator*, translated by David Dollenmayer. Originally published 2006. New York: New York University Press, 2014.

Beverly, John. '*Testimonio*, Subalternity, and Narrative Authority'. In *A Companion to Latin American Literature and Culture*, edited by Sara Castro-Klaren. Oxford: Wiley Blackwell, 2013.

Bewell, Alan. 'Romanticism and Colonial Natural History.' *Studies in Romanticism* 43.1 (2004): 5–34.

Bhabha, Homi K. 'Introduction: Narrating the Nation.' In *Nation and Narration*, edited by Homi K. Bhabha, 1–7. London: Routledge, 1990.

Bhabha, Homi K. *The Location of Culture*. London: Routledge, 1994.

Bhattacharyya, Deborah P. 'Mediating India: An Analysis of a Guidebook.' *Annals of Tourism Research* 24.2 (1997): 371–89.

Bischoff, Simon, ed. *Paul Bowles Photographs: 'How Could I Send a Picture into the Desert?'*. Zurich: Scalo Publishers, 1994.

Bitterli, Urs. *Cultures in Conflict: Encounters Between European and Non-European Cultures, 1492–1800*. Stanford, CA: Stanford University Press, 1986.

Blair, Hugh. *Lectures on Rhetoric and Belles Lettres*. 2 vols. 1783. Carbondale, IL: Southern Illinois University Press, 1965.

Blanding, Michael. *The Map Thief*. New York: Gotham Books, 2014.

Blanton, Casey. *Travel Writing: The Self and the World*. Originally published 1995. London: Routledge, 2002.

Blommaert, Jan. *Ethnography, Superdiversity and Linguistic Landscapes: Chronicles of Complexity*. Bristol: Multilingual Matters, 2013.

Blunt, Alison. *Travel, Gender, and Imperialism: Mary Kingsley and West Africa*. New York: The Guilford Press, 1994.

Boelhower, William. 'Mapping the Gift Path: Exchange and Rivalry in John Smith's "A True Relation".' *American Literary History* 15.4 (2003): 655–82.

Boellstorff, Tom. *Coming of Age in Second Life: An Anthropologist Explores the Virtually Human*. Princeton, NJ: Princeton University Press, 2008.

Bohls, Elizabeth A. *Women Travel Writers and the Language of Aesthetics, 1716–1818*. Cambridge: Cambridge University Press, 1995.

Bon, François. *Paysage fer*. Paris: Verdier, 2000.

Bora, Renu. 'Outing Texture.' In *Novel Gazing: Queer Readings in Fiction*, edited by Eve Kosofsky Sedgwick, 94–127. Durham, NC: Duke University Press, 1997.

Borodale, Sean. *Notes for an Atlas*. N.p.: Isinglass, 2003.

Bougainville, Louis-Antoine de. *The Pacific Journal of Louis-Antoine de Bougainville, 1767–1768*, translated and edited by John Dunmore. London: Hakluyt Society, 2002.

Bougainville, Louis-Antoine de. *Voyage autour du monde*. Originally published 1771. Paris: Presses de l'Université de Paris-Sorbonne, 2001.

Bougainville, Louis-Antoine de. *Voyage Round the World Performed by Order of His Most Christian Majesty in the Years 1766, 1767, 1768, 1769*. London, 1772.

Bough, Jill. *Donkey*. London: Reaktion, 2011.

Boulton, James T., ed. *The Letters of D.H. Lawrence, Volume I: September 1901–May 1913*. Cambridge: Cambridge University Press, 1979.

Bourguet, Marie-Noëlle. 'The Explorer.' In *Enlightenment Portraits*, edited by Michel Vovelle, translated by Lydia G. Cochrane, 257–315. Originally published 1992. Chicago, IL: University of Chicago Press, 1997.

Bourke, Eoin, trans. and ed. *'Poor Green Erin': German Travel Writers' Narratives on Ireland from Before the 1798 Rising to After the Great Famine*. Oxford: Peter Lang, 2012.

Bouvier, Nicolas and Hervé Guyader. *L'Oreille du voyageur: Nicolas Bouvier de Genève à Tokyo*. Geneva: Éditions Zoë, 2008.

Bowdich, T. Edward. *Mission from Cape Coast Castle to Ashantee*. London: John Murray, 1819.

Bowdich, Sarah and T. Edward. *Excursions in Madeira and Porto Santo, during the Autumn of 1823, while on his Third Voyage to Africa; by the Late T. Edward Bowdich . . . To which is added, By Mrs Bowdich, I. A Narrative of the Continuance of the Voyage to its Completion . . . II. A Description of the English Settlements on the River Gambia. III. Appendix: Containing Zoological and Botanical Descriptions, and Translations from the Arabic. Illustrated by Sections, Views, Costumes, and Zoological Figures*. London: George B. Whittaker, 1825.

Boyle, Robert. 'General Heads for the Natural History of a Country, Great and Small.' In *The Philosophical Works of the Hon. Robert Boyle Esq.* 3 vols. London: 1725.

Bracher, Frederick. 'The Maps in "Gulliver's Travels".' *Huntington Library Quarterly* 8.1 (1944): 59–74.

Branagan, Thomas. *The Guardian Genius of the Federal Union; or, Patriotic Admonitions on the Signs of the Times, in relation to the Evil Spirit of Party, Arising from the Root of all our Evils, Human Slavery, being the first part of the Beauties of Philanthropy*. New York: Published for the Author, n.d.

Brant, Clare. 'Scenting a Subject: Odour Poetics and the Politics of Space.' *Ethnos: Journal of Anthropology* 73.4 (2008): 544–63.

Bratton, J. S. *The Making of the West End Stage: Marriage, Management and the Mapping of Gender in London, 1830–1870*. Cambridge: Cambridge University Press, 2011.

Bravo, Michael. 'Geographies of Exploration and Improvement: William Scoresby and Arctic Whaling, 1782–1822.' *Journal of Historical Geography* 32.3 (2006): 512–38.

Brazell, Karen, trans. *The Confessions of Lady Nijō*. Stanford, CA: Stanford University Press, 1973.

Breen, T. H. *The Marketplace of Revolution: How Consumer Politics Shaped American Independence*. Oxford: Oxford University Press, 2004.

Brennan, Michael G. 'The Texts of Peter Martyr's *De orbe novo decades* (1504–1628).' *Connotations* 6.2 (1996/97): 227–43.

Brennan, Michael G., ed. *The Origins of the Grand Tour: The Travels of Robert Montagu, Lord Mandeville (1649–1654) William Hammond (1655–1658) Banaster Maynard (1660–1663)*. London: Hakluyt Society, 2004.

Brennan, Michael G., ed. *The Travel Diary of Robert Bargrave, Levant Merchant (1647–1656)*. London: The Hakluyt Society, 1999.

Brewer, John and Roy Porter, eds. *Consumption and the World of Goods*. New York: Routledge, 1993.

Bridges, R. C. and P. E. H. Hair. *Compassing the Vaste Globe of the Earth: Studies in the History of the Hakluyt Society 1846–1996*. London: The Hakluyt Society, 1996.

Brister, Lori. 'The Precise and the Subjective: The Guidebook Industry and Women's Travel Writing in Late Nineteenth-Century Europe and North Africa.' In *Women, Travel Writing, and Truth*, edited by Clare Broome Saunders, 61–76. London: Routledge, 2014.

British Antarctic Survey. 'The Antarctic Treaty.' Accessed 28 April 2015. www.bas.ac.uk/about/antarctica/the-antarctic-treaty.

Brody, Hugh. *Maps and Dreams: Indians and the British Columbia Frontier*. Vancouver: Douglas & McIntyre, 1981.

Brooks, Peter. *Reading for the Plot: Design and Intention in Narrative*. Cambridge, MA: Harvard University Press, 1992.

Bruce, James. *Travels to Discover the Source of the Nile*. 2nd ed. 7 vols. Edinburgh: James Ballantyne, 1804.

Bruno, Giuliana. *Atlas of Emotion: Journeys in Art, Architecture and Film*. London: Verso, 2002.

Buckton, Oliver. *Cruising with Robert Louis Stevenson: Travel, Narrative, and the Colonial Body*. Athens, OH: Ohio University Press, 2007.

Buell, Lawrence. *The Environmental Imagination*. Cambridge, MA: Harvard University Press, 1995.

Buell, Lawrence. *Writing for an Endangered World*. Cambridge, MA: Harvard University Press, 2001.

Buffon, Comte de. *Barr's Buffon: Buffon's Natural History*, 10 vols. London: n.p., 1797.

Burden, Robert. 'Home Thoughts from Abroad: Cultural Difference and the Critique of Modernity in D.H. Lawrence's *Twilight in Italy* (1916) and Other Travel Writing.' In *Landscapes and Englishness*, edited by Robert Burden and Stephan Kohl, 137–63. Amsterdam: Rodopi, 2006.

Burke, Edmund. *A Philosophical Enquiry into the Origin of Our Ideas of the Sublime and the Beautiful*. Originally published 1757. Oxford: Oxford University Press, 1990.

Burnett, D. Graham. *Masters of All They Surveyed: Exploration, Geography, and a British El Dorado*. Chicago, IL: University of Chicago Press, 2000.

Burrows, George Thomas. *Some Old English Inns*. London: T. Werner Laurie, 1907.

[Burt, Edmund.] *Letters from a Gentleman in the North of Scotland to his Friend in London*. 2 vols. London: 1754.

Burton, Stacy. *Travel Narrative and the Ends of Modernity*. Cambridge: Cambridge University Press, 2014.

Butcher, Tim. *Blood River: A Journey to Africa's Broken Heart*. London: Chatto & Windus, 2007.

Butler, Jon. *Becoming America: The Revolution Before 1776*. Cambridge, MA: Harvard University Press, 2000.

Butler, Judith. *Senses of the Subject*. New York: Fordham, 2015.

Butor, Michel. *Mobile*. Paris: Gallimard, 1962.

Buzard, James. *The Beaten Track: European Tourism, Literature, and the Ways to 'Culture', 1800–1918*. Oxford: Clarendon Press, 1993.

Byrne, Angela. '"My Little Readers": Catharine Parr Traill's Natural Histories for Children.' *Journal of Literature and Science* 8.1 (2015): 86–101.

Byrne, Angela. 'Scientific Practice and the Scientific Self in Rupert's Land, *c.* 1770–1830: Fur Trade Networks of Knowledge Exchange.' In *Spaces of Global Knowledge: Exhibition, Encounter and Exchange in an Age of Empire*, edited by Diarmid A. Finnegan and Jonathan J. Wright, 79–95. Aldershot: Ashgate, 2015.

Cachey, Theodore J. 'Maps and Literature in Renaissance Italy.' In *The History of Cartography*, vol. 3, *Cartography in the European Renaissance*, edited by David Woodward, 450–60. Chicago, IL: University of Chicago Press, 2007.

Caesar, Terry. *Forgiving the Boundaries: Home as Abroad in American Travel Writing*. Athens, GA: University of Georgia Press, 1995.

Calargé, Carla. 'Clandestine or Conquistadores? Beyond Sensational Headlines, or a Literature of Urgency.' *Research in African Literatures* 46.2 (2015): 1–14.

Callanan, Michelle and Sarah Thomas. 'Volunteer Tourism: Deconstructing Volunteer Activities within a Dynamic Environment.' In *Niche Tourism: Contemporary Issues, Trends and Cases*, edited by Marini Novelli, 183–200. Oxford: Elsevier, 2005.

Campbell, Mary Baine. 'Travel Writing and Its Theory.' In *The Cambridge Companion to Travel Writing*, edited by Peter Hulme and Tim Youngs, 261–78. Cambridge: Cambridge University Press, 2002.

Carlyle, Janice. *Common Scents: Comparative Encounters in High-Victorian Fiction*. Oxford: Oxford University Press, 2004.

Carroll, Lewis. *Alice's Adventures in Wonderland*. Originally published 1865. New York: Macmillan, 1920.

Carroll, Lewis. *Through the Looking-Glass*. New York: Macmillan, 1875.

Carroll, Siobhan. *An Empire of Air and Water: Uncolonizable Space in the British Imagination, 1750–1850*. Philadelphia, PA: University of Pennsylvania Press, 2015.

Carson, Cary, Ronald Hoffman and Peter J. Albert, eds. *Of Consuming Interests: The Style of Life in the Eighteenth Century*. Charlottesville, VA: University Press of Virginia, 1994.

Cartmill, Matt. *A View to a Death in the Morning: Hunting and Nature through History*. Cambridge, MA: Harvard University Press, 1993.

Caruth, Cathy. *Unclaimed Experience: Trauma, Narrative and History*. Baltimore, MD: Johns Hopkins University Press, 1996.

Cassin, Barbara, ed. *Vocabulaire européen des philosophies: dictionnaire des intraduisibles*. Paris: Seuil, 2004.

Cavell, Janice. 'Making Books for Mr Murray: The Case of Edward Parry's Third Arctic Narrative.' *The Library: Transactions of the Bibliographical Society* 14.1 (2013): 45–69.

Cavell, Janice. *Tracing the Connected Narrative: Arctic Exploration in British Print Culture, 1818–1860*. Toronto: University of Toronto Press, 2008.

Cervantes Saavedra, Miguel de. *Don Quixote de la Mancha*, edited by Francisco Rico. 2 vols. Madrid: Critica, 1998.

Cervantes Saavedra, Miguel de. *El ingenioso hidalgo Don Quixote de la Mancha*. Madrid: Don Joaquin Ibarra, 1780.

Chamarette, Jenny. 'Flesh, Folds and Texturality: Thinking Visual Ellipsis via Merleau-Ponty, Hélène Cixous and Robert Frank.' *Paragraph* 30.2 (2007): 34–49.

Chambers, Neil, ed. *The Scientific Correspondence of Sir Joseph Banks, 1765–1820*. 6 vols. London: Pickering and Chatto, 2007.

Champlain, Samuel de. *Les voyages du sieur de Champlain Xaintongeois, Capitaine ordinaire pour le Roy, en la marine. Divisez en deux livres. Ou, journal tres-fidele des observations faites és de descouvertures de la Nouvelle France: tant en la description des terres*. Paris: Iean Berjon, 1613.

Chapin, David. *Exploring Other Worlds: Margaret Fox, Elisha Kent Kane, and the Antebellum Culture of Curiosity*. Amherst, MA: University of Massachusetts Press, 2004.

Chatman, Seymour. *Story and Discourse*. Ithaca, NY: Cornell University Press, 1978.

Chatwin, Bruce. *In Patagonia*. Originally published 1977. London: Vintage-Random House, 2005.

Cherry-Garrard, Apsley. *The Worst Journey in the World: The Story of Scott's Last Expedition to the South Pole*. Originally published 1922. London: Picador, 1994.

Cherry-Garrard, Apsley. *The Worst Journey in the World: The Story of Scott's Last Expedition to the South Pole*. Originally published 1922. London: Vintage, 2010.

Cheyfitz, Eric. *The Poetics of Imperialism: Translation and Colonization from* The Tempest *to* Tarzan. Philadelphia, PA: University of Philadelphia Press, 1997.

Cheyfitz, Eric. '*Tarzan of the Apes*: US Foreign Policy in the Twentieth Century.' *American Literary History* 1.2 (1989): 339–60.

Chivers, Tom and Martin Kratz. *Mount London: Ascents in the Vertical City*. London: Penned in the Margins, 2014.

Chow, Rey. *Writing Diaspora: Tactics of Intervention in Contemporary Cultural Studies*. Bloomington, IN: Indiana University Press, 1993.

Churchyard, Thomas. *A Discourse of the Queenes Maiesties Entertainement* . . . . London, 1578; STC 5226.

Clapp, Susannah. *With Chatwin: Portrait of a Writer*. London: Jonathan Cape, 1997.

Clark, Steve. 'Introduction.' In *Travel Writing and Empire: Postcolonial Theory in Transit*, edited by Steve Clark, 1–28. London: Zed Books, 1999.

Classen, Constance, ed. *The Book of Touch*. New York: Berg, 2005.

Classen, Constance. *The Deepest Sense: A Cultural History of Touch*. Urbana, IL: University of Illinois Press, 2012.

Classen, Constance, David Howes and Anthony Synnott. *Aroma: The Cultural History of Smell*. London: Routledge, 1994.

Clastres, Pierre. 'The Last Frontier.' In *Archeology of Violence*, translated by Jeanine Herman, 9–27. New York: Semiotext(e), 1994.

Clayton, Daniel W. *Islands of Truth: The Imperial Fashioning of Vancouver Island*. Vancouver: University of British Columbia Press, 2000.

Clifford, James. 'Introduction: Partial Truths.' In *Writing Culture: The Poetics and Politics of Ethnography*, edited by James Clifford and George E. Marcus, 1–26. Berkeley, CA: University of California Press, 1986.

Clifford, James. *The Predicament of Culture*. Cambridge, MA: Harvard University Press, 1988.

Clifford, James. *Routes: Travel and Translation in the Late Twentieth Century*. Cambridge, MA: Harvard University Press, 1997.

Clifford, James. 'Traveling Cultures.' In *Cultural Studies*, edited by Lawrence Grossberg, Cary Nelson and Paula A. Reichler, 96–116. New York: Routledge, 1992.

Clifford, Susan and Angela King. 'Preface.' In *Second Nature*, edited by Richard Mabey, vii–viii. London: Cape, 1984.

Colbert, Benjamin. 'Introduction: Home Tourism.' In *Travel Writing and Tourism in Britain and Ireland*, edited by Benjamin Colbert, 1–12. Basingstoke: Palgrave Macmillan, 2012.

Colbert, Benjamin. 'Travel Narrative.' In *The Encyclopedia of Romantic Literature*, edited by Frederick Burwick, 3:1448–55. Chichester: Wiley-Blackwell, 2012.

Collini, Silvia and Antonella Vannoni, eds. *Les instructions scientifiques pour les voyageurs: XVIIe–XVIIIe siècle*. Paris: L'Harmattan, 2005.

Collis, Christy. 'Walking in Your Footsteps: "Footsteps of the Explorers" Expeditions and the Contest for Australian Desert Space.' In *New Spaces of Exploration: Geographies of Discovery in the Twentieth Century*, edited by Simon Naylor and James R. Ryan, 222–40. London: I. B. Tauris, 2010.

Columbus, Christopher. *The Journal of Christopher Columbus (During his First Voyage, 1492–93) and documents relating the voyages of John Cabot and Gaspar Corte Real*, translated with notes and an introduction by Clements R. Markham. London: Hakluyt Society, 1893.

The Complete Letter-Writer. London: 1756.

Condé, Maryse, *Guadeloupe*. Photographs by Jean Du Boisberranger. Paris: Richer/Hoa-Qui, 1988.

Conley, Timothy. 'Ante-Americanisms: Friendly Critiques of the Emerging Nation.' In *(Anti)-Americanisms*, edited by Michael Draxlbauer, Astrid M. Fellner, and Thomas Fröschl, 33–58. Vienna: Lit Verlag, 2004.

Conley, Tom. 'Early Modern Literature and Cartography: An Overview.' In *The History of Cartography*, vol. 3, *Cartography in the European Renaissance*, edited by David Woodward, 401–11. Chicago, IL: University of Chicago Press, 2007.

Conley, Tom. *The Self-Made Map: Cartographic Writing in Early Modern France*. Minneapolis, MN: University of Minnesota Press, 1996.

Connor, Steven. *The Book of Skin*. London: Reaktion Books, 2004.

Conroy, Jane. 'Changing Perspectives: French Travellers in Ireland, 1785–1835'. In *CrossCultural Travel*, edited by Jane Conroy, 131–42. Oxford: Peter Lang, 2003.

Constantine, Mary-Ann and Nigel Leask, eds. *Enlightenment Travel and British Identities: Thomas Pennant's Tours in Scotland and Wales*. London: Anthem Press, 2017.

Cook, Andrew S. 'Surveying the Seas: Establishing the Sea Routes to the East Indies.' In *Cartographies of Travel and Navigation*, edited by James R. Akerman, 69–96. Chicago, IL: University of Chicago Press, 2006.

Cook, James. *A Journal of a Voyage Round the World, in His Majesty's Ship Endeavour, in the Years 1768, 1769, 1770, and 1771*. London: T. Becket and P. A. DeHondt, 1771.

Cook, James. *Journal of the Resolution's Voyage, in 1772, 1773, 1774, and 1775*. London: F. Newbery, 1775.

Cook, James. *A Voyage to the Pacific Ocean . . . in the Years 1776, 1777, 1778, 1779, and 1780*. 3 vols + atlas. London: H. Hughs, G. Nicol, and T. Cadell, 1785.

Corbett, J. Martin. 'Scents of Identity: Organisation Studies and the Cultural Conundrum of the Nose.' *Culture and Organization* 12.3 (2006): 221–32.

Corbin, Alain. *The Foul and the Fragrant: Odor and the French Imagination*, translated by Miriam L. Kochan, Roy Porter and Christopher Prendergast. Originally published 1982. Cambridge, MA: Harvard University Press, 1988.

Coryate, Thomas. *Coryat's Crudities. Hastily Gobbled up in Five Months Travels*. Originally published 1611. Glasgow: James MacLehose and Sons, 1905.

Coulbert, Esme. '"The Romance of the Road": Narratives of Motoring in England, 1896–1930.' In *Travel Writing and Tourism in Britain and Ireland*, edited by Benjamin Colbert, 201–18. Houndmills: Palgrave Macmillan, 2012.

Cowart, David. *Literary Symbiosis: The Reconfigured Text in Twentieth-Century Writing*. Athens, GA: University of Georgia Press, 1993.

Cowley, Jason. 'Editors' Letter: The New Nature Writing.' *Granta* 102 (2008): 7–12.

Cox, John D. *Traveling South: Travel Narratives and the Construction of American Identity*. Athens, GA: University of Georgia Press, 2005.

Craciun, Adriana. 'Oceanic Voyages, Maritime Books, and Eccentric Inscriptions.' *Atlantic Studies* 10.2 (2013): 170–96.

Crapanzano, Vincent. 'Hermes' Dilemma: The Masking of Subversion in Ethnographic Description.' In *Writing Culture: The Poetics and Politics of Ethnography*, edited by James Clifford and George F. Marcus, 51–76. Berkeley, CA: University of California Press, 1986.

Cronin, Michael. *Across the Lines: Travel, Language and Translation*. Cork: Cork University Press, 2000.

Cronin, Michael. 'The Empire Talks Back: Orality, Heteronomy and the Cultural Turn in Interpreting Studies'. In *Translation and Power*, edited by Edwin Gentzler and Maria Tymoczko, 45–62. Boston, MA: University of Massachusetts Press, 2002.

Cronin, Michael. *The Expanding World: Towards a Politics of Microspection*. Winchester: Zero Books, 2011.

Crowley, Patrick, Noreen Humble and Silvia Ross. 'Introduction: The Mediterranean Turn.' In *Mediterranean Travels: Writing Self and Other from the Ancient World to Contemporary Society*, edited by Patrick Crowley, Noreen Humble and Silvia Ross, 1–13. London: Modern Humanities Research Association and Maney Publishing, 2011.

Cruikshank, Julie. *Do Glaciers Listen? Local Knowledge, Colonial Encounters and Social Imagination*. Vancouver: University of British Columbia Press, 2005.

Culbert, John. 'Breaking the Truth: Jamaica Kincaid and the Politics of Travel.' In *Women, Travel Writing, and Truth*, edited by Clare Broome Saunders, 141–55. London: Routledge, 2014.

Culler, Jonathan. 'Story and Discourse in the Analysis of Narrative.' In *The Pursuit of Signs: Semiotics, Literature, Deconstruction*, 169–87. Ithaca, NY: Cornell University Press, 2001.

The Curious Traveller, being a Choice Collection of very remarkable Histories, Voyages, Travels etc. digested into Familiar Letters. London: 1742.

Cushing, Frank Hamilton. *Zuni: Selected Writings of Frank Hamilton Cushing*, edited by Jesse Green. Lincoln, NE: Nebraska University Press, 1979.

Dann, Graham and Kristian Steen Jacobsen. 'Tourism Smellscapes.' *Tourism Geographies* 5.1 (2003): 3–25.

Danticat, Edwidge. *After the Dance: A Walk through Carnival in Jacmel, Haiti*. New York: Crown, 2002.

Danzer, Gerald A. and James R. Akerman. 'American Railroad Maps, 1828–1876.' In *Mapping Movement in American History and Culture*, edited by James R. Akerman and Peter Nekola, The Newberry Library. Accessed 26 September 2017. http://mappingmovement.newberry.org/essay/american–railroad–maps–1828–1876.

Das, Nandini and Tim Youngs, eds. *The Cambridge History of Travel Writing*. Cambridge: Cambridge University Press, 2019.

Das, Santanu. *Touch and Intimacy in First World War Literature*. Cambridge: Cambridge University Press, 2005.

Dassow Walls, Laura. *The Passage to Cosmos: Alexander von Humboldt and the Shaping of America*. Chicago, IL: University of Chicago Press, 2009.

Davidson, Robyn. *Tracks*. London: Picador-PanMacmillan, 1998.

Davies, Hugh William. *Bernhard von Breydenbach and His Journey to the Holy Land, 1483–4: A Bibliography*. London: J. & J. Leighton, 1911.

Davies, John. 'M62: In the Company of Ghosts.' In *In the Company of Ghosts: The Poetics of the Motorway*, edited by Alan Corkish with Edward Chell and Andrew Taylor, 19–24. Liverpool: erbacce-press, 2012.

Davis, Leonard J. *Factual Fictions: The Origins of the English Novel*. Philadelphia, PA: University of Pennsylvania Press, 1996.

Day, Jon. *Cyclogeography: Journeys of a London Bicycle Courier*. London: Notting Hill Editions, 2015.

Day, Matthew. 'Travelling in New Forms: Reissued and Reprinted Travel Literature in the Long Eighteenth-Century.' *Memoirs du livre/Studies in Book Culture* 4.2 (Spring 2013): 1–18.

Deakin, Roger. *Waterlog*. London: Chatto and Windus, 1999.

Deakin, Roger. *Wildwood: A Journey Through Trees*. London: Hamish Hamilton, 2007.

de Bellaigue, Eric. *British Book Publishing as a Business since the 1960s: Selected Essays*. London: British Library, 2004.

de Callias, Suzanne and Blanche Vogt. *Aux pays des femmes soldats: Finlande - Esthonie - Danemark – Lithuanie*. Paris: Fasquelle, 1931.

de Certeau, Michel. *The Practice of Everyday Life*, translated by Stephen Rendall. Originally published 1980. Berkeley, CA: University of California Press, 1988.

de Cherisey, Marie-Hélène and Laurent. *Passeurs d'espoir: 1. Une famille à la rencontre des bâtisseurs du XXIe siècle*. Paris: Presses de la Renaissance, 2005.

de Crèvecoeur, J. Hector St John. *Letters from an American Farmer*. London: 1782.

de Crèvecoeur, J. Hector St John. *Letters from an American Farmer and Sketches of Eighteenth-Century America*. New York: Penguin, 1986.

Deegan, Marilyn and Kathryn Sutherland, eds. *Text Editing, Print and the Digital World*. Farnham: Ashgate, 2009.

Delano-Smith, Catherine. 'Milieus of Mobility: Itineraries, Route Maps, and Road Maps.' In *Cartographies of Travel and Navigation*, edited by James R. Akerman, 16–69. Chicago, IL: University of Chicago Press, 2006.

Delanty, Gerard. 'The Cosmopolitan Imagination: Critical Cosmopolitanism and Social Theory.' *British Journal of Sociology* 57.1 (2006): 25–47.

de Lauretis, Theresa. 'Desire in Narrative.' In *Alice Doesn't: Feminism, Semiotics, Cinema*, 103–57. Bloomington, IN: Indiana University Press, 1984.

Deleuze, Gilles and Félix Guattari. '1440: The Smooth and the Striated.' In *A Thousand Plateaus: Capitalism and Schizophrenia*, translated by Brian Massumi, 523–51. Originally published 1980. Minneapolis, MN: University of Minnesota Press, 2004.

de Lima Martins, Luciana. 'Navigating in Tropical Waters: British Maritime Views of Rio de Janeiro.' *Imago Mundi* 50 (1998): 141–54.

Demleitner, Nora V. 'The Law at a Crossroads: The Construction of Migrant Women Trafficked into Prostitution.' In *Global Human Smuggling: Comparative Perspectives*, edited by Kyle David and Rey Koslowski, 257–93. Baltimore, MD: Johns Hopkins University Press, 2001.

Derrida, Jacques. '"Eating Well" or the Calculation of the Subject.' In *Points . . .: Interviews 1974–1994*, translated by Peggy Kamuf et al., edited by Elisabeth Weber, 255–87. Originally published 1989. Stanford, CA: Stanford University Press, 1995.

Derrida, Jacques. 'From Restricted to General Economy: A Hegelianism without Reserve.' In *Writing and Difference*, translated by Alan Bass. Originally published 1967. London: Routledge, 2003.

Derrida, Jacques. *The Gift of Death*, translated by David Wills. Originally published 1992. Chicago, IL: University of Chicago Press, 1995.

Derrida, Jacques. *Given Time: Counterfeit Money*, translated by Peggy Kamuf. Originally published 1991. Chicago, IL: University of Chicago, 1992.

Derrida, Jacques and Anne Dufourmantelle. *Of Hospitality: Anne Dufourmantelle Invites Jacques Derrida to Respond*, translated by Rachel Bowlby. Originally published 1997. Stanford, CA: Stanford University Press, 2000.

Derrida, Jacques. *On Touching – Jean-Luc Nancy*, translated by Christine Irizarry. Originally published 2000. Stanford, CA: Stanford University Press, 2005.

Desforges, Luke. 'Traveling the World: Identity and Travel Biography.' *Annals of Tourism Research* 27.4 (2000): 926–45.

Dessaix, Robert. *Night Letters: A Journey Through Switzerland and Italy*. Sydney: Macmillan, 1996.

Di Biase, Carmine G, ed. *Travel and Translation in the Early Modern Period*. Amsterdam: Rodopi, 2006.

Dickinson, Janet and Les Lumsdon. *Slow Travel and Tourism*. London: Earthscan, 2010.

Dikeç, Mustafa, Nigel Clark and Clive Barnett. 'Extending Hospitality: Giving Space, Taking Time.' *Paragraph* 32 (2009): 1–14.

Dobraszczyk, Paul, Carlos López Galviz and Bradley L. Garrett. *Global Undergrounds: Exploring Cities Within*. London: Reaktion, 2016.

Dooley, Alan C. *Author and Printer in Victorian England*. Charlottesville, VA: University Press of Virginia, 1992.

Dowland, Douglas. '"Macrocosm of Microcosm Me": Steinbeck's *Travels with Charley*.' *Literature Interpretation Theory* 16 (2005): 311–31.

Driver, Felix. '*Missionary Travels*: Livingstone, Africa and the Book.' *Scottish Geographical Journal* 129.3–4 (2013): 164–78.

Drobnick, Jim. 'Introduction: Olfactocentrism.' In *The Smell Culture Reader*, edited by Jim Drobnick, 1–17. Oxford: Berg, 2006.

Drobnick, Jim. 'Volatile Effects: Olfactory Dimensions of Art and Architecture.' In *The Empire of the Senses: The Sensual Culture Reader*, edited by David Howes, 265–80. Oxford and New York: Berg, 2005.

Dunaway, Finis. 'Hunting with the Camera: Nature Photography, Manliness, and Modern Memory, 1890–1930.' *Journal of American Studies* 34.2 (2000): 207–30.

Duncan, James and Derek Gregory. 'Introduction.' In *Writes of Passage: Reading Travel Writing*, edited by James Duncan and Derek Gregory, 1–13. London: Routledge, 1999.

Duncan, John. *Travels in Western Africa, in 1845 & 1846*. London: Richard Bentley, 1847.

Dunlop, Carol and Julio Cortázar. *Les Autonautes de la cosmoroute: ou, un voyage intemporel Paris-Marseille*. Paris: Gallimard, 1983.

Durkheim, Émile. *The Rules of Sociological Method*, translated by W. D. Halls, edited by Steven Lukes. Originally published 1895. Houndmills: Palgrave Macmillan, 2013.

Dym, Jordana. 'More Calculated to Mislead than Inform: The Cartography of Travel Writers in Central America, 1821–1950.' *Journal of Historical Geography* 30.2 (2004): 340–63.

Eco, Umberto. *The Infinity of Lists*, translated by Alastair McEwen. London: MacLehose Press, 2009.

Eddis, William. *Letters from America, Historical and Descriptive, comprising Occurrences from 1769–1777 Inclusive*. London, 1792.

Edney, M. H. *Mapping an Empire: The Geographical Construction of British India, 1765–1843*. Chicago, IL: Chicago University Press, 1997.

Edwards, Justin D. and Rune Graulund. *Mobility at Large: Globalization, Textuality and Innovative Travel Writing*. Liverpool: Liverpool University Press, 2012.

Edwards, Phillip. *The Story of the Voyage: Sea Narratives in Eighteenth-Century England*. Cambridge: Cambridge University Press, 1994.

Eggert, Paul. 'Discourse versus Authorship: The Baedeker Travel Guide and D. H. Lawrence's *Twilight in Italy*.' In *Texts and Textuality: Textual Instability, Theory and Interpretation*, edited by Philip G. Cohen, 207–34. New York: Routledge, 1997.

Elder, John and Robert Finch, eds. *The Norton Book of Nature Writing*. New York: W. W. Norton, 1990.

Ellis, Henry. *Journal of the Proceedings of the Late Embassy to China*. London: John Murray, 1817.

Elsner, Jaś and Joan-Pau Rubiés. 'Introduction.' In *Voyages and Visions: Towards a Cultural History of Travel*, edited by Jaś Elsner and Joan-Pau Rubiés, 1–56. London: Reaktion, 1999.

The Entertaining Correspondent, or Curious Relations, digested into familiar Letters and Conversations. London, 1739.

Erlmann, Veit. 'But What of the Ethnographic Ear? Anthropology, Sound, and the Senses.' In *Hearing Cultures: Essays on Sound, Listening, and Modernity*, edited by Veit Erlmann, 1–20. Oxford: Berg, 2004.

Ernst, Wolfgang. *Sonic Time Machines: Explicit Sound, Sirenic Voices, and Implicit Sonicity*. Amsterdam: Amsterdam University Press, 2016.

Ette, Ottmar. *Literature on the Move*, translated by Katharina Vester. Originally published 2001. Amsterdam: Rodopi, 2003.

Evelyn, John. *The Diary of John Evelyn*, ed. E. S. de Beer. Oxford: Clarendon Press, 1955.

'F.A.' 'English Hotel Life.' *London Society* 22.129 (September 1872): 256–61.

Fabian, Johannes. *Anthropology with an Attitude: Critical Essays*. Stanford, CA: Stanford University Press, 2001.

Fabian, Johannes. *Time and the Other: How Anthropology Makes Its Object*. New York: Columbia University Press, 1983.

Farber, Paul Lawrence. *Finding Order in Nature*. Baltimore, MD: Johns Hopkins University Press, 2000.

Farrier, David. *Postcolonial Asylum: Seeking Sanctuary before the Law*. Liverpool: Liverpool University Press, 2011.

Faucon, Jean-Claude. 'La Représentation de l'animal par Marco Polo.' *Médiévales* 32 (1997): 97–117.

Featherstone, Mike. 'Global Culture: An Introduction.' *Theory, Culture, Society* 7.2 (1990): 1–14.

Feest, Christian. 'The Collecting of American Indian Artifacts in Europe, 1493–1750.' In *America in European Consciousness, 1493–1750*, edited by Karen Ordahl Kupperman, 324–60. Chapel Hill, NC: University of North Carolina Press, 1995.

Felsenstein, Frank. Introduction to *Travels through France and Italy* by Tobias Smollett, edited by Frank Felstenstein, xv–lxvi. Oxford: Oxford University Press, 1981.

Fernández-Armesto, Felipe. *Food: A History*. London: Pan Books, 2001.

Fielding, Henry. 'Essay on Conversation.' In *Miscellanies by Henry Fielding Esq*. 3 vols, 1:178–240. London, 1743.

Fielding, Penny. *Scotland and the Fictions of Geography: North Britain, 1760–1830*. Cambridge: Cambridge University Press, 2009.

Filonova, Elena. 'Between Literacy and Non-Literacy: Interpreters in the Exploration and Colonization of Nineteenth-Century Alaska.' *The Translator* 12.2 (2006): 211–31.

Finkelstein, David. *The House of Blackwood: Author–Publisher Relations in the Victorian Era*. University Park, PA: Pennsylvania State University Press, 2002.

Finnegan, Diarmid A. 'Geographies of Scientific Speech in Mid-Victorian Edinburgh.' In *Geographies of Nineteenth-Century Science*, edited by David N. Livingstone and Charles W. J. Withers, 153–77. Chicago, IL: University of Chicago Press, 2011.

Fishman, Burton J. 'Defoe, Herman Moll and the Geography of South America.' *Huntington Library Quarterly* 36.3 (April 1973): 227–38.

Fleischman, Sid. *The Trouble Begins at 8: A Life of Mark Twain in the Wild, Wild West*. New York: Greenwillow Books, 2008.

Fleming, Fergus. *Barrow's Boys: A Stirring Story of Daring, Fortitude and Outright Lunacy*. London: Granta, 1998.

Flinders, Matthew. *Trim: The Story of a Brave, Seafaring Cat*. London: Collins, 1977.

Folks, Jeffrey J. 'Mediterranean Travel Writing: From *Etruscan Places* to *Under the Tuscan Sun*.' *Papers on Language and Literature* 40.1 (2004): 102–12.

Forsdick, Charles. 'Peter Fleming and Ella Maillart in China: Travel Writing as Stereoscopic and Polygraphic Form.' *Studies in Travel Writing* 13.4 (2009): 293–303.

Forsdick, Charles. 'Projected Journeys.' In *The Art of the Project: Projects and Experiments in Twentieth-Century French Culture*, edited by Johnnie Gratton and Michael Sheringham, 51–65. Oxford: Berghahn, 2005.

Forsdick, Charles. 'Traveling, Writing: Danticat's *After the Dance*.' In *Edwidge Danticat: A Reader's Guide*, edited by Martin Munro, 99–116. Charlottesville, VA: University of Virginia Press, 2010.

Forsdick, Charles. *Travel in Twentieth-Century French and Francophone Cultures: The Persistence of Diversity*. Oxford: Oxford University Press, 2005.

Forsdick, Charles. 'Travel Writing, Disability, Blindness: Venturing Beyond Visual Geographies.' In *New Directions in Travel Writing Studies*, edited by Julia Kuehn and Paul Smethurst, 113–28. London: Palgrave, 2015.

Forsdick, Charles, Corinne Fowler and Ludmilla Kostova. 'Introduction: Ethics on the Move.' In *Travel and Ethics: Theory and Practice*, edited by Corinne Fowler, Charles Forsdick and Ludmilla Kostova, 1–15. New York: Routledge, 2014.

Forster, E. M. *Where Angels Fear to Tread*. Originally published 1905. London: Penguin, 2007.

Forster, George. *A Voyage Round the World*, edited by Nicholas Thomas and Oliver Berghof. Originally published 1775. Honolulu, HI: University of Hawai'i Press, 2000.

Forster, John Reinhold. 'An Account of Some Curious Fishes, Sent from Hudson's Bay; By Mr. John Reinhold Forster, F.R.S. in a Letter to Thomas Pennant, Esq; F.R.S.' *Philosophical Transactions* 63 (1773–4): 149–60.

Fosbroke, Thomas Dudley. *Companion to the Wye Tour. Ariconensia; or Archæological Sketches of Ross, and Archenfield*. Ross: W. Farror, 1821.

Fosbroke, Thomas Dudley. *The Tourist's Grammar; or Rules Relating to the Scenery and Antiquities Incident to Travellers: Compiled from the First Authorities, and Including an Epitome of Gilpin's Principles of the Picturesque*. London: John Nichols and Son, 1826.

Fosbroke, Thomas Dudley. *The Wye Tour, or Gilpin on the Wye, with Historical and Archæological Additions*. Ross: W. Farror, 1818.

Fosbroke, Thomas Dudley. *The Wye Tour, or Gilpin on the Wye, with Picturesque, Historical, and Archæological Additions*. New ed. Ross: W. Farror, 1822.

Fosbroke, Thomas Dudley. *The Wye Tour, or Gilpin on 'The Wye,' with Picturesque Illustrations: to Which Is Added an Appendix [...]*. 5th ed. Ross: W. Farror, 1837.

Fosbroke, Thomas Dudley. *The Wye Tour, Containing an Account of Ross, Extracts Concerning the Wye, from the 'Tour of a German Prince.' And an Account of Goodrich Court, the Seat of Sir Samuel Rush Meyrick, K. H. Forming an Appendix to the Author's Prior Publication of 'Gilpin on The Wye,' or 'Wye Tour.'* New ed. Ross: W. Farror, 1837.

Fowler, Corinne, Charles Forsdick and Ludmilla Kostova, eds. *Travel and Ethics: Theory and Practice*. New York: Routledge, 2014.

Fowles, John. 'The Blinded Eye.' In *Second Nature*, edited by Richard Mabey, 77–89. London: Cape, 1984.

Fox, Adam. 'Printed Questionnaires, Research Networks, and the Discovery of the British Isles, 1650–1800.' *The Historical Journal* 53.3 (2010): 593–621.

Franklin, Adrian. *Nature and Social Theory*. London: Sage, 2002.

Fraser, Robert. *Victorian Quest Romance: Stevenson, Haggard, Kipling, and Conan Doyle*. Plymouth: Northcote House, 1998.

Frenzel, Fabian, Ko Koens and Malte Steinbruck. *Slum Tourism, Power and Ethics*. London: Routledge, 2012.

Freud, Sigmund. *Beyond the Pleasure Principle*, translated by James Strachey. Originally published 1920. New York: Norton, 1961.

Freud, Sigmund. *Three Essays on the Theory of Sexuality*. In *On Sexuality*, edited by Angela Richards, translated by James Strachey, 31–169. Originally published 1905. Harmondsworth: Penguin, 1977.

Frois, Luis, S. J. *The First European Description of Japan, 1585: A Critical English-Language Edition of Striking Contrasts in the Customs of Europe and Japan*, translated and edited by Richard K. Danford, Robin D. Gill and Daniel T. Reff. London: Routledge, 2014.

Fuller, Mary C. *Voyages in Print: English Travel to America, 1576–1624*. Cambridge: Cambridge University Press, 1995.

Fulton, Alice. *Feeling as a Foreign Language: The Good Strangeness of Poetry*. Saint Paul, MN: Graywolf Press, 1999.

Furlough, Ellen and Shelley Baronowski. *Being Elsewhere: Tourism, Consumer Culture and Identity in Modern Europe and North America*. Ann Arbor, MI: University of Michigan Press, 2001.

Fussell, Paul. *Abroad: British Literary Traveling Between the Wars*. New York: Oxford University Press, 1980.

Fyfe, Aileen. *Steam-Powered Knowledge: William Chambers and the Business of Publishing, 1820–1860*. Chicago, IL: University of Chicago Press, 2012.

Gardner, Thomas. *Pocket-Guide to the English Traveller*. London, 1719.

Garrett, Bradley L. *Subterranean London: Cracking the Capital*. London: Prestel, 2014.

Garrett, Bradley L., Alexander Moss and Scott Cadman. *London Rising: Illicit Photos from the City's Heights*. London: Prestel, 2016.

Garrington, Abbie. *Haptic Modernism: Touch and the Tactile in Modernist Writing*. Edinburgh: Edinburgh University Press, 2013.

Gascoigne, Joseph. *Science in the Service of Empire: Joseph Banks, the British State and the Uses of Science in the Age of Revolution*. Cambridge: Cambridge University Press, 1998.

Gates, Barbara T. *Kindred Nature: Victorian and Edwardian Women Embrace the Living World*. Chicago, IL: University of Chicago Press, 1998.

Gates, Barbara T. and Ann B. Shteir, eds. *Natural Eloquence: Women Reinscribe Science*. Madison, WI: University of Wisconsin Press, 1997.

Gazaï, Caroline and Geneviève Gaillet. *Vacances en Iran*. Paris: Berger-Levrault, 1961.

Geertz, Clifford. 'Thick Description: Toward an Interpretive Theory of Culture.' In *The Interpretation of Cultures: Selected Essays*, 3–30. New York: Basic Books, 1973.

Gellhorn, Martha. 'Cuba Revisited.' *Granta* 10. 'In Trouble Again: A Special Issue of Travel Writing' (1986): 105–34.

Genette, Gérard. *Narrative Discourse: An Essay in Method*, translated by Jane E. Lewin. Originally published 1972. Ithaca, NY: Cornell University Press, 1980.

George, Don. *Lonely Planet's Guide to Travel Writing*. Footscray, Vic.: Lonely Planet, 2009.

George, Rosemary Marangoly. *The Politics of Home: Postcolonial Relocations and Twentieth-Century Fiction*. Cambridge: Cambridge University Press, 1996.

George, Susan. *Lugano Report: On Preserving Capitalism in the Twenty-First Century*. London: Pluto Press, 1999.

Ghose, Indira. *Women Travellers in Colonial India: The Power of the Female Gaze*. Delhi: Oxford University Press, 1998.

Gibson, James J. *The Senses Considered as Perceptual Systems*. Boston, MA: Houghton Mifflin, 1966.

Giddens, Anthony. *Modernity and Self-Identity: Self and Society in the Late Modern Age*. Cambridge: Polity Press, 1991.

Gikandi, Simon. *Slavery and the Culture of Taste*. Princeton, NJ: Princeton University Press, 2012.

Gill, Robin D. *Topsy-Turvy 1585: The Short Version: A Translation and Popular Introduction of the Famous Treatise by Luis Frois S.J. Listing 611 Ways Europeans & Japanese are Contrary*. Key Biscayne: Paraverse Press, 2005.

Gillies, John. *Shakespeare and the Geography of Difference*. Cambridge: Cambridge University Press, 1994.

Gilpin, William. *Observations on the River Wye, and Several Parts of South Wales, &c. Relative Chiefly to Picturesque Beauty; Made in the Summer of the Year 1770*. 2nd ed. London: R. Blamire, 1789.

Gilpin, William. *Observations, Relative Chiefly to Picturesque Beauty . . . Particularly the High-Lands of Scotland*. London: Blamire, 1789.

Gilpin, William. *Three Essays*. London: R. Blamire, 1792.

Godelier, Maurice. *The Enigma of the Gift*, translated by Nora Scott. Originally published 1996. Chicago, IL: Chicago University Press, 1999.

Goethe, Johann Wolfgang von. *Italian Journey*, translated by W. H. Auden and Elizabeth Mayer. Originally published 1816–17. London: Penguin, 1970.

Goh, Irving and Ryan Bishop, eds. 'Special Issue: *Plus d'un toucher.* Touching Worlds.' *SubStance* 40.3 (2011).

Goldberg, Jonathan. *Writing Matter: From the Hands of the English Renaissance*. Stanford, CA: Stanford University Press, 1990.

Goodwin, Gráinne and Gordon Johnston. 'Guidebook Publishing in the Nineteenth Century: John Murray's *Handbooks for Travellers*.' *Studies in Travel Writing* 17 (2013): 43–61.

Gottlieb, Alma and Philip Graham. *Parallel Worlds: An Anthropologist and a Writer Encounter Africa*. New York: Crown, 1992.

Graeber, David. *Toward an Anthropological Theory of Value: The False Coin of Our Own Dreams*. New York: Palgrave, 2001.

Grann, David. *The Lost City of Z*. London: Simon & Schuster, 2009.

Grayson, James H. 'Basil Hall's *Account of a Voyage of Discovery*: The Value of a British Naval Officer's Account of Travels in the Seas of Eastern Asia in 1816.' *Sungkyun Journal of East Asian Studies* 7.1 (2007): 1–18.

Green, Toby. *Saddled with Darwin: A Journey Through South America*. London: Weidenfeld & Nicolson, 1999.

Greenblatt, Stephen. *Marvelous Possessions: The Wonder of the New World*. Oxford: Clarendon Press, 1991.

Greenblatt, Stephen, ed. *New World Encounters*. Berkeley, CA: University of California Press, 1993.

Greene, Barbara. *Too Late to Turn Back: Barbara and Graham Greene in Liberia*. Originally published 1936. London: Settle Bendall, 1981.

Greene, Graham. *Journey without Maps*. London: Heinemann, 1936.

Greene, John Patrick. 'French Encounters with Material Culture of the South Pacific.' *Eighteenth-Century Life* 26.3 (2002): 225–45.

Gregory, George. *Letters on Literature, Taste, and Composition, Addressed to His Son*. Philadelphia, PA: Bradford and Inskeep, 1809.

Grewal, Inderpal. *Home and Harem: Nation, Gender, Empire, and the Cultures of Travel*. Leicester: Leicester University Press, 1996.

Griffiths, Jay. *Wild: An Elemental Journey*. Harmondsworth: Penguin, 2008.

Groesen, Michiel van. *The Representations of the Overseas World in the De Bry Collection of Voyages (1590–1634)*. Leiden: Brill, 2008.

Gros, Frédéric. *A Philosophy of Walking*, translated by John Howe. Originally published 2014. London: Verso, 2015.

Grove, Richard H. *Green Imperialism: Colonial Expansion, Tropical Island Edens and the Origins of Environmentalism*. Cambridge: Cambridge University Press, 1995.

Grove, Richard and Vinita Damoradan. 'Imperialism, Intellectual Networks, and Environmental Change: Origins and Evolution of Global Environmental History, 1676–2000: Part I.' *Economic and Political Weekly* 41.41 (2006): 4345–54.

Grove, Richard and Vinita Damoradan. 'Imperialism, Intellectual Networks, and Environmental Change: Origins and Evolution of Global Environmental History, 1676–2000: Part II.' *Economic and Political Weekly* 41.42 (2006): 4497–505.

Guild, William. *A Chart and Description of the Boston and Worcester and Western Railroads*. Boston, MA: Bradbury & Guild, 1847.

Hagglund, Elizabeth. 'Travel Writing and Domestic Ritual.' In *Seuils et traverses: enjeux de l'écriture du voyage*. 2 vols, edited by Jean-Yves Le Disez and Jan Borm, 2:89–95. Brest: Centre de Recherche Bretonne et Celtique, 2002.

Hains, Brigid. *The Ice and the Inland: Mawson, Flynn, and the Myth of the Frontier*. Carlton South: Melbourne University Press, 2002.

Hakemulder, Frank. *The Moral Laboratory: Experiments Examining the Effects of Reading Literature on Social Perception and Moral Self-Concept*. Amsterdam: John Benjamins, 2000.

Hakluyt, Richard. *Hakluyt's Collection of the Early Voyages, Travels, and Discoveries of the English Nation*, edited by R. H. Evans, J. Mackinlay and R. Priestley. London: Evans, Mackinlay and Priestley, 1809–12.

Hakluyt, Richard. *The Principal Navigations*, edited by Edmund Goldsmid. Edinburgh: E. and G. Goldsmid, 1885–90.

Hakluyt, Richard. *The Principal Navigations, Voyages and Discoveries of the English Nation*, 3 vols. Originally published London, 1598–1600. Glasgow: James MacLehose and Sons, 1903–5.

'Hall, Basil.' In *The Supplement to the Penny Cyclopaedia of the Society for the Diffusion of Useful Knowledge*. Vol. 2: Habenaria–Zingiber, 9. London: Charles Knight, 1846.

Hall, Basil. *Account of a Voyage of Discovery to the West Coast of Corea, and the Great Loo-Choo Island*. London: John Murray, 1818.

Hall, Basil. *Extracts from a Journal, Written on the Coasts of Chili, Peru, and Mexico, in the Years 1820, 1821, 1822*. 2 vols. Edinburgh: Archibald Constance, 1826–7.

Hall, Basil. *Fragments of Voyages and Travels, Including Anecdotes of a Naval Life*. 3 vols. Edinburgh: Robert Cadell, 1831.

Hall, Basil. *Narrative of a Voyage to Java, China, and the Great Loo-Choo Island*. London: Edward Moxon, 1840.

Hall, Basil. *Voyage to Corea, and the Island of Loo-Choo*. London: John Murray, 1820.

Hall, Basil. *Voyage to Loo-Choo, and Other Places in the Eastern Seas, in the Year 1816*. Edinburgh: Archibald Constance, 1826.

Hall, Stuart and Paul du Gay. *Questions of Cultural Identity*. London: Sage, 1996.

Hallock, Thomas. '"On the Borders of a New World": Ecology, Frontier Plots, and Imperial Elegy in William Bartram's *Travels*.' *South Atlantic Review* 66.4 (2001): 109–33.

Hallock, Thomas. 'On the Borders of a New World: William Bartram's Travels.' In *From the Fallen Tree: Frontier Narratives, Environmental Politics, and the Roots of a National Pastoral, 1749–1826*, 149–73. Chapel Hill, NC: University of North Carolina Press, 2003.

Hamann, Horst. *New York Vertical*. Kempen: Te Neues, 2000.

Hamann, Horst. *Paris Vertical*. Kempen: Te Neues, 2005.

Hamilton-Paterson, James. 'The End of Travel.' *Granta* 94 (2006): 221–34.

Hammond, Wayne G. and Cristina Scull, eds. *J.R.R. Tolkien, Artist and Illustrator*. Boston, MA: Houghton Mifflin, 1995.

Hannerz, Ulf. 'Cosmopolitans and Locals in World Culture.' *Theory, Culture, Society* 7.2 (1990): 237–50.

Hanway, Mary Ann. *A Journey to the Highlands of Scotland by a Lady*. London, 1777.

Hao, Gao. 'The Amherst Embassy and British Discoveries in China.' *History* 99.337 (2014): 568–87.

Hariot, Thomas. *Admiranda narratio fida tamen, de commodis et incolarum ritibus Virginiae*. Frankfurt-am-Main: Theodor de Bry, 1590.

Harley, J. B. Introduction to *John Ogilby. Britannia, London 1675*. Amsterdam: Theatrum Orbis Terrarum, 1970.

Harper, Charles G. *The Old Inns of Old England: A Picturesque Account of the Ancient and Storied Hostelries of Our Own Country*. 2 vols. London: Chapman & Hall, 1906.

Harper, Francis, ed. *The Travels of William Bartram: Naturalist's Edition*. Athens, GA: University of Georgia Press, 1958.

Harper, Lila Marz. *Solitary Travellers: Nineteenth-Century Women's Travel Narratives and the Scientific Vocation*. London: Associated University Presses, 2001.

Harris, Andrew. 'Vertical Urbanisms Opening up Geographies of the Three-Dimensional City.' *Progress in Human Geography* 39.5 (2014): 601–20.

Harry, James Spence. *Atala. By Chateaubriand*. Chicago, IL: Belford-Clarke Co. 1891.

Hayden, Ferdinand Vandeveer. *Preliminary Report of the United States Geological Survey of Montana and Portions of Adjacent Territories; being a Fifth Annual Report of Progress*. 42nd Congress, 2nd Sess., House Ex. Doc. 326 (Serial Set 1520). Washington, DC: Government Printing Office, 1872.

Haywood, Eliza. *Epistles to the Ladies*. London, 1749.

Hazlitt, Sarah. 'Sarah Hazlitt's Journal of My Trip to Scotland.' Originally published 1822. *University of Buffalo Studies* 24 (1959): 171–252.

Heal, Felicity. *Hospitality in Early Modern England*. Oxford: Oxford University Press, 1990.

Healey, Kimberley J. *The Modernist Traveler: French Detours, 1900–1930*. Lincoln, NE: University of Nebraska Press, 2003.

Heffernan, James A. W. *Museum of Words: The Poetics of Ekphrasis from Homer to Ashbery*. Chicago, IL: University of Chicago Press, 1993.

Held, David. 'Democracy and the New International Order.' In *Cosmopolitan Democracy: An Agenda for a New World Order*, edited by Daniele Archibugi and David Held, 96–120. Cambridge: Polity, 1995.

Heldt, Gustav. 'Writing Like a Man: Poetic Literacy, Textual Property, and Gender in the *Tosa Diary*.' *Journal of Asian Studies* 64.1 (2005): 7–34.

Heldt, Gustav, trans., 'Tosa Diary.' In *Traditional Japanese Literature: An Anthology, Beginnings to 1600*, edited by Haruo Shirane, 204–13. New York: Columbia University Press, 2007.

Helfers, James P. 'The Explorer and the Pilgrim? Modern Critical Opinion and the Editorial Methods of Richard Hakluyt and Samuel Purchas.' *Studies in Philology* 94 (1997): 160–86.

Helgerson, Richard. *Forms of Nationhood: The Elizabethan Writing of England*. Chicago, IL: University of Chicago Press, 1992.

Helmers, Marguerite and Tilar J. Mazzeo. 'Introduction: Travel and the Body.' *Journal of Narrative Theory* 35.3 (2005): 267–76.

Helmreich, Stefan. 'An Anthropologist Underwater: Immersive Soundscapes, Submarine Cyborgs, and Transductive Ethnography.' *American Ethnologist* 34.4 (2007): 621–41.

Helms, Mary W. 'Essay on Objects: Interpretations of Distance Made Tangible.' In *Implicit Understandings*, edited by Stuart B. Schwartz, 355–76. Cambridge: Cambridge University Press, 1994.

Henderson, David. 'Traffic Patterns.' In *Theorizing Sound Writing*, edited by Deborah A. Kapchan, 142–62. Middletown, CT: Wesleyan University Press, 2017.

Henderson, Louise C. 'David Livingstone's *Missionary Travels* in Britain and America: Exploring the Wider Circulation of a Victorian Travel Narrative.' *Scottish Geographical Journal* 129.3–4 (2013): 179–93.

Henige, David. *Historical Evidence and Argument*. Madison, WI: University of Wisconsin Press, 2005.

Heringman, Noah. *Romantic Rocks, Aesthetic Geology*. Ithaca, NY: Cornell University Press, 2004.

Heringman, Noah, ed. *Romantic Science: The Literary Forms of Natural History*. Albany, NY: State University of New York Press, 2003.

Hess, Jillian M. 'Coleridge's Fly-Catchers: Adapting Commonplace-Book Form.' *Journal of the History of Ideas* 73.3 (2012): 463–83.

Hewitt, Lucy and Stephen Graham. 'Vertical Cities: Representations of Urban Verticality in 20th-Century Science Fiction Literature.' *Urban Studies* 52.5 (2014): 923–37.

Hibbert, Samuel. *A Description of the Shetland Islands, Comprising an Account of Their Geology, Scenery, Antiquities and Superstitions*. Edinburgh: Archibald Constable, 1822.

Hight, Eleanor M. and Gary D. Sampson. 'Introduction: Photography, "Race", and Post-Colonial Theory.' In *Colonialist Photography: Imag(in)ing Race and Place*, edited by Eleanor M. Hight and Gary D. Sampson, 1–19. London: Routledge, 2004.

Hikmet, Nâzim. *Paysages humains*. Paris: La Découverte, 2002.

Hissey, James John. *The Charm of the Road. England and Wales*. London: Macmillan and Co., 1910.

Hissey, James John. *Through Ten English Counties*. London: Richard Bentley & Son, 1894.

Hitchcock, Peter. *Imaginary States: Studies in Cultural Transnationalism*. Urbana, IL: University of Illinois Press, 2003.

Hodge, Stephen, Simon Persighetti, Phil Smith, Cathy Turner and Tony Weaver. *An Exeter Mis-Guide*. [Exeter]: Wrights & Sites, 2003.

Holland, Patrick and Graham Huggan. *Tourists with Typewriters: Critical Reflections on Contemporary Travel Writing*. Ann Arbor, MI: University of Michigan Press, 1998.

Holland Braund, Kathryn E. 'William Bartram's Gustatory Tour.' In *Fields of Vision: Essays on the Travels of William Bartram*, edited by Kathryn E. Holland Braund and Charlotte M. Porter, 33–53. Tuscaloosa, AL: University of Alabama Press, 2010.

Holman, James. *A Voyage Round the World, Including Travels in Africa, Asia, Australasia, America, etc. etc. from 1827 to 1832*. 4 vols. London: Smith, Elder & Co., 1834–5.

Holman, James. *The Narrative of a Journey, Undertaken in the Years 1819, 1820, & 1821, through France, Italy, Savoy, Switzerland etc. Comprising Incidents that Occurred to the Author Who Has Long Suffered under a Total Deprivation of Sight*. London: Rivington, 1822.

Holmes, Morgan. 'Donkeys, Englishmen and Other Animals: The Precarious Distinctions of Victorian Interspecies Morality.' In *European Stevenson*, edited by Richard Ambrosini and Richard Dury, 109–24. Newcastle-upon-Tyne: Cambridge Scholars, 2009.

Holmes, Richard. *Footsteps: Adventures of a Romantic Biographer*. Originally published 1985. New York: Vintage Departures, 1996.

Holtzman, Jon. *Uncertain Tastes: Memory, Ambivalence, and the Politics of Eating in Samburu, Northern Kenya*. Berkeley, CA: University of California Press, 2009.

Hooper, Glenn and Tim Youngs. 'Introduction.' In *Perspectives on Travel Writing*, edited by Glen Hooper and Tim Youngs, 1–11. Aldershot: Ashgate, 2004.

'Hotels.' *Chambers's Journal of Popular Literature, Science and Art* 19.491 (30 May 1863): 345–8.

Houston, Stuart, Mary Houston and Tim Ball. *Eighteenth-Century Naturalists of Hudson Bay*. Montréal: McGill-Queen's University Press, 2003.

Howitt, William. *The Book of the Seasons; or the Calendar of Nature*. London: Henry Colburn and Richard Bentley, 1831.

Huggan, Graham. 'Postcolonial Ecocriticism and the Limits of Green Romanticism.' *Journal of Postcolonial Writing* 45.1 (2009): 3–14.

Huggan, Graham and Helen Tiffin. *Postcolonial Ecocriticism: Literature, Animals, Environment*. London: Routledge, 2010.

Hughes, Charles. *Shakespeare's Europe: A Survey of the Condition of Europe at the End of the 16th Century: Being Unpublished Chapters of Fynes Moryson's Itinerary (1617)*. 2nd ed. New York: Blom, 1967.

Huhtamo, Erkki. *Illusions in Motion: Media Archaeology of the Moving Panorama and Related Spectacles*. Cambridge, MA: MIT Press, 2013.

Hulme, Peter. *Colonial Encounters: Europe and the Native Caribbean, 1492–1797*. London: Methuen, 1986.

Hulme, Peter. 'In the Wake of Columbus: Frederick Ober's Ambulant Gloss.' *Literature and History* 6.2 (1997): 18–36.

Hulme, Peter. 'Travelling to Write (1940–2000).' In *The Cambridge Companion to Travel Writing*, edited by Peter Hulme and Tim Youngs, 87–101. Cambridge: Cambridge University Press, 2002.

Hulme, Peter and Tim Youngs. *Talking about Travel Writing: A Conversation between Peter Hulme and Tim Youngs*. Leicester: English Association, 2007.

Humboldt, Alexander von. *Aspects of Nature*. Originally published 1808. Translated by Mrs Sabines. London: Longmans and John Murray, 1850.

Humboldt, Alexander von. *Cosmos: A Sketch of a Physical Description of the Universe*, translated by E. C. Otté. 2 vols. New York: Harper and Brothers, 1850.

Humboldt, Alexander von. *Personal Narrative*. Originally published 1814–29. Edited, abridged and translated by Jason Williams. Harmondsworth: Penguin, 1995.

Humphrey, Caroline and Stephen Hugh-Jones, eds. *Barter, Exchange and Value: An Anthropological Approach*. Cambridge: Cambridge University Press, 1992.

[Hunt, Leigh?]. Review of *Poems, with Illustrations*, by Louisa Anne Twamley. *Monthly Repository* 9.100 (Apr. 1835): 289–90.

Hunt, Lynn. *Inventing Human Rights*. New York: W. W. Norton, 2008.

Hurston, Zora Neale. *Mules and Men*. Originally published 1935. Bloomington, IN: Indiana University Press, 1978.

Iannini, Christopher. 'The Vertigo of Circum-Caribbean Empire: William Bartram's Florida.' *Mississippi Quarterly: The Journal of Southern Cultures* 57.1 (Winter 2003–4): 147–55.

Imazeki Toshiko. '"Tabi" no hyōgen to kyokō: Chūsei joryū nikki o chūshin ni.' In *Chūsei bungaku* 39 (1996): 25–33.

Inada Toshinori. 'Chūsei kikō bungaku no tabi no shosō to sono imi', in *Chūsei bungaku* 39 (1996): 14–24.

Ingold, Tim. 'Globes and Spheres.' In *The Perception of the Environment: Essays on Livelihood, Dwelling and Skill*, 209–18. London: Routledge, 2000.

The Invented Worlds of J.R.R. Tolkien: Drawings and Original Manuscripts from the Marquette University Collection, October 21, 2004–January 30, 2005, Patrick and Beatrice Haggerty Museum of Art, Marquette University, Milwaukee, Wisconsin. Milwaukee, WI: Haggerty Museum of Art, Marquette University, 2004.

Irvine, Margot. *Pour suivre un époux: Les récits de voyages des couples au dix-neuvième siècle*. Québec: Éditions Nota bene, 2008.

Irving, D. R. M. *Colonial Counterpoint: Music in Early Modern Manila*. New York: Oxford University Press, 2010.

Irving, Sarah. *Natural Science and the Origins of the British Empire*. London: Pickering and Chatto, 2008.

Iser, Wolfgang. 'The Reading Process: A Phenomenological Approach.' *New Literary History* 3.2 (1971): 279–99.

Jackson, Julian R. 'On Picturesque Description in Books of Travels.' *Journal of the Royal Geographical Society* 5 (1835): 381–7.

Jackson, Sarah. *Tactile Poetics: Touch and Contemporary Writing*. Edinburgh: Edinburgh University Press, 2015.

Jakobson, Roman. 'On Linguistic Aspects of Translation.' In *Theories of Translation: An Anthology of Essays from Dryden to Derrida*, edited by Rainer Schulte and John Biguenet, 144–51. Chicago, IL: University of Chicago Press, 1992.

James, Kevin J. '"[A] British Social Institution": The Visitors' Book and Hotel Culture in Victorian Britain and Ireland.' *Journeys: The International Journal of Travel and Travel Writing* 13.1 (2012): 42–69.

James, Kevin J. 'The Irishness of the Irish Inn: Narratives of Travel Accommodation in Ireland from Union to Home Rule.' *Studies in Travel Writing* 17.1 (2013): 22–42.

Jamie, Kathleen. *Findings*. London: Sort Of, 2005.

Jamie, Kathleen. 'A Lone Enraptured Male.' *London Review of Books*, 6 March 2008. Accessed 22 June 2017.

Jay, Martin. *Downcast Eyes: The Denigration of Vision in Twentieth-Century French Thought*. Berkeley, CA: University of California Press, 1994.

Jenner, Mark S. R. 'Follow Your Nose? Smell, Smelling, and Their Histories.' *American Historical Review* 116.2 (2011): 335–51.

Jerome, Jerome K. *Three Men in a Boat (To Say Nothing of the Dog)*. Bristol: J. W. Arrowsmith, 1889.

Joans, Barbara. *Bike Lust: Harleys, Women, and American Society*. Madison, WI: University of Wisconsin Press, 2001.

Johnson, Amryl. *Sequins for a Ragged Hem*. London: Virago, 1988.

Johnson, Nuala C. 'Global Knowledge in a Local World: Charlotte Wheeler Cuffe's Encounters with Burma 1901–1902.' In *Spaces of Global Knowledge: Exhibition, Encounter and Exchange in an Age of Empire*, edited by Diarmid A. Finnegan and Jonathan J. Wright, 19–38. Aldershot: Ashgate, 2015.

Jones, Kathryn N. '*Le voyageur étonné*: François Maspero's Alternative Itineraries.' *Studies in Travel Writing* 13.4 (2009): 335–44.

Jonson, Ben. *The Cambridge Edition of the Works of Ben Jonson*, edited by David Bevington, Martin Butler and Ian Donaldson. 7 vols. Cambridge: Cambridge University Press, 2012.

The Journals of the Lewis and Clark Expedition, University of Nebraska Press / University of Nebraska-Lincoln Libraries-Electronic Text Center. http://lewisandclarkjournals.unl.edu.

Justin Herman, Daniel. *Hunting and the American Imagination*. Washington, DC: Smithsonian Institution Press, 2001.

Kadushin, Raphael. 'Introduction.' In *Wonderlands: Good Gay Travel Writing*, edited by Raphael Kadushin, 3–7. Madison, WI: The University of Wisconsin Press, 2004.

Kaplan, Amy. *The Anarchy of Empire in the Making of U.S. Culture*. Cambridge, MA: Harvard University Press, 2002.

Kaplan, Amy and Donald E. Pease, eds. *Cultures of United States Imperialism*. Durham, NC: Duke University Press, 1993.

Kaplan, Caren. *Questions of Travel: Postmodern Discourses of Displacement*. Durham, NC: Duke University Press, 1996.

Kari, James, ed. *Ahtna Travel Narratives: A Demonstration of Shared Geographical Knowledge among Alaska Athabascans*, told by Jim McKinley, Frank Stickwan, Jake Tansy, Katie John and Adam Sanford; transcribed and edited by James Kari. Fairbanks, AK: Alaska Native Language Center, University of Alaska, 2010.

Kari, James. 'Introduction.' In *Ahtna Travel Narratives: A Demonstration of Shared Geographical Knowledge among Alaska Athabascans*, told by Jim McKinley, Frank Stickwan, Jake Tansy, Katie John and Adam Sanford; transcribed and edited by James Kari, ix–xv. Fairbanks, AK: Alaska Native Language Center, University of Alaska, 2010.

Karrow, Robert W., Jr. *Mapmakers of the Sixteenth Century and Their Maps*. Chicago, IL: Speculum Orbis, 1993.

Kaufman, Frederick. 'Gut Reaction: The Enteric Terrors of Washington Irving,' *Gastronomica: The Journal of Food and Culture* 3:2 (2003): 41–9.

Keates, Jonathan. *The Portable Paradise: Baedeker, Murray, and the Victorian Guidebook*. London: Notting Hill Editions, 2011.

Keene, Donald. *Seeds in the Heart: Japanese Literature from Earliest Times to the Late Sixteenth Century*. New York: Columbia University Press, 1999.

Keesey, William Monckton. *Tales of Old Inns. The History, Legend and Romance of Some of our Older Hostelries*. London: Trust Houses, 1927.

Keighren, Innes M., Charles W. J. Withers and Bill Bell. *Travels into Print: Exploration, Writing, and Publishing with John Murray, 1773–1859*. Chicago, IL: University of Chicago Press, 2015.

Kennedy, Valerie. 'Conradian Quest Versus Dubious Adventure: Graham and Barbara Greene in West Africa.' *Studies in Travel Writing* 19.1 (2015): 48–65.

Kerr, Julie. *Monastic Hospitality: The Benedictines in England, c. 1070–c. 1200*. Woodbridge: The Boydell Press, 2007.

Kerridge, Richard. 'Ecologies of Desire: Travel Writing and Nature Writing as Travelogue.' In *Travel Writing and Empire: Postcolonial Theory in Transit*, edited by Steve Clark, 164–82. London: Zed, 1999.

Khosravi, Shahram. *'Illegal' Traveller: An Auto-Ethnography of Borders*. Basingstoke: Palgrave Macmillan, 2010.

Kieran, Dan. *The Idle Traveller: The Art of Slow Travel*. Basingstoke: AA Publishing, 2012.

Kieran, Dan and Ian Vince. *Three Men in a Float: Across England at 15 MPH*. London: John Murray, 2008.

Kierstead, Christopher M. 'Convoluted Paths: Mapping Genre in Contemporary Footsteps Travel Writing.' *Genre* 46.3 (2013): 285–315.

Kincaid, Jamaica. *Among Flowers: A Walk in the Himalaya*. Washington, DC: National Geographic Society, 2005.

Kincaid, Jamaica. *A Small Place*. New York: Penguin, 1988.

Kincaid, Jamaica. 'In History.' In *My Garden (Book)*, 153–66. New York: Farrar, Straus and Giroux, 1999.

Kingsley, Mary. *Travels in West Africa: Congo Français, Corisco and Cameroons*. Originally published 1897. Boston, MA: Beacon Press, 1988.

Kinsley, Zoë. *Women Writing the Home Tour, 1682–1812*. Aldershot: Ashgate, 2008.

Kitson, Peter J., ed. *Nineteenth-Century Travels, Explorations and Empires: Writings from the Era of Imperial Consolidation, 1835–1910*, vol. 1, *North and South Poles*. London: Routledge, 2003.

Kitson, Peter J., ed. *Travels, Explorations and Empires: Writings from the Era of Imperial Expansion 1770–1835*, vol. 3, *North and South Poles*. London: Pickering and Chatto, 2001.

Klekar, Cynthia. '"Prisoners in Silken Bonds": Obligation, Trade, and Diplomacy in English Voyages to Japan and China.' *Journal for Early Modern Cultural Studies* 6.1 (2006): 84–105.

Knidler, Céline. *Le Paris souterrain dans le littérature*. Saarbrücken: Editions universitaires européennes, 2010.

Knox, Edward C. 'A Literature of Accommodation.' *French Politics, Culture & Society* 21.2 (2003): 95–110.

Koegel, John. 'Spanish and French Mission Music in Colonial North America.' *Journal of the Royal Musical Association* 126.1 (2001): 1–53.

Koelb, Janice. *The Poetics of Description: Imagined Places in European Literature*. New York: Palgrave Macmillan, 2006.

Koh, Grace. 'British Perceptions of Joseon Korea as Reflected in Travel Literature of the Late Eighteenth and Early Nineteenth Century.' *The Review of Korean Studies* 9.4 (2006): 103–33.

Kohnstamm, Thomas B. *Do Travel Writers Go to Hell? A Swashbuckling Tale of High Adventure, Questionable Ethics and Professional Hedonism*. Millers Point, NSW: Murdoch Books, 2008.

Koivunen, Leila. 'Africa on the Spot and from the Distance: David Livingstone's *Missionary Travels* and Nineteenth-Century Practices of Illustration.' *Scottish Geographical Journal* 129.3–4 (2013): 194–209.

Kopytoff, Igor. 'The Cultural Biography of Things: Commoditization as Process.' In *The Social Life of Things: Commodities in Cultural Perspective*, edited by Arjun Appadurai, 64–91. Cambridge: Cambridge University Press, 1986.

Korte, Barbara. *English Travel Writing from Pilgrimages to Postcolonial Explorations*. Houndmills: Macmillan, 2000.

Koshar, Rudy. *German Travel Cultures*. Oxford: Berg, 2000.

Kristeva, Julia. *Powers of Horror: An Essay on Abjection*, translated by Leon S. Roudiez. Originally published 1980. New York: Columbia University Press, 1982.

Kuehn, Julia and Paul Smethurst. 'Introduction.' In *New Directions in Travel Writing Studies*, edited by Julia Kuehn and Paul Smethurst, 1–13. Basingstoke: Palgrave Macmillan, 2015.

Kuehn, Julia and Paul Smethurst, eds. *New Directions in Travel Writing Studies*. Basingstoke: Palgrave Macmillan, 2015.

Kulikoff, Allan. *From British Peasants to Colonial American Farmers*. Chapel Hill, NC: University of North Carolina Press, 2000.

Kumar, Deepak. 'The Evolution of Colonial Science in India: Natural History and the East India Company.' In *Imperialism and the Natural World*, edited by John M. MacKenzie, 51–66. Manchester: Manchester University Press, 1990.

L.[eigh?] J.[ames?] *An Answer to the Untruths*. London: Thomas Cadman, 1589.

Lacarrière, Jacques. *Le Pays sous l'écorce*. Paris: Seuil, 1980.

Lackey, Kris. *RoadFrames: The American Highway Narrative*. Lincoln, NE: University of Nebraska Press, 1997.

Laderman, Scott. 'Guidebooks.' In *The Routledge Companion to Travel Writing*, edited by Carl Thompson, 258–68. Abingdon: Routledge, 2016.

Laffin, Christina, trans. 'Diary of the Sixteenth Night.' In *Traditional Japanese Literature: An Anthology, Beginnings to 1600*, edited by Haruo Shirane, 778–87. New York: Columbia University, 2007.

Laffin, Christina. *Rewriting Medieval Japanese Women: Politics, Personality, and Literary Production in the Life of Nun Abutsu*. Honolulu, HI: University of Hawai'i Press, 2013.

Laffin, Christina. 'Travel as Sacrifice: Abutsu's Poetic Journey in *Diary of the Sixteenth Night Moon*.' *Review of Japanese Culture and Society* 19 (2007): 71–86.

Laffin, Christina, Joan Piggott and Yoshida Sanae, eds. *Birth and Death in the Royal House: Selections from Fujiwara no Munetada's Journal Chūyūki*. Ithaca, NY: Cornell University Press, forthcoming.

Lang, Hans-Joachim and Benjamin Lease. 'Melville's Cosmopolitan: Bayard Taylor in The Confidence-Man.' *Amerikastudien* 22 (1977): 286–9.

La Pérouse, J. F. G. de. *The Journal of Jean-François de Galaup de la Pérouse, 1758–1788*, translated and edited by John Dunmore. London: The Hakluyt Society, 1994.

La Pérouse, J. F. G. de. *A Voyage Round the World, in the Years 1785, 1786, 1787, and 1788*, edited by M. L. A. Milet-Mureau. 3 vols. London, 1798.

Laplanche, Jean. *Essays on Otherness*, edited by John Fletcher. London: Routledge, 1999.

Laporte, Dominique. *History of Shit*, translated by Nadia Benabid and Rodolphe el-Khoury. Originally published 1978. Cambridge, MA: MIT Press, 2002.

Larabee, Mark D. 'Baedekers as Casualty: Great War Nationalism and the Fate of Travel Writing.' *Journal of the History of Ideas* 71.3 (2010): 457–80.

Lashley, Conrad, Paul Lynch and Alison Morrison. *Hospitality: A Social Lens*. Amsterdam: Elsevier, 2007.

Latour, Bruno. *Science in Action: How to Follow Scientists and Engineers through Society*. Cambridge, MA: Harvard University Press, 1987.

Lauritz Larson, John. *Internal Improvement: National Public Works and the Promise of Popular Government in the Early United States*. Chapel Hill, NC: University of North Carolina Press, 2001.

Lawrence, D. H. *Sea and Sardinia*. Originally published 1921. Harmondsworth: Penguin, 1996.

Lawrence, D. H. *Twilight in Italy and Other Essays*, edited by Paul Eggert. Cambridge: Cambridge University Press, 1994.

Leane, Elizabeth. 'Eggs, Emperors and Empire: Apsley Cherry-Garrard's "Worst Journey" as Imperial Quest Romance.' *Kunapipi* 31.2 (2009): 15–31.

Leane, Elizabeth and Steve Nicol. 'Filming the Frozen South: Animals in Early Antarctic Exploration Films.' In *Screening Nature: Cinema Beyond the Human*, edited by Anat Pick and Guinevere Narraway, 127–42. Oxford: Berghahn, 2013.

Leask, Nigel. *Curiosity and the Aesthetics of Travel Writing 1770–1840*. Oxford: Oxford University Press, 2002.

Le Bris, Michel. *Le Grand Dehors*. Paris: Payot, 1992.

Le Dantec, Bruno and Mahmoud Traoré. *Dem ak xabaar (Partir et raconter)*. Fécamp: Nouvelles Editions Lignes, 2012.

Le Disez, Jean-Yves. 'Animals as Figures of Otherness in Travel Narratives of Brittany, 1840–1895.' In *Perspectives on Travel Writing*, edited by Glen Hooper and Tim Youngs, 71–84. Aldershot: Ashgate, 2004.

Lee, Mrs R. *Elements of Natural History, for the Use of Schools and Young Persons*. London: Longman, Brown, Green and Longmans, 1844.

Lee, Mrs R. *Stories of Strange Lands; and Fragments from the Notes of a Traveller*. London: Edward Moxon, 1835.

Lee, Mrs R. *Trees, Plants, and Flowers: Their Beauties, Uses, and Influences*. London: Grant and Griffith, 1854.

Lefebvre, Henri. *The Production of Space*, translated by Donald Nicholson-Smith. Originally published 1974. Oxford: Blackwell, 1991.

Lefevere, André. *Translation, Rewriting and the Manipulation of Literary Fame*. London: Routledge, 1992.

Leigh Fermor, Patrick. *A Time of Gifts: On Foot to Constantinople – From the Hook of Holland to the Middle Danube*. London: John Murray, 2013.

Le May-Sheffield, Suzanne. 'Gendered Collaborations: Marrying Art and Science.' In *Figuring It Out: Science, Gender, and Visual Culture*, edited by Ann B. Shteir and Bernard Lightman, 240–60. Hanover, NH: Dartmouth College Press.

Lemmon, Alfred E. 'Jesuit Chroniclers and Historians of Colonial Spanish America: Sources for the Ethno-Musicologist.' *Inter-American Music Review* 10 (1989): 119–29.

Lennon, John and Malcolm Foley. *Dark Tourism: The Attraction of Death and Disaster*. London: Thompson Learning, 2004.

Leonard, Mathieu. 'Clandestins: l'odyssée invisible. Entretien avec Bruno Le Dantec.' *Article 11*, 21 November 2012. Accessed 24 May 2015. www.article11.info/?Clandestins-l-Odyssee-invisible.

Leonardi, Susan J. and Rebecca A. Pope. 'Screaming Divas: Collaboration as Feminist Practice.' *Tulsa Studies in Women's Literature* 13.2 (1994): 259–70.

Lessing, Gotthold Ephraim. *Laocoon: An Essay upon the Limits of Painting and Poetry*, translated by Ellen Frothingham. Originally published 1767. New York: Noonday Press, 1957.

Lévi-Strauss, Claude. *The Raw and the Cooked*, Introduction to a Science of Mythology: I, translated by John and Doreen Weightman. Originally published 1964. New York: Harper and Row, 1969.

Lewis, Meriwether and William Clark, and Members of the Corps of Discovery. *The Journals of the Lewis and Clark Expedition*, edited by Gary E. Moulton. 13 vols. Lincoln, NE: University of Nebraska Press, 1983–2001.

Lindgren Leavenworth, Maria. 'Destinations and Descriptions: Acts of Seeing in S. H. Kent's *Gath to the Cedars* and *Within the Arctic Circle*.' *Studies in Travel Writing* 15.3 (2011): 293–310.

Lindgren Leavenworth, Maria. *The Second Journey: Travelling in Literary Footsteps*. Second, revised edition. Umeå: Studier i språk och litteratur från Umeå universitet, 2010.

Linhard, Tabea Alexa. 'At Europe's End: Geographies of Mediterranean Crossings.' *Journal of Iberian and Latin American Research* 22.1 (2016): 1–14.

Lisle, Debbie. *The Global Politics of Contemporary Travel Writing*. Cambridge: Cambridge University Press, 2006.

Lisle, Debbie. 'Humanitarian Travels: Ethical Communication in Lonely Planet Guidebooks.' *Review of International Studies* 34.S1 (2008): 155–72.

'Literature and Maps.' In *The History of Cartography*, vol. 3, *Cartography in the European Renaissance*, edited by David Woodward, 401–76. Chicago, IL: University of Chicago Press, 2007.

Livingstone, David. *Missionary Travels and Researches in South Africa*. London: John Murray, 1857.

Livingstone, David N. *Putting Science in Its Place: Geographies of Scientific Knowledge*. Chicago, IL: University of Chicago Press, 2003.

Livingstone, Justin. 'The Meaning and Making of *Missionary Travels*: The Sedentary and Itinerant Discourses of a Victorian Bestseller.' *Studies in Travel Writing* 15.3 (2011): 267–92.

Lloyd, David Wharton. *Battlefield Tourism: Pilgrimage and the Commemoration of the Great War in Britain, Australia and Canada, 1919–1939*. Oxford: Berg, 1998.

Long, George. *English Inns and Road-Houses*. London: T. Werner Laurie, 1937.

Looby, Christopher. 'The Constitution of Nature: Taxonomy as Politics in Jefferson, Peale, and Bartram.' *Early American Literature* 22.3 (1987): 252–73.

Lopez, Barry. *Arctic Dreams*. Originally published 1986. New York: Random House, 2001.

Lorant, Stephan, ed. *The New World: The First Pictures of America, Made by John White and Jacques Le Moyne and Engraved by Theodore de Bry*. Rev. ed. New York: Duell, Sloan and Pearce, 1965.

Lotman, Jurij M. and Julian Graffy. 'The Origin of Plot in the Light of Typology.' *Poetics Today* 1.1–2 (1979): 161–84.

Low, Kelvin E. 'The Sensuous City: Sensory Methodologies in Urban Ethnographic Research.' *Ethnography* 16.3 (2015): 295–312.

Lowenthal, David. 'Tourists and Thermalists.' *The Geographical Review* 52 (1962): 124–7.

Lugones, Maria. 'Purity, Impurity, and Separation.' *Signs* 9.2 (1994): 458–79.

Lyons, Esther. *Esther Lyons' Glimpses of Alaska: A Collection of Views of the Interior of Alaska*. New York: Rand, McNally, 1897.

Lyotard, Jean-François. *The Postmodern Condition: A Report on Knowledge*, translated by Geoff Bennington and Brian Massumi. Originally published 1979. Minneapolis, MN: University of Minnesota Press, 1984.

Mabey, Richard, ed. *The Oxford Book of Nature Writing*. Oxford: Oxford University Press, 1995.

Mabey, Richard, ed. *Second Nature*. London: Cape, 1984.

MacCannell, Dean. *The Tourist: A New Theory of the Leisure Class*. Berkeley, CA: University of California Press, 1999.

McCarthy, James. *That Curious Fellow: Captain Basil Hall, R.N.* Dunbeath: Whittles Publishing, 2011.

McCleery, Alasdair. 'Dead Hands Keep a Closed Book.' *The Times Higher Education*. 5 June 2008. Accessed 3 March 2015. www.timeshighereducation.co.uk/features/dead-hands-keep-a-closed-book/402227.article.

MacCulloch, John. *A Description of the Western Islands of Scotland, Including the Isle of Man*. 3 vols. London: Archibald Constable, 1819.

McCullough, Helen Craig trans., 'A Tosa Journal.' In *Classical Japanese Prose: An Anthology*, edited by Helen Craig McCullough, 73–102. Stanford, CA: Stanford University Press, 1990.

McDermott, James. 'Charles Howard, Second Baron Howard of Effingham and First Earl of Nottingham (1536–1624).' In *Oxford Dictionary of National Biography*, edited by H. C. G. Matthew and Brian Harrison. Oxford: Oxford University Press, 2004, online edition.

MacEachren, Alan M. 'A Linear View of the World: Strip Maps as a Unique Form of Cartographic Representation.' *American Cartographer* 13.1 (1986): 7–25.

MacEachren, Alan M. and Gregory B. Johnson. 'The Evolution, Application and Implications of Strip Format Travel Maps.' *Cartographic Journal* 24 (1987): 147–58.

Macfarlane, Robert. *Landmarks*. London: Hamish Hamilton, 2015.

Macfarlane, Robert. *The Old Ways: A Journey on Foot*. London: Penguin, 2013.

Macfarlane, Robert. *The Wild Places*. London: Granta, 2007.

McGehee, Nancy Gard. 'Volunteer Tourism: Evolution, Issues, Futures.' *Journal of Sustainable Tourism* 22 (2014): 847–54.

Mackay, David. *In the Wake of Cook: Exploration, Science and Empire, 1780–1801*. Wellington: Victoria University Press, 1985.

MacKenzie, John. *Empire of Nature: Hunting, Conservation and British Imperialism*. Manchester: Manchester University Press, 1988.

McKinley, Jim. '"Atna" K'et Kayax "eł Tl'atina" Ngge': Ahtna Villages on the Copper River and in the Klutina River Drainage.' In *Ahtna Travel Narratives: A Demonstration of Shared Geographical Knowledge among Alaska Athabascans*, told by Jim McKinley, Frank Stickwan, Jake Tansy, Katie John and Adam Sanford; transcribed and edited by James Kari, 1–26. Fairbanks, AK: Alaska Native Language Center, University of Alaska, 2010.

McLane, Daisann. 'Ups and Downs of Vertical Travel.' *National Geographic Traveler*, November 2012. Accessed 19 July 2016. http://travel.nationalgeographic.com/travel/traveler-magazine/real-travel/traveler-highs.

McLane, Daisann. 'Want Memories? Follow Your Nose.' *National Geographic Traveler*. Accessed 2 February 2016. http://travel.nationalgeographic.com/travel/traveler-magazine/real-travel/smells.

MacLaren, Ian S. 'Creating Travel Literature: The Case of Paul Kane.' *Papers of the Bibliographical Society of Canada* 27.1 (1988): 80–95.

MacLaren, Ian S. 'Exploration/Travel Literature and the Evolution of the Author.' *International Journal of Canadian Studies* 5 (Spring 1992): 39–68.

MacLaren, Ian S. 'In Consideration of the Evolution of Explorers and Travellers into Authors: A Model.' *Studies in Travel Writing* 15.3 (2011): 221–41.

McLeod, John. *Narrative of a Voyage, in His Majesty's Late Ship* Alceste, *to the Yellow Sea*. London: John Murray, 1817.

Macnaghten, Phil and John Urry. *Contested Natures*. London: Sage, 1998.

McNee, Alan. *The Cockney Who Sold the Alps: Albert Smith and the Ascent of Mont Blanc*. Brighton: Victorian Secrets, 2015.

McNee, Alan. 'The Haptic Sublime and the "Cold Stony Reality" of Mountaineering.' *19: Interdisciplinary Studies in the Long Nineteenth Century* 19 (2014): 1–20.

McNee, Alan. *The New Mountaineer in Late Victorian Britain: Materiality, Modernity and the Haptic Sublime*. London: Palgrave Macmillan, 2016.

McQuillan, Martin. 'Toucher II: Keep Your Hands to Yourself, Jean-Luc Nancy.' *Derrida Today* 2.1 (2009): 84–108.

Magnone, Sophia. 'Bien Manger, Bien Mangé: Edible Reciprocity in Jean de Léry's *Histoire d'un voyage faict en la terre du Brésil*.' *Journal for Early Modern Cultural Studies* 14.3 (Summer 2014): 107–35.

Magris, Claudio. *Danube*, translated by Patrick Creagh. Originally published 1986. London: Harvill Secker, 1989.

Maillart, Ella. *Parmi la jeunesse russe*. Paris: Fasquelle, 1932.

Major, Emma. 'Femininity and National Identity: Elizabeth Montagu's Trip to France.' *ELH* 72.4 (2005): 901–18.

Malinowski, Bronislaw. *Argonauts of the Western Pacific*. Originally published 1922. London: Routledge, 1999.

Malinowski, Bronislaw. *A Diary in the Strict Sense of the Term*, translated by Norbert Guterman. Originally published 1967. Stanford, CA: Stanford University Press, 1989.

Mancall, Peter C. *Hakluyt's Promise: An Elizabethan's Obsession for an English America*. New Haven, CT: Yale University Press, 2007.

MarineBio. 'The Deep Sea.' Accessed 2 February 2016. http://marinebio.org/oceans/deep.

Marks, Laura. *The Skin of the Film: Intercultural Cinema, Embodiment, and the Senses*. Durham, NC: Duke University Press, 2000.

Marquis, Sarah. *Wild by Nature: From Siberia to Australia, Three Years Alone in the Wilderness on Foot*. Crows Nest, NSW: Allen & Unwin, 2016.

Marryat, Frederick. *Second Series of a Diary in America, with Remarks on Its Institutions*. Philadelphia, PA: T.K. & P.G. Collins, 1840.

Martin, Alison E. 'Outward Bound: Women Translators and Scientific Travel Writing, 1780–1800.' *Annals of Science* 73.2 (2016): 157–69.

Martin, Alison E. and Susan Pickford. 'Introduction.' In *Travel Narratives in Translation, 1750–1830: Nationalism, Ideology, Gender*, edited by Alison E. Martin and Susan Pickford, 1–24. New York: Routledge, 2012.

Martin, Steven. *Penguin*. London: Reaktion, 2009.

Martins, Luciana. 'The Art of Tropical Travel, 1768–1830.' In *Georgian Geographies: Essays on Space, Place and Landscape in the Eighteenth Century*, edited by Miles Ogborn and Charles W. J. Withers, 72–91. Manchester: Manchester University Press, 2004.

Marx, Karl. *Capital: A Critique of Political Economy*, vol. 1, translated by Ben Fowkes. Originally published 1867. London: Penguin, 1990.

Maskell, Henry P. and Edward W. Gregory. *Old Country Inns of England*. London: I. Pitman, 1910.

Maspero, François. *Balkans-Transit*, photographies de Klavdij Sluban. Paris: Seuil, 1997.

Maspero, François. *Les Passagers du Roissy-Express*, photographies d'Anaïk Frantz. Paris: Seuil, 1990.

Maspero, François. *Transit & Cie*. Paris: Quinzaine Littéraire/Louis Vuitton, 2004.

Matless, David. 'Sonic Geography in a Nature Region.' *Social & Cultural Geography* 6.5 (2005): 745–66.

Matos, Jacinta. 'Old Journeys Revisited: Aspects of Postwar English Travel Writing.' In *Temperamental Journeys: Essays on the Modern Literature of Travel*, edited by Michael Kowalewski, 215–29. Athens, GA: University of Georgia Press, 1992.

Matthiessen, Peter. *The Snow Leopard*. Originally published 1978. New York: Penguin, 2008.

Mauss, Marcel. *The Gift: The Form and Reason for Exchange in Archaic Societies*, translated by Ian Cunnison. Originally published 1925. London: Routledge & Kegan Paul, 1969.

Mawson, Douglas. *The Home of the Blizzard*. Originally published 1915. Edinburgh: Birlinn, 2000.

Mayes, Frances. *Bella Tuscany: The Sweet Life in Italy*. London: Bantam, 1999.

Mayes, Frances. *Every Day in Tuscany*. New York: Broadway, 2010.

Mayes, Frances. *Under the Tuscan Sun*. London: Bantam, 1996.

Mee, Catharine. *Interpersonal Encounters in Contemporary Travel Writing: French and Italian Perspectives*. London: Anthem, 2014.

Mendelson, Edward. 'Baedeker's Universe.' *Yale Review of Books* 74.3 (1985): 386–403.

Merchant, Carolyn. *The Death of Nature: Women, Ecology and the Scientific Revolution*. Originally published 1979. San Francisco: Harper & Row, 1990.

Merchant, Tanya. 'Narrating the Ichkari Soundscape: European and American Travelers on Central Asian Women's Lives and Music.' In *Writing Travel in Central Asian History*, edited by Nile Green, 193–212. Bloomington, IN: Indiana University Press, 2014.

Merleau-Ponty, Maurice. *Phenomenology of Perception*, translated by Colin Smith. Originally published 1945. London: Routledge, 2002.

Mettout, Eric. 'Omar Ba nous a tous bernés, ou pourquoi il faut être sceptique.' *L'Express*, 10 July 2009. Accessed 24 May 2015. http://blogs.lexpress.fr/nouvelleformule/2009/07/10/djeuner_avec_ma_copine_anne.

Meurer, Peter. 'Cartography in the German Lands.' In *The History of Cartography*, vol. 3, *Cartography in the European Renaissance*, edited by David Woodward, 1172–1245. Chicago, IL: University of Chicago Press, 2007.

Miller, Christopher L. and George R. Hamell. 'A New Perspective on Indian–White Contact: Cultural Symbols and Colonial Trade.' *Journal of American History* 73.2 (1986): 311–28.

Miller, David Phillip and Peter Hans Reill, eds. *Visions of Empire: Voyages, Botany and Representations of Nature*. Cambridge: Cambridge University Press, 1996.

Mills, Sara. *Discourses of Difference: An Analysis of Women's Travel Writing and Colonialism*. New York: Routledge, 1991.

'Mine Inn.' *Household Words* 8.189 (5 November 1853): 238–40.

Misztal, Barbara A. *Trust in Modern Societies: The Search for the Bases of Social Order*. Cambridge: Polity, 1996.

Mitford, Nancy. 'A Bad Time.' In *The Water Beetle*, 15–32. London: Hamish Hamilton, 1962.

Miyake, Lynne K. 'The Tosa Diary: In the Interstices of Gender and Criticism.' In *The Woman's Hand: Gender and Theory in Japanese Women's Writing*, edited by Paul Gordon Schalow and Janet A. Walker, 41–73. Stanford, CA: Stanford University Press, 1996.

Molz, Jennie Germann and Alison McIntosh. 'Hospitality at the Threshold.' *Hospitality & Society* 3.2 (2013): 87–91.

Mons. *The Cape Ann Trail*. Gloucester, MA: City of Gloucester and Gloucester Chamber of Commerce, 1930.

Moodie, Susanna. *Roughing It in the Bush: Or, Life in Canada*. 2 vols. Originally published 1852. Cambridge: Cambridge University Press, 2011.

Moore, Jim. *Underground Liverpool.* Liverpool: Bluecoat Press, 1998.

Moran, Joe. 'A Cultural History of the New Nature Writing.' *Literature and History* 23.1 (Spring 2014): 49–63.

Morgan, Mary. *Tour of Milford Haven in the Year 1791.* London, 1795.

Morgan, Robin. *The Anatomy of Freedom.* New York: Anchor/Doubleday, 1982.

Morris, Jan. *Hong Kong: The End of an Empire.* London: Penguin, 1990.

Morton, H. V. *In Search of England.* London: Methuen, 1927.

Morton, Timothy. *Ecology Without Nature: Rethinking Environmental Aesthetics.* Cambridge: MA: Harvard University Press, 2007.

Moryson, Fynes. *An Itinerary Written by Fynes Moryson Gent.* Originally published 1617. Glasgow: James MacLehose and Sons, 1907–8.

Moss, Kay and Kathryn Hoffman. *The Backcountry Housewife.* Gastonia, NC: Schiele Museum of Natural History, 2001.

Mostow, Joshua. 'The Ovular Journey: Women and Travel in Pre-Modern Japan.' In *Pacific Encounters: The Production of Self and Others,* edited by Eva-Marie Kröller, Allan Smith, Joshua Mostow and Robert Kramer, 124–44. Vancouver: Institute of Asian Research, University of British Columbia, 1997.

Mostow, Joshua S. *At the House of Gathered Leaves: Short Biographical and Autobiographical Narratives from Japanese Court Literature.* Honolulu, HI: University of Hawai'i Press, 2004.

Mostow, Joshua S. and Royall Tyler, trans. *The Ise Stories:* Ise monogatari. Honolulu, HI: University of Hawai'i Press, 2010.

Muir, John. *The Mountains of California.* New York: Century, 1894.

Muir, John. *My First Summer in the Sierra.* Boston, MA: Houghton Mifflin, 1911.

Munson, James and Richard Mullen. *The Smell of the Continent: The British Discover Europe.* London: Macmillan, 2009.

Murray, David. *Indian Giving: Economies of Power in Indian–White Exchanges.* Amherst, MA: Massachusetts University Press, 2000.

Murray, David. *Matter, Magic, and Spirit: Representing Indian and African American Belief.* Philadelphia, PA: University of Pennsylvania Press, 2007.

Musser, Charles. *High-Class Moving Pictures: Lyman H. Howe and the Forgotten Era of Traveling Exhibition 1880–1920.* Princeton, NJ: Princeton University Press, 1991.

Mylne, William. *Travels in the Colonies in 1773–1775,* edited by Ted Ruddock. Athens, GA: University of Georgia Press, 1993.

Nail, Thomas. 'Violence at the Borders: Nomadic Solidarity and Non-Status Migrant Resistance.' *Radical Philosophy Review* 15.1 (2012): 241–57.

Naipaul, V. S. *An Area of Darkness: An Experience of India.* London: André Deutsch, 1964.

NASA. 'A Brief History of Animals in Space.' Accessed 21 October 2015. http://history.nasa.gov/animals.html.

NASA Science. 'The Mysterious Smell of Moondust.' Accessed 2 February 2016. http://science.nasa.gov/science-news/science-at-nasa/2006/30jan_smellofmoondust.

Naude, Jacobus. 'The Role of Pseudo-Translations in Early Afrikaans Travel Writing. A Corpus-Based Translation Analysis.' *Southern African Linguistics and Applied Language Studies* 26.1 (2008): 97–106.

Naylor, Nicola. *Jasmine and Arnica.* London: Eye Books, 2001.

Nebenzahl, Kenneth. *Maps of the Holy Land: Images of* Terra Sancta *through Two Millennia.* New York: Abbeville, 1986.

Nehamas, Alexander. *The Art of Living: Socratic Reflections from Plato to Foucault.* Berkeley, CA: University of California Press, 1998.

Neidhart, Christoph. *Russia's Carnival: The Smells, Sights and Sounds of Transition.* Lanham, MD: Rowman and Littlefield, 2003.

Nettle, Daniel and Suzanne Romaine. *Vanishing Voices: The Extinction of the World's Languages.* Oxford: Oxford University Press, 2002.

Nicholl, Charles. *The Creature in the Map: A Journey to El Dorado.* Originally published 1995. New York: William Morrow and Company, Inc., 1996.

Nicholls, Peter. *Modernisms: A Literary Guide.* Berkeley, CA: University of California Press, 1995.

Niedenthal, Simon. 'Beyond the Snortal: Scented Media and Games.' University of Copenhagen, 30 November 2010. Accessed 2 February 2016. http://game.itu.dk/index.php/Game_Lecture:_Beyond_the_Snortal:_Scented_media_and_games.

Nield, Ted. *Underlands: A Journey through Britain's Lost Landscape.* London: Verso, 2014.

Nightingale, Devlin. 'What Does Travel Smell Like?' *Getaway*, 14 May 2012. Accessed 2 February 2016. http://blog.getaway.co.za/travel-news/travel-smell-like/#sthash.iwdXvPxN.dpuf.

Nishiki Hitoshi, 'Utamakura to meisho: waka no tsutsumareta kuni.' *Nihonjin wa naze, go shichi go shichi shichi no uta o aishite kita no ka.* Tokyo: Kasama Shoin, 2016.

Nixon, Angelique V. *Resisting Paradise: Tourism, Diaspora, and Sexuality in Caribbean Culture.* Jackson, MS: University of Mississippi Press, 2015.

'Nonhuman Empires.' Special section of *Comparative Studies of Asia, Africa and the Middle East* 35.1 (2015): 66–172.

Norton, Anne. *Alternative Americas: A Reading of Antebellum Political Culture.* Chicago, IL: University of Chicago Press, 1986.

Nussbaum, Martha C. *Love's Knowledge: Essays on Philosophy and Literature.* New York: Oxford University Press, 1990.

Nussbaum, Martha. *Not for Profit: Why Democracy Needs the Humanities.* Princeton, NJ: Princeton University Press, 2010.

Nyman, Jopi. 'Ethical Encounters with Animal Others in Travel Writing.' In *Travel and Ethics: Theory and Practice,* edited by Corinne Fowler, Charles Forsdick and Ludmilla Kostova, 108–27. New York: Routledge, 2014.

Oberholtzer Lee, Heidi. *Appetite and Desire in Early American Travel Narratives.* PhD diss. University of Notre Dame, 2005.

Oberholtzer Lee, Heidi. '"The Hungry Soul": Sacramental Appetite and the Transformation of Taste in Early American Travel Writing.' *Early American Studies* 3.1 (2005): 65–93.

Oberholtzer Lee, Heidi. 'Turtle Tears and Captive Appetites: The Problem of White Desire in the Caribbean.' *Journal of Narrative Theory* 35.3 (2005): 307–25.

Obeyesekere, Gananath. *The Apotheosis of Captain Cook: European Mythmaking in the Pacific.* Princeton, NJ: Princeton University Press, 1992.

O'Byrne, William R. *A Naval Biographical Dictionary.* London: John Murray, 1849.

Ó Fiannachta, Pádraig. *An Chomharsa Choimhthíoch.* Baile Átha Cliath: FÁS, 1957.

Ó Fiannachta, Pádraig. *Ó Mháigh go Fásach.* Má Nuad: An Sagart, 1977.

Ogilby, John. *Britannia.* London, 1675. Amsterdam: Theatrum Orbis Terrarum, 1970.

Ogilby, John. *Britannia, Volume the First.* London, 1675.

O'Gorman, Kevin D. *The Origins of Hospitality and Tourism.* Woodeaton, Oxfordshire: Goodfellows Publishers Limited, 2010.

Olsson, Anders. 'Exile and Literary Modernism.' In *Modernism,* edited by Ástráður Eysteinsson and Vivian Liska, 735–54. Amsterdam: John Benjamins, 2007.

O'Neill, Patrick. *Fictions of Discourse.* Toronto: University of Toronto Press, 1994.

'On the Word Picturesque' [signed 'A. P.']. *Belfast Monthly Magazine* 31 (February 1811): 116–21.

Orr, Mary. 'Fish with a Different Angle: "The Fresh-Water Fishes of Great Britain" by Mrs Sarah Bowdich (1791–1856).' *Annals of Science* 71.2 (2013): 1–35.

Orr, Mary. 'New Observations on a Geological Hotspot Track: "Excursions in Madeira and Porto Santo" (1825) by Mrs T. Edward Bowdich.' *Centaurus* 56.3 (2014): 135–66.

Orr, Mary. 'Pursuing Proper Protocol: Sarah Bowdich's Purview of the Sciences of Exploration.' *Victorian Studies* 49.2 (2007): 277–85.

Orwell, George. *The Road to Wigan Pier.* Originally published 1937. London: Penguin, 1989.

Osher Map Library and Smith Center for Cartographic Education, University of Southern Maine. 'The Basle 1494 Columbus Letter.' Accessed 5 June 2016. www.oshermaps.org/special-map-exhibits/columbus-letter.

Padron, Ricardo. 'Mapping Imaginary Worlds.' In *Maps: Finding Our Place in the World,* edited by James R. Akerman and Robert W. Karrow, Jr., 255–88. Chicago, IL: University of Chicago Press, 2007.

Padron, Ricardo. *The Spacious Word: Cartography, Literature, and Empire in Early Modern Spain.* Chicago, IL: University of Chicago Press, 2004.

Papadimitriou, Nick. *Scarp.* London: Sceptre, 2012.

Papayanis, Marilyn Adler. *Writing in the Margins: The Ethics of Expatriation from Lawrence to Ondaatje.* Nashville, TN: Vanderbilt University Press, 2005.

Parini, Jay. 'Introduction.' In John Steinbeck, *Travels with Charley, 50th Anniversary Edition,* vii–xxii. New York: Penguin, 2012.

Park, Mungo. *Travels in the Interior Districts of Africa: Performed under the Direction and Patronage of the African Association, in the Years 1795, 1796, and 1797.* London: W. Bulmer and Co., for the author, 1799.

Parker, John, *Van Meteren's Virginia, 1607–12*. Minneapolis, MN: University of Minnesota Press, 1961.

Parkes, Fanny. *Wanderings of a Pilgrim, In Search of the Picturesque, During Four-and-Twenty Years in the East . . .* London: Pelham Richardson, 1850.

Parkins, Wendy. 'At Home in Tuscany: Slow Living and the Cosmopolitan Subject.' *Home Cultures* 1.3 (2004): 257–74.

Parks, George Bruner. *Richard Hakluyt and the English Voyages*. Originally published 1928. New York: F. Ungar, 1961.

Parrish, Susan Scott. *American Curiosity: Cultures of Natural History in the Colonial British Atlantic World*. Chapel Hill, NC: University of North Carolina Press, 2006.

Parry, Benita. 'Directions and Dead Ends in Postcolonial Studies.' In *Relocating Postcolonialism*, edited by David Theo Goldberg and Ato Quayson, 66–81. Oxford: Blackwell, 2002.

Parsons, Nicholas T. *Worth the Detour: The History of the Guidebook*. Stroud: Sutton Publishing, 2007.

Paterson, Mark. 'Haptic Geographies: Ethnography, Haptic Knowledges and Sensuous Dispositions.' *Progress in Human Geography* 33.6 (2007): 766–88.

Paterson, Mark. *The Senses of Touch: Haptics, Affects and Technologies*. Oxford: Berg, 2007.

Patil, Vijayalaxmi N. 'A Seminar Report on Digital Smell.' Accessed 2 February 2016. http://sdmcse2006. pbworks.com/f/print1.pdf.

Patten, Robert L. *Charles Dickens and His Publishers*. Oxford: Clarendon Press, 1978.

Paumgarten, Nick. 'Up and Then Down: The Lives of Elevators.' *New Yorker*, 21 April 2008.

Payne, Anthony. *Richard Hakluyt: A Guide to His Books and to Those Associated with Him, 1580–1625*. London: Bernard Quaritch, 2008.

Payne, Anthony. 'Richard Hakluyt and the Earl of Essex: The Censorship of the Voyage to Cadiz in the Principal Navigations.' *Publishing History* 72 (2012): 7–52.

Pearl, Jason. 'Geography and Authority in the Royal Society's Instructions to Travellers.' In *Travel Narratives, the New Science and Literary Discourse, 1569–1750*, edited by Judy A. Hayden, 71–83. Aldershot: Ashgate, 2012.

Peat, Alexandra. *Travel and Modernist Literature: Sacred and Ethical Journeys*. New York: Routledge, 2011.

Peel, Victoria and Anders Sørensen. *Exploring the Use and Impact of Travel Guidebooks*. Bristol: Channel View Publications, 2016.

Pennant, Thomas. *A Tour in Scotland*. Chester: John Monk, 1771.

Pennant, Thomas. *A Tour in Scotland and Voyage to the Hebrides*. 2 vols. Chester: John Monk, 1774.

Pennant, Thomas. *Observations, Relative Chiefly to Picturesque Beauty . . . Particularly the High-Lands of Scotland*. London: Blamire, 1789.

Pennington, L. E., ed. *The Purchas Handbook: Studies of the Life, Times and Writings of Samuel Purchas, 1577–1626*, 2 vols. London: The Hakluyt Society, 1997.

Pennycook, Alastair and Emi Otsuji. *Metrolingualism: Language in the City*. London: Routledge, 2015.

Penrose, Boies. *Travel and Discovery in the Renaissance, 1420–1620*. Cambridge, MA: Harvard University Press, 1952.

Perec, Georges. *An Attempt at Exhausting a Place in Paris*, translated by Mark Lowenthal. Originally published 1975. Cambridge, MA: Wakefield Press, 2010.

Perec, Georges. *Species of Spaces and Other Places*, translated by John Sturrock. Originally published 1974. London: Penguin, 1999.

Perrot, Jean-Christophe and Diego Audemard, *Tandems africains: du Sahara au Kilimandjaro guides par des non-voyants*. Paris: Presses de la Renaissance, 2007.

Peters, Jeffrey N. *Mapping Discord: Allegorical Cartography in Early Modern French Writing*. Newark, DE: University of Delaware Press, 2004.

Petersen, Carl Emil. *Over den store bre. Alene i Nansens spor*. Oslo: Cappelens, 1988.

Peterson, Jennifer L. *Education in the School of Dreams: Travelogues and Early Nonfiction Film*. Durham, NC: Duke University Press, 2013.

Pettit, Don. 'The Smell of Space.' Accessed 2 February 2016. http://spaceflight.nasa.gov/station/crew/ exp6/spacechronicles4.html.

Pettitt, Clare. 'Exploration in Print: From the Miscellany to the Newspaper.' In *Reinterpreting Exploration: The West in the World*, edited by Dane Kennedy, 80–108. New York: Oxford University Press, 2014.

Philips, Deborah. 'Mapping Literary Britain: Tourist Guides to Literary Landscapes 1951–2007.' *Tourist Studies* 11.1 (2011): 21–35.

Phillips, Patricia. *The Scientific Lady: A Social History of Women's Scientific Interests 1520–1918*. London: Weidenfeld and Nicolson, 1990.

Phillips, Richard. 'Space for Curiosity.' *Progress in Human Geography* 38.4 (2014): 493–512.

Pier, John. 'Metalepsis.' In *The Living Handbook of Narratology*, edited by Peter Hühn, John Pier, Wolf Schmid and Jörg Schönert. Hamburg: Hamburg University Press. Accessed 18 March 2018. www.lhn. uni-hamburg.de/article/metalepsis-revised-version-uploaded-13-july-2016.

Pietz, William. 'Death of the Deodand: Accursed Objects and the Money Value of Human Life.' *Res: Anthropology and Aesthetics* 31.1 (1993): 97–108.

Pietz, William. 'The Fetish of Civilisation: Sacrificial Blood and Monetary Debt.' In *Colonial Subjects: Essays on the Practical History of Anthropology*, edited by Peter Pels and Oscar Salemink, 53–81. Ann Arbor, MI: Michigan University Press, 1999.

Pietz, William. 'The Problem of the Fetish, I.' *Res: Anthropology and Aesthetics* 9.1 (1985): 5–17.

Pietz, William. 'The Problem of the Fetish, II: The Origin of the Fetish.' *Res: Anthropology and Aesthetics* 13.1 (1987): 23–45.

Pietz, William. 'The Problem of the Fetish, IIIa: Bosman's Guinea and the Enlightenment Theory of Fetishism.' *Res: Anthropology and Aesthetics* 16.1 (1988): 105–23.

Piggott, Joan R. and Yoshida Sanae, eds. *Teishinkōki: Year 939 in the Journal of Regent Fujiwara no Tadahira*. Ithaca, NY: Cornell University Press, 2002.

Pike, David L. *Subterranean Cities: The World Beneath Paris and London, 1800–1945*. Ithaca, NY: Cornell University Press, 2005.

Pinet, Simon. *Archipelagoes: Insular Fictions from Chivalric Romance to the Novel*. Minneapolis, MN: University of Minnesota Press, 2011.

Pinet, Simone. 'Literature and Cartography in Early Modern Spain: Etymologies and Conjectures.' In *The History of Cartography*, vol. 3, *Cartography in the European Renaissance*, edited by David Woodward, 469–76. Chicago, IL: University of Chicago Press, 2007.

Platt, Charles. 'You've Got Smell.' *Wired*, 11 January 1999. Accessed 2 February 2016. www.wired.com/1999/11/digiscent.

Plutschow, Herbert Eugen. 'Japanese Travel Diaries of the Middle Ages.' *Oriens Extremus* 29.1–2 (1982): 1–136.

Plutschow, Herbert. 'Some Characteristics of Premodern Japanese Travel Literature.' *Proceedings of the Association for Japanese Literary Studies* 8 (2007): 26–34.

Pocrass, Kate and Patrick J. Kavanagh. *Mundane Journeys*. San Francisco, CA: Mundane Journeys, 2004.

Polezzi, Loredana. *Translating Travel: Contemporary Italian Travel Writing in English Translation*. London: Ashgate, 2001.

Polezzi, Loredana. 'Translation, Travel, Migration.' *The Translator* 12.2 (2006): 169–88.

'Popular Literature.' *Mechanics' Magazine* 176 (6 January 1827): 29–31.

Potts, Rolf. *Marco Polo Didn't Go There: Stories and Revelations from One Decade as a Post-Modern Travel Writer*. Palo Alto, CA: Travelers' Tales, 2008.

Poussin, Alexandre and Sylvain Tesson. *La marche dans le ciel*. Paris: France loisirs, 1997.

Poussin, Alexandre and Sylvain Tesson. *On a roulé sur la terre*. Paris: R. Laffont, 1996.

Pratt, Mary Louise. *Imperial Eyes: Travel Writing and Transculturation*. London: Routledge, 1992.

Prescott, Orville. 'Books of the Times,' *The New York Times*, 27 July 1962. Accessed 10 August 2014. http://query.nytimes.com/gst/abstract.html?res=9D07E5D8153DE63BBC4F51DFB1668389 679EDE.

Price, Richard and Sally Price. *Equatoria*. New York: Routledge, 1992.

Pueckler-Muskau, Hermann Ludwig Heinrich von. *Tour in England, Ireland, and France, in the Years 1828 & 1829; with Remarks on the Manners and Customs of the Inhabitants, and Anecdotes of Distinguished Public Characters. In a Series of Letters*, translated by Sarah Austin. 2 vols. London: Effingham Wilson, Royal Exchange, 1832.

Pugach, Sara. *Africa in Translation: A History of Colonial Linguistics in Africa and Beyond 1814–1945*. Ann Arbor, MI: University of Michigan Press, 2012.

Purchas, Samuel, ed. *Hakluytus Posthumus or, Purchas his Pilgrimes*, 20 vols. Originally published 1624–5. Glasgow: James MacLehose and Sons, 1905–7.

Quinn, D. B., ed. *The Hakluyt Handbook*, 2 vols. London: Hakluyt Society, 1974.

Quitt, Martin H. 'Trade and Acculturation at Jamestown, 1607–1609: The Limits of Understanding.' *William and Mary Quarterly* 52.2 (1995): 227–58.

Radison, Pierre-Esprit. *The Collected Writings, Volume 1. The Voyages*, edited by Germaine Warkentin. Toronto: The Champlain Society, 2012.

Rae-Ellis, Vivienne. *Louisa Anne Meredith: A Tigress in Exile*. Hobart: St. David's Park, 1990.

Rafael, Vicente L. *Contracting Colonialism: Translation and Christian Conversion in Tagalog Society under Early Spanish Rule*. Durham, NC: Duke University Press, 1993.

Rai, Alok. *George Orwell and the Politics of Despair: A Critical Study of the Writings of George Orwell*. Cambridge: Cambridge University Press, 1998.

Raj, Kapil. *Relocating Modern Science: Circulation and the Construction of Knowledge in South Asia and Europe 1650–1900*. Basingstoke: Palgrave Macmillan, 2007.

Rajamannar, Shifali. *Reading the Animal in the Literature of the British Raj*. New York: Palgrave Macmillan, 2012.

Raleigh, Walter. *The Discovery of the Large, Rich, and Beautiful Empire of Guiana, with a relation of the great and golden city of Manoa (which the Spaniards call El Dorado) of 1596*, edited by Robert H. Schomburgk. London: Hakluyt Society, 1848.

Raposo, Pedro M. P., Ana Simões, Manolis Patiniotis and José R. Bertomeu-Sánchez. 'Moving Localities and Creative Circulation: Travels as Knowledge Production in 18th-Century Europe.' *Centaurus* 56.3 (2014): 167–88.

Regis, Pamela. *Describing Early America: Bartram, Jefferson, Crèvecoeur, and the Influence of Natural History*. Philadelphia, PA: University of Pennsylvania Press, 1992.

Reinhartz, Dennis. *The Cartographer and the Literati*. Lewiston, NY: E. Mellen Press, 1997.

[*Report of the Secretary of War Communicating the Several Pacific Railroad Explorations*]. 33d Cong., 1st sess. House. Ex. doc. no. 129. 3 vols. + atlas. Washington, DC: A. O. P. Nicholson, 1855.

The Reveries of a Recluse; or, Sketches of Characters, Parties, Events, Writings, Opinions, &c. Edinburgh: Oliver & Boyd, 1824.

Review of *Account of a Voyage of Discovery to the West Coast of Corea*, by Basil Hall. *Quarterly Review* 18.36 (1818): 308–24.

Review of *Annual of British Landscape Scenery. An Autumn Ramble on the Banks of the Wye* [by Louisa Anne Twamley]. *Tait's Edinburgh Magazine* 5.60 (1838): 799–800.

Review of *Fragments of Voyages and Travels*, by Basil Hall. *Monthly Supplement of The Penny Magazine* (30 April 1832): 45.

Review of *Narrative of a Voyage to Java*, by Basil Hall. *United Service Journal and Naval and Military Magazine* 137 (April 1840): 554.

Review of *Voyage to Loo-Choo*, by Basil Hall. *The Monthly Review* 1.2 (February 1826): 126–38.

Reynolds, Dwight F. 'Music in Medieval Iberia: Contact, Influence and Hybridization.' *Medieval Encounters* 15.2–4 (2009): 236–55.

Rhys-Taylor, Alex. 'The Essences of Multiculture: A Sensory Exploration of an Inner-City Street Market.' *Identities: Global Studies in Culture and Power* 20.4 (2013): 393–406.

Richardson, A. E. *The Old Inns of England*. London: B.T. Batsford Ltd., 1934.

Richardson, Brian W. *Longitude and Empire: How Captain Cook's Voyages Changed the World*. Vancouver: University of British Columbia Press, 2005.

Richardson, James. *Wonders of the Yellowstone Region in the Rocky Mountains*. London: Blackie & Son, 1874.

Richardson, Lance. 'Come to Your Senses.' *Traveller*, 1 March 2014. Accessed 2 February 2016. www.traveller.com.au/come-to-your-senses-33h4z#ixzz2vYauI8VB.

Ricoeur, Paul. *Time and Narrative*, vol. 1, translated by Kathleen McLaughlin and David Pellauer. Originally published 1983. Chicago, IL: University of Chicago Press, 1984.

Rienarz, Jonathan. *Past Scents: Historical Perspectives on Smell*. Urbana, IL: University of Illinois Press, 2014.

Rindisbacher, Hans J. 'Smells of Switzerland.' In *From Multiculturalism to Hybridity: New Approaches to Teaching Modern Switzerland*, edited by Karin Baumgartner and Margitt Zinggeler, 229–52. Newcastle-upon-Tyne: Cambridge Scholars Press, 2010.

Robbins, Bruce. 'Comparative Cosmopolitanism.' *Social Text* 31/32 (1992): 169–86.

Robbins, Bruce. *Feeling Global: Internationalism in Distress*. New York: New York University Press, 1999.

Roberts, Jason. *A Sense of the World: How a Blind Man Became History's Greatest Traveller*. London: Pocket, 2006.

Roberts, Lissa. 'Situating Science in Global History: Local Exchanges and Networks of Circulation.' *Itinerario* 33.1 (2009): 9–30.

Robertson, Frances. *Print Culture: From Steam Press to Ebook*. Abingdon: Routledge, 2013.

Robinson, Douglas. *Translation and Empire: Postcolonial Theories Explained*. Manchester: St. Jerome, 1997.

Robinson, Michael. 'Linnaeus, Carl.' In *Literature of Travel and Exploration: an Encyclopedia*, edited by Jennifer Speake, 2:723–26. New York: Fitzroy Dearborn, 2003.

Rodaway, Paul. *Sensuous Geographies: Body, Sense and Place*. London: Routledge, 1994.

Rogers, Robert Vashon, Jr. *The Law of Hotel Life, or the Wrongs and Rights of Host and Guest*. San Francisco, CA: Sumer Whitney and Company, 1879.

Rogers, Robert Vashon, Jr. *Wrongs and Rights of a Traveller. By Boat — By Stage — By Rail.* Toronto: R. Carswell, 1875.

Rorty, Richard. *Philosophy and the Mirror of Nature.* Originally published 1979. Princeton, NJ: Princeton University Press, 2009.

Rosello, Mireille. *Postcolonial Hospitality: The Immigrant as Guest.* Stanford, CA: Stanford University Press, 2001.

Rosenbaum, Dan. 'MWC Day 2: Wearables to Gain a Sense of Smell.' *Wearable Tech Insider,* 3 March 2015. Accessed 2 February 2016. http://wearablesinsider.com/2015/03/03/mwc-day-2-wearables-to-gain-a-sense-of-smell.

Ross, Elizabeth. *Picturing Experience in the Early Printed Book: Breydenbach's* Peregrinatio *from Venice to Jerusalem.* University Park, PA: Penn State University Press, 2014.

Ross, Silvia. 'Home and Away: Tuscan Abodes and Italian Others in Contemporary Travel Writing.' *Studies in Travel Writing* 13.1 (2009): 45–60.

Roubaud, Jacques. *Tokyo intra-ordinaire.* Paris: Tripode, 2014.

Rowe, John Carlos. *Literary Culture and U.S. Imperialism: From the Revolution to World War II.* New York: Oxford University Press, 2000.

Royle, Nicholas. *The Uncanny.* London: Routledge, 2003.

Rubel, Paula G. and Abraham Rosman, eds. *Translating Cultures: Perspectives on Translation and Anthropology.* Oxford: Berg, 2003.

Rubiés, Joan-Pau. 'From the "History of Travayle" to the History of Travel Collections: The Rise of an Early Modern Genre.' In *Richard Hakluyt and Travel Writing in Early Modern Europe,* edited by Daniel Carey and Claire Jowitt, 25–41. London: The Hakluyt Society, 2013.

Russell, Alison. *Crossing Boundaries: Postmodern Travel Literature.* New York: Palgrave, 2000.

Rutkowska, Małgorzata. 'Travellers and Their Faithful Companions: Dogs in Contemporary American Travel Writing.' In *Animal Magic: Essays on Animals in the American Imagination,* edited by Jopi Nyman and Carol Smith, 124–36. Joensuu: University of Joensuu, 2004.

Sahlins, Marshall. *How 'Natives' Think: About Captain Cook, for Example.* Chicago, IL: University of Chicago Press, 1995.

Said, Edward W. *Beginnings: Intention and Method.* New York: Columbia University Press, 1985.

Said, Edward W. *Culture and Imperialism.* New York: Vintage, 1994.

Said, Edward W. *Orientalism.* London: Routledge & Kegan Paul, 1978.

Said, Edward W. 'Reflections on Exile'. In *Reflections on Exile and Other Essays,* 173–86. Cambridge, MA: Harvard University Press, 2000.

[Sala, George Augustus]. 'American Hotels and American Food. *Temple Bar: A London Magazine for Town and Country Readers* 2 (July 1861): 345–56.

Sandoval-Strausz, A. K. *Hotel: An American History.* New Haven, CT: Yale University Press, 2007.

Schafer, R. Murray. 'The Soundscape.' In *The Sound Studies Reader,* edited by Jonathan Sterne, 95–103. London: Routledge, 2012.

Schaff, Barbara. '"In the Footsteps of . . .": The Semiotics of Literary Tourism.' *KulturPoetik* (2011): 166–80.

Schilling, Derek. *Mémoires du quotidien: les lieux de Perec.* Villeneuve d'Ascq: Presses universitaires du Septentrion, 2006.

Schivelbusch, Wolfgang. *The Railway Journey: The Industrialization of Time and Space in the 19th Century.* Berkeley, CA: The University of California Press, 1986.

Schriber, Mary Suzanne. 'Edith Wharton and Travel Writing as Self-Discovery.' *American Literature* 59.2 (1987): 257–67.

Schueller, Malini Johar and Edward Watts. *Messy Beginnings: Postcoloniality and Early American Studies.* New Brunswick, NJ: Rutgers University Press, 2003.

Scott, David. *Semiologies of Travel from Gautier to Baudrillard.* Cambridge: Cambridge University Press, 2004.

Scott, Donald. 'The Popular Lecture and the Creation of a Public in the Mid-Nineteenth-Century United States.' *Journal of American History* 66.4 (1980): 791–809.

Seacole, Mary. *The Wonderful Adventures of Mrs Seacole in Many Lands,* edited by W. J. S. London: James Blackwood, 1857.

Seaton, A. V. 'In the Footsteps of Acerbi: Metempsychosis and the Repeated Journey.' In *Tutkimusmatkalla pohjoiseen: Giuseppe Acerbin Nordkapin matkan 200-vuotissymposiumi,* edited by Eero Jarva, Markku Mäkivuoti and Timo Sironen, 121–38. Oulu: Oulun yliopisto, 2001.

Seaton, A. V. 'Tourism as Metempsychosis and Metensomatosis: The Personae of Eternal Recurrence.' In *The Tourist as a Metaphor of the Social World,* edited by Graham M. S. Dann, 135–68. Cambridge, MA: CABI Publishing, 2002.

Secord, James A. *Victorian Sensation: The Extraordinary Publication, Reception, and Secret Authorship of* Vestiges of the Natural History of Creation. Chicago, IL: University of Chicago Press, 2000.

Segalen, Victor. *Equipée.* In *Oeuvres complètes*, vol. 2, edited by Henry Bouillier, 265–320. Originally published (abridged) 1929. Paris: Robert Laffont, 1995.

Segalen, Victor. *Essay on Exoticism: An Aesthetics of Diversity*, translated by Yaël Schlick. Originally published 1986. Durham, NC: Duke University Press, 2002.

Selinger, Evan and Kevin Outterson. 'The Ethics of Poverty Tourism.' *Environmental Philosophy* 7.2 (2010): 93–114.

Sellers, Charles. *The Market Revolution: Jacksonian America, 1815–1846.* New York: Oxford University Press, 1991.

Sensory Maps. 'Smellmap: Edinburgh.' Accessed 24 January 2016. http://sensorymaps.com/portfolio/smell-map-edinburgh.

Serres, Michel. *The Five Senses: A Philosophy of Mingled Bodies (I)*, translated by Margaret Sankey and Peter Cowley. Originally published 1985. London: Continuum, 2008.

Sève, Bernard. *De haut en bas: philosophie des listes.* Paris: Seuil, 2010.

Shand, Mark. *Travels on My Elephant.* London: Eland, 2012.

Shapinsky, Peter D. *Lords of the Sea: Pirates, Violence, and Commerce in Late Medieval Japan.* Ann Arbor, MI: Center for Japanese Studies Publications, University of Michigan, 2014.

Shapiro, Barbara. *A Culture of Fact: England 1550–1720.* Ithaca, NY: Cornell University Press, 2000.

Shepherd, Nan. *The Living Mountain.* Originally published 1977. Edinburgh: Canongate, 2011.

Sher, Richard B. *The Enlightenment and the Book: Scottish Authors and Their Publishers in Eighteenth-Century Britain, Ireland, and America.* Chicago, IL: University of Chicago Press, 2007.

Sheringham, Michael. *Everyday Life: Theories and Practices from Surrealism to the Present.* Oxford: Oxford University Press, 2006.

Sherman, William H. 'Distant Relations: Letters from America, 1492–1677.' *HLQ* 66: 3–4 (2003): 225–45.

Sherman, William H. 'Stirrings and Searchings (1500–1712).' In *The Cambridge Companion to Travel Writing*, edited by Peter Hulme and Tim Youngs, 17–36. Cambridge: Cambridge University Press, 2002.

Shirihai, Hadoram. *A Complete Guide to Antarctic Wildlife: The Birds and Marine Mammals of the Antarctic Continent and Southern Ocean.* 2nd ed. London: A & C Black, 2007.

Shteir, Ann B. *Cultivating Women, Cultivating Science: Flora's Daughters and Botany in England 1760–1860.* Baltimore, MD: Johns Hopkins University Press, 1996.

Silber, Ilana F. 'Bourdieu's Gift to Gift Theory: An Unacknowledged Trajectory.' *Sociological Theory* 27.2 (2009): 173–90.

Silverman, David J. '"We chuse to be bounded": Native American Animal Husbandry in Colonial New England.' *William and Mary Quarterly* 60.3 (July 2003): 511–48.

Silverman, Kaja. 'White Skins, Brown Masks: The Double Mimesis, or With Lawrence in Arabia.' In *Male Subjectivity at the Margins*, 299–338. New York: Routledge, 1992.

Siméus, Jenny, 'Collaboratively Writing a Self: Textual Strategies in Margaret McCord's *The Calling of Katie Makanya: A Memoir of South Africa.*' *Research in African Literatures* 46.2 (2015): 70–84.

Simon, Sherry. *Cities in Translation: Intersections of Language and Memory.* London: Routledge, 2011.

Simon, Sherry. *Translating Montreal: Episodes in the Life of a Divided City.* Montréal: McGill-Queen's University Press, 2006.

Simpson-Hausley, Paul. *Antarctica: Exploration, Perception, and Metaphor.* London: Routledge, 1992.

Sinclair, Iain. 'Into the Underworld.' *London Review of Books*, 22 January 2015.

Sinclair, Iain. *London Orbital: A Walk Around the M25.* London: Penguin, 2003.

Singer, Rita. 'Leisure, Refuge and Solidarity: Messages in Visitors' Books as Microforms of Travel Writing.' *Studies in Travel Writing* 20.4 (2016): 392–408.

Sissako, Abderrahmane. *En attendant le Bonheur.* DVD. 2002.

Sivils, Matthew Wynn. *American Environmental Fiction, 1782–1847.* Burlington, VT: Ashgate, 2014.

Skelton, R. A. *Explorers' Maps: Chapters in the Cartographic Record of Geographical Discovery.* New York: Frederick A. Praeger, 1958.

Skelton, R. A. 'Hakluyt's Maps.' In *The Hakluyt Handbook*, edited by D. B. Quinn, 2 vols, 1:48–73. London: Hakluyt Society, 1974.

Skey, Michael. 'What Does It Mean to Be a Cosmopolitan? An Examination of the Varying Meaningfulness and Commensurability of Everyday Cosmopolitan Practices.' *Identities: Global Studies in Culture and Power* 20.3 (2013): 235–52.

Slaughter, Thomas P. *Exploring Lewis and Clark: Reflections on Men and Wilderness*. New York: Alfred A. Knopf, 2003.

Slaughter, Thomas P. *The Natures of John and William Bartram*. New York: Alfred A. Knopf, 1996.

Smecca, Paola Daniela. *Representational Tactics in Travel Writing and Translation: A Focus on Sicily*. Rome: Carocci, 2005.

Smethurst, Paul. 'Introduction.' In *Travel Writing, Form and Empire: The Poetics and Politics of Mobility*, edited by Julia Kuehn and Paul Smethurst, 1–18. New York: Routledge, 2009.

Smethurst, Paul. *Travel Writing and the Natural World 1768–1840*. Basingstoke: Palgrave, 2013.

Smiles, Samuel. *A Publisher and His Friends: Memoir and Correspondence of the Late John Murray*. 2 vols. London: John Murray, 1891.

Smith, Albert. *The English Hotel Nuisance*. London: David Bryce, 1855.

Smith, Amy Elizabeth. 'Naming the Un-Familiar: Formal Letters and Travel Narratives in Late Seventeenth and Eighteenth-Century Britain.' *Review of English Studies* 54.214 (2003): 178–202.

Smith, Amy Elizabeth. 'Travel Narratives and the Familiar Letter Form in the Mid-Eighteenth-Century Authors.' *Studies in Philology* 95:1 (Winter 1998): 7–96.

Smith, Andrew. 'Migrancy, Hybridity, and Postcolonial Literary Studies.' In *Postcolonial Literary Studies*, edited by Neil Lazarus, 241–61. Cambridge: Cambridge University Press, 2004.

Smith, Keri. *How to Be an Explorer of the World*. New York: Perigee, 2008.

Smith, Mark M. 'Introduction: Onward to Audible Pasts.' In *Hearing History: A Reader*, edited by Mark M. Smith, ix–xx. Athens, GA: The University of Georgia Press, 2004.

Smith, Martha Nell. 'Electronic Scholarly Editing.' In *A Companion to Digital Humanities*, edited by Susan Schreibman, Ray Siemens and John Unsworth, 306–22. Oxford: Blackwell, 2004.

Smith, Peter J. *Between Two Stools: Scatology and Its Representation in English Literature, Chaucer to Swift*. Manchester: Manchester University Press, 2012.

Smith, Phil. *Counter-Tourism: The Handbook*. Axminster: Triarchy Press, 2012.

Smith, William. *A Natural History of Nevis and the Rest of the English Leeward Charibee Islands in America*. London, 1745.

Smollett, Tobias. *Travels through France and Italy*. Edited by Frank Felsenstein. Originally published 1776. Oxford: Oxford University Press, 1981.

Snyder, Gary. *The Practice of the Wild*. Originally published 1990. Berkeley, CA: Counterpoint, 2010.

Solis, Julia. *New York Underground: The Anatomy of a City*. New York: Routledge, 2005.

Solnit, Rebecca. *Wanderlust: A History of Walking*. London: Verso, 2002.

Soper, Kate. *What Is Nature?* Oxford: Blackwell, 1995.

Spivak, Gayatri Chakravorty. 'Can the Subaltern Speak?' In *Colonial Discourse and Post-Colonial Theory: A Reader*, edited by Patrick Williams and Laura Chrisman, 66–111. New York: Columbia University Press, 1994.

Spivak, Gayatri Chakravorty. 'Reading with Stuart Hall in "Pure" Literary Terms.' In *An Aesthetic Education in the Era of Globalization*, 351–71. Cambridge, MA: Harvard University Press, 2012.

Spufford, Francis. *I May Be Some Time: Ice and the English Imagination*. London: Faber, 1996.

Spufford, Francis, ed. *The Antarctic: An Anthology*. London: Granta, 2007.

Spurr, David. *The Rhetoric of Empire: Colonial Discourse in Journalism, Travel Writing, and Imperial Administration*. Durham, NC: Duke University Press, 1993.

Stafford, Barbara Maria. *Voyage into Substance: Art, Science, Nature, and the Illustrated Travel Account, 1760–1840*. Cambridge, MA: MIT Press, 1984.

Stallybrass, Peter. 'Marx's Coat.' In *Border Fetishisms: Material Objects in Unstable Spaces*, edited by Patricia Spyer, 183–207. London: Routledge, 1998.

Stanley, Henry Morton. *How I Found Livingstone: Travels, Adventures and Discoveries in Central Africa, Including Four Months Residence with Dr. Livingstone*. London: Sampson Low, Marston, Low, and Searle, 1872.

Starke, Mariana. *Letters from Italy, between the Years 1792 and 1798*. 2 vols. London: T. Gillet, 1800.

Statista, 'Global Travel and Tourism Industry – Statistics and Facts.' Accessed 29 August 2017. www.statista.com/topics/962/global-tourism.

Steigenwald, Bill. 'Sorry, Charley: Was John Steinbeck's *Travels with Charley* a Fraud?' *Reason*, April 2011. Accessed 15 August 2017. http://reason.com/archives/2011/04/04/sorry-charley.

Steinbeck, John and Robert Capa. *Russian Journal*. New York: Viking Press, 1948.

Steinbeck, John. *Travels with Charley in Search of America*. New York: Viking, 1962.

Steinbeck, John. *Travels with Charley: In Search of America*. In *Travels with Charley and Later Novels 1947–1962*, 765–931. New York: Library of America, 2007.

Steinitz, Rebecca. 'Diaries.' In *Encyclopedia of the Literature of Travel and Exploration*, edited by Jennifer Speake, 3 vols, 1:331–4. New York: Fitzroy Dearborn, 2003.

Sterne, Laurence. *A Sentimental Journey*, edited by Gradner D. Stout, Jr. Originally published 1768. Berkeley, CA: University of California Press, 1967.

Stevenson, Iain. *Book Makers: British Publishing in the Twentieth Century*. London: British Library, 2010.

Stevenson, Robert. 'Written Sources for Indian Music until 1882.' *Ethnomusicology* 17 (1973): 1–40.

Stevenson, Robert Louis. *Travels with a Donkey in the Cévennes*. London: Chatto & Windus, 1986.

Stibbe, Arran. *Ecolinguistics: Language, Ecology and the Stories We Live By*. London: Routledge, 2015.

Stiegler, Bernd. *Traveling in Place: A History of Armchair Travel*, translated by Peter Filkins. Originally published 2010. Chicago, IL: University of Chicago Press, 2013.

Still, Judith. *Enlightenment Hospitality: Cannibals, Harems and Adoption*. Oxford: Voltaire Foundation, 2011.

Stillinger, Jack. *Multiple Authorship and the Myth of Solitary Genius*. New York: Oxford University Press, 1991.

Stone, Marjorie and Judith Thompson. 'Contexts and Heterotexts: A Theoretical and Historical Introduction.' In *Literary Couplings: Writing Couples, Collaborators, and the Construction of Authorship*, edited by Marjorie Stone and Judith Thompson, 3–40. Madison, WI: University of Wisconsin Press, 2006.

Stowe, John. *Annales of England*. London: R. Newbery, 1600.

Strong, Pauline T. 'Fathoming the Primitive: Australian Aborigines in Four Explorers' Journals, 1697–1845.' *Ethnohistory* 3.2 (1986): 175–94.

Sutherland, J. A. *Victorian Novelists and Publishers*. London: Athlone Press, 1976.

Sutton, David E. *Remembrance of Repasts: An Anthropology of Food and Memory*. Oxford: Berg, 2001.

Sweet, Rosemary. *Cities and the Grand Tour: The British in Italy, c. 1690–1820*. Cambridge: Cambridge University Press, 2012.

Swift, Jonathan. 'Hints towards an Essay on Conversation.' In *The Works of Dr. Jonathan Swift*. 14 vols, 13:342–59. London, 1764.

Szerszynski, Bronislaw and John Urry. 'Cultures of Cosmopolitanism.' *Sociological Review* 50.4 (2002): 462–81.

Taylor, Andrew. 'M58 Poem.' In *In the Company of Ghosts: The Poetics of the Motorway*, edited by Alan Corkish with Edward Chell and Andrew Taylor, 27. Liverpool: erbacce-press, 2012.

Taylor, Andrew. 'Twitter Poem.' In *In the Company of Ghosts: The Poetics of the Motorway*, edited by Alan Corkish with Edward Chell and Andrew Taylor, 162. Liverpool: erbacce-press, 2012.

Taylor, Charles. *Sources of the Self: The Making of the Modern Identity*. Cambridge, MA: Harvard University Press, 1989.

Tegelberg, Matthew. 'Hidden Sights: Tourism, Representation and Lonely Planet Cambodia.' *International Journal of Cultural Studies* 13.5 (2010): 491–509.

Tenneriello, Susan. *Spectacle Culture and American Identity, 1815–1940*. New York: Palgrave Macmillan, 2013.

Terrie, Philip G. 'Tempests and Alligators: The Ambiguous Wilderness of William Bartram.' *North Dakota Quarterly* 59.2 (1991): 17–32.

Tesson, Sylvain. *The Consolations of the Forest: Alone in a Cabin on the Siberian Taiga*, translated by Linda Coverdale. Originally published 2011. London: Penguin, 2013.

Teukolsky, Rachel. *The Literate Eye: Victorian Art Writing and Modernist Aesthetics*. Oxford: Oxford University Press, 2009.

Thackeray, William Makepeace. *Little Travels and Roadside Sketches*. In *The Works of William Makepeace Thackeray*. 24 vols, 22:171–206. London: Smith, Elder & Co., 1869.

The Accomplished Letter-Writer. London, 1779.

Theroux, Paul. *The Happy Isles of Oceania: Paddling the Pacific*. Harmondsworth: Penguin, 1992.

Thiam, Bathie Ngoye. 'Soif d'Europe: l'imposture d'un immigré.' *Wal Fadjiri*, 16 July 2009. Accessed 20 January 2015. www.afriquechos.ch/spip.php?article3316&debut_articlesrescents=120.

Thomas, Dominic. *Black France: Colonialism, Immigration, and Transnationalism*. Bloomington, IN: Indiana University Press, 1997.

Thomas, Edward. *The South Country*. Originally published 1909. Wimborne Minster, Dorset: Little Toller Books, 2009.

Thomas, Keith. *Man and the Natural World*. New York: Pantheon, 1983.

Thomas, Nicholas. *Cook: The Extraordinary Voyages of James Cook*. New York: Walker and Company, 2003.

Thomas, Nicholas. *Entangled Objects: Exchange, Material Culture, and Colonialism in the Pacific*. Cambridge, MA: Harvard University Press, 1991.

Thompson, Carl. 'Earthquakes and Petticoats: Maria Graham, Geology, and Early Nineteenth-Century "Polite" Science.' *Journal of Victorian Culture* 17.3 (2012): 329–46.

Thompson, Carl. 'Introduction.' In *The Routledge Companion to Travel Writing*, edited by Carl Thompson, xvi–xx. Abingdon: Routledge, 2016.

Thompson, Carl, ed. *The Routledge Companion to Travel Writing*. Abingdon: Routledge, 2016.

Thompson, Carl. *The Suffering Traveller and the Romantic Imagination*. Oxford: Clarendon Press, 2007.

Thompson, Carl. *Travel Writing*. London: Routledge, 2011.

Thompson, Emily. 'Sound, Modernity and History.' In *The Sound Studies Reader*, edited by Jonathan Sterne, 117–29. London: Routledge, 2012.

Tilley, Heather, ed. 'Special Issue: The Victorian Tactile Imagination.' *19: Interdisciplinary Studies in the Long 19th Century* 19 (2014).

Tolias, George. 'Isolarii.' In *The History of Cartography*, vol. 3, *Cartography in the European Renaissance*, edited by David Woodward, 263–84. Chicago, IL: University of Chicago Press, 2007.

Tolkien, J. R. R. *The Art of the Hobbit*, edited by Wayne G. Hammond and Cristina Scull. London: HarperCollins, 2012.

Tolkien, J. R. R. *The Art of the Lord of the Rings*, edited by Wayne G. Hammond and Cristina Scull. London: HarperCollins, 2015.

Tomlinson, John. *Globalization and Culture*. Cambridge: Polity Press, 1999.

Torrens, H. S. 'Notes on "The Amateur" in the Development of British Geology.' *Proceedings of the Geologists' Association* 117.1 (2006): 1–8.

Totten, Gary. *African American Travel Narratives from Abroad: Mobility and Cultural Work in the Age of Jim Crow*. Amherst, MA: University of Massachusetts Press, 2015.

Tozier, Josephine. *Among English Inns. The Story of a Pilgrimage to Characteristic Spots of Rural England*. Boston, MA: L.C. Page & Company, 1904.

Triulzi, Alessandro and Robert L. McKenzie, eds. *Long Journeys: African Migrants on the Road*. Leiden: Brill, 2013.

Tucker Jones, Ryan. *Empire of Extinction: Russians and the North Pacific's Strange Beasts of the Sea, 1741–1867*. Oxford: Oxford University Press, 2014.

Tullett, William. 'The Macaroni's "Ambrosial Essences": Perfume, Identity and Public Space in Eighteenth-Century England.' *Journal for Eighteenth-Century Studies* 38.2 (2015): 163–80.

Turnbull, David. 'Local Knowledge and Comparative Scientific Traditions.' *Knowledge and Policy* 6.3–4 (1993–4): 29–54.

Turner, Katherine. *British Travel Writers in Europe 1750–1800*. Aldershot: Ashgate, 2001.

Twamley, Louisa Anne. *An Autumn Ramble on the Wye*. London: W. S. Orr and Co., 1838.

Twamley, Louisa Anne. *The Romance of Nature; or, the Flower-Seasons Illustrated*. London: Charles Tilt, 1836.

United Air Lines. *United Air Lines Maps of the Main Line Airway*. Chicago, IL: Rand McNally for United Air Lines, 1945.

Urbain, Jean-Didier. *Ethnologue, mais pas trop*. Originally published 2003. Paris: Payot & Rivages, 2008.

Urbain, Jean-Didier. 'I Travel Therefore I Am: The "Nomad Mind" and the Spirit of Travel,' translated by Charles Forsdick. *Studies in Travel Writing* 4 (2000): 141–64.

Urbain, Jean-Didier. *Secrets de voyage: menteurs, imposteurs, et autres voyageurs invisibles*. Paris: Éditions Payot & Rivages, 1998.

Urry, John and Jonas Larsen. *The Tourist Gaze 3.0*, 3rd ed. London: Sage, 2011.

Uusma, Bea. *Expeditionen: Min kärlekshistoria*. Stockholm: Norstedts, 2013.

Uusma, Bea. *The Expedition: A Love Story*. Translated by Agnes Broomé. London: Head of Zeus, 2014.

Vancouver, George. *A Voyage of Discovery to the North Pacific Ocean, and Round the World*. 3 vols. London: G. G. and J. Robinson, 1798.

Vernarde, Bruce L, ed. and trans. *The Rule of Saint Benedict*. Cambridge, MA: Dumbarton Oaks Medieval Library, University of Harvard Press, 2011.

Vilches, Elvira. 'Columbus's Gift: Representations of Grace and Wealth and the Enterprise of the Indies.' *MLN* 119.2 (2004): 201–25.

Vince, Ian. *The Lie of the Land: An Under-the-Field Guide to Great Britain*. London: Boxtree, 2010.

Viviès, Jean. *English Travel Narratives in the Eighteenth Century: Exploring Genres*. Aldershot: Ashgate, 2002.

Wadsworth, Sarah. 'Charles Knight and Sir Francis Bond Head: Two Early Victorian Perspectives on Printing and the Allied Trades.' *Victorian Periodicals Review* 31.4 (1998): 369–86.

Wærp, Henning Howlid. '"Innlandsisen, våre lengslers mål" Om Fridtjof Nansen: *På ski over Grønland* (1890) – og noen andre bøker i hans spor.' *Norsk Litteraturvitenskapelig Tidsskrift* 10.2 (2007): 97–116.

Waghenaer, Lucas Janszoon. *De Spieghel der Zeevaerdt*. Leyden: Christoffel Plantijn, 1584–5.

Walker, Jenny. 'From "Colour and Flair" to "A Corporate View": Evolutions in Guidebook Writing: An Interview with Jenny Walker.' *Studies in Travel Writing* 21.2 (2017): 208–20.

Walseth, Kristin. 'Young Muslim Women and Sport: The Impact of Identity Work.' *Leisure Studies* 25.1 (2006): 75–94.

Walters, Alice. 'Conversation Pieces: Science and Politeness in Eighteenth-Century England.' *History of Science* 35.2 (1997): 121–54.

Wang, Ning. 'Rethinking Authenticity in Tourism Experience.' *Annals of Tourism Research* 26.2 (1999): 349–70.

Ward, Charles Slegg. *The Eastern Counties*. London: Dulau & Co., 1883.

Warkentin, Germaine, ed. *Critical Issues in Editing Exploration Texts*. Toronto: University of Toronto Press, 1995.

Warner, Richard. *A Walk through Wales in August 1797*. Bath: R. Cruttell, 1798.

Warrender, Keith. *Underground Manchester: Secrets of the City Revealed*. Altrincham: Willow Publishing, 2007.

Watson, Nicola J. *The Literary Tourist: Readers and Places in Romantic and Victorian Britain*. Houndmills: Palgrave Macmillan, 2006.

Watts, Ruth. *Women in Science: A Social and Cultural History*. London: Routledge, 2007.

Webb, Ruth. *Ekphrasis, Imagination and Persuasion in Ancient Rhetorical Theory and Practice*. Aldershot: Ashgate, 2009.

Weedon, Alexis. *Victorian Publishing: The Economics of Book Production for a Mass Market, 1836–1916*. Aldershot: Ashgate, 2009.

Weedon, Alexis and Michael Bott. *British Book Trade Archives, 1830–1939: A Location Register*. Bristol: Simon Eliot and Michael Turner, 1996.

Weiner, Annette. *Inalienable Possessions: The Paradox of Keeping-While-Giving*. Berkeley, CA: University of California Press, 1992.

West, Rebecca. *Black Lamb and Grey Falcon: A Journey through Yugoslavia*. Originally published 1941. London: Penguin, 1994.

West, Rebecca. *Black Lamb and Grey Falcon: A Journey through Yugoslavia*. Originally published 1941. Edinburgh: Canongate, 2006.

Westover, Paul. *Necromanticism: Traveling to Meet the Dead, 1750–1860*. Houndmills: Palgrave Macmillan, 2012.

Weyler, Karen A. *Intricate Relations: Sexual and Economic Desire in American Fiction, 1789–1814*. Iowa City, IA: University of Iowa Press, 2004.

Wharton, Edith, *Italian Backgrounds*. New York: Scribner's, 1905.

Wheeler, Sara. *Terra Incognita: Travels in Antarctica*. New York: Random House, 1996.

White, Edmund. *States of Desire: Travels in Gay America*. London: Picador, 1986.

Whitney, Karl. *Hidden City: Adventures and Explorations in Dublin*. London: Penguin, 2015.

Whitney, Karl. 'what happens when nothing happens?' *3:AM Magazine*, 17 November 2010. Accessed 6 February 2018. www.3ammagazine.com/3am/what-happens-when-nothing-happens.

Whyte, William H. *City: Rediscovering the Center*. New York: Doubleday, 1988.

Williams, Glyndwyr. *The Great South Sea: English Voyages and Encounters 1570–1750*. New Haven, CT: Yale University Press, 1997.

Williams, Heather, Kathryn Jones and Carol Tully. 'Introduction: Wales and Travel Writing.' *Studies in Travel Writing* 18.2 (2014): 101–16.

Williams, Helen Maria. *A Tour in Switzerland*. 2 vols. London: G. G. and J. Robinson, 1797.

Williams, Raymond. *The Country and the City*. Originally published 1973. London: Hogarth, 1993.

Willis, Emma. *Theatricality, Dark Tourism and Ethical Spectatorship: Absent Others*. Basingstoke: Palgrave Macmillan, 2014.

Withers, Charles W. J. and Innes M. Keighren. 'Travels into Print: Authoring, Editing and Narratives of Travel and Exploration, c.1815–c.1857.' *Transactions of the Institute of British Geographers* 36.4 (2011): 560–73.

Wolff, Janet. 'On the Road Again: Metaphors of Travel in Cultural Criticism.' *Cultural Studies* 7.2 (1993): 224–39.

Wollstonecraft, Mary. *Letters Written During a Short Residence in Norway, Sweden and Denmark*. London, 1796.

Wood, Gordon S. *The Radicalism of the American Revolution*. New York: Knopf, 1992.

Woodfield, Denis B. *Surreptitious Printing in England 1550–1640*. New York: Bibliographical Society of America, 1973.

Woodward, David, ed. *Five Centuries of Map Printing*. Chicago, IL: University of Chicago Press, 1975.

Woodward, David. 'Roger Bacon's Terrestrial Coordinate System.' *Annals of the Association of American Geographers* 80.1 (1990): 109–22.

Woolley, Agnes. *Contemporary Asylum Narratives: Representing Refugees in the Twenty-First Century*. Basingstoke: Palgrave Macmillan, 2014.

Woolson, Abba Good. *Women in American Society*. Boston, MA: Roberts Brothers, 1873.

Wordsworth, Dorothy. 'Recollections of a Tour Made in Scotland A.D. 1820.' In *The Journals of Dorothy Wordsworth*, edited by E. de Selincourt, 2 vols, 1:195–409. London: Macmillan, 1941.

Wordsworth, William. *A Guide Through the Lakes of the North of England*. In *The Prose Works of Willliam Wordsworth*, edited by W. J. R. Owen and J. W. Smyser. 2 vols, 2:151–465. Originally published 1810. Oxford: Clarendon Press, 1974.

Worthen, John. *D.H. Lawrence: The Early Years, 1885–1912*. Cambridge: Cambridge University Press, 1991.

Wright, Sarah Bird. *Edith Wharton's Travel Writing: The Making of a Connoisseur*. Houndmills: Macmillan, 1997.

Wright, Thomas. *The Travels of Marco Polo, The Venetian. The Translation of Marsden Revised, with a Selection of his Notes*. London: Henry G. Bohn, 1854.

Wright, Tom F. *Lecturing the Atlantic: Speech, Print and an Anglo-American Commons 1830–1870*. Oxford: Oxford University Press, 2017.

Wright, Tom F. 'The Results of Locomotion: Bayard Taylor and the Travel Lecture in the Mid-Nineteenth-Century United States.' *Studies in Travel Writing* 14.2 (2010): 111–34.

Wurlitzer, Rudolph. *Hard Travel to Sacred Places*. Boston, MA: Shambhala, 1995.

'Wye-ator' [pseud.]. 'Wye and Wayfare.' *Punch* 45 (5 September 1863): 96.

York, Lorraine. *Rethinking Women's Collaborative Writing*. Toronto: University of Toronto Press, 2002.

Yost, Karl, ed. *The Ohio and Mississippi Navigator of Zadok Cramer: Third and Fourth Editions*. Morrison, IL: K. Yost, 1987.

Young, Iris Marion. *Justice and the Politics of Difference*. Princeton, NJ: Princeton University Press, 1990.

Youngs, Tim. 'Auden's Travel Writings.' In *The Cambridge Companion to W.H. Auden*, edited by Stan Smith, 68–81. Cambridge: Cambridge University Press, 2004.

Youngs, Tim. 'Digesting Africa: Representations of Eating by Nineteenth-Century British Travellers to Africa.' In *Food for Thought ou les Avatars de la Nourriture*, edited by Marie-Claire Rouyer, 91–106. Bordeaux: Université Michel de Montaigne-Bordeaux III, 1998.

Youngs, Tim. 'Making It Move: The Aboriginal in the Whitefella's Artifact.' In *Travel Writing, Form and Empire: The Poetics and Politics of Mobility*, edited by Julia Kuehn and Paul Smethurst, 148–66. New York: Routledge, 2009.

Youngs, Tim. *The Cambridge Introduction to Travel Writing*. Cambridge: Cambridge University Press, 2013.

Youngs, Tim. *Travellers in Africa: British Travelogues, 1850–1900*. Manchester: Manchester University Press, 1994.

Youngs, Tim. 'Urban Recesses: Memory, Nature and the City.' In *The Memory of Nature in Aboriginal, Canadian and American Contexts*, edited by Françoise Besson, Claire Omhovère and Héliane Ventura, 31–42. Newcastle-upon-Tyne: Cambridge Scholars Press, 2014.

Youngs, Tim. 'Where Are We Going? Cross-Border Approaches to Travel Writing.' In *Perspectives on Travel Writing*, edited by Glenn Hooper and Tim Youngs, 167–80. Aldershot: Ashgate, 2004.

Zamora, Margarita. *Reading Columbus*. Berkeley, CA: University of California Press, 1993.

Zeller, Suzanne. *Inventing Canada: Early Victorian Science and the Idea of a Transcontinental Nation*. Toronto: University of Toronto Press, 1987.

Zur, Dafna. 'Travel Across Time: Modern "Rewrites" of Pak Chiwŏn's *Yŏrha Ilgi*.' *Acta Koreana* 8.2 (2005): 49–64.

INDEX

Printed in Great Britain
by Amazon

17686593R00240